Table of Contents

BETA ESTIMATES FOR VALUATION AND COST OF CAPITAL

CAPM, Down-market, and Up-market Betas by Industry

Data for Common Stocks,
Preferred Stocks, and Mutual Funds
As of the End of the 3rd Quarter, 2018

G. Michael Phillips

William P. Jennings

James Chong

George Arzumanyan

WALNUT OAK PRESS

ISBN: 978-1-947572-31-7

Suggested Citation
Phillips, G. M., Jennings, W., Chong, J. & Arzumanyan, G. (2018). *Beta Estimates for Valuation & Cost of Capital: CAPM, Down-market, & Up-market Betas by Industry: Data for Common Stocks, Preferred Stocks, and Mutual Funds, As of the End of the 3rd Quarter, 2018*. Pasadena, CA: Walnut Oak Press.

Business Director: Robert Neff, CPA, ABV
Art Director: Austin Fuentes

A Note from the Authors

Valuation analysts are concerned with estimating the present value of future benefit streams (usually earnings or cash flows), using some risk-adjusted discount rate.

This may be computed using a "build-up" method, a "weighted average cost of capital" approach (when capital structure is assumed to be fixed), or it might be done using a statistical equation relating a discount rate to various external or market factors.

Perhaps the most common way to estimate a discount rate is to use a variation of the Capital Asset Pricing Model (CAPM), which relates expected returns of an asset to the expected returns of a broad stock market index. The original CAPM approach assumed that the expected responses by an asset to changes in the benchmark index were symmetrical in that a 1 unit increase in the index would be expected to generate the same absolute response as a 1 unit decrease.

Research has shown that such an assumption of strict symmetry is rarely maintained. Rather, the up-market response (when the benchmark goes up in value) might be larger or smaller than the associated down-market response (when the benchmark falls in value).

Two papers, attached as appendices in the main volumes of this series, explain in detail the use and computation of these different up-market and down-market beta statistics, their relationship to traditional CAPM Beta, and their use in estimating discount rates and cost of capital estimates. These papers in part discuss the use of a down-market beta rather than a traditional CAPM beta, which may give more accurate statements of an asset's expected loss when markets fall. Such "downside measures" might be better interpreted as what risk premia in discount rates are intended to capture in the sense that risk is usually associated with losses, and unexpected gains aren't usually considered as "risk".

The tables in this book provide up-market, down-market, and CAPM beta estimates by two-, three-, and four-digit SIC codes, using data for common stocks and preferred stocks in separate tables. In addition, tables are provided using Net Asset Value data (akin to prices) for mutual funds organized by fund type. For a given asset type and SIC code or fund category, the tables provide the mean, median, and various percentile values as well as a count of how many assets were in the analysis population.

This presentation of the up-market and down-market betas is among the most complete available. The use of common stock data provides a tool for general equity valuation. The use of preferred stocks provides a measure that can be used for somewhat more senior holdings and might be used by valuation analysts as a proxy for a wide range of private ownership structures.

The use of mutual fund-based beta estimates derived from mutual fund data provides a new resource for valuation analysts. There are many mutual fund categories, with descriptions based on the size of companies being targeted for investment, the geographical locations of the investments, and even other asset types, such as various types of bond funds, international holdings funds, and other more specific strategies, including "narrowness" and "broadness" of holdings. The sophisticated valuation analyst may find a reasonable proxy for a current exercise by selecting beta data for an appropriate corresponding mutual fund which may represent specific industry or holding company composition.

The data in this book are estimated using approximately one year of daily data, culminating on the date given for the table. These volumes are intended to be updated quarterly. Some beta estimations are performed using monthly data and a three- to five-year look-back period. However, the quality of estimates using the longer term monthly data are not as good as those obtained using a year of daily data. First, even five years of monthly data provides just 60 observations compared to the over 200 observations when using daily trading data. Second, the observed CAPM beta is essentially a weighted average of the up-market and down-market betas, where the proportions for weighting are based on the proportion of "up" versus "down" days (or months) for the benchmark. Consequently, even when there are an equal number of up and down months, the five years of monthly estimates would tend to have only 30 observations for estimating up-market or down-market betas compared to over 100 expected observations using daily data. Third, the mix of up and down days or months is not the same year to year, so there is a tendency to blur the up-market and down-market betas in the estimation process. The bottom line is that research indicates greater forecasting accuracy for future betas, whether CAPM, up-market, or down-market, when using daily rather than monthly data.

Finally, the valuation analyst should take careful note of the percentile values provided. As part of a valuation exercise, one might simply choose to use the midpoint (median) or perhaps the average. However, as the valuation proceeds, a better sense of how the target company compares to its industry may develop. For superior (or more financially stable, longer established, or better diversified) companies, it may be desirable to use a lower beta than just the midpoint; for relatively inferior (or smaller, newer, or otherwise riskier) companies, it may be desirable to use a higher beta than just the midpoint. We have provided a range of estimates facilitating the computation of 95% confidence intervals for valuation.

Each new volume will be available from www.WalnutOakPress.com and from select distributors soon after the new quarter. Several of the tables are also separately available for purchase in an e-book format. The data are generated using the www.MacroRisk.com online research platform and are used with permission.

How to Use this Book

Beta Estimates for Valuation and Cost of Capital assists in determining the cost of equity which would be used in valuing privately-held companies or thinly-traded stocks. The cost of equity is one of the components of the weighted average cost of capital (WACC). The WACC considers the different sources of capital a company uses to finance its operations. Each source of capital has its own cost (required rate of return). These sources may include equity, debt, preferred stock, etc. In this book, we focus primarily on equity capital and determining the required rate of return on equity.

Textbook example (using empirical betas from industry common stock data)

To estimate the required equity return, first determine what industry or SIC code the company you want to value belongs to. Let's say the company is in the coal mining industry (SIC code 12).

The next step is to determine which beta estimate is most appropriate for the company at hand. There are two parts to this computation, illustrated below. This book includes different beta estimates such as the mean, median and different percentiles to provide you with a range of potential estimates instead of providing just the average beta as found in many other valuation data sources. A judgment call is needed to determine whether the company at hand is as risky as the average company in the industry, less risky or more risky.

For the sake of illustration, let's assume that the target company is as risky as the average publicly traded company in the coal mining industry and therefore should correspond to the average beta estimate. (If the firm was perceived to be generally "better" or "worse" than the industry, one might choose to use a lower percentile or higher percentile of the reported betas.) Initially we focus on the gross riskiness of the target compared to its industry without adjusting for capital structure differences. The screenshot below shows data from Table 1 (March 30, 2018 edition). From the table we see that the empirical mean (average) beta is 0.94, a value based on eight publicly-traded companies in the coal mining industry.

Table 1

SIC Code	Description	Number of Companies	Equity Risk Premium	Mean	Median
12	COAL MINING	8	5.10%	0.944101	1.009107
122	BITUMINOUS COAL AND LIGNITE MINING	7	5.61%	1.038920	1.046510
1220	BITUMINOUS COAL & LIGNITE MINING	1	3.72%	0.688522	0.688522
1221	Bituminous Coal And Lignite Surface Mining	6	5.93%	1.097320	1.209890

After identifying the average beta, consider how the target company's capital structure may be different from the average capital structure in the coal mining industry. The beta estimate of 0.94 reflects the average capital structure (debt-to-equity ratio) in the coal mining industry, not necessarily the target company's capital structure which may be different from the industry average. If the company's capital structure is different from the average capital structure in the industry, adjust the industry's beta (in our case, ß=.94) to reflect the target company's leverage. This is a two-part calculation: first unlever the statistic then relever it to reflect the company's capital structure (which for this example we assume only consists of equity and debt). However, to the extent that the company's capital structure is like the average capital structure in the industry, the equity risk premium for the industry (presented in table 1) may be added to the risk-free rate to calculate the required return on equity for the company.

$$Required\ return\ for\ average\ company = risk\ free\ rate + industry\ equity\ risk\ premium$$

If the capital structures were similar, we would have used 5.10% (=.051) as the equity risk premium for the coal mining industry (presented in table 1) which would be added to our estimate of the risk-free rate to calculate the required rate of return. The equity risk premium in this book is calculated by multiplying the mean beta by an estimate of the U.S. market risk premium estimated by Pablo Fernandez et al. in "Market Risk Premium and Risk-Free Rate used for 59 countries in 2018: a survey". That academic study estimated the U.S. market risk premium as 5.40% (=.054).

To continue with our valuation, we'll assume that the capital structure of the company we want to value is different from the average capital structure in the industry. Review our section on debt-to-equity ratios and capital structures for different industries to get a sense of what a typical capital structure is for the company you are trying to value. Next, unlever the industry beta to compute a "pure" equity-only beta estimate. Then, relever the equity-only unlevered beta to reflect the actual capital structure of the firm being analyzed.

Part 1: *Unlever the empirical beta:* For this example, let's suppose that the average capital structure in the coal mining industry consists of 65% (=.65) equity and 35% (=.35) debt. If for some reason, the company's current capital structure does not represent the expected capital structure in the future, use the expected capital structure instead. To unlever the beta ($\mathrm{B_U}$):

$$B_U = \left(\frac{1}{1+\left(\frac{D}{E}\right)}\right) \times B_E = \left(\frac{1}{1+(0.35/0.65)}\right) \times 0.94 = 0.61$$

Part 2: *Relever the beta with target company data:* Also, let's suppose that our company's capital structure consists of 55% (=.55) equity and 45% (=.45) debt. To relever the beta ($\mathrm{B'_E}$):

$$B'_E = \left(1+\left(\frac{D'}{E'}\right)\right) \times B_U = \left(1+\left(\frac{0.45}{0.55}\right)\right) \times 0.61 = 1.11$$

We now have an estimated relevered beta for the firm reflecting its actual capital structure. The estimated value for $\mathrm{B'_E}$ is 1.11. In this case, $\mathrm{B'_E}$ is higher than the empirical estimate of 0.94, reported in Table 1, because the specific firm has greater leverage (debt to equity ratio) than the industry average. If the target firm had a lower debt to equity ratio than the industry, then the relevered beta would be expected to be lower than the industry estimate from Table 1. The unlevered, pure-equity, beta $\mathrm{B_U}$ is the lower bound beta estimate for firms in this industry.

After the Part 2 calculation, we can determine the required return on equity using the capital asset pricing model (although alternative asset pricing models can also be employed). Determine the appropriate risk-free rate. (While there are many sources and approaches, one is to use the forecasts of appropriate duration treasury yields which are available from the Philadelphia Federal Reserve.) For this example, assume that the risk-free rate is 2.8% (=.028) and the market risk premium is 5.4% (=.054). The required return on equity is estimated to be:

$$E(r) = 0.028 + 1.11 \times 0.054 = 0.0879 \; (= 8.79\%)$$

The rate of 8.79% (.0879) is the required return on equity.

The next step is to determine the cost of debt. This is usually the average yield-to-maturity (YTM) of new, not historical, debt in the coal mining industry or the borrowing cost of the company at hand if it's known. Let's assume the current cost of debt is five percent before any tax benefits. Any deductibility of interest is valued using the target company's effective income tax rate. For this example, assume the company's marginal tax rate is 30 percent (=.30).

Now, we are ready to calculate the WACC (assuming the company's capital structure consists of debt and equity only; if there are other sources of capital, add the product of the portion that capital represents from the total capital structure and its cost of capital to equation below):

$$WACC = (w_e \times r_e) + \big(w_d \times r_d \times (1 - t)\big)$$

$w_e = the\ percentage\ of\ equity\ capital\ in\ the\ company's\ capital\ structure$

$w_d = the\ percentage\ of\ debt\ capital\ in\ the\ company's\ capital\ structure$

$r_e = the\ company's\ cost\ of\ equity$

$r_d = the\ company's\ cost\ of\ debt$

$t = the\ company's\ effective\ income\ tax\ rate$

$$WACC = (0.55 \times 0.0879) + \big(0.45 \times 0.05 \times (1 - 0.3)\big)$$

$$WACC = 0.0497 \; (= 4.97\%)$$

We have calculated the WACC to be 4.97% (=.0497). This rate is the required return on capital given the company's capital structure and capital costs. This rate may now be used as the discount rate when calculating the present value of the company's expected free cash flows to the firm.

Please be aware that additional premiums may be needed in your case. Some valuation analysts add liquidity, control, and other premiums which are not reported here. The "textbook" example discussed above is illustrative and does not include many details that may be part of a professional business valuation or financial analysis.

Extensions (Multiple Line Companies)

What happens if a company is a blend across two or more industry groups? It is common for small firms to cross SIC lines. In such a case, one could compute the WACC separately for each product line or division, and then use the computed estimates of WACC to discount the future estimated cash flows of each business division or product. An alternative approach is discussed below in the context of Mutual Fund based estimates.

Extensions (Down-market Beta)

Depending on your application, it may be more appropriate to use a down-market beta. While the empirical beta looks at how a given industry's returns change with the stock market's overall fluctuations, the down-market beta focuses on relative performance just when the overall stock market is going down. Several papers discussing down-market beta and when and how to use it are included in the appendix to this volume.

It has been argued that company risk is associated with a failure to meet expected profits or to service debt, not the possibility of greater than expected or windfall profits. It has been shown (see appendix) that the empirical beta may be inaccurate as a measure of expected risk because it includes up-market (and presumably profitable) days along with down-market (and presumably unprofitable) days rather than focusing just on the down-market days. The down-market beta uses just the days when the market is losing money to quantify the firm's anticipated loss responses.

We propose that the down-market beta is a better measure of risk, the possibility of losing money, than is the traditional CAPM beta which is a blend of both the downside (unexpected losses) and upside (unexpected profits). This distinction is true whether discussing theoretical values, empirical estimates, or the unlevered or relevered versions of beta or down-market beta.

The computation of WACC using down-market beta is performed as previously discussed in the "textbook example" but utilizes the corresponding down-market beta (a mean, median, or some percentile as selected by the valuation analyst) rather than the corresponding traditional CAPM beta.

Extensions (Preferred Stocks)

It has been argued that the presence of seniority reduces the riskiness of investing in a company, potentially increasing the value of the preferred interest compared to a corresponding common stock position.

For computing the value of senior or control interests in privately held companies, it may be informative to utilize betas (or down-market betas) estimated from preferred stock data rather than common stock data.

When preferred stock is actually included in the capital structure, a third "preferred stock" component is added to the calculation of WACC. This would be just like the textbook example but adding the product of the portion that preferred capital represents from the total capital structure and the cost of preferred stock (which can be calculated using the CAPM as one of the approaches).

However, if the preferred stock is being used as a proxy for a more senior position (perhaps for a partnership interest or LLC membership) then one might use the preferred stock-based betas to find an industry risk premium and then use this alternative value rather than the common-stock based betas.

Table 2 presents the down-market beta for the construction industry (SIC Code 15).

Table 2

SIC Code	Description	Number of Companies	Equity Risk Premium	Mean	Median
	CONSTRUCTION				
15	CONSTRUCTION	1	2.36%	0.437062	0.437062
153	OPERATIVE BUILDERS	1	2.36%	0.437062	0.437062
1531	Operative Builders	1	2.36%	0.437062	0.437062

To calculate the cost of preferred stock in this case, assume again that the risk-free rate is 2.8% (=.028) and the market risk premium is 5.4% (=.054). The required return on preferred stock using the down-market beta and the CAPM approach is estimated to be:

$$E(r) = 0.028 + 0.437062 \times 0.054 = 0.0516\,(= 5.16\%)$$

To calculate the WACC for a company that has equity, preferred stock, and debt as part of its capital structure, the WACC formula would be:

$$WACC = (w_e \times r_e) + \left(w_{ps} \times r_{ps}\right) + \left(w_d \times r_d \times (1-t)\right)$$

We can also use the betas for preferred stocks to estimate the value of preferred stock itself. Assume that we have a preferred stock that is expected to pay $5 forever. To calculate the cost of preferred stock, we will use the same expected return on preferred stock we calculated earlier, 5.16% (=.0516), to calculate the value of preferred stock. The price of preferred stock is calculated to be:

$$P_{ps} = \frac{5}{0.0516} = 96.90$$

Extensions (Mutual Funds)

An alternative approach, particularly when valuing estates, larger wealth positions, multiple line businesses, holding companies, or investment pools, is to determine whether there is a category of mutual fund that corresponds to the characteristics of the privately held portfolio being valued.

The use of a mutual fund beta allows for an alternative measure of WACC by finding common combinations. Consider a valuation of a family's assets which includes substantial real estate holdings. In such a case, perhaps the use of a REIT-based mutual fund would provide an appropriate empirical mean beta for WACC applications. Similarly, suppose that a valuation target is comprised of substantial bond holdings as well as equity holdings. A balanced mutual fund, perhaps even a "life cycle" mutual fund, may provide appropriate benchmarking.

The use of Mutual Fund data is offered as an additional measure that could be used "stand-alone" or to bracket estimates based on other approaches.

For instance, let's assume we want to find the present value of future streams of cash flows from a rental property. This property is expected to provide an annual cash flow of $100,000 next year, and this cash flow is expected to increase by 2.5% (=.025) each year. To calculate the present value, we need to estimate a reasonable discount rate. Since we want to value a rental property, we might consider using the real estate group of mutual funds as a proxy for a beta estimate.

Table 3 presents the down-market betas for the real estate group of mutual funds.

Table 3

Peer Group	Number of Mutual Funds	Equity Risk Premium	Mean	Median
Real Estate	221	3.07%	0.568754	0.575317

Assuming the risk-free rate of 2.8% (=.028), the market risk premium of 5.4% (=.054) and the use of down-market mean beta, the required rate of return for the real estate category can be calculated as:

$$E(r) = 0.028 + 0.568754 \times 0.054 = 0.0587\ (= 5.87\%)$$

To calculate the present value of the rental property, we will implement the following formula:

$$Present\ Value = \frac{(Current\ Cash\ Flow) \times (1 + expected\ growth\ rate)}{required\ rate\ of\ return - expected\ growth\ rate}$$

In this case,

$$P = \frac{100{,}000(1 + 0.025)}{0.0587 - 0.025} = \$3{,}041{,}543$$

Debt-to-equity Ratios

Debt-to-equity Ratios

The table below presents debt-to-equity ratios for selected SIC codes. It includes all traded companies for which SEC Edgar information is available and the debt-to-equity ratios are positive or negative.

Source: SEC Edgar using Calcbench

Data as of the end of 2017

			Average			Median		
SIC	SIC Description	Number of Companies	Average Debt-to-equity Ratio	Debt Portion	Equity Portion	Median Debt-to-equity Ratio	Debt Portion	Equity Portion
010	AGRICULTURAL PRODUCTION-CROPS	6	0.562815	36.01%	63.99%	0.972059	49.29%	50.71%
020	AGRICULTURAL PROD-LIVESTOCK & ANIMAL SPECIALTIES	2	-0.775752	345.93%	-245.93%	-0.775752	345.93%	-245.93%
070	AGRICULTURAL SERVICES	5	2.886080	74.27%	25.73%	2.418669	70.75%	29.25%
090	FISHING, HUNTING AND TRAPPING	3	0.264783	20.94%	79.06%	0.319846	24.23%	75.77%
100	METAL MINING	17	-1.403512	347.82%	-247.82%	0.153731	13.32%	86.68%
104	GOLD AND SILVER ORES	24	0.042892	4.11%	95.89%	0.381641	27.62%	72.38%
109	MISCELLANEOUS METAL ORES	4	0.195775	16.37%	83.63%	0.330435	24.84%	75.16%
122	BITUMINOUS COAL & LIGNITE MINING	14	0.795933	44.32%	55.68%	1.066608	51.61%	48.39%
131	CRUDE PETROLEUM & NATURAL GAS	151	0.191799	16.09%	83.91%	0.652850	39.50%	60.50%
138	DRILLING OIL & GAS WELLS	65	-9.417897	111.88%	-11.88%	0.816712	44.96%	55.04%
140	MINING & QUARRYING OF NONMETALLIC MINERALS (NO FUELS)	19	0.611170	37.93%	62.07%	0.593763	37.26%	62.74%
152	GENERAL BLDG CONTRACTORS - RESIDENTIAL BLDGS	4	2.503789	71.46%	28.54%	1.928107	65.85%	34.15%
153	OPERATIVE BUILDERS	21	1.553966	60.85%	39.15%	1.081780	51.96%	48.04%
154	GENERAL BLDG CONTRACTORS - NONRESIDENTIAL BLDGS	2	1.739695	63.50%	36.50%	1.739695	63.50%	36.50%
160	HEAVY CONSTRUCTION OTHER THAN BLDG CONST - CONTRACTORS	8	4.324111	81.22%	18.78%	1.839932	64.79%	35.21%
162	WATER, SEWER, PIPELINE, COMM & POWER LINE CONSTRUCTION	8	1.258793	55.73%	44.27%	1.212859	54.81%	45.19%
170	CONSTRUCTION - SPECIAL TRADE CONTRACTORS	11	3.503863	77.80%	22.20%	1.312358	56.75%	43.25%
173	ELECTRICAL WORK	4	0.990993	49.77%	50.23%	0.943877	48.56%	51.44%
200	FOOD AND KINDRED PRODUCTS	7	1.916718	65.71%	34.29%	1.763700	63.82%	36.18%
201	MEAT PACKING PLANTS	7	0.603834	37.65%	62.35%	0.740693	42.55%	57.45%
202	DAIRY PRODUCTS	4	0.924446	48.04%	51.96%	0.440331	30.57%	69.43%
203	CANNED, FROZEN & PRESERVD FRUIT, VEG & FOOD SPECIALTIES	8	0.439033	30.51%	69.49%	0.560207	35.91%	64.09%
204	GRAIN MILL PRODUCTS	5	2.198312	68.73%	31.27%	1.071991	51.74%	48.26%
205	BAKERY PRODUCTS	4	0.684042	40.62%	59.38%	0.571851	36.38%	63.62%
206	SUGAR & CONFECTIONERY PRODUCTS	4	1.446322	59.12%	40.88%	0.374248	27.23%	72.77%
207	FATS & OILS	4	0.968348	49.20%	50.80%	1.154177	53.58%	46.42%
208	BEVERAGES	24	2.928240	74.54%	25.46%	0.678265	40.41%	59.59%
209	MISCELLANEOUS FOOD PREPARATIONS & KINDRED PRODUCTS	4	0.622091	38.35%	61.65%	0.458045	31.42%	68.58%
210	TOBACCO PRODUCTS	5	6.526795	86.71%	13.29%	3.364547	77.09%	22.91%
211	CIGARETTES	4	-2.085060	192.16%	-92.16%	-2.473274	167.88%	-67.88%
220	TEXTILE MILL PRODUCTS	2	3.327677	76.89%	23.11%	3.327677	76.89%	23.11%
222	BROADWOVEN FABRIC MILLS, MAN MADE FIBER & SILK	2	-1.892801	212.01%	-112.01%	-1.892801	212.01%	-112.01%
227	CARPETS & RUGS	3	1.567007	61.04%	38.96%	1.425391	58.77%	41.23%
230	APPAREL & OTHER FINISHD PRODS OF FABRICS & SIMILAR MATL	11	1.351643	57.48%	42.52%	0.984684	49.61%	50.39%
232	MEN'S & BOYS' FURNISHGS, WORK CLOTHG, & ALLIED GARMENTS	7	0.569516	36.29%	63.71%	0.679676	40.46%	59.54%

Debt-to-equity Ratios

SIC	SIC Description	Number of Companies	Average: Average Debt-to-equity Ratio	Average: Debt Portion	Average: Equity Portion	Median: Median Debt-to-equity Ratio	Median: Debt Portion	Median: Equity Portion
233	WOMEN'S, MISSES', AND JUNIORS OUTERWEAR	3	2.197424	68.72%	31.28%	2.332424	69.99%	30.01%
234	WOMEN'S, MISSES', CHILDREN'S & INFANTS' UNDERGARMENTS	2	0.414794	29.32%	70.68%	0.414794	29.32%	70.68%
239	MISCELLANEOUS FABRICATED TEXTILE PRODUCTS	2	2.008852	66.76%	33.24%	2.008852	66.76%	33.24%
240	LUMBER & WOOD PRODUCTS (NO FURNITURE)	6	2.891713	74.30%	25.70%	1.728136	63.34%	36.66%
242	SAWMILLS & PLANTING MILLS, GENERAL	2	0.251870	20.12%	79.88%	0.251870	20.12%	79.88%
243	MILLWOOD, VENEER, PLYWOOD, & STRUCTURAL WOOD MEMBERS	5	9.837507	90.77%	9.23%	2.614654	72.33%	27.67%
245	MOBILE HOMES	2	0.309111	23.61%	76.39%	0.309111	23.61%	76.39%
251	HOUSEHOLD FURNITURE	7	4.584039	82.09%	17.91%	1.662035	62.43%	37.57%
252	OFFICE FURNITURE	2	1.495128	59.92%	40.08%	1.495128	59.92%	40.08%
253	PUBLIC BLDG & RELATED FURNITURE	1	0.986357	49.66%	50.34%	0.986357	49.66%	50.34%
259	MISCELLANEOUS FURNITURE & FIXTURES	1	1.400254	58.34%	41.66%	1.400254	58.34%	41.66%
261	PULP MILLS	1	2.132043	68.07%	31.93%	2.132043	68.07%	31.93%
262	PAPER MILLS	11	1.611724	61.71%	38.29%	1.444053	59.08%	40.92%
263	PAPERBOARD MILLS	1	2.131987	68.07%	31.93%	2.131987	68.07%	31.93%
265	PAPERBOARD CONTAINERS & BOXES	5	2.059095	67.31%	32.69%	1.839503	64.78%	35.22%
267	CONVERTED PAPER & PAPERBOARD PRODS (NO CONTANERS/BOXES)	7	4.540119	81.95%	18.05%	2.388543	70.49%	29.51%
271	NEWSPAPERS: PUBLISHING OR PUBLISHING & PRINTING	9	0.172673	14.72%	85.28%	0.903261	47.46%	52.54%
273	BOOKS: PUBLISHING OR PUBLISHING & PRINTING	1	2.223860	68.98%	31.02%	2.223860	68.98%	31.02%
274	MISCELLANEOUS PUBLISHING	2	-3.959966	133.78%	-33.78%	-3.959966	133.78%	-33.78%
275	COMMERCIAL PRINTING	5	-1.265433	476.74%	-376.74%	2.817831	73.81%	26.19%
276	MANIFOLD BUSINESS FORMS	1	0.258822	20.56%	79.44%	0.258822	20.56%	79.44%
278	BLANKBOOKS, LOOSELEAF BINDERS & BOOKBINDG & RELATD WORK	2	1.896049	65.47%	34.53%	1.896049	65.47%	34.53%
280	CHEMICALS & ALLIED PRODUCTS	15	2.518445	71.58%	28.42%	2.345088	70.11%	29.89%
281	INDUSTRIAL INORGANIC CHEMICALS	12	1.563673	60.99%	39.01%	1.370462	57.81%	42.19%
282	PLASTIC MATERIAL, SYNTH RESIN/RUBBER, CELLULOS (NO GLASS)	19	3.326194	76.88%	23.12%	1.790869	64.17%	35.83%
283	MEDICINAL CHEMICALS & BOTANICAL PRODUCTS	355	0.969699	49.23%	50.77%	0.437072	30.41%	69.59%
284	SOAP, DETERGENTS, CLEANG PREPARATIONS, PERFUMES, COSMETICS	21	2.280302	69.52%	30.48%	0.362989	26.63%	73.37%
285	PAINTS, VARNISHES, LACQUERS, ENAMELS & ALLIED PRODS	3	3.161531	75.97%	24.03%	3.716277	78.80%	21.20%
286	INDUSTRIAL ORGANIC CHEMICALS	37	0.903078	47.45%	52.55%	0.398577	28.50%	71.50%
287	AGRICULTURAL CHEMICALS	17	1.991246	66.57%	33.43%	1.014213	50.35%	49.65%
289	MISCELLANEOUS CHEMICAL PRODUCTS	15	4.298708	81.13%	18.87%	1.037538	50.92%	49.08%
291	PETROLEUM REFINING	18	2.226151	69.00%	31.00%	1.056123	51.36%	48.64%
299	MISCELLANEOUS PRODUCTS OF PETROLEUM & COAL	3	-5.212941	123.74%	-23.74%	0.762925	43.28%	56.72%
301	TIRES & INNER TUBES	2	1.858784	65.02%	34.98%	1.858784	65.02%	34.98%
302	RUBBER & PLASTICS FOOTWEAR	2	0.643825	39.17%	60.83%	0.643825	39.17%	60.83%
305	GASKETS, PACKG & SEALG DEVICES & RUBBER & PLASTICS HOSE	2	3.825215	79.28%	20.72%	3.825215	79.28%	20.72%
306	FABRICATED RUBBER PRODUCTS, NEC	7	2.450341	71.02%	28.98%	0.455426	31.29%	68.71%
308	MISCELLANEOUS PLASTICS PRODUCTS	23	0.437819	30.45%	69.55%	0.472936	32.11%	67.89%
310	LEATHER & LEATHER PRODUCTS	4	-0.568762	131.89%	-31.89%	0.243720	19.60%	80.40%
314	FOOTWEAR, (NO RUBBER)	6	-2.326558	175.38%	-75.38%	0.355377	26.22%	73.78%

Debt-to-equity Ratios

SIC	SIC Description	Number of Companies	Average			Median		
			Average Debt-to-equity Ratio	Debt Portion	Equity Portion	Median Debt-to-equity Ratio	Debt Portion	Equity Portion
321	FLAT GLASS	1	2.846628	74.00%	26.00%	2.846628	74.00%	26.00%
322	GLASS & GLASSWARE, PRESSED OR BLOWN	4	2.638606	72.52%	27.48%	4.974424	83.26%	16.74%
323	GLASS PRODUCTS, MADE OF PURCHASED GLASS	3	1.416053	58.61%	41.39%	0.999237	49.98%	50.02%
324	CEMENT, HYDRAULIC	2	0.891215	47.12%	52.88%	0.891215	47.12%	52.88%
326	POTTERY & RELATED PRODUCTS	1	0.182588	15.44%	84.56%	0.182588	15.44%	84.56%
327	CONCRETE, GYPSUM & PLASTER PRODUCTS	7	1.086170	52.07%	47.93%	1.018495	50.46%	49.54%
328	CUT STONE & STONE PRODUCTS	1	0.354570	26.18%	73.82%	0.354570	26.18%	73.82%
329	ABRASIVE, ASBESTOS & MISC NONMETALLIC MINERAL PRODS	2	0.692788	40.93%	59.07%	0.692788	40.93%	59.07%
331	STEEL WORKS, BLAST FURNACES & ROLLING & FINISHING MILLS	19	2.954228	74.71%	25.29%	1.087798	52.10%	47.90%
333	PRIMARY SMELTING & REFINING OF NONFERROUS METALS	4	1.064218	51.56%	48.44%	1.019716	50.49%	49.51%
334	SECONDARY SMELTING & REFINING OF NONFERROUS METALS	2	13.894453	93.29%	6.71%	13.894453	93.29%	6.71%
335	ROLLING DRAWING & EXTRUDING OF NONFERROUS METALS	13	3.159248	75.96%	24.04%	1.198333	54.51%	45.49%
336	NONFERROUS FOUNDRIES (CASTINGS)	2	1.270420	55.96%	44.04%	1.270420	55.96%	44.04%
339	MISCELLANEOUS PRIMARY METAL PRODUCTS	3	1.463799	59.41%	40.59%	0.938737	48.42%	51.58%
341	METAL CANS	4	5.228923	83.95%	16.05%	4.153745	80.60%	19.40%
342	CUTLERY, HANDTOOLS & GENERAL HARDWARE	8	0.741113	42.57%	57.43%	0.837737	45.59%	54.41%
343	HEARING EQUIP, EXCEPT ELEC & WARM AIR; & PLUMBING FIXTURES	4	2.572502	72.01%	27.99%	1.990816	66.56%	33.44%
344	FABRICATED STRUCTURAL METAL PRODUCTS	14	2.964098	74.77%	25.23%	1.495333	59.93%	40.07%
346	METAL FORGINGS & STAMPINGS	5	1.928021	65.85%	34.15%	2.284726	69.56%	30.44%
347	COATING, ENGRAVING & ALLIED SERVICES	2	-0.502422	100.97%	-0.97%	-0.502422	100.97%	-0.97%
348	ORDNANCE & ACCESSORIES, (NO VEHICLES/GUIDED MISSILES)	4	0.631631	38.71%	61.29%	0.627309	38.55%	61.45%
349	MISCELLANEOUS FABRICATED METAL PRODUCTS	9	1.198614	54.52%	45.48%	1.094692	52.26%	47.74%
351	ENGINES & TURBINES	9	0.105558	9.55%	90.45%	1.213988	54.83%	45.17%
352	FARM MACHINERY & EQUIPMENT	6	1.783069	64.07%	35.93%	1.147249	53.43%	46.57%
353	CONSTRUCTION, MINING & MATERIALS HANDLING MACHINERY & EQUIP	24	0.537677	34.97%	65.03%	0.603421	37.63%	62.37%
354	METALWORKG MACHINERY & EQUIPMENT	8	1.493851	59.90%	40.10%	1.001646	50.04%	49.96%
355	SPECIAL INDUSTRY MACHINERY (NO METALWORKING MACHINERY)	19	-14.701356	107.30%	-7.30%	0.650131	39.40%	60.60%
356	GENERAL INDUSTRIAL MACHINERY & EQUIPMENT	25	1.384477	58.06%	41.94%	1.316793	56.84%	43.16%
357	COMPUTER & OFFICE EQUIPMENT	49	2.176452	68.52%	31.48%	0.921740	47.96%	52.04%
358	REFRIGERATION & SERVICE INDUSTRY MACHINERY	7	8.309527	89.26%	10.74%	1.453600	59.24%	40.76%
359	MISC INDUSTRIAL & COMMERCIAL MACHINERY & EQUIPMENT	7	0.801597	44.49%	55.51%	0.886813	47.00%	53.00%
360	ELECTRONIC & OTHER ELECTRICAL EQUIPMENT (NO COMPUTER EQUIP)	3	1.969203	66.32%	33.68%	1.233637	55.23%	44.77%
361	POWER, DISTRIBUTION & SPECIALTY TRANSFORMERS	4	1.494855	59.92%	40.08%	1.347281	57.40%	42.60%
362	ELECTRICAL INDUSTRIAL APPARATUS	15	0.940694	48.47%	51.53%	0.931133	48.22%	51.78%
363	HOUSEHOLD APPLIANCES	7	1.461450	59.37%	40.63%	0.775144	43.67%	56.33%
364	ELECTRIC LIGHTING & WIRING EQUIPMENT	11	0.121346	10.82%	89.18%	0.207695	17.20%	82.80%
365	HOUSEHOLD AUDIO & VIDEO EQUIPMENT	3	0.624343	38.44%	61.56%	0.368960	26.95%	73.05%
366	TELEPHONE & TELEGRAPH APPARATUS	63	1.532028	60.51%	39.49%	0.847454	45.87%	54.13%
367	ELECTRONIC COMPONENTS & ACCESSORIES	134	0.637485	38.93%	61.07%	0.641019	39.06%	60.94%
369	MISCELLANEOUS ELECTRICAL MACHINERY, EQUIPMENT & SUPPLIES	19	7.123369	87.69%	12.31%	1.925545	65.82%	34.18%

Debt-to-equity Ratios

SIC	SIC Description	Number of Companies	Average			Median		
			Average Debt-to-equity Ratio	Debt Portion	Equity Portion	Median Debt-to-equity Ratio	Debt Portion	Equity Portion
371	MOTOR VEHICLES & PASSENGER CAR BODIES	55	2.144406	68.20%	31.80%	1.747169	63.60%	36.40%
372	AIRCRAFT & PARTS	18	13.411446	93.06%	6.94%	1.318205	56.86%	43.14%
373	SHIP & BOAT BUILDING & REPAIRING	3	1.689435	62.82%	37.18%	2.064801	67.37%	32.63%
374	RAILROAD EQUIPMENT	5	0.958282	48.93%	51.07%	1.003198	50.08%	49.92%
375	MOTORCYCLES, BICYCLES & PARTS	5	0.853210	46.04%	53.96%	0.639690	39.01%	60.99%
376	GUIDED MISSILES & SPACE VEHICLES & PARTS	4	-13.389733	108.07%	-8.07%	1.386308	58.09%	41.91%
379	MISCELLANEOUS TRANSPORTATION EQUIPMENT	1	2.303650	69.73%	30.27%	2.303650	69.73%	30.27%
381	SEARCH, DETECTION, NAVAGATION, GUIDANCE, AERONAUTICAL SYS	7	1.381631	58.01%	41.99%	0.975247	49.37%	50.63%
382	LABORATORY APPARATUS & FURNITURE	72	1.116782	52.76%	47.24%	0.577382	36.60%	63.40%
384	SURGICAL & MEDICAL INSTRUMENTS & APPARATUS	152	1.031476	50.77%	49.23%	0.630122	38.65%	61.35%
385	OPHTHALMIC GOODS	3	0.837754	45.59%	54.41%	0.582168	36.80%	63.20%
386	PHOTOGRAPHIC EQUIPMENT & SUPPLIES	7	4.364429	81.36%	18.64%	0.678939	40.44%	59.56%
387	WATCHES, CLOCKS, CLOCKWORK OPERATED DEVICES/PARTS	2	1.113386	52.68%	47.32%	1.113386	52.68%	47.32%
391	JEWELRY, SILVERWARE & PLATED WARE	1	0.182797	15.45%	84.55%	0.182797	15.45%	84.55%
394	DOLLS & STUFFED TOYS	16	1.355622	57.55%	42.45%	0.925439	48.06%	51.94%
399	MISCELLANEOUS MANUFACTURING INDUSTRIES	12	12.668889	92.68%	7.32%	0.751125	42.89%	57.11%
401	RAILROADS, LINE-HAUL OPERATING	10	0.986481	49.66%	50.34%	1.122627	52.89%	47.11%
421	TRUCKING & COURIER SERVICES (NO AIR)	19	2.569205	71.98%	28.02%	0.661062	39.80%	60.20%
440	WATER TRANSPORTATION	22	1.252414	55.60%	44.40%	1.274853	56.04%	43.96%
441	DEEP SEA FOREIGN TRANSPORTATION OF FREIGHT	36	1.402759	58.38%	41.62%	1.054794	51.33%	48.67%
451	AIR TRANSPORTATION, SCHEDULED	11	3.162443	75.98%	24.02%	2.400468	70.59%	29.41%
452	AIR TRANSPORTATION, NONSCHEDULED	4	1.375201	57.90%	42.10%	1.481672	59.70%	40.30%
458	AIRPORTS, FLYING FIELDS & AIRPORT TERMINAL SERVICES	2	-2.304339	176.67%	-76.67%	-2.304339	176.67%	-76.67%
461	PIPE LINES (NO NATURAL GAS)	19	4.202136	80.78%	19.22%	1.324701	56.98%	43.02%
470	TRANSPORTATION SERVICES	13	-1.120374	930.75%	-830.75%	0.823887	45.17%	54.83%
473	ARRANGEMENT OF TRANSPORTATION OF FREIGHT & CARGO	8	1.952051	66.13%	33.87%	1.252864	55.61%	44.39%
481	RADIOTELEPHONE COMMUNICATIONS	39	6.716092	87.04%	12.96%	1.235086	55.26%	44.74%
482	TELEGRAPH & OTHER MESSAGE COMMUNICATIONS	3	1.786572	64.11%	35.89%	1.404274	58.41%	41.59%
483	RADIO BROADCASTING STATIONS	28	-7.153840	116.25%	-16.25%	1.233560	55.23%	44.77%
484	CABLE & OTHER PAY TELEVISION SERVICES	23	2.717492	73.10%	26.90%	1.672349	62.58%	37.42%
489	COMMUNICATIONS SERVICES, NEC	19	-2.142374	187.54%	-87.54%	1.035484	50.87%	49.13%
490	ELECTRIC, GAS & SANITARY SERVICES	1	4.888211	83.02%	16.98%	4.888211	83.02%	16.98%
491	ELECTRIC SERVICES	60	3.589097	78.21%	21.79%	2.310376	69.79%	30.21%
492	NATURAL GAS TRANSMISSION	51	-4.878255	125.78%	-25.78%	1.389651	58.15%	41.85%
493	ELECTRIC & OTHER SERVICES COMBINED	28	1.886316	65.35%	34.65%	2.152921	68.28%	31.72%
494	WATER SUPPLY	14	2.265628	69.38%	30.62%	1.920821	65.76%	34.24%
495	SANITARY SERVICES	13	-0.869646	667.14%	-567.14%	1.144729	53.37%	46.63%
499	COGENERATION SERVICES & SMALL POWER PRODUCERS	3	5.028053	83.41%	16.59%	5.661506	84.99%	15.01%
500	WHOLESALE-DURABLE GOODS	4	1.585697	61.33%	38.67%	1.925892	65.82%	34.18%
501	WHOLESALE-MOTOR VEHICLES & MOTOR VEHICLE PARTS & SUPPLIES	3	0.521361	34.27%	65.73%	1.231180	55.18%	44.82%

Debt-to-equity Ratios

			Average			Median		
SIC	SIC Description	Number of Companies	Average Debt-to-equity Ratio	Debt Portion	Equity Portion	Median Debt-to-equity Ratio	Debt Portion	Equity Portion
502	WHOLESALE-FURNITURE & HOME FURNISHINGS	3	-1.883876	213.14%	-113.14%	-1.580933	272.14%	-172.14%
503	WHOLESALE-LUMBER & OTHER CONSTRUCTION MATERIALS	9	3.319125	76.85%	23.15%	1.382618	58.03%	41.97%
504	WHOLESALE-PROFESSIONAL & COMMERCIAL EQUIPMENT & SUPPLIES	9	0.905128	47.51%	52.49%	1.470992	59.53%	40.47%
505	WHOLESALE-METALS & MINERALS (NO PETROLEUM)	5	-43.997516	102.33%	-2.33%	1.216418	54.88%	45.12%
506	WHOLESALE-ELECTRICAL APPARATUS & EQUIPMENT, WIRING SUPPLIES	17	0.491439	32.95%	67.05%	0.888493	47.05%	52.95%
507	WHOLESALE-HARDWARE & PLUMBING & HEATING EQUIPMENT & SUPPLIES	3	1.275074	56.05%	43.95%	1.699743	62.96%	37.04%
508	WHOLESALE-MACHINERY, EQUIPMENT & SUPPLIES	10	2.749202	73.33%	26.67%	1.491783	59.87%	40.13%
509	WHOLESALE-MISC DURABLE GOODS	5	0.467151	31.84%	68.16%	0.737241	42.44%	57.56%
511	WHOLESALE-PAPER & PAPER PRODUCTS	2	3.256009	76.50%	23.50%	3.256009	76.50%	23.50%
512	WHOLESALE-DRUGS, PROPRIETARIES & DRUGGISTS' SUNDRIES	9	0.045452	4.35%	95.65%	-1.028948	3554.47%	-3454.47%
513	WHOLESALE-APPAREL, PIECE GOODS & NOTIONS	3	0.105556	9.55%	90.45%	0.277999	21.75%	78.25%
514	WHOLESALE-GROCERIES & RELATED PRODUCTS	12	2.160844	68.36%	31.64%	1.807019	64.38%	35.62%
515	WHOLESALE-FARM PRODUCT RAW MATERIALS	5	1.256001	55.67%	44.33%	1.020504	50.51%	49.49%
516	WHOLESALE-CHEMICALS & ALLIED PRODUCTS	4	2.260262	69.33%	30.67%	1.714130	63.16%	36.84%
517	WHOLESALE-PETROLEUM BULK STATIONS & TERMINALS	10	3.329188	76.90%	23.10%	2.464235	71.13%	28.87%
518	WHOLESALE-BEER, WINE & DISTILLED ALCOHOLIC BEVERAGES	2	0.550368	35.50%	64.50%	0.550368	35.50%	64.50%
519	WHOLESALE-MISCELLANEOUS NONDURABLE GOODS	4	0.436700	30.40%	69.60%	0.905937	47.53%	52.47%
520	RETAIL-BUILDING MATERIALS, HARDWARE, GARDEN SUPPLY	4	1.509205	60.15%	39.85%	0.705075	41.35%	58.65%
521	RETAIL-LUMBER & OTHER BUILDING MATERIALS DEALERS	8	3.327511	76.89%	23.11%	1.243953	55.44%	44.56%
531	RETAIL-DEPARTMENT STORES	8	6.932166	87.39%	12.61%	1.941066	66.00%	34.00%
533	RETAIL-VARIETY STORES	11	1.096819	52.31%	47.69%	1.274034	56.03%	43.97%
540	RETAIL-FOOD STORES	2	-4.430059	129.15%	-29.15%	-4.430059	129.15%	-29.15%
541	RETAIL-GROCERY STORES	10	1.419242	58.66%	41.34%	1.093525	52.23%	47.77%
550	RETAIL-AUTO DEALERS & GASOLINE STATIONS	17	0.248578	19.91%	80.09%	3.323290	76.87%	23.13%
553	RETAIL-AUTO & HOME SUPPLY STORES	5	1.441680	59.04%	40.96%	1.483693	59.74%	40.26%
560	RETAIL-APPAREL & ACCESSORY STORES	12	76.888150	98.72%	1.28%	0.713471	41.64%	58.36%
562	RETAIL-WOMEN'S CLOTHING STORES	6	-0.626506	167.74%	-67.74%	1.012440	50.31%	49.69%
565	RETAIL-FAMILY CLOTHING STORES	13	2.309854	69.79%	30.21%	1.343426	57.33%	42.67%
566	RETAIL-SHOE STORES	6	0.705347	41.36%	58.64%	0.534614	34.84%	65.16%
570	RETAIL-HOME FURNITURE, FURNISHINGS & EQUIPMENT STORES	6	1.458886	59.33%	40.67%	1.380784	58.00%	42.00%
571	RETAIL-FURNITURE STORES	2	-118.322813	100.85%	-0.85%	-118.322813	100.85%	-0.85%
573	RETAIL-RADIO, TV & CONSUMER ELECTRONICS STORES	5	1.126021	52.96%	47.04%	1.276631	56.08%	43.92%
581	RETAIL-EATING & DRINKING PLACES	64	8.533082	89.51%	10.49%	0.831689	45.41%	54.59%
590	RETAIL-MISCELLANEOUS RETAIL	16	0.253429	20.22%	79.78%	0.411178	29.14%	70.86%
591	RETAIL-DRUG STORES AND PROPRIETARY STORES	7	2.566734	71.96%	28.04%	1.588953	61.37%	38.63%
594	RETAIL-MISCELLANEOUS SHOPPING GOODS STORES	11	0.946392	48.62%	51.38%	0.844933	45.80%	54.20%
596	RETAIL-NONSTORE RETAILERS	24	0.491799	32.97%	67.03%	1.352546	57.49%	42.51%
599	RETAIL-RETAIL STORES, NEC	12	0.986135	49.65%	50.35%	1.163710	53.78%	46.22%
602	NATIONAL COMMERCIAL BANKS	335	8.633553	89.62%	10.38%	8.351321	89.31%	10.69%
603	SAVINGS INSTITUTION, FEDERALLY CHARTERED	85	7.565504	88.33%	11.67%	7.576792	88.34%	11.66%

Debt-to-equity Ratios

SIC	SIC Description	Number of Companies	Average			Median		
			Average Debt-to-equity Ratio	Debt Portion	Equity Portion	Median Debt-to-equity Ratio	Debt Portion	Equity Portion
609	FUNCTIONS RELATED TO DEPOSITORY BANKING, NEC	3	1.240387	55.36%	44.64%	1.617829	61.80%	38.20%
611	FEDERAL & FEDERALLY-SPONSORED CREDIT AGENCIES	14	-517.943917	100.19%	-0.19%	18.487262	94.87%	5.13%
614	PERSONAL CREDIT INSTITUTIONS	15	2.648471	72.59%	27.41%	2.464682	71.14%	28.86%
615	SHORT-TERM BUSINESS CREDIT INSTITUTIONS	14	6.072158	85.86%	14.14%	6.593483	86.83%	13.17%
616	MORTGAGE BANKERS & LOAN CORRESPONDENTS	5	-0.811312	429.98%	-329.98%	3.284587	76.66%	23.34%
617	FINANCE LESSORS	1	11.386838	91.93%	8.07%	11.386838	91.93%	8.07%
619	FINANCE SERVICES	21	1.654754	62.33%	37.67%	1.709789	63.10%	36.90%
620	SECURITY & COMMODITY BROKERS, DEALERS, EXCHANGES & SERVICES	11	2.774112	73.50%	26.50%	1.681501	62.71%	37.29%
621	SECURITY BROKERS, DEALERS & FLOTATION COMPANIES	31	6.029739	85.77%	14.23%	2.817614	73.81%	26.19%
622	COMMODITY CONTRACTS BROKERS & DEALERS	47	0.236932	19.15%	80.85%	0.020928	2.05%	97.95%
628	INVESTMENT ADVICE	38	1.570647	61.10%	38.90%	0.734872	42.36%	57.64%
631	LIFE INSURANCE	42	11.996260	92.31%	7.69%	8.492675	89.47%	10.53%
632	ACCIDENT & HEALTH INSURANCE	17	4.223726	80.86%	19.14%	2.482414	71.28%	28.72%
633	FIRE, MARINE & CASUALTY INSURANCE	67	3.188780	76.13%	23.87%	2.835086	73.92%	26.08%
635	SURETY INSURANCE	8	3.196633	76.17%	23.83%	1.038666	50.95%	49.05%
636	TITLE INSURANCE	4	1.047555	51.16%	48.84%	1.021336	50.53%	49.47%
639	INSURANCE CARRIERS, NEC	3	4.523606	81.90%	18.10%	3.902579	79.60%	20.40%
641	INSURANCE AGENTS, BROKERS & SERVICE	11	2.515057	71.55%	28.45%	1.745095	63.57%	36.43%
650	REAL ESTATE	55	0.491034	32.93%	67.07%	0.525917	34.47%	65.53%
651	REAL ESTATE OPERATORS (NO DEVELOPERS) & LESSORS	17	0.655196	39.58%	60.42%	0.798409	44.40%	55.60%
653	REAL ESTATE AGENTS & MANAGERS (FOR OTHERS)	12	0.756731	43.08%	56.92%	1.225395	55.06%	44.94%
655	LAND SUBDIVIDERS & DEVELOPERS (NO CEMETERIES)	6	0.431128	30.13%	69.87%	0.354855	26.19%	73.81%
677	BLANK CHECKS	16	2.763124	73.43%	26.57%	-0.388923	63.65%	36.35%
679	OIL ROYALTY TRADERS	316	1.874556	65.21%	34.79%	1.163569	53.78%	46.22%
700	HOTELS, ROOMING HOUSES, CAMPS & OTHER LODGING PLACES	3	1.536074	60.57%	39.43%	0.792550	44.21%	55.79%
701	HOTELS & MOTELS	33	-0.426604	74.40%	25.60%	1.666690	62.50%	37.50%
720	SERVICES-PERSONAL SERVICES	14	1.036677	50.90%	49.10%	0.276921	21.69%	78.31%
731	SERVICES-ADVERTISING	26	-37.294189	102.76%	-2.76%	0.419817	29.57%	70.43%
732	SERVICES-CONSUMER CREDIT REPORTING, COLLECTION AGENCIES	7	-8.886042	112.68%	-12.68%	1.805272	64.35%	35.65%
733	SERVICES-MAILING, REPRODUCTION, COMMERCIAL ART & PHOTOGRAPHY	3	-1.449668	322.39%	-222.39%	-1.038686	2684.91%	-2584.91%
734	SERVICES-TO DWELLINGS & OTHER BUILDINGS	2	1.176049	54.05%	45.95%	1.176049	54.05%	45.95%
735	SERVICES-MISCELLANEOUS EQUIPMENT RENTAL & LEASING	42	1.093013	52.22%	47.78%	1.080992	51.95%	48.05%
736	SERVICES-EMPLOYMENT AGENCIES	24	1.518149	60.29%	39.71%	1.147228	53.43%	46.57%
737	SERVICES-COMPUTER PROGRAMMING, DATA PROCESSING, ETC.	310	-0.973031	3607.90%	-3507.90%	0.635148	38.84%	61.16%
738	SERVICES-MISCELLANEOUS BUSINESS SERVICES	123	-2.012781	198.74%	-98.74%	0.757771	43.11%	56.89%
750	SERVICES-AUTOMOTIVE REPAIR, SERVICES & PARKING	1	0.938708	48.42%	51.58%	0.938708	48.42%	51.58%
751	SERVICES-AUTO RENTAL & LEASING (NO DRIVERS)	6	8.385215	89.34%	10.66%	2.596184	72.19%	27.81%
760	SERVICES-MISCELLANEOUS REPAIR SERVICES	4	6.798905	87.18%	12.82%	1.478545	59.65%	40.35%
781	SERVICES-MOTION PICTURE & VIDEO TAPE PRODUCTION	10	0.086335	7.95%	92.05%	0.149088	12.97%	87.03%
782	SERVICES-MOTION PICTURE & VIDEO TAPE DISTRIBUTION	2	3.687433	78.67%	21.33%	3.687433	78.67%	21.33%

Debt-to-equity Ratios

SIC	SIC Description	Number of Companies	Average			Median		
			Average Debt-to-equity Ratio	Debt Portion	Equity Portion	Median Debt-to-equity Ratio	Debt Portion	Equity Portion
783	SERVICES-MOTION PICTURE THEATERS	7	0.536431	34.91%	65.09%	1.334052	57.16%	42.84%
784	SERVICES-VIDEO TAPE RENTAL	1	4.307921	81.16%	18.84%	4.307921	81.16%	18.84%
790	SERVICES-AMUSEMENT & RECREATION SERVICES	11	1.523920	60.38%	39.62%	0.355577	26.23%	73.77%
794	SERVICES-RACING, INCLUDING TRACK OPERATION	6	-1.269594	470.93%	-370.93%	0.425981	29.87%	70.13%
799	SERVICES-MISCELLANEOUS AMUSEMENT & RECREATION	19	1.322388	56.94%	43.06%	0.518768	34.16%	65.84%
800	SERVICES-HEALTH SERVICES	2	-5.136211	124.18%	-24.18%	-5.136211	124.18%	-24.18%
801	SERVICES-OFFICES & CLINICS OF DOCTORS OF MEDICINE	4	0.136528	12.01%	87.99%	0.237508	19.19%	80.81%
805	SERVICES-NURSING & PERSONAL CARE FACILITIES	10	6.254652	86.22%	13.78%	3.148969	75.90%	24.10%
806	SERVICES-HOSPITALS	14	1.776628	63.99%	36.01%	1.222903	55.01%	44.99%
807	SERVICES-MEDICAL LABORATORIES	19	-0.141727	16.51%	83.49%	0.733073	42.30%	57.70%
808	SERVICES-HOME HEALTH CARE SERVICES	8	-0.649160	185.03%	-85.03%	0.532979	34.77%	65.23%
809	SERVICES-MISC HEALTH & ALLIED SERVICES, NEC	18	-0.569011	132.02%	-32.02%	1.159751	53.70%	46.30%
811	SERVICES-LEGAL SERVICES	1	0.745687	42.72%	57.28%	0.745687	42.72%	57.28%
820	SERVICES-EDUCATIONAL SERVICES	26	0.357554	26.34%	73.66%	0.522591	34.32%	65.68%
830	SERVICES-SOCIAL SERVICES	1	0.418929	29.52%	70.48%	0.418929	29.52%	70.48%
835	SERVICES-CHILD DAY CARE SERVICES	1	2.295655	69.66%	30.34%	2.295655	69.66%	30.34%
870	SERVICES-ENGINEERING, ACCOUNTING, RESEARCH, MANAGEMENT	2	1.219076	54.94%	45.06%	1.219076	54.94%	45.06%
871	SERVICES-ENGINEERING SERVICES	10	2.183251	68.59%	31.41%	1.048236	51.18%	48.82%
873	SERVICES-COMMERCIAL PHYSICAL & BIOLOGICAL RESEARCH	23	0.756727	43.08%	56.92%	0.688278	40.77%	59.23%
874	SERVICES-MANAGEMENT SERVICES	45	-0.023577	2.41%	97.59%	0.520606	34.24%	65.76%
999	NON-OPERATING ESTABLISHMENTS	1	-0.903143	932.45%	-832.45%	-0.903143	932.45%	-832.45%

Positive Debt-to-equity Ratios

Positive Debt-to-equity Ratios

The table below presents debt-to-equity ratios for selected SIC codes. It includes all traded companies for which SEC Edgar information is available and the debt-to-equity ratios are positive.

Source: SEC Edgar using Calcbench

Data as of the end of 2017

			Average			Median		
SIC	SIC Description	Number of Companies	Average Debt-to-equity Ratio	Debt Portion	Equity Portion	Median Debt-to-equity Ratio	Debt Portion	Equity Portion
010	AGRICULTURAL PRODUCTION-CROPS	5	1.158828	53.68%	46.32%	1.399399	58.32%	41.68%
020	AGRICULTURAL PROD-LIVESTOCK & ANIMAL SPECIALTIES	1	0.038841	3.74%	96.26%	0.038841	3.74%	96.26%
070	AGRICULTURAL SERVICES	5	2.886080	74.27%	25.73%	2.418669	70.75%	29.25%
090	FISHING, HUNTING AND TRAPPING	3	0.264783	20.94%	79.06%	0.319846	24.23%	75.77%
100	METAL MINING	10	0.878110	46.75%	53.25%	0.839984	45.65%	54.35%
104	GOLD AND SILVER ORES	20	0.714633	41.68%	58.32%	0.494121	33.07%	66.93%
109	MISCELLANEOUS METAL ORES	3	0.612941	38.00%	62.00%	0.413781	29.27%	70.73%
122	BITUMINOUS COAL & LIGNITE MINING	12	1.720674	63.24%	36.76%	1.158134	53.66%	46.34%
131	CRUDE PETROLEUM & NATURAL GAS	123	1.623266	61.88%	38.12%	0.873027	46.61%	53.39%
138	DRILLING OIL & GAS WELLS	59	2.494086	71.38%	28.62%	0.931966	48.24%	51.76%
140	MINING & QUARRYING OF NONMETALLIC MINERALS (NO FUELS)	15	1.260144	55.76%	44.24%	0.825946	45.23%	54.77%
152	GENERAL BLDG CONTRACTORS - RESIDENTIAL BLDGS	4	2.503789	71.46%	28.54%	1.928107	65.85%	34.15%
153	OPERATIVE BUILDERS	19	2.043889	67.15%	32.85%	1.204554	54.64%	45.36%
154	GENERAL BLDG CONTRACTORS - NONRESIDENTIAL BLDGS	2	1.739695	63.50%	36.50%	1.739695	63.50%	36.50%
160	HEAVY CONSTRUCTION OTHER THAN BLDG CONST - CONTRACTORS	8	4.324111	81.22%	18.78%	1.839932	64.79%	35.21%
162	WATER, SEWER, PIPELINE, COMM & POWER LINE CONSTRUCTION	8	1.258793	55.73%	44.27%	1.212859	54.81%	45.19%
170	CONSTRUCTION - SPECIAL TRADE CONTRACTORS	8	5.161045	83.77%	16.23%	1.749260	63.63%	36.37%
173	ELECTRICAL WORK	4	0.990993	49.77%	50.23%	0.943877	48.56%	51.44%
200	FOOD AND KINDRED PRODUCTS	7	1.916718	65.71%	34.29%	1.763700	63.82%	36.18%
201	MEAT PACKING PLANTS	6	1.497626	59.96%	40.04%	1.199355	54.53%	45.47%
202	DAIRY PRODUCTS	3	1.232594	55.21%	44.79%	0.495837	33.15%	66.85%
203	CANNED, FROZEN & PRESERVD FRUIT, VEG & FOOD SPECIALTIES	6	1.987274	66.52%	33.48%	1.184231	54.22%	45.78%
204	GRAIN MILL PRODUCTS	5	2.198312	68.73%	31.27%	1.071991	51.74%	48.26%
205	BAKERY PRODUCTS	4	0.684042	40.62%	59.38%	0.571851	36.38%	63.62%
206	SUGAR & CONFECTIONERY PRODUCTS	4	1.446322	59.12%	40.88%	0.374248	27.23%	72.77%
207	FATS & OILS	3	1.291131	56.35%	43.65%	1.178255	54.09%	45.91%
208	BEVERAGES	21	4.022082	80.09%	19.91%	1.251350	55.58%	44.42%
209	MISCELLANEOUS FOOD PREPARATIONS & KINDRED PRODUCTS	3	1.318614	56.87%	43.13%	0.572126	36.39%	63.61%
210	TOBACCO PRODUCTS	3	11.813716	92.20%	7.80%	4.293620	81.11%	18.89%
211	CIGARETTES	2	0.931843	48.24%	51.76%	0.931843	48.24%	51.76%
220	TEXTILE MILL PRODUCTS	2	3.327677	76.89%	23.11%	3.327677	76.89%	23.11%
222	BROADWOVEN FABRIC MILLS, MAN MADE FIBER & SILK	1	1.375501	57.90%	42.10%	1.375501	57.90%	42.10%
227	CARPETS & RUGS	3	1.567007	61.04%	38.96%	1.425391	58.77%	41.23%
230	APPAREL & OTHER FINISHD PRODS OF FABRICS & SIMILAR MATL	11	1.351643	57.48%	42.52%	0.984684	49.61%	50.39%
232	MEN'S & BOYS' FURNISHGS, WORK CLOTHG, & ALLIED GARMENTS	6	0.843487	45.75%	54.25%	0.728266	42.14%	57.86%

Positive Debt-to-equity Ratios

SIC	SIC Description	Number of Companies	Average			Median		
			Average Debt-to-equity Ratio	Debt Portion	Equity Portion	Median Debt-to-equity Ratio	Debt Portion	Equity Portion
233	WOMEN'S, MISSES', AND JUNIORS OUTERWEAR	3	2.197424	68.72%	31.28%	2.332424	69.99%	30.01%
234	WOMEN'S, MISSES', CHILDREN'S & INFANTS' UNDERGARMENTS	2	0.414794	29.32%	70.68%	0.414794	29.32%	70.68%
239	MISCELLANEOUS FABRICATED TEXTILE PRODUCTS	2	2.008852	66.76%	33.24%	2.008852	66.76%	33.24%
240	LUMBER & WOOD PRODUCTS (NO FURNITURE)	6	2.891713	74.30%	25.70%	1.728136	63.34%	36.66%
242	SAWMILLS & PLANTING MILLS, GENERAL	1	0.503739	33.50%	66.50%	0.503739	33.50%	66.50%
243	MILLWOOD, VENEER, PLYWOOD, & STRUCTURAL WOOD MEMBERS	4	12.296883	92.48%	7.52%	8.861226	89.86%	10.14%
245	MOBILE HOMES	2	0.309111	23.61%	76.39%	0.309111	23.61%	76.39%
251	HOUSEHOLD FURNITURE	7	4.584039	82.09%	17.91%	1.662035	62.43%	37.57%
252	OFFICE FURNITURE	2	1.495128	59.92%	40.08%	1.495128	59.92%	40.08%
253	PUBLIC BLDG & RELATED FURNITURE	1	0.986357	49.66%	50.34%	0.986357	49.66%	50.34%
259	MISCELLANEOUS FURNITURE & FIXTURES	1	1.400254	58.34%	41.66%	1.400254	58.34%	41.66%
261	PULP MILLS	1	2.132043	68.07%	31.93%	2.132043	68.07%	31.93%
262	PAPER MILLS	10	1.772896	63.94%	36.06%	1.517964	60.29%	39.71%
263	PAPERBOARD MILLS	1	2.131987	68.07%	31.93%	2.131987	68.07%	31.93%
265	PAPERBOARD CONTAINERS & BOXES	5	2.059095	67.31%	32.69%	1.839503	64.78%	35.22%
267	CONVERTED PAPER & PAPERBOARD PRODS (NO CONTANERS/BOXES)	6	5.639414	84.94%	15.06%	3.149299	75.90%	24.10%
271	NEWSPAPERS: PUBLISHING OR PUBLISHING & PRINTING	7	2.532944	71.69%	28.31%	1.028472	50.70%	49.30%
273	BOOKS: PUBLISHING OR PUBLISHING & PRINTING	1	2.223860	68.98%	31.02%	2.223860	68.98%	31.02%
274	MISCELLANEOUS PUBLISHING	1	4.173967	80.67%	19.33%	4.173967	80.67%	19.33%
275	COMMERCIAL PRINTING	4	3.479076	77.67%	22.33%	3.256159	76.50%	23.50%
276	MANIFOLD BUSINESS FORMS	1	0.258822	20.56%	79.44%	0.258822	20.56%	79.44%
278	BLANKBOOKS, LOOSELEAF BINDERS & BOOKBINDG & RELATD WORK	2	1.896049	65.47%	34.53%	1.896049	65.47%	34.53%
280	CHEMICALS & ALLIED PRODUCTS	14	2.801091	73.69%	26.31%	2.346347	70.12%	29.88%
281	INDUSTRIAL INORGANIC CHEMICALS	12	1.563673	60.99%	39.01%	1.370462	57.81%	42.19%
282	PLASTIC MATERIAL, SYNTH RESIN/RUBBER, CELLULOS (NO GLASS)	15	4.573563	82.06%	17.94%	1.919525	65.75%	34.25%
283	MEDICINAL CHEMICALS & BOTANICAL PRODUCTS	302	2.115654	67.90%	32.10%	0.581552	36.77%	63.23%
284	SOAP, DETERGENTS, CLEANG PREPARATIONS, PERFUMES, COSMETICS	16	4.177121	80.68%	19.32%	0.796583	44.34%	55.66%
285	PAINTS, VARNISHES, LACQUERS, ENAMELS & ALLIED PRODS	3	3.161531	75.97%	24.03%	3.716277	78.80%	21.20%
286	INDUSTRIAL ORGANIC CHEMICALS	31	1.374224	57.88%	42.12%	0.771719	43.56%	56.44%
287	AGRICULTURAL CHEMICALS	15	2.495813	71.39%	28.61%	1.047211	51.15%	48.85%
289	MISCELLANEOUS CHEMICAL PRODUCTS	13	5.040568	83.45%	16.55%	1.652449	62.30%	37.70%
291	PETROLEUM REFINING	18	2.226151	69.00%	31.00%	1.056123	51.36%	48.64%
299	MISCELLANEOUS PRODUCTS OF PETROLEUM & COAL	2	0.864349	46.36%	53.64%	0.864349	46.36%	53.64%
301	TIRES & INNER TUBES	2	1.858784	65.02%	34.98%	1.858784	65.02%	34.98%
302	RUBBER & PLASTICS FOOTWEAR	2	0.643825	39.17%	60.83%	0.643825	39.17%	60.83%
305	GASKETS, PACKG & SEALG DEVICES & RUBBER & PLASTICS HOSE	2	3.825215	79.28%	20.72%	3.825215	79.28%	20.72%
306	FABRICATED RUBBER PRODUCTS, NEC	5	3.912653	79.64%	20.36%	1.096191	52.29%	47.71%
308	MISCELLANEOUS PLASTICS PRODUCTS	19	1.406597	58.45%	41.55%	0.990066	49.75%	50.25%
310	LEATHER & LEATHER PRODUCTS	3	0.498451	33.26%	66.74%	0.258244	20.52%	79.48%
314	FOOTWEAR, (NO RUBBER)	5	0.704685	41.34%	58.66%	0.403894	28.77%	71.23%

Positive Debt-to-equity Ratios

SIC	SIC Description	Number of Companies	Average			Median		
			Average Debt-to-equity Ratio	Debt Portion	Equity Portion	Median Debt-to-equity Ratio	Debt Portion	Equity Portion
321	FLAT GLASS	1	2.846628	74.00%	26.00%	2.846628	74.00%	26.00%
322	GLASS & GLASSWARE, PRESSED OR BLOWN	3	6.556957	86.77%	13.23%	9.524271	90.50%	9.50%
323	GLASS PRODUCTS, MADE OF PURCHASED GLASS	2	2.698168	72.96%	27.04%	2.698168	72.96%	27.04%
324	CEMENT, HYDRAULIC	2	0.891215	47.12%	52.88%	0.891215	47.12%	52.88%
326	POTTERY & RELATED PRODUCTS	1	0.182588	15.44%	84.56%	0.182588	15.44%	84.56%
327	CONCRETE, GYPSUM & PLASTER PRODUCTS	6	3.202864	76.21%	23.79%	1.052879	51.29%	48.71%
328	CUT STONE & STONE PRODUCTS	1	0.354570	26.18%	73.82%	0.354570	26.18%	73.82%
329	ABRASIVE, ASBESTOS & MISC NONMETALLIC MINERAL PRODS	2	0.692788	40.93%	59.07%	0.692788	40.93%	59.07%
331	STEEL WORKS, BLAST FURNACES & ROLLING & FINISHING MILLS	19	2.954228	74.71%	25.29%	1.087798	52.10%	47.90%
333	PRIMARY SMELTING & REFINING OF NONFERROUS METALS	4	1.064218	51.56%	48.44%	1.019716	50.49%	49.51%
334	SECONDARY SMELTING & REFINING OF NONFERROUS METALS	2	13.894453	93.29%	6.71%	13.894453	93.29%	6.71%
335	ROLLING DRAWING & EXTRUDING OF NONFERROUS METALS	13	3.159248	75.96%	24.04%	1.198333	54.51%	45.49%
336	NONFERROUS FOUNDRIES (CASTINGS)	2	1.270420	55.96%	44.04%	1.270420	55.96%	44.04%
339	MISCELLANEOUS PRIMARY METAL PRODUCTS	3	1.463799	59.41%	40.59%	0.938737	48.42%	51.58%
341	METAL CANS	4	5.228923	83.95%	16.05%	4.153745	80.60%	19.40%
342	CUTLERY, HANDTOOLS & GENERAL HARDWARE	8	0.741113	42.57%	57.43%	0.837737	45.59%	54.41%
343	HEARING EQUIP, EXCEPT ELEC & WARM AIR; & PLUMBING FIXTURES	4	2.572502	72.01%	27.99%	1.990816	66.56%	33.44%
344	FABRICATED STRUCTURAL METAL PRODUCTS	14	2.964098	74.77%	25.23%	1.495333	59.93%	40.07%
346	METAL FORGINGS & STAMPINGS	5	1.928021	65.85%	34.15%	2.284726	69.56%	30.44%
347	COATING, ENGRAVING & ALLIED SERVICES	1	0.094640	8.65%	91.35%	0.094640	8.65%	91.35%
348	ORDNANCE & ACCESSORIES, (NO VEHICLES/GUIDED MISSILES)	4	0.631631	38.71%	61.29%	0.627309	38.55%	61.45%
349	MISCELLANEOUS FABRICATED METAL PRODUCTS	9	1.198614	54.52%	45.48%	1.094692	52.26%	47.74%
351	ENGINES & TURBINES	6	1.996209	66.62%	33.38%	1.460854	59.36%	40.64%
352	FARM MACHINERY & EQUIPMENT	6	1.783069	64.07%	35.93%	1.147249	53.43%	46.57%
353	CONSTRUCTION, MINING & MATERIALS HANDLING MACHINERY & EQUIP	23	1.346709	57.39%	42.61%	0.648856	39.35%	60.65%
354	METALWORKG MACHINERY & EQUIPMENT	8	1.493851	59.90%	40.10%	1.001646	50.04%	49.96%
355	SPECIAL INDUSTRY MACHINERY (NO METALWORKING MACHINERY)	18	0.892886	47.17%	52.83%	0.676748	40.36%	59.64%
356	GENERAL INDUSTRIAL MACHINERY & EQUIPMENT	24	1.442163	59.05%	40.95%	1.318776	56.87%	43.13%
357	COMPUTER & OFFICE EQUIPMENT	44	2.757832	73.39%	26.61%	1.054715	51.33%	48.67%
358	REFRIGERATION & SERVICE INDUSTRY MACHINERY	7	8.309527	89.26%	10.74%	1.453600	59.24%	40.76%
359	MISC INDUSTRIAL & COMMERCIAL MACHINERY & EQUIPMENT	6	1.118703	52.80%	47.20%	1.002551	50.06%	49.94%
360	ELECTRONIC & OTHER ELECTRICAL EQUIPMENT (NO COMPUTER EQUIP)	3	1.969203	66.32%	33.68%	1.233637	55.23%	44.77%
361	POWER, DISTRIBUTION & SPECIALTY TRANSFORMERS	4	1.494855	59.92%	40.08%	1.347281	57.40%	42.60%
362	ELECTRICAL INDUSTRIAL APPARATUS	13	1.251546	55.59%	44.41%	0.935644	48.34%	51.66%
363	HOUSEHOLD APPLIANCES	6	1.953343	66.14%	33.86%	0.857156	46.15%	53.85%
364	ELECTRIC LIGHTING & WIRING EQUIPMENT	7	0.767096	43.41%	56.59%	0.740874	42.56%	57.44%
365	HOUSEHOLD AUDIO & VIDEO EQUIPMENT	3	0.624343	38.44%	61.56%	0.368960	26.95%	73.05%
366	TELEPHONE & TELEGRAPH APPARATUS	56	2.159018	68.34%	31.66%	0.853769	46.06%	53.94%
367	ELECTRONIC COMPONENTS & ACCESSORIES	123	1.152344	53.54%	46.46%	0.706684	41.41%	58.59%
369	MISCELLANEOUS ELECTRICAL MACHINERY, EQUIPMENT & SUPPLIES	19	7.123369	87.69%	12.31%	1.925545	65.82%	34.18%

Positive Debt-to-equity Ratios

SIC	SIC Description	Number of Companies	Average			Median		
			Average Debt-to-equity Ratio	Debt Portion	Equity Portion	Median Debt-to-equity Ratio	Debt Portion	Equity Portion
371	MOTOR VEHICLES & PASSENGER CAR BODIES	50	2.618736	72.37%	27.63%	1.884635	65.33%	34.67%
372	AIRCRAFT & PARTS	15	16.585363	94.31%	5.69%	1.716486	63.19%	36.81%
373	SHIP & BOAT BUILDING & REPAIRING	3	1.689435	62.82%	37.18%	2.064801	67.37%	32.63%
374	RAILROAD EQUIPMENT	5	0.958282	48.93%	51.07%	1.003198	50.08%	49.92%
375	MOTORCYCLES, BICYCLES & PARTS	4	1.474817	59.59%	40.41%	0.704149	41.32%	58.68%
376	GUIDED MISSILES & SPACE VEHICLES & PARTS	3	7.943411	88.82%	11.18%	1.770660	63.91%	36.09%
379	MISCELLANEOUS TRANSPORTATION EQUIPMENT	1	2.303650	69.73%	30.27%	2.303650	69.73%	30.27%
381	SEARCH, DETECTION, NAVAGATION, GUIDANCE, AERONAUTICAL SYS	7	1.381631	58.01%	41.99%	0.975247	49.37%	50.63%
382	LABORATORY APPARATUS & FURNITURE	65	1.479692	59.67%	40.33%	0.700023	41.18%	58.82%
384	SURGICAL & MEDICAL INSTRUMENTS & APPARATUS	127	2.178428	68.54%	31.46%	0.765287	43.35%	56.65%
385	OPHTHALMIC GOODS	3	0.837754	45.59%	54.41%	0.582168	36.80%	63.20%
386	PHOTOGRAPHIC EQUIPMENT & SUPPLIES	7	4.364429	81.36%	18.64%	0.678939	40.44%	59.56%
387	WATCHES, CLOCKS, CLOCKWORK OPERATED DEVICES/PARTS	2	1.113386	52.68%	47.32%	1.113386	52.68%	47.32%
391	JEWELRY, SILVERWARE & PLATED WARE	1	0.182797	15.45%	84.55%	0.182797	15.45%	84.55%
394	DOLLS & STUFFED TOYS	15	1.521070	60.33%	39.67%	1.038400	50.94%	49.06%
399	MISCELLANEOUS MANUFACTURING INDUSTRIES	9	20.436399	95.34%	4.66%	1.361663	57.66%	42.34%
401	RAILROADS, LINE-HAUL OPERATING	9	1.389180	58.14%	41.86%	1.182957	54.19%	45.81%
421	TRUCKING & COURIER SERVICES (NO AIR)	17	3.499795	77.78%	22.22%	0.761982	43.25%	56.75%
440	WATER TRANSPORTATION	21	1.363399	57.69%	42.31%	1.318717	56.87%	43.13%
441	DEEP SEA FOREIGN TRANSPORTATION OF FREIGHT	36	1.402759	58.38%	41.62%	1.054794	51.33%	48.67%
451	AIR TRANSPORTATION, SCHEDULED	11	3.162443	75.98%	24.02%	2.400468	70.59%	29.41%
452	AIR TRANSPORTATION, NONSCHEDULED	4	1.375201	57.90%	42.10%	1.481672	59.70%	40.30%
458	AIRPORTS, FLYING FIELDS & AIRPORT TERMINAL SERVICES	1	0.265005	20.95%	79.05%	0.265005	20.95%	79.05%
461	PIPE LINES (NO NATURAL GAS)	17	5.848924	85.40%	14.60%	1.404095	58.40%	41.60%
470	TRANSPORTATION SERVICES	8	1.777705	64.00%	36.00%	2.080049	67.53%	32.47%
473	ARRANGEMENT OF TRANSPORTATION OF FREIGHT & CARGO	8	1.952051	66.13%	33.87%	1.252864	55.61%	44.39%
481	RADIOTELEPHONE COMMUNICATIONS	30	11.021083	91.68%	8.32%	2.226739	69.01%	30.99%
482	TELEGRAPH & OTHER MESSAGE COMMUNICATIONS	3	1.786572	64.11%	35.89%	1.404274	58.41%	41.59%
483	RADIO BROADCASTING STATIONS	20	3.567745	78.11%	21.89%	1.556000	60.88%	39.12%
484	CABLE & OTHER PAY TELEVISION SERVICES	21	3.645767	78.48%	21.52%	1.903018	65.55%	34.45%
489	COMMUNICATIONS SERVICES, NEC	11	2.029303	66.99%	33.01%	1.982436	66.47%	33.53%
490	ELECTRIC, GAS & SANITARY SERVICES	1	4.888211	83.02%	16.98%	4.888211	83.02%	16.98%
491	ELECTRIC SERVICES	57	3.777996	79.07%	20.93%	2.380080	70.41%	29.59%
492	NATURAL GAS TRANSMISSION	49	2.572471	72.01%	27.99%	1.493647	59.90%	40.10%
493	ELECTRIC & OTHER SERVICES COMBINED	26	2.204767	68.80%	31.20%	2.189007	68.64%	31.36%
494	WATER SUPPLY	12	2.796988	73.66%	26.34%	2.104273	67.79%	32.21%
495	SANITARY SERVICES	10	1.522007	60.35%	39.65%	1.438794	59.00%	41.00%
499	COGENERATION SERVICES & SMALL POWER PRODUCERS	3	5.028053	83.41%	16.59%	5.661506	84.99%	15.01%
500	WHOLESALE-DURABLE GOODS	4	1.585697	61.33%	38.67%	1.925892	65.82%	34.18%
501	WHOLESALE-MOTOR VEHICLES & MOTOR VEHICLE PARTS & SUPPLIES	2	1.907135	65.60%	34.40%	1.907135	65.60%	34.40%

Positive Debt-to-equity Ratios

SIC	SIC Description	Number of Companies	Average			Median		
			Average Debt-to-equity Ratio	Debt Portion	Equity Portion	Median Debt-to-equity Ratio	Debt Portion	Equity Portion
503	WHOLESALE-LUMBER & OTHER CONSTRUCTION MATERIALS	9	3.319125	76.85%	23.15%	1.382618	58.03%	41.97%
504	WHOLESALE-PROFESSIONAL & COMMERCIAL EQUIPMENT & SUPPLIES	7	1.796448	64.24%	35.76%	1.653569	62.31%	37.69%
505	WHOLESALE-METALS & MINERALS (NO PETROLEUM)	4	3.087564	75.54%	24.46%	1.461836	59.38%	40.62%
506	WHOLESALE-ELECTRICAL APPARATUS & EQUIPMENT, WIRING SUPPLIES	16	1.020068	50.50%	49.50%	0.939170	48.43%	51.57%
507	WHOLESALE-HARDWARE & PLUMBING & HEATING EQUIPMENT & SUPPLIES	3	1.275074	56.05%	43.95%	1.699743	62.96%	37.04%
508	WHOLESALE-MACHINERY, EQUIPMENT & SUPPLIES	9	3.295275	76.72%	23.28%	1.603776	61.59%	38.41%
509	WHOLESALE-MISC DURABLE GOODS	4	1.448640	59.16%	40.84%	0.839797	45.65%	54.35%
511	WHOLESALE-PAPER & PAPER PRODUCTS	2	3.256009	76.50%	23.50%	3.256009	76.50%	23.50%
512	WHOLESALE-DRUGS, PROPRIETARIES & DRUGGISTS' SUNDRIES	4	5.833320	85.37%	14.63%	3.057617	75.35%	24.65%
513	WHOLESALE-APPAREL, PIECE GOODS & NOTIONS	2	0.658334	39.70%	60.30%	0.658334	39.70%	60.30%
514	WHOLESALE-GROCERIES & RELATED PRODUCTS	11	2.476003	71.23%	28.77%	1.847561	64.88%	35.12%
515	WHOLESALE-FARM PRODUCT RAW MATERIALS	5	1.256001	55.67%	44.33%	1.020504	50.51%	49.49%
516	WHOLESALE-CHEMICALS & ALLIED PRODUCTS	4	2.260262	69.33%	30.67%	1.714130	63.16%	36.84%
517	WHOLESALE-PETROLEUM BULK STATIONS & TERMINALS	10	3.329188	76.90%	23.10%	2.464235	71.13%	28.87%
518	WHOLESALE-BEER, WINE & DISTILLED ALCOHOLIC BEVERAGES	2	0.550368	35.50%	64.50%	0.550368	35.50%	64.50%
519	WHOLESALE-MISCELLANEOUS NONDURABLE GOODS	3	1.277398	56.09%	43.91%	1.051200	51.25%	48.75%
520	RETAIL-BUILDING MATERIALS, HARDWARE, GARDEN SUPPLY	4	1.509205	60.15%	39.85%	0.705075	41.35%	58.65%
521	RETAIL-LUMBER & OTHER BUILDING MATERIALS DEALERS	7	6.458549	86.59%	13.41%	1.411579	58.53%	41.47%
531	RETAIL-DEPARTMENT STORES	7	8.343986	89.30%	10.70%	2.423600	70.79%	29.21%
533	RETAIL-VARIETY STORES	10	1.370868	57.82%	42.18%	1.370409	57.81%	42.19%
540	RETAIL-FOOD STORES	1	1.501717	60.03%	39.97%	1.501717	60.03%	39.97%
541	RETAIL-GROCERY STORES	9	1.699565	62.96%	37.04%	1.240695	55.37%	44.63%
550	RETAIL-AUTO DEALERS & GASOLINE STATIONS	14	4.658801	82.33%	17.67%	3.333923	76.93%	23.07%
553	RETAIL-AUTO & HOME SUPPLY STORES	4	3.672782	78.60%	21.40%	1.489313	59.83%	40.17%
560	RETAIL-APPAREL & ACCESSORY STORES	10	93.009711	98.94%	1.06%	0.812151	44.82%	55.18%
562	RETAIL-WOMEN'S CLOTHING STORES	5	1.618366	61.81%	38.19%	1.367910	57.77%	42.23%
565	RETAIL-FAMILY CLOTHING STORES	13	2.309854	69.79%	30.21%	1.343426	57.33%	42.67%
566	RETAIL-SHOE STORES	6	0.705347	41.36%	58.64%	0.534614	34.84%	65.16%
570	RETAIL-HOME FURNITURE, FURNISHINGS & EQUIPMENT STORES	6	1.458886	59.33%	40.67%	1.380784	58.00%	42.00%
571	RETAIL-FURNITURE STORES	1	0.568388	36.24%	63.76%	0.568388	36.24%	63.76%
573	RETAIL-RADIO, TV & CONSUMER ELECTRONICS STORES	4	1.752164	63.66%	36.34%	1.914537	65.69%	34.31%
581	RETAIL-EATING & DRINKING PLACES	48	12.906495	92.81%	7.19%	1.284017	56.22%	43.78%
590	RETAIL-MISCELLANEOUS RETAIL	10	1.436049	58.95%	41.05%	1.003146	50.08%	49.92%
591	RETAIL-DRUG STORES AND PROPRIETARY STORES	7	2.566734	71.96%	28.04%	1.588953	61.37%	38.63%
594	RETAIL-MISCELLANEOUS SHOPPING GOODS STORES	9	1.658139	62.38%	37.62%	1.090567	52.17%	47.83%
596	RETAIL-NONSTORE RETAILERS	19	2.238371	69.12%	30.88%	1.603399	61.59%	38.41%
599	RETAIL-RETAIL STORES, NEC	11	1.691474	62.85%	37.15%	1.201853	54.58%	45.42%
602	NATIONAL COMMERCIAL BANKS	335	8.633553	89.62%	10.38%	8.351321	89.31%	10.69%
603	SAVINGS INSTITUTION, FEDERALLY CHARTERED	84	7.655570	88.45%	11.55%	7.622099	88.40%	11.60%
609	FUNCTIONS RELATED TO DEPOSITORY BANKING, NEC	2	2.878220	74.21%	25.79%	2.878220	74.21%	25.79%

Positive Debt-to-equity Ratios

SIC	SIC Description	Number of Companies	Average: Average Debt-to-equity Ratio	Average: Debt Portion	Average: Equity Portion	Median: Median Debt-to-equity Ratio	Median: Debt Portion	Median: Equity Portion
611	FEDERAL & FEDERALLY-SPONSORED CREDIT AGENCIES	12	19.017612	95.00%	5.00%	18.929725	94.98%	5.02%
614	PERSONAL CREDIT INSTITUTIONS	14	3.750578	78.95%	21.05%	2.790405	73.62%	26.38%
615	SHORT-TERM BUSINESS CREDIT INSTITUTIONS	12	7.445716	88.16%	11.84%	7.009256	87.51%	12.49%
616	MORTGAGE BANKERS & LOAN CORRESPONDENTS	4	7.118995	87.68%	12.32%	6.379227	86.45%	13.55%
617	FINANCE LESSORS	1	11.386838	91.93%	8.07%	11.386838	91.93%	8.07%
619	FINANCE SERVICES	17	4.269137	81.02%	18.98%	2.108121	67.83%	32.17%
620	SECURITY & COMMODITY BROKERS, DEALERS, EXCHANGES & SERVICES	11	2.774112	73.50%	26.50%	1.681501	62.71%	37.29%
621	SECURITY BROKERS, DEALERS & FLOTATION COMPANIES	28	6.796458	87.17%	12.83%	3.992258	79.97%	20.03%
622	COMMODITY CONTRACTS BROKERS & DEALERS	41	0.271605	21.36%	78.64%	0.026661	2.60%	97.40%
628	INVESTMENT ADVICE	34	2.282278	69.53%	30.47%	0.938774	48.42%	51.58%
631	LIFE INSURANCE	42	11.996260	92.31%	7.69%	8.492675	89.47%	10.53%
632	ACCIDENT & HEALTH INSURANCE	17	4.223726	80.86%	19.14%	2.482414	71.28%	28.72%
633	FIRE, MARINE & CASUALTY INSURANCE	67	3.188780	76.13%	23.87%	2.835086	73.92%	26.08%
635	SURETY INSURANCE	8	3.196633	76.17%	23.83%	1.038666	50.95%	49.05%
636	TITLE INSURANCE	4	1.047555	51.16%	48.84%	1.021336	50.53%	49.47%
639	INSURANCE CARRIERS, NEC	3	4.523606	81.90%	18.10%	3.902579	79.60%	20.40%
641	INSURANCE AGENTS, BROKERS & SERVICE	11	2.515057	71.55%	28.45%	1.745095	63.57%	36.43%
650	REAL ESTATE	48	1.504443	60.07%	39.93%	0.719290	41.84%	58.16%
651	REAL ESTATE OPERATORS (NO DEVELOPERS) & LESSORS	15	1.237380	55.30%	44.70%	0.972553	49.30%	50.70%
653	REAL ESTATE AGENTS & MANAGERS (FOR OTHERS)	9	1.655549	62.34%	37.66%	1.441318	59.04%	40.96%
655	LAND SUBDIVIDERS & DEVELOPERS (NO CEMETERIES)	4	0.862729	46.32%	53.68%	0.479217	32.40%	67.60%
677	BLANK CHECKS	8	19.115702	95.03%	4.97%	1.236417	55.29%	44.71%
679	OIL ROYALTY TRADERS	304	2.146359	68.22%	31.78%	1.199052	54.53%	45.47%
700	HOTELS, ROOMING HOUSES, CAMPS & OTHER LODGING PLACES	3	1.536074	60.57%	39.43%	0.792550	44.21%	55.79%
701	HOTELS & MOTELS	28	3.004742	75.03%	24.97%	1.804023	64.34%	35.66%
720	SERVICES-PERSONAL SERVICES	10	2.059528	67.32%	32.68%	0.461205	31.56%	68.44%
731	SERVICES-ADVERTISING	14	2.438531	70.92%	29.08%	0.757581	43.10%	56.90%
732	SERVICES-CONSUMER CREDIT REPORTING, COLLECTION AGENCIES	5	3.530646	77.93%	22.07%	2.242374	69.16%	30.84%
733	SERVICES-MAILING, REPRODUCTION, COMMERCIAL ART & PHOTOGRAPHY	1	1.466554	59.46%	40.54%	1.466554	59.46%	40.54%
734	SERVICES-TO DWELLINGS & OTHER BUILDINGS	2	1.176049	54.05%	45.95%	1.176049	54.05%	45.95%
735	SERVICES-MISCELLANEOUS EQUIPMENT RENTAL & LEASING	39	2.083745	67.57%	32.43%	1.469997	59.51%	40.49%
736	SERVICES-EMPLOYMENT AGENCIES	22	2.349160	70.14%	29.86%	1.408141	58.47%	41.53%
737	SERVICES-COMPUTER PROGRAMMING, DATA PROCESSING, ETC.	253	3.266451	76.56%	23.44%	0.868290	46.48%	53.52%
738	SERVICES-MISCELLANEOUS BUSINESS SERVICES	96	3.333886	76.93%	23.07%	1.250082	55.56%	44.44%
750	SERVICES-AUTOMOTIVE REPAIR, SERVICES & PARKING	1	0.938708	48.42%	51.58%	0.938708	48.42%	51.58%
751	SERVICES-AUTO RENTAL & LEASING (NO DRIVERS)	6	8.385215	89.34%	10.66%	2.596184	72.19%	27.81%
760	SERVICES-MISCELLANEOUS REPAIR SERVICES	3	9.550381	90.52%	9.48%	1.649093	62.25%	37.75%
781	SERVICES-MOTION PICTURE & VIDEO TAPE PRODUCTION	7	0.678869	40.44%	59.56%	0.273492	21.48%	78.52%
782	SERVICES-MOTION PICTURE & VIDEO TAPE DISTRIBUTION	1	8.495528	89.47%	10.53%	8.495528	89.47%	10.53%
783	SERVICES-MOTION PICTURE THEATERS	5	2.119645	67.95%	32.05%	2.155368	68.31%	31.69%

Positive Debt-to-equity Ratios

SIC	SIC Description	Number of Companies	Average			Median		
			Average Debt-to-equity Ratio	Debt Portion	Equity Portion	Median Debt-to-equity Ratio	Debt Portion	Equity Portion
784	SERVICES-VIDEO TAPE RENTAL	1	4.307921	81.16%	18.84%	4.307921	81.16%	18.84%
790	SERVICES-AMUSEMENT & RECREATION SERVICES	7	3.642246	78.46%	21.54%	0.474393	32.18%	67.82%
794	SERVICES-RACING, INCLUDING TRACK OPERATION	4	1.028739	50.71%	49.29%	0.545350	35.29%	64.71%
799	SERVICES-MISCELLANEOUS AMUSEMENT & RECREATION	12	4.123397	80.48%	19.52%	2.239455	69.13%	30.87%
800	SERVICES-HEALTH SERVICES	1	0.535449	34.87%	65.13%	0.535449	34.87%	65.13%
801	SERVICES-OFFICES & CLINICS OF DOCTORS OF MEDICINE	2	0.880247	46.82%	53.18%	0.880247	46.82%	53.18%
805	SERVICES-NURSING & PERSONAL CARE FACILITIES	9	7.377358	88.06%	11.94%	4.015679	80.06%	19.94%
806	SERVICES-HOSPITALS	11	6.051201	85.82%	14.18%	1.405944	58.44%	41.56%
807	SERVICES-MEDICAL LABORATORIES	16	2.023069	66.92%	33.08%	0.948877	48.69%	51.31%
808	SERVICES-HOME HEALTH CARE SERVICES	5	1.557003	60.89%	39.11%	0.575215	36.52%	63.48%
809	SERVICES-MISC HEALTH & ALLIED SERVICES, NEC	12	2.308040	69.77%	30.23%	1.413771	58.57%	41.43%
811	SERVICES-LEGAL SERVICES	1	0.745687	42.72%	57.28%	0.745687	42.72%	57.28%
820	SERVICES-EDUCATIONAL SERVICES	19	1.254061	55.64%	44.36%	0.740784	42.55%	57.45%
830	SERVICES-SOCIAL SERVICES	1	0.418929	29.52%	70.48%	0.418929	29.52%	70.48%
835	SERVICES-CHILD DAY CARE SERVICES	1	2.295655	69.66%	30.34%	2.295655	69.66%	30.34%
870	SERVICES-ENGINEERING, ACCOUNTING, RESEARCH, MANAGEMENT	2	1.219076	54.94%	45.06%	1.219076	54.94%	45.06%
871	SERVICES-ENGINEERING SERVICES	10	2.183251	68.59%	31.41%	1.048236	51.18%	48.82%
873	SERVICES-COMMERCIAL PHYSICAL & BIOLOGICAL RESEARCH	19	1.308258	56.68%	43.32%	0.802366	44.52%	55.48%
874	SERVICES-MANAGEMENT SERVICES	33	1.792628	64.19%	35.81%	0.893704	47.19%	52.81%

Table of Contents for SIC Codes

Table of Contents for SIC Codes

Sorted by description

Disclaimer: some SIC codes may not appear in this book.
Sorted by description

SIC Code	Description	Dvision Description
3291	Abrasive Products	Manufacturing
3290	Abrasive, Asbestos & Misc Nonmetallic Mineral Prods	Manufacturing
329	Abrasive, Asbestos, And Miscellaneous Nonmetallic Mineral Products	Manufacturing
6321	Accident & Health Insurance	Finance, Insurance, And Real Estate
6321	Accident And Health Insurance	Finance, Insurance, And Real Estate
632	Accident And Health Insurance And Medical Service Plans	Finance, Insurance, And Real Estate
872	Accounting, Auditing, And Bookkeeping Services	Services
8721	Accounting, Auditing, And Bookkeeping Services	Services
2282	Acetate Filament Yarn: Throwing, Twisting, Winding, Or Spooling	Manufacturing
2891	Adhesives & Sealants	Manufacturing
2891	Adhesives And Sealants	Manufacturing
7322	Adjustment And Collection Services	Services
96	Administration Of Economic Programs	Public Adminstration
941	Administration Of Educational Programs	Public Adminstration
9411	Administration Of Educational Programs	Public Adminstration
95	Administration Of Environmental Quality And Housing Programs	Public Adminstration
951	Administration Of Environmental Quality Programs	Public Adminstration
961	Administration Of General Economic Programs	Public Adminstration
9611	Administration Of General Economic Programs	Public Adminstration
953	Administration Of Housing And Urban Development Programs	Public Adminstration
9531	Administration Of Housing Programs	Public Adminstration
94	Administration Of Human Resource Programs	Public Adminstration
943	Administration Of Public Health Programs	Public Adminstration
9431	Administration Of Public Health Programs	Public Adminstration
944	Administration Of Social, Human Resource And Income Maintenance Programs	Public Adminstration
9441	Administration Of Social, Human Resource And Income Maintenance Programs	Public Adminstration
9532	Administration Of Urban Planning And Community And Rural Developmemt	Public Adminstration
945	Administration Of Veterans' Affairs, Except Health And Insurance	Public Adminstration
9451	Administration Of Veterans' Affairs, Except Health And Insurance	Public Adminstration
731	Advertising	Services
7311	Advertising Agencies	Services
7319	Advertising, Not Elsewhere Classified	Services
287	Agricultural Chemicals	Manufacturing
2870	Agricultural Chemicals	Manufacturing
01	Agricultural Production-Crops	Agriculture, Forestry, And Fishing
02	Agricultural Production-Livestock And Animal Specialties	Agriculture, Forestry, And Fishing
07	Agricultural Services	Agriculture, Forestry, And Fishing
3563	Air And Gas Compressors	Manufacturing
9511	Air And Water Resource And Solid Waste Management	Public Adminstration
4513	Air Courier Services	Transportation, Communications, Electric, Gas, And Sanitary Service
4513	Air Courier Services	Transportation, Communications, Electric, Gas, And Sanitary Service
452	Air Transportation, Nonscheduled	Transportation, Communications, Electric, Gas, And Sanitary Service
4522	Air Transportation, Nonscheduled	Transportation, Communications, Electric, Gas, And Sanitary Service
4522	Air Transportation, Nonscheduled	Transportation, Communications, Electric, Gas, And Sanitary Service
4512	Air Transportation, Scheduled	Transportation, Communications, Electric, Gas, And Sanitary Service
4512	Air Transportation, Scheduled	Transportation, Communications, Electric, Gas, And Sanitary Service
451	Air Transportation, Scheduled, And Air Courier Services	Transportation, Communications, Electric, Gas, And Sanitary Service
3585	Air-Cond & Warm Air Heatg Equip & Comm & Indl Refrig Equip	Manufacturing
3585	Air-Conditioning And Warm Air Heating Equipment	Manufacturing
3721	Aircraft	Manufacturing
3721	Aircraft	Manufacturing
3720	Aircraft & Parts	Manufacturing
372	Aircraft And Parts	Manufacturing
3724	Aircraft Engines & Engine Parts	Manufacturing
3724	Aircraft Engines And Engine Parts	Manufacturing
3728	Aircraft Parts & Auxiliary Equipment, Nec	Manufacturing
3728	Aircraft Parts And Auxiliary Equipment, Not Elsewhere Classified	Manufacturing
4581	Airports, Flying Fields & Airport Terminal Services	Transportation, Communications, Electric, Gas, And Sanitary Service
458	Airports, Flying Fields, And Airport Terminal Services	Transportation, Communications, Electric, Gas, And Sanitary Service
4581	Airports, Flying Fields, And Airport Terminal Services	Transportation, Communications, Electric, Gas, And Sanitary Service
2812	Alkalies And Chlorine	Manufacturing
3363	Aluminum Die-Castings	Manufacturing
3354	Aluminum Extruded Products	Manufacturing

Table of Contents for SIC Codes

Sorted by description

SIC Code	Description	Dvision Description
3365	Aluminum Foundries	Manufacturing
3355	Aluminum Rolling And Drawing, Not Elsewhere Classified	Manufacturing
3353	Aluminum Sheet, Plate, And Foil	Manufacturing
8880	American Depositary Receipts	Services
3483	Ammunition, Except For Small Arms	Manufacturing
79	Amusement And Recreation Services	Services
7999	Amusement And Recreation Services, Not Elsewhere Classified	Services
7996	Amusement Parks	Services
2077	Animal And Marine Fats And Oils	Manufacturing
0273	Animal Aquaculture	Agriculture, Forestry, And Fishing
075	Animal Services, Except Veterinary	Agriculture, Forestry, And Fishing
027	Animal Specialties	Agriculture, Forestry, And Fishing
0279	Animal Specialties, Not Elsewhere Classified	Agriculture, Forestry, And Fishing
0752	Animal Specialty Services, Except Veterinary	Agriculture, Forestry, And Fishing
123	Anthracite Mining	Mining
1231	Anthracite Mining	Mining
2300	Apparel & Other Finishd Prods Of Fabrics & Similar Matl	Manufacturing
2389	Apparel And Accessories, Not Elsewhere Classified	Manufacturing
56	Apparel And Accessory Stores	Retail Trade
23	Apparel And Other Finished Products Made From Fabrics And Similar Material	Manufacturing
2387	Apparel Belts	Manufacturing
513	Apparel, Piece Goods, And Notions	Wholesale Trade
842	Arboreta And Botanical Or Zoological Gardens	Services
8422	Arboreta And Botanical Or Zoological Gardens	Services
3446	Architectural And Ornamental Metalwork	Manufacturing
8712	Architectural Services	Services
7694	Armature Rewinding Shops	Services
472	Arrangement Of Passenger Transportation	Transportation, Communications, Electric, Gas, And Sanitary Service
4729	Arrangement Of Passenger Transportation, Not Elsewhere Classified	Transportation, Communications, Electric, Gas, And Sanitary Service
4731	Arrangement Of Transportation Of Freight & Cargo	Transportation, Communications, Electric, Gas, And Sanitary Service
473	Arrangement Of Transportation Of Freight And Cargo	Transportation, Communications, Electric, Gas, And Sanitary Service
4731	Arrangement Of Transportation Of Freight And Cargo	Transportation, Communications, Electric, Gas, And Sanitary Service
3292	Asbestos Products	Manufacturing
2952	Asphalt Felts And Coatings	Manufacturing
2950	Asphalt Paving & Roofing Materials	Manufacturing
295	Asphalt Paving And Roofing Materials	Manufacturing
2951	Asphalt Paving Mixtures And Blocks	Manufacturing
6189	Asset-Backed Securities	Finance, Insurance, And Real Estate
553	Auto And Home Supply Stores	Retail Trade
5531	Auto And Home Supply Stores	Retail Trade
3822	Auto Controls For Regulating Residential & Comml Environments	Manufacturing
3822	Automatic Controls For Regulating Residential And Commercial Environment	Manufacturing
5962	Automatic Merchandising Machine Operators	Retail Trade
3581	Automatic Vending Machines	Manufacturing
752	Automobile Parking	Services
7521	Automobile Parking	Services
5012	Automobiles And Other Motor Vehicles	Wholesale Trade
55	Automotive Dealers And Gasoline Service Stations	Retail Trade
559	Automotive Dealers, Not Elsewhere Classified	Retail Trade
5599	Automotive Dealers, Not Elsewhere Classified	Retail Trade
7533	Automotive Exhaust System Repair Shops	Services
7536	Automotive Glass Replacement Shops	Services
751	Automotive Rental And Leasing, Without Drivers	Services
753	Automotive Repair Shops	Services
7539	Automotive Repair Shops, Not Elsewhere Classified	Services
75	Automotive Repair, Services, And Parking	Services
754	Automotive Services, Except Repair	Services
7549	Automotive Services, Except Repair And Carwashes	Services
3465	Automotive Stampings	Manufacturing
7537	Automotive Transmission Repair Shops	Services
2396	Automotive Trimmings, Apparel Findings, And Related Products	Manufacturing
205	Bakery Products	Manufacturing
2050	Bakery Products	Manufacturing
3562	Ball & Roller Bearings	Manufacturing
3562	Ball And Roller Bearings	Manufacturing
7929	Bands, Orchestras, Actors, And Other Entertainers And Entertainment	Services

Table of Contents for SIC Codes

Sorted by description

SIC Code	Description	Dvision Description
724	Barber Shops	Services
7241	Barber Shops	Services
723	Beauty Shops	Services
7231	Beauty Shops	Services
0211	Beef Cattle Feedlots	Agriculture, Forestry, And Fishing
0212	Beef Cattle, Except Feedlots	Agriculture, Forestry, And Fishing
5181	Beer And Ale	Wholesale Trade
518	Beer, Wine, And Distilled Alcoholic Beverages	Wholesale Trade
2063	Beet Sugar	Manufacturing
0171	Berry Crops	Agriculture, Forestry, And Fishing
208	Beverages	Manufacturing
2080	Beverages	Manufacturing
2836	Biological Products, (No Disgnostic Substances)	Manufacturing
2836	Biological Products, Except Diagnostic Substances	Manufacturing
1220	Bituminous Coal & Lignite Mining	Mining
1221	Bituminous Coal & Lignite Surface Mining	Mining
122	Bituminous Coal And Lignite Mining	Mining
1221	Bituminous Coal And Lignite Surface Mining	Mining
1222	Bituminous Coal Underground Mining	Mining
6770	Blank Checks	Finance, Insurance, And Real Estate
2780	Blankbooks, Looseleaf Binders & Bookbindg & Relatd Work	Manufacturing
2782	Blankbooks, Looseleaf Binders And Devices	Manufacturing
278	Blankbooks, Looseleaf Binders, And Bookbinding And Related Work	Manufacturing
3524	Blowers, Residential Lawn	Manufacturing
3732	Boat Building And Repairing	Manufacturing
555	Boat Dealers	Retail Trade
5551	Boat Dealers	Retail Trade
3452	Bolts, Nuts, Screws, Rivets & Washers	Manufacturing
3452	Bolts, Nuts, Screws, Rivets, And Washers	Manufacturing
2732	Book Printing	Manufacturing
2732	Book Printing	Manufacturing
5942	Book Stores	Retail Trade
2789	Bookbinding And Related Work	Manufacturing
273	Books	Manufacturing
5192	Books, Periodicals, And Newspapers	Wholesale Trade
2731	Books: Publishing Or Publishing & Printing	Manufacturing
2731	Books: Publishing, Or Publishing And Printing	Manufacturing
313	Boot And Shoe Cut Stock And Findings	Manufacturing
3131	Boot And Shoe Cut Stock And Findings	Manufacturing
2086	Bottled & Canned Soft Drinks & Carbonated Waters	Manufacturing
2086	Bottled And Canned Soft Drinks And Carbonated Waters	Manufacturing
793	Bowling Centers	Services
7933	Bowling Centers	Services
6081	Branches And Agencies Of Foreign Banks	Finance, Insurance, And Real Estate
2342	Brassieres, Girdles, And Allied Garments	Manufacturing
2051	Bread And Other Bakery Products, Except Cookies And Crackers	Manufacturing
3251	Brick And Structural Clay Tile	Manufacturing
5032	Brick, Stone, And Related Construction Materials	Wholesale Trade
1622	Bridge, Tunnel, And Elevated Highway Construction	Construction
221	Broadwoven Fabric Mills, Cotton	Manufacturing
2211	Broadwoven Fabric Mills, Cotton	Manufacturing
2211	Broadwoven Fabric Mills, Cotton	Manufacturing
2221	Broadwoven Fabric Mills, Man Made Fiber & Silk	Manufacturing
222	Broadwoven Fabric Mills, Manmade Fiber And Silk	Manufacturing
2221	Broadwoven Fabric Mills, Manmade Fiber And Silk	Manufacturing
223	Broadwoven Fabric Mills, Wool (Including Dyeing And Finishing)	Manufacturing
2231	Broadwoven Fabric Mills, Wool (Including Dyeing And Finishing)	Manufacturing
0251	Broiler, Fryer, And Roaster Chickens	Agriculture, Forestry, And Fishing
3991	Brooms And Brushes	Manufacturing
7349	Building Cleaning And Maintenance Services, Not Elsewhere Classified	Services
15	Building Construction-General Contractors And Operative Builders	Construction
52	Building Materials, Hardware, Garden Supply, And Mobile Home Dealers	Retail Trade
3995	Burial Caskets	Manufacturing
414	Bus Charter Service	Transportation, Communications, Electric, Gas, And Sanitary Service
4142	Bus Charter Service, Except Local	Transportation, Communications, Electric, Gas, And Sanitary Service
8244	Business And Secretarial Schools	Services

Table of Contents for SIC Codes

Sorted by description

SIC Code	Description	Dvision Description
861	Business Associations	Services
8611	Business Associations	Services
8748	Business Consulting Services, Not Elsewhere Classified	Services
615	Business Credit Institutions	Finance, Insurance, And Real Estate
73	Business Services	Services
7389	Business Services, Not Elsewhere Classified	Services
4841	Cable & Other Pay Television Services	Transportation, Communications, Electric, Gas, And Sanitary Service
484	Cable And Other Pay Television Services	Transportation, Communications, Electric, Gas, And Sanitary Service
4841	Cable And Other Pay Television Services	Transportation, Communications, Electric, Gas, And Sanitary Service
3578	Calculating & Accounting Machines (No Electronic Computers)	Manufacturing
3578	Calculating And Accounting Machines, Except Electronic Computers	Manufacturing
5946	Camera And Photographic Supply Stores	Retail Trade
703	Camps And Recreational Vehicle Parks	Services
2064	Candy And Other Confectionery Products	Manufacturing
544	Candy, Nut, And Confectionery Stores	Retail Trade
5441	Candy, Nut, And Confectionery Stores	Retail Trade
2062	Cane Sugar Refining	Manufacturing
2061	Cane Sugar, Except Refining	Manufacturing
2091	Canned And Cured Fish And Seafoods	Manufacturing
2033	Canned Fruits, Vegetables, Preserves, Jams, And Jellies	Manufacturing
2032	Canned Specialties	Manufacturing
2030	Canned, Frozen & Preservd Fruit, Veg & Food Specialties	Manufacturing
203	Canned, Frozen, And Preserved Fruits, Vegetables, And Food Special	Manufacturing
2033	Canned, Fruits, Veg, Preserves, Jams & Jellies	Manufacturing
2394	Canvas And Related Products	Manufacturing
3624	Carbon And Graphite Products	Manufacturing
2895	Carbon Black	Manufacturing
3955	Carbon Paper And Inked Ribbons	Manufacturing
3592	Carburetors, Pistons, Piston Rings, And Valves	Manufacturing
4785	Cargo Checkers And Surveyors, Marine	Transportation, Communications, Electric, Gas, And Sanitary Service
175	Carpentry And Floor Work	Construction
1751	Carpentry Work	Construction
7217	Carpet And Upholstery Cleaning	Services
2273	Carpets & Rugs	Manufacturing
227	Carpets And Rugs	Manufacturing
2273	Carpets And Rugs	Manufacturing
7542	Carwashes	Services
011	Cash Grains	Agriculture, Forestry, And Fishing
0119	Cash Grains, Not Elsewhere Classified	Agriculture, Forestry, And Fishing
5961	Catalog And Mail-Order Houses	Retail Trade
2823	Cellulosic Manmade Fibers	Manufacturing
324	Cement, Hydraulic	Manufacturing
3241	Cement, Hydraulic	Manufacturing
3241	Cement, Hydraulic	Manufacturing
6553	Cemetery Subdividers And Developers	Finance, Insurance, And Real Estate
601	Central Reserve Depository Institutions	Finance, Insurance, And Real Estate
6019	Central Reserve Depository Institutions, Not Elsewhere Classified	Finance, Insurance, And Real Estate
3253	Ceramic Wall And Floor Tile	Manufacturing
2043	Cereal Breakfast Foods	Manufacturing
147	Chemical And Fertilizer Mineral Mining	Mining
1479	Chemical And Fertilizer Mineral Mining, Not Elsewhere Classified	Mining
2800	Chemicals & Allied Products	Manufacturing
28	Chemicals And Allied Products	Manufacturing
516	Chemicals And Allied Products	Wholesale Trade
5169	Chemicals And Allied Products, Not Elsewhere Classified	Wholesale Trade
2899	Chemicals And Chemical Preparations, Not Elsewhere Classified	Manufacturing
213	Chewing And Smoking Tobacco And Snuff	Manufacturing
2131	Chewing And Smoking Tobacco And Snuff	Manufacturing
2067	Chewing Gum	Manufacturing
0252	Chicken Eggs	Agriculture, Forestry, And Fishing
835	Child Day Care Services	Services
8351	Child Day Care Services	Services
564	Children's And Infants' Wear Stores	Retail Trade
5641	Children's And Infants' Wear Stores	Retail Trade
2066	Chocolate And Cocoa Products	Manufacturing
211	Cigarettes	Manufacturing

Table of Contents for SIC Codes

Sorted by description

SIC Code	Description	Dvision Description
2111	Cigarettes	Manufacturing
2111	Cigarettes	Manufacturing
212	Cigars	Manufacturing
2121	Cigars	Manufacturing
0174	Citrus Fruits	Agriculture, Forestry, And Fishing
864	Civic, Social, And Fraternal Associations	Services
8641	Civic, Social, And Fraternal Associations	Services
3255	Clay Refractories	Manufacturing
145	Clay, Ceramic, And Refractory Minerals	Mining
1459	Clay, Ceramic, And Refractory Minerals, Not Elsewhere Classified	Mining
5052	Coal And Other Minerals And Ores	Wholesale Trade
12	Coal Mining	Mining
124	Coal Mining Services	Mining
1241	Coal Mining Services	Mining
2672	Coated And Laminated Paper, Not Elsewhere Classified	Manufacturing
2295	Coated Fabrics, Not Rubberized	Manufacturing
3470	Coating, Engraving & Allied Services	Manufacturing
347	Coating, Engraving, And Allied Services	Manufacturing
3479	Coating, Engraving, And Allied Services, Not Elsewhere Classified	Manufacturing
4991	Cogeneration Services & Small Power Producers	Transportation, Communications, Electric, Gas, And Sanitary Service
7993	Coin-Operated Amusement Devices	Services
7215	Coin-Operated Laundries And Drycleaning	Services
3316	Cold-Rolled Steel Sheet, Strip, And Bars	Manufacturing
8221	Colleges, Universities, And Professional Schools	Services
822	Colleges, Universities, Professional Schools, And Junior Colleges	Services
493	Combination Electric And Gas, And Other Utility Services	Transportation, Communications, Electric, Gas, And Sanitary Service
4939	Combination Utilities, Not Elsewhere Classified	Transportation, Communications, Electric, Gas, And Sanitary Service
7336	Commercial Art And Graphic Design	Services
602	Commercial Banks	Finance, Insurance, And Real Estate
6029	Commercial Banks, Nec	Finance, Insurance, And Real Estate
6029	Commercial Banks, Not Elsewhere Classified	Finance, Insurance, And Real Estate
8732	Commercial Economic, Sociological, And Educational Research	Services
5046	Commercial Equipment, Not Elsewhere Classified	Wholesale Trade
091	Commercial Fishing	Agriculture, Forestry, And Fishing
3582	Commercial Laundry, Drycleaning, And Pressing Machines	Manufacturing
7335	Commercial Photography	Services
8731	Commercial Physical And Biological Research	Services
275	Commercial Printing	Manufacturing
2750	Commercial Printing	Manufacturing
2754	Commercial Printing, Gravure	Manufacturing
2752	Commercial Printing, Lithographic	Manufacturing
2759	Commercial Printing, Not Elsewhere Classified	Manufacturing
794	Commercial Sports	Services
3646	Commercial, Industrial, And Institutional Electric Lighting Fixtures	Manufacturing
6221	Commodity Contracts Brokers & Dealers	Finance, Insurance, And Real Estate
622	Commodity Contracts Brokers And Dealers	Finance, Insurance, And Real Estate
6221	Commodity Contracts Brokers And Dealers	Finance, Insurance, And Real Estate
48	Communications	Transportation, Communications, Electric, Gas, And Sanitary Service
366	Communications Equipment	Manufacturing
3669	Communications Equipment, Nec	Manufacturing
3669	Communications Equipment, Not Elsewhere Classified	Manufacturing
4899	Communications Services, Nec	Transportation, Communications, Electric, Gas, And Sanitary Service
489	Communications Services, Not Elsewhere Classified	Transportation, Communications, Electric, Gas, And Sanitary Service
4899	Communications Services, Not Elsewhere Classified	Transportation, Communications, Electric, Gas, And Sanitary Service
3570	Computer & Office Equipment	Manufacturing
5734	Computer And Computer Software Stores	Retail Trade
357	Computer And Office Equipment	Manufacturing
3576	Computer Communications Equipment	Manufacturing
7376	Computer Facilities Management Services	Services
7373	Computer Integrated Systems Design	Services
7378	Computer Maintenance And Repair	Services
3577	Computer Peripheral Equipment, Nec	Manufacturing
3577	Computer Peripheral Equipment, Not Elsewhere Classified	Manufacturing
7374	Computer Processing And Data Preparation And Processing Services	Services
7371	Computer Programming Services	Services
737	Computer Programming, Data Processing, And Other Computer Related	Services

Table of Contents for SIC Codes

Sorted by description

SIC Code	Description	Dvision Description
861	Business Associations	Services
8611	Business Associations	Services
8748	Business Consulting Services, Not Elsewhere Classified	Services
615	Business Credit Institutions	Finance, Insurance, And Real Estate
73	Business Services	Services
7389	Business Services, Not Elsewhere Classified	Services
4841	Cable & Other Pay Television Services	Transportation, Communications, Electric, Gas, And Sanitary Service
484	Cable And Other Pay Television Services	Transportation, Communications, Electric, Gas, And Sanitary Service
4841	Cable And Other Pay Television Services	Transportation, Communications, Electric, Gas, And Sanitary Service
3578	Calculating & Accounting Machines (No Electronic Computers)	Manufacturing
3578	Calculating And Accounting Machines, Except Electronic Computers	Manufacturing
5946	Camera And Photographic Supply Stores	Retail Trade
703	Camps And Recreational Vehicle Parks	Services
2064	Candy And Other Confectionery Products	Manufacturing
544	Candy, Nut, And Confectionery Stores	Retail Trade
5441	Candy, Nut, And Confectionery Stores	Retail Trade
2062	Cane Sugar Refining	Manufacturing
2061	Cane Sugar, Except Refining	Manufacturing
2091	Canned And Cured Fish And Seafoods	Manufacturing
2033	Canned Fruits, Vegetables, Preserves, Jams, And Jellies	Manufacturing
2032	Canned Specialties	Manufacturing
2030	Canned, Frozen & Preservd Fruit, Veg & Food Specialties	Manufacturing
203	Canned, Frozen, And Preserved Fruits, Vegetables, And Food Special	Manufacturing
2033	Canned, Fruits, Veg, Preserves, Jams & Jellies	Manufacturing
2394	Canvas And Related Products	Manufacturing
3624	Carbon And Graphite Products	Manufacturing
2895	Carbon Black	Manufacturing
3955	Carbon Paper And Inked Ribbons	Manufacturing
3592	Carburetors, Pistons, Piston Rings, And Valves	Manufacturing
4785	Cargo Checkers And Surveyors, Marine	Transportation, Communications, Electric, Gas, And Sanitary Service
175	Carpentry And Floor Work	Construction
1751	Carpentry Work	Construction
7217	Carpet And Upholstery Cleaning	Services
2273	Carpets & Rugs	Manufacturing
227	Carpets And Rugs	Manufacturing
2273	Carpets And Rugs	Manufacturing
7542	Carwashes	Services
011	Cash Grains	Agriculture, Forestry, And Fishing
0119	Cash Grains, Not Elsewhere Classified	Agriculture, Forestry, And Fishing
5961	Catalog And Mail-Order Houses	Retail Trade
2823	Cellulosic Manmade Fibers	Manufacturing
324	Cement, Hydraulic	Manufacturing
3241	Cement, Hydraulic	Manufacturing
3241	Cement, Hydraulic	Manufacturing
6553	Cemetery Subdividers And Developers	Finance, Insurance, And Real Estate
601	Central Reserve Depository Institutions	Finance, Insurance, And Real Estate
6019	Central Reserve Depository Institutions, Not Elsewhere Classified	Finance, Insurance, And Real Estate
3253	Ceramic Wall And Floor Tile	Manufacturing
2043	Cereal Breakfast Foods	Manufacturing
147	Chemical And Fertilizer Mineral Mining	Mining
1479	Chemical And Fertilizer Mineral Mining, Not Elsewhere Classified	Mining
2800	Chemicals & Allied Products	Manufacturing
28	Chemicals And Allied Products	Manufacturing
516	Chemicals And Allied Products	Wholesale Trade
5169	Chemicals And Allied Products, Not Elsewhere Classified	Wholesale Trade
2899	Chemicals And Chemical Preparations, Not Elsewhere Classified	Manufacturing
213	Chewing And Smoking Tobacco And Snuff	Manufacturing
2131	Chewing And Smoking Tobacco And Snuff	Manufacturing
2067	Chewing Gum	Manufacturing
0252	Chicken Eggs	Agriculture, Forestry, And Fishing
835	Child Day Care Services	Services
8351	Child Day Care Services	Services
564	Children's And Infants' Wear Stores	Retail Trade
5641	Children's And Infants' Wear Stores	Retail Trade
2066	Chocolate And Cocoa Products	Manufacturing
211	Cigarettes	Manufacturing

Table of Contents for SIC Codes

Sorted by description

SIC Code	Description	Dvision Description
2111	Cigarettes	Manufacturing
2111	Cigarettes	Manufacturing
212	Cigars	Manufacturing
2121	Cigars	Manufacturing
0174	Citrus Fruits	Agriculture, Forestry, And Fishing
864	Civic, Social, And Fraternal Associations	Services
8641	Civic, Social, And Fraternal Associations	Services
3255	Clay Refractories	Manufacturing
145	Clay, Ceramic, And Refractory Minerals	Mining
1459	Clay, Ceramic, And Refractory Minerals, Not Elsewhere Classified	Mining
5052	Coal And Other Minerals And Ores	Wholesale Trade
12	Coal Mining	Mining
124	Coal Mining Services	Mining
1241	Coal Mining Services	Mining
2672	Coated And Laminated Paper, Not Elsewhere Classified	Manufacturing
2295	Coated Fabrics, Not Rubberized	Manufacturing
3470	Coating, Engraving & Allied Services	Manufacturing
347	Coating, Engraving, And Allied Services	Manufacturing
3479	Coating, Engraving, And Allied Services, Not Elsewhere Classified	Manufacturing
4991	Cogeneration Services & Small Power Producers	Transportation, Communications, Electric, Gas, And Sanitary Service
7993	Coin-Operated Amusement Devices	Services
7215	Coin-Operated Laundries And Drycleaning	Services
3316	Cold-Rolled Steel Sheet, Strip, And Bars	Manufacturing
8221	Colleges, Universities, And Professional Schools	Services
822	Colleges, Universities, Professional Schools, And Junior Colleges	Services
493	Combination Electric And Gas, And Other Utility Services	Transportation, Communications, Electric, Gas, And Sanitary Service
4939	Combination Utilities, Not Elsewhere Classified	Transportation, Communications, Electric, Gas, And Sanitary Service
7336	Commercial Art And Graphic Design	Services
602	Commercial Banks	Finance, Insurance, And Real Estate
6029	Commercial Banks, Nec	Finance, Insurance, And Real Estate
6029	Commercial Banks, Not Elsewhere Classified	Finance, Insurance, And Real Estate
8732	Commercial Economic, Sociological, And Educational Research	Services
5046	Commercial Equipment, Not Elsewhere Classified	Wholesale Trade
091	Commercial Fishing	Agriculture, Forestry, And Fishing
3582	Commercial Laundry, Drycleaning, And Pressing Machines	Manufacturing
7335	Commercial Photography	Services
8731	Commercial Physical And Biological Research	Services
275	Commercial Printing	Manufacturing
2750	Commercial Printing	Manufacturing
2754	Commercial Printing, Gravure	Manufacturing
2752	Commercial Printing, Lithographic	Manufacturing
2759	Commercial Printing, Not Elsewhere Classified	Manufacturing
794	Commercial Sports	Services
3646	Commercial, Industrial, And Institutional Electric Lighting Fixtures	Manufacturing
6221	Commodity Contracts Brokers & Dealers	Finance, Insurance, And Real Estate
622	Commodity Contracts Brokers And Dealers	Finance, Insurance, And Real Estate
6221	Commodity Contracts Brokers And Dealers	Finance, Insurance, And Real Estate
48	Communications	Transportation, Communications, Electric, Gas, And Sanitary Service
366	Communications Equipment	Manufacturing
3669	Communications Equipment, Nec	Manufacturing
3669	Communications Equipment, Not Elsewhere Classified	Manufacturing
4899	Communications Services, Nec	Transportation, Communications, Electric, Gas, And Sanitary Service
489	Communications Services, Not Elsewhere Classified	Transportation, Communications, Electric, Gas, And Sanitary Service
4899	Communications Services, Not Elsewhere Classified	Transportation, Communications, Electric, Gas, And Sanitary Service
3570	Computer & Office Equipment	Manufacturing
5734	Computer And Computer Software Stores	Retail Trade
357	Computer And Office Equipment	Manufacturing
3576	Computer Communications Equipment	Manufacturing
7376	Computer Facilities Management Services	Services
7373	Computer Integrated Systems Design	Services
7378	Computer Maintenance And Repair	Services
3577	Computer Peripheral Equipment, Nec	Manufacturing
3577	Computer Peripheral Equipment, Not Elsewhere Classified	Manufacturing
7374	Computer Processing And Data Preparation And Processing Services	Services
7371	Computer Programming Services	Services
737	Computer Programming, Data Processing, And Other Computer Related	Services

Table of Contents for SIC Codes

Sorted by description

SIC Code	Description	Dvision Description
7379	Computer Related Services, Not Elsewhere Classified	Services
7377	Computer Rental And Leasing	Services
3572	Computer Storage Devices	Manufacturing
3572	Computer Storage Devices	Manufacturing
3575	Computer Terminals	Manufacturing
3575	Computer Terminals	Manufacturing
5045	Computers And Computer Peripheral Equipment And Software	Wholesale Trade
3271	Concrete Block And Brick	Manufacturing
3272	Concrete Products, Except Block & Brick	Manufacturing
3272	Concrete Products, Except Block And Brick	Manufacturing
177	Concrete Work	Construction
1771	Concrete Work	Construction
3270	Concrete, Gypsum & Plaster Products	Manufacturing
327	Concrete, Gypsum, And Plaster Products	Manufacturing
5145	Confectionery	Wholesale Trade
15	Construction	Construction
1700	Construction - Special Trade Contractors	Construction
5082	Construction And Mining (Except Petroleum) Machinery And Equipment	Wholesale Trade
3531	Construction Machinery & Equip	Manufacturing
3531	Construction Machinery And Equipment	Manufacturing
5039	Construction Materials, Not Elsewhere Classified	Wholesale Trade
1442	Construction Sand And Gravel	Mining
3530	Construction, Mining & Materials Handling Machinery & Equip	Manufacturing
353	Construction, Mining, And Materials Handling Machinery And Equipment	Manufacturing
17	Construction-Special Trade Contractors	Construction
732	Consumer Credit Reporting Agencies, Mercantile Reporting Agencies	Services
2670	Converted Paper & Paperboard Prods (No Contaners/Boxes)	Manufacturing
267	Converted Paper And Paperboard Products, Except Containers And Boxes	Manufacturing
2679	Converted Paper And Paperboard Products, Not Elsewhere Classified	Manufacturing
3535	Conveyors And Conveying Equipment	Manufacturing
2052	Cookies & Crackers	Manufacturing
2052	Cookies And Crackers	Manufacturing
3366	Copper Foundries	Manufacturing
102	Copper Ores	Mining
1021	Copper Ores	Mining
2298	Cordage And Twine	Manufacturing
0115	Corn	Agriculture, Forestry, And Fishing
9223	Correctional Institutions	Public Adminstration
2653	Corrugated And Solid Fiber Boxes	Manufacturing
3960	Costume Jewelry & Novelties	Manufacturing
3961	Costume Jewelry And Costume Novelties, Except Precious Metal	Manufacturing
396	Costume Jewelry, Costume Novelties, Buttons, And Miscellaneous	Manufacturing
0131	Cotton	Agriculture, Forestry, And Fishing
0724	Cotton Ginning	Agriculture, Forestry, And Fishing
2074	Cottonseed Oil Mills	Manufacturing
4215	Courier Services, Except By Air	Transportation, Communications, Electric, Gas, And Sanitary Service
921	Courts	Public Adminstration
9211	Courts	Public Adminstration
2021	Creamery Butter	Manufacturing
7323	Credit Reporting Services	Services
606	Credit Unions	Finance, Insurance, And Real Estate
6061	Credit Unions, Federally Chartered	Finance, Insurance, And Real Estate
6062	Credit Unions, Not Federally Chartered	Finance, Insurance, And Real Estate
0722	Crop Harvesting, Primarily By Machine	Agriculture, Forestry, And Fishing
0721	Crop Planting, Cultivating, And Protecting	Agriculture, Forestry, And Fishing
0723	Crop Preparation Services For Market, Except Cotton Ginning	Agriculture, Forestry, And Fishing
072	Crop Services	Agriculture, Forestry, And Fishing
3466	Crowns And Closures	Manufacturing
1311	Crude Petroleum & Natural Gas	Mining
131	Crude Petroleum And Natural Gas	Mining
1311	Crude Petroleum And Natural Gas	Mining
4612	Crude Petroleum Pipelines	Transportation, Communications, Electric, Gas, And Sanitary Service
1423	Crushed And Broken Granite	Mining
1422	Crushed And Broken Limestone	Mining
142	Crushed And Broken Stone, Including Riprap	Mining
1429	Crushed And Broken Stone, Not Elsewhere Classified	Mining

Table of Contents for SIC Codes

Sorted by description

SIC Code	Description	Dvision Description
3643	Current-Carrying Wiring Devices	Manufacturing
2391	Curtains And Draperies	Manufacturing
3087	Custom Compounding Of Purchased Plastics Resins	Manufacturing
3281	Cut Stone & Stone Products	Manufacturing
328	Cut Stone And Stone Products	Manufacturing
3281	Cut Stone And Stone Products	Manufacturing
3421	Cutlery	Manufacturing
3420	Cutlery, Handtools & General Hardware	Manufacturing
342	Cutlery, Handtools, And General Hardware	Manufacturing
3545	Cutting Tools, Machine Tool Accessories, And Machinists' Precision Tools	Manufacturing
2865	Cyclic Organic Crudes And Intermediates, And Organic Dyes And Pigments	Manufacturing
024	Dairy Farms	Agriculture, Forestry, And Fishing
0241	Dairy Farms	Agriculture, Forestry, And Fishing
202	Dairy Products	Manufacturing
2020	Dairy Products	Manufacturing
545	Dairy Products Stores	Retail Trade
5451	Dairy Products Stores	Retail Trade
5143	Dairy Products, Except Dried Or Canned	Wholesale Trade
791	Dance Studios, Schools, And Halls	Services
7911	Dance Studios, Schools, And Halls	Services
8243	Data Processing Schools	Services
0175	Deciduous Tree Fruits	Agriculture, Forestry, And Fishing
442	Deep Sea Domestic Transportation Of Freight	Transportation, Communications, Electric, Gas, And Sanitary Service
4424	Deep Sea Domestic Transportation Of Freight	Transportation, Communications, Electric, Gas, And Sanitary Service
441	Deep Sea Foreign Transportation Of Freight	Transportation, Communications, Electric, Gas, And Sanitary Service
4412	Deep Sea Foreign Transportation Of Freight	Transportation, Communications, Electric, Gas, And Sanitary Service
4412	Deep Sea Foreign Transportation Of Freight	Transportation, Communications, Electric, Gas, And Sanitary Service
4481	Deep Sea Transportation Of Passengers, Except By Ferry	Transportation, Communications, Electric, Gas, And Sanitary Service
3843	Dental Equipment & Supplies	Manufacturing
3843	Dental Equipment And Supplies	Manufacturing
8072	Dental Laboratories	Services
531	Department Stores	Retail Trade
5311	Department Stores	Retail Trade
60	Depository Institutions	Finance, Insurance, And Real Estate
7381	Detective, Guard, And Armored Car Services	Services
2675	Die-Cut Paper And Paperboard And Cardboard	Manufacturing
141	Dimension Stone	Mining
1411	Dimension Stone	Mining
7331	Direct Mail Advertising Services	Services
5963	Direct Selling Establishments	Retail Trade
7342	Disinfecting And Pest Control Services	Services
2085	Distilled And Blended Liquors	Manufacturing
2047	Dog And Cat Food	Manufacturing
3942	Dolls & Stuffed Toys	Manufacturing
3942	Dolls And Stuffed Toys	Manufacturing
394	Dolls, Toys, Games And Sporting And Athletic Goods	Manufacturing
2591	Drapery Hardware And Window Blinds And Shades	Manufacturing
5714	Drapery, Curtain, And Upholstery Stores	Retail Trade
3357	Drawing & Insulating Of Nonferrous Wire	Manufacturing
3357	Drawing And Insulating Of Nonferrous Wire	Manufacturing
2381	Dress And Work Gloves, Except Knit And All-Leather	Manufacturing
2034	Dried And Dehydrated Fruits, Vegetables, And Soup Mixes	Manufacturing
1381	Drilling Oil & Gas Wells	Mining
1381	Drilling Oil And Gas Wells	Mining
5813	Drinking Places (Alcoholic Beverages)	Retail Trade
7833	Drive-In Motion Picture Theaters	Services
591	Drug Stores And Proprietary Stores	Retail Trade
5912	Drug Stores And Proprietary Stores	Retail Trade
283	Drugs	Manufacturing
512	Drugs, Drug Proprietaries, And Druggists' Sundries	Wholesale Trade
5122	Drugs, Drug Proprietaries, And Druggists' Sundries	Wholesale Trade
2023	Dry, Condensed, And Evaporated Dairy Products	Manufacturing
7216	Drycleaning Plants, Except Rug Cleaning	Services
5099	Durable Goods, Not Elsewhere Classified	Wholesale Trade
226	Dyeing And Finishing Textiles, Except Wool Fabrics And Knit Goods	Manufacturing
58	Eating And Drinking Places	Retail Trade

SIC Code	Description	Dvision Description
581	Eating And Drinking Places	Retail Trade
5812	Eating Places	Retail Trade
82	Educational Services	Services
6732	Educational, Religious, And Charitable Trusts	Finance, Insurance, And Real Estate
4931	Electric & Other Services Combined	Transportation, Communications, Electric, Gas, And Sanitary Service
3548	Electric And Gas Welding And Soldering Equipment	Manufacturing
4931	Electric And Other Services Combined	Transportation, Communications, Electric, Gas, And Sanitary Service
3634	Electric Housewares & Fans	Manufacturing
3634	Electric Housewares And Fans	Manufacturing
3641	Electric Lamp Bulbs And Tubes	Manufacturing
3640	Electric Lighting & Wiring Equipment	Manufacturing
364	Electric Lighting And Wiring Equipment	Manufacturing
491	Electric Services	Transportation, Communications, Electric, Gas, And Sanitary Service
4911	Electric Services	Transportation, Communications, Electric, Gas, And Sanitary Service
4911	Electric Services	Transportation, Communications, Electric, Gas, And Sanitary Service
361	Electric Transmission And Distribution Equipment	Manufacturing
4900	Electric, Gas & Sanitary Services	Transportation, Communications, Electric, Gas, And Sanitary Service
49	Electric, Gas, And Sanitary Services	Transportation, Communications, Electric, Gas, And Sanitary Service
7629	Electrical And Electronic Repair Shops, Not Elsewhere Classified	Services
5063	Electrical Apparatus And Equipment, Wiring Supplies, And Construction	Wholesale Trade
5064	Electrical Appliances, Television And Radio Sets	Wholesale Trade
3694	Electrical Equipment For Internal Combustion Engines	Manufacturing
506	Electrical Goods	Wholesale Trade
362	Electrical Industrial Apparatus	Manufacturing
3620	Electrical Industrial Apparatus	Manufacturing
3629	Electrical Industrial Apparatus, Not Elsewhere Classified	Manufacturing
3699	Electrical Machinery, Equipment, And Supplies, Not Elsewhere Classified	Manufacturing
762	Electrical Repair Shops	Services
173	Electrical Work	Construction
1731	Electrical Work	Construction
1731	Electrical Work	Construction
3845	Electromedical & Electrotherapeutic Apparatus	Manufacturing
3845	Electromedical And Electrotherapeutic Apparatus	Manufacturing
3313	Electrometallurgical Products, Except Steel	Manufacturing
3671	Electron Tubes	Manufacturing
3600	Electronic & Other Electrical Equipment (No Computer Equip)	Manufacturing
36	Electronic And Other Electrical Equipment And Components, Except Computer	Manufacturing
3675	Electronic Capacitors	Manufacturing
3677	Electronic Coils, Transformers & Other Inductors	Manufacturing
3677	Electronic Coils, Transformers, And Other Inductors	Manufacturing
3670	Electronic Components & Accessories	Manufacturing
367	Electronic Components And Accessories	Manufacturing
3679	Electronic Components, Nec	Manufacturing
3679	Electronic Components, Not Elsewhere Classified	Manufacturing
3571	Electronic Computers	Manufacturing
3571	Electronic Computers	Manufacturing
3678	Electronic Connectors	Manufacturing
3678	Electronic Connectors	Manufacturing
5065	Electronic Parts And Equipment, Not Elsewhere Classified	Wholesale Trade
3676	Electronic Resistors	Manufacturing
3471	Electroplating, Plating, Polishing, Anodizing, And Coloring	Manufacturing
821	Elementary And Secondary Schools	Services
8211	Elementary And Secondary Schools	Services
3534	Elevators And Moving Stairways	Manufacturing
7361	Employment Agencies	Services
3431	Enameled Iron And Metal Sanitary Ware	Manufacturing
8711	Engineering Services	Services
87	Engineering, Accounting, Research, Management, And Related Services	Services
871	Engineering, Architectural, And Surveying Services	Services
3510	Engines & Turbines	Manufacturing
351	Engines And Turbines	Manufacturing
2677	Envelopes	Manufacturing
7359	Equipment Rental And Leasing, Not Elsewhere Classified	Services
1794	Excavation Work	Construction
913	Executive And Legislative Offices Combined	Public Adminstration
9131	Executive And Legislative Offices Combined	Public Adminstration

Sorted by description

SIC Code	Description	Dvision Description
911	Executive Offices	Public Adminstration
9111	Executive Offices	Public Adminstration
91	Executive, Legislative, And General Government, Except Finance	Public Adminstration
2892	Explosives	Manufacturing
34	Fabricated Metal Products, Except Machinery And Transportation Equipment	Manufacturing
3499	Fabricated Metal Products, Not Elsewhere Classified	Manufacturing
3498	Fabricated Pipe And Pipe Fittings	Manufacturing
3443	Fabricated Plate Work (Boiler Shops)	Manufacturing
3443	Fabricated Plate Work (Boiler Shops)	Manufacturing
3060	Fabricated Rubber Products, Nec	Manufacturing
306	Fabricated Rubber Products, Not Elsewhere Classified	Manufacturing
3069	Fabricated Rubber Products, Not Elsewhere Classified	Manufacturing
3441	Fabricated Structural Metal	Manufacturing
344	Fabricated Structural Metal Products	Manufacturing
3440	Fabricated Structural Metal Products	Manufacturing
2399	Fabricated Textile Products, Not Elsewhere Classified	Manufacturing
8744	Facilities Support Management Services	Services
565	Family Clothing Stores	Retail Trade
5651	Family Clothing Stores	Retail Trade
352	Farm And Garden Machinery And Equipment	Manufacturing
5083	Farm And Garden Machinery And Equipment	Wholesale Trade
076	Farm Labor And Management Services	Agriculture, Forestry, And Fishing
0761	Farm Labor Contractors And Crew Leaders	Agriculture, Forestry, And Fishing
3523	Farm Machinery & Equipment	Manufacturing
3523	Farm Machinery And Equipment	Manufacturing
0762	Farm Management Services	Agriculture, Forestry, And Fishing
4221	Farm Product Warehousing And Storage	Transportation, Communications, Electric, Gas, And Sanitary Service
5191	Farm Supplies	Wholesale Trade
515	Farm-Product Raw Materials	Wholesale Trade
5159	Farm-Product Raw Materials, Not Elsewhere Classified	Wholesale Trade
3965	Fasteners, Buttons, Needles, And Pins	Manufacturing
2070	Fats & Oils	Manufacturing
207	Fats And Oils	Manufacturing
6111	Federal & Federally-Sponsored Credit Agencies	Finance, Insurance, And Real Estate
611	Federal And Federally-Sponsored Credit Agencies	Finance, Insurance, And Real Estate
6111	Federal And Federally-Sponsored Credit Agencies	Finance, Insurance, And Real Estate
6011	Federal Reserve Banks	Finance, Insurance, And Real Estate
4482	Ferries	Transportation, Communications, Electric, Gas, And Sanitary Service
106	Ferroalloy Ores, Except Vanadium	Mining
1061	Ferroalloy Ores, Except Vanadium	Mining
2875	Fertilizers, Mixing Only	Manufacturing
2655	Fiber Cans, Tubes, Drums, And Similar Products	Manufacturing
013	Field Crops, Except Cash Grains	Agriculture, Forestry, And Fishing
0139	Field Crops, Except Cash Grains, Not Elsewhere Classified	Agriculture, Forestry, And Fishing
6172	Finance Lessors	Finance, Insurance, And Real Estate
6199	Finance Services	Finance, Insurance, And Real Estate
3263	Fine Earthenware (Whiteware) Table And Kitchen Articles	Manufacturing
0912	Finfish	Agriculture, Forestry, And Fishing
2261	Finishers Of Broadwoven Fabrics Of Cotton	Manufacturing
2262	Finishers Of Broadwoven Fabrics Of Manmade Fiber And Silk	Manufacturing
2269	Finishers Of Textiles, Not Elsewhere Classified	Manufacturing
9224	Fire Protection	Public Adminstration
6331	Fire, Marine & Casualty Insurance	Finance, Insurance, And Real Estate
633	Fire, Marine, And Casualty Insurance	Finance, Insurance, And Real Estate
6331	Fire, Marine, And Casualty Insurance	Finance, Insurance, And Real Estate
5146	Fish And Seafoods	Wholesale Trade
092	Fish Hatcheries And Preserves	Agriculture, Forestry, And Fishing
0921	Fish Hatcheries And Preserves	Agriculture, Forestry, And Fishing
09	Fishing, Hunting, And Trapping	Agriculture, Forestry, And Fishing
4785	Fixed Facilities And Inspection And Weighing Services For Motor Vehicles	Transportation, Communications, Electric, Gas, And Sanitary Service
321	Flat Glass	Manufacturing
3211	Flat Glass	Manufacturing
3211	Flat Glass	Manufacturing
2087	Flavoring Extracts And Flavoring Syrups, Not Elsewhere Classified	Manufacturing
5713	Floor Covering Stores	Retail Trade
1752	Floor Laying And Other Floor Work, Not Elsewhere Classified	Construction

SIC Code	Description	Dvision Description
5992	Florists	Retail Trade
2041	Flour And Other Grain Mill Products	Manufacturing
5193	Flowers, Nursery Stock, And Florists' Supplies	Wholesale Trade
2026	Fluid Milk	Manufacturing
3593	Fluid Power Cylinders And Actuators	Manufacturing
3594	Fluid Power Pumps And Motors	Manufacturing
3492	Fluid Power Valves And Hose Fittings	Manufacturing
2657	Folding Paperboard Boxes, Including Sanitary	Manufacturing
20	Food And Kindred Products	Manufacturing
2000	Food And Kindred Products	Manufacturing
0182	Food Crops Grown Under Cover	Agriculture, Forestry, And Fishing
2099	Food Preparations, Not Elsewhere Classified	Manufacturing
3556	Food Products Machinery	Manufacturing
54	Food Stores	Retail Trade
5139	Footwear	Wholesale Trade
3140	Footwear, (No Rubber)	Manufacturing
314	Footwear, Except Rubber	Manufacturing
3149	Footwear, Except Rubber, Not Elsewhere Classified	Manufacturing
608	Foreign Banking And Branches And Agencies Of Foreign Banks	Finance, Insurance, And Real Estate
8888	Foreign Governments	Services
6082	Foreign Trade And International Banking Institutions	Finance, Insurance, And Real Estate
083	Forest Nurseries And Gathering Of Forest Products	Agriculture, Forestry, And Fishing
0831	Forest Nurseries And Gathering Of Forest Products	Agriculture, Forestry, And Fishing
08	Forestry	Agriculture, Forestry, And Fishing
085	Forestry Services	Agriculture, Forestry, And Fishing
0851	Forestry Services	Agriculture, Forestry, And Fishing
443	Freight Transportation On The Great Lakes¨St. Lawrence Seaway	Transportation, Communications, Electric, Gas, And Sanitary Service
4432	Freight Transportation On The Great Lakes¨St. Lawrence Seaway	Transportation, Communications, Electric, Gas, And Sanitary Service
5148	Fresh Fruits And Vegetables	Wholesale Trade
2053	Frozen Bakery Products, Except Bread	Manufacturing
2037	Frozen Fruits, Fruit Juices, And Vegetables	Manufacturing
2038	Frozen Specialties, Not Elsewhere Classified	Manufacturing
543	Fruit And Vegetable Markets	Retail Trade
5431	Fruit And Vegetable Markets	Retail Trade
017	Fruits And Tree Nuts	Agriculture, Forestry, And Fishing
0179	Fruits And Tree Nuts, Not Elsewhere Classified	Agriculture, Forestry, And Fishing
598	Fuel Dealers	Retail Trade
5989	Fuel Dealers, Not Elsewhere Classified	Retail Trade
5983	Fuel Oil Dealers	Retail Trade
609	Functions Related To Depository Banking	Finance, Insurance, And Real Estate
6099	Functions Related To Depository Banking, Nec	Finance, Insurance, And Real Estate
6099	Functions Related To Depository Banking, Not Elsewhere Classified	Finance, Insurance, And Real Estate
726	Funeral Service And Crematories	Services
7261	Funeral Service And Crematories	Services
237	Fur Goods	Manufacturing
2371	Fur Goods	Manufacturing
0271	Fur-Bearing Animals And Rabbits	Agriculture, Forestry, And Fishing
5021	Furniture	Wholesale Trade
25	Furniture And Fixtures	Manufacturing
2599	Furniture And Fixtures, Not Elsewhere Classified	Manufacturing
502	Furniture And Homefurnishings	Wholesale Trade
5712	Furniture Stores	Retail Trade
3944	Games, Toys & Children's Vehicles (No Dolls & Bicycles)	Manufacturing
3944	Games, Toys, And Children's Vehicles, Except Dolls And Bicycles	Manufacturing
7212	Garment Pressing, And Agents For Laundries And Drycleaners	Services
4932	Gas & Other Services Combined	Transportation, Communications, Electric, Gas, And Sanitary Service
4932	Gas And Other Services Combined	Transportation, Communications, Electric, Gas, And Sanitary Service
492	Gas Production And Distribution	Transportation, Communications, Electric, Gas, And Sanitary Service
3050	Gaskets, Packg & Sealg Devices & Rubber & Plastics Hose	Manufacturing
3053	Gaskets, Packing, And Sealing Devices	Manufacturing
305	Gaskets, Packing, And Sealing Devices And Rubber And Plastics Hose	Manufacturing
554	Gasoline Service Stations	Retail Trade
5541	Gasoline Service Stations	Retail Trade
7538	General Automotive Repair Shops	Services
1540	General Bldg Contractors - Nonresidential Bldgs	Construction
1520	General Bldg Contractors - Residential Bldgs	Construction

Table of Contents for SIC Codes

Sorted by description

SIC Code	Description	Dvision Description
154	General Building Contractors-Nonresidential Buildings	Construction
152	General Building Contractors-Residential Buildings	Construction
1541	General Contractors-Industrial Buildings And Warehouses	Construction
1542	General Contractors-Nonresidential Buildings, Other Than Industrial	Construction
1522	General Contractors-Residential Buildings, Other Than Single-Family	Construction
1521	General Contractors-Single-Family Houses	Construction
019	General Farms, Primarily Crop	Agriculture, Forestry, And Fishing
0191	General Farms, Primarily Crop	Agriculture, Forestry, And Fishing
029	General Farms, Primarily Livestock And Animal Specialties	Agriculture, Forestry, And Fishing
0291	General Farms, Primarily Livestock And Animal Specialties	Agriculture, Forestry, And Fishing
919	General Government, Not Elsewhere Classified	Public Adminstration
9199	General Government, Not Elsewhere Classified	Public Adminstration
3560	General Industrial Machinery & Equipment	Manufacturing
3569	General Industrial Machinery & Equipment, Nec	Manufacturing
356	General Industrial Machinery And Equipment	Manufacturing
3569	General Industrial Machinery And Equipment, Not Elsewhere Classified	Manufacturing
0219	General Livestock, Except Dairy And Poultry	Agriculture, Forestry, And Fishing
8062	General Medical And Surgical Hospitals	Services
53	General Merchandise Stores	Retail Trade
4225	General Warehousing And Storage	Transportation, Communications, Electric, Gas, And Sanitary Service
5947	Gift, Novelty, And Souvenir Shops	Retail Trade
2361	Girls', Children's, And Infants' Dresses, Blouses, And Shirts	Manufacturing
236	Girls', Children's, And Infants' Outerwear	Manufacturing
2369	Girls', Children's, And Infants' Outerwear, Not Elsewhere Classified	Manufacturing
3220	Glass & Glassware, Pressed Or Blown	Manufacturing
322	Glass And Glassware, Pressed Or Blown	Manufacturing
1793	Glass And Glazing Work	Construction
3221	Glass Containers	Manufacturing
3221	Glass Containers	Manufacturing
1793	Glass Installation, Except Automotive-Contractors	Construction
323	Glass Products, Made Of Purchased Glass	Manufacturing
3231	Glass Products, Made Of Purchased Glass	Manufacturing
3231	Glass Products, Made Of Purchased Glass	Manufacturing
104	Gold And Silver Ores	Mining
1040	Gold And Silver Ores	Mining
1041	Gold Ores	Mining
5153	Grain And Field Beans	Wholesale Trade
204	Grain Mill Products	Manufacturing
2040	Grain Mill Products	Manufacturing
0172	Grapes	Agriculture, Forestry, And Fishing
3321	Gray And Ductile Iron Foundries	Manufacturing
277	Greeting Cards	Manufacturing
2771	Greeting Cards	Manufacturing
2771	Greeting Cards	Manufacturing
514	Groceries And Related Products	Wholesale Trade
5149	Groceries And Related Products, Not Elsewhere Classified	Wholesale Trade
5141	Groceries, General Line	Wholesale Trade
541	Grocery Stores	Retail Trade
5411	Grocery Stores	Retail Trade
3769	Guided Missile And Space Vehicle Parts And Auxiliary Equipment, Not Elsewhere Classified	Manufacturing
3764	Guided Missile And Space Vehicle Propulsion Units And Propulsion	Manufacturing
3760	Guided Missiles & Space Vehicles & Parts	Manufacturing
3761	Guided Missiles And Space Vehicles	Manufacturing
376	Guided Missiles And Space Vehicles And Parts	Manufacturing
2861	Gum And Wood Chemicals	Manufacturing
3275	Gypsum Products	Manufacturing
3423	Hand And Edge Tools, Except Machine Tools And Handsaws	Manufacturing
317	Handbags And Other Personal Leather Goods	Manufacturing
5072	Hardware	Wholesale Trade
525	Hardware Stores	Retail Trade
5251	Hardware Stores	Retail Trade
507	Hardware, And Plumbing And Heating Equipment And Supplies	Wholesale Trade
3429	Hardware, Not Elsewhere Classified	Manufacturing
2426	Hardwood Dimension And Flooring Mills	Manufacturing
2435	Hardwood Veneer And Plywood	Manufacturing

Table of Contents for SIC Codes

Sorted by description

SIC Code	Description	Dvision Description
235	Hats, Caps, And Millinery	Manufacturing
2353	Hats, Caps, And Millinery	Manufacturing
4955	Hazardous Waste Management	Transportation, Communications, Electric, Gas, And Sanitary Service
8099	Health And Allied Services, Not Elsewhere Classified	Services
80	Health Services	Services
3430	Heating Equip, Except Elec & Warm Air; & Plumbing Fixtures	Manufacturing
3433	Heating Equipment, Except Electric & Warm Air Furnaces	Manufacturing
3433	Heating Equipment, Except Electric And Warm Air Furnaces	Manufacturing
343	Heating Equipment, Except Electric And Warm Air; And Plumbing Fixtures	Manufacturing
7353	Heavy Construction Equipment Rental And Leasing	Services
1600	Heavy Construction Other Than Bldg Const - Contractors	Construction
16	Heavy Construction Other Than Building Construction-Contractors	Construction
162	Heavy Construction, Except Highway And Street Construction	Construction
1629	Heavy Construction, Not Elsewhere Classified	Construction
7363	Help Supply Services	Services
161	Highway And Street Construction, Except Elevated Highways	Construction
1611	Highway And Street Construction, Except Elevated Highways	Construction
5945	Hobby, Toy, And Game Shops	Retail Trade
0213	Hogs	Agriculture, Forestry, And Fishing
67	Holding And Other Investment Offices	Finance, Insurance, And Real Estate
671	Holding Offices	Finance, Insurance, And Real Estate
571	Home Furniture And Furnishings Stores	Retail Trade
57	Home Furniture, Furnishings, And Equipment Stores	Retail Trade
808	Home Health Care Services	Services
8082	Home Health Care Services	Services
5023	Homefurnishings	Wholesale Trade
0272	Horses And Other Equines	Agriculture, Forestry, And Fishing
018	Horticultural Specialties	Agriculture, Forestry, And Fishing
2252	Hosiery, Not Elsewhere Classified	Manufacturing
6324	Hospital & Medical Service Plans	Finance, Insurance, And Real Estate
6324	Hospital And Medical Service Plans	Finance, Insurance, And Real Estate
806	Hospitals	Services
7011	Hotels & Motels	Services
701	Hotels And Motels	Services
7011	Hotels And Motels	Services
7000	Hotels, Rooming Houses, Camps & Other Lodging Places	Services
70	Hotels, Rooming Houses, Camps, And Other Lodging Places	Services
3142	House Slippers	Manufacturing
2392	Housefurnishings, Except Curtains And Draperies	Manufacturing
572	Household Appliance Stores	Retail Trade
5722	Household Appliance Stores	Retail Trade
363	Household Appliances	Manufacturing
3630	Household Appliances	Manufacturing
3639	Household Appliances, Not Elsewhere Classified	Manufacturing
3651	Household Audio & Video Equipment	Manufacturing
3651	Household Audio And Video Equipment	Manufacturing
365	Household Audio And Video Equipment, And Audio Recordings	Manufacturing
3631	Household Cooking Equipment	Manufacturing
251	Household Furniture	Manufacturing
2510	Household Furniture	Manufacturing
2519	Household Furniture, Not Elsewhere Classified	Manufacturing
3633	Household Laundry Equipment	Manufacturing
3632	Household Refrigerators And Home And Farm Freezers	Manufacturing
3635	Household Vacuum Cleaners	Manufacturing
097	Hunting And Trapping, And Game Propagation	Agriculture, Forestry, And Fishing
0971	Hunting And Trapping, And Game Propagation	Agriculture, Forestry, And Fishing
2024	Ice Cream & Frozen Desserts	Manufacturing
2024	Ice Cream And Frozen Desserts	Manufacturing
2835	In Vitro & In Vivo Diagnostic Substances	Manufacturing
2835	In Vitro And In Vivo Diagnostic Substances	Manufacturing
832	Individual And Family Social Services	Services
8322	Individual And Family Social Services	Services
3564	Industrial & Commercial Fans & Blowers & Air Purifing Equip	Manufacturing
3564	Industrial And Commercial Fans And Blowers And Air Purification Equipment	Manufacturing
35	Industrial And Commercial Machinery And Computer Equipment	Manufacturing

Table of Contents for SIC Codes

Sorted by description

SIC Code	Description	Dvision Description
3599	Industrial And Commercial Machinery And Equipment, Not Elsewhere Classified	Manufacturing
5113	Industrial And Personal Service Paper	Wholesale Trade
2813	Industrial Gases	Manufacturing
281	Industrial Inorganic Chemicals	Manufacturing
2810	Industrial Inorganic Chemicals	Manufacturing
2819	Industrial Inorganic Chemicals, Not Elsewhere Classified	Manufacturing
3823	Industrial Instruments For Measurement, Display, And Control	Manufacturing
3823	Industrial Instruments For Measurement, Display, And Control Of Processes	Manufacturing
7218	Industrial Launderers	Services
5084	Industrial Machinery And Equipment	Wholesale Trade
286	Industrial Organic Chemicals	Manufacturing
2860	Industrial Organic Chemicals	Manufacturing
2869	Industrial Organic Chemicals, Not Elsewhere Classified	Manufacturing
3543	Industrial Patterns	Manufacturing
3567	Industrial Process Furnaces & Ovens	Manufacturing
3567	Industrial Process Furnaces And Ovens	Manufacturing
1446	Industrial Sand	Mining
5085	Industrial Supplies	Wholesale Trade
3537	Industrial Trucks, Tractors, Trailers, And Stackers	Manufacturing
3537	Industrial Trucks, Tractors, Trailors & Stackers	Manufacturing
3491	Industrial Valves	Manufacturing
7375	Information Retrieval Services	Services
2816	Inorganic Pigments	Manufacturing
1796	Installation Or Erection Of Building Equipment, Not Elsewhere Classified	Construction
3825	Instruments For Meas & Testing Of Electricity & Elec Signals	Manufacturing
3825	Instruments For Measuring And Testing Of Electricity And Electric	Manufacturing
6411	Insurance Agents, Brokers & Service	Finance, Insurance, And Real Estate
64	Insurance Agents, Brokers, And Service	Finance, Insurance, And Real Estate
641	Insurance Agents, Brokers, And Service	Finance, Insurance, And Real Estate
6411	Insurance Agents, Brokers, And Service	Finance, Insurance, And Real Estate
63	Insurance Carriers	Finance, Insurance, And Real Estate
6399	Insurance Carriers, Nec	Finance, Insurance, And Real Estate
639	Insurance Carriers, Not Elsewhere Classified	Finance, Insurance, And Real Estate
6399	Insurance Carriers, Not Elsewhere Classified	Finance, Insurance, And Real Estate
413	Intercity And Rural Bus Transportation	Transportation, Communications, Electric, Gas, And Sanitary Service
4131	Intercity And Rural Bus Transportation	Transportation, Communications, Electric, Gas, And Sanitary Service
8052	Intermediate Care Facilities	Services
3519	Internal Combustion Engines, Not Elsewhere Classified	Manufacturing
972	International Affairs	Public Adminstration
9721	International Affairs	Public Adminstration
9721	International Affairs	Public Adminstration
6282	Investment Advice	Finance, Insurance, And Real Estate
6282	Investment Advice	Finance, Insurance, And Real Estate
672	Investment Offices	Finance, Insurance, And Real Estate
6799	Investors, Nec	Finance, Insurance, And Real Estate
6799	Investors, Not Elsewhere Classified	Finance, Insurance, And Real Estate
0134	Irish Potatoes	Agriculture, Forestry, And Fishing
3320	Iron & Steel Foundries	Manufacturing
3462	Iron And Steel Forgings	Manufacturing
332	Iron And Steel Foundries	Manufacturing
101	Iron Ores	Mining
1011	Iron Ores	Mining
497	Irrigation Systems	Transportation, Communications, Electric, Gas, And Sanitary Service
4971	Irrigation Systems	Transportation, Communications, Electric, Gas, And Sanitary Service
3915	Jewelers' Findings And Materials, And Lapidary Work	Manufacturing
5944	Jewelry Stores	Retail Trade
3911	Jewelry, Precious Metal	Manufacturing
3911	Jewelry, Precious Metal	Manufacturing
3910	Jewelry, Silverware & Plated Ware	Manufacturing
391	Jewelry, Silverware, And Plated Ware	Manufacturing
5094	Jewelry, Watches, Precious Stones, And Precious Metals	Wholesale Trade
833	Job Training And Vocational Rehabilitation Services	Services
8331	Job Training And Vocational Rehabilitation Services	Services
8222	Junior Colleges And Technical Institutes	Services
92	Justice, Public Order, And Safety	Public Adminstration

Table of Contents for SIC Codes

Sorted by description

SIC Code	Description	Dvision Description
1455	Kaolin And Ball Clay	Mining
8092	Kidney Dialysis Centers	Services
2253	Knit Outerwear Mills	Manufacturing
2253	Knit Outerwear Mills	Manufacturing
2254	Knit Underwear And Nightwear Mills	Manufacturing
225	Knitting Mills	Manufacturing
2250	Knitting Mills	Manufacturing
2259	Knitting Mills, Not Elsewhere Classified	Manufacturing
863	Labor Unions And Similar Labor Organizations	Services
8631	Labor Unions And Similar Labor Organizations	Services
3826	Laboratory Analytical Instruments	Manufacturing
3826	Laboratory Analytical Instruments	Manufacturing
3821	Laboratory Apparatus & Furniture	Manufacturing
382	Laboratory Apparatus And Analytical, Optical, Measuring, And Control	Manufacturing
3821	Laboratory Apparatus And Furniture	Manufacturing
2258	Lace And Warp Knit Fabric Mills	Manufacturing
3083	Laminated Plastics Plate, Sheet, And Profile Shapes	Manufacturing
6552	Land Subdividers & Developers (No Cemeteries)	Finance, Insurance, And Real Estate
655	Land Subdividers And Developers	Finance, Insurance, And Real Estate
6552	Land Subdividers And Developers, Except Cemeteries	Finance, Insurance, And Real Estate
9512	Land, Mineral, Wildlife, And Forest Conservation	Public Adminstration
078	Landscape And Horticultural Services	Agriculture, Forestry, And Fishing
0781	Landscape Counseling And Planning	Agriculture, Forestry, And Fishing
7219	Laundry And Garment Services, Not Elsewhere Classified	Services
721	Laundry, Cleaning, And Garment Services	Services
3524	Lawn & Garden Tractors & Home Lawn & Gardens Equip	Manufacturing
0782	Lawn And Garden Services	Agriculture, Forestry, And Fishing
3524	Lawn And Garden Tractors And Home Lawn And Garden Equipment	Manufacturing
103	Lead And Zinc Ores	Mining
1031	Lead And Zinc Ores	Mining
3952	Lead Pencils, Crayons, And Artists' Materials	Manufacturing
3100	Leather & Leather Products	Manufacturing
31	Leather And Leather Products	Manufacturing
2386	Leather And Sheep-Lined Clothing	Manufacturing
315	Leather Gloves And Mittens	Manufacturing
3151	Leather Gloves And Mittens	Manufacturing
319	Leather Goods, Not Elsewhere Classified	Manufacturing
3199	Leather Goods, Not Elsewhere Classified	Manufacturing
311	Leather Tanning And Finishing	Manufacturing
3111	Leather Tanning And Finishing	Manufacturing
9222	Legal Counsel And Prosecution	Public Adminstration
81	Legal Services	Services
811	Legal Services	Services
8111	Legal Services	Services
912	Legislative Bodies	Public Adminstration
9121	Legislative Bodies	Public Adminstration
6517	Lessors Of Railroad Property	Finance, Insurance, And Real Estate
6519	Lessors Of Real Property, Nec	Finance, Insurance, And Real Estate
6519	Lessors Of Real Property, Not Elsewhere Classified	Finance, Insurance, And Real Estate
823	Libraries	Services
8231	Libraries	Services
631	Life Insurance	Finance, Insurance, And Real Estate
6311	Life Insurance	Finance, Insurance, And Real Estate
6311	Life Insurance	Finance, Insurance, And Real Estate
3648	Lighting Equipment, Not Elsewhere Classified	Manufacturing
3274	Lime	Manufacturing
7213	Linen Supply	Services
3996	Linoleum, Asphalted-Felt-Base, And Other Hard Surface Floor Cover	Manufacturing
5984	Liquefied Petroleum Gas (Bottled Gas) Dealers	Retail Trade
592	Liquor Stores	Retail Trade
5921	Liquor Stores	Retail Trade
5154	Livestock	Wholesale Trade
0751	Livestock Services, Except Veterinary	Agriculture, Forestry, And Fishing
021	Livestock, Except Dairy And Poultry	Agriculture, Forestry, And Fishing
6163	Loan Brokers	Finance, Insurance, And Real Estate
6163	Loan Brokers	Finance, Insurance, And Real Estate

Table of Contents for SIC Codes

Sorted by description

SIC Code	Description	Dvision Description
4100	Local & Suburban Transit & Interurban Hwy Passenger Trans	Transportation, Communications, Electric, Gas, And Sanitary Service
411	Local And Suburban Passenger Transportation	Transportation, Communications, Electric, Gas, And Sanitary Service
4111	Local And Suburban Transit	Transportation, Communications, Electric, Gas, And Sanitary Service
41	Local And Suburban Transit And Interurban Highway Passenger Transportation	Transportation, Communications, Electric, Gas, And Sanitary Service
4141	Local Bus Charter Service	Transportation, Communications, Electric, Gas, And Sanitary Service
4119	Local Passenger Transportation, Not Elsewhere Classified	Transportation, Communications, Electric, Gas, And Sanitary Service
4214	Local Trucking With Storage	Transportation, Communications, Electric, Gas, And Sanitary Service
4212	Local Trucking Without Storage	Transportation, Communications, Electric, Gas, And Sanitary Service
241	Logging	Manufacturing
2411	Logging	Manufacturing
2992	Lubricating Oils And Greases	Manufacturing
316	Luggage	Manufacturing
3161	Luggage	Manufacturing
5948	Luggage And Leather Goods Stores	Retail Trade
2400	Lumber & Wood Products (No Furniture)	Manufacturing
521	Lumber And Other Building Materials Dealers	Retail Trade
5211	Lumber And Other Building Materials Dealers	Retail Trade
503	Lumber And Other Construction Materials	Wholesale Trade
24	Lumber And Wood Products, Except Furniture	Manufacturing
5031	Lumber, Plywood, Millwork, And Wood Panels	Wholesale Trade
2098	Macaroni, Spaghetti, Vermicelli, And Noodles	Manufacturing
3541	Machine Tools, Metal Cutting Types	Manufacturing
3541	Machine Tools, Metal Cutting Types	Manufacturing
3542	Machine Tools, Metal Forming Types	Manufacturing
508	Machinery, Equipment, And Supplies	Wholesale Trade
3695	Magnetic & Optical Recording Media	Manufacturing
3695	Magnetic And Optical Recording Media	Manufacturing
733	Mailing, Reproduction, Commercial Art And Photography, And Stenography	Services
3322	Malleable Iron Foundries	Manufacturing
2083	Malt	Manufacturing
2082	Malt Beverages	Manufacturing
2082	Malt Beverages	Manufacturing
874	Management And Public Relations Services	Services
8742	Management Consulting Services	Services
6722	Management Investment Offices, Open-End	Finance, Insurance, And Real Estate
8741	Management Services	Services
276	Manifold Business Forms	Manufacturing
2761	Manifold Business Forms	Manufacturing
2761	Manifold Business Forms	Manufacturing
2824	Manmade Organic Fibers, Except Cellulosic	Manufacturing
2097	Manufactured Ice	Manufacturing
3999	Manufacturing Industries, Not Elsewhere Classified	Manufacturing
4493	Marinas	Transportation, Communications, Electric, Gas, And Sanitary Service
4491	Marine Cargo Handling	Transportation, Communications, Electric, Gas, And Sanitary Service
3953	Marking Devices	Manufacturing
1741	Masonry, Stone Setting, And Other Stone Work	Construction
174	Masonry, Stonework, Tile Setting, And Plastering	Construction
2515	Mattresses, Foundations, And Convertible Beds	Manufacturing
3829	Measuring & Controlling Devices, Nec	Manufacturing
3829	Measuring And Controlling Devices, Not Elsewhere Classified	Manufacturing
3586	Measuring And Dispensing Pumps	Manufacturing
38	Measuring, Analyzing, And Controlling Instruments; Photographic, Medical	Manufacturing
542	Meat And Fish (Seafood) Markets, Including Freezer Provisioners	Retail Trade
5421	Meat And Fish (Seafood) Markets, Including Freezer Provisioners	Retail Trade
2011	Meat Packing Plants	Manufacturing
2011	Meat Packing Plants	Manufacturing
201	Meat Products	Manufacturing
5147	Meats And Meat Products	Wholesale Trade
3568	Mechanical Power Transmission Equipment, Not Elsewhere Classified	Manufacturing
807	Medical And Dental Laboratories	Services
7352	Medical Equipment Rental And Leasing	Services
8071	Medical Laboratories	Services
5047	Medical, Dental, And Hospital Equipment And Supplies	Wholesale Trade
2833	Medicinal Chemicals & Botanical Products	Manufacturing
2833	Medicinal Chemicals And Botanical Products	Manufacturing
86	Membership Organizations	Services

Table of Contents for SIC Codes

Sorted by description

SIC Code	Description	Dvision Description
869	Membership Organizations, Not Elsewhere Classified	Services
8699	Membership Organizations, Not Elsewhere Classified	Services
7997	Membership Sports And Recreation Clubs	Services
2320	Men's & Boys' Furnishgs, Work Clothg, & Allied Garments	Manufacturing
561	Men's And Boys' Clothing And Accessory Stores	Retail Trade
5611	Men's And Boys' Clothing And Accessory Stores	Retail Trade
5136	Men's And Boys' Clothing And Furnishings	Wholesale Trade
2329	Men's And Boys' Clothing, Not Elsewhere Classified	Manufacturing
232	Men's And Boys' Furnishings, Work Clothing, And Allied Garments	Manufacturing
2323	Men's And Boys' Neckwear	Manufacturing
2325	Men's And Boys' Separate Trousers And Slacks	Manufacturing
2321	Men's And Boys' Shirts, Except Work Shirts	Manufacturing
231	Men's And Boys' Suits, Coats, And Overcoats	Manufacturing
2311	Men's And Boys' Suits, Coats, And Overcoats	Manufacturing
2322	Men's And Boys' Underwear And Nightwear	Manufacturing
2326	Men's And Boys' Work Clothing	Manufacturing
3143	Men's Footwear, Except Athletic	Manufacturing
3411	Metal Cans	Manufacturing
3411	Metal Cans	Manufacturing
341	Metal Cans And Shipping Containers	Manufacturing
3442	Metal Doors, Sash, Frames, Molding, And Trim	Manufacturing
3442	Metal Doors, Sash, Frames, Moldings & Trim	Manufacturing
3497	Metal Foil And Leaf	Manufacturing
3460	Metal Forgings & Stampings	Manufacturing
346	Metal Forgings And Stampings	Manufacturing
3398	Metal Heat Treating	Manufacturing
2514	Metal Household Furniture	Manufacturing
10	Metal Mining	Mining
1000	Metal Mining	Mining
108	Metal Mining Services	Mining
1081	Metal Mining Services	Mining
3412	Metal Shipping Barrels, Drums, Kegs & Pails	Manufacturing
3412	Metal Shipping Barrels, Drums, Kegs, And Pails	Manufacturing
3469	Metal Stampings, Not Elsewhere Classified	Manufacturing
505	Metals And Minerals, Except Petroleum	Wholesale Trade
5051	Metals Service Centers And Offices	Wholesale Trade
3540	Metalworkg Machinery & Equipment	Manufacturing
354	Metalworking Machinery And Equipment	Manufacturing
3549	Metalworking Machinery, Not Elsewhere Classified	Manufacturing
2430	Millwood, Veneer, Plywood, & Structural Wood Members	Manufacturing
2431	Millwork	Manufacturing
243	Millwork, Veneer, Plywood, And Structural Wood Members	Manufacturing
6795	Mineral Royalty Traders	Finance, Insurance, And Real Estate
3296	Mineral Wool	Manufacturing
3295	Minerals And Earths, Ground Or Otherwise Treated	Manufacturing
1400	Mining & Quarrying Of Nonmetallic Minerals (No Fuels)	Mining
14	Mining And Quarrying Of Nonmetallic Minerals, Except Fuels	Mining
3532	Mining Machinery & Equip (No Oil & Gas Field Mach & Equip)	Manufacturing
3532	Mining Machinery And Equipment, Except Oil And Gas Field Machinery	Manufacturing
3590	Misc Industrial & Commercial Machinery & Equipment	Manufacturing
799	Miscellaneous Amusement And Recreation Services	Services
238	Miscellaneous Apparel And Accessories	Manufacturing
569	Miscellaneous Apparel And Accessory Stores	Retail Trade
5699	Miscellaneous Apparel And Accessory Stores	Retail Trade
6159	Miscellaneous Business Credit Institution	Finance, Insurance, And Real Estate
6159	Miscellaneous Business Credit Institutions	Finance, Insurance, And Real Estate
738	Miscellaneous Business Services	Services
289	Miscellaneous Chemical Products	Manufacturing
2890	Miscellaneous Chemical Products	Manufacturing
509	Miscellaneous Durable Goods	Wholesale Trade
3690	Miscellaneous Electrical Machinery, Equipment & Supplies	Manufacturing
369	Miscellaneous Electrical Machinery, Equipment, And Supplies	Manufacturing
735	Miscellaneous Equipment Rental And Leasing	Services
349	Miscellaneous Fabricated Metal Products	Manufacturing
3490	Miscellaneous Fabricated Metal Products	Manufacturing
239	Miscellaneous Fabricated Textile Products	Manufacturing

Table of Contents for SIC Codes

Sorted by description

SIC Code	Description	Dvision Description
2390	Miscellaneous Fabricated Textile Products	Manufacturing
3496	Miscellaneous Fabricated Wire Products	Manufacturing
2090	Miscellaneous Food Preparations & Kindred Products	Manufacturing
209	Miscellaneous Food Preparations And Kindred Products	Manufacturing
549	Miscellaneous Food Stores	Retail Trade
5499	Miscellaneous Food Stores	Retail Trade
2590	Miscellaneous Furniture & Fixtures	Manufacturing
259	Miscellaneous Furniture And Fixtures	Manufacturing
539	Miscellaneous General Merchandise Stores	Retail Trade
5399	Miscellaneous General Merchandise Stores	Retail Trade
809	Miscellaneous Health And Allied Services, Not Elsewhere Classified	Services
5719	Miscellaneous Homefurnishings Stores	Retail Trade
359	Miscellaneous Industrial And Commercial Machinery And Equipment	Manufacturing
679	Miscellaneous Investing	Finance, Insurance, And Real Estate
39	Miscellaneous Manufacturing Industries	Manufacturing
399	Miscellaneous Manufacturing Industries	Manufacturing
3990	Miscellaneous Manufacturing Industries	Manufacturing
0919	Miscellaneous Marine Products	Agriculture, Forestry, And Fishing
109	Miscellaneous Metal Ores	Mining
1090	Miscellaneous Metal Ores	Mining
1099	Miscellaneous Metal Ores, Not Elsewhere Classified	Mining
519	Miscellaneous Nondurable Goods	Wholesale Trade
149	Miscellaneous Nonmetallic Minerals, Except Fuels	Mining
1499	Miscellaneous Nonmetallic Minerals, Except Fuels	Mining
729	Miscellaneous Personal Services	Services
7299	Miscellaneous Personal Services, Not Elsewhere Classified	Services
308	Miscellaneous Plastics Products	Manufacturing
3080	Miscellaneous Plastics Products	Manufacturing
339	Miscellaneous Primary Metal Products	Manufacturing
3390	Miscellaneous Primary Metal Products	Manufacturing
2990	Miscellaneous Products Of Petroleum & Coal	Manufacturing
299	Miscellaneous Products Of Petroleum And Coal	Manufacturing
274	Miscellaneous Publishing	Manufacturing
2741	Miscellaneous Publishing	Manufacturing
2741	Miscellaneous Publishing	Manufacturing
76	Miscellaneous Repair Services	Services
769	Miscellaneous Repair Shops And Related Services	Services
59	Miscellaneous Retail	Retail Trade
5999	Miscellaneous Retail Stores, Not Elsewhere Classified	Retail Trade
478	Miscellaneous Services Incidental To Transportation	Transportation, Communications, Electric, Gas, And Sanitary Service
594	Miscellaneous Shopping Goods Stores	Retail Trade
179	Miscellaneous Special Trade Contractors	Construction
3449	Miscellaneous Structural Metalwork	Manufacturing
229	Miscellaneous Textile Goods	Manufacturing
379	Miscellaneous Transportation Equipment	Manufacturing
3790	Miscellaneous Transportation Equipment	Manufacturing
249	Miscellaneous Wood Products	Manufacturing
4925	Mixed, Manufactured, Or Liquefied Petroleum Gas Production	Transportation, Communications, Electric, Gas, And Sanitary Service
527	Mobile Home Dealers	Retail Trade
5271	Mobile Home Dealers	Retail Trade
2451	Mobile Homes	Manufacturing
2451	Mobile Homes	Manufacturing
3061	Molded, Extruded, And Lathe-Cut Mechanical Rubber Goods	Manufacturing
6162	Mortgage Bankers & Loan Correspondents	Finance, Insurance, And Real Estate
616	Mortgage Bankers And Brokers	Finance, Insurance, And Real Estate
6162	Mortgage Bankers And Loan Correspondents	Finance, Insurance, And Real Estate
7822	Motion Picture And Video Tape Distribution	Services
7812	Motion Picture And Video Tape Production	Services
782	Motion Picture Distribution And Allied Services	Services
781	Motion Picture Production And Allied Services	Services
783	Motion Picture Theaters	Services
7832	Motion Picture Theaters, Except Drive-In	Services
78	Motion Pictures	Services
42	Motor Freight Transportation And Warehousing	Transportation, Communications, Electric, Gas, And Sanitary Service
3716	Motor Homes	Manufacturing
3716	Motor Homes	Manufacturing

Table of Contents for SIC Codes

Sorted by description

SIC Code	Description	Dvision Description
551	Motor Vehicle Dealers (New And Used)	Retail Trade
5511	Motor Vehicle Dealers (New And Used)	Retail Trade
552	Motor Vehicle Dealers (Used Only)	Retail Trade
5521	Motor Vehicle Dealers (Used Only)	Retail Trade
3714	Motor Vehicle Parts & Accessories	Manufacturing
3714	Motor Vehicle Parts And Accessories	Manufacturing
5015	Motor Vehicle Parts, Used	Wholesale Trade
5013	Motor Vehicle Supplies And New Parts	Wholesale Trade
3711	Motor Vehicles & Passenger Car Bodies	Manufacturing
371	Motor Vehicles And Motor Vehicle Equipment	Manufacturing
501	Motor Vehicles And Motor Vehicle Parts And Supplies	Wholesale Trade
3711	Motor Vehicles And Passenger Car Bodies	Manufacturing
557	Motorcycle Dealers	Retail Trade
5571	Motorcycle Dealers	Retail Trade
3751	Motorcycles, Bicycles & Parts	Manufacturing
375	Motorcycles, Bicycles, And Parts	Manufacturing
3751	Motorcycles, Bicycles, And Parts	Manufacturing
3621	Motors & Generators	Manufacturing
3621	Motors And Generators	Manufacturing
841	Museums And Art Galleries	Services
8412	Museums And Art Galleries	Services
84	Museums, Art Galleries, And Botanical And Zoological Gardens	Services
5736	Musical Instrument Stores	Retail Trade
393	Musical Instruments	Manufacturing
3931	Musical Instruments	Manufacturing
3931	Musical Instruments	Manufacturing
2441	Nailed And Lock Corner Wood Boxes And Shook	Manufacturing
224	Narrow Fabric And Other Smallwares Mills: Cotton, Wool, Silk	Manufacturing
2241	Narrow Fabric And Other Smallwares Mills: Cotton, Wool, Silk	Manufacturing
6021	National Commercial Banks	Finance, Insurance, And Real Estate
6021	National Commercial Banks	Finance, Insurance, And Real Estate
971	National Security	Public Adminstration
9711	National Security	Public Adminstration
97	National Security And International Affairs	Public Adminstration
4924	Natural Gas Distribution	Transportation, Communications, Electric, Gas, And Sanitary Service
4924	Natural Gas Distribution	Transportation, Communications, Electric, Gas, And Sanitary Service
132	Natural Gas Liquids	Mining
1321	Natural Gas Liquids	Mining
4923	Natural Gas Transmisison & Distribution	Transportation, Communications, Electric, Gas, And Sanitary Service
4922	Natural Gas Transmission	Transportation, Communications, Electric, Gas, And Sanitary Service
4922	Natural Gas Transmission	Transportation, Communications, Electric, Gas, And Sanitary Service
4923	Natural Gas Transmission And Distribution	Transportation, Communications, Electric, Gas, And Sanitary Service
2022	Natural, Processed, And Imitation Cheese	Manufacturing
5994	News Dealers And Newsstands	Retail Trade
7383	News Syndicates	Services
2711	Newspapers: Publishing Or Publishing & Printing	Manufacturing
271	Newspapers: Publishing, Or Publishing And Printing	Manufacturing
2711	Newspapers: Publishing, Or Publishing And Printing	Manufacturing
2873	Nitrogenous Fertilizers	Manufacturing
99	Nonclassifiable Establishments	Nonclassifiable Establishments
99	Nonclassifiable Establishments	Nonclassifiable Establishments
999	Nonclassifiable Establishments	Nonclassifiable Establishments
9999	Nonclassifiable Establishments	Nonclassifiable Establishments
3297	Nonclay Refractories	Manufacturing
8733	Noncommercial Research Organizations	Services
3644	Noncurrent-Carrying Wiring Devices	Manufacturing
6091	Nondeposit Trust Facilities	Finance, Insurance, And Real Estate
61	Nondepository Credit Institutions	Finance, Insurance, And Real Estate
5199	Nondurable Goods, Not Elsewhere Classified	Wholesale Trade
3364	Nonferrous Die-Castings, Except Aluminum	Manufacturing
3463	Nonferrous Forgings	Manufacturing
336	Nonferrous Foundries (Castings)	Manufacturing
3360	Nonferrous Foundries (Castings)	Manufacturing
3369	Nonferrous Foundries, Except Aluminum And Copper	Manufacturing
3299	Nonmetallic Mineral Products, Not Elsewhere Classified	Manufacturing
148	Nonmetallic Minerals Services, Except Fuels	Mining

Table of Contents for SIC Codes

Sorted by description

SIC Code	Description	Dvision Description
1481	Nonmetallic Minerals Services, Except Fuels	Mining
9995	Non-Operating Establishments	Nonclassifiable Establishments
596	Nonstore Retailers	Retail Trade
2297	Nonwoven Fabrics	Manufacturing
805	Nursing And Personal Care Facilities	Services
8059	Nursing And Personal Care Facilities, Not Elsewhere Classified	Services
2542	Office And Store Fixtures, Partitions, Shelving, And Lockers, Except Wood	Manufacturing
5044	Office Equipment	Wholesale Trade
252	Office Furniture	Manufacturing
2520	Office Furniture	Manufacturing
2522	Office Furniture (No Wood)	Manufacturing
2522	Office Furniture, Except Wood	Manufacturing
3579	Office Machines, Nec	Manufacturing
3579	Office Machines, Not Elsewhere Classified	Manufacturing
8041	Offices And Clinics Of Chiropractors	Services
802	Offices And Clinics Of Dentists	Services
8021	Offices And Clinics Of Dentists	Services
801	Offices And Clinics Of Doctors Of Medicine	Services
8011	Offices And Clinics Of Doctors Of Medicine	Services
803	Offices And Clinics Of Doctors Of Osteopathy	Services
8031	Offices And Clinics Of Doctors Of Osteopathy	Services
8049	Offices And Clinics Of Health Practitioners, Not Elsewhere Classified	Services
8042	Offices And Clinics Of Optometrists	Services
804	Offices And Clinics Of Other Health Practitioners	Services
8043	Offices And Clinics Of Podiatrists	Services
6712	Offices Of Bank Holding Companies	Finance, Insurance, And Real Estate
6719	Offices Of Holding Companies, Not Elsewhere Classified	Finance, Insurance, And Real Estate
1382	Oil & Gas Field Exploration Services	Mining
3533	Oil & Gas Field Machinery & Equipment	Manufacturing
1389	Oil & Gas Field Services, Nec	Mining
13	Oil And Gas Extraction	Mining
1382	Oil And Gas Field Exploration Services	Mining
3533	Oil And Gas Field Machinery And Equipment	Manufacturing
138	Oil And Gas Field Services	Mining
1389	Oil And Gas Field Services, Not Elsewhere Classified	Mining
6792	Oil Royalty Traders	Finance, Insurance, And Real Estate
6792	Oil Royalty Traders	Finance, Insurance, And Real Estate
153	Operative Builders	Construction
1531	Operative Builders	Construction
1531	Operative Builders	Construction
6513	Operators Of Apartment Buildings	Finance, Insurance, And Real Estate
6513	Operators Of Apartment Buildings	Finance, Insurance, And Real Estate
6514	Operators Of Dwellings Other Than Apartment Buildings	Finance, Insurance, And Real Estate
6512	Operators Of Nonresidential Buildings	Finance, Insurance, And Real Estate
6512	Operators Of Nonresidential Buildings	Finance, Insurance, And Real Estate
6515	Operators Of Residential Mobile Home Sites	Finance, Insurance, And Real Estate
385	Ophthalmic Goods	Manufacturing
3851	Ophthalmic Goods	Manufacturing
3851	Ophthalmic Goods	Manufacturing
5048	Ophthalmic Goods	Wholesale Trade
5995	Optical Goods Stores	Retail Trade
3827	Optical Instruments & Lenses	Manufacturing
3827	Optical Instruments And Lenses	Manufacturing
3480	Ordnance & Accessories, (No Vehicles/Guided Missiles)	Manufacturing
348	Ordnance And Accessories, Except Vehicles And Guided Missiles	Manufacturing
3489	Ordnance And Accessories, Not Elsewhere Classified	Manufacturing
704	Organization Hotels And Lodging Houses, On Membership Basis	Services
7041	Organization Hotels And Lodging Houses, On Membership Basis	Services
0181	Ornamental Floriculture And Nursery Products	Agriculture, Forestry, And Fishing
0783	Ornamental Shrub And Tree Services	Agriculture, Forestry, And Fishing
3842	Orthopedic, Prosthetic & Surgical Appliances & Supplies	Manufacturing
3842	Orthopedic, Prosthetic, And Surgical Appliances And Supplies	Manufacturing
7312	Outdoor Advertising Services	Services
3536	Overhead Traveling Cranes, Hoists, And Monorail Systems	Manufacturing
5142	Packaged Frozen Foods	Wholesale Trade
3565	Packaging Machinery	Manufacturing

Table of Contents for SIC Codes

Sorted by description

SIC Code	Description	Dvision Description
2671	Packaging Paper And Plastics Film, Coated And Laminated	Manufacturing
4783	Packing And Crating	Transportation, Communications, Electric, Gas, And Sanitary Service
523	Paint, Glass, And Wallpaper Stores	Retail Trade
5231	Paint, Glass, And Wallpaper Stores	Retail Trade
172	Painting And Paper Hanging	Construction
1721	Painting And Paper Hanging	Construction
5198	Paints, Varnishes, And Supplies	Wholesale Trade
2851	Paints, Varnishes, Lacquers, Enamels & Allied Prods	Manufacturing
285	Paints, Varnishes, Lacquers, Enamels, And Allied Products	Manufacturing
2851	Paints, Varnishes, Lacquers, Enamels, And Allied Products	Manufacturing
26	Paper And Allied Products	Manufacturing
511	Paper And Paper Products	Wholesale Trade
3554	Paper Industries Machinery	Manufacturing
262	Paper Mills	Manufacturing
2621	Paper Mills	Manufacturing
2621	Paper Mills	Manufacturing
2650	Paperboard Containers & Boxes	Manufacturing
265	Paperboard Containers And Boxes	Manufacturing
263	Paperboard Mills	Manufacturing
2631	Paperboard Mills	Manufacturing
2631	Paperboard Mills	Manufacturing
2600	Papers & Allied Products	Manufacturing
2540	Partitions, Shelvg, Lockers, & Office & Store Fixtures	Manufacturing
254	Partitions, Shelving, Lockers, And Office And Store Fixtures	Manufacturing
7515	Passenger Car Leasing	Services
7514	Passenger Car Rental	Services
6794	Patent Owners & Lessors	Finance, Insurance, And Real Estate
6794	Patent Owners And Lessors	Finance, Insurance, And Real Estate
3951	Pens, Mechanical Pencils, And Parts	Manufacturing
3950	Pens, Pencils & Other Artists' Materials	Manufacturing
395	Pens, Pencils, And Other Artists' Materials	Manufacturing
637	Pension, Health, And Welfare Funds	Finance, Insurance, And Real Estate
6371	Pension, Health, And Welfare Funds	Finance, Insurance, And Real Estate
2844	Perfumes, Cosmetics & Other Toilet Preparations	Manufacturing
2844	Perfumes, Cosmetics, And Other Toilet Preparations	Manufacturing
2721	Periodicals: Publishing Or Publishing & Printing	Manufacturing
272	Periodicals: Publishing, Or Publishing And Printing	Manufacturing
2721	Periodicals: Publishing, Or Publishing And Printing	Manufacturing
614	Personal Credit Institutions	Finance, Insurance, And Real Estate
6141	Personal Credit Institutions	Finance, Insurance, And Real Estate
6141	Personal Credit Institutions	Finance, Insurance, And Real Estate
3172	Personal Leather Goods, Except Women's Handbags And Purses	Manufacturing
72	Personal Services	Services
736	Personnel Supply Services	Services
2879	Pesticides And Agricultural Chemicals, Not Elsewhere Classified	Manufacturing
517	Petroleum And Petroleum Products	Wholesale Trade
5172	Petroleum And Petroleum Products Wholesalers, Except Bulk Station	Wholesale Trade
5171	Petroleum Bulk Stations And Terminals	Wholesale Trade
291	Petroleum Refining	Manufacturing
2911	Petroleum Refining	Manufacturing
2911	Petroleum Refining	Manufacturing
29	Petroleum Refining And Related Industries	Manufacturing
2834	Pharmaceutical Preparations	Manufacturing
2834	Pharmaceutical Preparations	Manufacturing
3652	Phonograph Records & Prerecorded Audio Tapes & Disks	Manufacturing
3652	Phonograph Records And Prerecorded Audio Tapes And Disks	Manufacturing
1475	Phosphate Rock	Mining
2874	Phosphatic Fertilizers	Manufacturing
7334	Photocopying And Duplicating Services	Services
7384	Photofinishing Laboratories	Services
3861	Photographic Equipment & Supplies	Manufacturing
386	Photographic Equipment And Supplies	Manufacturing
3861	Photographic Equipment And Supplies	Manufacturing
5043	Photographic Equipment And Supplies	Wholesale Trade
722	Photographic Studios, Portrait	Services
7221	Photographic Studios, Portrait	Services

Table of Contents for SIC Codes

Sorted by description

SIC Code	Description	Dvision Description
7991	Physical Fitness Facilities	Services
2035	Pickled Fruits And Vegetables, Vegetable Sauces And Seasonings	Manufacturing
5131	Piece Goods, Notions, And Other Dry Goods	Wholesale Trade
4610	Pipe Lines (No Natural Gas)	Transportation, Communications, Electric, Gas, And Sanitary Service
46	Pipelines, Except Natural Gas	Transportation, Communications, Electric, Gas, And Sanitary Service
461	Pipelines, Except Natural Gas	Transportation, Communications, Electric, Gas, And Sanitary Service
4619	Pipelines, Not Elsewhere Classified	Transportation, Communications, Electric, Gas, And Sanitary Service
1742	Plastering, Drywall, Acoustical, And Insulation Work	Construction
2820	Plastic Material, Synth Resin/Rubber, Cellulos (No Glass)	Manufacturing
2821	Plastic Materials, Synth Resins & Nonvulcan Elastomers	Manufacturing
3085	Plastics Bottles	Manufacturing
3086	Plastics Foam Products	Manufacturing
3086	Plastics Foam Products	Manufacturing
5162	Plastics Materials And Basic Forms And Shapes	Wholesale Trade
282	Plastics Materials And Synthetic Resins, Synthetic Rubber, Cellulosic Manmade Fibers	Manufacturing
2821	Plastics Materials, Synthetic Resins, And Nonvulcanizable Elastomers	Manufacturing
3084	Plastics Pipe	Manufacturing
3088	Plastics Plumbing Fixtures	Manufacturing
3089	Plastics Products, Nec	Manufacturing
3089	Plastics Products, Not Elsewhere Classified	Manufacturing
2673	Plastics, Foil & Coated Paper Bags	Manufacturing
2673	Plastics, Foil, And Coated Paper Bags	Manufacturing
2796	Platemaking And Related Services	Manufacturing
2395	Pleating, Decorative And Novelty Stitching, And Tucking	Manufacturing
5074	Plumbing And Heating Equipment And Supplies (Hydronics)	Wholesale Trade
3432	Plumbing Fixture Fittings And Trim	Manufacturing
171	Plumbing, Heating And Air-Conditioning	Construction
1711	Plumbing, Heating And Air-Conditioning	Construction
9221	Police Protection	Public Adminstration
865	Political Organizations	Services
8651	Political Organizations	Services
3264	Porcelain Electrical Supplies	Manufacturing
1474	Potash, Soda, And Borate Minerals	Mining
2096	Potato Chips, Corn Chips, And Similar Snacks	Manufacturing
3260	Pottery & Related Products	Manufacturing
326	Pottery And Related Products	Manufacturing
3269	Pottery Products, Not Elsewhere Classified	Manufacturing
025	Poultry And Eggs	Agriculture, Forestry, And Fishing
0259	Poultry And Eggs, Not Elsewhere Classified	Agriculture, Forestry, And Fishing
5144	Poultry And Poultry Products	Wholesale Trade
0254	Poultry Hatcheries	Agriculture, Forestry, And Fishing
2015	Poultry Slaughtering And Processing	Manufacturing
2015	Poultry Slaughtering And Processing	Manufacturing
7211	Power Laundries, Family And Commercial	Services
3612	Power, Distribution & Specialty Transformers	Manufacturing
3612	Power, Distribution, And Specialty Transformers	Manufacturing
3546	Power-Driven Handtools	Manufacturing
3448	Prefabricated Metal Buildings & Components	Manufacturing
3448	Prefabricated Metal Buildings And Components	Manufacturing
2452	Prefabricated Wood Bldgs & Components	Manufacturing
2452	Prefabricated Wood Buildings And Components	Manufacturing
7372	Prepackaged Software	Services
2048	Prepared Feeds And Feed Ingredients For Animals And Fowls, Except Dog And Cat	Manufacturing
2045	Prepared Flour Mixes And Doughs	Manufacturing
2092	Prepared Fresh Or Frozen Fish & Seafoods	Manufacturing
2092	Prepared Fresh Or Frozen Fish And Seafoods	Manufacturing
3229	Pressed And Blown Glass And Glassware, Not Elsewhere Classified	Manufacturing
3692	Primary Batteries, Dry And Wet	Manufacturing
33	Primary Metal Industries	Manufacturing
3399	Primary Metal Products, Not Elsewhere Classified	Manufacturing
3334	Primary Production Of Aluminum	Manufacturing
3334	Primary Production Of Aluminum	Manufacturing
3330	Primary Smelting & Refining Of Nonferrous Metals	Manufacturing
3331	Primary Smelting And Refining Of Copper	Manufacturing

SIC Code	Description	Dvision Description
333	Primary Smelting And Refining Of Nonferrous Metals	Manufacturing
3339	Primary Smelting And Refining Of Nonferrous Metals, Except Copper	Manufacturing
3672	Printed Circuit Boards	Manufacturing
3672	Printed Circuit Boards	Manufacturing
5111	Printing And Writing Paper	Wholesale Trade
2893	Printing Ink	Manufacturing
3555	Printing Trades Machinery & Equipment	Manufacturing
3555	Printing Trades Machinery And Equipment	Manufacturing
27	Printing, Publishing, And Allied Industries	Manufacturing
88	Private Households	Services
881	Private Households	Services
8811	Private Households	Services
2999	Products Of Petroleum And Coal, Not Elsewhere Classified	Manufacturing
504	Professional And Commercial Equipment And Supplies	Wholesale Trade
5049	Professional Equipment And Supplies, Not Elsewhere Classified	Wholesale Trade
862	Professional Membership Organizations	Services
8621	Professional Membership Organizations	Services
7941	Professional Sports Clubs And Promoters	Services
8063	Psychiatric Hospitals	Services
2531	Public Bldg & Related Furniture	Manufacturing
253	Public Building And Related Furniture	Manufacturing
2531	Public Building And Related Furniture	Manufacturing
93	Public Finance, Taxation, And Monetary Policy	Public Adminstration
931	Public Finance, Taxation, And Monetary Policy	Public Adminstration
9311	Public Finance, Taxation, And Monetary Policy	Public Adminstration
7992	Public Golf Courses	Services
922	Public Order And Safety	Public Adminstration
9229	Public Order And Safety, Not Elsewhere Classified	Public Adminstration
8743	Public Relations Services	Services
4220	Public Warehousing & Storage	Transportation, Communications, Electric, Gas, And Sanitary Service
422	Public Warehousing And Storage	Transportation, Communications, Electric, Gas, And Sanitary Service
261	Pulp Mills	Manufacturing
2611	Pulp Mills	Manufacturing
2611	Pulp Mills	Manufacturing
3561	Pumps & Pumping Equipment	Manufacturing
3561	Pumps And Pumping Equipment	Manufacturing
7948	Racing, Including Track Operation	Services
3663	Radio & Tv Broadcasting & Communications Equipment	Manufacturing
3663	Radio And Television Broadcasting And Communications Equipment	Manufacturing
483	Radio And Television Broadcasting Stations	Transportation, Communications, Electric, Gas, And Sanitary Service
7622	Radio And Television Repair Shops	Services
4832	Radio Broadcasting Stations	Transportation, Communications, Electric, Gas, And Sanitary Service
4832	Radio Broadcasting Stations	Transportation, Communications, Electric, Gas, And Sanitary Service
5731	Radio, Television, And Consumer Electronics Stores	Retail Trade
7313	Radio, Television, And Publishers' Advertising Representatives	Services
573	Radio, Television, Consumer Electronics, And Music Stores	Retail Trade
4812	Radiotelephone Communications	Transportation, Communications, Electric, Gas, And Sanitary Service
4812	Radiotelephone Communications	Transportation, Communications, Electric, Gas, And Sanitary Service
374	Railroad Equipment	Manufacturing
3743	Railroad Equipment	Manufacturing
3743	Railroad Equipment	Manufacturing
4013	Railroad Switching & Terminal Establishments	Transportation, Communications, Electric, Gas, And Sanitary Service
4013	Railroad Switching And Terminal Establishments	Transportation, Communications, Electric, Gas, And Sanitary Service
40	Railroad Transportation	Transportation, Communications, Electric, Gas, And Sanitary Service
401	Railroads	Transportation, Communications, Electric, Gas, And Sanitary Service
4011	Railroads, Line-Haul Operating	Transportation, Communications, Electric, Gas, And Sanitary Service
4011	Railroads, Line-Haul Operating	Transportation, Communications, Electric, Gas, And Sanitary Service
3273	Ready-Mixed Concrete	Manufacturing
65	Real Estate	Finance, Insurance, And Real Estate
6500	Real Estate	Finance, Insurance, And Real Estate
6531	Real Estate Agents & Managers (For Others)	Finance, Insurance, And Real Estate
653	Real Estate Agents And Managers	Finance, Insurance, And Real Estate
6531	Real Estate Agents And Managers	Finance, Insurance, And Real Estate
6532	Real Estate Dealers (For Their Own Account)	Finance, Insurance, And Real Estate
6798	Real Estate Investment Trusts	Finance, Insurance, And Real Estate
6798	Real Estate Investment Trusts	Finance, Insurance, And Real Estate

Sorted by description

SIC Code	Description	Dvision Description
651	Real Estate Operators (Except Developers) And Lessors	Finance, Insurance, And Real Estate
6510	Real Estate Operators (No Developers) & Lessors	Finance, Insurance, And Real Estate
2493	Reconstituted Wood Products	Manufacturing
5735	Record And Prerecorded Tape Stores	Retail Trade
556	Recreational Vehicle Dealers	Retail Trade
5561	Recreational Vehicle Dealers	Retail Trade
7033	Recreational Vehicle Parks And Campsites	Services
4613	Refined Petroleum Pipelines	Transportation, Communications, Electric, Gas, And Sanitary Service
4222	Refrigerated Warehousing And Storage	Transportation, Communications, Electric, Gas, And Sanitary Service
3580	Refrigeration & Service Industry Machinery	Manufacturing
7623	Refrigeration And Air-Conditioning Service And Repair Shops	Services
358	Refrigeration And Service Industry Machinery	Manufacturing
5078	Refrigeration Equipment And Supplies	Wholesale Trade
4953	Refuse Systems	Transportation, Communications, Electric, Gas, And Sanitary Service
4953	Refuse Systems	Transportation, Communications, Electric, Gas, And Sanitary Service
963	Regulation And Administration Of Communications, Electric, Gas	Public Adminstration
9631	Regulation And Administration Of Communications, Electric, Gas	Public Adminstration
962	Regulation And Administration Of Transportation Programs	Public Adminstration
9621	Regulation And Administration Of Transportation Programs	Public Adminstration
964	Regulation Of Agricultural Marketing And Commodities	Public Adminstration
9641	Regulation Of Agricultural Marketing And Commodities	Public Adminstration
965	Regulation, Licensing, And Inspection Of Miscellaneous Commercial	Public Adminstration
9651	Regulation, Licensing, And Inspection Of Miscellaneous Commercial	Public Adminstration
3625	Relays And Industrial Controls	Manufacturing
866	Religious Organizations	Services
8661	Religious Organizations	Services
474	Rental Of Railroad Cars	Transportation, Communications, Electric, Gas, And Sanitary Service
4741	Rental Of Railroad Cars	Transportation, Communications, Electric, Gas, And Sanitary Service
7699	Repair Shops And Related Services, Not Elsewhere Classified	Services
873	Research, Development, And Testing Services	Services
836	Residential Care	Services
8361	Residential Care	Services
3645	Residential Electric Lighting Fixtures	Manufacturing
546	Retail Bakeries	Retail Trade
5461	Retail Bakeries	Retail Trade
526	Retail Nurseries, Lawn And Garden Supply Stores	Retail Trade
5261	Retail Nurseries, Lawn And Garden Supply Stores	Retail Trade
599	Retail Stores, Not Elsewhere Classified	Retail Trade
52	Retail Trade	Retail Trade
5600	Retail-Apparel & Accessory Stores	Retail Trade
5531	Retail-Auto & Home Supply Stores	Retail Trade
5500	Retail-Auto Dealers & Gasoline Stations	Retail Trade
5200	Retail-Building Materials, Hardware, Garden Supply	Retail Trade
5961	Retail-Catalog & Mail-Order Houses	Retail Trade
5734	Retail-Computer & Computer Software Stores	Retail Trade
5412	Retail-Convenience Stores	Retail Trade
5311	Retail-Department Stores	Retail Trade
5912	Retail-Drug Stores And Proprietary Stores	Retail Trade
5810	Retail-Eating & Drinking Places	Retail Trade
5812	Retail-Eating Places	Retail Trade
5651	Retail-Family Clothing Stores	Retail Trade
5400	Retail-Food Stores	Retail Trade
5712	Retail-Furniture Stores	Retail Trade
5411	Retail-Grocery Stores	Retail Trade
5945	Retail-Hobby, Toy & Game Shops	Retail Trade
5700	Retail-Home Furniture, Furnishings & Equipment Stores	Retail Trade
5944	Retail-Jewelry Stores	Retail Trade
5211	Retail-Lumber & Other Building Materials Dealers	Retail Trade
5399	Retail-Misc General Merchandise Stores	Retail Trade
5900	Retail-Miscellaneous Retail	Retail Trade
5940	Retail-Miscellaneous Shopping Goods Stores	Retail Trade
5271	Retail-Mobile Home Dealers	Retail Trade
5960	Retail-Nonstore Retailers	Retail Trade
5731	Retail-Radio, Tv & Consumer Electronics Stores	Retail Trade
5735	Retail-Record & Prerecorded Tape Stores	Retail Trade
5990	Retail-Retail Stores, Nec	Retail Trade

Sorted by description

Sorted by description

SIC Code	Description	Dvision Description
7382	Security Systems Services	Services
3674	Semiconductors & Related Devices	Manufacturing
3674	Semiconductors And Related Devices	Manufacturing
5087	Service Establishment Equipment And Supplies	Wholesale Trade
279	Service Industries For The Printing Trade	Manufacturing
2790	Service Industries For The Printing Trade	Manufacturing
3589	Service Industry Machinery, Not Elsewhere Classified	Manufacturing
7829	Services Allied To Motion Picture Distribution	Services
7819	Services Allied To Motion Picture Production	Services
628	Services Allied With The Exchange Of Securities Or Commodities	Finance, Insurance, And Real Estate
6289	Services Allied With The Exchange Of Securities Or Commodities	Finance, Insurance, And Real Estate
449	Services Incidental To Water Transportation	Transportation, Communications, Electric, Gas, And Sanitary Service
734	Services To Dwellings And Other Buildings	Services
89	Services, Not Elsewhere Classified	Services
899	Services, Not Elsewhere Classified	Services
8999	Services, Not Elsewhere Classified	Services
7310	Services-Advertising	Services
7311	Services-Advertising Agencies	Services
7829	Services-Allied To Motion Picture Distribution	Services
7819	Services-Allied To Motion Picture Production	Services
7900	Services-Amusement & Recreation Services	Services
7510	Services-Auto Rental & Leasing (No Drivers)	Services
7500	Services-Automotive Repair, Services & Parking	Services
7389	Services-Business Services, Nec	Services
8351	Services-Child Day Care Services	Services
8731	Services-Commercial Physical & Biological Research	Services
7373	Services-Computer Integrated Systems Design	Services
7374	Services-Computer Processing & Data Preparation	Services
7371	Services-Computer Programming Services	Services
7370	Services-Computer Programming, Data Processing, Etc.	Services
7377	Services-Computer Rental & Leasing	Services
7320	Services-Consumer Credit Reporting, Collection Agencies	Services
7381	Services-Detective, Guard & Armored Car Services	Services
7331	Services-Direct Mail Advertising Services	Services
8200	Services-Educational Services	Services
7361	Services-Employment Agencies	Services
8711	Services-Engineering Services	Services
8700	Services-Engineering, Accounting, Research, Management	Services
7359	Services-Equipment Rental & Leasing, Nec	Services
8744	Services-Facilities Support Management Services	Services
8062	Services-General Medical & Surgical Hospitals, Nec	Services
8000	Services-Health Services	Services
7363	Services-Help Supply Services	Services
8082	Services-Home Health Care Services	Services
8060	Services-Hospitals	Services
8111	Services-Legal Services	Services
7330	Services-Mailing, Reproduction, Commercial Art & Photography	Services
8742	Services-Management Consulting Services	Services
8741	Services-Management Services	Services
8071	Services-Medical Laboratories	Services
8600	Services-Membership Organizations	Services
7997	Services-Membership Sports & Recreation Clubs	Services
8090	Services-Misc Health & Allied Services, Nec	Services
7990	Services-Miscellaneous Amusement & Recreation	Services
7380	Services-Miscellaneous Business Services	Services
7350	Services-Miscellaneous Equipment Rental & Leasing	Services
7600	Services-Miscellaneous Repair Services	Services
7822	Services-Motion Picture & Video Tape Distribution	Services
7812	Services-Motion Picture & Video Tape Production	Services
7830	Services-Motion Picture Theaters	Services
8050	Services-Nursing & Personal Care Facilities	Services
8011	Services-Offices & Clinics Of Doctors Of Medicine	Services
7200	Services-Personal Services	Services
7384	Services-Photofinishing Laboratories	Services
7372	Services-Prepackaged Software	Services
7948	Services-Racing, Including Track Operation	Services

Table of Contents for SIC Codes

Sorted by description

Table of Contents for SIC Codes

Sorted by description

Table of Contents for SIC Codes

Sorted by description

SIC Code	Description	Dvision Description
0811	Timber Tracts	Agriculture, Forestry, And Fishing
2296	Tire Cord And Fabrics	Manufacturing
7534	Tire Retreading And Repair Shops	Services
3011	Tires & Inner Tubes	Manufacturing
301	Tires And Inner Tubes	Manufacturing
3011	Tires And Inner Tubes	Manufacturing
5014	Tires And Tubes	Wholesale Trade
654	Title Abstract Offices	Finance, Insurance, And Real Estate
6541	Title Abstract Offices	Finance, Insurance, And Real Estate
636	Title Insurance	Finance, Insurance, And Real Estate
6361	Title Insurance	Finance, Insurance, And Real Estate
6361	Title Insurance	Finance, Insurance, And Real Estate
0132	Tobacco	Agriculture, Forestry, And Fishing
5194	Tobacco And Tobacco Products	Wholesale Trade
21	Tobacco Products	Manufacturing
2100	Tobacco Products	Manufacturing
214	Tobacco Stemming And Redrying	Manufacturing
2141	Tobacco Stemming And Redrying	Manufacturing
5993	Tobacco Stores And Stands	Retail Trade
7532	Top, Body, And Upholstery Repair Shops And Paint Shops	Services
3824	Totalizing Fluid Meters & Counting Devices	Manufacturing
3824	Totalizing Fluid Meters And Counting Devices	Manufacturing
4725	Tour Operators	Transportation, Communications, Electric, Gas, And Sanitary Service
4492	Towing And Tugboat Services	Transportation, Communications, Electric, Gas, And Sanitary Service
5092	Toys And Hobby Goods And Supplies	Wholesale Trade
45	Transportation By Air	Transportation, Communications, Electric, Gas, And Sanitary Service
37	Transportation Equipment	Manufacturing
5088	Transportation Equipment And Supplies, Except Motor Vehicles	Wholesale Trade
3799	Transportation Equipment, Not Elsewhere Classified	Manufacturing
47	Transportation Services	Transportation, Communications, Electric, Gas, And Sanitary Service
4700	Transportation Services	Transportation, Communications, Electric, Gas, And Sanitary Service
4789	Transportation Services, Not Elsewhere Classified	Transportation, Communications, Electric, Gas, And Sanitary Service
4724	Travel Agencies	Transportation, Communications, Electric, Gas, And Sanitary Service
3792	Travel Trailers And Campers	Manufacturing
0173	Tree Nuts	Agriculture, Forestry, And Fishing
3713	Truck & Bus Bodies	Manufacturing
3713	Truck And Bus Bodies	Manufacturing
7513	Truck Rental And Leasing, Without Drivers	Services
3715	Truck Trailers	Manufacturing
3715	Truck Trailers	Manufacturing
4210	Trucking & Courier Services (No Air)	Transportation, Communications, Electric, Gas, And Sanitary Service
4213	Trucking (No Local)	Transportation, Communications, Electric, Gas, And Sanitary Service
421	Trucking And Courier Services, Except Air	Transportation, Communications, Electric, Gas, And Sanitary Service
4213	Trucking, Except Local	Transportation, Communications, Electric, Gas, And Sanitary Service
673	Trusts	Finance, Insurance, And Real Estate
6733	Trusts, Except Educational, Religious, And Charitable	Finance, Insurance, And Real Estate
0253	Turkeys And Turkey Eggs	Agriculture, Forestry, And Fishing
2791	Typesetting	Manufacturing
2674	Uncoated Paper And Multiwall Bags	Manufacturing
6726	Unit Investment Trusts, Face-Amount Certificate Offices	Finance, Insurance, And Real Estate
43	United States Postal Service	Transportation, Communications, Electric, Gas, And Sanitary Service
431	United States Postal Service	Transportation, Communications, Electric, Gas, And Sanitary Service
4311	United States Postal Service	Transportation, Communications, Electric, Gas, And Sanitary Service
3081	Unsupported Plastics Film & Sheet	Manufacturing
3081	Unsupported Plastics Film And Sheet	Manufacturing
3082	Unsupported Plastics Profile Shapes	Manufacturing
1094	Uranium-Radium-Vanadium Ores	Mining
593	Used Merchandise Stores	Retail Trade
5932	Used Merchandise Stores	Retail Trade
7519	Utility Trailer And Recreational Vehicle Rental	Services
3494	Valves And Pipe Fittings, Not Elsewhere Classified	Manufacturing
533	Variety Stores	Retail Trade
5331	Variety Stores	Retail Trade
2076	Vegetable Oil Mills, Except Corn, Cottonseed, And Soybean	Manufacturing
016	Vegetables And Melons	Agriculture, Forestry, And Fishing
0161	Vegetables And Melons	Agriculture, Forestry, And Fishing

Table of Contents for SIC Codes

Sorted by description

SIC Code	Description	Dvision Description
3647	Vehicular Lighting Equipment	Manufacturing
074	Veterinary Services	Agriculture, Forestry, And Fishing
0742	Veterinary Services For Animal Specialties	Agriculture, Forestry, And Fishing
0741	Veterinary Services For Livestock	Agriculture, Forestry, And Fishing
784	Video Tape Rental	Services
7841	Video Tape Rental	Services
3261	Vitreous China Plumbing Fixtures And China And Earthenware Fittings	Manufacturing
3262	Vitreous China Table And Kitchen Articles	Manufacturing
824	Vocational Schools	Services
8249	Vocational Schools, Not Elsewhere Classified	Services
5075	Warm Air Heating And Air-Conditioning Equipment And Supplies	Wholesale Trade
763	Watch, Clock, And Jewelry Repair	Services
7631	Watch, Clock, And Jewelry Repair	Services
387	Watches, Clocks, Clockwork Operated Devices, And Parts	Manufacturing
3873	Watches, Clocks, Clockwork Operated Devices, And Parts	Manufacturing
3873	Watches, Clocks, Clockwork Operated Devices/Parts	Manufacturing
494	Water Supply	Transportation, Communications, Electric, Gas, And Sanitary Service
4941	Water Supply	Transportation, Communications, Electric, Gas, And Sanitary Service
4941	Water Supply	Transportation, Communications, Electric, Gas, And Sanitary Service
44	Water Transportation	Transportation, Communications, Electric, Gas, And Sanitary Service
4400	Water Transportation	Transportation, Communications, Electric, Gas, And Sanitary Service
444	Water Transportation Of Freight, Not Elsewhere Classified	Transportation, Communications, Electric, Gas, And Sanitary Service
4449	Water Transportation Of Freight, Not Elsewhere Classified	Transportation, Communications, Electric, Gas, And Sanitary Service
448	Water Transportation Of Passengers	Transportation, Communications, Electric, Gas, And Sanitary Service
4489	Water Transportation Of Passengers, Not Elsewhere Classified	Transportation, Communications, Electric, Gas, And Sanitary Service
4499	Water Transportation Services, Not Elsewhere Classified	Transportation, Communications, Electric, Gas, And Sanitary Service
178	Water Well Drilling	Construction
1781	Water Well Drilling	Construction
1623	Water, Sewer, Pipeline, And Communications And Power Line Construction	Construction
1623	Water, Sewer, Pipeline, Comm & Power Line Construction	Construction
2385	Waterproof Outerwear	Manufacturing
2257	Weft Knit Fabric Mills	Manufacturing
7692	Welding Repair	Services
2046	Wet Corn Milling	Manufacturing
0111	Wheat	Agriculture, Forestry, And Fishing
50	Wholesale Trade¨Durable Goods	Wholesale Trade
51	Wholesale Trade¨Nondurable Goods	Wholesale Trade
5130	Wholesale-Apparel, Piece Goods & Notions	Wholesale Trade
5180	Wholesale-Beer, Wine & Distilled Alcoholic Beverages	Wholesale Trade
5160	Wholesale-Chemicals & Allied Products	Wholesale Trade
5045	Wholesale-Computers & Peripheral Equipment & Software	Wholesale Trade
5082	Wholesale-Construction & Mining (No Petro) Machinery & Equip	Wholesale Trade
5122	Wholesale-Drugs, Proprietaries & Druggists' Sundries	Wholesale Trade
5000	Wholesale-Durable Goods	Wholesale Trade
5099	Wholesale-Durable Goods, Nec	Wholesale Trade
5063	Wholesale-Electrical Apparatus & Equipment, Wiring Supplies	Wholesale Trade
5064	Wholesale-Electrical Appliances, Tv & Radio Sets	Wholesale Trade
5065	Wholesale-Electronic Parts & Equipment, Nec	Wholesale Trade
5150	Wholesale-Farm Product Raw Materials	Wholesale Trade
5020	Wholesale-Furniture & Home Furnishings	Wholesale Trade
5140	Wholesale-Groceries & Related Products	Wholesale Trade
5141	Wholesale-Groceries, General Line	Wholesale Trade
5072	Wholesale-Hardware	Wholesale Trade
5070	Wholesale-Hardware & Plumbing & Heating Equipment & Supplies	Wholesale Trade
5084	Wholesale-Industrial Machinery & Equipment	Wholesale Trade
5094	Wholesale-Jewelry, Watches, Precious Stones & Metals	Wholesale Trade
5030	Wholesale-Lumber & Other Construction Materials	Wholesale Trade
5031	Wholesale-Lumber, Plywood, Millwork & Wood Panels	Wholesale Trade
5080	Wholesale-Machinery, Equipment & Supplies	Wholesale Trade
5047	Wholesale-Medical, Dental & Hospital Equipment & Supplies	Wholesale Trade
5050	Wholesale-Metals & Minerals (No Petroleum)	Wholesale Trade
5051	Wholesale-Metals Service Centers & Offices	Wholesale Trade
5090	Wholesale-Misc Durable Goods	Wholesale Trade
5190	Wholesale-Miscellaneous Nondurable Goods	Wholesale Trade
5013	Wholesale-Motor Vehicle Supplies & New Parts	Wholesale Trade
5010	Wholesale-Motor Vehicles & Motor Vehicle Parts & Supplies	Wholesale Trade

Table of Contents for SIC Codes

Sorted by description

Common Stocks by SIC Codes

Betas of Common Stocks by SIC Codes as of September 28, 2018

Details:
Benchmark: S&P 500 Index
Returns period and frequency: 1 year of daily returns
Risk-free rate for betas: Federal Funds Rate
Expected US Equity Risk Premium: 5.40% (Fernandez, Pablo and Pershin, Vitaly and Fernández Acín, Isabel, Market Risk Premium and Risk-Free Rate used for 59 Countries in 2018: A Survey (April 3, 2018). Available at SSRN: https://ssrn.com/abstract=3155709)

SIC Code	Description	Number of Companies	Equity Risk Premium	Mean	Median	1st Percentile	2.5th Percentile	5th Percentile	40th Percentile	50th Percentile	60th Percentile	95th Percentile	97.5th Percentile	99th Percentile
	AGRICULTURE, FORESTRY, AND FISHING													
01	AGRICULTURAL PRODUCTION-CROPS	9	2.93%	0.543482	0.579645	-0.066171	-0.050572	-0.024573	0.439192	0.579645	0.698799	1.197898	1.317569	1.389372
011	CASH GRAINS	2	4.23%	0.783737	0.783737	0.729691	0.731345	0.734103	0.772707	0.783737	0.794766	0.833370	0.836128	0.837782
0115	Corn	1	4.53%	0.838885	0.838885	0.838885	0.838885	0.838885	0.838885	0.838885	0.838885	0.838885	0.838885	0.838885
0116	Soybeans	1	3.93%	0.728588	0.728588	0.728588	0.728588	0.728588	0.728588	0.728588	0.728588	0.728588	0.728588	0.728588
013	FIELD CROPS, EXCEPT CASH GRAINS	1	0.29%	0.053422	0.053422	0.053422	0.053422	0.053422	0.053422	0.053422	0.053422	0.053422	0.053422	0.053422
0131	Cotton	1	0.29%	0.053422	0.053422	0.053422	0.053422	0.053422	0.053422	0.053422	0.053422	0.053422	0.053422	0.053422
016	VEGETABLES AND MELONS	1	7.76%	1.437240	1.437240	1.437240	1.437240	1.437240	1.437240	1.437240	1.437240	1.437240	1.437240	1.437240
0161	Vegetables And Melons	1	7.76%	1.437240	1.437240	1.437240	1.437240	1.437240	1.437240	1.437240	1.437240	1.437240	1.437240	1.437240
017	FRUITS AND TREE NUTS	2	2.50%	0.463026	0.463026	0.176064	0.184849	0.199490	0.404462	0.463026	0.521590	0.726562	0.741203	0.749988
0174	Citrus Fruits	2	2.50%	0.463026	0.463026	0.176064	0.184849	0.199490	0.404462	0.463026	0.521590	0.726562	0.741203	0.749988
018	HORTICULTURAL SPECIALTIES	1	-0.41%	-0.076570	-0.076570	-0.076570	-0.076570	-0.076570	-0.076570	-0.076570	-0.076570	-0.076570	-0.076570	-0.076570
0181	Ornamental Floriculture And Nursery Products	1	-0.41%	-0.076570	-0.076570	-0.076570	-0.076570	-0.076570	-0.076570	-0.076570	-0.076570	-0.076570	-0.076570	-0.076570
019	GENERAL FARMS, PRIMARILY CROP	1	2.18%	0.404079	0.404079	0.404079	0.404079	0.404079	0.404079	0.404079	0.404079	0.404079	0.404079	0.404079
0191	General Farms, Primarily Crop	1	2.18%	0.404079	0.404079	0.404079	0.404079	0.404079	0.404079	0.404079	0.404079	0.404079	0.404079	0.404079
02	AGRICULTURAL PRODUCTION-LIVESTOCK AND ANIMAL SPECIALTIES	2	0.31%	0.056826	0.056826	-0.308621	-0.297434	-0.278789	-0.017755	0.056826	0.131406	0.392440	0.411085	0.422272
021	LIVESTOCK, EXCEPT DAIRY AND POULTRY	1	-1.71%	-0.316079	-0.316079	-0.316079	-0.316079	-0.316079	-0.316079	-0.316079	-0.316079	-0.316079	-0.316079	-0.316079
0213	Hogs	1	-1.71%	-0.316079	-0.316079	-0.316079	-0.316079	-0.316079	-0.316079	-0.316079	-0.316079	-0.316079	-0.316079	-0.316079
025	POULTRY AND EGGS	1	2.32%	0.429730	0.429730	0.429730	0.429730	0.429730	0.429730	0.429730	0.429730	0.429730	0.429730	0.429730
0252	Chicken Eggs	1	2.32%	0.429730	0.429730	0.429730	0.429730	0.429730	0.429730	0.429730	0.429730	0.429730	0.429730	0.429730
07	AGRICULTURAL SERVICES	5	2.63%	0.487309	0.701490	-0.831268	-0.744383	-0.599575	0.644450	0.701490	0.794408	1.092013	1.111791	1.123659
074	VETERINARY SERVICES	1	3.02%	0.558890	0.558890	0.558890	0.558890	0.558890	0.558890	0.558890	0.558890	0.558890	0.558890	0.558890
0742	Veterinary Services For Animal Specialties	1	3.02%	0.558890	0.558890	0.558890	0.558890	0.558890	0.558890	0.558890	0.558890	0.558890	0.558890	0.558890
075	ANIMAL SERVICES, EXCEPT VETERINARY	1	-4.80%	-0.889191	-0.889191	-0.889191	-0.889191	-0.889191	-0.889191	-0.889191	-0.889191	-0.889191	-0.889191	-0.889191
0752	Animal Specialty Services, Except Veterinary	1	-4.80%	-0.889191	-0.889191	-0.889191	-0.889191	-0.889191	-0.889191	-0.889191	-0.889191	-0.889191	-0.889191	-0.889191
076	FARM LABOR AND MANAGEMENT SERVICES	1	5.04%	0.933784	0.933784	0.933784	0.933784	0.933784	0.933784	0.933784	0.933784	0.933784	0.933784	0.933784
0762	Farm Management Services	1	5.04%	0.933784	0.933784	0.933784	0.933784	0.933784	0.933784	0.933784	0.933784	0.933784	0.933784	0.933784
078	LANDSCAPE AND HORTICULTURAL SERVICES	1	3.79%	0.701490	0.701490	0.701490	0.701490	0.701490	0.701490	0.701490	0.701490	0.701490	0.701490	0.701490
0782	Lawn And Garden Services	1	3.79%	0.701490	0.701490	0.701490	0.701490	0.701490	0.701490	0.701490	0.701490	0.701490	0.701490	0.701490
08	FORESTRY	1	2.83%	0.524506	0.524506	0.524506	0.524506	0.524506	0.524506	0.524506	0.524506	0.524506	0.524506	0.524506
085	FORESTRY SERVICES	1	2.83%	0.524506	0.524506	0.524506	0.524506	0.524506	0.524506	0.524506	0.524506	0.524506	0.524506	0.524506
0851	Forestry Services	1	2.83%	0.524506	0.524506	0.524506	0.524506	0.524506	0.524506	0.524506	0.524506	0.524506	0.524506	0.524506
09	FISHING, HUNTING, AND TRAPPING	2	0.94%	0.173698	0.173698	-0.899326	-0.866478	-0.811732	-0.045286	0.173698	0.392682	1.159128	1.213874	1.246722
	MINING													
10	METAL MINING	218	2.53%	0.468866	0.447739	-0.922960	-0.476219	-0.153134	0.324466	0.447739	0.562070	1.302041	1.416184	1.645182
1000	METAL MINING	5	0.17%	0.032374	0.196183	-1.694146	-1.585661	-1.404852	0.134357	0.196183	0.302789	1.074811	1.151326	1.197234
101	IRON ORES	6	2.83%	0.524980	0.596061	0.143170	0.173369	0.223701	0.582887	0.596061	0.609234	0.670087	0.677873	0.682545
1011	Iron Ores	6	2.83%	0.524980	0.596061	0.143170	0.173369	0.223701	0.582887	0.596061	0.609234	0.670087	0.677873	0.682545
102	COPPER ORES	20	4.20%	0.778116	0.636588	0.101784	0.165620	0.272014	0.572700	0.636588	0.749115	1.586892	1.619396	1.638898
1021	Copper Ores	20	4.20%	0.778116	0.636588	0.101784	0.165620	0.272014	0.572700	0.636588	0.749115	1.586892	1.619396	1.638898
103	LEAD AND ZINC ORES	2	5.37%	0.994314	0.994314	0.592969	0.605255	0.625732	0.912407	0.994314	1.076221	1.362896	1.383373	1.395659

Betas of Common Stocks by SIC Codes as of September 28, 2018

SIC Code	Description	Number of Companies	Equity Risk Premium	Mean	Median	1st Percentile	2.5th Percentile	5th Percentile	40th Percentile	50th Percentile	60th Percentile	95th Percentile	97.5th Percentile	99th Percentile
1031	Lead And Zinc Ores	2	5.37%	0.994314	0.994314	0.592969	0.605255	0.625732	0.912407	0.994314	1.076221	1.362896	1.383373	1.395659
104	GOLD AND SILVER ORES	123	2.00%	0.370738	0.349243	-0.922653	-0.434163	-0.263254	0.295223	0.349243	0.454493	0.938683	0.991771	1.238612
1040	GOLD AND SILVER ORES	3	1.59%	0.293737	0.325581	0.201579	0.205375	0.211701	0.300274	0.325581	0.331781	0.353483	0.355033	0.355963
1041	Gold Ores	110	1.95%	0.360188	0.344596	-0.923450	-0.570426	-0.306430	0.262079	0.344596	0.438278	0.936659	0.993145	1.279200
1044	Silver Ores	10	2.75%	0.509894	0.518818	0.112495	0.139954	0.185719	0.436421	0.518818	0.547805	0.922682	0.951151	0.968232
106	FERROALLOY ORES, EXCEPT VANADIUM	6	4.17%	0.773120	0.771457	0.187371	0.203692	0.230893	0.737123	0.771457	0.805791	1.437493	1.524937	1.577403
1061	Ferroalloy Ores, Except Vanadium	6	4.17%	0.773120	0.771457	0.187371	0.203692	0.230893	0.737123	0.771457	0.805791	1.437493	1.524937	1.577403
108	METAL MINING SERVICES	27	1.90%	0.351041	0.164276	-0.409561	-0.267907	-0.139915	0.128749	0.164276	0.225919	1.223010	1.262428	1.287965
1081	Metal Mining Services	27	1.90%	0.351041	0.164276	-0.409561	-0.267907	-0.139915	0.128749	0.164276	0.225919	1.223010	1.262428	1.287965
109	MISCELLANEOUS METAL ORES	29	4.03%	0.745948	0.669409	-0.570405	-0.325274	-0.133266	0.555126	0.669409	0.867306	1.335018	1.879737	2.611079
1090	MISCELLANEOUS METAL ORES	1	7.03%	1.301520	1.301520	1.301520	1.301520	1.301520	1.301520	1.301520	1.301520	1.301520	1.301520	1.301520
1094	Uranium-Radium-Vanadium Ores	14	5.11%	0.946345	0.959995	-0.095280	-0.012929	0.124324	0.640915	0.959995	1.038722	1.966802	2.532721	2.872272
1099	Miscellaneous Metal Ores, Not Elsewhere Classified	14	2.73%	0.505867	0.576628	-0.652454	-0.530397	-0.326969	0.494219	0.576628	0.661126	1.097803	1.107937	1.114017
12	COAL MINING	9	4.55%	0.841857	0.914405	0.094552	0.133086	0.197309	0.858639	0.914405	1.073201	1.199256	1.209548	1.215723
122	BITUMINOUS COAL AND LIGNITE MINING	8	5.07%	0.938481	1.013653	0.413867	0.449698	0.509417	0.900464	1.013653	1.115604	1.201829	1.210835	1.216238
1220	BITUMINOUS COAL & LIGNITE MINING	2	5.02%	0.928825	0.928825	0.735181	0.741109	0.750989	0.889305	0.928825	0.968344	1.106660	1.116540	1.122468
1221	Bituminous Coal And Lignite Surface Mining	6	5.09%	0.941700	1.013653	0.412715	0.446819	0.503659	0.914405	1.013653	1.112900	1.206975	1.213408	1.217267
124	COAL MINING SERVICES	1	0.37%	0.068863	0.068863	0.068863	0.068863	0.068863	0.068863	0.068863	0.068863	0.068863	0.068863	0.068863
1241	Coal Mining Services	1	0.37%	0.068863	0.068863	0.068863	0.068863	0.068863	0.068863	0.068863	0.068863	0.068863	0.068863	0.068863
13	OIL AND GAS EXTRACTION	216	4.84%	0.895740	0.979356	-0.625844	-0.317070	-0.055868	0.873534	0.979356	1.125260	1.603140	1.784299	2.031143
131	CRUDE PETROLEUM AND NATURAL GAS	147	4.80%	0.888065	0.958015	-0.532878	-0.211167	-0.036942	0.859497	0.958015	1.014338	1.619063	1.890414	2.170509
1311	Crude Petroleum And Natural Gas	147	4.80%	0.888065	0.958015	-0.532878	-0.211167	-0.036942	0.859497	0.958015	1.014338	1.619063	1.890414	2.170509
132	NATURAL GAS LIQUIDS	4	6.79%	1.257610	1.211485	1.103823	1.104818	1.106475	1.159750	1.211485	1.263220	1.473320	1.488815	1.498112
1321	Natural Gas Liquids	4	6.79%	1.257610	1.211485	1.103823	1.104818	1.106475	1.159750	1.211485	1.263220	1.473320	1.488815	1.498112
138	OIL AND GAS FIELD SERVICES	65	4.81%	0.890828	1.132880	-1.625555	-0.345903	-0.053912	0.916034	1.132880	1.203908	1.553552	1.637634	1.709281
1381	Drilling Oil And Gas Wells	19	5.82%	1.078483	1.220330	-0.113856	-0.002353	0.183486	1.179084	1.220330	1.292938	1.685252	1.726841	1.751794
1382	Oil And Gas Field Exploration Services	19	2.82%	0.522828	0.734270	-2.867676	-1.949295	-0.418661	0.557403	0.734270	0.906456	1.318565	1.400038	1.448921
1389	Oil And Gas Field Services, Not Elsewhere Classified	27	5.50%	1.017736	1.192960	-0.398648	-0.122918	0.161393	1.069270	1.192960	1.247962	1.539713	1.578913	1.598795
14	MINING AND QUARRYING OF NONMETALLIC MINERALS, EXCEPT FUELS	28	-12.78%	-2.367050	0.506845	-58.970237	-26.653993	-0.578273	0.389131	0.506845	0.755441	1.266693	1.311935	1.353476
1400	MINING & QUARRYING OF NONMETALLIC MINERALS (NO FUELS)	2	4.40%	0.814137	0.814137	0.358963	0.372897	0.396120	0.721244	0.814137	0.907030	1.232154	1.255377	1.269311
141	DIMENSION STONE	2	0.04%	0.007993	0.007993	-0.206044	-0.199492	-0.188572	-0.035688	0.007993	0.051673	0.204557	0.215477	0.222029
1411	Dimension Stone	2	0.04%	0.007993	0.007993	-0.206044	-0.199492	-0.188572	-0.035688	0.007993	0.051673	0.204557	0.215477	0.222029
142	CRUSHED AND BROKEN STONE, INCLUDING RIPRAP	2	5.21%	0.964481	0.964481	0.871715	0.874555	0.879288	0.945549	0.964481	0.983413	1.049674	1.054407	1.057247
1422	Crushed And Broken Limestone	1	5.72%	1.059140	1.059140	1.059140	1.059140	1.059140	1.059140	1.059140	1.059140	1.059140	1.059140	1.059140
1423	Crushed And Broken Granite	1	4.70%	0.869822	0.869822	0.869822	0.869822	0.869822	0.869822	0.869822	0.869822	0.869822	0.869822	0.869822
144	SAND AND GRAVEL	5	3.05%	0.564513	0.752144	-0.268007	-0.226504	-0.157332	0.609704	0.752144	0.803455	1.047788	1.068709	1.081262
1442	Construction Sand And Gravel	2	4.41%	0.816283	0.816283	0.753427	0.755351	0.758558	0.803455	0.816283	0.829110	0.874007	0.877214	0.879138
1446	Industrial Sand	3	2.14%	0.396666	0.396045	-0.281842	-0.261090	-0.226504	0.257701	0.396045	0.534762	1.020272	1.054951	1.075758
147	CHEMICAL AND FERTILIZER MINERAL MINING	8	-50.43%	-9.338558	0.748902	-74.853089	-66.361122	-52.207844	0.676942	0.748902	0.785483	1.333364	1.357267	1.371609

Betas of Common Stocks by SIC Codes as of September 28, 2018

SIC Code	Description	Number of Companies	Equity Risk Premium	Mean	Median	1st Percentile	2.5th Percentile	5th Percentile	40th Percentile	50th Percentile	60th Percentile	95th Percentile	97.5th Percentile	99th Percentile
1474	Potash, Soda, And Borate Minerals	5	-84.44%	-15.637422	0.468013	-77.279365	-72.426813	-64.339225	0.425397	0.468013	0.572477	0.760739	0.764684	0.767052
1479	Chemical And Fertilizer Mineral Mining, Not Elsewhere Classified	3	6.26%	1.159549	1.244580	0.860730	0.872480	0.892064	1.166243	1.244580	1.271898	1.367511	1.374341	1.378438
148	NONMETALLIC MINERALS SERVICES, EXCEPT FUELS	2	-1.05%	-0.194688	-0.194688	-0.710674	-0.694878	-0.668552	-0.299991	-0.194688	-0.089384	0.279177	0.305503	0.321299
1481	Nonmetallic Minerals Services, Except Fuels	2	-1.05%	-0.194688	-0.194688	-0.710674	-0.694878	-0.668552	-0.299991	-0.194688	-0.089384	0.279177	0.305503	0.321299
149	MISCELLANEOUS NONMETALLIC MINERALS, EXCEPT FUELS	7	1.87%	0.346381	0.420520	-0.301207	-0.283771	-0.254712	0.098516	0.420520	0.495614	1.029758	1.049619	1.061536
1499	Miscellaneous Nonmetallic Minerals, Except Fuels	7	1.87%	0.346381	0.420520	-0.301207	-0.283771	-0.254712	0.098516	0.420520	0.495614	1.029758	1.049619	1.061536
	CONSTRUCTION													
15	CONSTRUCTION	24	5.00%	0.926277	1.024388	-0.100400	0.184091	0.534550	0.955087	1.024388	1.082496	1.352090	1.385630	1.401500
152	GENERAL BUILDING CONTRACTORS-RESIDENTIAL BUILDINGS	2	6.17%	1.142925	1.142925	1.113844	1.114734	1.116218	1.136990	1.142925	1.148860	1.169633	1.171116	1.172007
1521	General Contractors-Single-Family Houses	2	6.17%	1.142925	1.142925	1.113844	1.114734	1.116218	1.136990	1.142925	1.148860	1.169633	1.171116	1.172007
153	OPERATIVE BUILDERS	16	4.95%	0.916859	1.009996	-0.156664	0.043429	0.376919	0.954428	1.009996	1.071240	1.245480	1.305780	1.341960
1531	Operative Builders	16	4.95%	0.916859	1.009996	-0.156664	0.043429	0.376919	0.954428	1.009996	1.071240	1.245480	1.305780	1.341960
154	GENERAL BUILDING CONTRACTORS-NONRESIDENTIAL BUILDINGS	6	4.75%	0.879174	0.760528	0.534550	0.534550	0.534550	0.534550	0.760528	0.986505	1.377263	1.394671	1.405117
1541	General Contractors-Industrial Buildings And Warehouses	5	4.63%	0.857708	0.534550	0.534550	0.534550	0.534550	0.534550	0.534550	0.829854	1.384226	1.398153	1.406509
1542	General Contractors-Nonresidential Buildings, Other Than Industrial	1	5.33%	0.986505	0.986505	0.986505	0.986505	0.986505	0.986505	0.986505	0.986505	0.986505	0.986505	0.986505
16	HEAVY CONSTRUCTION OTHER THAN BUILDING CONSTRUCTION-CONTRACTORS	20	4.87%	0.901803	0.994883	0.124830	0.126172	0.128409	0.884930	0.994883	1.148752	1.303157	1.783063	2.071007
161	HIGHWAY AND STREET CONSTRUCTION, EXCEPT ELEVATED HIGHWAYS	3	7.61%	1.408755	1.227770	0.745371	0.760138	0.784750	1.129321	1.227770	1.434810	2.159450	2.211210	2.242266
1611	Highway And Street Construction, Except Elevated Highways	3	7.61%	1.408755	1.227770	0.745371	0.760138	0.784750	1.129321	1.227770	1.434810	2.159450	2.211210	2.242266
162	HEAVY CONSTRUCTION, EXCEPT HIGHWAY AND STREET CONSTRUCTION	17	4.39%	0.812341	0.932305	0.124688	0.125819	0.127702	0.864027	0.932305	1.108100	1.230912	1.241776	1.248294
1622	Bridge, Tunnel, And Elevated Highway Construction	1	6.39%	1.184190	1.184190	1.184190	1.184190	1.184190	1.184190	1.184190	1.184190	1.184190	1.184190	1.184190
1623	Water, Sewer, Pipeline, And Communications And Power Line Construction	9	4.08%	0.755980	0.926738	0.141862	0.144872	0.149888	0.712113	0.926738	0.931192	1.216884	1.234762	1.245489
1629	Heavy Construction, Not Elsewhere Classified	7	4.49%	0.831684	1.141860	0.124218	0.124641	0.125348	0.950075	1.141860	1.152198	1.224004	1.224742	1.225185
17	CONSTRUCTION-SPECIAL TRADE CONTRACTORS	9	4.68%	0.866621	0.791936	0.604377	0.609387	0.617735	0.717970	0.791936	0.862328	1.228658	1.268694	1.292716
171	PLUMBING, HEATING AND AIR-CONDITIONING	1	4.28%	0.791936	0.791936	0.791936	0.791936	0.791936	0.791936	0.791936	0.791936	0.791936	0.791936	0.791936
1711	Plumbing, Heating And Air-Conditioning	1	4.28%	0.791936	0.791936	0.791936	0.791936	0.791936	0.791936	0.791936	0.791936	0.791936	0.791936	0.791936
173	ELECTRICAL WORK	5	4.21%	0.780393	0.699478	0.602708	0.605212	0.609387	0.676799	0.699478	0.771657	1.038977	1.058859	1.070787
1731	Electrical Work	5	4.21%	0.780393	0.699478	0.602708	0.605212	0.609387	0.676799	0.699478	0.771657	1.038977	1.058859	1.070787

Betas of Common Stocks by SIC Codes as of September 28, 2018

SIC Code	Description	Number of Companies	Equity Risk Premium	Mean	Median	1st Percentile	2.5th Percentile	5th Percentile	40th Percentile	50th Percentile	60th Percentile	95th Percentile	97.5th Percentile	99th Percentile
174	MASONRY, STONEWORK, TILE SETTING, AND PLASTERING	2	6.53%	1.208640	1.208640	1.110552	1.113555	1.118559	1.188622	1.208640	1.228658	1.298721	1.303726	1.306728
1742	Plastering, Drywall, Acoustical, And Insulation Work	2	6.53%	1.208640	1.208640	1.110552	1.113555	1.118559	1.188622	1.208640	1.228658	1.298721	1.303726	1.306728
177	CONCRETE WORK	1	3.72%	0.688411	0.688411	0.688411	0.688411	0.688411	0.688411	0.688411	0.688411	0.688411	0.688411	0.688411
1771	Concrete Work	1	3.72%	0.688411	0.688411	0.688411	0.688411	0.688411	0.688411	0.688411	0.688411	0.688411	0.688411	0.688411
	MANUFACTURING													
20	FOOD AND KINDRED PRODUCTS	87	3.55%	0.657823	0.515858	-0.170635	-0.107033	-0.002178	0.466117	0.515858	0.577573	1.222139	1.294586	2.914940
2000	FOOD AND KINDRED PRODUCTS	2	1.33%	0.246885	0.246885	0.124579	0.128323	0.134563	0.221924	0.246885	0.271845	0.359206	0.365446	0.369190
201	MEAT PRODUCTS	7	2.24%	0.413925	0.479126	0.110923	0.117581	0.128679	0.391326	0.479126	0.509213	0.641361	0.646381	0.649393
2011	Meat Packing Plants	2	1.92%	0.354869	0.354869	0.183954	0.189186	0.197906	0.319988	0.354869	0.389749	0.511831	0.520551	0.525783
2013	Sausages And Other Prepared Meat Products	2	1.19%	0.219638	0.219638	0.108747	0.112142	0.117799	0.197007	0.219638	0.242269	0.321477	0.327134	0.330529
2015	Poultry Slaughtering And Processing	3	3.15%	0.582821	0.617935	0.481902	0.486066	0.493007	0.590173	0.617935	0.624628	0.648054	0.649728	0.650732
202	DAIRY PRODUCTS	7	3.00%	0.556456	0.514867	-0.089028	-0.054450	0.003182	0.418862	0.514867	0.653340	1.144913	1.208686	1.246951
2022	Natural, Processed, And Imitation Cheese	2	4.30%	0.796479	0.796479	0.746671	0.748196	0.750737	0.786314	0.796479	0.806643	0.842220	0.844761	0.846286
2023	Dry, Condensed, And Evaporated Dairy Products	1	1.92%	0.354858	0.354858	0.354858	0.354858	0.354858	0.354858	0.354858	0.354858	0.354858	0.354858	0.354858
2024	Ice Cream And Frozen Desserts	1	-0.61%	-0.112081	-0.112081	-0.112081	-0.112081	-0.112081	-0.112081	-0.112081	-0.112081	-0.112081	-0.112081	-0.112081
2026	Fluid Milk	3	3.71%	0.686485	0.514867	0.276984	0.284266	0.296403	0.466319	0.514867	0.666386	1.196701	1.234580	1.257308
203	CANNED, FROZEN, AND PRESERVED FRUITS, VEGETABLES, AND FOOD SPECIAL	9	3.85%	0.713321	0.577900	0.356940	0.370521	0.393158	0.561544	0.577900	0.652047	1.208822	1.235456	1.251436
2030	CANNED, FROZEN & PRESERVD FRUIT, VEG & FOOD SPECIALTIES	2	5.22%	0.966337	0.966337	0.676499	0.685372	0.700159	0.907186	0.966337	1.025488	1.232515	1.247302	1.256175
2032	Canned Specialties	2	2.50%	0.462893	0.462893	0.350185	0.353635	0.359386	0.439891	0.462893	0.485894	0.566399	0.572150	0.575600
2033	Canned Fruits, Vegetables, Preserves, Jams, And Jellies	3	4.58%	0.847635	0.901125	0.520626	0.532274	0.551687	0.823472	0.901125	0.946684	1.106141	1.117530	1.124364
2034	Dried And Dehydrated Fruits, Vegetables, And Soup Mixes	1	2.49%	0.461067	0.461067	0.461067	0.461067	0.461067	0.461067	0.461067	0.461067	0.461067	0.461067	0.461067
2037	Frozen Fruits, Fruit Juices, And Vegetables	1	3.01%	0.557455	0.557455	0.557455	0.557455	0.557455	0.557455	0.557455	0.557455	0.557455	0.557455	0.557455
204	GRAIN MILL PRODUCTS	7	3.15%	0.582621	0.623693	0.248432	0.267175	0.298414	0.570420	0.623693	0.640171	0.834125	0.864044	0.881996
2041	Flour And Other Grain Mill Products	2	3.13%	0.579299	0.579299	0.535792	0.537124	0.539343	0.570420	0.579299	0.588177	0.619254	0.621473	0.622805
2043	Cereal Breakfast Foods	1	2.40%	0.444195	0.444195	0.444195	0.444195	0.444195	0.444195	0.444195	0.444195	0.444195	0.444195	0.444195
2044	Rice Milling	1	1.27%	0.235936	0.235936	0.235936	0.235936	0.235936	0.235936	0.235936	0.235936	0.235936	0.235936	0.235936
2046	Wet Corn Milling	2	3.63%	0.672828	0.672828	0.651589	0.652240	0.653323	0.668493	0.672828	0.677162	0.692332	0.693415	0.694066
2047	Dog And Cat Food	1	4.83%	0.893964	0.893964	0.893964	0.893964	0.893964	0.893964	0.893964	0.893964	0.893964	0.893964	0.893964
205	BAKERY PRODUCTS	5	2.33%	0.431006	0.390119	0.102468	0.115258	0.136576	0.356919	0.390119	0.503562	0.686844	0.688483	0.689467
2051	Bread And Other Bakery Products, Except Cookies And Crackers	2	1.88%	0.348619	0.348619	0.307948	0.309193	0.311268	0.340318	0.348619	0.356919	0.385969	0.388044	0.389289
2052	Cookies And Crackers	3	2.62%	0.485930	0.673727	0.105536	0.122930	0.151919	0.557770	0.673727	0.677006	0.688483	0.689303	0.689795
206	SUGAR AND CONFECTIONERY PRODUCTS	4	2.58%	0.478127	0.479591	0.117637	0.133419	0.159723	0.466533	0.479591	0.492649	0.794480	0.820344	0.835862
2061	Cane Sugar, Except Refining	1	4.57%	0.846208	0.846208	0.846208	0.846208	0.846208	0.846208	0.846208	0.846208	0.846208	0.846208	0.846208
2066	Chocolate And Cocoa Products	2	1.53%	0.282472	0.282472	0.110623	0.115884	0.124652	0.247401	0.282472	0.317543	0.440292	0.449060	0.454321
2068	Salted And Roasted Nuts And Seeds	1	2.71%	0.501354	0.501354	0.501354	0.501354	0.501354	0.501354	0.501354	0.501354	0.501354	0.501354	0.501354
207	FATS AND OILS	2	3.47%	0.643040	0.643040	0.394650	0.402254	0.414927	0.592348	0.643040	0.693732	0.871153	0.883826	0.891430
2075	Soybean Oil Mills	1	2.10%	0.389581	0.389581	0.389581	0.389581	0.389581	0.389581	0.389581	0.389581	0.389581	0.389581	0.389581
2077	Animal And Marine Fats And Oils	1	4.84%	0.896499	0.896499	0.896499	0.896499	0.896499	0.896499	0.896499	0.896499	0.896499	0.896499	0.896499

Betas of Common Stocks by SIC Codes as of September 28, 2018

SIC Code	Description	Number of Companies	Equity Risk Premium	Mean	Median	1st Percentile	2.5th Percentile	5th Percentile	40th Percentile	50th Percentile	60th Percentile	95th Percentile	97.5th Percentile	99th Percentile
208	BEVERAGES	32	2.61%	0.482606	0.482011	-0.313258	-0.192677	-0.103585	0.421700	0.482011	0.530065	1.177611	1.328861	1.391626
2080	BEVERAGES	1	-0.10%	-0.018415	-0.018415	-0.018415	-0.018415	-0.018415	-0.018415	-0.018415	-0.018415	-0.018415	-0.018415	-0.018415
2082	Malt Beverages	5	4.06%	0.751272	0.576888	0.473930	0.474288	0.474885	0.537998	0.576888	0.663193	1.305306	1.369388	1.407837
2084	Wines, Brandy, And Brandy Spirits	5	0.96%	0.177200	0.164619	-0.376241	-0.350135	-0.306625	0.115354	0.164619	0.292515	0.568241	0.578726	0.585017
2085	Distilled And Blended Liquors	5	3.50%	0.647957	0.685632	0.300912	0.310618	0.326794	0.593860	0.685632	0.715123	0.987192	1.015671	1.032758
2086	Bottled And Canned Soft Drinks And Carbonated Waters	14	2.08%	0.385826	0.390175	-0.127064	-0.116163	-0.097995	0.326158	0.390175	0.478380	0.845238	0.961974	1.032016
2087	Flavoring Extracts And Flavoring Syrups, Not Elsewhere Classified	2	5.88%	1.089050	1.089050	0.883799	0.890082	0.900554	1.047162	1.089050	1.130938	1.277546	1.288018	1.294301
209	MISCELLANEOUS FOOD PREPARATIONS AND KINDRED PRODUCTS	12	8.39%	1.554077	0.585738	0.184917	0.203659	0.234896	0.570645	0.585738	0.618566	5.944355	8.979877	10.801191
2095	Roasted Coffee	5	4.16%	0.770420	0.977136	0.299958	0.320878	0.355745	0.840154	0.977136	0.977136	0.977136	0.977136	0.977136
2097	Manufactured Ice	1	0.93%	0.172422	0.172422	0.172422	0.172422	0.172422	0.172422	0.172422	0.172422	0.172422	0.172422	0.172422
2099	Food Preparations, Not Elsewhere Classified	6	13.16%	2.437401	0.571718	0.332895	0.350011	0.378537	0.566353	0.571718	0.577082	9.160148	10.587774	11.444350
21	TOBACCO PRODUCTS	9	3.61%	0.668439	0.555345	0.187514	0.200308	0.221632	0.499330	0.555345	0.574590	1.511236	1.600768	1.654487
2100	TOBACCO PRODUCTS	2	4.85%	0.898993	0.898993	0.562218	0.572527	0.589710	0.830263	0.898993	0.967722	1.208275	1.225458	1.235767
211	CIGARETTES	7	3.25%	0.602567	0.485326	0.185381	0.194977	0.210970	0.424215	0.485326	0.541771	1.367674	1.528987	1.625775
2111	Cigarettes	7	3.25%	0.602567	0.485326	0.185381	0.194977	0.210970	0.424215	0.485326	0.541771	1.367674	1.528987	1.625775
22	TEXTILE MILL PRODUCTS	11	3.29%	0.609486	0.701898	-0.643131	-0.469481	-0.180065	0.606143	0.701898	0.739993	1.086448	1.159849	1.203890
221	BROADWOVEN FABRIC MILLS, COTTON	2	3.07%	0.569381	0.569381	0.402181	0.407300	0.415830	0.535259	0.569381	0.603503	0.722932	0.731462	0.736581
2211	Broadwoven Fabric Mills, Cotton	2	3.07%	0.569381	0.569381	0.402181	0.407300	0.415830	0.535259	0.569381	0.603503	0.722932	0.731462	0.736581
222	BROADWOVEN FABRIC MILLS, MANMADE FIBER AND SILK	2	0.49%	0.090374	0.090374	-0.741913	-0.716434	-0.673971	-0.079481	0.090374	0.260228	0.854718	0.897181	0.922660
2221	Broadwoven Fabric Mills, Manmade Fiber And Silk	2	0.49%	0.090374	0.090374	-0.741913	-0.716434	-0.673971	-0.079481	0.090374	0.260228	0.854718	0.897181	0.922660
225	KNITTING MILLS	3	4.57%	0.845943	0.701898	0.604666	0.607643	0.612604	0.682055	0.701898	0.808168	1.180115	1.206682	1.222623
2252	Hosiery, Not Elsewhere Classified	1	3.25%	0.602682	0.602682	0.602682	0.602682	0.602682	0.602682	0.602682	0.602682	0.602682	0.602682	0.602682
2253	Knit Outerwear Mills	2	5.22%	0.967574	0.967574	0.707212	0.715182	0.728466	0.914439	0.967574	1.020709	1.206682	1.219966	1.227936
227	CARPETS AND RUGS	3	4.11%	0.760302	0.830415	0.610628	0.617357	0.628570	0.785561	0.830415	0.833202	0.842955	0.843651	0.844069
2273	Carpets And Rugs	3	4.11%	0.760302	0.830415	0.610628	0.617357	0.628570	0.785561	0.830415	0.833202	0.842955	0.843651	0.844069
228	YARN AND THREAD MILLS	1	3.06%	0.566103	0.566103	0.566103	0.566103	0.566103	0.566103	0.566103	0.566103	0.566103	0.566103	0.566103
2282	Yarn Texturizing, Throwing, Twisting, And Winding Mills	1	3.06%	0.566103	0.566103	0.566103	0.566103	0.566103	0.566103	0.566103	0.566103	0.566103	0.566103	0.566103
23	APPAREL AND OTHER FINISHED PRODUCTS MADE FROM FABRICS AND SIMILAR MATERIAL	19	3.17%	0.587945	0.759321	-2.024871	-1.373092	-0.286794	0.725386	0.759321	0.904571	1.069388	1.184579	1.253694
2300	APPAREL & OTHER FINISHD PRODS OF FABRICS & SIMILAR MATL	2	6.28%	1.162305	1.162305	1.027589	1.031713	1.038587	1.134812	1.162305	1.189798	1.286024	1.292897	1.297021
232	MEN'S AND BOYS' FURNISHINGS, WORK CLOTHING, AND ALLIED GARMENTS	6	4.39%	0.812418	0.916518	0.449933	0.463870	0.487099	0.911293	0.916518	0.921742	1.015486	1.029638	1.038129
2321	Men's And Boys' Shirts, Except Work Shirts	2	3.68%	0.681192	0.681192	0.445452	0.452669	0.464696	0.633081	0.681192	0.729302	0.897687	0.909714	0.916931
2325	Men's And Boys' Separate Trousers And Slacks	1	3.38%	0.626472	0.626472	0.626472	0.626472	0.626472	0.626472	0.626472	0.626472	0.626472	0.626472	0.626472
2326	Men's And Boys' Work Clothing	1	5.03%	0.930572	0.930572	0.930572	0.930572	0.930572	0.930572	0.930572	0.930572	0.930572	0.930572	0.930572
2329	Men's And Boys' Clothing, Not Elsewhere Classified	2	5.28%	0.977542	0.977542	0.912618	0.914605	0.917918	0.964292	0.977542	0.990791	1.037165	1.040478	1.042465
233	WOMEN'S, MISSES', AND JUNIORS' OUTERWEAR	8	1.21%	0.224490	0.628397	-2.290410	-2.036941	-1.614491	0.491876	0.628397	0.748203	0.938420	0.942009	0.944163

Betas of Common Stocks by SIC Codes as of September 28, 2018

SIC Code	Description	Number of Companies	Equity Risk Premium	Mean	Median	1st Percentile	2.5th Percentile	5th Percentile	40th Percentile	50th Percentile	60th Percentile	95th Percentile	97.5th Percentile	99th Percentile
2330	WOMEN'S, MISSES', AND JUNIORS OUTERWEAR	1	4.03%	0.745424	0.745424	0.745424	0.745424	0.745424	0.745424	0.745424	0.745424	0.745424	0.745424	0.745424
2337	Women's, Misses', And Juniors' Suits, Skirts, And Coats	1	5.00%	0.925087	0.925087	0.925087	0.925087	0.925087	0.925087	0.925087	0.925087	0.925087	0.925087	0.925087
2339	Women's, Misses', And Juniors' Outerwear, Not Elsewhere Classified	6	0.11%	0.020901	0.462636	-2.338690	-2.157641	-1.855891	0.413903	0.462636	0.511369	0.899030	0.922314	0.936285
234	WOMEN'S, MISSES', CHILDREN'S, AND INFANTS' UNDERGARMENTS	1	3.89%	0.720377	0.720377	0.720377	0.720377	0.720377	0.720377	0.720377	0.720377	0.720377	0.720377	0.720377
2341	Women's, Misses', Children's, And Infants' Underwear And Nightwear	1	3.89%	0.720377	0.720377	0.720377	0.720377	0.720377	0.720377	0.720377	0.720377	0.720377	0.720377	0.720377
238	MISCELLANEOUS APPAREL AND ACCESSORIES	2	3.93%	0.727766	0.727766	0.580847	0.585345	0.592841	0.697782	0.727766	0.757749	0.862690	0.870186	0.874684
2385	Waterproof Outerwear	1	4.74%	0.877682	0.877682	0.877682	0.877682	0.877682	0.877682	0.877682	0.877682	0.877682	0.877682	0.877682
2389	Apparel And Accessories, Not Elsewhere Classified	1	3.12%	0.577849	0.577849	0.577849	0.577849	0.577849	0.577849	0.577849	0.577849	0.577849	0.577849	0.577849
24	LUMBER AND WOOD PRODUCTS, EXCEPT FURNITURE	12	5.02%	0.929636	0.951187	0.128422	0.231885	0.404325	0.923223	0.951187	0.996884	1.421329	1.454995	1.475194
2400	LUMBER & WOOD PRODUCTS (NO FURNITURE)	1	4.20%	0.778454	0.778454	0.778454	0.778454	0.778454	0.778454	0.778454	0.778454	0.778454	0.778454	0.778454
241	LOGGING	1	3.99%	0.739357	0.739357	0.739357	0.739357	0.739357	0.739357	0.739357	0.739357	0.739357	0.739357	0.739357
2411	Logging	1	3.99%	0.739357	0.739357	0.739357	0.739357	0.739357	0.739357	0.739357	0.739357	0.739357	0.739357	0.739357
242	SAWMILLS AND PLANING MILLS	2	2.62%	0.485368	0.485368	0.067965	0.080742	0.102038	0.400183	0.485368	0.570552	0.868697	0.889993	0.902771
2421	Sawmills And Planing Mills, General	2	2.62%	0.485368	0.485368	0.067965	0.080742	0.102038	0.400183	0.485368	0.570552	0.868697	0.889993	0.902771
243	MILLWORK, VENEER, PLYWOOD, AND STRUCTURAL WOOD MEMBERS	3	5.66%	1.047931	1.050980	0.943320	0.946616	0.952109	1.029009	1.050980	1.071122	1.141619	1.146655	1.149676
2430	MILLWOOD, VENEER, PLYWOOD, & STRUCTURAL WOOD MEMBERS	1	5.08%	0.941123	0.941123	0.941123	0.941123	0.941123	0.941123	0.941123	0.941123	0.941123	0.941123	0.941123
2434	Wood Kitchen Cabinets	1	6.22%	1.151690	1.151690	1.151690	1.151690	1.151690	1.151690	1.151690	1.151690	1.151690	1.151690	1.151690
2439	Structural Wood Members, Not Elsewhere Classified	1	5.68%	1.050980	1.050980	1.050980	1.050980	1.050980	1.050980	1.050980	1.050980	1.050980	1.050980	1.050980
245	WOOD BUILDINGS AND MOBILE HOMES	2	7.71%	1.427450	1.427450	1.367464	1.369301	1.372361	1.415208	1.427450	1.439692	1.482539	1.485600	1.487436
2451	Mobile Homes	2	7.71%	1.427450	1.427450	1.367464	1.369301	1.372361	1.415208	1.427450	1.439692	1.482539	1.485600	1.487436
249	MISCELLANEOUS WOOD PRODUCTS	3	4.80%	0.889463	0.961250	0.691993	0.700236	0.713973	0.906300	0.961250	0.973128	1.014701	1.017671	1.019452
2491	Wood Preserving	1	3.71%	0.686498	0.686498	0.686498	0.686498	0.686498	0.686498	0.686498	0.686498	0.686498	0.686498	0.686498
2493	Reconstituted Wood Products	1	5.51%	1.020640	1.020640	1.020640	1.020640	1.020640	1.020640	1.020640	1.020640	1.020640	1.020640	1.020640
2499	Wood Products, Not Elsewhere Classified	1	5.19%	0.961250	0.961250	0.961250	0.961250	0.961250	0.961250	0.961250	0.961250	0.961250	0.961250	0.961250
25	FURNITURE AND FIXTURES	20	3.85%	0.713459	0.734611	0.150491	0.244759	0.401872	0.635772	0.734611	0.827357	1.056454	1.068082	1.075059
251	HOUSEHOLD FURNITURE	12	3.50%	0.648435	0.637440	0.124030	0.178606	0.269566	0.550497	0.637440	0.738736	1.000388	1.027809	1.044262
2511	Wood Household Furniture, Except Upholstered	7	2.74%	0.506852	0.529319	0.107492	0.137261	0.186875	0.511608	0.529319	0.537867	0.742861	0.749049	0.752762
2512	Wood Household Furniture, Upholstered	1	3.03%	0.560895	0.560895	0.560895	0.560895	0.560895	0.560895	0.560895	0.560895	0.560895	0.560895	0.560895
2515	Mattresses, Foundations, And Convertible Beds	3	5.15%	0.952932	0.955517	0.850199	0.853423	0.858797	0.934024	0.955517	0.975460	1.045259	1.050244	1.053236
2519	Household Furniture, Not Elsewhere Classified	1	4.39%	0.813562	0.813562	0.813562	0.813562	0.813562	0.813562	0.813562	0.813562	0.813562	0.813562	0.813562
252	OFFICE FURNITURE	7	4.65%	0.861875	0.924941	0.495476	0.513688	0.544042	0.910522	0.924941	0.937438	1.059628	1.069669	1.075694

Betas of Common Stocks by SIC Codes as of September 28, 2018

SIC Code	Description	Number of Companies	Equity Risk Premium	Mean	Median	1st Percentile	2.5th Percentile	5th Percentile	40th Percentile	50th Percentile	60th Percentile	95th Percentile	97.5th Percentile	99th Percentile
2521	Wood Office Furniture	3	4.31%	0.799005	0.900909	0.491686	0.504214	0.525092	0.817394	0.900909	0.923281	1.001584	1.007177	1.010533
2522	Office Furniture, Except Wood	4	4.91%	0.909028	0.935355	0.692868	0.703634	0.721578	0.929107	0.935355	0.941603	1.059619	1.069664	1.075692
253	PUBLIC BUILDING AND RELATED FURNITURE	1	2.46%	0.454842	0.454842	0.454842	0.454842	0.454842	0.454842	0.454842	0.454842	0.454842	0.454842	0.454842
2531	Public Building And Related Furniture	1	2.46%	0.454842	0.454842	0.454842	0.454842	0.454842	0.454842	0.454842	0.454842	0.454842	0.454842	0.454842
26	PAPER AND ALLIED PRODUCTS	27	4.12%	0.762999	0.728423	0.098589	0.112101	0.149619	0.659916	0.728423	0.871380	1.270230	1.279218	1.289233
261	PULP MILLS	2	3.78%	0.699263	0.699263	0.670686	0.671561	0.673019	0.693431	0.699263	0.705095	0.725507	0.726965	0.727840
2611	Pulp Mills	2	3.78%	0.699263	0.699263	0.670686	0.671561	0.673019	0.693431	0.699263	0.705095	0.725507	0.726965	0.727840
262	PAPER MILLS	10	3.36%	0.621417	0.638763	0.092700	0.097377	0.105172	0.578562	0.638763	0.690047	1.115442	1.121706	1.125464
2621	Paper Mills	10	3.36%	0.621417	0.638763	0.092700	0.097377	0.105172	0.578562	0.638763	0.690047	1.115442	1.121706	1.125464
263	PAPERBOARD MILLS	4	4.30%	0.795656	0.738241	0.584442	0.588745	0.595916	0.701613	0.738241	0.774868	1.075777	1.100174	1.114811
2631	Paperboard Mills	4	4.30%	0.795656	0.738241	0.584442	0.588745	0.595916	0.701613	0.738241	0.774868	1.075777	1.100174	1.114811
265	PAPERBOARD CONTAINERS AND BOXES	2	5.50%	1.018315	1.018315	1.018291	1.018291	1.018293	1.018310	1.018315	1.018320	1.018338	1.018339	1.018340
2655	Fiber Cans, Tubes, Drums, And Similar Products	2	5.50%	1.018315	1.018315	1.018291	1.018291	1.018293	1.018310	1.018315	1.018320	1.018338	1.018339	1.018340
267	CONVERTED PAPER AND PAPERBOARD PRODUCTS, EXCEPT CONTAINERS AND BOXES	9	4.66%	0.863224	1.012780	0.228767	0.258615	0.308362	0.601124	1.012780	1.218740	1.285638	1.290774	1.293856
2671	Packaging Paper And Plastics Film, Coated And Laminated	5	4.84%	0.895432	1.270230	0.218817	0.233742	0.258615	0.945179	1.270230	1.270230	1.270230	1.270230	1.270230
2673	Plastics, Foil, And Coated Paper Bags	2	4.81%	0.890434	0.890434	0.493067	0.505231	0.525505	0.809338	0.890434	0.971529	1.255362	1.275636	1.287800
2679	Converted Paper And Paperboard Products, Not Elsewhere Classified	2	4.08%	0.755495	0.755495	0.503356	0.511074	0.523939	0.704038	0.755495	0.806952	0.987052	0.999916	1.007634
27	PRINTING, PUBLISHING, AND ALLIED INDUSTRIES	40	3.36%	0.621454	0.620380	-0.016890	0.001942	0.019396	0.570110	0.620380	0.698219	1.120336	1.257370	1.620304
271	NEWSPAPERS: PUBLISHING, OR PUBLISHING AND PRINTING	18	2.89%	0.535619	0.539028	0.005726	0.010195	0.017644	0.487116	0.539028	0.622274	0.958280	0.966918	0.972102
2711	Newspapers: Publishing, Or Publishing And Printing	18	2.89%	0.535619	0.539028	0.005726	0.010195	0.017644	0.487116	0.539028	0.622274	0.958280	0.966918	0.972102
272	PERIODICALS: PUBLISHING, OR PUBLISHING AND PRINTING	2	3.61%	0.667983	0.667983	0.639356	0.640233	0.641693	0.662140	0.667983	0.673825	0.694272	0.695732	0.696609
2721	Periodicals: Publishing, Or Publishing And Printing	2	3.61%	0.667983	0.667983	0.639356	0.640233	0.641693	0.662140	0.667983	0.673825	0.694272	0.695732	0.696609
273	BOOKS	4	3.63%	0.672328	0.699152	0.408035	0.419002	0.437279	0.666315	0.699152	0.731989	0.869823	0.880053	0.886191
2731	Books: Publishing, Or Publishing And Printing	4	3.63%	0.672328	0.699152	0.408035	0.419002	0.437279	0.666315	0.699152	0.731989	0.869823	0.880053	0.886191
274	MISCELLANEOUS PUBLISHING	5	4.29%	0.793632	0.616759	-0.010942	0.016811	0.063068	0.543303	0.616759	0.804243	1.706902	1.784581	1.831188
2741	Miscellaneous Publishing	5	4.29%	0.793632	0.616759	-0.010942	0.016811	0.063068	0.543303	0.616759	0.804243	1.706902	1.784581	1.831188
275	COMMERCIAL PRINTING	8	3.74%	0.693056	0.661880	0.111890	0.126434	0.150674	0.616401	0.661880	0.747004	1.197088	1.219474	1.232906
2750	COMMERCIAL PRINTING	1	6.02%	1.113940	1.113940	1.113940	1.113940	1.113940	1.113940	1.113940	1.113940	1.113940	1.113940	1.113940
2752	Commercial Printing, Lithographic	2	2.54%	0.470233	0.470233	0.245298	0.252183	0.263660	0.424327	0.470233	0.516138	0.676805	0.688282	0.695167
2754	Commercial Printing, Gravure	3	4.10%	0.760014	0.935988	0.118870	0.143884	0.185573	0.769229	0.935988	0.997162	1.211273	1.226566	1.235743
2759	Commercial Printing, Not Elsewhere Classified	2	3.27%	0.605002	0.605002	0.586382	0.586952	0.587902	0.601202	0.605002	0.608801	0.622101	0.623051	0.623621
276	MANIFOLD BUSINESS FORMS	1	3.18%	0.589266	0.589266	0.589266	0.589266	0.589266	0.589266	0.589266	0.589266	0.589266	0.589266	0.589266
2761	Manifold Business Forms	1	3.18%	0.589266	0.589266	0.589266	0.589266	0.589266	0.589266	0.589266	0.589266	0.589266	0.589266	0.589266
277	GREETING CARDS	1	2.06%	0.381911	0.381911	0.381911	0.381911	0.381911	0.381911	0.381911	0.381911	0.381911	0.381911	0.381911
2771	Greeting Cards	1	2.06%	0.381911	0.381911	0.381911	0.381911	0.381911	0.381911	0.381911	0.381911	0.381911	0.381911	0.381911

Betas of Common Stocks by SIC Codes as of September 28, 2018

SIC Code	Description	Number of Companies	Equity Risk Premium	Mean	Median	1st Percentile	2.5th Percentile	5th Percentile	40th Percentile	50th Percentile	60th Percentile	95th Percentile	97.5th Percentile	99th Percentile
278	BLANKBOOKS, LOOSELEAF BINDERS, AND BOOKBINDING AND RELATED WORK	1	3.82%	0.707943	0.707943	0.707943	0.707943	0.707943	0.707943	0.707943	0.707943	0.707943	0.707943	0.707943
2782	Blankbooks, Looseleaf Binders And Devices	1	3.82%	0.707943	0.707943	0.707943	0.707943	0.707943	0.707943	0.707943	0.707943	0.707943	0.707943	0.707943
28	CHEMICALS AND ALLIED PRODUCTS	503	4.31%	0.799034	0.883131	-1.139677	-0.375347	-0.132542	0.759138	0.883131	1.003270	1.635365	1.837625	1.994738
2800	CHEMICALS & ALLIED PRODUCTS	1	6.51%	1.205420	1.205420	1.205420	1.205420	1.205420	1.205420	1.205420	1.205420	1.205420	1.205420	1.205420
281	INDUSTRIAL INORGANIC CHEMICALS	15	5.09%	0.942546	1.105090	-0.593374	-0.375311	-0.011872	0.989527	1.105090	1.134024	1.566166	1.611498	1.638697
2810	INDUSTRIAL INORGANIC CHEMICALS	1	5.24%	0.970337	0.970337	0.970337	0.970337	0.970337	0.970337	0.970337	0.970337	0.970337	0.970337	0.970337
2812	Alkalies And Chlorine	1	5.98%	1.108260	1.108260	1.108260	1.108260	1.108260	1.108260	1.108260	1.108260	1.108260	1.108260	1.108260
2813	Industrial Gases	2	5.75%	1.065440	1.065440	0.960355	0.963572	0.968933	1.043994	1.065440	1.086886	1.161947	1.167309	1.170525
2816	Inorganic Pigments	4	6.90%	1.276920	1.224265	1.008711	1.018297	1.034273	1.218910	1.224265	1.229620	1.593284	1.625057	1.644121
2819	Industrial Inorganic Chemicals, Not Elsewhere Classified	7	3.72%	0.688718	0.894426	-0.676445	-0.582990	-0.427231	0.543450	0.894426	1.020824	1.496269	1.511790	1.521102
282	PLASTICS MATERIALS AND SYNTHETIC RESINS, SYNTHETIC RUBBER, CELLULOSIC MANMADE FIBERS	14	5.39%	0.997950	1.123865	-0.507828	-0.259607	0.154093	1.000629	1.123865	1.194754	1.470316	1.530818	1.567119
2821	Plastics Materials, Synthetic Resins, And Nonvulcanizable Elastomers	14	5.39%	0.997950	1.123865	-0.507828	-0.259607	0.154093	1.000629	1.123865	1.194754	1.470316	1.530818	1.567119
283	DRUGS	403	4.36%	0.808120	0.864799	-0.918662	-0.332445	-0.093539	0.757255	0.864799	1.017922	1.673970	1.871363	2.130112
2833	Medicinal Chemicals And Botanical Products	12	4.19%	0.776745	0.865857	0.146466	0.213770	0.325944	0.706764	0.865857	0.930950	1.082824	1.084097	1.084861
2834	Pharmaceutical Preparations	308	4.25%	0.786268	0.849026	-0.910417	-0.357977	-0.141512	0.729311	0.849026	0.992409	1.725670	1.895544	2.123266
2835	In Vitro And In Vivo Diagnostic Substances	22	4.70%	0.870377	0.861594	-0.062536	-0.016138	0.057568	0.775697	0.861594	0.945173	1.655637	1.909576	2.072353
2836	Biological Products, Except Diagnostic Substances	61	4.87%	0.902173	1.012960	-0.792125	-0.063560	0.114445	0.903357	1.012960	1.126010	1.508150	1.563755	1.703724
284	SOAP, DETERGENTS, AND CLEANING PREPARATIONS; PERFUMES, COSMETICS	20	2.41%	0.446917	0.415149	-0.144325	-0.133877	-0.116462	0.382044	0.415149	0.446802	1.023472	1.023681	1.023806
2841	Soap And Other Detergents, Except Specialty Cleaners	5	3.31%	0.613309	0.528082	0.362585	0.363205	0.364240	0.465855	0.528082	0.628804	0.975089	0.999490	1.014130
2842	Specialty Cleaning, Polishing, And Sanitation Preparations	4	1.10%	0.203841	0.268526	-0.140192	-0.123544	-0.095798	0.238609	0.268526	0.298442	0.412922	0.421264	0.426268
2844	Perfumes, Cosmetics, And Other Toilet Preparations	11	2.48%	0.459676	0.423636	-0.090636	-0.054646	0.005337	0.406662	0.423636	0.472598	0.886519	0.954984	0.996064
285	PAINTS, VARNISHES, LACQUERS, ENAMELS, AND ALLIED PRODUCTS	4	5.06%	0.936308	0.940944	0.897569	0.898896	0.901106	0.932074	0.940944	0.949813	0.965019	0.965839	0.966331
2851	Paints, Varnishes, Lacquers, Enamels, And Allied Products	4	5.06%	0.936308	0.940944	0.897569	0.898896	0.901106	0.932074	0.940944	0.949813	0.965019	0.965839	0.966331
286	INDUSTRIAL ORGANIC CHEMICALS	21	4.32%	0.800854	0.836716	-0.129381	-0.087651	-0.018101	0.790670	0.836716	0.961143	1.366040	1.581995	1.711568
2860	INDUSTRIAL ORGANIC CHEMICALS	1	9.71%	1.797950	1.797950	1.797950	1.797950	1.797950	1.797950	1.797950	1.797950	1.797950	1.797950	1.797950
2861	Gum And Wood Chemicals	2	2.69%	0.498885	0.498885	-0.007761	0.007749	0.033598	0.395488	0.498885	0.602282	0.964171	0.990021	1.005530
2865	Cyclic Organic Crudes And Intermediates, And Organic Dyes And Pigments	1	3.58%	0.662050	0.662050	0.662050	0.662050	0.662050	0.662050	0.662050	0.662050	0.662050	0.662050	0.662050
2869	Industrial Organic Chemicals, Not Elsewhere Classified	17	4.24%	0.785892	0.836716	-0.108602	-0.035703	0.085796	0.802397	0.836716	0.955707	1.178264	1.272152	1.328485
287	AGRICULTURAL CHEMICALS	13	4.40%	0.814783	1.010400	-1.029813	-0.765127	-0.323984	0.835142	1.010400	1.102208	1.569848	1.584284	1.592946
2870	AGRICULTURAL CHEMICALS	3	6.14%	1.137842	1.550600	0.289935	0.328527	0.392846	1.293321	1.550600	1.560224	1.593908	1.596314	1.597758

Betas of Common Stocks by SIC Codes as of September 28, 2018

SIC Code	Description	Number of Companies	Equity Risk Premium	Mean	Median	1st Percentile	2.5th Percentile	5th Percentile	40th Percentile	50th Percentile	60th Percentile	95th Percentile	97.5th Percentile	99th Percentile
2873	Nitrogenous Fertilizers	5	2.89%	0.534997	1.010400	-1.140607	-1.042112	-0.877955	0.780362	1.010400	1.034164	1.306554	1.336147	1.353903
2874	Phosphatic Fertilizers	2	5.75%	1.064917	1.064917	0.901371	0.906377	0.914721	1.031540	1.064917	1.098293	1.215112	1.223456	1.228462
2879	Pesticides And Agricultural Chemicals, Not Elsewhere Classified	3	4.27%	0.791276	0.583578	0.311238	0.319575	0.333470	0.527998	0.583578	0.763776	1.394471	1.439520	1.466550
289	MISCELLANEOUS CHEMICAL PRODUCTS	12	3.08%	0.569449	0.917897	-1.112395	-0.987857	-0.780293	0.816779	0.917897	0.992056	1.152791	1.158095	1.161278
2890	MISCELLANEOUS CHEMICAL PRODUCTS	2	-0.14%	-0.025655	-0.025655	-1.172025	-1.136932	-1.078444	-0.259608	-0.025655	0.208298	1.027134	1.085622	1.120715
2891	Adhesives And Sealants	1	5.85%	1.082500	1.082500	1.082500	1.082500	1.082500	1.082500	1.082500	1.082500	1.082500	1.082500	1.082500
2893	Printing Ink	1	5.27%	0.975460	0.975460	0.975460	0.975460	0.975460	0.975460	0.975460	0.975460	0.975460	0.975460	0.975460
2895	Carbon Black	1	6.28%	1.163400	1.163400	1.163400	1.163400	1.163400	1.163400	1.163400	1.163400	1.163400	1.163400	1.163400
2899	Chemicals And Chemical Preparations, Not Elsewhere Classified	7	2.83%	0.523335	0.787742	-0.430906	-0.416298	-0.391952	0.698022	0.787742	0.831297	1.065980	1.079450	1.087532
29	PETROLEUM REFINING AND RELATED INDUSTRIES	20	4.73%	0.875802	0.844295	0.435428	0.441785	0.452381	0.832865	0.844295	0.877297	1.360869	1.378334	1.388814
291	PETROLEUM REFINING	17	4.98%	0.922864	0.862667	0.497096	0.562495	0.671494	0.844294	0.862667	0.914598	1.366384	1.381092	1.389917
2911	Petroleum Refining	17	4.98%	0.922864	0.862667	0.497096	0.562495	0.671494	0.844294	0.862667	0.914598	1.366384	1.381092	1.389917
295	ASPHALT PAVING AND ROOFING MATERIALS	1	4.45%	0.823738	0.823738	0.823738	0.823738	0.823738	0.823738	0.823738	0.823738	0.823738	0.823738	0.823738
2951	Asphalt Paving Mixtures And Blocks	1	4.45%	0.823738	0.823738	0.823738	0.823738	0.823738	0.823738	0.823738	0.823738	0.823738	0.823738	0.823738
299	MISCELLANEOUS PRODUCTS OF PETROLEUM AND COAL	2	2.71%	0.501815	0.501815	0.432602	0.434721	0.438252	0.487690	0.501815	0.515939	0.565377	0.568908	0.571027
2990	MISCELLANEOUS PRODUCTS OF PETROLEUM & COAL	1	3.09%	0.572439	0.572439	0.572439	0.572439	0.572439	0.572439	0.572439	0.572439	0.572439	0.572439	0.572439
2999	Products Of Petroleum And Coal, Not Elsewhere Classified	1	2.33%	0.431190	0.431190	0.431190	0.431190	0.431190	0.431190	0.431190	0.431190	0.431190	0.431190	0.431190
30	RUBBER AND MISCELLANEOUS PLASTICS PRODUCTS	39	4.20%	0.778491	0.833091	0.125687	0.183451	0.289752	0.726229	0.833091	0.893401	1.154806	1.219814	1.474985
301	TIRES AND INNER TUBES	2	5.02%	0.930439	0.930439	0.920973	0.921263	0.921746	0.928507	0.930439	0.932370	0.939131	0.939614	0.939904
3011	Tires And Inner Tubes	2	5.02%	0.930439	0.930439	0.920973	0.921263	0.921746	0.928507	0.930439	0.932370	0.939131	0.939614	0.939904
302	RUBBER AND PLASTICS FOOTWEAR	5	4.49%	0.831761	0.791166	0.636724	0.646377	0.662464	0.791166	0.791166	0.846881	0.998675	1.007202	1.012319
3021	Rubber And Plastics Footwear	5	4.49%	0.831761	0.791166	0.636724	0.646377	0.662464	0.791166	0.791166	0.846881	0.998675	1.007202	1.012319
305	GASKETS, PACKING, AND SEALING DEVICES AND RUBBER AND PLASTICS HOSE	3	3.69%	0.683855	0.927880	0.203305	0.225486	0.262454	0.780008	0.927880	0.929338	0.934439	0.934804	0.935022
3052	Rubber And Plastics Hose And Belting	1	5.01%	0.927880	0.927880	0.927880	0.927880	0.927880	0.927880	0.927880	0.927880	0.927880	0.927880	0.927880
3053	Gaskets, Packing, And Sealing Devices	2	3.03%	0.561843	0.561843	0.195985	0.207184	0.225851	0.487178	0.561843	0.636508	0.897836	0.916502	0.927702
306	FABRICATED RUBBER PRODUCTS, NOT ELSEWHERE CLASSIFIED	3	2.00%	0.369532	0.369163	0.092817	0.101277	0.115376	0.312766	0.369163	0.425781	0.623946	0.638100	0.646593
3069	Fabricated Rubber Products, Not Elsewhere Classified	3	2.00%	0.369532	0.369163	0.092817	0.101277	0.115376	0.312766	0.369163	0.425781	0.623946	0.638100	0.646593
308	MISCELLANEOUS PLASTICS PRODUCTS	26	4.40%	0.814666	0.842359	0.309600	0.322499	0.357896	0.715104	0.842359	0.851627	1.185590	1.365306	1.533183
3081	Unsupported Plastics Film And Sheet	3	3.80%	0.704297	0.833091	0.311642	0.327605	0.354209	0.726673	0.833091	0.862233	0.964229	0.971515	0.975886
3084	Plastics Pipe	1	3.86%	0.715104	0.715104	0.715104	0.715104	0.715104	0.715104	0.715104	0.715104	0.715104	0.715104	0.715104
3086	Plastics Foam Products	3	3.62%	0.670795	0.614523	0.484860	0.488829	0.495445	0.588061	0.614523	0.674748	0.885536	0.900593	0.909626
3089	Plastics Products, Not Elsewhere Classified	19	4.64%	0.860049	0.851627	0.351597	0.375895	0.416392	0.786909	0.851627	0.893401	1.242197	1.443649	1.564519
31	LEATHER AND LEATHER PRODUCTS	7	4.40%	0.815612	0.778428	0.117758	0.153732	0.213688	0.656989	0.778428	0.801684	1.575882	1.651401	1.696712

Betas of Common Stocks by SIC Codes as of September 28, 2018

SIC Code	Description	Number of Companies	Equity Risk Premium	Mean	Median	1st Percentile	2.5th Percentile	5th Percentile	40th Percentile	50th Percentile	60th Percentile	95th Percentile	97.5th Percentile	99th Percentile
314	FOOTWEAR, EXCEPT RUBBER	4	5.86%	1.085899	1.020324	0.583264	0.594116	0.612203	0.898442	1.020324	1.142206	1.651401	1.689161	1.711816
3142	House Slippers	1	4.41%	0.817188	0.817188	0.817188	0.817188	0.817188	0.817188	0.817188	0.817188	0.817188	0.817188	0.817188
3143	Men's Footwear, Except Athletic	1	6.61%	1.223460	1.223460	1.223460	1.223460	1.223460	1.223460	1.223460	1.223460	1.223460	1.223460	1.223460
3149	Footwear, Except Rubber, Not Elsewhere Classified	2	6.22%	1.151475	1.151475	0.587538	0.604801	0.633574	1.036385	1.151475	1.266564	1.669375	1.698148	1.715411
317	HANDBAGS AND OTHER PERSONAL LEATHER GOODS	1	2.66%	0.493486	0.493486	0.493486	0.493486	0.493486	0.493486	0.493486	0.493486	0.493486	0.493486	0.493486
3171	Women's Handbags And Purses	1	2.66%	0.493486	0.493486	0.493486	0.493486	0.493486	0.493486	0.493486	0.493486	0.493486	0.493486	0.493486
319	LEATHER GOODS, NOT ELSEWHERE CLASSIFIED	2	2.35%	0.436102	0.436102	0.100622	0.110892	0.128008	0.367636	0.436102	0.504567	0.744195	0.761312	0.771581
3199	Leather Goods, Not Elsewhere Classified	2	2.35%	0.436102	0.436102	0.100622	0.110892	0.128008	0.367636	0.436102	0.504567	0.744195	0.761312	0.771581
32	STONE, CLAY, GLASS, AND CONCRETE PRODUCTS	14	4.22%	0.781878	0.863555	0.041947	0.067049	0.108886	0.774027	0.863555	0.906923	1.248317	1.391779	1.477855
322	GLASS AND GLASSWARE, PRESSED OR BLOWN	3	4.50%	0.832517	0.908616	0.503384	0.515789	0.536464	0.825916	0.908616	0.945657	1.075300	1.084560	1.090116
3221	Glass Containers	2	4.29%	0.794467	0.794467	0.501101	0.510082	0.525049	0.734596	0.794467	0.854338	1.063885	1.078852	1.087833
3229	Pressed And Blown Glass And Glassware, Not Elsewhere Classified	1	4.91%	0.908616	0.908616	0.908616	0.908616	0.908616	0.908616	0.908616	0.908616	0.908616	0.908616	0.908616
323	GLASS PRODUCTS, MADE OF PURCHASED GLASS	1	4.11%	0.760794	0.760794	0.760794	0.760794	0.760794	0.760794	0.760794	0.760794	0.760794	0.760794	0.760794
3231	Glass Products, Made Of Purchased Glass	1	4.11%	0.760794	0.760794	0.760794	0.760794	0.760794	0.760794	0.760794	0.760794	0.760794	0.760794	0.760794
324	CEMENT, HYDRAULIC	2	2.84%	0.526111	0.526111	0.035231	0.050258	0.075303	0.425932	0.526111	0.626291	0.976920	1.001965	1.016992
3241	Cement, Hydraulic	2	2.84%	0.526111	0.526111	0.035231	0.050258	0.075303	0.425932	0.526111	0.626291	0.976920	1.001965	1.016992
325	STRUCTURAL CLAY PRODUCTS	1	3.59%	0.665562	0.665562	0.665562	0.665562	0.665562	0.665562	0.665562	0.665562	0.665562	0.665562	0.665562
3253	Ceramic Wall And Floor Tile	1	3.59%	0.665562	0.665562	0.665562	0.665562	0.665562	0.665562	0.665562	0.665562	0.665562	0.665562	0.665562
326	POTTERY AND RELATED PRODUCTS	1	5.46%	1.011050	1.011050	1.011050	1.011050	1.011050	1.011050	1.011050	1.011050	1.011050	1.011050	1.011050
3264	Porcelain Electrical Supplies	1	5.46%	1.011050	1.011050	1.011050	1.011050	1.011050	1.011050	1.011050	1.011050	1.011050	1.011050	1.011050
327	CONCRETE, GYPSUM, AND PLASTER PRODUCTS	6	4.46%	0.826519	0.863555	0.170633	0.195673	0.237406	0.826959	0.863555	0.900151	1.415185	1.475213	1.511229
3272	Concrete Products, Except Block And Brick	3	3.39%	0.627017	0.826959	0.167400	0.187591	0.221242	0.692355	0.826959	0.841597	0.892832	0.896491	0.898687
3273	Ready-Mixed Concrete	1	8.29%	1.535240	1.535240	1.535240	1.535240	1.535240	1.535240	1.535240	1.535240	1.535240	1.535240	1.535240
3274	Lime	1	2.63%	0.487805	0.487805	0.487805	0.487805	0.487805	0.487805	0.487805	0.487805	0.487805	0.487805	0.487805
3275	Gypsum Products	1	5.70%	1.055020	1.055020	1.055020	1.055020	1.055020	1.055020	1.055020	1.055020	1.055020	1.055020	1.055020
33	PRIMARY METAL INDUSTRIES	37	5.38%	0.996152	1.151090	-0.664768	-0.228301	-0.005963	1.001680	1.151090	1.211730	1.546910	1.574801	1.705108
331	STEEL WORKS, BLAST FURNACES, AND ROLLING AND FINISHING MILLS	18	6.22%	1.151647	1.250620	0.251532	0.392631	0.627794	1.183418	1.250620	1.318026	1.582872	1.687426	1.750158
3312	Steel Works, Blast Furnaces (Including Coke Ovens), And Rolling Mills	13	6.55%	1.213883	1.318020	0.233400	0.347300	0.537134	1.278220	1.318020	1.322696	1.644374	1.718177	1.762459
3313	Electrometallurgical Products, Except Steel	1	3.84%	0.710793	0.710793	0.710793	0.710793	0.710793	0.710793	0.710793	0.710793	0.710793	0.710793	0.710793
3315	Steel Wiredrawing And Steel Nails And Spikes	1	4.62%	0.855128	0.855128	0.855128	0.855128	0.855128	0.855128	0.855128	0.855128	0.855128	0.855128	0.855128
3317	Steel Pipe And Tubes	3	6.09%	1.127749	1.151090	0.763154	0.775030	0.794822	1.071919	1.151090	1.216256	1.444337	1.460629	1.470403
332	IRON AND STEEL FOUNDRIES	1	5.20%	0.963549	0.963549	0.963549	0.963549	0.963549	0.963549	0.963549	0.963549	0.963549	0.963549	0.963549
3324	Steel Investment Foundries	1	5.20%	0.963549	0.963549	0.963549	0.963549	0.963549	0.963549	0.963549	0.963549	0.963549	0.963549	0.963549
333	PRIMARY SMELTING AND REFINING OF NONFERROUS METALS	6	4.32%	0.799742	1.170650	-0.880407	-0.767400	-0.579053	1.118350	1.170650	1.222950	1.457288	1.470464	1.478370
3334	Primary Production Of Aluminum	3	7.16%	1.326740	1.378230	1.123548	1.131344	1.144338	1.326254	1.378230	1.399312	1.473099	1.478370	1.481532

Betas of Common Stocks by SIC Codes as of September 28, 2018

SIC Code	Description	Number of Companies	Equity Risk Premium	Mean	Median	1st Percentile	2.5th Percentile	5th Percentile	40th Percentile	50th Percentile	60th Percentile	95th Percentile	97.5th Percentile	99th Percentile
3339	Primary Smelting And Refining Of Nonferrous Metals, Except Copper	3	1.47%	0.272743	0.551025	-0.925611	-0.880407	-0.805069	0.249671	0.551025	0.685410	1.155758	1.189354	1.209512
334	SECONDARY SMELTING AND REFINING OF NONFERROUS METALS	1	0.78%	0.144038	0.144038	0.144038	0.144038	0.144038	0.144038	0.144038	0.144038	0.144038	0.144038	0.144038
3341	Secondary Smelting And Refining Of Nonferrous Metals	1	0.78%	0.144038	0.144038	0.144038	0.144038	0.144038	0.144038	0.144038	0.144038	0.144038	0.144038	0.144038
335	ROLLING, DRAWING, AND EXTRUDING OF NONFERROUS METALS	11	5.02%	0.929269	1.025410	-0.129785	-0.103252	-0.059029	0.985860	1.025410	1.087460	1.514830	1.532750	1.543502
3351	Rolling, Drawing, And Extruding Of Copper	3	5.07%	0.939785	0.943914	0.851908	0.854724	0.859418	0.925137	0.943914	0.960213	1.017260	1.021335	1.023780
3353	Aluminum Sheet, Plate, And Foil	1	8.37%	1.550670	1.550670	1.550670	1.550670	1.550670	1.550670	1.550670	1.550670	1.550670	1.550670	1.550670
3356	Rolling, Drawing, And Extruding Of Nonferrous Metals, Except Copper	1	6.57%	1.216470	1.216470	1.216470	1.216470	1.216470	1.216470	1.216470	1.216470	1.216470	1.216470	1.216470
3357	Drawing And Insulating Of Nonferrous Wire	6	4.17%	0.772577	1.036660	-0.138630	-0.125363	-0.103252	0.985860	1.036660	1.087460	1.409545	1.444268	1.465101
34	FABRICATED METAL PRODUCTS, EXCEPT MACHINERY AND TRANSPORTATION EQUIPMENT	48	3.85%	0.713053	0.759104	-0.127057	-0.003944	0.045495	0.645189	0.759104	0.809381	1.220790	1.313916	1.744187
341	METAL CANS AND SHIPPING CONTAINERS	7	4.44%	0.822296	0.819005	0.145540	0.178627	0.233773	0.723660	0.819005	1.060076	1.220790	1.220790	1.220790
3411	Metal Cans	6	5.07%	0.938765	1.019898	0.499566	0.512240	0.533362	0.819005	1.019898	1.220790	1.220790	1.220790	1.220790
3412	Metal Shipping Barrels, Drums, Kegs, And Pails	1	0.67%	0.123482	0.123482	0.123482	0.123482	0.123482	0.123482	0.123482	0.123482	0.123482	0.123482	0.123482
342	CUTLERY, HANDTOOLS, AND GENERAL HARDWARE	7	3.12%	0.577554	0.797693	-0.216470	-0.196843	-0.164130	0.664578	0.797693	0.801369	1.078599	1.097589	1.108984
3421	Cutlery	2	0.93%	0.173140	0.173140	-0.221501	-0.209420	-0.189286	0.092601	0.173140	0.253679	0.535566	0.555700	0.567781
3423	Hand And Edge Tools, Except Machine Tools And Handsaws	1	4.31%	0.797693	0.797693	0.797693	0.797693	0.797693	0.797693	0.797693	0.797693	0.797693	0.797693	0.797693
3429	Hardware, Not Elsewhere Classified	4	3.91%	0.724726	0.896898	0.012986	0.049674	0.110821	0.841051	0.896898	0.952745	1.097589	1.107085	1.112782
343	HEATING EQUIPMENT, EXCEPT ELECTRIC AND WARM AIR; AND PLUMBING FIXTURES	2	2.15%	0.397452	0.397452	0.107663	0.116534	0.131319	0.338311	0.397452	0.456592	0.663584	0.678369	0.687240
3433	Heating Equipment, Except Electric And Warm Air Furnaces	2	2.15%	0.397452	0.397452	0.107663	0.116534	0.131319	0.338311	0.397452	0.456592	0.663584	0.678369	0.687240
344	FABRICATED STRUCTURAL METAL PRODUCTS	10	4.92%	0.911974	0.887887	0.653158	0.664348	0.682998	0.822675	0.887887	0.958367	1.216130	1.274900	1.310162
3441	Fabricated Structural Metal	2	4.62%	0.856154	0.856154	0.786026	0.788173	0.791751	0.841842	0.856154	0.870465	0.920556	0.924134	0.926281
3442	Metal Doors, Sash, Frames, Molding, And Trim	3	4.44%	0.822183	0.733613	0.728687	0.728837	0.729089	0.732608	0.733613	0.787760	0.977276	0.990813	0.998935
3443	Fabricated Plate Work (Boiler Shops)	3	5.09%	0.942476	0.848061	0.649745	0.655816	0.665934	0.807588	0.848061	0.945183	1.285109	1.309390	1.323958
3448	Prefabricated Metal Buildings And Components	2	5.71%	1.056725	1.056725	1.041295	1.041767	1.042555	1.053576	1.056725	1.059874	1.070896	1.071683	1.072155
345	SCREW MACHINE PRODUCTS, AND BOLTS, NUTS, SCREWS, RIVETS, AND WASHERS	4	1.45%	0.269004	0.200657	0.033898	0.037422	0.043295	0.146181	0.200657	0.255133	0.590397	0.616774	0.632601
3451	Screw Machine Products	1	1.57%	0.291451	0.291451	0.291451	0.291451	0.291451	0.291451	0.291451	0.291451	0.291451	0.291451	0.291451
3452	Bolts, Nuts, Screws, Rivets, And Washers	3	1.41%	0.261521	0.109863	0.033114	0.035464	0.039380	0.094200	0.109863	0.216521	0.589823	0.616488	0.632486

Betas of Common Stocks by SIC Codes as of September 28, 2018

SIC Code	Description	Number of Companies	Equity Risk Premium	Mean	Median	1st Percentile	2.5th Percentile	5th Percentile	40th Percentile	50th Percentile	60th Percentile	95th Percentile	97.5th Percentile	99th Percentile
346	METAL FORGINGS AND STAMPINGS	5	5.22%	0.967180	0.785413	0.404376	0.419216	0.443950	0.727977	0.785413	0.833629	1.867775	1.988002	2.060139
3463	Nonferrous Forgings	1	4.89%	0.905953	0.905953	0.905953	0.905953	0.905953	0.905953	0.905953	0.905953	0.905953	0.905953	0.905953
3465	Automotive Stampings	2	3.85%	0.713618	0.713618	0.643259	0.645413	0.649003	0.699259	0.713618	0.727977	0.778234	0.781823	0.783977
3469	Metal Stampings, Not Elsewhere Classified	2	6.76%	1.251356	1.251356	0.411619	0.437326	0.480169	1.079981	1.251356	1.422731	2.022543	2.065386	2.091093
347	COATING, ENGRAVING, AND ALLIED SERVICES	2	2.18%	0.403292	0.403292	0.280414	0.284175	0.290445	0.378215	0.403292	0.428369	0.516139	0.522409	0.526170
3471	Electroplating, Plating, Polishing, Anodizing, And Coloring	1	1.50%	0.277906	0.277906	0.277906	0.277906	0.277906	0.277906	0.277906	0.277906	0.277906	0.277906	0.277906
3479	Coating, Engraving, And Allied Services, Not Elsewhere Classified	1	2.85%	0.528678	0.528678	0.528678	0.528678	0.528678	0.528678	0.528678	0.528678	0.528678	0.528678	0.528678
348	ORDNANCE AND ACCESSORIES, EXCEPT VEHICLES AND GUIDED MISSILES	2	3.05%	0.565631	0.565631	0.530750	0.531818	0.533597	0.558512	0.565631	0.572749	0.597664	0.599443	0.600511
3484	Small Arms	2	3.05%	0.565631	0.565631	0.530750	0.531818	0.533597	0.558512	0.565631	0.572749	0.597664	0.599443	0.600511
349	MISCELLANEOUS FABRICATED METAL PRODUCTS	9	4.00%	0.740354	0.911894	0.097462	0.136560	0.201724	0.827959	0.911894	0.922358	1.031220	1.031250	1.031268
3490	MISCELLANEOUS FABRICATED METAL PRODUCTS	2	2.58%	0.478056	0.478056	0.398832	0.401257	0.405299	0.461888	0.478056	0.494224	0.550813	0.554855	0.557280
3491	Industrial Valves	3	4.77%	0.882764	0.911894	0.809073	0.812221	0.817467	0.890910	0.911894	0.915400	0.927671	0.928548	0.929073
3495	Wire Springs	1	4.99%	0.924974	0.924974	0.924974	0.924974	0.924974	0.924974	0.924974	0.924974	0.924974	0.924974	0.924974
3499	Fabricated Metal Products, Not Elsewhere Classified	3	3.84%	0.711269	1.031130	0.090591	0.119383	0.167370	0.839183	1.031130	1.031160	1.031265	1.031273	1.031277
35	INDUSTRIAL AND COMMERCIAL MACHINERY AND COMPUTER EQUIPMENT	168	4.74%	0.877284	0.951788	-0.125060	-0.057524	0.079585	0.825162	0.951788	1.001376	1.639007	1.718970	1.937644
351	ENGINES AND TURBINES	10	4.91%	0.909855	0.829271	0.475520	0.488764	0.510839	0.754020	0.829271	0.886614	1.581842	1.617871	1.639488
3510	ENGINES & TURBINES	1	5.12%	0.948698	0.948698	0.948698	0.948698	0.948698	0.948698	0.948698	0.948698	0.948698	0.948698	0.948698
3511	Steam, Gas, And Hydraulic Turbines, And Turbine Generator Set Units	5	4.45%	0.824347	0.623027	0.470614	0.476501	0.486312	0.599735	0.623027	0.699143	1.485784	1.569842	1.620277
3519	Internal Combustion Engines, Not Elsewhere Classified	4	5.44%	1.007029	0.934637	0.670477	0.678583	0.692095	0.880989	0.934637	0.988285	1.423312	1.458541	1.479678
352	FARM AND GARDEN MACHINERY AND EQUIPMENT	9	5.14%	0.951431	0.924544	0.457860	0.474325	0.501767	0.912752	0.924544	0.989613	1.342888	1.353044	1.359138
3523	Farm Machinery And Equipment	7	5.38%	0.996129	0.924544	0.468749	0.501549	0.556215	0.915700	0.924544	1.092656	1.347966	1.355583	1.360153
3524	Lawn And Garden Tractors And Home Lawn And Garden Equipment	2	4.29%	0.794987	0.794987	0.588312	0.594639	0.605183	0.752808	0.794987	0.837166	0.984791	0.995335	1.001662
353	CONSTRUCTION, MINING, AND MATERIALS HANDLING MACHINERY AND EQUIPMENT	24	5.09%	0.941720	0.982082	0.042630	0.182295	0.364318	0.978453	0.982082	1.062106	1.462695	1.602458	1.708611
3531	Construction Machinery And Equipment	7	3.76%	0.696238	0.642114	0.358335	0.364318	0.374289	0.546199	0.642114	0.791952	1.064798	1.082539	1.093184
3532	Mining Machinery And Equipment, Except Oil And Gas Field Machinery	2	7.10%	1.314725	1.314725	1.219670	1.222580	1.227430	1.295326	1.314725	1.334124	1.402021	1.406870	1.409780
3533	Oil And Gas Field Machinery And Equipment	9	5.25%	0.971593	0.998172	0.030022	0.150776	0.352033	0.985360	0.998172	1.062106	1.368378	1.420034	1.451028
3535	Conveyors And Conveying Equipment	1	5.28%	0.978130	0.978130	0.978130	0.978130	0.978130	0.978130	0.978130	0.978130	0.978130	0.978130	0.978130
3536	Overhead Traveling Cranes, Hoists, And Monorail Systems	1	9.61%	1.779380	1.779380	1.779380	1.779380	1.779380	1.779380	1.779380	1.779380	1.779380	1.779380	1.779380

Betas of Common Stocks by SIC Codes as of September 28, 2018

SIC Code	Description	Number of Companies	Equity Risk Premium	Mean	Median	1st Percentile	2.5th Percentile	5th Percentile	40th Percentile	50th Percentile	60th Percentile	95th Percentile	97.5th Percentile	99th Percentile
3537	Industrial Trucks, Tractors, Trailers, And Stackers	4	4.86%	0.899079	0.865469	0.536769	0.541258	0.548738	0.726298	0.865469	1.004640	1.296473	1.314037	1.324575
354	METALWORKING MACHINERY AND EQUIPMENT	8	3.94%	0.729201	0.913899	-0.088925	-0.085548	-0.079921	0.748542	0.913899	1.035374	1.306075	1.343718	1.366303
3541	Machine Tools, Metal Cutting Types	4	4.11%	0.761570	0.861969	-0.040517	-0.012766	0.033486	0.679394	0.861969	1.044543	1.349095	1.365228	1.374907
3542	Machine Tools, Metal Forming Types	1	4.30%	0.796258	0.796258	0.796258	0.796258	0.796258	0.796258	0.796258	0.796258	0.796258	0.796258	0.796258
3545	Cutting Tools, Machine Tool Accessories, And Machinists' Precision Tools	1	5.67%	1.050710	1.050710	1.050710	1.050710	1.050710	1.050710	1.050710	1.050710	1.050710	1.050710	1.050710
3546	Power-Driven Handtools	1	-0.49%	-0.091176	-0.091176	-0.091176	-0.091176	-0.091176	-0.091176	-0.091176	-0.091176	-0.091176	-0.091176	-0.091176
3549	Metalworking Machinery, Not Elsewhere Classified	1	5.57%	1.031540	1.031540	1.031540	1.031540	1.031540	1.031540	1.031540	1.031540	1.031540	1.031540	1.031540
355	SPECIAL INDUSTRY MACHINERY, EXCEPT METALWORKING MACHINERY	18	5.08%	0.941389	0.910917	0.072633	0.082482	0.098898	0.672295	0.910917	1.197992	1.726456	1.788013	1.824947
3554	Paper Industries Machinery	1	3.80%	0.703684	0.703684	0.703684	0.703684	0.703684	0.703684	0.703684	0.703684	0.703684	0.703684	0.703684
3555	Printing Trades Machinery And Equipment	1	7.20%	1.333280	1.333280	1.333280	1.333280	1.333280	1.333280	1.333280	1.333280	1.333280	1.333280	1.333280
3556	Food Products Machinery	1	0.57%	0.104692	0.104692	0.104692	0.104692	0.104692	0.104692	0.104692	0.104692	0.104692	0.104692	0.104692
3559	Special Industry Machinery, Not Elsewhere Classified	15	5.33%	0.986889	1.118150	0.123499	0.209647	0.353227	0.659376	1.118150	1.206534	1.748182	1.798876	1.829292
356	GENERAL INDUSTRIAL MACHINERY AND EQUIPMENT	29	4.75%	0.879462	0.924507	0.176878	0.178472	0.195301	0.893371	0.924507	0.998865	1.214966	1.524193	1.954613
3560	GENERAL INDUSTRIAL MACHINERY & EQUIPMENT	1	6.45%	1.195360	1.195360	1.195360	1.195360	1.195360	1.195360	1.195360	1.195360	1.195360	1.195360	1.195360
3561	Pumps And Pumping Equipment	9	5.17%	0.957362	0.968764	0.609943	0.623071	0.644950	0.957655	0.968764	1.020249	1.185158	1.200954	1.210432
3562	Ball And Roller Bearings	4	4.71%	0.871774	0.918937	0.444755	0.456489	0.476046	0.786191	0.918937	1.051683	1.201474	1.206882	1.210127
3564	Industrial And Commercial Fans And Blowers And Air Purification Equipment	6	3.53%	0.653735	0.670851	0.177966	0.181193	0.186570	0.474592	0.670851	0.867110	1.124420	1.140115	1.149532
3566	Speed Changers, Industrial High-Speed Drives, And Gears	1	4.01%	0.742802	0.742802	0.742802	0.742802	0.742802	0.742802	0.742802	0.742802	0.742802	0.742802	0.742802
3568	Mechanical Power Transmission Equipment, Not Elsewhere Classified	1	5.43%	1.006390	1.006390	1.006390	1.006390	1.006390	1.006390	1.006390	1.006390	1.006390	1.006390	1.006390
3569	General Industrial Machinery And Equipment, Not Elsewhere Classified	7	5.04%	0.933441	0.915153	0.189295	0.203821	0.228030	0.898816	0.915153	0.920765	1.882388	2.061974	2.169726
357	COMPUTER AND OFFICE EQUIPMENT	55	4.91%	0.909664	0.978934	-0.074199	0.065603	0.142439	0.896713	0.978934	1.005641	1.653233	1.716060	1.903387
3571	Electronic Computers	12	4.32%	0.799450	0.831583	0.039633	0.057487	0.087244	0.810560	0.831583	0.984494	1.335644	1.342857	1.347185
3572	Computer Storage Devices	7	6.44%	1.193498	1.225320	0.593853	0.641582	0.721131	1.208844	1.225320	1.234248	1.593113	1.649182	1.682823
3576	COMPUTER COMMUNICATIONS EQUIPMENT	7	4.58%	0.847607	0.783899	-0.160414	-0.110252	-0.026649	0.620002	0.783899	0.932418	1.877846	1.997153	2.068737
3577	Computer Peripheral Equipment, Not Elsewhere Classified	22	4.62%	0.855576	0.917060	0.162267	0.187830	0.227303	0.896463	0.917060	0.984763	1.416244	1.562690	1.658204
3578	Calculating And Accounting Machines, Except Electronic Computers	5	5.82%	1.078034	1.234450	0.311741	0.352561	0.420594	1.126614	1.234450	1.250826	1.559830	1.595385	1.616718
3579	Office Machines, Not Elsewhere Classified	2	5.23%	0.968771	0.968771	0.958811	0.959116	0.959624	0.966738	0.968771	0.970804	0.977918	0.978426	0.978731
358	REFRIGERATION AND SERVICE INDUSTRY MACHINERY	10	3.59%	0.665051	0.727157	-0.011285	0.043778	0.135550	0.707048	0.727157	0.762390	1.035780	1.050315	1.059036

Betas of Common Stocks by SIC Codes as of September 28, 2018

SIC Code	Description	Number of Companies	Equity Risk Premium	Mean	Median	1st Percentile	2.5th Percentile	5th Percentile	40th Percentile	50th Percentile	60th Percentile	95th Percentile	97.5th Percentile	99th Percentile
3580	REFRIGERATION & SERVICE INDUSTRY MACHINERY	2	2.04%	0.377040	0.377040	-0.039493	-0.026742	-0.005490	0.292033	0.377040	0.462046	0.759570	0.780821	0.793572
3585	Air-Conditioning And Warm Air Heating Equipment	3	4.53%	0.839721	0.739607	0.715204	0.715951	0.717196	0.734627	0.739607	0.804656	1.032326	1.048588	1.058345
3589	Service Industry Machinery, Not Elsewhere Classified	5	3.65%	0.675453	0.695562	0.366486	0.376394	0.392906	0.627340	0.695562	0.735963	0.959513	0.979882	0.992103
359	MISCELLANEOUS INDUSTRIAL AND COMMERCIAL MACHINERY AND EQUIPMENT	5	2.33%	0.431204	0.916969	-0.962612	-0.907762	-0.816346	0.516174	0.916969	1.005185	1.176094	1.180917	1.183811
3590	MISC INDUSTRIAL & COMMERCIAL MACHINERY & EQUIPMENT	1	-5.40%	-0.999178	-0.999178	-0.999178	-0.999178	-0.999178	-0.999178	-0.999178	-0.999178	-0.999178	-0.999178	-0.999178
3592	Carburetors, Pistons, Piston Rings, And Valves	1	6.14%	1.137510	1.137510	1.137510	1.137510	1.137510	1.137510	1.137510	1.137510	1.137510	1.137510	1.137510
3594	Fluid Power Pumps And Motors	1	6.40%	1.185740	1.185740	1.185740	1.185740	1.185740	1.185740	1.185740	1.185740	1.185740	1.185740	1.185740
3596	Scales And Balances, Except Laboratory	1	-0.46%	-0.085020	-0.085020	-0.085020	-0.085020	-0.085020	-0.085020	-0.085020	-0.085020	-0.085020	-0.085020	-0.085020
3599	Industrial And Commercial Machinery And Equipment, Not Elsewhere Classified	1	4.95%	0.916969	0.916969	0.916969	0.916969	0.916969	0.916969	0.916969	0.916969	0.916969	0.916969	0.916969
36	ELECTRONIC AND OTHER ELECTRICAL EQUIPMENT AND COMPONENTS, EXCEPT COMPUTER	265	3.90%	0.722571	0.802767	-0.604905	-0.295606	-0.065291	0.675006	0.802767	0.930478	1.639398	1.811528	2.054806
361	ELECTRIC TRANSMISSION AND DISTRIBUTION EQUIPMENT	5	3.50%	0.647742	0.656903	0.155442	0.176043	0.210376	0.588160	0.656903	0.731103	1.058601	1.085625	1.101840
3612	Power, Distribution, And Specialty Transformers	3	2.31%	0.427886	0.485046	0.148576	0.158876	0.176043	0.416379	0.485046	0.519417	0.639717	0.648310	0.653466
3613	Switchgear And Switchboard Apparatus	2	5.28%	0.977527	0.977527	0.845106	0.849160	0.855916	0.950502	0.977527	1.004552	1.099138	1.105894	1.109948
362	ELECTRICAL INDUSTRIAL APPARATUS	18	3.96%	0.733223	0.952926	-0.242226	-0.204911	-0.142718	0.864165	0.952926	1.014976	1.192556	1.209573	1.219783
3621	Motors And Generators	13	3.58%	0.662685	0.964580	-0.249543	-0.223203	-0.179302	0.821563	0.964580	1.026756	1.202566	1.214578	1.221785
3625	Relays And Industrial Controls	2	4.67%	0.863901	0.863901	0.863470	0.863483	0.863505	0.863813	0.863901	0.863989	0.864297	0.864319	0.864332
3629	Electrical Industrial Apparatus, Not Elsewhere Classified	3	5.14%	0.951768	1.015400	0.694866	0.704678	0.721032	0.949985	1.015400	1.042636	1.137962	1.144771	1.148856
363	HOUSEHOLD APPLIANCES	7	4.50%	0.833747	0.836601	0.423330	0.432545	0.447903	0.803939	0.836601	0.960986	1.135293	1.147967	1.155571
3630	HOUSEHOLD APPLIANCES	1	6.27%	1.160640	1.160640	1.160640	1.160640	1.160640	1.160640	1.160640	1.160640	1.160640	1.160640	1.160640
3632	Household Refrigerators And Home And Farm Freezers	1	5.64%	1.043910	1.043910	1.043910	1.043910	1.043910	1.043910	1.043910	1.043910	1.043910	1.043910	1.043910
3633	Household Laundry Equipment	2	5.16%	0.956376	0.956376	0.838996	0.842590	0.848578	0.932421	0.956376	0.980330	1.064173	1.070161	1.073755
3634	Electric Housewares And Fans	3	3.09%	0.572975	0.519574	0.419235	0.422306	0.427426	0.499097	0.519574	0.572092	0.755906	0.769035	0.776913
364	ELECTRIC LIGHTING AND WIRING EQUIPMENT	9	2.55%	0.472820	0.591467	-0.267334	-0.238296	-0.189901	0.152014	0.591467	0.782020	1.124708	1.186604	1.223742
3640	ELECTRIC LIGHTING & WIRING EQUIPMENT	3	2.80%	0.517758	0.591467	-0.269129	-0.242784	-0.198876	0.415835	0.591467	0.722874	1.182797	1.215648	1.235359
3641	Electric Lamp Bulbs And Tubes	3	1.69%	0.312152	0.042151	-0.042976	-0.040370	-0.036027	0.024778	0.042151	0.221525	0.849332	0.894176	0.921082
3643	Current-Carrying Wiring Devices	1	4.83%	0.894770	0.894770	0.894770	0.894770	0.894770	0.894770	0.894770	0.894770	0.894770	0.894770	0.894770
3645	Residential Electric Lighting Fixtures	1	0.22%	0.041218	0.041218	0.041218	0.041218	0.041218	0.041218	0.041218	0.041218	0.041218	0.041218	0.041218
3646	Commercial, Industrial, And Institutional Electric Lighting Fixtures	1	4.48%	0.829658	0.829658	0.829658	0.829658	0.829658	0.829658	0.829658	0.829658	0.829658	0.829658	0.829658
365	HOUSEHOLD AUDIO AND VIDEO EQUIPMENT, AND AUDIO RECORDINGS	7	2.20%	0.407322	0.426651	-0.739028	-0.636183	-0.464774	0.407141	0.426651	0.499790	1.070893	1.141172	1.183339

Betas of Common Stocks by SIC Codes as of September 28, 2018

SIC Code	Description	Number of Companies	Equity Risk Premium	Mean	Median	1st Percentile	2.5th Percentile	5th Percentile	40th Percentile	50th Percentile	60th Percentile	95th Percentile	97.5th Percentile	99th Percentile
3651	Household Audio And Video Equipment	6	3.29%	0.609808	0.487600	0.338084	0.342509	0.349884	0.426651	0.487600	0.548549	1.094319	1.152885	1.188024
3652	Phonograph Records And Prerecorded Audio Tapes And Disks	1	-4.36%	-0.807592	-0.807592	-0.807592	-0.807592	-0.807592	-0.807592	-0.807592	-0.807592	-0.807592	-0.807592	-0.807592
366	COMMUNICATIONS EQUIPMENT	67	1.70%	0.314303	0.615227	-6.493114	-0.435359	-0.254683	0.543143	0.615227	0.694738	1.091132	1.296209	1.483907
3661	Telephone And Telegraph Apparatus	17	3.56%	0.658901	0.607736	0.183774	0.184650	0.186110	0.558874	0.607736	0.807634	1.102198	1.235574	1.315600
3663	Radio And Television Broadcasting And Communications Equipment	35	0.47%	0.087149	0.630023	-12.073053	-3.041481	-0.080745	0.566619	0.630023	0.704422	0.950162	1.087686	1.459311
3669	Communications Equipment, Not Elsewhere Classified	15	2.45%	0.453786	0.449892	-0.499297	-0.472970	-0.429091	0.345792	0.449892	0.675722	1.157591	1.207316	1.237150
367	ELECTRONIC COMPONENTS AND ACCESSORIES	132	5.11%	0.945663	0.983847	-0.269513	-0.128741	0.068770	0.845061	0.983847	1.097474	1.812672	2.010211	2.170043
3671	Electron Tubes	1	0.63%	0.116577	0.116577	0.116577	0.116577	0.116577	0.116577	0.116577	0.116577	0.116577	0.116577	0.116577
3672	Printed Circuit Boards	14	2.94%	0.544195	0.589108	-0.132809	-0.105737	-0.060616	0.470487	0.589108	0.610852	0.999891	1.036371	1.058258
3674	Semiconductors And Related Devices	96	5.71%	1.057642	1.124390	-0.331601	0.094668	0.151468	0.985160	1.124390	1.240650	1.834105	1.995513	2.094095
3675	Electronic Capacitors	1	1.58%	0.292622	0.292622	0.292622	0.292622	0.292622	0.292622	0.292622	0.292622	0.292622	0.292622	0.292622
3676	Electronic Resistors	1	5.31%	0.982534	0.982534	0.982534	0.982534	0.982534	0.982534	0.982534	0.982534	0.982534	0.982534	0.982534
3677	Electronic Coils, Transformers, And Other Inductors	2	4.47%	0.827051	0.827051	0.581404	0.588924	0.601457	0.776919	0.827051	0.877182	1.052644	1.065177	1.072697
3678	Electronic Connectors	4	4.50%	0.833054	0.938093	0.416351	0.438750	0.476081	0.914735	0.938093	0.961450	1.042972	1.048791	1.052282
3679	Electronic Components, Not Elsewhere Classified	13	3.86%	0.715166	0.357408	-0.168326	-0.148303	-0.114931	0.191456	0.357408	0.889544	1.902298	2.060389	2.155244
369	MISCELLANEOUS ELECTRICAL MACHINERY, EQUIPMENT, AND SUPPLIES	20	4.38%	0.810791	0.824949	-0.022446	0.065698	0.212603	0.743233	0.824949	0.888573	1.466277	1.522768	1.556663
3690	MISCELLANEOUS ELECTRICAL MACHINERY, EQUIPMENT & SUPPLIES	2	2.21%	0.409676	0.409676	-0.071390	-0.056664	-0.032120	0.311499	0.409676	0.507853	0.851472	0.876016	0.890742
3691	Storage Batteries	8	4.67%	0.864029	0.813469	0.440252	0.444019	0.450296	0.721733	0.813469	0.926051	1.363069	1.411699	1.440878
3692	Primary Batteries, Dry And Wet	1	5.32%	0.985027	0.985027	0.985027	0.985027	0.985027	0.985027	0.985027	0.985027	0.985027	0.985027	0.985027
3694	Electrical Equipment For Internal Combustion Engines	1	3.70%	0.684870	0.684870	0.684870	0.684870	0.684870	0.684870	0.684870	0.684870	0.684870	0.684870	0.684870
3695	Magnetic And Optical Recording Media	4	4.31%	0.798298	0.692933	0.236383	0.248858	0.269649	0.580343	0.692933	0.805522	1.474458	1.526859	1.558300
3699	Electrical Machinery, Equipment, And Supplies, Not Elsewhere Classified	4	4.89%	0.905287	0.865804	0.722603	0.725319	0.729846	0.815013	0.865804	0.916594	1.136006	1.152378	1.162201
37	TRANSPORTATION EQUIPMENT	102	4.62%	0.856220	0.926396	-0.461278	-0.161331	0.073560	0.833148	0.926396	0.982049	1.413919	1.484377	1.844726
371	MOTOR VEHICLES AND MOTOR VEHICLE EQUIPMENT	54	5.35%	0.991390	1.044185	-0.088988	0.019641	0.316828	0.981865	1.044185	1.143754	1.423262	1.455752	1.746189
3711	Motor Vehicles And Passenger Car Bodies	19	4.93%	0.912991	0.992590	-0.001359	0.037744	0.102915	0.877904	0.992590	1.051170	1.442521	1.452876	1.459088
3713	Truck And Bus Bodies	1	2.86%	0.530147	0.530147	0.530147	0.530147	0.530147	0.530147	0.530147	0.530147	0.530147	0.530147	0.530147
3714	Motor Vehicle Parts And Accessories	31	5.60%	1.036748	1.094630	0.016379	0.278559	0.463188	0.987474	1.094630	1.147030	1.380655	1.576915	1.869928
3715	Truck Trailers	1	5.87%	1.087150	1.087150	1.087150	1.087150	1.087150	1.087150	1.087150	1.087150	1.087150	1.087150	1.087150
3716	Motor Homes	2	6.57%	1.215880	1.215880	1.209461	1.209658	1.209985	1.214570	1.215880	1.217190	1.221775	1.222103	1.222299
372	AIRCRAFT AND PARTS	29	4.04%	0.748808	0.828804	-0.056829	0.104771	0.248006	0.664854	0.828804	0.850361	1.328174	1.391620	1.461298
3721	Aircraft	10	4.80%	0.888400	0.942009	0.437183	0.454888	0.484396	0.898737	0.942009	0.961379	1.206166	1.274008	1.314713
3724	Aircraft Engines And Engine Parts	8	2.87%	0.530983	0.525336	-0.132763	-0.085064	-0.005565	0.499283	0.525336	0.588471	0.937740	0.960796	0.974629

Betas of Common Stocks by SIC Codes as of September 28, 2018

SIC Code	Description	Number of Companies	Equity Risk Premium	Mean	Median	1st Percentile	2.5th Percentile	5th Percentile	40th Percentile	50th Percentile	60th Percentile	95th Percentile	97.5th Percentile	99th Percentile
3728	Aircraft Parts And Auxiliary Equipment, Not Elsewhere Classified	11	4.21%	0.780324	0.754501	0.234546	0.256066	0.291932	0.642442	0.754501	0.815271	1.407705	1.457728	1.487741
373	SHIP AND BOAT BUILDING AND REPAIRING	5	4.35%	0.805055	0.777099	0.084472	0.104303	0.137353	0.626962	0.777099	0.837074	1.663911	1.756021	1.811286
3730	SHIP & BOAT BUILDING & REPAIRING	1	9.98%	1.848130	1.848130	1.848130	1.848130	1.848130	1.848130	1.848130	1.848130	1.848130	1.848130	1.848130
3731	Ship Building And Repairing	2	2.70%	0.499145	0.499145	0.079810	0.092647	0.114042	0.413566	0.499145	0.584723	0.884248	0.905642	0.918479
3732	Boat Building And Repairing	2	3.18%	0.589428	0.589428	0.405510	0.411141	0.420524	0.551894	0.589428	0.626962	0.758332	0.767715	0.773346
374	RAILROAD EQUIPMENT	5	4.23%	0.783007	0.809180	0.559676	0.574946	0.600397	0.807108	0.809180	0.825119	0.892472	0.897903	0.901161
3743	Railroad Equipment	5	4.23%	0.783007	0.809180	0.559676	0.574946	0.600397	0.807108	0.809180	0.825119	0.892472	0.897903	0.901161
375	MOTORCYCLES, BICYCLES, AND PARTS	3	3.42%	0.633837	0.596391	0.467970	0.471901	0.478453	0.570183	0.596391	0.645067	0.815434	0.827603	0.834904
3751	Motorcycles, Bicycles, And Parts	3	3.42%	0.633837	0.596391	0.467970	0.471901	0.478453	0.570183	0.596391	0.645067	0.815434	0.827603	0.834904
376	GUIDED MISSILES AND SPACE VEHICLES AND PARTS	3	-0.90%	-0.166708	-0.464275	-0.812796	-0.802127	-0.784346	-0.535402	-0.464275	-0.214608	0.659227	0.721644	0.759094
3761	Guided Missiles And Space Vehicles	1	4.23%	0.784061	0.784061	0.784061	0.784061	0.784061	0.784061	0.784061	0.784061	0.784061	0.784061	0.784061
3764	Guided Missile And Space Vehicle Propulsion Units And Propulsion	1	-2.51%	-0.464275	-0.464275	-0.464275	-0.464275	-0.464275	-0.464275	-0.464275	-0.464275	-0.464275	-0.464275	-0.464275
3769	Guided Missile And Space Vehicle Parts And Auxiliary Equipment, Not Elsewhere Classified	1	-4.43%	-0.819909	-0.819909	-0.819909	-0.819909	-0.819909	-0.819909	-0.819909	-0.819909	-0.819909	-0.819909	-0.819909
379	MISCELLANEOUS TRANSPORTATION EQUIPMENT	3	4.94%	0.914093	0.977480	0.767493	0.773922	0.784635	0.934626	0.977480	0.982302	0.999179	1.000385	1.001108
3790	MISCELLANEOUS TRANSPORTATION EQUIPMENT	1	5.28%	0.977480	0.977480	0.977480	0.977480	0.977480	0.977480	0.977480	0.977480	0.977480	0.977480	0.977480
3795	Tanks And Tank Components	1	4.12%	0.763208	0.763208	0.763208	0.763208	0.763208	0.763208	0.763208	0.763208	0.763208	0.763208	0.763208
3799	Transportation Equipment, Not Elsewhere Classified	1	5.41%	1.001590	1.001590	1.001590	1.001590	1.001590	1.001590	1.001590	1.001590	1.001590	1.001590	1.001590
38	MEASURING, ANALYZING, AND CONTROLLING INSTRUMENTS; PHOTOGRAPHIC, MEDICAL	263	3.64%	0.674427	0.777392	-0.786724	-0.362819	-0.121490	0.647065	0.777392	0.870012	1.389707	1.449448	1.612859
381	SEARCH, DETECTION, NAVIGATION, GUIDANCE, AERONAUTICAL, AND NAUTICAL	11	4.09%	0.757675	0.746117	0.345263	0.345924	0.347025	0.724073	0.746117	0.762978	1.155130	1.198230	1.224090
3812	Search, Detection, Navigation, Guidance, Aeronautical, And Nautical	11	4.09%	0.757675	0.746117	0.345263	0.345924	0.347025	0.724073	0.746117	0.762978	1.155130	1.198230	1.224090
382	LABORATORY APPARATUS AND ANALYTICAL, OPTICAL, MEASURING, AND CONTROL	91	4.07%	0.753027	0.840167	-0.478916	-0.118539	0.043770	0.728718	0.840167	0.971498	1.423575	1.435765	1.547329
3821	Laboratory Apparatus And Furniture	3	1.55%	0.286219	0.306849	0.056423	0.064089	0.076866	0.255742	0.306849	0.345578	0.481130	0.490812	0.496621
3822	Automatic Controls For Regulating Residential And Commercial Environment	4	0.40%	0.073225	0.815785	-2.538670	-2.396950	-2.160749	0.636027	0.815785	0.995542	1.267615	1.281048	1.289107
3823	Industrial Instruments For Measurement, Display, And Control Of Processes	17	4.69%	0.867663	0.945637	0.180854	0.219317	0.283422	0.858850	0.945637	0.991164	1.422186	1.480498	1.515485
3824	Totalizing Fluid Meters And Counting Devices	1	4.46%	0.825207	0.825207	0.825207	0.825207	0.825207	0.825207	0.825207	0.825207	0.825207	0.825207	0.825207
3825	Instruments For Measuring And Testing Of Electricity And Electric	20	4.01%	0.742283	0.818487	-0.187158	-0.108559	0.022439	0.696784	0.818487	0.932466	1.355914	1.389672	1.409927

Betas of Common Stocks by SIC Codes as of September 28, 2018

SIC Code	Description	Number of Companies	Equity Risk Premium	Mean	Median	1st Percentile	2.5th Percentile	5th Percentile	40th Percentile	50th Percentile	60th Percentile	95th Percentile	97.5th Percentile	99th Percentile
3826	Laboratory Analytical Instruments	18	4.61%	0.853976	0.925326	0.114200	0.164431	0.248149	0.825145	0.925326	1.071234	1.425859	1.431920	1.435556
3827	Optical Instruments And Lenses	10	5.59%	1.034984	0.949960	0.619391	0.629008	0.645037	0.868321	0.949960	1.075438	1.536304	1.580152	1.606461
3829	Measuring And Controlling Devices, Not Elsewhere Classified	18	3.37%	0.623964	0.619488	-0.120208	-0.114887	-0.106018	0.515520	0.619488	0.815177	1.266265	1.288238	1.301421
384	SURGICAL, MEDICAL, AND DENTAL INSTRUMENTS AND SUPPLIES	152	3.28%	0.608089	0.732931	-0.827710	-0.477792	-0.217822	0.582678	0.732931	0.826613	1.318338	1.436263	1.542963
3841	Surgical And Medical Instruments And Apparatus	92	3.49%	0.646981	0.736026	-0.678668	-0.565389	-0.119047	0.618797	0.736026	0.867147	1.329420	1.444203	1.493499
3842	Orthopedic, Prosthetic, And Surgical Appliances And Supplies	23	2.69%	0.497729	0.793942	-1.690363	-1.019793	-0.104749	0.484714	0.793942	0.808091	1.115161	1.203975	1.266774
3843	Dental Equipment And Supplies	5	3.13%	0.580516	0.658431	-0.274768	-0.257574	-0.228918	0.395193	0.658431	0.702852	1.562345	1.661452	1.720917
3844	X-Ray Apparatus And Tubes And Related Irradiation Apparatus	2	4.76%	0.881221	0.881221	0.870222	0.870559	0.871120	0.878976	0.881221	0.883466	0.891322	0.891883	0.892220
3845	Electromedical And Electrotherapeutic Apparatus	30	3.02%	0.559814	0.631644	-0.404270	-0.359069	-0.254604	0.570869	0.631644	0.748227	1.211419	1.302917	1.337047
385	OPHTHALMIC GOODS	2	5.21%	0.964660	0.964660	0.923559	0.924817	0.926914	0.956272	0.964660	0.973048	1.002406	1.004503	1.005761
3851	Ophthalmic Goods	2	5.21%	0.964660	0.964660	0.923559	0.924817	0.926914	0.956272	0.964660	0.973048	1.002406	1.004503	1.005761
386	PHOTOGRAPHIC EQUIPMENT AND SUPPLIES	5	3.50%	0.648896	0.636172	0.032065	0.050970	0.082479	0.515525	0.636172	0.703213	1.321171	1.385845	1.424650
3861	Photographic Equipment And Supplies	5	3.50%	0.648896	0.636172	0.032065	0.050970	0.082479	0.515525	0.636172	0.703213	1.321171	1.385845	1.424650
387	WATCHES, CLOCKS, CLOCKWORK OPERATED DEVICES, AND PARTS	2	7.86%	1.455561	1.455561	0.895452	0.912598	0.941175	1.341253	1.455561	1.569868	1.969946	1.998523	2.015669
3873	Watches, Clocks, Clockwork Operated Devices, And Parts	2	7.86%	1.455561	1.455561	0.895452	0.912598	0.941175	1.341253	1.455561	1.569868	1.969946	1.998523	2.015669
39	MISCELLANEOUS MANUFACTURING INDUSTRIES	29	2.19%	0.405800	0.540606	-0.921479	-0.777012	-0.651455	0.492545	0.540606	0.567867	0.986374	1.135503	1.336369
391	JEWELRY, SILVERWARE, AND PLATED WARE	3	1.43%	0.265050	0.204715	0.022430	0.028010	0.037310	0.167514	0.204715	0.278117	0.535024	0.553375	0.564385
3911	Jewelry, Precious Metal	3	1.43%	0.265050	0.204715	0.022430	0.028010	0.037310	0.167514	0.204715	0.278117	0.535024	0.553375	0.564385
394	DOLLS, TOYS, GAMES AND SPORTING AND ATHLETIC GOODS	20	2.09%	0.386688	0.524086	-0.952436	-0.854405	-0.691020	0.481193	0.524086	0.546954	1.002513	1.236397	1.376727
3942	Dolls And Stuffed Toys	3	0.76%	0.140151	0.198119	-0.656383	-0.630225	-0.586628	0.023731	0.198119	0.337727	0.826353	0.861255	0.882196
3944	Games, Toys, And Children's Vehicles, Except Dolls And Bicycles	9	2.23%	0.412420	0.464823	-0.941716	-0.827604	-0.637419	0.368081	0.464823	0.534914	1.273326	1.371803	1.430889
3949	Sporting And Athletic Goods, Not Elsewhere Classified	8	2.43%	0.450191	0.541952	-0.518849	-0.404709	-0.214475	0.533998	0.541952	0.564971	0.732782	0.735307	0.736822
399	MISCELLANEOUS MANUFACTURING INDUSTRIES	6	2.92%	0.539882	0.724660	-0.562295	-0.478879	-0.339853	0.651169	0.724660	0.798150	0.974408	0.983218	0.988503
3990	MISCELLANEOUS MANUFACTURING INDUSTRIES	1	2.67%	0.494302	0.494302	0.494302	0.494302	0.494302	0.494302	0.494302	0.494302	0.494302	0.494302	0.494302
3993	Signs And Advertising Specialties	1	-3.34%	-0.617905	-0.617905	-0.617905	-0.617905	-0.617905	-0.617905	-0.617905	-0.617905	-0.617905	-0.617905	-0.617905
3996	Linoleum, Asphalted-Felt-Base, And Other Hard Surface Floor Cover	1	3.52%	0.651169	0.651169	0.651169	0.651169	0.651169	0.651169	0.651169	0.651169	0.651169	0.651169	0.651169
3999	Manufacturing Industries, Not Elsewhere Classified	3	4.88%	0.903909	0.921551	0.800618	0.804320	0.810490	0.896871	0.921551	0.935646	0.984979	0.988503	0.990617
	TRANSPORTATION, COMMUNICATIONS, ELECTRIC, GAS, AND SANITARY SERVICE													
40	RAILROAD TRANSPORTATION	7	5.21%	0.963920	1.036070	0.653087	0.663365	0.680495	0.977672	1.036070	1.077068	1.135732	1.139446	1.141674
401	RAILROADS	7	5.21%	0.963920	1.036070	0.653087	0.663365	0.680495	0.977672	1.036070	1.077068	1.135732	1.139446	1.141674
4011	Railroads, Line-Haul Operating	7	5.21%	0.963920	1.036070	0.653087	0.663365	0.680495	0.977672	1.036070	1.077068	1.135732	1.139446	1.141674

Betas of Common Stocks by SIC Codes as of September 28, 2018

SIC Code	Description	Number of Companies	Equity Risk Premium	Mean	Median	1st Percentile	2.5th Percentile	5th Percentile	40th Percentile	50th Percentile	60th Percentile	95th Percentile	97.5th Percentile	99th Percentile
41	LOCAL AND SUBURBAN TRANSIT AND INTERURBAN HIGHWAY PASSENGER TRANSPORTATION	1	0.04%	0.008308	0.008308	0.008308	0.008308	0.008308	0.008308	0.008308	0.008308	0.008308	0.008308	0.008308
415	SCHOOL BUSES	1	0.04%	0.008308	0.008308	0.008308	0.008308	0.008308	0.008308	0.008308	0.008308	0.008308	0.008308	0.008308
4151	School Buses	1	0.04%	0.008308	0.008308	0.008308	0.008308	0.008308	0.008308	0.008308	0.008308	0.008308	0.008308	0.008308
42	MOTOR FREIGHT TRANSPORTATION AND WAREHOUSING	25	5.35%	0.991664	0.951486	0.217435	0.283413	0.369775	0.857980	0.951486	0.982725	1.828750	1.828750	1.828750
421	TRUCKING AND COURIER SERVICES, EXCEPT AIR	23	5.62%	1.040557	0.962002	0.371081	0.392617	0.433771	0.895643	0.962002	1.015096	1.828750	1.828750	1.828750
4213	Trucking, Except Local	23	5.62%	1.040557	0.962002	0.371081	0.392617	0.433771	0.895643	0.962002	1.015096	1.828750	1.828750	1.828750
422	PUBLIC WAREHOUSING AND STORAGE	2	2.32%	0.429397	0.429397	0.178568	0.186246	0.199044	0.378207	0.429397	0.480586	0.659749	0.672547	0.680225
4221	Farm Product Warehousing And Storage	1	0.94%	0.173449	0.173449	0.173449	0.173449	0.173449	0.173449	0.173449	0.173449	0.173449	0.173449	0.173449
4225	General Warehousing And Storage	1	3.70%	0.685344	0.685344	0.685344	0.685344	0.685344	0.685344	0.685344	0.685344	0.685344	0.685344	0.685344
44	WATER TRANSPORTATION	44	3.89%	0.720004	0.779697	-1.537010	-0.710929	0.072878	0.687847	0.779697	0.904726	1.263206	1.618946	1.656260
4400	WATER TRANSPORTATION	2	-3.62%	-0.670298	-0.670298	-2.083529	-2.040266	-1.968163	-0.958712	-0.670298	-0.381884	0.627567	0.699670	0.742933
441	DEEP SEA FOREIGN TRANSPORTATION OF FREIGHT	32	4.13%	0.765269	0.768133	-0.512294	-0.119250	0.078063	0.639654	0.768133	0.909195	1.437534	1.651012	1.658085
4412	Deep Sea Foreign Transportation Of Freight	32	4.13%	0.765269	0.768133	-0.512294	-0.119250	0.078063	0.639654	0.768133	0.909195	1.437534	1.651012	1.658085
442	DEEP SEA DOMESTIC TRANSPORTATION OF FREIGHT	1	5.41%	1.002130	1.002130	1.002130	1.002130	1.002130	1.002130	1.002130	1.002130	1.002130	1.002130	1.002130
4424	Deep Sea Domestic Transportation Of Freight	1	5.41%	1.002130	1.002130	1.002130	1.002130	1.002130	1.002130	1.002130	1.002130	1.002130	1.002130	1.002130
444	WATER TRANSPORTATION OF FREIGHT, NOT ELSEWHERE CLASSIFIED	1	4.33%	0.801325	0.801325	0.801325	0.801325	0.801325	0.801325	0.801325	0.801325	0.801325	0.801325	0.801325
4449	Water Transportation Of Freight, Not Elsewhere Classified	1	4.33%	0.801325	0.801325	0.801325	0.801325	0.801325	0.801325	0.801325	0.801325	0.801325	0.801325	0.801325
448	WATER TRANSPORTATION OF PASSENGERS	3	5.08%	0.941080	0.901687	0.709838	0.715711	0.725499	0.862534	0.901687	0.964476	1.184236	1.199933	1.209351
4481	Deep Sea Transportation Of Passengers, Except By Ferry	3	5.08%	0.941080	0.901687	0.709838	0.715711	0.725499	0.862534	0.901687	0.964476	1.184236	1.199933	1.209351
449	SERVICES INCIDENTAL TO WATER TRANSPORTATION	5	4.22%	0.781094	0.687751	0.364009	0.376775	0.398052	0.639959	0.687751	0.870675	1.148124	1.148507	1.148737
4491	Marine Cargo Handling	1	6.18%	1.145060	1.145060	1.145060	1.145060	1.145060	1.145060	1.145060	1.145060	1.145060	1.145060	1.145060
4492	Towing And Tugboat Services	1	3.71%	0.687751	0.687751	0.687751	0.687751	0.687751	0.687751	0.687751	0.687751	0.687751	0.687751	0.687751
4499	Water Transportation Services, Not Elsewhere Classified	3	3.73%	0.690886	0.568270	0.359753	0.366137	0.376775	0.525716	0.568270	0.684394	1.090828	1.119859	1.137278
45	TRANSPORTATION BY AIR	22	3.90%	0.722809	0.827411	-0.507875	-0.258102	0.122539	0.787964	0.827411	0.873929	1.102189	1.130030	1.145534
451	AIR TRANSPORTATION, SCHEDULED, AND AIR COURIER SERVICES	17	4.29%	0.794283	0.846046	0.131335	0.150527	0.182512	0.802570	0.846046	0.883702	1.116494	1.136182	1.147995
4512	Air Transportation, Scheduled	13	4.36%	0.806922	0.808776	0.248631	0.323820	0.449135	0.794943	0.808776	0.854370	1.072800	1.114335	1.139256
4513	Air Courier Services	4	4.07%	0.753206	0.893816	0.141318	0.175482	0.232424	0.884182	0.893816	0.903449	1.077133	1.091892	1.100747
452	AIR TRANSPORTATION, NONSCHEDULED	4	4.15%	0.768343	0.780725	0.529726	0.537313	0.549958	0.728249	0.780725	0.833201	0.969395	0.978325	0.983683
4522	Air Transportation, Nonscheduled	4	4.15%	0.768343	0.780725	0.529726	0.537313	0.549958	0.728249	0.780725	0.833201	0.969395	0.978325	0.983683
458	AIRPORTS, FLYING FIELDS, AND AIRPORT TERMINAL SERVICES	1	-3.64%	-0.674391	-0.674391	-0.674391	-0.674391	-0.674391	-0.674391	-0.674391	-0.674391	-0.674391	-0.674391	-0.674391
4581	Airports, Flying Fields, And Airport Terminal Services	1	-3.64%	-0.674391	-0.674391	-0.674391	-0.674391	-0.674391	-0.674391	-0.674391	-0.674391	-0.674391	-0.674391	-0.674391

Betas of Common Stocks by SIC Codes as of September 28, 2018

SIC Code	Description	Number of Companies	Equity Risk Premium	Mean	Median	1st Percentile	2.5th Percentile	5th Percentile	40th Percentile	50th Percentile	60th Percentile	95th Percentile	97.5th Percentile	99th Percentile
46	PIPELINES, EXCEPT NATURAL GAS	11	4.56%	0.845122	0.778768	0.606279	0.616742	0.634180	0.777860	0.778768	0.828203	1.121740	1.124055	1.125444
461	PIPELINES, EXCEPT NATURAL GAS	11	4.56%	0.845122	0.778768	0.606279	0.616742	0.634180	0.777860	0.778768	0.828203	1.121740	1.124055	1.125444
4612	Crude Petroleum Pipelines	6	4.28%	0.792445	0.765870	0.602792	0.608023	0.616742	0.753879	0.765870	0.777860	1.051828	1.089099	1.111462
4613	Refined Petroleum Pipelines	1	6.03%	1.117110	1.117110	1.117110	1.117110	1.117110	1.117110	1.117110	1.117110	1.117110	1.117110	1.117110
4619	Pipelines, Not Elsewhere Classified	4	4.62%	0.856139	0.841619	0.760076	0.760943	0.762389	0.803908	0.841619	0.879329	0.970217	0.976019	0.979499
47	TRANSPORTATION SERVICES	20	4.13%	0.765544	0.744847	0.320280	0.337417	0.365978	0.672527	0.744847	0.837482	1.234641	1.322526	1.375256
4700	TRANSPORTATION SERVICES	5	2.49%	0.461657	0.368984	0.368984	0.368984	0.368984	0.368984	0.368984	0.441437	0.630996	0.641106	0.647172
472	ARRANGEMENT OF PASSENGER TRANSPORTATION	3	3.93%	0.728646	0.742621	0.317531	0.330544	0.352233	0.655868	0.742621	0.820989	1.095276	1.114868	1.126623
4724	Travel Agencies	1	4.01%	0.742621	0.742621	0.742621	0.742621	0.742621	0.742621	0.742621	0.742621	0.742621	0.742621	0.742621
4725	Tour Operators	2	3.90%	0.721658	0.721658	0.317112	0.329496	0.350136	0.639098	0.721658	0.804218	1.093180	1.113820	1.126204
473	ARRANGEMENT OF TRANSPORTATION OF FREIGHT AND CARGO	10	5.05%	0.935513	0.901800	0.625421	0.634517	0.649677	0.855315	0.901800	0.916353	1.327151	1.368781	1.393758
4731	Arrangement Of Transportation Of Freight And Cargo	10	5.05%	0.935513	0.901800	0.625421	0.634517	0.649677	0.855315	0.901800	0.916353	1.327151	1.368781	1.393758
478	MISCELLANEOUS SERVICES INCIDENTAL TO TRANSPORTATION	2	3.95%	0.730770	0.730770	0.514857	0.521467	0.532483	0.686706	0.730770	0.774833	0.929056	0.940072	0.946682
4789	Transportation Services, Not Elsewhere Classified	2	3.95%	0.730770	0.730770	0.514857	0.521467	0.532483	0.686706	0.730770	0.774833	0.929056	0.940072	0.946682
48	COMMUNICATIONS	126	3.97%	0.735651	0.730327	-0.342062	-0.070461	0.150552	0.661702	0.730327	0.801680	1.384210	1.463536	1.720658
481	TELEPHONE COMMUNICATIONS	55	4.05%	0.749119	0.747092	-0.252859	-0.077761	0.095025	0.630299	0.747092	0.790457	1.417427	1.581967	1.841866
4812	Radiotelephone Communications	14	3.74%	0.692986	0.643626	0.218391	0.242631	0.283032	0.580261	0.643626	0.727651	1.292849	1.685644	1.921322
4813	Telephone Communications, Except Radiotelephone	41	4.15%	0.768287	0.769898	-0.295922	-0.111364	-0.015356	0.703869	0.769898	0.870529	1.393370	1.473560	1.573628
482	TELEGRAPH AND OTHER MESSAGE COMMUNICATIONS	2	5.98%	1.107692	1.107692	0.914045	0.919973	0.929853	1.068172	1.107692	1.147211	1.285530	1.295410	1.301338
4822	Telegraph And Other Message Communications	2	5.98%	1.107692	1.107692	0.914045	0.919973	0.929853	1.068172	1.107692	1.147211	1.285530	1.295410	1.301338
483	RADIO AND TELEVISION BROADCASTING STATIONS	25	3.50%	0.647892	0.661702	-0.021295	0.064263	0.169315	0.615074	0.661702	0.703481	1.173166	1.239578	1.293891
4832	Radio Broadcasting Stations	12	3.11%	0.576171	0.673523	-0.052190	-0.012977	0.052380	0.503378	0.673523	0.772056	1.042854	1.095882	1.127699
4833	Television Broadcasting Stations	13	3.86%	0.714096	0.661702	0.345420	0.380138	0.438001	0.626797	0.661702	0.683278	1.239578	1.284839	1.311996
484	CABLE AND OTHER PAY TELEVISION SERVICES	25	3.92%	0.725075	0.722745	0.314054	0.355384	0.416285	0.697724	0.722745	0.777673	0.972655	0.990885	1.003572
4841	Cable And Other Pay Television Services	25	3.92%	0.725075	0.722745	0.314054	0.355384	0.416285	0.697724	0.722745	0.777673	0.972655	0.990885	1.003572
489	COMMUNICATIONS SERVICES, NOT ELSEWHERE CLASSIFIED	19	4.25%	0.786888	0.888471	-0.458258	-0.258759	0.073739	0.740905	0.888471	0.977380	1.295918	1.521674	1.657128
4899	Communications Services, Not Elsewhere Classified	19	4.25%	0.786888	0.888471	-0.458258	-0.258759	0.073739	0.740905	0.888471	0.977380	1.295918	1.521674	1.657128
49	ELECTRIC, GAS, AND SANITARY SERVICES	127	2.50%	0.462993	0.330223	-0.439209	-0.136605	0.037681	0.279785	0.330223	0.413413	0.871187	1.060710	2.288969
491	ELECTRIC SERVICES	45	1.74%	0.322351	0.260082	0.031584	0.044659	0.084248	0.242743	0.260082	0.298657	0.779435	0.871420	0.993812
4911	Electric Services	45	1.74%	0.322351	0.260082	0.031584	0.044659	0.084248	0.242743	0.260082	0.298657	0.779435	0.871420	0.993812
492	GAS PRODUCTION AND DISTRIBUTION	22	2.99%	0.553122	0.527128	0.077513	0.090902	0.117933	0.478188	0.527128	0.573658	0.931978	1.154462	1.301527
4922	Natural Gas Transmission	6	3.27%	0.605194	0.662277	0.089654	0.121254	0.173920	0.585502	0.662277	0.739051	0.903375	0.918037	0.926833
4923	Natural Gas Transmission And Distribution	7	4.13%	0.765685	0.791807	0.394207	0.403810	0.419816	0.661724	0.791807	0.792403	1.255191	1.327381	1.370694
4924	Natural Gas Distribution	9	1.91%	0.353081	0.300085	0.122038	0.138460	0.165830	0.280683	0.300085	0.362535	0.566885	0.569264	0.570691
493	COMBINATION ELECTRIC AND GAS, AND OTHER UTILITY SERVICES	24	1.60%	0.295974	0.275826	-0.374353	-0.149168	0.135641	0.235229	0.275826	0.285891	0.743272	0.817457	0.837470

Betas of Common Stocks by SIC Codes as of September 28, 2018

SIC Code	Description	Number of Companies	Equity Risk Premium	Mean	Median	1st Percentile	2.5th Percentile	5th Percentile	40th Percentile	50th Percentile	60th Percentile	95th Percentile	97.5th Percentile	99th Percentile
4931	Electric And Other Services Combined	18	1.25%	0.232358	0.237487	-0.413516	-0.247075	0.030327	0.217930	0.237487	0.274276	0.449878	0.456237	0.460052
4932	Gas And Other Services Combined	5	2.24%	0.414024	0.351343	0.228524	0.231681	0.236942	0.322419	0.351343	0.379013	0.718346	0.755575	0.777912
4939	Combination Utilities, Not Elsewhere Classified	1	4.59%	0.850812	0.850812	0.850812	0.850812	0.850812	0.850812	0.850812	0.850812	0.850812	0.850812	0.850812
494	WATER SUPPLY	15	2.79%	0.515834	0.569012	0.164296	0.183310	0.215000	0.500587	0.569012	0.596161	0.801261	0.810558	0.816137
4941	Water Supply	15	2.79%	0.515834	0.569012	0.164296	0.183310	0.215000	0.500587	0.569012	0.596161	0.801261	0.810558	0.816137
495	SANITARY SERVICES	21	4.44%	0.823083	0.636355	-0.466039	-0.364971	-0.196524	0.399735	0.636355	0.679519	2.601460	4.957325	6.370844
4950	SANITARY SERVICES	2	6.49%	1.202468	1.202468	-0.168544	-0.126574	-0.056625	0.922670	1.202468	1.482266	2.461561	2.531510	2.573480
4953	Refuse Systems	16	2.34%	0.432715	0.652807	-0.474459	-0.386021	-0.238625	0.567993	0.652807	0.679519	0.794699	0.796542	0.797648
4955	HAZARDOUS WASTE MANAGEMENT	2	20.72%	3.837259	3.837259	0.430847	0.535125	0.708921	3.142073	3.837259	4.532445	6.965597	7.139393	7.243671
4959	Sanitary Services, Not Elsewhere Classified	1	1.52%	0.281841	0.281841	0.281841	0.281841	0.281841	0.281841	0.281841	0.281841	0.281841	0.281841	0.281841
	WHOLESALE TRADE													
50	WHOLESALE TRADE"DURABLE GOODS	73	3.98%	0.737243	0.831337	-0.366287	-0.132365	0.051161	0.782473	0.831337	0.894220	1.276976	1.386738	1.548776
501	MOTOR VEHICLES AND MOTOR VEHICLE PARTS AND SUPPLIES	9	3.99%	0.739666	0.834303	-0.048737	0.015966	0.123804	0.813035	0.834303	0.867684	1.068126	1.099653	1.118569
5012	Automobiles And Other Motor Vehicles	2	4.33%	0.801559	0.801559	0.769469	0.770451	0.772088	0.795010	0.801559	0.808107	0.831029	0.832666	0.833648
5013	Motor Vehicle Supplies And New Parts	6	4.15%	0.767760	0.892994	-0.046892	0.020577	0.133026	0.876029	0.892994	0.909959	1.091771	1.111476	1.123298
5015	Motor Vehicle Parts, Used	1	2.42%	0.447317	0.447317	0.447317	0.447317	0.447317	0.447317	0.447317	0.447317	0.447317	0.447317	0.447317
503	LUMBER AND OTHER CONSTRUCTION MATERIALS	9	4.16%	0.769673	0.825061	0.279092	0.316545	0.378967	0.777457	0.825061	0.878059	1.031765	1.046032	1.054593
5030	WHOLESALE-LUMBER & OTHER CONSTRUCTION MATERIALS	3	3.54%	0.655324	0.634184	0.567592	0.569631	0.573028	0.620594	0.634184	0.660458	0.752419	0.758987	0.762929
5031	Lumber, Plywood, Millwork, And Wood Panels	4	4.38%	0.811179	0.965147	0.274739	0.305664	0.357204	0.950858	0.965147	0.979436	1.049599	1.054950	1.058160
5033	Roofing, Siding, And Insulation Materials	1	4.81%	0.891308	0.891308	0.891308	0.891308	0.891308	0.891308	0.891308	0.891308	0.891308	0.891308	0.891308
5039	Construction Materials, Not Elsewhere Classified	1	4.46%	0.825061	0.825061	0.825061	0.825061	0.825061	0.825061	0.825061	0.825061	0.825061	0.825061	0.825061
504	PROFESSIONAL AND COMMERCIAL EQUIPMENT AND SUPPLIES	16	4.40%	0.814498	0.829587	0.138097	0.150388	0.170873	0.801682	0.829587	0.874760	1.282363	1.361386	1.408801
5044	Office Equipment	1	0.70%	0.129903	0.129903	0.129903	0.129903	0.129903	0.129903	0.129903	0.129903	0.129903	0.129903	0.129903
5045	Computers And Computer Peripheral Equipment And Software	9	5.18%	0.958444	0.888511	0.569468	0.581543	0.601668	0.877510	0.888511	0.956306	1.356118	1.398264	1.423552
5047	Medical, Dental, And Hospital Equipment And Supplies	6	3.85%	0.712679	0.792917	0.205420	0.236757	0.288985	0.784151	0.792917	0.801682	1.020396	1.054753	1.075367
505	METALS AND MINERALS, EXCEPT PETROLEUM	6	5.28%	0.978494	1.085610	0.239604	0.249590	0.266233	1.011250	1.085610	1.159970	1.688893	1.758161	1.799723
5051	Metals Service Centers And Offices	6	5.28%	0.978494	1.085610	0.239604	0.249590	0.266233	1.011250	1.085610	1.159970	1.688893	1.758161	1.799723
506	ELECTRICAL GOODS	17	3.52%	0.651709	0.675630	0.107182	0.107758	0.108717	0.442543	0.675630	0.910615	1.094396	1.096468	1.097711
5063	Electrical Apparatus And Equipment, Wiring Supplies, And Construction	5	4.35%	0.806118	0.913778	0.272018	0.311633	0.377660	0.910615	0.913778	0.927088	1.004035	1.011157	1.015431
5065	Electronic Parts And Equipment, Not Elsewhere Classified	12	3.17%	0.587373	0.446088	0.107062	0.107458	0.108117	0.413896	0.446088	0.590902	1.095691	1.097116	1.097970
507	HARDWARE, AND PLUMBING AND HEATING EQUIPMENT AND SUPPLIES	3	5.62%	1.039986	0.958467	0.791577	0.796686	0.805201	0.924408	0.958467	1.041438	1.331835	1.352577	1.365023

Betas of Common Stocks by SIC Codes as of September 28, 2018

SIC Code	Description	Number of Companies	Equity Risk Premium	Mean	Median	1st Percentile	2.5th Percentile	5th Percentile	40th Percentile	50th Percentile	60th Percentile	95th Percentile	97.5th Percentile	99th Percentile
5074	Plumbing And Heating Equipment And Supplies (Hydronics)	2	6.30%	1.165894	1.165894	0.962616	0.968838	0.979210	1.124408	1.165894	1.207379	1.352577	1.362949	1.369171
5075	Warm Air Heating And Air-Conditioning Equipment And Supplies	1	4.26%	0.788171	0.788171	0.788171	0.788171	0.788171	0.788171	0.788171	0.788171	0.788171	0.788171	0.788171
508	MACHINERY, EQUIPMENT, AND SUPPLIES	8	3.68%	0.682296	0.822977	-0.252807	-0.190512	-0.086685	0.793234	0.822977	0.866287	1.068063	1.092631	1.107373
5084	Industrial Machinery And Equipment	6	3.34%	0.617634	0.822977	-0.264673	-0.220176	-0.146015	0.797602	0.822977	0.848352	1.072407	1.094804	1.108241
5085	Industrial Supplies	1	5.27%	0.976808	0.976808	0.976808	0.976808	0.976808	0.976808	0.976808	0.976808	0.976808	0.976808	0.976808
5087	Service Establishment Equipment And Supplies	1	4.19%	0.775761	0.775761	0.775761	0.775761	0.775761	0.775761	0.775761	0.775761	0.775761	0.775761	0.775761
509	MISCELLANEOUS DURABLE GOODS	5	1.81%	0.334874	0.144106	-0.530539	-0.499398	-0.447498	0.073546	0.144106	0.418998	1.192283	1.237402	1.264473
5091	Sporting And Recreational Goods And Supplies	2	5.71%	1.056929	1.056929	0.835849	0.842617	0.853896	1.011810	1.056929	1.102047	1.259961	1.271240	1.278008
5094	Jewelry, Watches, Precious Stones, And Precious Metals	2	0.30%	0.055906	0.055906	-0.030530	-0.027884	-0.023474	0.038266	0.055906	0.073546	0.135286	0.139696	0.142342
5099	Durable Goods, Not Elsewhere Classified	1	-2.98%	-0.551299	-0.551299	-0.551299	-0.551299	-0.551299	-0.551299	-0.551299	-0.551299	-0.551299	-0.551299	-0.551299
51	WHOLESALE TRADE¨NONDURABLE GOODS	63	3.74%	0.692036	0.709994	-0.513302	-0.285402	-0.069989	0.623191	0.709994	0.782068	1.499553	1.720230	1.925442
511	PAPER AND PAPER PRODUCTS	1	-0.55%	-0.101431	-0.101431	-0.101431	-0.101431	-0.101431	-0.101431	-0.101431	-0.101431	-0.101431	-0.101431	-0.101431
5112	Stationery And Office Supplies	1	-0.55%	-0.101431	-0.101431	-0.101431	-0.101431	-0.101431	-0.101431	-0.101431	-0.101431	-0.101431	-0.101431	-0.101431
512	DRUGS, DRUG PROPRIETARIES, AND DRUGGISTS' SUNDRIES	23	4.42%	0.818176	0.739696	-0.347573	-0.103549	0.243581	0.702895	0.739696	0.825400	1.595903	1.720230	1.804116
5122	Drugs, Drug Proprietaries, And Druggists' Sundries	23	4.42%	0.818176	0.739696	-0.347573	-0.103549	0.243581	0.702895	0.739696	0.825400	1.595903	1.720230	1.804116
513	APPAREL, PIECE GOODS, AND NOTIONS	2	2.73%	0.505446	0.505446	0.465312	0.466541	0.468588	0.497255	0.505446	0.513637	0.542304	0.544351	0.545580
5136	Men's And Boys' Clothing And Furnishings	1	2.51%	0.464493	0.464493	0.464493	0.464493	0.464493	0.464493	0.464493	0.464493	0.464493	0.464493	0.464493
5139	Footwear	1	2.95%	0.546399	0.546399	0.546399	0.546399	0.546399	0.546399	0.546399	0.546399	0.546399	0.546399	0.546399
514	GROCERIES AND RELATED PRODUCTS	14	2.86%	0.529040	0.519261	-0.062595	-0.033337	0.015427	0.472088	0.519261	0.657040	0.924832	0.957084	0.976434
5140	WHOLESALE-GROCERIES & RELATED PRODUCTS	2	2.59%	0.479021	0.479021	0.076164	0.088496	0.109050	0.396806	0.479021	0.561237	0.848992	0.869546	0.881878
5141	Groceries, General Line	8	2.67%	0.494664	0.519261	-0.052918	-0.009145	0.063810	0.470900	0.519261	0.578202	0.815623	0.848619	0.868417
5145	Confectionery	1	5.34%	0.989335	0.989335	0.989335	0.989335	0.989335	0.989335	0.989335	0.989335	0.989335	0.989335	0.989335
5148	Fresh Fruits And Vegetables	1	2.53%	0.468460	0.468460	0.468460	0.468460	0.468460	0.468460	0.468460	0.468460	0.468460	0.468460	0.468460
5149	Groceries And Related Products, Not Elsewhere Classified	2	2.79%	0.516707	0.516707	0.328109	0.333882	0.343505	0.478218	0.516707	0.555196	0.689909	0.699532	0.705305
515	FARM-PRODUCT RAW MATERIALS	4	2.75%	0.509532	0.539300	0.068789	0.075685	0.087177	0.346174	0.539300	0.732426	0.890212	0.892774	0.894311
5153	Grain And Field Beans	2	2.59%	0.479764	0.479764	0.072504	0.084971	0.105749	0.396650	0.479764	0.562879	0.853779	0.874557	0.887025
5159	Farm-Product Raw Materials, Not Elsewhere Classified	2	2.91%	0.539300	0.539300	0.223861	0.233517	0.249611	0.474925	0.539300	0.603675	0.828989	0.845083	0.854739
516	CHEMICALS AND ALLIED PRODUCTS	5	5.41%	1.002042	0.986579	0.655987	0.670671	0.695143	0.948317	0.986579	1.011631	1.359682	1.398491	1.421776
5162	Plastics Materials And Basic Forms And Shapes	1	3.49%	0.646198	0.646198	0.646198	0.646198	0.646198	0.646198	0.646198	0.646198	0.646198	0.646198	0.646198
5169	Chemicals And Allied Products, Not Elsewhere Classified	4	5.89%	1.091003	1.017895	0.893794	0.898098	0.905272	0.999105	1.017895	1.036684	1.379087	1.408193	1.425657
517	PETROLEUM AND PETROLEUM PRODUCTS	7	4.93%	0.912151	0.782068	0.329150	0.372514	0.444788	0.782068	0.782068	0.818343	1.681686	1.856918	1.962057

Betas of Common Stocks by SIC Codes as of September 28, 2018

SIC Code	Description	Number of Companies	Equity Risk Premium	Mean	Median	1st Percentile	2.5th Percentile	5th Percentile	40th Percentile	50th Percentile	60th Percentile	95th Percentile	97.5th Percentile	99th Percentile
5172	Petroleum And Petroleum Products Wholesalers, Except Bulk Station	7	4.93%	0.912151	0.782068	0.329150	0.372514	0.444788	0.782068	0.782068	0.818343	1.681686	1.856918	1.962057
518	BEER, WINE, AND DISTILLED ALCOHOLIC BEVERAGES	1	2.14%	0.396731	0.396731	0.396731	0.396731	0.396731	0.396731	0.396731	0.396731	0.396731	0.396731	0.396731
5180	WHOLESALE-BEER, WINE & DISTILLED ALCOHOLIC BEVERAGES	1	2.14%	0.396731	0.396731	0.396731	0.396731	0.396731	0.396731	0.396731	0.396731	0.396731	0.396731	0.396731
519	MISCELLANEOUS NONDURABLE GOODS	6	2.37%	0.439014	0.567147	-0.490408	-0.448612	-0.378950	0.424300	0.567147	0.709994	1.039001	1.063741	1.078584
5190	WHOLESALE-MISCELLANEOUS NONDURABLE GOODS	1	-2.80%	-0.518273	-0.518273	-0.518273	-0.518273	-0.518273	-0.518273	-0.518273	-0.518273	-0.518273	-0.518273	-0.518273
5191	Farm Supplies	2	2.51%	0.464791	0.464791	0.047533	0.060306	0.081595	0.379637	0.464791	0.549946	0.847988	0.869276	0.882050
5192	Books, Periodicals, And Newspapers	1	3.83%	0.709994	0.709994	0.709994	0.709994	0.709994	0.709994	0.709994	0.709994	0.709994	0.709994	0.709994
5199	Nondurable Goods, Not Elsewhere Classified	2	4.08%	0.756390	0.756390	0.430942	0.440905	0.457509	0.689972	0.756390	0.822808	1.055271	1.071876	1.081838
	RETAIL TRADE													
52	RETAIL TRADE	14	3.91%	0.724456	0.908529	-0.248825	-0.193243	-0.100607	0.844703	0.908529	0.944551	1.150219	1.172690	1.186172
521	LUMBER AND OTHER BUILDING MATERIALS DEALERS	12	4.14%	0.766165	0.908529	-0.236971	-0.163610	-0.041340	0.856355	0.908529	0.961186	1.157133	1.176147	1.187555
5211	Lumber And Other Building Materials Dealers	12	4.14%	0.766165	0.908529	-0.236971	-0.163610	-0.041340	0.856355	0.908529	0.961186	1.157133	1.176147	1.187555
523	PAINT, GLASS, AND WALLPAPER STORES	1	5.13%	0.949252	0.949252	0.949252	0.949252	0.949252	0.949252	0.949252	0.949252	0.949252	0.949252	0.949252
5231	Paint, Glass, And Wallpaper Stores	1	5.13%	0.949252	0.949252	0.949252	0.949252	0.949252	0.949252	0.949252	0.949252	0.949252	0.949252	0.949252
526	RETAIL NURSERIES, LAWN AND GARDEN SUPPLY STORES	1	0.00%	-0.000846	-0.000846	-0.000846	-0.000846	-0.000846	-0.000846	-0.000846	-0.000846	-0.000846	-0.000846	-0.000846
5261	Retail Nurseries, Lawn And Garden Supply Stores	1	0.00%	-0.000846	-0.000846	-0.000846	-0.000846	-0.000846	-0.000846	-0.000846	-0.000846	-0.000846	-0.000846	-0.000846
53	GENERAL MERCHANDISE STORES	18	3.81%	0.706389	0.710988	0.245676	0.285097	0.350798	0.633979	0.710988	0.740924	1.001614	1.072607	1.115203
531	DEPARTMENT STORES	8	4.19%	0.775572	0.768194	0.462616	0.472954	0.490184	0.619400	0.768194	0.917336	1.085135	1.114368	1.131907
5311	Department Stores	8	4.19%	0.775572	0.768194	0.462616	0.472954	0.490184	0.619400	0.768194	0.917336	1.085135	1.114368	1.131907
533	VARIETY STORES	8	3.37%	0.623812	0.685993	0.230217	0.246449	0.273503	0.631036	0.685993	0.738118	0.859587	0.889850	0.908007
5331	Variety Stores	8	3.37%	0.623812	0.685993	0.230217	0.246449	0.273503	0.631036	0.685993	0.738118	0.859587	0.889850	0.908007
539	MISCELLANEOUS GENERAL MERCHANDISE STORES	2	4.10%	0.759962	0.759962	0.685684	0.687958	0.691747	0.744803	0.759962	0.775120	0.828176	0.831965	0.834239
5399	Miscellaneous General Merchandise Stores	2	4.10%	0.759962	0.759962	0.685684	0.687958	0.691747	0.744803	0.759962	0.775120	0.828176	0.831965	0.834239
54	FOOD STORES	23	3.51%	0.650471	0.468303	-0.174936	-0.164823	-0.133560	0.405213	0.468303	0.608564	1.096272	2.971348	4.335023
541	GROCERY STORES	18	2.23%	0.412527	0.426703	-0.176468	-0.168654	-0.155630	0.336985	0.426703	0.561716	0.888159	0.922384	0.942918
5411	Grocery Stores	18	2.23%	0.412527	0.426703	-0.176468	-0.168654	-0.155630	0.336985	0.426703	0.561716	0.888159	0.922384	0.942918
544	CANDY, NUT, AND CONFECTIONERY STORES	1	2.53%	0.468303	0.468303	0.468303	0.468303	0.468303	0.468303	0.468303	0.468303	0.468303	0.468303	0.468303
5441	Candy, Nut, And Confectionery Stores	1	2.53%	0.468303	0.468303	0.468303	0.468303	0.468303	0.468303	0.468303	0.468303	0.468303	0.468303	0.468303
546	RETAIL BAKERIES	1	28.32%	5.244140	5.244140	5.244140	5.244140	5.244140	5.244140	5.244140	5.244140	5.244140	5.244140	5.244140
5461	Retail Bakeries	1	28.32%	5.244140	5.244140	5.244140	5.244140	5.244140	5.244140	5.244140	5.244140	5.244140	5.244140	5.244140
549	MISCELLANEOUS FOOD STORES	3	3.28%	0.607636	0.605220	0.115884	0.130864	0.155830	0.505356	0.605220	0.706534	1.061133	1.086462	1.101659
5499	Miscellaneous Food Stores	3	3.28%	0.607636	0.605220	0.115884	0.130864	0.155830	0.505356	0.605220	0.706534	1.061133	1.086462	1.101659
55	AUTOMOTIVE DEALERS AND GASOLINE SERVICE STATIONS	20	4.72%	0.874756	0.968738	0.014587	0.097296	0.235144	0.887960	0.968738	1.017660	1.441289	1.490205	1.519554
5500	RETAIL-AUTO DEALERS & GASOLINE STATIONS	2	7.52%	1.393110	1.393110	1.350941	1.352232	1.354383	1.384504	1.393110	1.401716	1.431837	1.433989	1.435279

Betas of Common Stocks by SIC Codes as of September 28, 2018

SIC Code	Description	Number of Companies	Equity Risk Premium	Mean	Median	1st Percentile	2.5th Percentile	5th Percentile	40th Percentile	50th Percentile	60th Percentile	95th Percentile	97.5th Percentile	99th Percentile
551	MOTOR VEHICLE DEALERS (NEW AND USED)	8	5.50%	1.019045	1.029575	0.884767	0.889851	0.898324	1.019984	1.029575	1.041496	1.107222	1.109091	1.110212
5511	Motor Vehicle Dealers (New And Used)	8	5.50%	1.019045	1.029575	0.884767	0.889851	0.898324	1.019984	1.029575	1.041496	1.107222	1.109091	1.110212
552	MOTOR VEHICLE DEALERS (USED ONLY)	2	4.18%	0.774222	0.774222	0.539181	0.546376	0.558368	0.726254	0.774222	0.822190	0.990076	1.002068	1.009263
5521	Motor Vehicle Dealers (Used Only)	2	4.18%	0.774222	0.774222	0.539181	0.546376	0.558368	0.726254	0.774222	0.822190	0.990076	1.002068	1.009263
553	AUTO AND HOME SUPPLY STORES	3	4.80%	0.889544	0.797839	0.340997	0.354982	0.378291	0.704606	0.797839	0.946095	1.464992	1.502056	1.524294
5531	Auto And Home Supply Stores	3	4.80%	0.889544	0.797839	0.340997	0.354982	0.378291	0.704606	0.797839	0.946095	1.464992	1.502056	1.524294
554	GASOLINE SERVICE STATIONS	4	2.21%	0.408621	0.391345	-0.031846	-0.018787	0.002978	0.306330	0.391345	0.476359	0.838451	0.865400	0.881569
5541	Gasoline Service Stations	4	2.21%	0.408621	0.391345	-0.031846	-0.018787	0.002978	0.306330	0.391345	0.476359	0.838451	0.865400	0.881569
555	BOAT DEALERS	1	3.81%	0.704984	0.704984	0.704984	0.704984	0.704984	0.704984	0.704984	0.704984	0.704984	0.704984	0.704984
5551	Boat Dealers	1	3.81%	0.704984	0.704984	0.704984	0.704984	0.704984	0.704984	0.704984	0.704984	0.704984	0.704984	0.704984
56	APPAREL AND ACCESSORY STORES	34	4.10%	0.759768	0.810554	-0.220633	0.066497	0.188958	0.755792	0.810554	0.906220	1.185824	1.292101	1.303248
5600	RETAIL-APPAREL & ACCESSORY STORES	1	4.97%	0.919627	0.919627	0.919627	0.919627	0.919627	0.919627	0.919627	0.919627	0.919627	0.919627	0.919627
561	MEN'S AND BOYS' CLOTHING AND ACCESSORY STORES	2	6.41%	1.186630	1.186630	1.087131	1.090177	1.095253	1.166324	1.186630	1.206936	1.278007	1.283084	1.286129
5611	Men's And Boys' Clothing And Accessory Stores	2	6.41%	1.186630	1.186630	1.087131	1.090177	1.095253	1.166324	1.186630	1.206936	1.278007	1.283084	1.286129
562	WOMEN'S CLOTHING STORES	8	2.78%	0.514503	0.610236	-0.369193	-0.304902	-0.197751	0.465476	0.610236	0.755792	0.970758	1.004944	1.025456
5621	Women's Clothing Stores	8	2.78%	0.514503	0.610236	-0.369193	-0.304902	-0.197751	0.465476	0.610236	0.755792	0.970758	1.004944	1.025456
563	WOMEN'S ACCESSORY AND SPECIALTY STORES	1	5.79%	1.072140	1.072140	1.072140	1.072140	1.072140	1.072140	1.072140	1.072140	1.072140	1.072140	1.072140
5632	Women's Accessory And Specialty Stores	1	5.79%	1.072140	1.072140	1.072140	1.072140	1.072140	1.072140	1.072140	1.072140	1.072140	1.072140	1.072140
565	FAMILY CLOTHING STORES	15	4.09%	0.756975	0.777327	0.196379	0.238937	0.309867	0.711783	0.777327	0.862316	1.148196	1.229438	1.278183
5651	Family Clothing Stores	15	4.09%	0.756975	0.777327	0.196379	0.238937	0.309867	0.711783	0.777327	0.862316	1.148196	1.229438	1.278183
566	SHOE STORES	6	4.57%	0.846770	0.828784	0.612636	0.617575	0.625808	0.722703	0.828784	0.934865	1.099988	1.115354	1.124574
5661	Shoe Stores	6	4.57%	0.846770	0.828784	0.612636	0.617575	0.625808	0.722703	0.828784	0.934865	1.099988	1.115354	1.124574
569	MISCELLANEOUS APPAREL AND ACCESSORY STORES	1	4.95%	0.915808	0.915808	0.915808	0.915808	0.915808	0.915808	0.915808	0.915808	0.915808	0.915808	0.915808
5699	Miscellaneous Apparel And Accessory Stores	1	4.95%	0.915808	0.915808	0.915808	0.915808	0.915808	0.915808	0.915808	0.915808	0.915808	0.915808	0.915808
57	HOME FURNITURE, FURNISHINGS, AND EQUIPMENT STORES	11	3.83%	0.709655	0.794061	-0.408088	-0.364230	-0.291133	0.776095	0.794061	0.825420	1.316035	1.404328	1.457303
5700	RETAIL-HOME FURNITURE, FURNISHINGS & EQUIPMENT STORES	1	5.19%	0.960700	0.960700	0.960700	0.960700	0.960700	0.960700	0.960700	0.960700	0.960700	0.960700	0.960700
571	HOME FURNITURE AND FURNISHINGS STORES	6	4.39%	0.813549	0.785078	0.583731	0.598631	0.623466	0.776095	0.785078	0.794061	1.060943	1.100196	1.123749
5712	Furniture Stores	3	4.84%	0.896006	0.776095	0.772544	0.772653	0.772834	0.775370	0.776095	0.848766	1.103115	1.121282	1.132183
5713	Floor Covering Stores	1	4.29%	0.794061	0.794061	0.794061	0.794061	0.794061	0.794061	0.794061	0.794061	0.794061	0.794061	0.794061
5719	Miscellaneous Homefurnishings Stores	2	3.78%	0.699609	0.699609	0.576313	0.580088	0.586378	0.674446	0.699609	0.724771	0.812839	0.819129	0.822904
572	HOUSEHOLD APPLIANCE STORES	1	-0.78%	-0.144939	-0.144939	-0.144939	-0.144939	-0.144939	-0.144939	-0.144939	-0.144939	-0.144939	-0.144939	-0.144939
5722	Household Appliance Stores	1	-0.78%	-0.144939	-0.144939	-0.144939	-0.144939	-0.144939	-0.144939	-0.144939	-0.144939	-0.144939	-0.144939	-0.144939
573	RADIO, TELEVISION, CONSUMER ELECTRONICS, AND MUSIC STORES	3	3.80%	0.703051	1.053860	-0.407503	-0.362768	-0.288208	0.755623	1.053860	1.141612	1.448744	1.470682	1.483845
5731	Radio, Television, And Consumer Electronics Stores	2	6.88%	1.273240	1.273240	1.058248	1.064829	1.075798	1.229364	1.273240	1.317116	1.470682	1.481651	1.488232
5735	Record And Prerecorded Tape Stores	1	-2.36%	-0.437327	-0.437327	-0.437327	-0.437327	-0.437327	-0.437327	-0.437327	-0.437327	-0.437327	-0.437327	-0.437327
58	EATING AND DRINKING PLACES	66	3.40%	0.628959	0.659513	-0.100722	-0.031104	0.066654	0.591338	0.659513	0.710734	1.091770	1.271613	1.737663

Betas of Common Stocks by SIC Codes as of September 28, 2018

SIC Code	Description	Number of Companies	Equity Risk Premium	Mean	Median	1st Percentile	2.5th Percentile	5th Percentile	40th Percentile	50th Percentile	60th Percentile	95th Percentile	97.5th Percentile	99th Percentile
581	EATING AND DRINKING PLACES	66	3.40%	0.628959	0.659513	-0.100722	-0.031104	0.066654	0.591338	0.659513	0.710734	1.091770	1.271613	1.737663
5810	RETAIL-EATING & DRINKING PLACES	2	1.35%	0.249232	0.249232	0.168227	0.170707	0.174840	0.232700	0.249232	0.265763	0.323623	0.327756	0.330236
5812	Eating Places	63	3.45%	0.637966	0.660223	-0.104886	-0.033629	0.062347	0.592043	0.660223	0.712843	1.091770	1.283809	1.768898
5813	Drinking Places (Alcoholic Beverages)	1	4.43%	0.820953	0.820953	0.820953	0.820953	0.820953	0.820953	0.820953	0.820953	0.820953	0.820953	0.820953
59	MISCELLANEOUS RETAIL	73	2.95%	0.545939	0.695471	-1.707920	-1.525298	-1.114887	0.596152	0.695471	0.762552	1.482742	1.686974	2.064551
5900	RETAIL-MISCELLANEOUS RETAIL	1	-7.60%	-1.407560	-1.407560	-1.407560	-1.407560	-1.407560	-1.407560	-1.407560	-1.407560	-1.407560	-1.407560	-1.407560
591	DRUG STORES AND PROPRIETARY STORES	8	4.68%	0.866293	0.840512	0.588561	0.600631	0.620749	0.792134	0.840512	0.884736	1.192216	1.233838	1.258811
5912	Drug Stores And Proprietary Stores	8	4.68%	0.866293	0.840512	0.588561	0.600631	0.620749	0.792134	0.840512	0.884736	1.192216	1.233838	1.258811
592	LIQUOR STORES	1	2.48%	0.458769	0.458769	0.458769	0.458769	0.458769	0.458769	0.458769	0.458769	0.458769	0.458769	0.458769
5921	Liquor Stores	1	2.48%	0.458769	0.458769	0.458769	0.458769	0.458769	0.458769	0.458769	0.458769	0.458769	0.458769	0.458769
593	USED MERCHANDISE STORES	3	3.24%	0.600574	0.617113	0.427207	0.433020	0.442709	0.578357	0.617113	0.645946	0.746862	0.754071	0.758396
5932	Used Merchandise Stores	3	3.24%	0.600574	0.617113	0.427207	0.433020	0.442709	0.578357	0.617113	0.645946	0.746862	0.754071	0.758396
594	MISCELLANEOUS SHOPPING GOODS STORES	14	4.06%	0.751676	0.752335	0.256593	0.257353	0.258619	0.707431	0.752335	0.783712	1.202673	1.316341	1.384543
5941	Sporting Goods Stores And Bicycle Shops	3	3.08%	0.570786	0.413714	0.263058	0.267670	0.275356	0.382968	0.413714	0.538703	0.976165	1.007413	1.026161
5942	Book Stores	2	4.29%	0.793755	0.793755	0.789762	0.789884	0.790088	0.792940	0.793755	0.794570	0.797423	0.797626	0.797749
5943	Stationery Stores	1	7.72%	1.430010	1.430010	1.430010	1.430010	1.430010	1.430010	1.430010	1.430010	1.430010	1.430010	1.430010
5944	Jewelry Stores	3	3.06%	0.565845	0.681607	0.264596	0.277362	0.298638	0.596503	0.681607	0.697254	0.752018	0.755929	0.758276
5945	Hobby, Toy, And Game Shops	3	4.44%	0.821827	0.698081	0.687359	0.687687	0.688234	0.695893	0.698081	0.774517	1.042042	1.061151	1.072616
5947	Gift, Novelty, And Souvenir Shops	2	4.40%	0.815284	0.815284	0.746238	0.748352	0.751875	0.801193	0.815284	0.829375	0.878694	0.882216	0.884330
596	NONSTORE RETAILERS	30	2.59%	0.480451	0.599742	-1.830578	-1.706494	-1.570252	0.565487	0.599742	0.796518	1.805701	2.062655	2.227646
5960	RETAIL-NONSTORE RETAILERS	2	-2.51%	-0.465645	-0.465645	-1.478931	-1.447912	-1.396213	-0.672438	-0.465645	-0.258851	0.464924	0.516623	0.547642
5961	Catalog And Mail-Order Houses	28	2.96%	0.548030	0.644454	-1.836283	-1.720756	-1.380152	0.587238	0.644454	0.852808	1.839623	2.081619	2.235232
598	FUEL DEALERS	4	0.29%	0.053598	0.068853	-0.018461	-0.015356	-0.010181	0.056626	0.068853	0.081079	0.096021	0.096620	0.096979
5983	Fuel Oil Dealers	4	0.29%	0.053598	0.068853	-0.018461	-0.015356	-0.010181	0.056626	0.068853	0.081079	0.096021	0.096620	0.096979
599	RETAIL STORES, NOT ELSEWHERE CLASSIFIED	12	3.11%	0.576571	0.736405	-0.590777	-0.478057	-0.290191	0.668190	0.736405	0.772800	1.052119	1.110529	1.145576
5992	Florists	1	4.15%	0.767644	0.767644	0.767644	0.767644	0.767644	0.767644	0.767644	0.767644	0.767644	0.767644	0.767644
5995	Optical Goods Stores	1	4.73%	0.875519	0.875519	0.875519	0.875519	0.875519	0.875519	0.875519	0.875519	0.875519	0.875519	0.875519
5999	Miscellaneous Retail Stores, Not Elsewhere Classified	10	2.85%	0.527569	0.674353	-0.604440	-0.512215	-0.358506	0.542573	0.674353	0.733594	1.073359	1.121150	1.149824
	FINANCE, INSURANCE, AND REAL ESTATE													
60	DEPOSITORY INSTITUTIONS	382	3.07%	0.569237	0.621320	-0.112587	-0.077027	-0.035183	0.533619	0.621320	0.702086	1.077206	1.184110	1.225070
602	COMMERCIAL BANKS	292	3.21%	0.594964	0.652559	-0.108979	-0.062811	-0.023356	0.571112	0.652559	0.723227	1.072561	1.132281	1.203778
6021	National Commercial Banks	106	3.48%	0.643668	0.710198	-0.058175	-0.050044	-0.011061	0.628707	0.710198	0.750228	1.103860	1.147113	1.190768
6022	State Commercial Banks	161	3.10%	0.573452	0.632196	-0.114400	-0.094543	-0.037395	0.541758	0.632196	0.696061	1.043230	1.119180	1.237498
6029	Commercial Banks, Not Elsewhere Classified	25	2.85%	0.527000	0.577156	-0.014295	-0.003907	0.018367	0.551184	0.577156	0.623191	0.968973	0.988111	1.003338
603	SAVINGS INSTITUTIONS	80	2.40%	0.443584	0.480174	-0.152345	-0.101939	-0.076396	0.367425	0.480174	0.570736	1.019497	1.177997	1.225070
6035	Savings Institutions, Federally Chartered	60	2.33%	0.432003	0.423365	-0.166181	-0.120338	-0.077557	0.315586	0.423365	0.570736	1.027137	1.202137	1.225070
6036	Savings Institutions, Not Federally Chartered	20	2.58%	0.478326	0.507999	-0.068940	-0.055642	-0.033478	0.481769	0.507999	0.561619	0.901488	0.962739	0.999490
606	CREDIT UNIONS	1	4.89%	0.904664	0.904664	0.904664	0.904664	0.904664	0.904664	0.904664	0.904664	0.904664	0.904664	0.904664
6061	Credit Unions, Federally Chartered	1	4.89%	0.904664	0.904664	0.904664	0.904664	0.904664	0.904664	0.904664	0.904664	0.904664	0.904664	0.904664
608	FOREIGN BANKING AND BRANCHES AND AGENCIES OF FOREIGN BANKS	2	2.84%	0.526380	0.526380	0.445752	0.448221	0.452334	0.509925	0.526380	0.542835	0.600426	0.604539	0.607008

Betas of Common Stocks by SIC Codes as of September 28, 2018

SIC Code	Description	Number of Companies	Equity Risk Premium	Mean	Median	1st Percentile	2.5th Percentile	5th Percentile	40th Percentile	50th Percentile	60th Percentile	95th Percentile	97.5th Percentile	99th Percentile
6081	Branches And Agencies Of Foreign Banks	2	2.84%	0.526380	0.526380	0.445752	0.448221	0.452334	0.509925	0.526380	0.542835	0.600426	0.604539	0.607008
609	FUNCTIONS RELATED TO DEPOSITORY BANKING	7	4.84%	0.896381	0.828661	0.524947	0.534039	0.549193	0.825106	0.828661	0.893939	1.295654	1.312262	1.322227
6099	Functions Related To Depository Banking, Not Elsewhere Classified	7	4.84%	0.896381	0.828661	0.524947	0.534039	0.549193	0.825106	0.828661	0.893939	1.295654	1.312262	1.322227
61	NONDEPOSITORY CREDIT INSTITUTIONS	46	3.07%	0.569085	0.585697	-0.246074	-0.135436	0.008234	0.398056	0.585697	0.721176	1.166903	1.207046	1.264862
611	FEDERAL AND FEDERALLY-SPONSORED CREDIT AGENCIES	5	1.75%	0.324929	0.256503	0.003559	0.018394	0.043119	0.250269	0.256503	0.343755	0.622065	0.640494	0.651551
6111	Federal And Federally-Sponsored Credit Agencies	5	1.75%	0.324929	0.256503	0.003559	0.018394	0.043119	0.250269	0.256503	0.343755	0.622065	0.640494	0.651551
614	PERSONAL CREDIT INSTITUTIONS	16	3.99%	0.738055	0.895625	-0.244934	-0.130078	0.061350	0.777886	0.895625	0.927583	1.201028	1.204639	1.206806
6141	Personal Credit Institutions	16	3.99%	0.738055	0.895625	-0.244934	-0.130078	0.061350	0.777886	0.895625	0.927583	1.201028	1.204639	1.206806
615	BUSINESS CREDIT INSTITUTIONS	12	2.64%	0.489614	0.360262	0.067999	0.086108	0.116289	0.300735	0.360262	0.558010	0.948394	0.953637	0.956784
6153	Short-Term Business Credit Institutions, Except Agricultural	8	2.32%	0.429603	0.360262	0.063609	0.075133	0.094339	0.320762	0.360262	0.445731	0.787460	0.805305	0.816013
6159	Miscellaneous Business Credit Institutions	4	3.29%	0.609636	0.610209	0.259886	0.260847	0.262449	0.412446	0.610209	0.807971	0.956021	0.957451	0.958309
616	MORTGAGE BANKERS AND BROKERS	10	2.91%	0.539132	0.500486	-0.135357	-0.107573	-0.061266	0.397657	0.500486	0.677949	1.087771	1.199476	1.266498
6162	Mortgage Bankers And Loan Correspondents	6	2.56%	0.473277	0.499987	-0.127161	-0.087083	-0.020285	0.397058	0.499987	0.602915	0.810625	0.812670	0.813898
6163	Loan Brokers	4	3.44%	0.637916	0.594278	0.062312	0.077888	0.103848	0.476545	0.594278	0.712010	1.233078	1.272129	1.295560
6199	FINANCE SERVICES	3	2.66%	0.492571	0.534485	0.352909	0.358467	0.367731	0.497429	0.534485	0.546393	0.588071	0.591048	0.592834
62	SECURITY AND COMMODITY BROKERS, DEALERS, EXCHANGES, AND SERVICES	100	3.97%	0.734854	0.783738	-0.182042	-0.140547	-0.005270	0.670113	0.783738	0.909236	1.354428	1.378686	1.409415
621	SECURITY BROKERS, DEALERS, AND FLOTATION COMPANIES	33	4.56%	0.844533	0.893409	-0.372090	-0.162171	0.039635	0.760937	0.893409	1.092450	1.392042	1.418822	1.442587
6211	Security Brokers, Dealers, And Flotation Companies	33	4.56%	0.844533	0.893409	-0.372090	-0.162171	0.039635	0.760937	0.893409	1.092450	1.392042	1.418822	1.442587
622	COMMODITY CONTRACTS BROKERS AND DEALERS	2	4.29%	0.794205	0.794205	0.256846	0.273295	0.300712	0.684539	0.794205	0.903870	1.287697	1.315114	1.331563
6221	Commodity Contracts Brokers And Dealers	2	4.29%	0.794205	0.794205	0.256846	0.273295	0.300712	0.684539	0.794205	0.903870	1.287697	1.315114	1.331563
623	SECURITY AND COMMODITY EXCHANGES	6	3.36%	0.621849	0.716304	0.085636	0.104265	0.135312	0.629536	0.716304	0.803072	0.959354	0.963112	0.965368
6231	Security And Commodity Exchanges	6	3.36%	0.621849	0.716304	0.085636	0.104265	0.135312	0.629536	0.716304	0.803072	0.959354	0.963112	0.965368
628	SERVICES ALLIED WITH THE EXCHANGE OF SECURITIES OR COMMODITIES	59	3.69%	0.682989	0.723372	-0.174706	-0.142193	-0.012054	0.519446	0.723372	0.865803	1.258183	1.291308	1.317683
6282	Investment Advice	58	3.73%	0.690299	0.743449	-0.174775	-0.143838	-0.017273	0.521230	0.743449	0.873080	1.259460	1.291769	1.318113
6289	Services Allied With The Exchange Of Securities Or Commodities	1	1.40%	0.259021	0.259021	0.259021	0.259021	0.259021	0.259021	0.259021	0.259021	0.259021	0.259021	0.259021
63	INSURANCE CARRIERS	142	2.66%	0.493301	0.567546	-0.842187	-0.162329	-0.006038	0.470952	0.567546	0.625433	1.126248	1.201968	1.276628
631	LIFE INSURANCE	35	3.14%	0.581060	0.518668	-0.108185	-0.064414	-0.048646	0.448780	0.518668	0.705216	1.276265	1.288690	1.327960
6311	Life Insurance	35	3.14%	0.581060	0.518668	-0.108185	-0.064414	-0.048646	0.448780	0.518668	0.705216	1.276265	1.288690	1.327960
632	ACCIDENT AND HEALTH INSURANCE AND MEDICAL SERVICE PLANS	18	3.66%	0.678635	0.708949	0.209294	0.234412	0.276276	0.655592	0.708949	0.771075	1.168945	1.185053	1.194717
6321	Accident And Health Insurance	9	3.51%	0.650518	0.672638	0.200428	0.212249	0.231949	0.446340	0.672638	0.717766	1.186000	1.193580	1.198128
6324	Hospital And Medical Service Plans	9	3.82%	0.706751	0.763025	0.426790	0.427119	0.427667	0.703684	0.763025	0.795224	0.926818	0.948835	0.962045

Betas of Common Stocks by SIC Codes as of September 28, 2018

SIC Code	Description	Number of Companies	Equity Risk Premium	Mean	Median	1st Percentile	2.5th Percentile	5th Percentile	40th Percentile	50th Percentile	60th Percentile	95th Percentile	97.5th Percentile	99th Percentile
633	FIRE, MARINE, AND CASUALTY INSURANCE	73	2.25%	0.416985	0.519975	-1.163448	-0.194372	0.012883	0.449645	0.519975	0.583126	0.932197	1.065584	1.143916
6331	Fire, Marine, And Casualty Insurance	73	2.25%	0.416985	0.519975	-1.163448	-0.194372	0.012883	0.449645	0.519975	0.583126	0.932197	1.065584	1.143916
635	SURETY INSURANCE	8	2.08%	0.386100	0.608726	-1.173147	-1.012882	-0.745774	0.585487	0.608726	0.645280	0.834189	0.861843	0.878436
6351	Surety Insurance	8	2.08%	0.386100	0.608726	-1.173147	-1.012882	-0.745774	0.585487	0.608726	0.645280	0.834189	0.861843	0.878436
636	TITLE INSURANCE	5	2.97%	0.549612	0.590560	0.206308	0.229880	0.269165	0.587716	0.590560	0.624736	0.701163	0.704308	0.706195
6361	Title Insurance	5	2.97%	0.549612	0.590560	0.206308	0.229880	0.269165	0.587716	0.590560	0.624736	0.701163	0.704308	0.706195
637	PENSION, HEALTH, AND WELFARE FUNDS	1	4.12%	0.762217	0.762217	0.762217	0.762217	0.762217	0.762217	0.762217	0.762217	0.762217	0.762217	0.762217
6371	Pension, Health, And Welfare Funds	1	4.12%	0.762217	0.762217	0.762217	0.762217	0.762217	0.762217	0.762217	0.762217	0.762217	0.762217	0.762217
639	INSURANCE CARRIERS, NOT ELSEWHERE CLASSIFIED	2	1.23%	0.228579	0.228579	0.177635	0.179194	0.181793	0.218182	0.228579	0.238976	0.275365	0.277964	0.279523
6399	Insurance Carriers, Not Elsewhere Classified	2	1.23%	0.228579	0.228579	0.177635	0.179194	0.181793	0.218182	0.228579	0.238976	0.275365	0.277964	0.279523
64	INSURANCE AGENTS, BROKERS, AND SERVICE	14	3.78%	0.699673	0.720062	0.240689	0.310643	0.427233	0.669895	0.720062	0.744166	0.992488	1.076089	1.126250
641	INSURANCE AGENTS, BROKERS, AND SERVICE	14	3.78%	0.699673	0.720062	0.240689	0.310643	0.427233	0.669895	0.720062	0.744166	0.992488	1.076089	1.126250
6411	Insurance Agents, Brokers, And Service	14	3.78%	0.699673	0.720062	0.240689	0.310643	0.427233	0.669895	0.720062	0.744166	0.992488	1.076089	1.126250
65	REAL ESTATE	43	3.12%	0.577121	0.556703	-0.059065	-0.045540	-0.009440	0.488705	0.556703	0.603606	1.212696	1.384887	1.427476
6500	REAL ESTATE	3	3.29%	0.609523	0.424227	-0.037986	-0.023837	-0.000254	0.329898	0.424227	0.629734	1.349007	1.400383	1.431209
651	REAL ESTATE OPERATORS (EXCEPT DEVELOPERS) AND LESSORS	16	2.46%	0.454902	0.532317	-0.009237	-0.008325	-0.006805	0.400152	0.532317	0.572211	0.874028	0.910807	0.932874
6510	REAL ESTATE OPERATORS (NO DEVELOPERS) & LESSORS	2	2.06%	0.380963	0.380963	0.268042	0.271498	0.277260	0.357917	0.380963	0.404008	0.484665	0.490427	0.493883
6512	Operators Of Nonresidential Buildings	9	2.76%	0.511803	0.572211	0.000879	0.016964	0.043774	0.569198	0.572211	0.614505	0.834364	0.841936	0.846480
6513	Operators Of Apartment Buildings	3	0.68%	0.126427	0.095675	-0.003762	-0.000718	0.004355	0.075382	0.095675	0.134419	0.270025	0.279711	0.285523
6519	Lessors Of Real Property, Not Elsewhere Classified	2	4.13%	0.765502	0.765502	0.587059	0.592521	0.601625	0.729085	0.765502	0.801918	0.929378	0.938482	0.943944
653	REAL ESTATE AGENTS AND MANAGERS	20	3.70%	0.684377	0.629054	0.287895	0.301546	0.324296	0.554711	0.629054	0.713998	1.221924	1.307932	1.359537
6531	Real Estate Agents And Managers	20	3.70%	0.684377	0.629054	0.287895	0.301546	0.324296	0.554711	0.629054	0.713998	1.221924	1.307932	1.359537
655	LAND SUBDIVIDERS AND DEVELOPERS	4	2.73%	0.505416	0.453926	-0.052053	-0.028884	0.009731	0.449990	0.453926	0.457862	1.073186	1.127248	1.159685
6552	Land Subdividers And Developers, Except Cemeteries	4	2.73%	0.505416	0.453926	-0.052053	-0.028884	0.009731	0.449990	0.453926	0.457862	1.073186	1.127248	1.159685
67	HOLDING AND OTHER INVESTMENT OFFICES	242	5.76%	1.067497	0.435770	-0.693117	-0.253353	-0.045773	0.371335	0.435770	0.541654	1.140551	1.300235	2.001458
671	HOLDING OFFICES	54	2.66%	0.493060	0.556218	-0.290281	-0.024961	-0.012326	0.391952	0.556218	0.622922	0.978290	1.114635	1.212872
6712	Offices Of Bank Holding Companies	44	2.98%	0.551381	0.587743	-0.023942	-0.017706	-0.001763	0.503795	0.587743	0.648993	0.983375	1.162685	1.220483
6719	Offices Of Holding Companies, Not Elsewhere Classified	10	1.28%	0.236445	0.145038	-0.527827	-0.440697	-0.295482	0.141442	0.145038	0.216808	0.768596	0.809793	0.834510
672	INVESTMENT OFFICES	27	1.84%	0.339829	0.360254	-0.135183	-0.082125	-0.014943	0.317063	0.360254	0.383342	0.525744	0.762331	1.007292
6722	Management Investment Offices, Open-End	2	4.63%	0.856547	0.856547	0.548775	0.558197	0.573899	0.793736	0.856547	0.919358	1.139195	1.154897	1.164319
6726	Unit Investment Trusts, Face-Amount Certificate Offices	25	1.61%	0.298492	0.324269	-0.137904	-0.088927	-0.021465	0.311754	0.324269	0.367362	0.472740	0.481565	0.484622
673	TRUSTS	8	2.92%	0.540229	0.504314	0.005015	0.007345	0.011230	0.183646	0.504314	0.806143	1.219468	1.259884	1.284134

Betas of Common Stocks by SIC Codes as of September 28, 2018

SIC Code	Description	Number of Companies	Equity Risk Premium	Mean	Median	1st Percentile	2.5th Percentile	5th Percentile	40th Percentile	50th Percentile	60th Percentile	95th Percentile	97.5th Percentile	99th Percentile
6733	Trusts, Except Educational, Religious, And Charitable	8	2.92%	0.540229	0.504314	0.005015	0.007345	0.011230	0.183646	0.504314	0.806143	1.219468	1.259884	1.284134
6770	BLANK CHECKS	6	0.77%	0.142483	0.027610	-0.024163	-0.023512	-0.022428	0.003613	0.027610	0.051607	0.541500	0.602201	0.638622
679	MISCELLANEOUS INVESTING	147	7.98%	1.478619	0.460237	-0.823889	-0.400723	-0.086019	0.413509	0.460237	0.554404	1.194763	1.924839	8.539184
6794	Patent Owners And Lessors	10	1.88%	0.348329	0.549761	-0.941820	-0.840000	-0.670299	0.491827	0.549761	0.585430	0.879571	0.934018	0.966687
6798	Real Estate Investment Trusts	58	3.61%	0.668114	0.421331	-0.065008	-0.043212	0.034167	0.397341	0.421331	0.455895	0.996492	1.230894	6.831035
6799	Investors, Not Elsewhere Classified	79	11.97%	2.216747	0.511940	-0.790541	-0.586793	-0.167226	0.434257	0.511940	0.629116	1.357567	1.979723	30.817729
	SERVICES													
70	HOTELS, ROOMING HOUSES, CAMPS, AND OTHER LODGING PLACES	29	4.31%	0.798731	0.803812	0.163388	0.238913	0.364409	0.728403	0.803812	0.832355	1.235798	1.253841	1.259456
7000	HOTELS, ROOMING HOUSES, CAMPS & OTHER LODGING PLACES	1	4.37%	0.808334	0.808334	0.808334	0.808334	0.808334	0.808334	0.808334	0.808334	0.808334	0.808334	0.808334
701	HOTELS AND MOTELS	28	4.31%	0.798388	0.796145	0.161590	0.234417	0.355465	0.719570	0.796145	0.838496	1.237552	1.254175	1.259590
7011	Hotels And Motels	28	4.31%	0.798388	0.796145	0.161590	0.234417	0.355465	0.719570	0.796145	0.838496	1.237552	1.254175	1.259590
72	PERSONAL SERVICES	16	3.28%	0.607614	0.622502	-0.485041	-0.455383	-0.405951	0.515921	0.622502	0.650620	1.588333	1.594111	1.597579
7200	SERVICES-PERSONAL SERVICES	4	4.23%	0.783061	0.515921	0.515921	0.515921	0.515921	0.515921	0.515921	0.515921	1.424196	1.504338	1.552423
721	LAUNDRY, CLEANING, AND GARMENT SERVICES	3	3.05%	0.565258	0.828924	0.007827	0.032963	0.074855	0.661353	0.828924	0.838295	0.871094	0.873436	0.874842
7211	Power Laundries, Family And Commercial	1	-0.05%	-0.008930	-0.008930	-0.008930	-0.008930	-0.008930	-0.008930	-0.008930	-0.008930	-0.008930	-0.008930	-0.008930
7215	Coin-Operated Laundries And Drycleaning	1	4.48%	0.828924	0.828924	0.828924	0.828924	0.828924	0.828924	0.828924	0.828924	0.828924	0.828924	0.828924
7218	Industrial Launderers	1	4.73%	0.875779	0.875779	0.875779	0.875779	0.875779	0.875779	0.875779	0.875779	0.875779	0.875779	0.875779
723	BEAUTY SHOPS	2	3.36%	0.622502	0.622502	0.622455	0.622456	0.622459	0.622492	0.622502	0.622512	0.622545	0.622548	0.622549
7231	Beauty Shops	2	3.36%	0.622502	0.622502	0.622455	0.622456	0.622459	0.622492	0.622502	0.622512	0.622545	0.622548	0.622549
726	FUNERAL SERVICE AND CREMATORIES	2	3.01%	0.557734	0.557734	0.387319	0.392536	0.401230	0.522955	0.557734	0.592512	0.714237	0.722931	0.728148
7261	Funeral Service And Crematories	2	3.01%	0.557734	0.557734	0.387319	0.392536	0.401230	0.522955	0.557734	0.592512	0.714237	0.722931	0.728148
729	MISCELLANEOUS PERSONAL SERVICES	5	2.74%	0.506666	0.650620	-0.499541	-0.491632	-0.478451	0.241173	0.650620	0.854624	1.512038	1.555964	1.582320
7299	Miscellaneous Personal Services, Not Elsewhere Classified	5	2.74%	0.506666	0.650620	-0.499541	-0.491632	-0.478451	0.241173	0.650620	0.854624	1.512038	1.555964	1.582320
73	BUSINESS SERVICES	451	4.15%	0.768157	0.810587	-0.984003	-0.316108	-0.117920	0.689552	0.810587	0.907805	1.490150	1.759163	1.989435
731	ADVERTISING	18	4.39%	0.813116	0.593891	-0.096206	-0.057546	0.006888	0.549296	0.593891	0.763181	2.409977	2.913594	3.215763
7311	Advertising Agencies	12	5.04%	0.932684	0.549296	0.052030	0.071320	0.103469	0.549296	0.549296	0.660248	2.765471	3.091341	3.286862
7312	Outdoor Advertising Services	3	2.84%	0.525306	0.638485	0.041806	0.060072	0.090515	0.516714	0.638485	0.692349	0.880873	0.894339	0.902419
7313	Radio, Television, And Publishers' Advertising Representatives	2	2.25%	0.417353	0.417353	-0.111193	-0.095013	-0.068047	0.309486	0.417353	0.525220	0.902753	0.929719	0.945899
7319	Advertising, Not Elsewhere Classified	1	5.58%	1.033250	1.033250	1.033250	1.033250	1.033250	1.033250	1.033250	1.033250	1.033250	1.033250	1.033250
732	CONSUMER CREDIT REPORTING AGENCIES, MERCANTILE REPORTING AGENCIES	9	4.47%	0.827901	0.833217	0.175669	0.246058	0.363371	0.830062	0.833217	0.859708	1.153632	1.156036	1.157478
7320	SERVICES-CONSUMER CREDIT REPORTING, COLLECTION AGENCIES	1	6.19%	1.146420	1.146420	1.146420	1.146420	1.146420	1.146420	1.146420	1.146420	1.146420	1.146420	1.146420
7322	Adjustment And Collection Services	2	4.63%	0.857202	0.857202	0.718150	0.722407	0.729501	0.828824	0.857202	0.885580	0.984903	0.991998	0.996254
7323	Credit Reporting Services	6	4.13%	0.765047	0.831245	0.161021	0.209436	0.290127	0.829273	0.831245	0.833217	1.085413	1.121926	1.143835
733	MAILING, REPRODUCTION, COMMERCIAL ART AND PHOTOGRAPHY, AND STENOGRAPHY	4	-3.52%	-0.652226	0.170234	-3.653960	-3.490489	-3.218039	-0.010065	0.170234	0.350533	0.762142	0.787854	0.803282

Betas of Common Stocks by SIC Codes as of September 28, 2018

SIC Code	Description	Number of Companies	Equity Risk Premium	Mean	Median	1st Percentile	2.5th Percentile	5th Percentile	40th Percentile	50th Percentile	60th Percentile	95th Percentile	97.5th Percentile	99th Percentile
7331	Direct Mail Advertising Services	2	0.92%	0.170234	0.170234	-0.124255	-0.115240	-0.100215	0.110134	0.170234	0.230334	0.440683	0.455708	0.464723
7336	Commercial Art And Graphic Design	1	-20.32%	-3.762940	-3.762940	-3.762940	-3.762940	-3.762940	-3.762940	-3.762940	-3.762940	-3.762940	-3.762940	-3.762940
7338	Secretarial And Court Reporting Services	1	4.39%	0.813567	0.813567	0.813567	0.813567	0.813567	0.813567	0.813567	0.813567	0.813567	0.813567	0.813567
734	SERVICES TO DWELLINGS AND OTHER BUILDINGS	3	3.69%	0.682637	0.891456	0.244113	0.263930	0.296957	0.759345	0.891456	0.898276	0.922144	0.923849	0.924872
7342	Disinfecting And Pest Control Services	1	4.81%	0.891456	0.891456	0.891456	0.891456	0.891456	0.891456	0.891456	0.891456	0.891456	0.891456	0.891456
7349	Building Cleaning And Maintenance Services, Not Elsewhere Classified	2	3.12%	0.578228	0.578228	0.237849	0.248268	0.265635	0.508763	0.578228	0.647693	0.890821	0.908188	0.918607
735	MISCELLANEOUS EQUIPMENT RENTAL AND LEASING	19	4.27%	0.791500	0.841992	-0.338974	-0.247131	-0.094060	0.635938	0.841992	1.064015	1.475887	1.545534	1.587321
7350	SERVICES-MISCELLANEOUS EQUIPMENT RENTAL & LEASING	1	6.39%	1.183410	1.183410	1.183410	1.183410	1.183410	1.183410	1.183410	1.183410	1.183410	1.183410	1.183410
7353	Heavy Construction Equipment Rental And Leasing	1	4.90%	0.906837	0.906837	0.906837	0.906837	0.906837	0.906837	0.906837	0.906837	0.906837	0.906837	0.906837
7359	Equipment Rental And Leasing, Not Elsewhere Classified	17	4.11%	0.761662	0.816818	-0.345777	-0.264139	-0.128076	0.589977	0.816818	0.998783	1.491364	1.553272	1.590417
736	PERSONNEL SUPPLY SERVICES	24	4.09%	0.757809	0.753579	-0.200999	-0.062965	0.127014	0.673417	0.753579	0.884700	1.398716	1.537749	1.644934
7361	Employment Agencies	5	5.03%	0.931655	0.765826	0.513376	0.522347	0.537298	0.722257	0.765826	0.864200	1.575464	1.645927	1.688205
7363	Help Supply Services	19	3.85%	0.712060	0.741332	-0.221004	-0.112977	0.067066	0.636745	0.741332	0.884700	1.363743	1.384727	1.397317
737	COMPUTER PROGRAMMING, DATA PROCESSING, AND OTHER COMPUTER RELATED	285	4.29%	0.794495	0.852038	-0.783692	-0.200432	-0.112691	0.728694	0.852038	0.958901	1.491146	1.733443	1.857369
7370	SERVICES-COMPUTER PROGRAMMING, DATA PROCESSING, ETC.	3	2.65%	0.490484	0.671497	-0.376065	-0.343997	-0.290550	0.457709	0.671497	0.776678	1.144810	1.171105	1.186882
7371	Computer Programming Services	54	4.22%	0.781226	0.824835	-0.660746	-0.259174	0.185347	0.719677	0.824835	0.902642	1.374268	1.549378	1.733612
7372	Prepackaged Software	136	4.18%	0.774614	0.862928	-0.930294	-0.398685	-0.113859	0.716249	0.862928	0.974933	1.593850	1.764929	1.922487
7373	Computer Integrated Systems Design	34	4.67%	0.864453	0.826160	-0.021513	0.232656	0.328519	0.792242	0.826160	0.943253	1.426632	1.533311	1.716124
7374	Computer Processing And Data Preparation And Processing Services	41	4.18%	0.774351	0.807421	-0.171103	-0.139578	-0.108018	0.764900	0.807421	0.906707	1.475400	1.475400	1.592304
7375	Information Retrieval Services	11	5.92%	1.096698	1.193690	0.107589	0.216279	0.397430	1.193690	1.193690	1.193690	1.450445	1.451343	1.451881
7376	Computer Facilities Management Services	1	7.97%	1.476580	1.476580	1.476580	1.476580	1.476580	1.476580	1.476580	1.476580	1.476580	1.476580	1.476580
7379	Computer Related Services, Not Elsewhere Classified	5	2.97%	0.549173	0.721563	-0.112570	-0.092067	-0.057894	0.519131	0.721563	0.815827	0.973711	0.975772	0.977009
738	MISCELLANEOUS BUSINESS SERVICES	89	3.96%	0.733209	0.685680	-1.496139	-0.310886	-0.236022	0.560916	0.685680	0.811993	1.373270	1.773450	3.149510
7380	SERVICES-MISCELLANEOUS BUSINESS SERVICES	1	5.01%	0.927134	0.927134	0.927134	0.927134	0.927134	0.927134	0.927134	0.927134	0.927134	0.927134	0.927134
7381	Detective, Guard, And Armored Car Services	2	4.56%	0.843797	0.843797	-0.070674	-0.042680	0.003977	0.657170	0.843797	1.030423	1.683617	1.730273	1.758267
7382	Security Systems Services	2	5.62%	1.040065	1.040065	1.021891	1.022447	1.023375	1.036356	1.040065	1.043774	1.056756	1.057683	1.058239
7384	Photofinishing Laboratories	1	3.20%	0.593021	0.593021	0.593021	0.593021	0.593021	0.593021	0.593021	0.593021	0.593021	0.593021	0.593021
7389	Business Services, Not Elsewhere Classified	83	3.90%	0.722503	0.684384	-1.544434	-0.320575	-0.248471	0.528184	0.684384	0.793879	1.301183	1.742586	3.713926
75	AUTOMOTIVE REPAIR, SERVICES, AND PARKING	6	5.31%	0.983172	1.200080	-0.092858	-0.038798	0.051304	1.129090	1.200080	1.271070	1.558630	1.578980	1.591190
751	AUTOMOTIVE RENTAL AND LEASING, WITHOUT DRIVERS	4	6.61%	1.224711	1.353800	0.612287	0.642849	0.693786	1.304162	1.353800	1.403438	1.574910	1.587120	1.594446

Betas of Common Stocks by SIC Codes as of September 28, 2018

SIC Code	Description	Number of Companies	Equity Risk Premium	Mean	Median	1st Percentile	2.5th Percentile	5th Percentile	40th Percentile	50th Percentile	60th Percentile	95th Percentile	97.5th Percentile	99th Percentile
7510	SERVICES-AUTO RENTAL & LEASING (NO DRIVERS)	1	7.76%	1.436530	1.436530	1.436530	1.436530	1.436530	1.436530	1.436530	1.436530	1.436530	1.436530	1.436530
7513	Truck Rental And Leasing, Without Drivers	2	5.03%	0.931491	0.931491	0.598704	0.608891	0.625870	0.863575	0.931491	0.999407	1.237112	1.254091	1.264278
7514	Passenger Car Rental	1	8.64%	1.599330	1.599330	1.599330	1.599330	1.599330	1.599330	1.599330	1.599330	1.599330	1.599330	1.599330
753	AUTOMOTIVE REPAIR SHOPS	1	6.10%	1.129090	1.129090	1.129090	1.129090	1.129090	1.129090	1.129090	1.129090	1.129090	1.129090	1.129090
7538	General Automotive Repair Shops	1	6.10%	1.129090	1.129090	1.129090	1.129090	1.129090	1.129090	1.129090	1.129090	1.129090	1.129090	1.129090
754	AUTOMOTIVE SERVICES, EXCEPT REPAIR	1	-0.70%	-0.128899	-0.128899	-0.128899	-0.128899	-0.128899	-0.128899	-0.128899	-0.128899	-0.128899	-0.128899	-0.128899
7542	Carwashes	1	-0.70%	-0.128899	-0.128899	-0.128899	-0.128899	-0.128899	-0.128899	-0.128899	-0.128899	-0.128899	-0.128899	-0.128899
76	MISCELLANEOUS REPAIR SERVICES	2	1.19%	0.219765	0.219765	0.117389	0.120523	0.125746	0.198872	0.219765	0.240657	0.313783	0.319006	0.322140
762	ELECTRICAL REPAIR SHOPS	2	1.19%	0.219765	0.219765	0.117389	0.120523	0.125746	0.198872	0.219765	0.240657	0.313783	0.319006	0.322140
7623	Refrigeration And Air-Conditioning Service And Repair Shops	2	1.19%	0.219765	0.219765	0.117389	0.120523	0.125746	0.198872	0.219765	0.240657	0.313783	0.319006	0.322140
78	MOTION PICTURES	18	3.38%	0.625994	0.646785	-0.274709	-0.181366	-0.025794	0.497679	0.646785	0.693619	1.687416	1.869388	1.978571
781	MOTION PICTURE PRODUCTION AND ALLIED SERVICES	13	2.49%	0.460575	0.617932	-0.293012	-0.227122	-0.117307	0.474339	0.617932	0.693619	0.804514	0.835477	0.854056
7812	Motion Picture And Video Tape Production	11	2.56%	0.474266	0.617932	-0.300333	-0.245425	-0.153912	0.498195	0.617932	0.683928	0.814835	0.840638	0.856120
7819	Services Allied To Motion Picture Production	2	2.08%	0.385279	0.385279	0.045120	0.055533	0.072888	0.315859	0.385279	0.454700	0.697671	0.715026	0.725439
782	MOTION PICTURE DISTRIBUTION AND ALLIED SERVICES	1	11.08%	2.051360	2.051360	2.051360	2.051360	2.051360	2.051360	2.051360	2.051360	2.051360	2.051360	2.051360
7822	Motion Picture And Video Tape Distribution	1	11.08%	2.051360	2.051360	2.051360	2.051360	2.051360	2.051360	2.051360	2.051360	2.051360	2.051360	2.051360
783	MOTION PICTURE THEATERS	3	2.89%	0.535288	0.495614	0.435834	0.437664	0.440714	0.483414	0.495614	0.531619	0.657635	0.666636	0.672037
7832	Motion Picture Theaters, Except Drive-In	3	2.89%	0.535288	0.495614	0.435834	0.437664	0.440714	0.483414	0.495614	0.531619	0.657635	0.666636	0.672037
784	VIDEO TAPE RENTAL	1	8.77%	1.623190	1.623190	1.623190	1.623190	1.623190	1.623190	1.623190	1.623190	1.623190	1.623190	1.623190
7841	Video Tape Rental	1	8.77%	1.623190	1.623190	1.623190	1.623190	1.623190	1.623190	1.623190	1.623190	1.623190	1.623190	1.623190
79	AMUSEMENT AND RECREATION SERVICES	33	3.16%	0.584370	0.444756	-1.129599	-1.071082	-0.863432	0.362661	0.444756	0.562439	2.594280	3.247636	3.303618
7900	SERVICES-AMUSEMENT & RECREATION SERVICES	3	0.39%	0.071593	0.254764	-0.283759	-0.267273	-0.239798	0.144861	0.254764	0.254764	0.254764	0.254764	0.254764
792	THEATRICAL PRODUCERS (EXCEPT MOTION PICTURE), BANDS, ORCHESTRAS	3	0.71%	0.131913	0.376870	-1.137700	-1.091336	-1.014062	0.067774	0.376870	0.538992	1.106419	1.146950	1.171268
7922	Theatrical Producers (Except Motion Picture) And Miscellaneous Theater	2	0.05%	0.009435	0.009435	-1.145049	-1.109708	-1.050806	-0.226174	0.009435	0.245044	1.069676	1.128578	1.163919
7929	Bands, Orchestras, Actors, And Other Entertainers And Entertainment	1	2.04%	0.376870	0.376870	0.376870	0.376870	0.376870	0.376870	0.376870	0.376870	0.376870	0.376870	0.376870
793	BOWLING CENTERS	1	-1.34%	-0.247671	-0.247671	-0.247671	-0.247671	-0.247671	-0.247671	-0.247671	-0.247671	-0.247671	-0.247671	-0.247671
7933	Bowling Centers	1	-1.34%	-0.247671	-0.247671	-0.247671	-0.247671	-0.247671	-0.247671	-0.247671	-0.247671	-0.247671	-0.247671	-0.247671
794	COMMERCIAL SPORTS	8	1.38%	0.255289	0.341279	-0.958848	-0.827069	-0.607438	0.251054	0.341279	0.449084	0.738924	0.768199	0.785765
7941	Professional Sports Clubs And Promoters	2	1.84%	0.341279	0.341279	0.259252	0.261763	0.265948	0.324538	0.341279	0.358019	0.416609	0.420794	0.423305
7948	Racing, Including Track Operation	6	1.22%	0.226626	0.385230	-0.983948	-0.889821	-0.732942	0.224958	0.385230	0.545502	0.755653	0.776564	0.789111
799	MISCELLANEOUS AMUSEMENT AND RECREATION SERVICES	18	5.06%	0.937725	0.717250	-0.621416	-0.441661	-0.142070	0.472711	0.717250	0.932772	3.241805	3.291372	3.321113
7990	SERVICES-MISCELLANEOUS AMUSEMENT & RECREATION	3	12.09%	2.238133	2.174260	1.218701	1.247953	1.296706	1.979248	2.174260	2.407596	3.224272	3.282606	3.317606

Betas of Common Stocks by SIC Codes as of September 28, 2018

SIC Code	Description	Number of Companies	Equity Risk Premium	Mean	Median	1st Percentile	2.5th Percentile	5th Percentile	40th Percentile	50th Percentile	60th Percentile	95th Percentile	97.5th Percentile	99th Percentile
7993	Coin-Operated Amusement Devices	1	2.04%	0.377533	0.377533	0.377533	0.377533	0.377533	0.377533	0.377533	0.377533	0.377533	0.377533	0.377533
7996	Amusement Parks	3	2.90%	0.536717	0.477248	0.455017	0.455697	0.456832	0.472711	0.477248	0.517466	0.658231	0.668285	0.674318
7997	Membership Sports And Recreation Clubs	3	4.14%	0.766656	0.931413	0.318336	0.337103	0.368383	0.806295	0.931413	0.957676	1.049598	1.056164	1.060104
7999	Amusement And Recreation Services, Not Elsewhere Classified	8	3.97%	0.734624	0.600458	-0.691908	-0.617892	-0.494530	0.364135	0.600458	0.792569	2.533123	2.878717	3.086073
80	HEALTH SERVICES	80	3.71%	0.686435	0.649229	-0.644509	-0.267720	0.063592	0.542487	0.649229	0.731056	1.470960	1.917080	2.035988
801	OFFICES AND CLINICS OF DOCTORS OF MEDICINE	15	4.75%	0.878800	0.892431	0.255669	0.268680	0.290367	0.861224	0.892431	1.032174	1.382512	1.428446	1.456006
8011	Offices And Clinics Of Doctors Of Medicine	15	4.75%	0.878800	0.892431	0.255669	0.268680	0.290367	0.861224	0.892431	1.032174	1.382512	1.428446	1.456006
804	OFFICES AND CLINICS OF OTHER HEALTH PRACTITIONERS	1	2.29%	0.424117	0.424117	0.424117	0.424117	0.424117	0.424117	0.424117	0.424117	0.424117	0.424117	0.424117
8041	Offices And Clinics Of Chiropractors	1	2.29%	0.424117	0.424117	0.424117	0.424117	0.424117	0.424117	0.424117	0.424117	0.424117	0.424117	0.424117
805	NURSING AND PERSONAL CARE FACILITIES	8	2.99%	0.553889	0.563710	0.239864	0.256452	0.284099	0.523146	0.563710	0.608298	0.793477	0.820545	0.836785
8051	Skilled Nursing Care Facilities	8	2.99%	0.553889	0.563710	0.239864	0.256452	0.284099	0.523146	0.563710	0.608298	0.793477	0.820545	0.836785
806	HOSPITALS	16	4.12%	0.762270	0.729491	-0.227632	-0.176075	-0.090147	0.634043	0.729491	0.865416	1.392258	1.654604	1.812012
8062	General Medical And Surgical Hospitals	11	3.00%	0.556301	0.560943	-0.239089	-0.204718	-0.147432	0.541119	0.560943	0.634043	1.082230	1.098195	1.107774
8069	Specialty Hospitals, Except Psychiatric	5	6.56%	1.215402	1.140710	0.739210	0.760313	0.795484	1.115166	1.140710	1.171370	1.777032	1.846991	1.888966
807	MEDICAL AND DENTAL LABORATORIES	18	2.33%	0.432407	0.473637	-1.098695	-0.911893	-0.600556	0.369948	0.473637	0.564295	1.299982	1.307751	1.312412
8071	Medical Laboratories	18	2.33%	0.432407	0.473637	-1.098695	-0.911893	-0.600556	0.369948	0.473637	0.564295	1.299982	1.307751	1.312412
808	HOME HEALTH CARE SERVICES	7	3.05%	0.563984	0.543399	0.306949	0.309709	0.314309	0.510241	0.543399	0.666660	0.766098	0.768183	0.769435
8082	Home Health Care Services	7	3.05%	0.563984	0.543399	0.306949	0.309709	0.314309	0.510241	0.543399	0.666660	0.766098	0.768183	0.769435
809	MISCELLANEOUS HEALTH AND ALLIED SERVICES, NOT ELSEWHERE CLASSIFIED	15	4.66%	0.863337	0.678405	0.114357	0.152769	0.216787	0.623867	0.678405	0.695172	2.084772	2.274486	2.388314
8090	SERVICES-MISC HEALTH & ALLIED SERVICES, NEC	1	3.74%	0.691985	0.691985	0.691985	0.691985	0.691985	0.691985	0.691985	0.691985	0.691985	0.691985	0.691985
8093	Specialty Outpatient Facilities, Not Elsewhere Classified	6	5.74%	1.062497	0.659893	0.113317	0.150167	0.211584	0.641380	0.659893	0.678405	2.328690	2.396445	2.437098
8099	Health And Allied Services, Not Elsewhere Classified	8	3.97%	0.735386	0.648775	0.277522	0.286315	0.300970	0.588889	0.648775	0.727216	1.340087	1.405433	1.444641
81	LEGAL SERVICES	1	4.54%	0.840006	0.840006	0.840006	0.840006	0.840006	0.840006	0.840006	0.840006	0.840006	0.840006	0.840006
811	LEGAL SERVICES	1	4.54%	0.840006	0.840006	0.840006	0.840006	0.840006	0.840006	0.840006	0.840006	0.840006	0.840006	0.840006
8111	Legal Services	1	4.54%	0.840006	0.840006	0.840006	0.840006	0.840006	0.840006	0.840006	0.840006	0.840006	0.840006	0.840006
82	EDUCATIONAL SERVICES	15	2.59%	0.480046	0.565476	-0.677464	-0.582564	-0.424398	0.518702	0.565476	0.673778	1.009897	1.069009	1.104475
8200	SERVICES-EDUCATIONAL SERVICES	3	3.99%	0.738686	0.869882	0.231092	0.250646	0.283238	0.739517	0.869882	0.921530	1.102296	1.115208	1.122955
821	ELEMENTARY AND SECONDARY SCHOOLS	4	2.80%	0.518062	0.508831	0.414257	0.416355	0.419851	0.479215	0.508831	0.538446	0.629196	0.635461	0.639220
8211	Elementary And Secondary Schools	4	2.80%	0.518062	0.508831	0.414257	0.416355	0.419851	0.479215	0.508831	0.538446	0.629196	0.635461	0.639220
822	COLLEGES, UNIVERSITIES, PROFESSIONAL SCHOOLS, AND JUNIOR COLLEGES	3	1.41%	0.261325	0.565476	-0.714606	-0.675420	-0.610109	0.304235	0.565476	0.644227	0.919855	0.939542	0.951355
8221	Colleges, Universities, And Professional Schools	3	1.41%	0.261325	0.565476	-0.714606	-0.675420	-0.610109	0.304235	0.565476	0.644227	0.919855	0.939542	0.951355
823	LIBRARIES	1	4.87%	0.902543	0.902543	0.902543	0.902543	0.902543	0.902543	0.902543	0.902543	0.902543	0.902543	0.902543
8231	Libraries	1	4.87%	0.902543	0.902543	0.902543	0.902543	0.902543	0.902543	0.902543	0.902543	0.902543	0.902543	0.902543

Betas of Common Stocks by SIC Codes as of September 28, 2018

SIC Code	Description	Number of Companies	Equity Risk Premium	Mean	Median	1st Percentile	2.5th Percentile	5th Percentile	40th Percentile	50th Percentile	60th Percentile	95th Percentile	97.5th Percentile	99th Percentile
824	VOCATIONAL SCHOOLS	3	0.81%	0.150208	0.017596	-0.282699	-0.273506	-0.258185	-0.043689	0.017596	0.158448	0.651429	0.686642	0.707770
8249	Vocational Schools, Not Elsewhere Classified	3	0.81%	0.150208	0.017596	-0.282699	-0.273506	-0.258185	-0.043689	0.017596	0.158448	0.651429	0.686642	0.707770
829	SCHOOLS AND EDUCATIONAL SERVICES, NOT ELSEWHERE CLASSIFIED	1	4.19%	0.775249	0.775249	0.775249	0.775249	0.775249	0.775249	0.775249	0.775249	0.775249	0.775249	0.775249
8299	Schools And Educational Services, Not Elsewhere Classified	1	4.19%	0.775249	0.775249	0.775249	0.775249	0.775249	0.775249	0.775249	0.775249	0.775249	0.775249	0.775249
83	SOCIAL SERVICES	4	3.99%	0.739583	0.846001	-0.013474	0.020553	0.077267	0.770410	0.846001	0.921592	1.252914	1.277702	1.292575
832	INDIVIDUAL AND FAMILY SOCIAL SERVICES	1	5.25%	0.971986	0.971986	0.971986	0.971986	0.971986	0.971986	0.971986	0.971986	0.971986	0.971986	0.971986
8322	Individual And Family Social Services	1	5.25%	0.971986	0.971986	0.971986	0.971986	0.971986	0.971986	0.971986	0.971986	0.971986	0.971986	0.971986
833	JOB TRAINING AND VOCATIONAL REHABILITATION SERVICES	1	7.03%	1.302490	1.302490	1.302490	1.302490	1.302490	1.302490	1.302490	1.302490	1.302490	1.302490	1.302490
8331	Job Training And Vocational Rehabilitation Services	1	7.03%	1.302490	1.302490	1.302490	1.302490	1.302490	1.302490	1.302490	1.302490	1.302490	1.302490	1.302490
835	CHILD DAY CARE SERVICES	1	3.89%	0.720016	0.720016	0.720016	0.720016	0.720016	0.720016	0.720016	0.720016	0.720016	0.720016	0.720016
8351	Child Day Care Services	1	3.89%	0.720016	0.720016	0.720016	0.720016	0.720016	0.720016	0.720016	0.720016	0.720016	0.720016	0.720016
836	RESIDENTIAL CARE	1	-0.20%	-0.036160	-0.036160	-0.036160	-0.036160	-0.036160	-0.036160	-0.036160	-0.036160	-0.036160	-0.036160	-0.036160
8361	Residential Care	1	-0.20%	-0.036160	-0.036160	-0.036160	-0.036160	-0.036160	-0.036160	-0.036160	-0.036160	-0.036160	-0.036160	-0.036160
87	ENGINEERING, ACCOUNTING, RESEARCH, MANAGEMENT, AND RELATED SERVICES	167	3.76%	0.696806	0.706179	-0.683336	-0.426102	-0.256407	0.606990	0.706179	0.888110	1.624180	1.745727	2.073143
871	ENGINEERING, ARCHITECTURAL, AND SURVEYING SERVICES	19	4.36%	0.806733	0.927543	0.129039	0.148261	0.180297	0.779519	0.927543	0.965400	1.276705	1.460778	1.571221
8711	Engineering Services	19	4.36%	0.806733	0.927543	0.129039	0.148261	0.180297	0.779519	0.927543	0.965400	1.276705	1.460778	1.571221
872	ACCOUNTING, AUDITING, AND BOOKKEEPING SERVICES	4	3.20%	0.593332	0.548234	0.123111	0.139581	0.167032	0.506176	0.548234	0.590291	1.082770	1.123750	1.148338
8721	Accounting, Auditing, And Bookkeeping Services	4	3.20%	0.593332	0.548234	0.123111	0.139581	0.167032	0.506176	0.548234	0.590291	1.082770	1.123750	1.148338
873	RESEARCH, DEVELOPMENT, AND TESTING SERVICES	95	4.07%	0.754623	0.838312	-0.470139	-0.366960	-0.224106	0.652726	0.838312	0.964405	1.711334	1.744429	1.937984
8731	Commercial Physical And Biological Research	79	4.14%	0.767144	0.854667	-0.579239	-0.409437	-0.281726	0.664650	0.854667	0.972737	1.724289	1.754737	2.019433
8732	Commercial Economic, Sociological, And Educational Research	8	3.16%	0.584670	0.501276	-0.072735	-0.055663	-0.027209	0.300938	0.501276	0.692699	1.464827	1.585683	1.658197
8733	Noncommercial Research Organizations	6	4.37%	0.809134	0.931553	0.063041	0.096913	0.153368	0.899937	0.931553	0.963169	1.283940	1.311125	1.327436
8734	Testing Laboratories	2	4.19%	0.776339	0.776339	0.504397	0.512722	0.526596	0.720840	0.776339	0.831837	1.026081	1.039955	1.048280
874	MANAGEMENT AND PUBLIC RELATIONS SERVICES	49	2.97%	0.550533	0.605972	-1.027301	-0.458251	-0.375883	0.462161	0.605972	0.670710	1.250288	1.878408	2.093485
8741	Management Services	12	2.70%	0.499531	0.626581	-0.407219	-0.359005	-0.278649	0.480516	0.626581	0.773415	0.998725	1.031907	1.051817
8742	Management Consulting Services	33	2.90%	0.536771	0.591608	-1.200941	-0.680022	-0.353588	0.427896	0.591608	0.658473	1.565784	2.057322	2.111567
8743	Public Relations Services	1	1.91%	0.354544	0.354544	0.354544	0.354544	0.354544	0.354544	0.354544	0.354544	0.354544	0.354544	0.354544
8744	Facilities Support Management Services	1	3.27%	0.605972	0.605972	0.605972	0.605972	0.605972	0.605972	0.605972	0.605972	0.605972	0.605972	0.605972
8748	Business Consulting Services, Not Elsewhere Classified	2	6.23%	1.153890	1.153890	1.109084	1.110456	1.112742	1.144746	1.153890	1.163034	1.195038	1.197324	1.198696
88	PRIVATE HOUSEHOLDS	3	2.29%	0.423423	0.355082	0.135849	0.142560	0.153746	0.310341	0.355082	0.440828	0.740940	0.762376	0.775238
8880	AMERICAN DEPOSITARY RECEIPTS	3	2.29%	0.423423	0.355082	0.135849	0.142560	0.153746	0.310341	0.355082	0.440828	0.740940	0.762376	0.775238
89	SERVICES, NOT ELSEWHERE CLASSIFIED	15	3.64%	0.674415	0.754801	-0.888484	-0.691240	-0.362499	0.507400	0.754801	0.873220	1.746790	2.093255	2.301134

Betas of Common Stocks by SIC Codes as of September 28, 2018

SIC Code	Description	Number of Companies	Equity Risk Premium	Mean	Median	1st Percentile	2.5th Percentile	5th Percentile	40th Percentile	50th Percentile	60th Percentile	95th Percentile	97.5th Percentile	99th Percentile
899	SERVICES, NOT ELSEWHERE CLASSIFIED	15	3.64%	0.674415	0.754801	-0.888484	-0.691240	-0.362499	0.507400	0.754801	0.873220	1.746790	2.093255	2.301134
8999	Services, Not Elsewhere Classified	15	3.64%	0.674415	0.754801	-0.888484	-0.691240	-0.362499	0.507400	0.754801	0.873220	1.746790	2.093255	2.301134
	PUBLIC ADMINISTRATION													
94	ADMINISTRATION OF HUMAN RESOURCE PROGRAMS	1	4.87%	0.902207	0.902207	0.902207	0.902207	0.902207	0.902207	0.902207	0.902207	0.902207	0.902207	0.902207
943	ADMINISTRATION OF PUBLIC HEALTH PROGRAMS	1	4.87%	0.902207	0.902207	0.902207	0.902207	0.902207	0.902207	0.902207	0.902207	0.902207	0.902207	0.902207
9431	Administration Of Public Health Programs	1	4.87%	0.902207	0.902207	0.902207	0.902207	0.902207	0.902207	0.902207	0.902207	0.902207	0.902207	0.902207
96	ADMINISTRATION OF ECONOMIC PROGRAMS	2	8.62%	1.595460	1.595460	0.790908	0.815538	0.856586	1.431265	1.595460	1.759654	2.334333	2.375381	2.400011
961	ADMINISTRATION OF GENERAL ECONOMIC PROGRAMS	1	4.18%	0.774489	0.774489	0.774489	0.774489	0.774489	0.774489	0.774489	0.774489	0.774489	0.774489	0.774489
9611	Administration Of General Economic Programs	1	4.18%	0.774489	0.774489	0.774489	0.774489	0.774489	0.774489	0.774489	0.774489	0.774489	0.774489	0.774489
963	REGULATION AND ADMINISTRATION OF COMMUNICATIONS, ELECTRIC, GAS	1	13.05%	2.416430	2.416430	2.416430	2.416430	2.416430	2.416430	2.416430	2.416430	2.416430	2.416430	2.416430
9631	Regulation And Administration Of Communications, Electric, Gas	1	13.05%	2.416430	2.416430	2.416430	2.416430	2.416430	2.416430	2.416430	2.416430	2.416430	2.416430	2.416430
	NONCLASSIFIABLE ESTABLISHMENTS													
99	NONCLASSIFIABLE ESTABLISHMENTS	70	2.33%	0.431187	0.465059	-5.091094	-0.964969	-0.619790	0.328979	0.465059	0.696845	2.307893	2.911982	3.259567
999	NONCLASSIFIABLE ESTABLISHMENTS	70	2.33%	0.431187	0.465059	-5.091094	-0.964969	-0.619790	0.328979	0.465059	0.696845	2.307893	2.911982	3.259567
9995	NON-OPERATING ESTABLISHMENTS	2	6.29%	1.165717	1.165717	-0.111295	-0.072202	-0.007049	0.905102	1.165717	1.426332	2.338483	2.403636	2.442729
9999	Nonclassifiable Establishments	68	2.21%	0.409584	0.465059	-5.353831	-0.968673	-0.629632	0.332141	0.465059	0.696298	2.012540	2.931092	3.264115

Down-market Betas of Common Stocks by SIC Codes as of September 28, 2018

Details:
Benchmark: S&P 500 Index
Returns period and frequency: 1 year of daily returns
Risk-free rate for betas: Federal Funds Rate
Expected US Equity Risk Premium: 5.40% (Fernandez, Pablo and Pershin, Vitaly and Fernández Acín, Isabel, Market Risk Premium and Risk-Free Rate used for 59 Countries in 2018: A Survey (April 3, 2018). Available at SSRN: https://ssrn.com/abstract=3155709)

SIC Code	Description	Number of Companies	Equity Risk Premium	Mean	Median	1st Percentile	2.5th Percentile	5th Percentile	40th Percentile	50th Percentile	60th Percentile	95th Percentile	97.5th Percentile	99th Percentile
	AGRICULTURE, FORESTRY, AND FISHING													
01	AGRICULTURAL PRODUCTION-CROPS	9	4.25%	0.786563	0.804933	-0.013856	0.005834	0.038651	0.531348	0.804933	0.917948	1.821064	2.031732	2.158133
011	CASH GRAINS	2	4.46%	0.826006	0.826006	0.470213	0.481105	0.499257	0.753395	0.826006	0.898617	1.152755	1.170907	1.181799
0115	Corn	1	6.42%	1.189060	1.189060	1.189060	1.189060	1.189060	1.189060	1.189060	1.189060	1.189060	1.189060	1.189060
0116	Soybeans	1	2.50%	0.462952	0.462952	0.462952	0.462952	0.462952	0.462952	0.462952	0.462952	0.462952	0.462952	0.462952
013	FIELD CROPS, EXCEPT CASH GRAINS	1	-0.15%	-0.026983	-0.026983	-0.026983	-0.026983	-0.026983	-0.026983	-0.026983	-0.026983	-0.026983	-0.026983	-0.026983
0131	Cotton	1	-0.15%	-0.026983	-0.026983	-0.026983	-0.026983	-0.026983	-0.026983	-0.026983	-0.026983	-0.026983	-0.026983	-0.026983
016	VEGETABLES AND MELONS	1	12.11%	2.242400	2.242400	2.242400	2.242400	2.242400	2.242400	2.242400	2.242400	2.242400	2.242400	2.242400
0161	Vegetables And Melons	1	12.11%	2.242400	2.242400	2.242400	2.242400	2.242400	2.242400	2.242400	2.242400	2.242400	2.242400	2.242400
017	FRUITS AND TREE NUTS	2	2.54%	0.471017	0.471017	0.143779	0.153797	0.170493	0.404234	0.471017	0.537800	0.771541	0.788237	0.798255
0174	Citrus Fruits	2	2.54%	0.471017	0.471017	0.143779	0.153797	0.170493	0.404234	0.471017	0.537800	0.771541	0.788237	0.798255
018	HORTICULTURAL SPECIALTIES	1	0.97%	0.178919	0.178919	0.178919	0.178919	0.178919	0.178919	0.178919	0.178919	0.178919	0.178919	0.178919
0181	Ornamental Floriculture And Nursery Products	1	0.97%	0.178919	0.178919	0.178919	0.178919	0.178919	0.178919	0.178919	0.178919	0.178919	0.178919	0.178919
019	GENERAL FARMS, PRIMARILY CROP	1	6.18%	1.144480	1.144480	1.144480	1.144480	1.144480	1.144480	1.144480	1.144480	1.144480	1.144480	1.144480
0191	General Farms, Primarily Crop	1	6.18%	1.144480	1.144480	1.144480	1.144480	1.144480	1.144480	1.144480	1.144480	1.144480	1.144480	1.144480
02	AGRICULTURAL PRODUCTION-LIVESTOCK AND ANIMAL SPECIALTIES	2	-1.00%	-0.184740	-0.184740	-0.747200	-0.729982	-0.701285	-0.299527	-0.184740	-0.069952	0.331806	0.360503	0.377721
021	LIVESTOCK, EXCEPT DAIRY AND POULTRY	1	-4.10%	-0.758679	-0.758679	-0.758679	-0.758679	-0.758679	-0.758679	-0.758679	-0.758679	-0.758679	-0.758679	-0.758679
0213	Hogs	1	-4.10%	-0.758679	-0.758679	-0.758679	-0.758679	-0.758679	-0.758679	-0.758679	-0.758679	-0.758679	-0.758679	-0.758679
025	POULTRY AND EGGS	1	2.10%	0.389200	0.389200	0.389200	0.389200	0.389200	0.389200	0.389200	0.389200	0.389200	0.389200	0.389200
0252	Chicken Eggs	1	2.10%	0.389200	0.389200	0.389200	0.389200	0.389200	0.389200	0.389200	0.389200	0.389200	0.389200	0.389200
07	AGRICULTURAL SERVICES	5	2.46%	0.456328	0.654744	-0.620295	-0.541558	-0.410328	0.648650	0.654744	0.674548	0.905586	0.930753	0.945852
074	VETERINARY SERVICES	1	3.45%	0.639508	0.639508	0.639508	0.639508	0.639508	0.639508	0.639508	0.639508	0.639508	0.639508	0.639508
0742	Veterinary Services For Animal Specialties	1	3.45%	0.639508	0.639508	0.639508	0.639508	0.639508	0.639508	0.639508	0.639508	0.639508	0.639508	0.639508
075	ANIMAL SERVICES, EXCEPT VETERINARY	1	-3.63%	-0.672787	-0.672787	-0.672787	-0.672787	-0.672787	-0.672787	-0.672787	-0.672787	-0.672787	-0.672787	-0.672787
0752	Animal Specialty Services, Except Veterinary	1	-3.63%	-0.672787	-0.672787	-0.672787	-0.672787	-0.672787	-0.672787	-0.672787	-0.672787	-0.672787	-0.672787	-0.672787
076	FARM LABOR AND MANAGEMENT SERVICES	1	3.80%	0.704254	0.704254	0.704254	0.704254	0.704254	0.704254	0.704254	0.704254	0.704254	0.704254	0.704254
0762	Farm Management Services	1	3.80%	0.704254	0.704254	0.704254	0.704254	0.704254	0.704254	0.704254	0.704254	0.704254	0.704254	0.704254
078	LANDSCAPE AND HORTICULTURAL SERVICES	1	3.54%	0.654744	0.654744	0.654744	0.654744	0.654744	0.654744	0.654744	0.654744	0.654744	0.654744	0.654744
0782	Lawn And Garden Services	1	3.54%	0.654744	0.654744	0.654744	0.654744	0.654744	0.654744	0.654744	0.654744	0.654744	0.654744	0.654744
08	FORESTRY	1	1.13%	0.209226	0.209226	0.209226	0.209226	0.209226	0.209226	0.209226	0.209226	0.209226	0.209226	0.209226
085	FORESTRY SERVICES	1	1.13%	0.209226	0.209226	0.209226	0.209226	0.209226	0.209226	0.209226	0.209226	0.209226	0.209226	0.209226
0851	Forestry Services	1	1.13%	0.209226	0.209226	0.209226	0.209226	0.209226	0.209226	0.209226	0.209226	0.209226	0.209226	0.209226
09	FISHING, HUNTING, AND TRAPPING	2	1.76%	0.326507	0.326507	-0.883502	-0.846461	-0.784726	0.079566	0.326507	0.573448	1.437740	1.499475	1.536516
	MINING													
10	METAL MINING	218	2.41%	0.446687	0.440422	-1.528382	-0.989698	-0.513455	0.266059	0.440422	0.592359	1.474210	2.058245	2.236753
1000	METAL MINING	5	-1.29%	-0.239090	0.364331	-2.300980	-2.197870	-2.026020	-0.041889	0.364331	0.481564	0.774480	0.789113	0.797893
101	IRON ORES	6	3.72%	0.688897	0.577922	-0.101169	-0.061317	0.005105	0.494621	0.577922	0.661223	1.419880	1.454410	1.475128
1011	Iron Ores	6	3.72%	0.688897	0.577922	-0.101169	-0.061317	0.005105	0.494621	0.577922	0.661223	1.419880	1.454410	1.475128
102	COPPER ORES	20	3.80%	0.703815	0.617534	-0.124753	-0.047625	0.080922	0.566533	0.617534	0.742576	1.444445	1.480777	1.502577
1021	Copper Ores	20	3.80%	0.703815	0.617534	-0.124753	-0.047625	0.080922	0.566533	0.617534	0.742576	1.444445	1.480777	1.502577
103	LEAD AND ZINC ORES	2	5.58%	1.033574	1.033574	0.962018	0.964209	0.967860	1.018971	1.033574	1.048177	1.099288	1.102939	1.105130

Down-market Betas of Common Stocks by SIC Codes as of September 28, 2018

SIC Code	Description	Number of Companies	Equity Risk Premium	Mean	Median	1st Percentile	2.5th Percentile	5th Percentile	40th Percentile	50th Percentile	60th Percentile	95th Percentile	97.5th Percentile	99th Percentile
1031	Lead And Zinc Ores	2	5.58%	1.033574	1.033574	0.962018	0.964209	0.967860	1.018971	1.033574	1.048177	1.099288	1.102939	1.105130
104	GOLD AND SILVER ORES	123	1.63%	0.301965	0.252868	-1.427023	-1.014247	-0.505367	0.130982	0.252868	0.411367	1.378142	1.915233	2.228000
1040	GOLD AND SILVER ORES	3	2.95%	0.547142	0.368769	0.149650	0.156358	0.167537	0.324051	0.368769	0.520511	1.051609	1.089544	1.112306
1041	Gold Ores	110	1.60%	0.296926	0.285368	-1.492784	-1.021629	-0.527839	0.135562	0.285368	0.426187	1.386448	2.000447	2.233785
1044	Silver Ores	10	1.53%	0.283844	0.116998	-0.329760	-0.293188	-0.232233	0.114248	0.116998	0.140331	1.093732	1.135016	1.159786
106	FERROALLOY ORES, EXCEPT VANADIUM	6	4.01%	0.742410	0.999944	-0.133131	-0.083800	-0.001581	0.996848	0.999944	1.003040	1.088385	1.100363	1.107549
1061	Ferroalloy Ores, Except Vanadium	6	4.01%	0.742410	0.999944	-0.133131	-0.083800	-0.001581	0.996848	0.999944	1.003040	1.088385	1.100363	1.107549
108	METAL MINING SERVICES	27	3.42%	0.632823	0.475506	-0.568093	-0.502519	-0.385406	0.235299	0.475506	0.545289	1.933508	3.057515	3.977720
1081	Metal Mining Services	27	3.42%	0.632823	0.475506	-0.568093	-0.502519	-0.385406	0.235299	0.475506	0.545289	1.933508	3.057515	3.977720
109	MISCELLANEOUS METAL ORES	29	3.65%	0.676345	0.745861	-1.273914	-0.964921	-0.548288	0.687471	0.745861	0.813514	1.714196	1.959653	2.076879
1090	MISCELLANEOUS METAL ORES	1	7.56%	1.400120	1.400120	1.400120	1.400120	1.400120	1.400120	1.400120	1.400120	1.400120	1.400120	1.400120
1094	Uranium-Radium-Vanadium Ores	14	4.62%	0.854810	0.833780	-0.226086	-0.183608	-0.112812	0.793971	0.833780	1.002884	1.613119	1.744519	1.823360
1099	Miscellaneous Metal Ores, Not Elsewhere Classified	14	2.41%	0.446181	0.562786	-1.384269	-1.240808	-1.001706	0.390508	0.562786	0.696237	1.646600	1.900815	2.053344
12	COAL MINING	9	4.86%	0.899898	0.886893	0.312852	0.314888	0.318281	0.812515	0.886893	0.933061	1.652822	1.845706	1.961436
122	BITUMINOUS COAL AND LIGNITE MINING	8	5.26%	0.973449	0.915748	0.354973	0.394743	0.461026	0.868299	0.915748	0.958428	1.701043	1.869817	1.971081
1220	BITUMINOUS COAL & LIGNITE MINING	2	5.64%	1.043950	1.043950	1.014334	1.015241	1.016752	1.037906	1.043950	1.049994	1.071148	1.072659	1.073566
1221	Bituminous Coal And Lignite Surface Mining	6	5.13%	0.949948	0.840407	0.347398	0.375805	0.423150	0.793921	0.840407	0.886893	1.765093	1.901842	1.983891
124	COAL MINING SERVICES	1	1.68%	0.311495	0.311495	0.311495	0.311495	0.311495	0.311495	0.311495	0.311495	0.311495	0.311495	0.311495
1241	Coal Mining Services	1	1.68%	0.311495	0.311495	0.311495	0.311495	0.311495	0.311495	0.311495	0.311495	0.311495	0.311495	0.311495
13	OIL AND GAS EXTRACTION	216	4.49%	0.832206	0.896482	-1.043640	-0.396755	-0.219404	0.770314	0.896482	1.030580	1.758790	1.974173	2.518987
131	CRUDE PETROLEUM AND NATURAL GAS	147	4.27%	0.791105	0.841091	-0.583575	-0.283119	-0.212872	0.711733	0.841091	0.959106	1.716481	2.126199	2.434205
1311	Crude Petroleum And Natural Gas	147	4.27%	0.791105	0.841091	-0.583575	-0.283119	-0.212872	0.711733	0.841091	0.959106	1.716481	2.126199	2.434205
132	NATURAL GAS LIQUIDS	4	6.45%	1.194729	1.005619	0.973521	0.973825	0.974332	0.990294	1.005619	1.020944	1.679880	1.737120	1.771464
1321	Natural Gas Liquids	4	6.45%	1.194729	1.005619	0.973521	0.973825	0.974332	0.990294	1.005619	1.020944	1.679880	1.737120	1.771464
138	OIL AND GAS FIELD SERVICES	65	4.88%	0.902849	0.970237	-1.627552	-0.955470	-0.351485	0.896545	0.970237	1.080188	1.784432	1.820146	2.411460
1381	Drilling Oil And Gas Wells	19	5.71%	1.058251	1.155760	-0.949436	-0.764045	-0.455060	1.000610	1.155760	1.181688	1.997374	2.714062	3.144075
1382	Oil And Gas Field Exploration Services	19	3.28%	0.607403	0.792454	-2.300841	-1.832047	-1.050724	0.668269	0.792454	0.926881	1.590614	1.651922	1.688707
1389	Oil And Gas Field Services, Not Elsewhere Classified	27	5.41%	1.001398	0.994145	-0.167663	-0.101398	0.000713	0.951623	0.994145	1.091072	1.734040	1.773704	1.783002
14	MINING AND QUARRYING OF NONMETALLIC MINERALS, EXCEPT FUELS	28	-34.73%	-6.431921	0.501181	-143.071352	-64.492879	-1.157073	0.444000	0.501181	0.862512	1.379116	1.418656	1.457430
1400	MINING & QUARRYING OF NONMETALLIC MINERALS (NO FUELS)	2	3.68%	0.682204	0.682204	0.254074	0.267180	0.289024	0.594830	0.682204	0.769577	1.075383	1.097227	1.110333
141	DIMENSION STONE	2	1.40%	0.260079	0.260079	0.171941	0.174639	0.179136	0.242092	0.260079	0.278066	0.341022	0.345519	0.348217
1411	Dimension Stone	2	1.40%	0.260079	0.260079	0.171941	0.174639	0.179136	0.242092	0.260079	0.278066	0.341022	0.345519	0.348217
142	CRUSHED AND BROKEN STONE, INCLUDING RIPRAP	2	4.74%	0.877579	0.877579	0.855094	0.855782	0.856929	0.872990	0.877579	0.882167	0.898228	0.899375	0.900063
1422	Crushed And Broken Limestone	1	4.86%	0.900522	0.900522	0.900522	0.900522	0.900522	0.900522	0.900522	0.900522	0.900522	0.900522	0.900522
1423	Crushed And Broken Granite	1	4.62%	0.854635	0.854635	0.854635	0.854635	0.854635	0.854635	0.854635	0.854635	0.854635	0.854635	0.854635
144	SAND AND GRAVEL	5	3.63%	0.671619	0.894019	-0.580864	-0.493786	-0.348654	0.861370	0.894019	0.907262	1.276201	1.319836	1.346016
1442	Construction Sand And Gravel	2	6.18%	1.145298	1.145298	0.931489	0.938035	0.948943	1.101664	1.145298	1.188932	1.341653	1.352561	1.359107
1446	Industrial Sand	3	1.92%	0.355833	0.812397	-0.609891	-0.566351	-0.493786	0.522134	0.812397	0.828721	0.885857	0.889938	0.892387
147	CHEMICAL AND FERTILIZER MINERAL MINING	8	-127.50%	-23.611825	0.731256	-181.747348	-161.182869	-126.908738	0.502258	0.731256	1.034531	1.449771	1.466526	1.476578

Down-market Betas of Common Stocks by SIC Codes as of September 28, 2018

SIC Code	Description	Number of Companies	Equity Risk Premium	Mean	Median	1st Percentile	2.5th Percentile	5th Percentile	40th Percentile	50th Percentile	60th Percentile	95th Percentile	97.5th Percentile	99th Percentile
1474	Potash, Soda, And Borate Minerals	5	-208.55%	-38.620745	0.495584	-187.622913	-175.871782	-156.286564	0.455422	0.495584	0.498921	0.867654	0.913120	0.940400
1479	Chemical And Fertilizer Mineral Mining, Not Elsewhere Classified	3	7.58%	1.403043	1.387540	1.339295	1.340772	1.343233	1.377694	1.387540	1.406688	1.473706	1.478493	1.481365
148	NONMETALLIC MINERALS SERVICES, EXCEPT FUELS	2	-0.74%	-0.137277	-0.137277	-0.344896	-0.338540	-0.327947	-0.179648	-0.137277	-0.094906	0.053394	0.063987	0.070342
1481	Nonmetallic Minerals Services, Except Fuels	2	-0.74%	-0.137277	-0.137277	-0.344896	-0.338540	-0.327947	-0.179648	-0.137277	-0.094906	0.053394	0.063987	0.070342
149	MISCELLANEOUS NONMETALLIC MINERALS, EXCEPT FUELS	7	1.60%	0.296792	0.456206	-1.343016	-1.203420	-0.970760	0.259397	0.456206	0.481544	1.165472	1.171151	1.174558
1499	Miscellaneous Nonmetallic Minerals, Except Fuels	7	1.60%	0.296792	0.456206	-1.343016	-1.203420	-0.970760	0.259397	0.456206	0.481544	1.165472	1.171151	1.174558
	CONSTRUCTION													
15	CONSTRUCTION	24	5.51%	1.021115	0.989167	0.374346	0.465505	0.600727	0.887594	0.989167	1.059774	1.538959	1.654350	1.734804
152	GENERAL BUILDING CONTRACTORS-RESIDENTIAL BUILDINGS	2	6.44%	1.191780	1.191780	1.175953	1.176438	1.177245	1.188550	1.191780	1.195010	1.206315	1.207123	1.207607
1521	General Contractors-Single-Family Houses	2	6.44%	1.191780	1.191780	1.175953	1.176438	1.177245	1.188550	1.191780	1.195010	1.206315	1.207123	1.207607
153	OPERATIVE BUILDERS	16	5.23%	0.968826	0.989167	0.353208	0.412659	0.511744	0.847734	0.989167	1.018710	1.473835	1.514538	1.538959
1531	Operative Builders	16	5.23%	0.968826	0.989167	0.353208	0.412659	0.511744	0.847734	0.989167	1.018710	1.473835	1.514538	1.538959
154	GENERAL BUILDING CONTRACTORS-NONRESIDENTIAL BUILDINGS	6	5.96%	1.103663	0.899345	0.879760	0.879760	0.879760	0.879760	0.899345	0.918930	1.660163	1.724301	1.762785
1541	General Contractors-Industrial Buildings And Warehouses	5	6.16%	1.140610	0.879760	0.879760	0.879760	0.879760	0.879760	0.879760	1.037988	1.685818	1.737129	1.767916
1542	General Contractors-Nonresidential Buildings, Other Than Industrial	1	4.96%	0.918930	0.918930	0.918930	0.918930	0.918930	0.918930	0.918930	0.918930	0.918930	0.918930	0.918930
16	HEAVY CONSTRUCTION OTHER THAN BUILDING CONSTRUCTION-CONTRACTORS	20	5.64%	1.044709	1.118260	-0.131717	0.009362	0.244493	0.909547	1.118260	1.202832	1.758921	2.433425	2.838128
161	HIGHWAY AND STREET CONSTRUCTION, EXCEPT ELEVATED HIGHWAYS	3	9.48%	1.756052	1.687920	0.496618	0.533087	0.593867	1.444797	1.687920	1.971922	2.965929	3.036930	3.079530
1611	Highway And Street Construction, Except Elevated Highways	3	9.48%	1.756052	1.687920	0.496618	0.533087	0.593867	1.444797	1.687920	1.971922	2.965929	3.036930	3.079530
162	HEAVY CONSTRUCTION, EXCEPT HIGHWAY AND STREET CONSTRUCTION	17	4.96%	0.919178	1.101420	-0.146567	-0.027764	0.170241	0.894686	1.101420	1.169096	1.468966	1.485218	1.494969
1622	Bridge, Tunnel, And Elevated Highway Construction	1	7.89%	1.460840	1.460840	1.460840	1.460840	1.460840	1.460840	1.460840	1.460840	1.460840	1.460840	1.460840
1623	Water, Sewer, Pipeline, And Communications And Power Line Construction	9	5.01%	0.927857	0.939268	0.302398	0.352128	0.435012	0.879826	0.939268	1.095934	1.245094	1.251202	1.254867
1629	Heavy Construction, Not Elsewhere Classified	7	4.49%	0.830639	1.101420	-0.195845	-0.150959	-0.076149	0.762675	1.101420	1.155624	1.481763	1.491617	1.497529
17	CONSTRUCTION-SPECIAL TRADE CONTRACTORS	9	5.37%	0.994329	0.947518	0.566765	0.595635	0.643752	0.942981	0.947518	0.992984	1.377272	1.438996	1.476030
171	PLUMBING, HEATING AND AIR-CONDITIONING	1	5.12%	0.947518	0.947518	0.947518	0.947518	0.947518	0.947518	0.947518	0.947518	0.947518	0.947518	0.947518
1711	Plumbing, Heating And Air-Conditioning	1	5.12%	0.947518	0.947518	0.947518	0.947518	0.947518	0.947518	0.947518	0.947518	0.947518	0.947518	0.947518
173	ELECTRICAL WORK	5	4.83%	0.894784	0.941847	0.557141	0.571577	0.595635	0.880349	0.941847	0.966848	1.154550	1.173325	1.184590
1731	Electrical Work	5	4.83%	0.894784	0.941847	0.557141	0.571577	0.595635	0.880349	0.941847	0.966848	1.154550	1.173325	1.184590

Down-market Betas of Common Stocks by SIC Codes as of September 28, 2018

SIC Code	Description	Number of Companies	Equity Risk Premium	Mean	Median	1st Percentile	2.5th Percentile	5th Percentile	40th Percentile	50th Percentile	60th Percentile	95th Percentile	97.5th Percentile	99th Percentile
174	MASONRY, STONEWORK, TILE SETTING, AND PLASTERING	2	7.19%	1.330690	1.330690	1.164061	1.169162	1.177663	1.296684	1.330690	1.364696	1.483717	1.492219	1.497319
1742	Plastering, Drywall, Acoustical, And Insulation Work	2	7.19%	1.330690	1.330690	1.164061	1.169162	1.177663	1.296684	1.330690	1.364696	1.483717	1.492219	1.497319
177	CONCRETE WORK	1	4.68%	0.866141	0.866141	0.866141	0.866141	0.866141	0.866141	0.866141	0.866141	0.866141	0.866141	0.866141
1771	Concrete Work	1	4.68%	0.866141	0.866141	0.866141	0.866141	0.866141	0.866141	0.866141	0.866141	0.866141	0.866141	0.866141
	MANUFACTURING													
20	FOOD AND KINDRED PRODUCTS	87	2.99%	0.554400	0.471021	-0.578636	-0.420040	-0.244904	0.441644	0.471021	0.542056	1.494007	1.842681	3.271560
2000	FOOD AND KINDRED PRODUCTS	2	1.39%	0.256579	0.256579	0.012932	0.020390	0.032821	0.206855	0.256579	0.306303	0.480337	0.492768	0.500227
201	MEAT PRODUCTS	7	1.42%	0.263770	0.442210	-0.399890	-0.349889	-0.266556	0.254802	0.442210	0.450971	0.592954	0.614522	0.627463
2011	Meat Packing Plants	2	1.52%	0.282273	0.282273	0.125534	0.130332	0.138329	0.250285	0.282273	0.314260	0.426216	0.434213	0.439011
2013	Sausages And Other Prepared Meat Products	2	-0.82%	-0.151680	-0.151680	-0.427592	-0.419146	-0.405069	-0.207988	-0.151680	-0.095371	0.101710	0.115787	0.124233
2015	Poultry Slaughtering And Processing	3	2.85%	0.528401	0.492302	0.457522	0.458587	0.460361	0.485204	0.492302	0.521060	0.621711	0.628901	0.633214
202	DAIRY PRODUCTS	7	3.91%	0.724746	0.553571	0.226055	0.232212	0.242472	0.527836	0.553571	0.696703	1.564999	1.724544	1.820272
2022	Natural, Processed, And Imitation Cheese	2	4.35%	0.806289	0.806289	0.792407	0.792832	0.793540	0.803456	0.806289	0.809121	0.819037	0.819745	0.820170
2023	Dry, Condensed, And Evaporated Dairy Products	1	2.76%	0.510679	0.510679	0.510679	0.510679	0.510679	0.510679	0.510679	0.510679	0.510679	0.510679	0.510679
2024	Ice Cream And Frozen Desserts	1	1.20%	0.221951	0.221951	0.221951	0.221951	0.221951	0.221951	0.221951	0.221951	0.221951	0.221951	0.221951
2026	Fluid Milk	3	4.91%	0.909339	0.553571	0.295619	0.303516	0.316677	0.500928	0.553571	0.819675	1.751038	1.817564	1.857480
203	CANNED, FROZEN, AND PRESERVED FRUITS, VEGETABLES, AND FOOD SPECIAL	9	6.17%	1.141835	0.538705	0.192799	0.197291	0.204777	0.515018	0.538705	0.687428	3.565908	4.218534	4.610110
2030	CANNED, FROZEN & PRESERVD FRUIT, VEG & FOOD SPECIALTIES	2	14.42%	2.670960	2.670960	0.514764	0.580770	0.690780	2.230920	2.670960	3.111000	4.651140	4.761150	4.827156
2032	Canned Specialties	2	2.47%	0.457207	0.457207	0.195153	0.203175	0.216545	0.403727	0.457207	0.510687	0.697869	0.711239	0.719261
2033	Canned Fruits, Vegetables, Preserves, Jams, And Jellies	3	5.35%	0.990795	1.137120	0.245432	0.272728	0.318223	0.955143	1.137120	1.231302	1.560939	1.584485	1.598612
2034	Dried And Dehydrated Fruits, Vegetables, And Soup Mixes	1	2.75%	0.509096	0.509096	0.509096	0.509096	0.509096	0.509096	0.509096	0.509096	0.509096	0.509096	0.509096
2037	Frozen Fruits, Fruit Juices, And Vegetables	1	2.91%	0.538705	0.538705	0.538705	0.538705	0.538705	0.538705	0.538705	0.538705	0.538705	0.538705	0.538705
204	GRAIN MILL PRODUCTS	7	2.52%	0.466631	0.557092	-0.098437	-0.060390	0.003021	0.403019	0.557092	0.568452	0.898302	0.950331	0.981548
2041	Flour And Other Grain Mill Products	2	2.31%	0.428698	0.428698	0.302871	0.306723	0.313142	0.403019	0.428698	0.454376	0.544253	0.550672	0.554524
2043	Cereal Breakfast Foods	1	1.61%	0.298940	0.298940	0.298940	0.298940	0.298940	0.298940	0.298940	0.298940	0.298940	0.298940	0.298940
2044	Rice Milling	1	-0.67%	-0.123801	-0.123801	-0.123801	-0.123801	-0.123801	-0.123801	-0.123801	-0.123801	-0.123801	-0.123801	-0.123801
2046	Wet Corn Milling	2	3.33%	0.615763	0.615763	0.576820	0.578012	0.579999	0.607815	0.615763	0.623711	0.651527	0.653514	0.654706
2047	Dog And Cat Food	1	5.41%	1.002360	1.002360	1.002360	1.002360	1.002360	1.002360	1.002360	1.002360	1.002360	1.002360	1.002360
205	BAKERY PRODUCTS	5	1.56%	0.288450	0.135559	-0.040366	-0.036176	-0.029191	0.092009	0.135559	0.322403	0.696934	0.708717	0.715787
2051	Bread And Other Bakery Products, Except Cookies And Crackers	2	0.25%	0.046199	0.046199	-0.041373	-0.038692	-0.034224	0.028328	0.046199	0.064071	0.126623	0.131091	0.133772
2052	Cookies And Crackers	3	2.43%	0.449951	0.602669	0.038204	0.055484	0.084283	0.487472	0.602669	0.626235	0.708717	0.714608	0.718143
206	SUGAR AND CONFECTIONERY PRODUCTS	4	2.40%	0.444198	0.494673	0.175899	0.188408	0.209258	0.465200	0.494673	0.524146	0.608472	0.614179	0.617603
2061	Cane Sugar, Except Refining	1	3.35%	0.619886	0.619886	0.619886	0.619886	0.619886	0.619886	0.619886	0.619886	0.619886	0.619886	0.619886
2066	Chocolate And Cocoa Products	2	1.66%	0.306555	0.306555	0.170339	0.174509	0.181459	0.278756	0.306555	0.334354	0.431651	0.438601	0.442771
2068	Salted And Roasted Nuts And Seeds	1	2.94%	0.543795	0.543795	0.543795	0.543795	0.543795	0.543795	0.543795	0.543795	0.543795	0.543795	0.543795
207	FATS AND OILS	2	2.58%	0.477354	0.477354	-0.015495	-0.000408	0.024737	0.376772	0.477354	0.577935	0.929970	0.955116	0.970203
2075	Soybean Oil Mills	1	-0.14%	-0.025554	-0.025554	-0.025554	-0.025554	-0.025554	-0.025554	-0.025554	-0.025554	-0.025554	-0.025554	-0.025554
2077	Animal And Marine Fats And Oils	1	5.29%	0.980261	0.980261	0.980261	0.980261	0.980261	0.980261	0.980261	0.980261	0.980261	0.980261	0.980261

Down-market Betas of Common Stocks by SIC Codes as of September 28, 2018

SIC Code	Description	Number of Companies	Equity Risk Premium	Mean	Median	1st Percentile	2.5th Percentile	5th Percentile	40th Percentile	50th Percentile	60th Percentile	95th Percentile	97.5th Percentile	99th Percentile
208	BEVERAGES	32	2.56%	0.474909	0.536956	-0.784750	-0.610490	-0.426711	0.411199	0.536956	0.715463	1.133881	1.324760	1.490444
2080	BEVERAGES	1	-2.84%	-0.526170	-0.526170	-0.526170	-0.526170	-0.526170	-0.526170	-0.526170	-0.526170	-0.526170	-0.526170	-0.526170
2082	Malt Beverages	5	4.62%	0.854766	0.825070	0.344798	0.358216	0.380580	0.718839	0.825070	0.876048	1.471223	1.536061	1.574965
2084	Wines, Brandy, And Brandy Spirits	5	0.52%	0.097215	0.391154	-0.869319	-0.821911	-0.742899	0.190374	0.391154	0.440460	0.576663	0.584444	0.589112
2085	Distilled And Blended Liquors	5	3.37%	0.623333	0.741995	0.186960	0.189208	0.192954	0.534368	0.741995	0.820242	1.010459	1.019564	1.025028
2086	Bottled And Canned Soft Drinks And Carbonated Waters	14	2.30%	0.425419	0.458121	-0.335646	-0.321111	-0.296886	0.254815	0.458121	0.664494	1.051927	1.148258	1.206057
2087	Flavoring Extracts And Flavoring Syrups, Not Elsewhere Classified	2	5.11%	0.945409	0.945409	0.849475	0.852412	0.857306	0.925830	0.945409	0.964987	1.033511	1.038405	1.041342
209	MISCELLANEOUS FOOD PREPARATIONS AND KINDRED PRODUCTS	12	3.55%	0.657191	0.464897	0.311406	0.328866	0.357964	0.447086	0.464897	0.467760	1.651718	2.331439	2.739272
2095	Roasted Coffee	5	2.48%	0.459661	0.467760	0.434154	0.435896	0.438800	0.465470	0.467760	0.467760	0.467760	0.467760	0.467760
2097	Manufactured Ice	1	2.36%	0.437121	0.437121	0.437121	0.437121	0.437121	0.437121	0.437121	0.437121	0.437121	0.437121	0.437121
2099	Food Preparations, Not Elsewhere Classified	6	4.64%	0.858477	0.447454	0.305058	0.312994	0.326220	0.423886	0.447454	0.471021	2.393232	2.702196	2.887574
21	TOBACCO PRODUCTS	9	2.79%	0.516763	0.507232	-0.752186	-0.639168	-0.450805	0.502156	0.507232	0.642686	1.318798	1.468629	1.558528
2100	TOBACCO PRODUCTS	2	-0.32%	-0.058453	-0.058453	-0.812149	-0.789077	-0.750623	-0.212268	-0.058453	0.095363	0.633718	0.672172	0.695244
211	CIGARETTES	7	3.68%	0.681110	0.507232	0.136289	0.169298	0.224313	0.503425	0.507232	0.608823	1.393714	1.506087	1.573511
2111	Cigarettes	7	3.68%	0.681110	0.507232	0.136289	0.169298	0.224313	0.503425	0.507232	0.608823	1.393714	1.506087	1.573511
22	TEXTILE MILL PRODUCTS	11	3.09%	0.571527	0.807892	-1.600282	-1.283559	-0.755688	0.781744	0.807892	0.828353	1.220965	1.311798	1.366297
221	BROADWOVEN FABRIC MILLS, COTTON	2	4.29%	0.794818	0.794818	0.782005	0.782398	0.783051	0.792203	0.794818	0.797433	0.806585	0.807238	0.807631
2211	Broadwoven Fabric Mills, Cotton	2	4.29%	0.794818	0.794818	0.782005	0.782398	0.783051	0.792203	0.794818	0.797433	0.806585	0.807238	0.807631
222	BROADWOVEN FABRIC MILLS, MANMADE FIBER AND SILK	2	-2.08%	-0.386065	-0.386065	-1.782923	-1.740162	-1.668894	-0.671138	-0.386065	-0.100992	0.896764	0.968032	1.010793
2221	Broadwoven Fabric Mills, Manmade Fiber And Silk	2	-2.08%	-0.386065	-0.386065	-1.782923	-1.740162	-1.668894	-0.671138	-0.386065	-0.100992	0.896764	0.968032	1.010793
225	KNITTING MILLS	3	5.33%	0.986278	0.866201	0.693526	0.698812	0.707622	0.830961	0.866201	0.973487	1.348987	1.375809	1.391901
2252	Hosiery, Not Elsewhere Classified	1	4.68%	0.866201	0.866201	0.866201	0.866201	0.866201	0.866201	0.866201	0.866201	0.866201	0.866201	0.866201
2253	Knit Outerwear Mills	2	5.65%	1.046316	1.046316	0.697128	0.707818	0.725633	0.975053	1.046316	1.117579	1.366999	1.384814	1.395504
227	CARPETS AND RUGS	3	3.57%	0.660980	0.828353	0.310621	0.326470	0.352885	0.722693	0.828353	0.833589	0.851913	0.853222	0.854007
2273	Carpets And Rugs	3	3.57%	0.660980	0.828353	0.310621	0.326470	0.352885	0.722693	0.828353	0.833589	0.851913	0.853222	0.854007
228	YARN AND THREAD MILLS	1	2.85%	0.527521	0.527521	0.527521	0.527521	0.527521	0.527521	0.527521	0.527521	0.527521	0.527521	0.527521
2282	Yarn Texturizing, Throwing, Twisting, And Winding Mills	1	2.85%	0.527521	0.527521	0.527521	0.527521	0.527521	0.527521	0.527521	0.527521	0.527521	0.527521	0.527521
23	APPAREL AND OTHER FINISHED PRODUCTS MADE FROM FABRICS AND SIMILAR MATERIAL	19	2.65%	0.490345	0.727925	-2.251847	-1.793592	-1.029833	0.622465	0.727925	0.812885	1.278428	1.607369	1.804734
2300	APPAREL & OTHER FINISHD PRODS OF FABRICS & SIMILAR MATL	2	7.51%	1.391066	1.391066	0.856727	0.873084	0.900346	1.282017	1.391066	1.500115	1.881786	1.909048	1.925405
232	MEN'S AND BOYS' FURNISHINGS, WORK CLOTHING, AND ALLIED GARMENTS	6	4.68%	0.867533	0.829033	0.577096	0.584615	0.597146	0.727925	0.829033	0.930140	1.178345	1.191838	1.199933
2321	Men's And Boys' Shirts, Except Work Shirts	2	3.51%	0.650005	0.650005	0.573642	0.575980	0.579876	0.634420	0.650005	0.665589	0.720133	0.724029	0.726367
2325	Men's And Boys' Separate Trousers And Slacks	1	3.63%	0.672331	0.672331	0.672331	0.672331	0.672331	0.672331	0.672331	0.672331	0.672331	0.672331	0.672331
2326	Men's And Boys' Work Clothing	1	5.02%	0.930140	0.930140	0.930140	0.930140	0.930140	0.930140	0.930140	0.930140	0.930140	0.930140	0.930140
2329	Men's And Boys' Clothing, Not Elsewhere Classified	2	6.22%	1.151360	1.151360	1.098469	1.100089	1.102787	1.140566	1.151360	1.162154	1.199933	1.202632	1.204251
233	WOMEN'S, MISSES', AND JUNIORS' OUTERWEAR	8	-0.72%	-0.133409	0.204349	-2.438543	-2.260333	-1.963316	-0.189036	0.204349	0.584688	0.817155	0.838324	0.851026

Down-market Betas of Common Stocks by SIC Codes as of September 28, 2018

SIC Code	Description	Number of Companies	Equity Risk Premium	Mean	Median	1st Percentile	2.5th Percentile	5th Percentile	40th Percentile	50th Percentile	60th Percentile	95th Percentile	97.5th Percentile	99th Percentile
2330	WOMEN'S, MISSES', AND JUNIORS OUTERWEAR	1	-1.44%	-0.266530	-0.266530	-0.266530	-0.266530	-0.266530	-0.266530	-0.266530	-0.266530	-0.266530	-0.266530	-0.266530
2337	Women's, Misses', And Juniors' Suits, Skirts, And Coats	1	4.64%	0.859494	0.859494	0.859494	0.859494	0.859494	0.859494	0.859494	0.859494	0.859494	0.859494	0.859494
2339	Women's, Misses', And Juniors' Outerwear, Not Elsewhere Classified	6	-1.49%	-0.276706	0.204349	-2.472488	-2.345195	-2.133040	-0.169662	0.204349	0.578360	0.706393	0.722458	0.732098
234	WOMEN'S, MISSES', CHILDREN'S, AND INFANTS' UNDERGARMENTS	1	4.49%	0.831475	0.831475	0.831475	0.831475	0.831475	0.831475	0.831475	0.831475	0.831475	0.831475	0.831475
2341	Women's, Misses', Children's, And Infants' Underwear And Nightwear	1	4.49%	0.831475	0.831475	0.831475	0.831475	0.831475	0.831475	0.831475	0.831475	0.831475	0.831475	0.831475
238	MISCELLANEOUS APPAREL AND ACCESSORIES	2	4.23%	0.782510	0.782510	0.478278	0.487591	0.503113	0.720421	0.782510	0.844598	1.061906	1.077428	1.086741
2385	Waterproof Outerwear	1	5.90%	1.092950	1.092950	1.092950	1.092950	1.092950	1.092950	1.092950	1.092950	1.092950	1.092950	1.092950
2389	Apparel And Accessories, Not Elsewhere Classified	1	2.55%	0.472069	0.472069	0.472069	0.472069	0.472069	0.472069	0.472069	0.472069	0.472069	0.472069	0.472069
24	LUMBER AND WOOD PRODUCTS, EXCEPT FURNITURE	12	4.71%	0.872264	0.887024	0.366461	0.371568	0.380080	0.856369	0.887024	0.969160	1.415781	1.452241	1.474116
2400	LUMBER & WOOD PRODUCTS (NO FURNITURE)	1	2.56%	0.474560	0.474560	0.474560	0.474560	0.474560	0.474560	0.474560	0.474560	0.474560	0.474560	0.474560
241	LOGGING	1	1.96%	0.363056	0.363056	0.363056	0.363056	0.363056	0.363056	0.363056	0.363056	0.363056	0.363056	0.363056
2411	Logging	1	1.96%	0.363056	0.363056	0.363056	0.363056	0.363056	0.363056	0.363056	0.363056	0.363056	0.363056	0.363056
242	SAWMILLS AND PLANING MILLS	2	3.42%	0.633514	0.633514	0.398798	0.405983	0.417959	0.585612	0.633514	0.681415	0.849068	0.861044	0.868229
2421	Sawmills And Planing Mills, General	2	3.42%	0.633514	0.633514	0.398798	0.405983	0.417959	0.585612	0.633514	0.681415	0.849068	0.861044	0.868229
243	MILLWORK, VENEER, PLYWOOD, AND STRUCTURAL WOOD MEMBERS	3	5.45%	1.010130	1.088470	0.850133	0.857429	0.869589	1.039830	1.088470	1.090106	1.095832	1.096241	1.096486
2430	MILLWOOD, VENEER, PLYWOOD, & STRUCTURAL WOOD MEMBERS	1	4.56%	0.845269	0.845269	0.845269	0.845269	0.845269	0.845269	0.845269	0.845269	0.845269	0.845269	0.845269
2434	Wood Kitchen Cabinets	1	5.92%	1.096650	1.096650	1.096650	1.096650	1.096650	1.096650	1.096650	1.096650	1.096650	1.096650	1.096650
2439	Structural Wood Members, Not Elsewhere Classified	1	5.88%	1.088470	1.088470	1.088470	1.088470	1.088470	1.088470	1.088470	1.088470	1.088470	1.088470	1.088470
245	WOOD BUILDINGS AND MOBILE HOMES	2	7.68%	1.422410	1.422410	1.357446	1.359435	1.362749	1.409152	1.422410	1.435668	1.482071	1.485386	1.487374
2451	Mobile Homes	2	7.68%	1.422410	1.422410	1.357446	1.359435	1.362749	1.409152	1.422410	1.435668	1.482071	1.485386	1.487374
249	MISCELLANEOUS WOOD PRODUCTS	3	4.48%	0.829106	0.901029	0.578294	0.588174	0.604640	0.835165	0.901029	0.923739	1.003225	1.008902	1.012309
2491	Wood Preserving	1	3.09%	0.571708	0.571708	0.571708	0.571708	0.571708	0.571708	0.571708	0.571708	0.571708	0.571708	0.571708
2493	Reconstituted Wood Products	1	4.87%	0.901029	0.901029	0.901029	0.901029	0.901029	0.901029	0.901029	0.901029	0.901029	0.901029	0.901029
2499	Wood Products, Not Elsewhere Classified	1	5.48%	1.014580	1.014580	1.014580	1.014580	1.014580	1.014580	1.014580	1.014580	1.014580	1.014580	1.014580
25	FURNITURE AND FIXTURES	20	4.88%	0.903108	0.904158	0.233106	0.256983	0.296776	0.859634	0.904158	0.945322	1.489306	1.606973	1.677573
251	HOUSEHOLD FURNITURE	12	3.88%	0.718436	0.836894	0.226404	0.240227	0.263266	0.708601	0.836894	0.859634	1.000497	1.003274	1.004939
2511	Wood Household Furniture, Except Upholstered	7	3.18%	0.588694	0.576657	0.222216	0.229755	0.242322	0.553045	0.576657	0.612385	0.954145	0.975049	0.987592
2512	Wood Household Furniture, Upholstered	1	4.88%	0.903889	0.903889	0.903889	0.903889	0.903889	0.903889	0.903889	0.903889	0.903889	0.903889	0.903889
2515	Mattresses, Foundations, And Convertible Beds	3	4.92%	0.911605	0.911567	0.819086	0.821917	0.826636	0.892693	0.911567	0.930464	0.996602	1.001326	1.004160
2519	Household Furniture, Not Elsewhere Classified	1	4.65%	0.861664	0.861664	0.861664	0.861664	0.861664	0.861664	0.861664	0.861664	0.861664	0.861664	0.861664
252	OFFICE FURNITURE	7	6.37%	1.179469	1.257220	0.441042	0.485408	0.559353	1.233376	1.257220	1.261366	1.650324	1.687482	1.709777

Down-market Betas of Common Stocks by SIC Codes as of September 28, 2018

SIC Code	Description	Number of Companies	Equity Risk Premium	Mean	Median	1st Percentile	2.5th Percentile	5th Percentile	40th Percentile	50th Percentile	60th Percentile	95th Percentile	97.5th Percentile	99th Percentile
2521	Wood Office Furniture	3	5.03%	0.930937	0.904427	0.421323	0.436112	0.460760	0.805834	0.904427	1.018926	1.419671	1.448295	1.465470
2522	Office Furniture, Except Wood	4	7.38%	1.365868	1.260675	1.218672	1.220461	1.223441	1.258602	1.260675	1.262748	1.655564	1.690102	1.710825
253	PUBLIC BUILDING AND RELATED FURNITURE	1	6.40%	1.184640	1.184640	1.184640	1.184640	1.184640	1.184640	1.184640	1.184640	1.184640	1.184640	1.184640
2531	Public Building And Related Furniture	1	6.40%	1.184640	1.184640	1.184640	1.184640	1.184640	1.184640	1.184640	1.184640	1.184640	1.184640	1.184640
26	PAPER AND ALLIED PRODUCTS	27	4.46%	0.825464	0.817687	-0.069869	-0.035813	0.130006	0.786788	0.817687	0.937850	1.356055	1.474589	1.580243
261	PULP MILLS	2	4.12%	0.762061	0.762061	0.451931	0.461425	0.477248	0.698769	0.762061	0.825353	1.046874	1.062697	1.072191
2611	Pulp Mills	2	4.12%	0.762061	0.762061	0.451931	0.461425	0.477248	0.698769	0.762061	0.825353	1.046874	1.062697	1.072191
262	PAPER MILLS	10	5.03%	0.931458	0.987095	0.057018	0.150419	0.306087	0.898112	0.987095	1.001530	1.528771	1.589725	1.626298
2621	Paper Mills	10	5.03%	0.931458	0.987095	0.057018	0.150419	0.306087	0.898112	0.987095	1.001530	1.528771	1.589725	1.626298
263	PAPERBOARD MILLS	4	4.46%	0.826652	0.766469	0.680672	0.682714	0.686118	0.741401	0.766469	0.791536	1.051443	1.072902	1.085777
2631	Paperboard Mills	4	4.46%	0.826652	0.766469	0.680672	0.682714	0.686118	0.741401	0.766469	0.791536	1.051443	1.072902	1.085777
265	PAPERBOARD CONTAINERS AND BOXES	2	5.34%	0.988683	0.988683	0.874163	0.877669	0.883512	0.965312	0.988683	1.012054	1.093854	1.099697	1.103203
2655	Fiber Cans, Tubes, Drums, And Similar Products	2	5.34%	0.988683	0.988683	0.874163	0.877669	0.883512	0.965312	0.988683	1.012054	1.093854	1.099697	1.103203
267	CONVERTED PAPER AND PAPERBOARD PRODUCTS, EXCEPT CONTAINERS AND BOXES	9	3.70%	0.684983	0.817687	-0.048477	0.017667	0.127907	0.587120	0.817687	0.817687	1.176803	1.238761	1.275937
2671	Packaging Paper And Plastics Film, Coated And Laminated	5	3.72%	0.688233	0.817687	0.461459	0.465710	0.472796	0.702403	0.817687	0.817687	0.817687	0.817687	0.817687
2673	Plastics, Foil, And Coated Paper Bags	2	3.26%	0.604074	0.604074	-0.078640	-0.057740	-0.022908	0.464745	0.604074	0.743403	1.231055	1.265888	1.286787
2679	Converted Paper And Paperboard Products, Not Elsewhere Classified	2	4.09%	0.757767	0.757767	0.529269	0.536264	0.547922	0.711134	0.757767	0.804399	0.967611	0.979269	0.986264
27	PRINTING, PUBLISHING, AND ALLIED INDUSTRIES	40	3.58%	0.662529	0.650651	-0.057598	-0.031431	0.008202	0.559607	0.650651	0.717357	1.517564	1.657702	1.747371
271	NEWSPAPERS: PUBLISHING, OR PUBLISHING AND PRINTING	18	3.10%	0.574818	0.653342	-0.060546	-0.038802	-0.002562	0.555852	0.653342	0.706074	1.116039	1.206389	1.260600
2711	Newspapers: Publishing, Or Publishing And Printing	18	3.10%	0.574818	0.653342	-0.060546	-0.038802	-0.002562	0.555852	0.653342	0.706074	1.116039	1.206389	1.260600
272	PERIODICALS: PUBLISHING, OR PUBLISHING AND PRINTING	2	2.72%	0.504530	0.504530	0.352803	0.357448	0.365189	0.473565	0.504530	0.535494	0.643870	0.651611	0.656256
2721	Periodicals: Publishing, Or Publishing And Printing	2	2.72%	0.504530	0.504530	0.352803	0.357448	0.365189	0.473565	0.504530	0.535494	0.643870	0.651611	0.656256
273	BOOKS	4	3.72%	0.688228	0.594931	0.294565	0.307663	0.329495	0.584122	0.594931	0.605739	1.177579	1.227399	1.257292
2731	Books: Publishing, Or Publishing And Printing	4	3.72%	0.688228	0.594931	0.294565	0.307663	0.329495	0.584122	0.594931	0.605739	1.177579	1.227399	1.257292
274	MISCELLANEOUS PUBLISHING	5	3.98%	0.737711	0.557340	-0.009373	0.022037	0.074387	0.531678	0.557340	0.740192	1.525990	1.589930	1.628294
2741	Miscellaneous Publishing	5	3.98%	0.737711	0.557340	-0.009373	0.022037	0.074387	0.531678	0.557340	0.740192	1.525990	1.589930	1.628294
275	COMMERCIAL PRINTING	8	4.63%	0.857930	0.802543	0.183894	0.195732	0.215464	0.600475	0.802543	0.978806	1.703284	1.755217	1.786377
2750	COMMERCIAL PRINTING	1	8.16%	1.510390	1.510390	1.510390	1.510390	1.510390	1.510390	1.510390	1.510390	1.510390	1.510390	1.510390
2752	Commercial Printing, Lithographic	2	3.99%	0.738029	0.738029	0.303408	0.316713	0.338887	0.649331	0.738029	0.826727	1.137171	1.159345	1.172650
2754	Commercial Printing, Gravure	3	5.44%	1.008009	0.928127	0.301539	0.320720	0.352689	0.800252	0.928127	1.103932	1.719248	1.763199	1.789570
2759	Commercial Printing, Not Elsewhere Classified	2	2.30%	0.426480	0.426480	0.181011	0.188525	0.201049	0.376384	0.426480	0.476576	0.651911	0.664435	0.671949
276	MANIFOLD BUSINESS FORMS	1	1.30%	0.240957	0.240957	0.240957	0.240957	0.240957	0.240957	0.240957	0.240957	0.240957	0.240957	0.240957
2761	Manifold Business Forms	1	1.30%	0.240957	0.240957	0.240957	0.240957	0.240957	0.240957	0.240957	0.240957	0.240957	0.240957	0.240957
277	GREETING CARDS	1	4.57%	0.846076	0.846076	0.846076	0.846076	0.846076	0.846076	0.846076	0.846076	0.846076	0.846076	0.846076
2771	Greeting Cards	1	4.57%	0.846076	0.846076	0.846076	0.846076	0.846076	0.846076	0.846076	0.846076	0.846076	0.846076	0.846076

Down-market Betas of Common Stocks by SIC Codes as of September 28, 2018

SIC Code	Description	Number of Companies	Equity Risk Premium	Mean	Median	1st Percentile	2.5th Percentile	5th Percentile	40th Percentile	50th Percentile	60th Percentile	95th Percentile	97.5th Percentile	99th Percentile
278	BLANKBOOKS, LOOSELEAF BINDERS, AND BOOKBINDING AND RELATED WORK	1	4.07%	0.753429	0.753429	0.753429	0.753429	0.753429	0.753429	0.753429	0.753429	0.753429	0.753429	0.753429
2782	Blankbooks, Looseleaf Binders And Devices	1	4.07%	0.753429	0.753429	0.753429	0.753429	0.753429	0.753429	0.753429	0.753429	0.753429	0.753429	0.753429
28	CHEMICALS AND ALLIED PRODUCTS	503	4.28%	0.792106	0.865887	-1.291555	-0.524447	-0.186759	0.718157	0.865887	0.999692	1.930935	2.175948	2.675704
2800	CHEMICALS & ALLIED PRODUCTS	1	5.91%	1.094420	1.094420	1.094420	1.094420	1.094420	1.094420	1.094420	1.094420	1.094420	1.094420	1.094420
281	INDUSTRIAL INORGANIC CHEMICALS	15	4.31%	0.797344	0.981608	-2.153078	-1.617560	-0.725030	0.899512	0.981608	1.030306	1.712436	1.886078	1.990263
2810	INDUSTRIAL INORGANIC CHEMICALS	1	3.78%	0.700419	0.700419	0.700419	0.700419	0.700419	0.700419	0.700419	0.700419	0.700419	0.700419	0.700419
2812	Alkalies And Chlorine	1	5.63%	1.042660	1.042660	1.042660	1.042660	1.042660	1.042660	1.042660	1.042660	1.042660	1.042660	1.042660
2813	Industrial Gases	2	5.10%	0.944432	0.944432	0.907999	0.909114	0.910973	0.936996	0.944432	0.951867	0.977890	0.979749	0.980864
2816	Inorganic Pigments	4	7.40%	1.369752	1.292835	0.839272	0.847752	0.861886	1.130376	1.292835	1.455294	1.985302	2.022511	2.044836
2819	Industrial Inorganic Chemicals, Not Elsewhere Classified	7	2.20%	0.407031	0.887898	-2.357085	-2.127577	-1.745064	0.877952	0.887898	1.041337	1.230734	1.247612	1.257739
282	PLASTICS MATERIALS AND SYNTHETIC RESINS, SYNTHETIC RUBBER, CELLULOSIC MANMADE FIBERS	14	4.71%	0.871904	0.957468	-0.573300	-0.366056	-0.020650	0.872177	0.957468	1.058820	1.454638	1.589724	1.670776
2821	Plastics Materials, Synthetic Resins, And Nonvulcanizable Elastomers	14	4.71%	0.871904	0.957468	-0.573300	-0.366056	-0.020650	0.872177	0.957468	1.058820	1.454638	1.589724	1.670776
283	DRUGS	403	4.36%	0.807717	0.871920	-1.141550	-0.483131	-0.188520	0.723641	0.871920	1.029948	2.004248	2.251657	2.853334
2833	Medicinal Chemicals And Botanical Products	12	4.16%	0.769899	0.678190	0.224678	0.252526	0.298940	0.631826	0.678190	0.798562	1.420553	1.423177	1.424751
2834	Pharmaceutical Preparations	308	4.26%	0.788124	0.878039	-1.471471	-0.596079	-0.188115	0.724463	0.878039	1.041542	2.026091	2.371257	2.844319
2835	In Vitro And In Vivo Diagnostic Substances	22	3.95%	0.730670	0.726074	-0.127891	-0.099065	-0.052762	0.698034	0.726074	0.791573	1.440151	1.485164	1.511640
2836	Biological Products, Except Diagnostic Substances	61	5.09%	0.941872	0.958939	-0.515646	-0.426273	-0.283805	0.832171	0.958939	1.048700	1.785810	2.149440	4.144334
284	SOAP, DETERGENTS, AND CLEANING PREPARATIONS; PERFUMES, COSMETICS	20	2.80%	0.517714	0.517794	-0.098824	-0.025983	0.095419	0.453760	0.517794	0.599952	1.017872	1.080211	1.117614
2841	Soap And Other Detergents, Except Specialty Cleaners	5	3.30%	0.610285	0.584890	0.249900	0.255372	0.264494	0.485920	0.584890	0.699538	0.983350	0.997330	1.005718
2842	Specialty Cleaning, Polishing, And Sanitation Preparations	4	3.48%	0.643682	0.657539	0.566169	0.568784	0.573143	0.636542	0.657539	0.678536	0.694821	0.695023	0.695144
2844	Perfumes, Cosmetics, And Other Toilet Preparations	11	2.32%	0.429830	0.437183	-0.121827	-0.083489	-0.019594	0.396154	0.437183	0.464812	0.935045	1.038797	1.101049
285	PAINTS, VARNISHES, LACQUERS, ENAMELS, AND ALLIED PRODUCTS	4	4.45%	0.823526	0.823860	0.767718	0.768103	0.768745	0.795156	0.823860	0.852563	0.877839	0.878380	0.878705
2851	Paints, Varnishes, Lacquers, Enamels, And Allied Products	4	4.45%	0.823526	0.823860	0.767718	0.768103	0.768745	0.795156	0.823860	0.852563	0.877839	0.878380	0.878705
286	INDUSTRIAL ORGANIC CHEMICALS	21	3.74%	0.693314	0.812454	-0.265833	-0.212478	-0.123552	0.680347	0.812454	0.916316	1.149930	1.459700	1.645562
2860	INDUSTRIAL ORGANIC CHEMICALS	1	0.08%	0.014834	0.014834	0.014834	0.014834	0.014834	0.014834	0.014834	0.014834	0.014834	0.014834	0.014834
2861	Gum And Wood Chemicals	2	2.39%	0.442314	0.442314	-0.112235	-0.095259	-0.066965	0.329141	0.442314	0.555487	0.951593	0.979887	0.996863
2865	Cyclic Organic Crudes And Intermediates, And Organic Dyes And Pigments	1	3.67%	0.680347	0.680347	0.680347	0.680347	0.680347	0.680347	0.680347	0.680347	0.680347	0.680347	0.680347
2869	Industrial Organic Chemicals, Not Elsewhere Classified	17	4.12%	0.763517	0.817652	-0.222727	-0.104713	0.091977	0.748912	0.817652	0.966174	1.273838	1.521654	1.670344
287	AGRICULTURAL CHEMICALS	13	4.29%	0.794730	0.783942	-1.098449	-0.804207	-0.313803	0.752489	0.783942	1.076388	1.416790	1.457845	1.482478
2870	AGRICULTURAL CHEMICALS	3	4.42%	0.819085	0.755137	0.348369	0.360821	0.381575	0.672123	0.755137	0.876520	1.301359	1.331704	1.349912

Down-market Betas of Common Stocks by SIC Codes as of September 28, 2018

SIC Code	Description	Number of Companies	Equity Risk Premium	Mean	Median	1st Percentile	2.5th Percentile	5th Percentile	40th Percentile	50th Percentile	60th Percentile	95th Percentile	97.5th Percentile	99th Percentile
2873	Nitrogenous Fertilizers	5	3.17%	0.586366	0.783942	-1.213150	-1.090959	-0.887308	0.767125	0.783942	0.951045	1.439460	1.469180	1.487012
2874	Phosphatic Fertilizers	2	4.61%	0.854130	0.854130	0.667019	0.672747	0.682293	0.815944	0.854130	0.892316	1.025967	1.035514	1.041241
2879	Pesticides And Agricultural Chemicals, Not Elsewhere Classified	3	5.82%	1.078049	1.230600	0.682071	0.698863	0.726849	1.118655	1.230600	1.251014	1.322463	1.327567	1.330629
289	MISCELLANEOUS CHEMICAL PRODUCTS	12	4.10%	0.759914	0.868531	-0.080842	0.003623	0.144396	0.717833	0.868531	0.886573	1.313733	1.332362	1.343539
2890	MISCELLANEOUS CHEMICAL PRODUCTS	2	5.88%	1.089558	1.089558	0.899739	0.905550	0.915234	1.050819	1.089558	1.128296	1.263881	1.273565	1.279376
2891	Adhesives And Sealants	1	4.67%	0.864427	0.864427	0.864427	0.864427	0.864427	0.864427	0.864427	0.864427	0.864427	0.864427	0.864427
2893	Printing Ink	1	6.18%	1.144670	1.144670	1.144670	1.144670	1.144670	1.144670	1.144670	1.144670	1.144670	1.144670	1.144670
2895	Carbon Black	1	7.30%	1.350990	1.350990	1.350990	1.350990	1.350990	1.350990	1.350990	1.350990	1.350990	1.350990	1.350990
2899	Chemicals And Chemical Preparations, Not Elsewhere Classified	7	2.76%	0.511395	0.498932	-0.106437	-0.060365	0.016420	0.456401	0.498932	0.571635	0.907502	0.914974	0.919456
29	PETROLEUM REFINING AND RELATED INDUSTRIES	20	4.53%	0.838448	0.908859	0.091933	0.129512	0.192145	0.840862	0.908859	0.930944	1.215906	1.251868	1.273445
291	PETROLEUM REFINING	17	4.78%	0.884605	0.923599	0.252203	0.332400	0.466062	0.873368	0.923599	0.931193	1.227262	1.257546	1.275716
2911	Petroleum Refining	17	4.78%	0.884605	0.923599	0.252203	0.332400	0.466062	0.873368	0.923599	0.931193	1.227262	1.257546	1.275716
295	ASPHALT PAVING AND ROOFING MATERIALS	1	5.10%	0.944715	0.944715	0.944715	0.944715	0.944715	0.944715	0.944715	0.944715	0.944715	0.944715	0.944715
2951	Asphalt Paving Mixtures And Blocks	1	5.10%	0.944715	0.944715	0.944715	0.944715	0.944715	0.944715	0.944715	0.944715	0.944715	0.944715	0.944715
299	MISCELLANEOUS PRODUCTS OF PETROLEUM AND COAL	2	2.12%	0.392979	0.392979	0.073402	0.083185	0.099490	0.327759	0.392979	0.458199	0.686469	0.702774	0.712557
2990	MISCELLANEOUS PRODUCTS OF PETROLEUM & COAL	1	3.88%	0.719079	0.719079	0.719079	0.719079	0.719079	0.719079	0.719079	0.719079	0.719079	0.719079	0.719079
2999	Products Of Petroleum And Coal, Not Elsewhere Classified	1	0.36%	0.066880	0.066880	0.066880	0.066880	0.066880	0.066880	0.066880	0.066880	0.066880	0.066880	0.066880
30	RUBBER AND MISCELLANEOUS PLASTICS PRODUCTS	39	3.49%	0.645404	0.720377	-1.221632	-0.120696	0.066932	0.614397	0.720377	0.863688	1.328245	1.434944	1.457555
301	TIRES AND INNER TUBES	2	5.90%	1.091935	1.091935	1.041039	1.042597	1.045194	1.081548	1.091935	1.102322	1.138677	1.141273	1.142831
3011	Tires And Inner Tubes	2	5.90%	1.091935	1.091935	1.041039	1.042597	1.045194	1.081548	1.091935	1.102322	1.138677	1.141273	1.142831
302	RUBBER AND PLASTICS FOOTWEAR	5	4.67%	0.865442	0.898633	0.506408	0.530922	0.571779	0.898633	0.898633	0.934724	1.038588	1.044804	1.048534
3021	Rubber And Plastics Footwear	5	4.67%	0.865442	0.898633	0.506408	0.530922	0.571779	0.898633	0.898633	0.934724	1.038588	1.044804	1.048534
305	GASKETS, PACKING, AND SEALING DEVICES AND RUBBER AND PLASTICS HOSE	3	-1.81%	-0.335305	0.077049	-1.914937	-1.853958	-1.752326	-0.329479	0.077049	0.236165	0.793069	0.832848	0.856715
3052	Rubber And Plastics Hose And Belting	1	-10.56%	-1.955590	-1.955590	-1.955590	-1.955590	-1.955590	-1.955590	-1.955590	-1.955590	-1.955590	-1.955590	-1.955590
3053	Gaskets, Packing, And Sealing Devices	2	2.56%	0.474838	0.474838	0.085005	0.096939	0.116828	0.395280	0.474838	0.554396	0.832848	0.852738	0.864671
306	FABRICATED RUBBER PRODUCTS, NOT ELSEWHERE CLASSIFIED	3	2.58%	0.478484	0.440225	0.172756	0.180943	0.194590	0.385639	0.440225	0.517766	0.789160	0.808546	0.820177
3069	Fabricated Rubber Products, Not Elsewhere Classified	3	2.58%	0.478484	0.440225	0.172756	0.180943	0.194590	0.385639	0.440225	0.517766	0.789160	0.808546	0.820177
308	MISCELLANEOUS PLASTICS PRODUCTS	26	3.79%	0.701158	0.637436	0.017010	0.078710	0.146969	0.614397	0.637436	0.810518	1.403873	1.447836	1.462713
3081	Unsupported Plastics Film And Sheet	3	3.75%	0.694327	0.810518	0.247287	0.264528	0.293265	0.695573	0.810518	0.855748	1.014055	1.025362	1.032147
3084	Plastics Pipe	1	1.95%	0.360584	0.360584	0.360584	0.360584	0.360584	0.360584	0.360584	0.360584	0.360584	0.360584	0.360584
3086	Plastics Foam Products	3	4.06%	0.752685	0.497049	0.331427	0.336497	0.344947	0.463249	0.497049	0.684231	1.339369	1.386164	1.414242
3089	Plastics Products, Not Elsewhere Classified	19	3.84%	0.712026	0.660474	0.005493	0.049917	0.123956	0.614397	0.660474	0.802842	1.332212	1.402421	1.444546
31	LEATHER AND LEATHER PRODUCTS	7	3.84%	0.710316	0.730630	0.032726	0.076753	0.150131	0.723749	0.730630	0.773286	1.176731	1.224995	1.253954

Down-market Betas of Common Stocks by SIC Codes as of September 28, 2018

SIC Code	Description	Number of Companies	Equity Risk Premium	Mean	Median	1st Percentile	2.5th Percentile	5th Percentile	40th Percentile	50th Percentile	60th Percentile	95th Percentile	97.5th Percentile	99th Percentile
314	FOOTWEAR, EXCEPT RUBBER	4	4.64%	0.859120	0.835329	0.499361	0.509558	0.526553	0.765629	0.835329	0.905029	1.224995	1.249128	1.263607
3142	House Slippers	1	5.14%	0.951496	0.951496	0.951496	0.951496	0.951496	0.951496	0.951496	0.951496	0.951496	0.951496	0.951496
3143	Men's Footwear, Except Athletic	1	6.88%	1.273260	1.273260	1.273260	1.273260	1.273260	1.273260	1.273260	1.273260	1.273260	1.273260	1.273260
3149	Footwear, Except Rubber, Not Elsewhere Classified	2	3.27%	0.605863	0.605863	0.494829	0.498228	0.503893	0.583203	0.605863	0.628522	0.707832	0.713497	0.716896
317	HANDBAGS AND OTHER PERSONAL LEATHER GOODS	1	3.95%	0.730630	0.730630	0.730630	0.730630	0.730630	0.730630	0.730630	0.730630	0.730630	0.730630	0.730630
3171	Women's Handbags And Purses	1	3.95%	0.730630	0.730630	0.730630	0.730630	0.730630	0.730630	0.730630	0.730630	0.730630	0.730630	0.730630
319	LEATHER GOODS, NOT ELSEWHERE CLASSIFIED	2	2.17%	0.402550	0.402550	0.011359	0.023334	0.043293	0.322715	0.402550	0.482384	0.761807	0.781765	0.793741
3199	Leather Goods, Not Elsewhere Classified	2	2.17%	0.402550	0.402550	0.011359	0.023334	0.043293	0.322715	0.402550	0.482384	0.761807	0.781765	0.793741
32	STONE, CLAY, GLASS, AND CONCRETE PRODUCTS	14	4.99%	0.923244	0.872828	0.197844	0.218675	0.253395	0.816588	0.872828	0.912442	1.754869	1.912464	2.007022
322	GLASS AND GLASSWARE, PRESSED OR BLOWN	3	5.68%	1.051244	1.244600	0.587100	0.607228	0.640774	1.110416	1.244600	1.262770	1.326365	1.330908	1.333633
3221	Glass Containers	2	4.91%	0.909141	0.909141	0.580391	0.590455	0.607228	0.842049	0.909141	0.976233	1.211054	1.227827	1.237891
3229	Pressed And Blown Glass And Glassware, Not Elsewhere Classified	1	7.21%	1.335450	1.335450	1.335450	1.335450	1.335450	1.335450	1.335450	1.335450	1.335450	1.335450	1.335450
323	GLASS PRODUCTS, MADE OF PURCHASED GLASS	1	4.89%	0.906446	0.906446	0.906446	0.906446	0.906446	0.906446	0.906446	0.906446	0.906446	0.906446	0.906446
3231	Glass Products, Made Of Purchased Glass	1	4.89%	0.906446	0.906446	0.906446	0.906446	0.906446	0.906446	0.906446	0.906446	0.906446	0.906446	0.906446
324	CEMENT, HYDRAULIC	2	2.96%	0.548949	0.548949	0.191256	0.202206	0.220455	0.475950	0.548949	0.621947	0.877442	0.895691	0.906641
3241	Cement, Hydraulic	2	2.96%	0.548949	0.548949	0.191256	0.202206	0.220455	0.475950	0.548949	0.621947	0.877442	0.895691	0.906641
325	STRUCTURAL CLAY PRODUCTS	1	8.56%	1.585150	1.585150	1.585150	1.585150	1.585150	1.585150	1.585150	1.585150	1.585150	1.585150	1.585150
3253	Ceramic Wall And Floor Tile	1	8.56%	1.585150	1.585150	1.585150	1.585150	1.585150	1.585150	1.585150	1.585150	1.585150	1.585150	1.585150
326	POTTERY AND RELATED PRODUCTS	1	11.18%	2.070060	2.070060	2.070060	2.070060	2.070060	2.070060	2.070060	2.070060	2.070060	2.070060	2.070060
3264	Porcelain Electrical Supplies	1	11.18%	2.070060	2.070060	2.070060	2.070060	2.070060	2.070060	2.070060	2.070060	2.070060	2.070060	2.070060
327	CONCRETE, GYPSUM, AND PLASTER PRODUCTS	6	3.70%	0.685354	0.618137	0.292263	0.294479	0.298173	0.425342	0.618137	0.810932	1.278943	1.352231	1.396205
3272	Concrete Products, Except Block And Brick	3	2.56%	0.474018	0.320336	0.291376	0.292263	0.293740	0.314426	0.320336	0.418455	0.761872	0.786402	0.801120
3273	Ready-Mixed Concrete	1	7.70%	1.425520	1.425520	1.425520	1.425520	1.425520	1.425520	1.425520	1.425520	1.425520	1.425520	1.425520
3274	Lime	1	2.30%	0.425342	0.425342	0.425342	0.425342	0.425342	0.425342	0.425342	0.425342	0.425342	0.425342	0.425342
3275	Gypsum Products	1	4.53%	0.839210	0.839210	0.839210	0.839210	0.839210	0.839210	0.839210	0.839210	0.839210	0.839210	0.839210
33	PRIMARY METAL INDUSTRIES	37	4.90%	0.908022	1.047100	-0.855426	-0.601484	-0.218796	1.012660	1.047100	1.179820	1.574322	1.605998	1.621701
331	STEEL WORKS, BLAST FURNACES, AND ROLLING AND FINISHING MILLS	18	5.40%	0.999976	1.092470	0.171364	0.194492	0.233039	1.036928	1.092470	1.160420	1.400426	1.410388	1.416365
3312	Steel Works, Blast Furnaces (Including Coke Ovens), And Rolling Mills	13	5.90%	1.092700	1.199220	0.268615	0.301573	0.356501	1.119692	1.199220	1.274046	1.406286	1.413318	1.417537
3313	Electrometallurgical Products, Except Steel	1	0.84%	0.155945	0.155945	0.155945	0.155945	0.155945	0.155945	0.155945	0.155945	0.155945	0.155945	0.155945
3315	Steel Wiredrawing And Steel Nails And Spikes	1	6.21%	1.150720	1.150720	1.150720	1.150720	1.150720	1.150720	1.150720	1.150720	1.150720	1.150720	1.150720
3317	Steel Pipe And Tubes	3	4.48%	0.829265	0.877894	0.604697	0.613061	0.626999	0.822140	0.877894	0.904471	0.997491	1.004136	1.008122
332	IRON AND STEEL FOUNDRIES	1	5.61%	1.038750	1.038750	1.038750	1.038750	1.038750	1.038750	1.038750	1.038750	1.038750	1.038750	1.038750
3324	Steel Investment Foundries	1	5.61%	1.038750	1.038750	1.038750	1.038750	1.038750	1.038750	1.038750	1.038750	1.038750	1.038750	1.038750
333	PRIMARY SMELTING AND REFINING OF NONFERROUS METALS	6	4.08%	0.754954	1.035471	-0.533479	-0.502011	-0.449564	0.855251	1.035471	1.215690	1.603115	1.617643	1.626359
3334	Primary Production Of Aluminum	3	7.21%	1.334457	1.515950	0.868465	0.888286	0.921321	1.383810	1.515950	1.539194	1.620548	1.626359	1.629846

Down-market Betas of Common Stocks by SIC Codes as of September 28, 2018

SIC Code	Description	Number of Companies	Equity Risk Premium	Mean	Median	1st Percentile	2.5th Percentile	5th Percentile	40th Percentile	50th Percentile	60th Percentile	95th Percentile	97.5th Percentile	99th Percentile
3339	Primary Smelting And Refining Of Nonferrous Metals, Except Copper	3	0.95%	0.175451	-0.134880	-0.546066	-0.533479	-0.512500	-0.218796	-0.134880	0.135234	1.080633	1.148162	1.188679
334	SECONDARY SMELTING AND REFINING OF NONFERROUS METALS	1	-5.53%	-1.024720	-1.024720	-1.024720	-1.024720	-1.024720	-1.024720	-1.024720	-1.024720	-1.024720	-1.024720	-1.024720
3341	Secondary Smelting And Refining Of Nonferrous Metals	1	-5.53%	-1.024720	-1.024720	-1.024720	-1.024720	-1.024720	-1.024720	-1.024720	-1.024720	-1.024720	-1.024720	-1.024720
335	ROLLING, DRAWING, AND EXTRUDING OF NONFERROUS METALS	11	5.43%	1.004865	1.063170	-0.018849	0.045971	0.154005	0.951146	1.063170	1.215070	1.585110	1.594100	1.599494
3351	Rolling, Drawing, And Extruding Of Copper	3	4.82%	0.891783	0.871412	0.743379	0.747298	0.753831	0.845283	0.871412	0.909764	1.043994	1.053582	1.059335
3353	Aluminum Sheet, Plate, And Foil	1	8.66%	1.603090	1.603090	1.603090	1.603090	1.603090	1.603090	1.603090	1.603090	1.603090	1.603090	1.603090
3356	Rolling, Drawing, And Extruding Of Nonferrous Metals, Except Copper	1	7.21%	1.335850	1.335850	1.335850	1.335850	1.335850	1.335850	1.335850	1.335850	1.335850	1.335850	1.335850
3357	Drawing And Insulating Of Nonferrous Wire	6	4.90%	0.906538	1.083108	-0.040456	-0.008046	0.045971	0.951146	1.083108	1.215070	1.524815	1.545973	1.558667
34	FABRICATED METAL PRODUCTS, EXCEPT MACHINERY AND TRANSPORTATION EQUIPMENT	48	3.76%	0.696595	0.838833	-0.462476	-0.120944	-0.083793	0.688896	0.838833	0.913119	1.186770	1.186770	1.241789
341	METAL CANS AND SHIPPING CONTAINERS	7	4.44%	0.823053	0.880466	0.222949	0.244981	0.281699	0.747755	0.880466	1.064248	1.186770	1.186770	1.186770
3411	Metal Cans	6	5.00%	0.925518	1.033618	0.463363	0.478831	0.504609	0.880466	1.033618	1.186770	1.186770	1.186770	1.186770
3412	Metal Shipping Barrels, Drums, Kegs, And Pails	1	1.12%	0.208262	0.208262	0.208262	0.208262	0.208262	0.208262	0.208262	0.208262	0.208262	0.208262	0.208262
342	CUTLERY, HANDTOOLS, AND GENERAL HARDWARE	7	3.51%	0.649365	0.790013	-0.122495	-0.116715	-0.107081	0.784861	0.790013	0.918159	1.097664	1.111287	1.119461
3421	Cutlery	2	1.77%	0.327539	0.327539	-0.117271	-0.103655	-0.080960	0.236761	0.327539	0.418317	0.736038	0.758733	0.772349
3423	Hand And Edge Tools, Except Machine Tools And Handsaws	1	5.58%	1.034090	1.034090	1.034090	1.034090	1.034090	1.034090	1.034090	1.034090	1.034090	1.034090	1.034090
3429	Hardware, Not Elsewhere Classified	4	3.86%	0.714097	0.896802	-0.036559	0.001787	0.065697	0.832728	0.896802	0.960875	1.106712	1.115811	1.121270
343	HEATING EQUIPMENT, EXCEPT ELECTRIC AND WARM AIR; AND PLUMBING FIXTURES	2	2.64%	0.489808	0.489808	0.053997	0.067339	0.089574	0.400867	0.489808	0.578749	0.890043	0.912278	0.925619
3433	Heating Equipment, Except Electric And Warm Air Furnaces	2	2.64%	0.489808	0.489808	0.053997	0.067339	0.089574	0.400867	0.489808	0.578749	0.890043	0.912278	0.925619
344	FABRICATED STRUCTURAL METAL PRODUCTS	10	4.95%	0.916493	0.933917	0.575551	0.576646	0.578469	0.867388	0.933917	1.009070	1.224174	1.257377	1.277299
3441	Fabricated Structural Metal	2	5.52%	1.021322	1.021322	0.961288	0.963126	0.966189	1.009070	1.021322	1.033573	1.076454	1.079517	1.081355
3442	Metal Doors, Sash, Frames, Molding, And Trim	3	4.12%	0.763136	0.806816	0.579462	0.586422	0.598021	0.760417	0.806816	0.827007	0.897675	0.902722	0.905751
3443	Fabricated Plate Work (Boiler Shops)	3	4.63%	0.856602	0.696300	0.585194	0.588596	0.594264	0.673625	0.696300	0.815156	1.231152	1.260866	1.278694
3448	Prefabricated Metal Buildings And Components	2	6.11%	1.131535	1.131535	1.120290	1.120634	1.121208	1.129240	1.131535	1.133830	1.141863	1.142436	1.142781
345	SCREW MACHINE PRODUCTS, AND BOLTS, NUTS, SCREWS, RIVETS, AND WASHERS	4	2.69%	0.498188	0.518229	0.264843	0.274139	0.289632	0.486424	0.518229	0.550034	0.678685	0.688165	0.693854
3451	Screw Machine Products	1	3.08%	0.571238	0.571238	0.571238	0.571238	0.571238	0.571238	0.571238	0.571238	0.571238	0.571238	0.571238
3452	Bolts, Nuts, Screws, Rivets, And Washers	3	2.56%	0.473837	0.465220	0.262777	0.268975	0.279303	0.423905	0.465220	0.511705	0.674403	0.686025	0.692997

Down-market Betas of Common Stocks by SIC Codes as of September 28, 2018

SIC Code	Description	Number of Companies	Equity Risk Premium	Mean	Median	1st Percentile	2.5th Percentile	5th Percentile	40th Percentile	50th Percentile	60th Percentile	95th Percentile	97.5th Percentile	99th Percentile
346	METAL FORGINGS AND STAMPINGS	5	1.94%	0.359173	0.631983	-0.727601	-0.678179	-0.595807	0.404456	0.631983	0.736035	0.953748	0.961452	0.966074
3463	Nonferrous Forgings	1	4.82%	0.892114	0.892114	0.892114	0.892114	0.892114	0.892114	0.892114	0.892114	0.892114	0.892114	0.892114
3465	Automotive Stampings	2	4.32%	0.800570	0.800570	0.635355	0.640412	0.648842	0.766852	0.800570	0.834287	0.952297	0.960727	0.965784
3469	Metal Stampings, Not Elsewhere Classified	2	-1.88%	-0.348693	-0.348693	-0.752313	-0.739957	-0.719364	-0.431064	-0.348693	-0.266321	0.021979	0.042572	0.054927
347	COATING, ENGRAVING, AND ALLIED SERVICES	2	1.54%	0.284673	0.284673	0.189902	0.192803	0.197638	0.265332	0.284673	0.304013	0.371707	0.376542	0.379443
3471	Electroplating, Plating, Polishing, Anodizing, And Coloring	1	1.02%	0.187968	0.187968	0.187968	0.187968	0.187968	0.187968	0.187968	0.187968	0.187968	0.187968	0.187968
3479	Coating, Engraving, And Allied Services, Not Elsewhere Classified	1	2.06%	0.381377	0.381377	0.381377	0.381377	0.381377	0.381377	0.381377	0.381377	0.381377	0.381377	0.381377
348	ORDNANCE AND ACCESSORIES, EXCEPT VEHICLES AND GUIDED MISSILES	2	4.29%	0.794552	0.794552	0.577267	0.583919	0.595005	0.750208	0.794552	0.838895	0.994098	1.005184	1.011836
3484	Small Arms	2	4.29%	0.794552	0.794552	0.577267	0.583919	0.595005	0.750208	0.794552	0.838895	0.994098	1.005184	1.011836
349	MISCELLANEOUS FABRICATED METAL PRODUCTS	9	4.22%	0.782002	0.950365	-0.064750	-0.018683	0.058096	0.906947	0.950365	0.950479	1.078892	1.089516	1.095890
3490	MISCELLANEOUS FABRICATED METAL PRODUCTS	2	2.31%	0.427523	0.427523	-0.085002	-0.069313	-0.043163	0.322926	0.427523	0.532119	0.898209	0.924358	0.940047
3491	Industrial Valves	3	5.13%	0.950428	0.950365	0.872440	0.874826	0.878802	0.934462	0.950365	0.966306	1.022100	1.026085	1.028476
3495	Wire Springs	1	4.84%	0.896092	0.896092	0.896092	0.896092	0.896092	0.896092	0.896092	0.896092	0.896092	0.896092	0.896092
3499	Fabricated Metal Products, Not Elsewhere Classified	3	4.38%	0.811864	1.047020	0.303605	0.326362	0.364292	0.895303	1.047020	1.057644	1.094828	1.097484	1.099078
35	INDUSTRIAL AND COMMERCIAL MACHINERY AND COMPUTER EQUIPMENT	168	4.99%	0.923170	0.905142	-0.321999	-0.148136	0.125414	0.802518	0.905142	0.983249	1.665563	2.151591	3.041119
351	ENGINES AND TURBINES	10	4.52%	0.836189	0.708677	0.296483	0.322376	0.365531	0.637173	0.708677	0.784442	1.625466	1.719273	1.775557
3510	ENGINES & TURBINES	1	1.51%	0.279221	0.279221	0.279221	0.279221	0.279221	0.279221	0.279221	0.279221	0.279221	0.279221	0.279221
3511	Steam, Gas, And Hydraulic Turbines, And Turbine Generator Set Units	5	4.87%	0.902550	0.766538	0.478212	0.489000	0.506979	0.720249	0.766538	0.784442	1.612723	1.712902	1.773009
3519	Internal Combustion Engines, Not Elsewhere Classified	4	4.82%	0.892480	0.798670	0.577629	0.579442	0.582463	0.689493	0.798670	0.907846	1.333831	1.364995	1.383694
352	FARM AND GARDEN MACHINERY AND EQUIPMENT	9	5.16%	0.955374	1.073820	0.057426	0.135716	0.266198	0.839052	1.073820	1.157940	1.478838	1.498284	1.509952
3523	Farm Machinery And Equipment	7	4.90%	0.906510	0.780360	0.044378	0.103095	0.200957	0.778581	0.780360	1.024170	1.488561	1.503146	1.511896
3524	Lawn And Garden Tractors And Home Lawn And Garden Equipment	2	6.08%	1.126395	1.126395	1.074872	1.076449	1.079078	1.115880	1.126395	1.136910	1.173713	1.176341	1.177919
353	CONSTRUCTION, MINING, AND MATERIALS HANDLING MACHINERY AND EQUIPMENT	24	5.16%	0.956217	0.979899	0.214121	0.271209	0.373353	0.920785	0.979899	1.011176	1.569128	1.606241	1.620520
3531	Construction Machinery And Equipment	7	4.71%	0.872002	0.876093	0.354262	0.373353	0.405173	0.719441	0.876093	0.936737	1.457625	1.523138	1.562445
3532	Mining Machinery And Equipment, Except Oil And Gas Field Machinery	2	5.15%	0.953785	0.953785	0.756241	0.762288	0.772367	0.913469	0.953785	0.994100	1.135202	1.145281	1.151328
3533	Oil And Gas Field Machinery And Equipment	9	5.31%	0.982813	0.985721	0.218235	0.281493	0.386923	0.953152	0.985721	1.011176	1.526248	1.578144	1.609282
3535	Conveyors And Conveying Equipment	1	5.31%	0.982631	0.982631	0.982631	0.982631	0.982631	0.982631	0.982631	0.982631	0.982631	0.982631	0.982631
3536	Overhead Traveling Cranes, Hoists, And Monorail Systems	1	7.88%	1.458500	1.458500	1.458500	1.458500	1.458500	1.458500	1.458500	1.458500	1.458500	1.458500	1.458500

Down-market Betas of Common Stocks by SIC Codes as of September 28, 2018

SIC Code	Description	Number of Companies	Equity Risk Premium	Mean	Median	1st Percentile	2.5th Percentile	5th Percentile	40th Percentile	50th Percentile	60th Percentile	95th Percentile	97.5th Percentile	99th Percentile
3537	Industrial Trucks, Tractors, Trailers, And Stackers	4	4.93%	0.912795	0.950771	0.677308	0.686353	0.701427	0.903672	0.950771	0.997870	1.070997	1.074678	1.076887
354	METALWORKING MACHINERY AND EQUIPMENT	8	3.96%	0.732518	0.814692	-0.152415	-0.133448	-0.101837	0.734718	0.814692	0.909158	1.346328	1.354644	1.359634
3541	Machine Tools, Metal Cutting Types	4	4.39%	0.812795	1.026640	-0.137972	-0.097342	-0.029624	0.853359	1.026640	1.199920	1.355832	1.359396	1.361534
3542	Machine Tools, Metal Forming Types	1	3.90%	0.722232	0.722232	0.722232	0.722232	0.722232	0.722232	0.722232	0.722232	0.722232	0.722232	0.722232
3545	Cutting Tools, Machine Tool Accessories, And Machinists' Precision Tools	1	5.29%	0.979616	0.979616	0.979616	0.979616	0.979616	0.979616	0.979616	0.979616	0.979616	0.979616	0.979616
3546	Power-Driven Handtools	1	0.08%	0.015575	0.015575	0.015575	0.015575	0.015575	0.015575	0.015575	0.015575	0.015575	0.015575	0.015575
3549	Metalworking Machinery, Not Elsewhere Classified	1	4.81%	0.891544	0.891544	0.891544	0.891544	0.891544	0.891544	0.891544	0.891544	0.891544	0.891544	0.891544
355	SPECIAL INDUSTRY MACHINERY, EXCEPT METALWORKING MACHINERY	18	4.82%	0.891752	0.908439	0.229517	0.264997	0.324130	0.779810	0.908439	0.970862	1.431373	1.558032	1.634027
3554	Paper Industries Machinery	1	4.24%	0.785173	0.785173	0.785173	0.785173	0.785173	0.785173	0.785173	0.785173	0.785173	0.785173	0.785173
3555	Printing Trades Machinery And Equipment	1	9.10%	1.684690	1.684690	1.684690	1.684690	1.684690	1.684690	1.684690	1.684690	1.684690	1.684690	1.684690
3556	Food Products Machinery	1	1.11%	0.205864	0.205864	0.205864	0.205864	0.205864	0.205864	0.205864	0.205864	0.205864	0.205864	0.205864
3559	Special Industry Machinery, Not Elsewhere Classified	15	4.82%	0.891721	0.927974	0.362759	0.389398	0.433795	0.836684	0.927974	0.990464	1.378487	1.382579	1.385033
356	GENERAL INDUSTRIAL MACHINERY AND EQUIPMENT	29	5.96%	1.104442	1.027040	0.146759	0.219686	0.349970	0.922903	1.027040	1.068118	2.362836	3.434450	4.030976
3560	GENERAL INDUSTRIAL MACHINERY & EQUIPMENT	1	5.73%	1.060910	1.060910	1.060910	1.060910	1.060910	1.060910	1.060910	1.060910	1.060910	1.060910	1.060910
3561	Pumps And Pumping Equipment	9	5.16%	0.956070	0.964267	0.482948	0.506477	0.545691	0.924774	0.964267	1.066237	1.244894	1.252752	1.257467
3562	Ball And Roller Bearings	4	5.22%	0.966493	1.186640	0.127295	0.171025	0.243909	1.116608	1.186640	1.256672	1.380872	1.387711	1.391814
3564	Industrial And Commercial Fans And Blowers And Air Purification Equipment	6	7.73%	1.431850	0.929247	0.503720	0.521757	0.551818	0.903582	0.929247	0.954912	3.591513	4.010086	4.261231
3566	Speed Changers, Industrial High-Speed Drives, And Gears	1	3.91%	0.724667	0.724667	0.724667	0.724667	0.724667	0.724667	0.724667	0.724667	0.724667	0.724667	0.724667
3568	Mechanical Power Transmission Equipment, Not Elsewhere Classified	1	5.87%	1.087080	1.087080	1.087080	1.087080	1.087080	1.087080	1.087080	1.087080	1.087080	1.087080	1.087080
3569	General Industrial Machinery And Equipment, Not Elsewhere Classified	7	6.24%	1.156350	1.027040	0.291455	0.320974	0.370173	0.954903	1.027040	1.036562	2.477189	2.742775	2.902126
357	COMPUTER AND OFFICE EQUIPMENT	55	4.81%	0.890002	0.824124	-0.227649	-0.051494	0.201459	0.793248	0.824124	0.924214	1.931353	2.459398	2.890442
3571	Electronic Computers	12	4.77%	0.884197	0.827867	-0.098343	0.021623	0.221566	0.792407	0.827867	0.885178	1.605685	1.753278	1.841833
3572	Computer Storage Devices	7	6.53%	1.209085	1.031050	0.610307	0.615205	0.623369	0.944812	1.031050	1.053370	2.505593	2.806612	2.987223
3576	COMPUTER COMMUNICATIONS EQUIPMENT	7	5.47%	1.012375	1.053480	0.451299	0.452152	0.453574	0.927543	1.053480	1.067184	1.761682	1.882081	1.954320
3577	Computer Peripheral Equipment, Not Elsewhere Classified	22	4.36%	0.807088	0.798446	0.189265	0.197104	0.211292	0.694842	0.798446	0.813853	1.220913	1.928084	2.394491
3578	Calculating And Accounting Machines, Except Electronic Computers	5	3.74%	0.692385	1.117520	-0.260474	-0.222847	-0.160136	0.807132	1.117520	1.123848	1.150724	1.152897	1.154201
3579	Office Machines, Not Elsewhere Classified	2	4.24%	0.785838	0.785838	0.770755	0.771217	0.771986	0.782759	0.785838	0.788916	0.799689	0.800458	0.800920
358	REFRIGERATION AND SERVICE INDUSTRY MACHINERY	10	5.04%	0.934255	0.893645	-0.427613	-0.251000	0.043356	0.886414	0.893645	0.910572	1.794236	1.988728	2.105423

Down-market Betas of Common Stocks by SIC Codes as of September 28, 2018

SIC Code	Description	Number of Companies	Equity Risk Premium	Mean	Median	1st Percentile	2.5th Percentile	5th Percentile	40th Percentile	50th Percentile	60th Percentile	95th Percentile	97.5th Percentile	99th Percentile
3580	REFRIGERATION & SERVICE INDUSTRY MACHINERY	2	0.92%	0.170219	0.170219	-0.531044	-0.509576	-0.473798	0.027104	0.170219	0.313333	0.814235	0.850013	0.871481
3585	Air-Conditioning And Warm Air Heating Equipment	3	5.37%	0.994054	0.900461	0.765642	0.769770	0.776648	0.872947	0.900461	0.984131	1.276975	1.297893	1.310443
3589	Service Industry Machinery, Not Elsewhere Classified	5	6.50%	1.203990	0.925739	0.807813	0.812752	0.820983	0.910175	0.925739	1.043299	1.990504	2.086862	2.144677
359	MISCELLANEOUS INDUSTRIAL AND COMMERCIAL MACHINERY AND EQUIPMENT	5	3.19%	0.589970	0.965340	-0.382879	-0.363221	-0.330459	0.551861	0.965340	1.039720	1.268306	1.282933	1.291709
3590	MISC INDUSTRIAL & COMMERCIAL MACHINERY & EQUIPMENT	1	-2.14%	-0.395984	-0.395984	-0.395984	-0.395984	-0.395984	-0.395984	-0.395984	-0.395984	-0.395984	-0.395984	-0.395984
3592	Carburetors, Pistons, Piston Rings, And Valves	1	7.01%	1.297560	1.297560	1.297560	1.297560	1.297560	1.297560	1.297560	1.297560	1.297560	1.297560	1.297560
3594	Fluid Power Pumps And Motors	1	6.22%	1.151290	1.151290	1.151290	1.151290	1.151290	1.151290	1.151290	1.151290	1.151290	1.151290	1.151290
3596	Scales And Balances, Except Laboratory	1	-0.37%	-0.068357	-0.068357	-0.068357	-0.068357	-0.068357	-0.068357	-0.068357	-0.068357	-0.068357	-0.068357	-0.068357
3599	Industrial And Commercial Machinery And Equipment, Not Elsewhere Classified	1	5.21%	0.965340	0.965340	0.965340	0.965340	0.965340	0.965340	0.965340	0.965340	0.965340	0.965340	0.965340
36	ELECTRONIC AND OTHER ELECTRICAL EQUIPMENT AND COMPONENTS, EXCEPT COMPUTER	265	5.06%	0.936298	0.798988	-0.989914	-0.297594	-0.003872	0.689153	0.798988	0.944754	1.703594	2.032634	2.928104
361	ELECTRIC TRANSMISSION AND DISTRIBUTION EQUIPMENT	5	4.23%	0.783498	0.838434	0.413310	0.421574	0.435348	0.721274	0.838434	0.901797	1.102472	1.115676	1.123598
3612	Power, Distribution, And Specialty Transformers	3	3.75%	0.694072	0.545534	0.410556	0.414688	0.421574	0.517987	0.545534	0.662203	1.070545	1.099713	1.117213
3613	Switchgear And Switchboard Apparatus	2	4.96%	0.917638	0.917638	0.840018	0.842394	0.846354	0.901797	0.917638	0.933478	0.988921	0.992881	0.995257
362	ELECTRICAL INDUSTRIAL APPARATUS	18	5.07%	0.938640	0.987454	0.022507	0.060772	0.124548	0.880632	0.987454	1.064792	1.620328	1.810069	1.923914
3621	Motors And Generators	13	4.84%	0.895528	1.030080	0.015004	0.042015	0.087033	0.800156	1.030080	1.064792	1.731940	1.865875	1.946236
3625	Relays And Industrial Controls	2	5.75%	1.064229	1.064229	0.793003	0.801306	0.815144	1.008877	1.064229	1.119581	1.313314	1.327152	1.335455
3629	Electrical Industrial Apparatus, Not Elsewhere Classified	3	5.63%	1.041729	0.944828	0.894193	0.895743	0.898327	0.934494	0.944828	1.013302	1.252963	1.270081	1.280353
363	HOUSEHOLD APPLIANCES	7	6.00%	1.110907	0.707062	0.223280	0.245313	0.282034	0.655991	0.707062	0.930249	2.775265	3.091848	3.281797
3630	HOUSEHOLD APPLIANCES	1	18.41%	3.408430	3.408430	3.408430	3.408430	3.408430	3.408430	3.408430	3.408430	3.408430	3.408430	3.408430
3632	Household Refrigerators And Home And Farm Freezers	1	5.83%	1.079040	1.079040	1.079040	1.079040	1.079040	1.079040	1.079040	1.079040	1.079040	1.079040	1.079040
3633	Household Laundry Equipment	2	5.41%	1.002471	1.002471	0.712970	0.721832	0.736603	0.943389	1.002471	1.061553	1.268339	1.283110	1.291972
3634	Electric Housewares And Fans	3	2.31%	0.427979	0.453402	0.213487	0.220832	0.233072	0.404440	0.453402	0.487110	0.605090	0.613517	0.618573
364	ELECTRIC LIGHTING AND WIRING EQUIPMENT	9	3.02%	0.559661	0.585707	-0.214137	-0.175076	-0.109975	0.241771	0.585707	0.713471	1.291292	1.369106	1.415794
3640	ELECTRIC LIGHTING & WIRING EQUIPMENT	3	3.81%	0.705985	0.585707	0.095335	0.110346	0.135365	0.485631	0.585707	0.757950	1.360799	1.403859	1.429696
3641	Electric Lamp Bulbs And Tubes	3	2.44%	0.451969	0.155787	0.152555	0.152654	0.152819	0.155127	0.155787	0.334156	0.958446	1.003038	1.029793
3643	Current-Carrying Wiring Devices	1	5.71%	1.057850	1.057850	1.057850	1.057850	1.057850	1.057850	1.057850	1.057850	1.057850	1.057850	1.057850
3645	Residential Electric Lighting Fixtures	1	-1.30%	-0.240177	-0.240177	-0.240177	-0.240177	-0.240177	-0.240177	-0.240177	-0.240177	-0.240177	-0.240177	-0.240177
3646	Commercial, Industrial, And Institutional Electric Lighting Fixtures	1	4.03%	0.745412	0.745412	0.745412	0.745412	0.745412	0.745412	0.745412	0.745412	0.745412	0.745412	0.745412
365	HOUSEHOLD AUDIO AND VIDEO EQUIPMENT, AND AUDIO RECORDINGS	7	2.72%	0.503301	0.550034	-0.527749	-0.453398	-0.329479	0.532426	0.550034	0.672436	1.095869	1.157699	1.194798

Down-market Betas of Common Stocks by SIC Codes as of September 28, 2018

SIC Code	Description	Number of Companies	Equity Risk Premium	Mean	Median	1st Percentile	2.5th Percentile	5th Percentile	40th Percentile	50th Percentile	60th Percentile	95th Percentile	97.5th Percentile	99th Percentile
3651	Household Audio And Video Equipment	6	3.69%	0.683404	0.652036	0.262404	0.282795	0.316779	0.550034	0.652036	0.754038	1.116479	1.168004	1.198920
3652	Phonograph Records And Prerecorded Audio Tapes And Disks	1	-3.12%	-0.577317	-0.577317	-0.577317	-0.577317	-0.577317	-0.577317	-0.577317	-0.577317	-0.577317	-0.577317	-0.577317
366	COMMUNICATIONS EQUIPMENT	67	5.83%	1.079589	0.629012	-0.975719	-0.377819	-0.048287	0.562798	0.629012	0.705729	1.517093	2.022340	11.931015
3661	Telephone And Telegraph Apparatus	17	3.07%	0.568131	0.612118	-1.225108	-0.896515	-0.348860	0.573607	0.612118	0.633381	1.666478	1.822994	1.916904
3663	Radio And Television Broadcasting And Communications Equipment	35	8.35%	1.545836	0.654010	-0.547878	-0.268103	0.145848	0.625411	0.654010	0.763278	1.576355	6.438263	21.181965
3669	Communications Equipment, Not Elsewhere Classified	15	3.09%	0.571331	0.450566	0.036682	0.070525	0.126931	0.430728	0.450566	0.612463	1.139459	1.141360	1.142500
367	ELECTRONIC COMPONENTS AND ACCESSORIES	132	4.97%	0.920530	0.960928	-1.645149	-0.295660	0.019205	0.801080	0.960928	1.089166	1.719270	1.911786	2.484884
3671	Electron Tubes	1	1.80%	0.332536	0.332536	0.332536	0.332536	0.332536	0.332536	0.332536	0.332536	0.332536	0.332536	0.332536
3672	Printed Circuit Boards	14	3.34%	0.618220	0.538934	0.000269	0.008785	0.022978	0.473654	0.538934	0.599989	1.340562	1.535526	1.652504
3674	Semiconductors And Related Devices	96	4.99%	0.923264	1.002040	-2.144447	-0.489986	0.072616	0.896886	1.002040	1.147620	1.685730	1.906101	2.127649
3675	Electronic Capacitors	1	2.18%	0.403175	0.403175	0.403175	0.403175	0.403175	0.403175	0.403175	0.403175	0.403175	0.403175	0.403175
3676	Electronic Resistors	1	6.09%	1.127630	1.127630	1.127630	1.127630	1.127630	1.127630	1.127630	1.127630	1.127630	1.127630	1.127630
3677	Electronic Coils, Transformers, And Other Inductors	2	4.95%	0.916185	0.916185	0.727628	0.733400	0.743021	0.877704	0.916185	0.954666	1.089350	1.098970	1.104742
3678	Electronic Connectors	4	4.78%	0.884972	0.913779	0.730940	0.737756	0.749118	0.892240	0.913779	0.935318	0.980495	0.983214	0.984845
3679	Electronic Components, Not Elsewhere Classified	13	7.06%	1.306614	1.009430	-0.025017	0.032717	0.128939	0.761822	1.009430	1.088968	3.724128	5.218854	6.115690
369	MISCELLANEOUS ELECTRICAL MACHINERY, EQUIPMENT, AND SUPPLIES	20	4.62%	0.856358	0.768800	-0.080216	-0.015602	0.092088	0.712237	0.768800	0.918349	1.664887	1.873378	1.998473
3690	MISCELLANEOUS ELECTRICAL MACHINERY, EQUIPMENT & SUPPLIES	2	3.31%	0.612617	0.612617	0.113608	0.128884	0.154343	0.510778	0.612617	0.714456	1.070891	1.096350	1.111626
3691	Storage Batteries	8	3.62%	0.670891	0.631535	-0.093766	-0.049478	0.024336	0.612097	0.631535	0.667541	1.396910	1.519925	1.593734
3692	Primary Batteries, Dry And Wet	1	11.24%	2.081870	2.081870	2.081870	2.081870	2.081870	2.081870	2.081870	2.081870	2.081870	2.081870	2.081870
3694	Electrical Equipment For Internal Combustion Engines	1	3.83%	0.709541	0.709541	0.709541	0.709541	0.709541	0.709541	0.709541	0.709541	0.709541	0.709541	0.709541
3695	Magnetic And Optical Recording Media	4	5.12%	0.948749	0.808976	0.578856	0.585127	0.595579	0.752011	0.808976	0.865941	1.497602	1.549986	1.581416
3699	Electrical Machinery, Equipment, And Supplies, Not Elsewhere Classified	4	5.33%	0.987098	1.036832	0.751162	0.761892	0.779776	1.004204	1.036832	1.069459	1.124794	1.127757	1.129535
37	TRANSPORTATION EQUIPMENT	102	4.61%	0.853820	0.901861	-0.767655	-0.104594	0.148489	0.791677	0.901861	0.979717	1.629704	1.977352	2.054229
371	MOTOR VEHICLES AND MOTOR VEHICLE EQUIPMENT	54	4.69%	0.869392	0.937023	-0.285611	0.177194	0.266840	0.825644	0.937023	1.001044	1.512378	1.624168	1.733913
3711	Motor Vehicles And Passenger Car Bodies	19	4.29%	0.795133	0.944493	-0.589041	-0.315040	0.141628	0.924189	0.944493	0.986746	1.231286	1.231988	1.232409
3713	Truck And Bus Bodies	1	1.51%	0.279617	0.279617	0.279617	0.279617	0.279617	0.279617	0.279617	0.279617	0.279617	0.279617	0.279617
3714	Motor Vehicle Parts And Accessories	31	4.95%	0.917214	0.848622	0.193551	0.265693	0.361752	0.797883	0.848622	1.005340	1.620645	1.685605	1.784416
3715	Truck Trailers	1	6.55%	1.213850	1.213850	1.213850	1.213850	1.213850	1.213850	1.213850	1.213850	1.213850	1.213850	1.213850
3716	Motor Homes	2	5.16%	0.956265	0.956265	0.908270	0.909739	0.912188	0.946470	0.956265	0.966060	1.000343	1.002791	1.004261
372	AIRCRAFT AND PARTS	29	4.17%	0.771883	0.769965	-0.979737	-0.621953	-0.137389	0.681209	0.769965	0.975996	1.501874	1.662950	1.862030
3721	Aircraft	10	4.32%	0.800873	0.981818	-1.077812	-0.867140	-0.516021	0.856597	0.981818	0.996809	1.717348	1.856049	1.939270
3724	Aircraft Engines And Engine Parts	8	2.66%	0.492658	0.630500	-0.326317	-0.266204	-0.166014	0.484136	0.630500	0.719880	0.943097	0.955777	0.963385

Down-market Betas of Common Stocks by SIC Codes as of September 28, 2018

SIC Code	Description	Number of Companies	Equity Risk Premium	Mean	Median	1st Percentile	2.5th Percentile	5th Percentile	40th Percentile	50th Percentile	60th Percentile	95th Percentile	97.5th Percentile	99th Percentile
3728	Aircraft Parts And Auxiliary Equipment, Not Elsewhere Classified	11	5.12%	0.948600	1.041980	0.408756	0.414144	0.423125	0.749403	1.041980	1.114740	1.497155	1.508953	1.516031
373	SHIP AND BOAT BUILDING AND REPAIRING	5	4.94%	0.914538	0.670671	0.153142	0.177886	0.219124	0.622015	0.670671	0.748991	2.053190	2.201530	2.290534
3730	SHIP & BOAT BUILDING & REPAIRING	1	12.69%	2.349870	2.349870	2.349870	2.349870	2.349870	2.349870	2.349870	2.349870	2.349870	2.349870	2.349870
3731	Ship Building And Repairing	2	2.71%	0.501559	0.501559	0.143945	0.154893	0.173138	0.428576	0.501559	0.574541	0.829979	0.848224	0.859172
3732	Boat Building And Repairing	2	3.29%	0.609852	0.609852	0.550248	0.552073	0.555114	0.597688	0.609852	0.622015	0.664589	0.667630	0.669455
374	RAILROAD EQUIPMENT	5	5.06%	0.936676	0.896431	0.789545	0.792553	0.797567	0.872930	0.896431	0.942115	1.123000	1.137045	1.145472
3743	Railroad Equipment	5	5.06%	0.936676	0.896431	0.789545	0.792553	0.797567	0.872930	0.896431	0.942115	1.123000	1.137045	1.145472
375	MOTORCYCLES, BICYCLES, AND PARTS	3	4.01%	0.742352	0.865672	0.365168	0.380490	0.406026	0.763528	0.865672	0.893824	0.992354	0.999392	1.003615
3751	Motorcycles, Bicycles, And Parts	3	4.01%	0.742352	0.865672	0.365168	0.380490	0.406026	0.763528	0.865672	0.893824	0.992354	0.999392	1.003615
376	GUIDED MISSILES AND SPACE VEHICLES AND PARTS	3	5.66%	1.047540	0.955517	0.148737	0.173434	0.214597	0.790868	0.955517	1.175380	1.944899	1.999864	2.032844
3761	Guided Missiles And Space Vehicles	1	5.16%	0.955517	0.955517	0.955517	0.955517	0.955517	0.955517	0.955517	0.955517	0.955517	0.955517	0.955517
3764	Guided Missile And Space Vehicle Propulsion Units And Propulsion	1	11.10%	2.054830	2.054830	2.054830	2.054830	2.054830	2.054830	2.054830	2.054830	2.054830	2.054830	2.054830
3769	Guided Missile And Space Vehicle Parts And Auxiliary Equipment, Not Elsewhere Classified	1	0.71%	0.132272	0.132272	0.132272	0.132272	0.132272	0.132272	0.132272	0.132272	0.132272	0.132272	0.132272
379	MISCELLANEOUS TRANSPORTATION EQUIPMENT	3	5.64%	1.044037	0.931484	0.252866	0.273640	0.308264	0.792991	0.931484	1.137509	1.858597	1.910104	1.941007
3790	MISCELLANEOUS TRANSPORTATION EQUIPMENT	1	10.59%	1.961610	1.961610	1.961610	1.961610	1.961610	1.961610	1.961610	1.961610	1.961610	1.961610	1.961610
3795	Tanks And Tank Components	1	1.29%	0.239017	0.239017	0.239017	0.239017	0.239017	0.239017	0.239017	0.239017	0.239017	0.239017	0.239017
3799	Transportation Equipment, Not Elsewhere Classified	1	5.03%	0.931484	0.931484	0.931484	0.931484	0.931484	0.931484	0.931484	0.931484	0.931484	0.931484	0.931484
38	MEASURING, ANALYZING, AND CONTROLLING INSTRUMENTS; PHOTOGRAPHIC, MEDICAL	263	4.03%	0.746709	0.794117	-1.469509	-0.766999	-0.440451	0.667795	0.794117	0.913563	1.611889	1.782864	2.330251
381	SEARCH, DETECTION, NAVIGATION, GUIDANCE, AERONAUTICAL, AND NAUTICAL	11	4.57%	0.845523	0.888904	0.379595	0.384922	0.393801	0.765714	0.888904	0.937414	1.318360	1.345965	1.362528
3812	Search, Detection, Navigation, Guidance, Aeronautical, And Nautical	11	4.57%	0.845523	0.888904	0.379595	0.384922	0.393801	0.765714	0.888904	0.937414	1.318360	1.345965	1.362528
382	LABORATORY APPARATUS AND ANALYTICAL, OPTICAL, MEASURING, AND CONTROL	91	4.22%	0.782184	0.862583	-1.317816	-0.451791	-0.339519	0.749870	0.862583	0.972403	1.597205	1.944975	2.123402
3821	Laboratory Apparatus And Furniture	3	0.78%	0.144086	0.123373	0.047794	0.050108	0.053964	0.107949	0.123373	0.151225	0.248706	0.255669	0.259847
3822	Automatic Controls For Regulating Residential And Commercial Environment	4	0.71%	0.132232	0.556958	-1.736447	-1.633018	-1.460637	0.518597	0.556958	0.595319	1.130482	1.175446	1.202424
3823	Industrial Instruments For Measurement, Display, And Control Of Processes	17	4.30%	0.795995	0.911644	-0.348706	-0.210761	0.019148	0.834655	0.911644	0.968739	1.271230	1.321130	1.351070
3824	Totalizing Fluid Meters And Counting Devices	1	4.24%	0.785696	0.785696	0.785696	0.785696	0.785696	0.785696	0.785696	0.785696	0.785696	0.785696	0.785696
3825	Instruments For Measuring And Testing Of Electricity And Electric	20	3.51%	0.649692	0.868692	-1.110093	-0.879773	-0.495905	0.622190	0.868692	0.911315	1.416289	1.499405	1.549274

Down-market Betas of Common Stocks by SIC Codes as of September 28, 2018

SIC Code	Description	Number of Companies	Equity Risk Premium	Mean	Median	1st Percentile	2.5th Percentile	5th Percentile	40th Percentile	50th Percentile	60th Percentile	95th Percentile	97.5th Percentile	99th Percentile
3826	Laboratory Analytical Instruments	18	5.84%	1.080671	1.094995	-0.168211	-0.059683	0.121195	0.960711	1.094995	1.174542	2.085037	2.308664	2.442839
3827	Optical Instruments And Lenses	10	4.25%	0.787570	0.764357	-0.359196	-0.240278	-0.042081	0.726833	0.764357	0.812340	1.512108	1.546229	1.566702
3829	Measuring And Controlling Devices, Not Elsewhere Classified	18	4.67%	0.865462	0.825842	-0.051887	-0.032901	-0.001258	0.606167	0.825842	1.034417	1.681802	1.879886	1.998736
384	SURGICAL, MEDICAL, AND DENTAL INSTRUMENTS AND SUPPLIES	152	3.85%	0.713705	0.743499	-1.592192	-0.863630	-0.688910	0.595689	0.743499	0.889214	1.621263	1.770648	2.418477
3841	Surgical And Medical Instruments And Apparatus	92	3.19%	0.591010	0.779188	-2.146804	-1.078204	-0.766999	0.631734	0.779188	0.914585	1.470485	1.592825	1.774589
3842	Orthopedic, Prosthetic, And Surgical Appliances And Supplies	23	6.32%	1.170339	0.688654	-0.380766	-0.290261	-0.157627	0.529710	0.688654	0.894694	1.769746	6.341278	9.682571
3843	Dental Equipment And Supplies	5	3.91%	0.723294	0.788810	-0.622299	-0.538853	-0.399778	0.758417	0.788810	0.955774	1.510476	1.548508	1.571327
3844	X-Ray Apparatus And Tubes And Related Irradiation Apparatus	2	5.21%	0.964763	0.964763	0.842549	0.846290	0.852526	0.939821	0.964763	0.989704	1.076999	1.083235	1.086976
3845	Electromedical And Electrotherapeutic Apparatus	30	3.90%	0.721546	0.665529	-0.186016	-0.069161	0.008674	0.572393	0.665529	0.751613	1.753184	2.006483	2.386107
385	OPHTHALMIC GOODS	2	5.28%	0.978492	0.978492	0.869018	0.872369	0.877955	0.956150	0.978492	1.000834	1.079029	1.084615	1.087966
3851	Ophthalmic Goods	2	5.28%	0.978492	0.978492	0.869018	0.872369	0.877955	0.956150	0.978492	1.000834	1.079029	1.084615	1.087966
386	PHOTOGRAPHIC EQUIPMENT AND SUPPLIES	5	3.80%	0.704600	0.307539	0.083651	0.089405	0.098995	0.254810	0.307539	0.656039	1.660670	1.720905	1.757046
3861	Photographic Equipment And Supplies	5	3.80%	0.704600	0.307539	0.083651	0.089405	0.098995	0.254810	0.307539	0.656039	1.660670	1.720905	1.757046
387	WATCHES, CLOCKS, CLOCKWORK OPERATED DEVICES, AND PARTS	2	5.24%	0.970976	0.970976	0.535529	0.548859	0.571075	0.882109	0.970976	1.059843	1.370877	1.393093	1.406423
3873	Watches, Clocks, Clockwork Operated Devices, And Parts	2	5.24%	0.970976	0.970976	0.535529	0.548859	0.571075	0.882109	0.970976	1.059843	1.370877	1.393093	1.406423
39	MISCELLANEOUS MANUFACTURING INDUSTRIES	29	2.39%	0.442450	0.567695	-1.295427	-1.217618	-0.795411	0.473137	0.567695	0.713379	1.044998	1.098832	1.167519
391	JEWELRY, SILVERWARE, AND PLATED WARE	3	1.76%	0.326256	0.332462	0.183595	0.188152	0.195748	0.302081	0.332462	0.359119	0.452420	0.459085	0.463083
3911	Jewelry, Precious Metal	3	1.76%	0.326256	0.332462	0.183595	0.188152	0.195748	0.302081	0.332462	0.359119	0.452420	0.459085	0.463083
394	DOLLS, TOYS, GAMES AND SPORTING AND ATHLETIC GOODS	20	2.43%	0.449856	0.599705	-0.987891	-0.726668	-0.291296	0.471222	0.599705	0.736888	0.940557	0.995164	1.027927
3942	Dolls And Stuffed Toys	3	1.36%	0.252735	0.183987	-0.236878	-0.223994	-0.202522	0.098096	0.183987	0.311126	0.756114	0.787899	0.806970
3944	Games, Toys, And Children's Vehicles, Except Dolls And Bicycles	9	1.80%	0.333054	0.502687	-1.068215	-0.927477	-0.692915	0.329454	0.502687	0.721248	0.876958	0.905884	0.923239
3949	Sporting And Athletic Goods, Not Elsewhere Classified	8	3.54%	0.655179	0.688435	0.277357	0.293917	0.321515	0.627998	0.688435	0.733449	0.970993	1.010382	1.034015
399	MISCELLANEOUS MANUFACTURING INDUSTRIES	6	2.57%	0.475858	0.691801	-1.251550	-1.107926	-0.868551	0.620728	0.691801	0.762874	1.169443	1.191376	1.204537
3990	MISCELLANEOUS MANUFACTURING INDUSTRIES	1	6.55%	1.213310	1.213310	1.213310	1.213310	1.213310	1.213310	1.213310	1.213310	1.213310	1.213310	1.213310
3993	Signs And Advertising Specialties	1	-7.28%	-1.347300	-1.347300	-1.347300	-1.347300	-1.347300	-1.347300	-1.347300	-1.347300	-1.347300	-1.347300	-1.347300
3996	Linoleum, Asphalted-Felt-Base, And Other Hard Surface Floor Cover	1	3.35%	0.620728	0.620728	0.620728	0.620728	0.620728	0.620728	0.620728	0.620728	0.620728	0.620728	0.620728
3999	Manufacturing Industries, Not Elsewhere Classified	3	4.26%	0.789470	0.762874	0.571599	0.577454	0.587213	0.723838	0.762874	0.817867	1.010343	1.024092	1.032341
	TRANSPORTATION, COMMUNICATIONS, ELECTRIC, GAS, AND SANITARY SERVICE													
40	RAILROAD TRANSPORTATION	7	5.59%	1.034770	1.075130	0.564434	0.596076	0.648812	1.023563	1.075130	1.084298	1.348071	1.365221	1.375510
401	RAILROADS	7	5.59%	1.034770	1.075130	0.564434	0.596076	0.648812	1.023563	1.075130	1.084298	1.348071	1.365221	1.375510
4011	Railroads, Line-Haul Operating	7	5.59%	1.034770	1.075130	0.564434	0.596076	0.648812	1.023563	1.075130	1.084298	1.348071	1.365221	1.375510

Down-market Betas of Common Stocks by SIC Codes as of September 28, 2018

SIC Code	Description	Number of Companies	Equity Risk Premium	Mean	Median	1st Percentile	2.5th Percentile	5th Percentile	40th Percentile	50th Percentile	60th Percentile	95th Percentile	97.5th Percentile	99th Percentile
41	LOCAL AND SUBURBAN TRANSIT AND INTERURBAN HIGHWAY PASSENGER TRANSPORTATION	1	2.80%	0.517977	0.517977	0.517977	0.517977	0.517977	0.517977	0.517977	0.517977	0.517977	0.517977	0.517977
415	SCHOOL BUSES	1	2.80%	0.517977	0.517977	0.517977	0.517977	0.517977	0.517977	0.517977	0.517977	0.517977	0.517977	0.517977
4151	School Buses	1	2.80%	0.517977	0.517977	0.517977	0.517977	0.517977	0.517977	0.517977	0.517977	0.517977	0.517977	0.517977
42	MOTOR FREIGHT TRANSPORTATION AND WAREHOUSING	25	6.25%	1.158036	1.158030	-0.250988	-0.073090	0.167606	1.012351	1.158030	1.232196	2.769560	2.769560	2.769560
421	TRUCKING AND COURIER SERVICES, EXCEPT AIR	23	6.69%	1.238547	1.170290	-0.206018	0.039335	0.374074	1.068066	1.170290	1.257480	2.769560	2.769560	2.769560
4213	Trucking, Except Local	23	6.69%	1.238547	1.170290	-0.206018	0.039335	0.374074	1.068066	1.170290	1.257480	2.769560	2.769560	2.769560
422	PUBLIC WAREHOUSING AND STORAGE	2	1.25%	0.232155	0.232155	0.126726	0.129953	0.135332	0.210638	0.232155	0.253671	0.328977	0.334356	0.337583
4221	Farm Product Warehousing And Storage	1	1.83%	0.339735	0.339735	0.339735	0.339735	0.339735	0.339735	0.339735	0.339735	0.339735	0.339735	0.339735
4225	General Warehousing And Storage	1	0.67%	0.124574	0.124574	0.124574	0.124574	0.124574	0.124574	0.124574	0.124574	0.124574	0.124574	0.124574
44	WATER TRANSPORTATION	44	3.46%	0.641274	0.712238	-3.176072	-1.880496	0.055565	0.614777	0.712238	0.865111	1.557283	1.813641	2.368716
4400	WATER TRANSPORTATION	2	-9.67%	-1.791080	-1.791080	-3.990220	-3.922899	-3.810698	-2.239884	-1.791080	-1.342276	0.228538	0.340739	0.408060
441	DEEP SEA FOREIGN TRANSPORTATION OF FREIGHT	32	4.08%	0.755284	0.732247	-1.388987	-0.416428	0.059300	0.638014	0.732247	0.883026	1.686223	2.044927	2.481339
4412	Deep Sea Foreign Transportation Of Freight	32	4.08%	0.755284	0.732247	-1.388987	-0.416428	0.059300	0.638014	0.732247	0.883026	1.686223	2.044927	2.481339
442	DEEP SEA DOMESTIC TRANSPORTATION OF FREIGHT	1	3.83%	0.709078	0.709078	0.709078	0.709078	0.709078	0.709078	0.709078	0.709078	0.709078	0.709078	0.709078
4424	Deep Sea Domestic Transportation Of Freight	1	3.83%	0.709078	0.709078	0.709078	0.709078	0.709078	0.709078	0.709078	0.709078	0.709078	0.709078	0.709078
444	WATER TRANSPORTATION OF FREIGHT, NOT ELSEWHERE CLASSIFIED	1	2.24%	0.414647	0.414647	0.414647	0.414647	0.414647	0.414647	0.414647	0.414647	0.414647	0.414647	0.414647
4449	Water Transportation Of Freight, Not Elsewhere Classified	1	2.24%	0.414647	0.414647	0.414647	0.414647	0.414647	0.414647	0.414647	0.414647	0.414647	0.414647	0.414647
448	WATER TRANSPORTATION OF PASSENGERS	3	5.18%	0.959370	0.965204	0.845304	0.848974	0.855092	0.940735	0.965204	0.986173	1.059565	1.064808	1.067953
4481	Deep Sea Transportation Of Passengers, Except By Ferry	3	5.18%	0.959370	0.965204	0.845304	0.848974	0.855092	0.940735	0.965204	0.986173	1.059565	1.064808	1.067953
449	SERVICES INCIDENTAL TO WATER TRANSPORTATION	5	3.92%	0.725458	0.626215	0.298397	0.300284	0.303429	0.507165	0.626215	0.742647	1.349899	1.403975	1.436420
4491	Marine Cargo Handling	1	7.87%	1.458050	1.458050	1.458050	1.458050	1.458050	1.458050	1.458050	1.458050	1.458050	1.458050	1.458050
4492	Towing And Tugboat Services	1	1.60%	0.297139	0.297139	0.297139	0.297139	0.297139	0.297139	0.297139	0.297139	0.297139	0.297139	0.297139
4499	Water Transportation Services, Not Elsewhere Classified	3	3.37%	0.624034	0.626215	0.334543	0.343472	0.358353	0.566690	0.626215	0.684431	0.888188	0.902742	0.911474
45	TRANSPORTATION BY AIR	22	3.83%	0.709064	0.885862	-1.174146	-0.693316	0.033497	0.849909	0.885862	0.919018	1.209377	1.244396	1.265302
451	AIR TRANSPORTATION, SCHEDULED, AND AIR COURIER SERVICES	17	4.57%	0.845941	0.916503	0.037348	0.045752	0.059759	0.883383	0.916503	0.941520	1.226144	1.252692	1.268621
4512	Air Transportation, Scheduled	13	4.76%	0.881225	0.920694	0.143411	0.258384	0.450007	0.886333	0.920694	0.959236	1.197502	1.238371	1.262892
4513	Air Courier Services	4	3.95%	0.731265	0.840222	0.053712	0.086660	0.141575	0.794453	0.840222	0.885990	1.168415	1.190642	1.203979
452	AIR TRANSPORTATION, NONSCHEDULED	4	3.66%	0.678278	0.701846	0.278649	0.289835	0.308479	0.592604	0.701846	0.811087	1.015083	1.026656	1.033601
4522	Air Transportation, Nonscheduled	4	3.66%	0.678278	0.701846	0.278649	0.289835	0.308479	0.592604	0.701846	0.811087	1.015083	1.026656	1.033601
458	AIRPORTS, FLYING FIELDS, AND AIRPORT TERMINAL SERVICES	1	-8.07%	-1.494700	-1.494700	-1.494700	-1.494700	-1.494700	-1.494700	-1.494700	-1.494700	-1.494700	-1.494700	-1.494700
4581	Airports, Flying Fields, And Airport Terminal Services	1	-8.07%	-1.494700	-1.494700	-1.494700	-1.494700	-1.494700	-1.494700	-1.494700	-1.494700	-1.494700	-1.494700	-1.494700

Down-market Betas of Common Stocks by SIC Codes as of September 28, 2018

SIC Code	Description	Number of Companies	Equity Risk Premium	Mean	Median	1st Percentile	2.5th Percentile	5th Percentile	40th Percentile	50th Percentile	60th Percentile	95th Percentile	97.5th Percentile	99th Percentile
46	PIPELINES, EXCEPT NATURAL GAS	11	4.31%	0.798609	0.707938	0.622267	0.625790	0.631661	0.663131	0.707938	0.746341	1.182105	1.193563	1.200437
461	PIPELINES, EXCEPT NATURAL GAS	11	4.31%	0.798609	0.707938	0.622267	0.625790	0.631661	0.663131	0.707938	0.746341	1.182105	1.193563	1.200437
4612	Crude Petroleum Pipelines	6	4.33%	0.801928	0.727140	0.621405	0.623635	0.627351	0.707938	0.727140	0.746341	1.101525	1.130358	1.147657
4613	Refined Petroleum Pipelines	1	6.51%	1.205020	1.205020	1.205020	1.205020	1.205020	1.205020	1.205020	1.205020	1.205020	1.205020	1.205020
4619	Pipelines, Not Elsewhere Classified	4	3.74%	0.692027	0.659222	0.643761	0.644297	0.645190	0.656877	0.659222	0.661567	0.784790	0.795524	0.801965
47	TRANSPORTATION SERVICES	20	3.74%	0.693501	0.595989	-0.056855	0.030905	0.177171	0.528854	0.595989	0.778663	1.359626	1.474538	1.543485
4700	TRANSPORTATION SERVICES	5	2.64%	0.489424	0.355435	0.355435	0.355435	0.355435	0.355435	0.355435	0.378426	0.856906	0.912405	0.945704
472	ARRANGEMENT OF PASSENGER TRANSPORTATION	3	2.08%	0.385156	0.347787	0.195671	0.200328	0.208089	0.316743	0.347787	0.401252	0.588381	0.601748	0.609767
4724	Travel Agencies	1	3.32%	0.615114	0.615114	0.615114	0.615114	0.615114	0.615114	0.615114	0.615114	0.615114	0.615114	0.615114
4725	Tour Operators	2	1.46%	0.270177	0.270177	0.194119	0.196448	0.200328	0.254655	0.270177	0.285699	0.340026	0.343907	0.346235
473	ARRANGEMENT OF TRANSPORTATION OF FREIGHT AND CARGO	10	4.65%	0.861121	0.944765	-0.063502	0.014286	0.143933	0.754587	0.944765	1.036844	1.480586	1.535018	1.567677
4731	Arrangement Of Transportation Of Freight And Cargo	10	4.65%	0.861121	0.944765	-0.063502	0.014286	0.143933	0.754587	0.944765	1.036844	1.480586	1.535018	1.567677
478	MISCELLANEOUS SERVICES INCIDENTAL TO TRANSPORTATION	2	4.47%	0.828107	0.828107	0.717973	0.721344	0.726963	0.805631	0.828107	0.850583	0.929251	0.934870	0.938241
4789	Transportation Services, Not Elsewhere Classified	2	4.47%	0.828107	0.828107	0.717973	0.721344	0.726963	0.805631	0.828107	0.850583	0.929251	0.934870	0.938241
48	COMMUNICATIONS	126	4.05%	0.750290	0.695480	-0.385495	-0.077592	0.164838	0.631199	0.695480	0.839087	1.516695	1.983266	2.067930
481	TELEPHONE COMMUNICATIONS	55	4.15%	0.767636	0.664752	-0.603508	0.098675	0.152814	0.577398	0.664752	0.823637	1.896594	2.059354	2.499639
4812	Radiotelephone Communications	14	3.04%	0.562084	0.534026	0.212989	0.229950	0.258220	0.454245	0.534026	0.603269	0.871416	0.874751	0.876752
4813	Telephone Communications, Except Radiotelephone	41	4.52%	0.837825	0.768740	-0.810356	0.076136	0.140532	0.632471	0.768740	0.894685	2.003610	2.089370	2.624504
482	TELEGRAPH AND OTHER MESSAGE COMMUNICATIONS	2	3.67%	0.678994	0.678994	0.435596	0.443047	0.455466	0.629321	0.678994	0.728667	0.902523	0.914941	0.922392
4822	Telegraph And Other Message Communications	2	3.67%	0.678994	0.678994	0.435596	0.443047	0.455466	0.629321	0.678994	0.728667	0.902523	0.914941	0.922392
483	RADIO AND TELEVISION BROADCASTING STATIONS	25	3.47%	0.643235	0.653628	-0.158458	0.053512	0.292642	0.618529	0.653628	0.738489	0.990861	1.007312	1.016959
4832	Radio Broadcasting Stations	12	3.08%	0.570424	0.569653	-0.235003	-0.137850	0.024072	0.519914	0.569653	0.639308	0.959204	0.963567	0.966186
4833	Television Broadcasting Stations	13	3.84%	0.710445	0.727933	0.362061	0.366442	0.373743	0.693230	0.727933	0.771921	1.007312	1.015351	1.020174
484	CABLE AND OTHER PAY TELEVISION SERVICES	25	3.71%	0.687650	0.646471	-0.031232	0.071250	0.210531	0.627264	0.646471	0.728315	1.041550	1.279262	1.488487
4841	Cable And Other Pay Television Services	25	3.71%	0.687650	0.646471	-0.031232	0.071250	0.210531	0.627264	0.646471	0.728315	1.041550	1.279262	1.488487
489	COMMUNICATIONS SERVICES, NOT ELSEWHERE CLASSIFIED	19	5.03%	0.930864	0.932495	-0.254226	-0.014461	0.385147	0.849577	0.932495	1.071345	1.525542	1.763871	1.906868
4899	Communications Services, Not Elsewhere Classified	19	5.03%	0.930864	0.932495	-0.254226	-0.014461	0.385147	0.849577	0.932495	1.071345	1.525542	1.763871	1.906868
49	ELECTRIC, GAS, AND SANITARY SERVICES	127	2.43%	0.449243	0.335404	-0.495535	-0.330850	-0.072613	0.264237	0.335404	0.473899	1.056313	1.108385	2.653103
491	ELECTRIC SERVICES	45	1.75%	0.324577	0.265055	-0.068154	-0.041107	0.044825	0.224157	0.265055	0.325990	0.805990	0.901072	1.021918
4911	Electric Services	45	1.75%	0.324577	0.265055	-0.068154	-0.041107	0.044825	0.224157	0.265055	0.325990	0.805990	0.901072	1.021918
492	GAS PRODUCTION AND DISTRIBUTION	22	2.83%	0.524861	0.487671	0.090675	0.096482	0.107215	0.406607	0.487671	0.643855	0.913552	0.977122	1.017333
4922	Natural Gas Transmission	6	3.60%	0.666723	0.750229	0.181754	0.196400	0.220809	0.696269	0.750229	0.804188	1.012227	1.028183	1.037757
4923	Natural Gas Transmission And Distribution	7	3.80%	0.703057	0.784646	0.369138	0.394300	0.436237	0.704937	0.784646	0.785071	0.857706	0.857748	0.857774
4924	Natural Gas Distribution	9	1.58%	0.291688	0.280203	0.088278	0.090490	0.094177	0.270961	0.280203	0.294898	0.488509	0.490184	0.491189
493	COMBINATION ELECTRIC AND GAS, AND OTHER UTILITY SERVICES	24	1.36%	0.252720	0.228016	-0.378185	-0.154282	0.123250	0.211946	0.228016	0.261424	0.570876	0.725063	0.831863

Down-market Betas of Common Stocks by SIC Codes as of September 28, 2018

SIC Code	Description	Number of Companies	Equity Risk Premium	Mean	Median	1st Percentile	2.5th Percentile	5th Percentile	40th Percentile	50th Percentile	60th Percentile	95th Percentile	97.5th Percentile	99th Percentile
4931	Electric And Other Services Combined	18	1.39%	0.257532	0.228016	0.126682	0.134394	0.147248	0.211015	0.228016	0.259800	0.465314	0.529405	0.567860
4932	Gas And Other Services Combined	5	2.11%	0.391433	0.289204	0.136076	0.140785	0.148632	0.258088	0.289204	0.341741	0.806560	0.854811	0.883762
4939	Combination Utilities, Not Elsewhere Classified	1	-2.85%	-0.527454	-0.527454	-0.527454	-0.527454	-0.527454	-0.527454	-0.527454	-0.527454	-0.527454	-0.527454	-0.527454
494	WATER SUPPLY	15	3.46%	0.640227	0.661893	0.087475	0.100954	0.123418	0.620608	0.661893	0.694727	0.983435	1.022483	1.045911
4941	Water Supply	15	3.46%	0.640227	0.661893	0.087475	0.100954	0.123418	0.620608	0.661893	0.694727	0.983435	1.022483	1.045911
495	SANITARY SERVICES	21	3.92%	0.725344	0.710768	-0.642205	-0.553136	-0.404687	0.543426	0.710768	0.820807	3.165100	3.313365	3.402324
4950	SANITARY SERVICES	2	8.57%	1.586899	1.586899	-0.250337	-0.194095	-0.100359	1.211953	1.586899	1.961845	3.274157	3.367893	3.424135
4953	Refuse Systems	16	3.75%	0.693864	0.751511	-0.657049	-0.590248	-0.478911	0.660675	0.751511	0.820807	1.688185	2.426643	2.869717
4955	HAZARDOUS WASTE MANAGEMENT	2	-0.30%	-0.056192	-0.056192	-0.332796	-0.324329	-0.310216	-0.112642	-0.056192	0.000258	0.197832	0.211945	0.220412
4959	Sanitary Services, Not Elsewhere Classified	1	5.77%	1.069000	1.069000	1.069000	1.069000	1.069000	1.069000	1.069000	1.069000	1.069000	1.069000	1.069000
	WHOLESALE TRADE													
50	WHOLESALE TRADE¨DURABLE GOODS	73	4.29%	0.795052	0.851666	-0.077408	0.005059	0.095525	0.763337	0.851666	0.916320	1.278634	1.438462	1.739568
501	MOTOR VEHICLES AND MOTOR VEHICLE PARTS AND SUPPLIES	9	4.26%	0.788231	0.877349	0.490014	0.490380	0.490990	0.857179	0.877349	0.891368	1.021373	1.053636	1.072995
5012	Automobiles And Other Motor Vehicles	2	4.01%	0.742741	0.742741	0.564537	0.569992	0.579084	0.706373	0.742741	0.779109	0.906398	0.915490	0.920945
5013	Motor Vehicle Supplies And New Parts	6	4.60%	0.852630	0.886111	0.507888	0.535066	0.580362	0.877349	0.886111	0.894873	1.043363	1.064632	1.077393
5015	Motor Vehicle Parts, Used	1	2.66%	0.492819	0.492819	0.492819	0.492819	0.492819	0.492819	0.492819	0.492819	0.492819	0.492819	0.492819
503	LUMBER AND OTHER CONSTRUCTION MATERIALS	9	4.07%	0.754615	0.846999	0.039746	0.077835	0.141318	0.746734	0.846999	0.850733	1.418490	1.537460	1.608842
5030	WHOLESALE-LUMBER & OTHER CONSTRUCTION MATERIALS	3	2.83%	0.523970	0.388477	0.332901	0.334603	0.337438	0.377135	0.388477	0.481115	0.805347	0.828507	0.842402
5031	Lumber, Plywood, Millwork, And Wood Panels	4	4.64%	0.859093	0.882796	0.039332	0.076801	0.139249	0.861318	0.882796	0.904273	1.545754	1.601092	1.634295
5033	Roofing, Siding, And Insulation Materials	1	5.73%	1.061580	1.061580	1.061580	1.061580	1.061580	1.061580	1.061580	1.061580	1.061580	1.061580	1.061580
5039	Construction Materials, Not Elsewhere Classified	1	3.90%	0.721668	0.721668	0.721668	0.721668	0.721668	0.721668	0.721668	0.721668	0.721668	0.721668	0.721668
504	PROFESSIONAL AND COMMERCIAL EQUIPMENT AND SUPPLIES	16	4.97%	0.920742	0.983026	0.130242	0.170892	0.238642	0.830920	0.983026	1.109810	1.318833	1.351401	1.370943
5044	Office Equipment	1	1.53%	0.283808	0.283808	0.283808	0.283808	0.283808	0.283808	0.283808	0.283808	0.283808	0.283808	0.283808
5045	Computers And Computer Peripheral Equipment And Software	9	5.45%	1.010106	1.077730	0.711534	0.725726	0.749380	0.926203	1.077730	1.103394	1.228788	1.228904	1.228974
5047	Medical, Dental, And Hospital Equipment And Supplies	6	4.82%	0.892852	0.985900	0.128039	0.165385	0.227627	0.826150	0.985900	1.145650	1.362258	1.373114	1.379628
505	METALS AND MINERALS, EXCEPT PETROLEUM	6	5.80%	1.073683	1.165460	0.400773	0.413342	0.434291	1.157500	1.165460	1.173420	1.766375	1.859863	1.915955
5051	Metals Service Centers And Offices	6	5.80%	1.073683	1.165460	0.400773	0.413342	0.434291	1.157500	1.165460	1.173420	1.766375	1.859863	1.915955
506	ELECTRICAL GOODS	17	4.12%	0.762255	0.820385	0.332404	0.336635	0.343686	0.622299	0.820385	0.937117	1.198898	1.206754	1.211468
5063	Electrical Apparatus And Equipment, Wiring Supplies, And Construction	5	4.65%	0.861255	0.872217	0.453601	0.476525	0.514731	0.851484	0.872217	0.915484	1.152053	1.173511	1.186387
5065	Electronic Parts And Equipment, Not Elsewhere Classified	12	3.89%	0.721005	0.637596	0.331523	0.334432	0.339279	0.506793	0.637596	0.906763	1.154490	1.184550	1.202586
507	HARDWARE, AND PLUMBING AND HEATING EQUIPMENT AND SUPPLIES	3	3.98%	0.737458	0.773366	0.577043	0.583053	0.593069	0.733300	0.773366	0.791887	0.856711	0.861341	0.864119

Down-market Betas of Common Stocks by SIC Codes as of September 28, 2018

SIC Code	Description	Number of Companies	Equity Risk Premium	Mean	Median	1st Percentile	2.5th Percentile	5th Percentile	40th Percentile	50th Percentile	60th Percentile	95th Percentile	97.5th Percentile	99th Percentile
5074	Plumbing And Heating Equipment And Supplies (Hydronics)	2	3.64%	0.673201	0.673201	0.575039	0.578044	0.583053	0.653168	0.673201	0.693234	0.763350	0.768358	0.771363
5075	Warm Air Heating And Air-Conditioning Equipment And Supplies	1	4.68%	0.865971	0.865971	0.865971	0.865971	0.865971	0.865971	0.865971	0.865971	0.865971	0.865971	0.865971
508	MACHINERY, EQUIPMENT, AND SUPPLIES	8	4.04%	0.748070	0.899141	-0.173470	-0.142865	-0.091856	0.821280	0.899141	0.986303	1.233109	1.249710	1.259670
5084	Industrial Machinery And Equipment	6	3.73%	0.689962	0.899141	-0.179299	-0.157438	-0.121004	0.845795	0.899141	0.952486	1.242595	1.254453	1.261567
5085	Industrial Supplies	1	6.06%	1.121570	1.121570	1.121570	1.121570	1.121570	1.121570	1.121570	1.121570	1.121570	1.121570	1.121570
5087	Service Establishment Equipment And Supplies	1	3.91%	0.723220	0.723220	0.723220	0.723220	0.723220	0.723220	0.723220	0.723220	0.723220	0.723220	0.723220
509	MISCELLANEOUS DURABLE GOODS	5	1.97%	0.364789	0.167738	-0.027136	-0.019664	-0.007212	0.137606	0.167738	0.317728	0.951103	1.002151	1.032781
5091	Sporting And Recreational Goods And Supplies	2	3.30%	0.610469	0.610469	0.176593	0.189875	0.212011	0.521923	0.610469	0.699015	1.008927	1.031063	1.044345
5094	Jewelry, Watches, Precious Stones, And Precious Metals	2	1.71%	0.317561	0.317561	0.096911	0.103665	0.114923	0.272530	0.317561	0.362592	0.520199	0.531456	0.538211
5099	Durable Goods, Not Elsewhere Classified	1	-0.17%	-0.032117	-0.032117	-0.032117	-0.032117	-0.032117	-0.032117	-0.032117	-0.032117	-0.032117	-0.032117	-0.032117
51	WHOLESALE TRADE¨NONDURABLE GOODS	63	3.41%	0.631404	0.710347	-1.873478	-0.808551	-0.082404	0.536986	0.710347	0.808564	1.233529	1.515098	2.623816
511	PAPER AND PAPER PRODUCTS	1	23.41%	4.334470	4.334470	4.334470	4.334470	4.334470	4.334470	4.334470	4.334470	4.334470	4.334470	4.334470
5112	Stationery And Office Supplies	1	23.41%	4.334470	4.334470	4.334470	4.334470	4.334470	4.334470	4.334470	4.334470	4.334470	4.334470	4.334470
512	DRUGS, DRUG PROPRIETARIES, AND DRUGGISTS' SUNDRIES	23	3.45%	0.639697	0.806527	-1.921846	-1.195240	-0.192458	0.675678	0.806527	0.881213	1.442827	1.515098	1.551249
5122	Drugs, Drug Proprietaries, And Druggists' Sundries	23	3.45%	0.639697	0.806527	-1.921846	-1.195240	-0.192458	0.675678	0.806527	0.881213	1.442827	1.515098	1.551249
513	APPAREL, PIECE GOODS, AND NOTIONS	2	1.65%	0.304673	0.304673	0.053371	0.061064	0.073886	0.253387	0.304673	0.355959	0.535460	0.548281	0.555974
5136	Men's And Boys' Clothing And Furnishings	1	0.26%	0.048243	0.048243	0.048243	0.048243	0.048243	0.048243	0.048243	0.048243	0.048243	0.048243	0.048243
5139	Footwear	1	3.03%	0.561103	0.561103	0.561103	0.561103	0.561103	0.561103	0.561103	0.561103	0.561103	0.561103	0.561103
514	GROCERIES AND RELATED PRODUCTS	14	2.33%	0.431906	0.360588	-0.044145	-0.019801	0.020772	0.322219	0.360588	0.530674	0.864099	0.881674	0.892219
5140	WHOLESALE-GROCERIES & RELATED PRODUCTS	2	1.90%	0.352598	0.352598	-0.052115	-0.039726	-0.019077	0.270004	0.352598	0.435193	0.724274	0.744922	0.757312
5141	Groceries, General Line	8	2.13%	0.395067	0.332301	0.073012	0.084691	0.104155	0.311023	0.332301	0.393348	0.722794	0.754750	0.773924
5145	Confectionery	1	4.86%	0.899249	0.899249	0.899249	0.899249	0.899249	0.899249	0.899249	0.899249	0.899249	0.899249	0.899249
5148	Fresh Fruits And Vegetables	1	2.01%	0.372071	0.372071	0.372071	0.372071	0.372071	0.372071	0.372071	0.372071	0.372071	0.372071	0.372071
5149	Groceries And Related Products, Not Elsewhere Classified	2	2.46%	0.454819	0.454819	0.072273	0.083984	0.103501	0.376748	0.454819	0.532890	0.806137	0.825654	0.837365
515	FARM-PRODUCT RAW MATERIALS	4	1.56%	0.288476	0.194844	0.007313	0.010699	0.016343	0.126119	0.194844	0.263569	0.691695	0.725428	0.745668
5153	Grain And Field Beans	2	2.89%	0.534273	0.534273	0.313883	0.320629	0.331874	0.489295	0.534273	0.579251	0.736672	0.747917	0.754663
5159	Farm-Product Raw Materials, Not Elsewhere Classified	2	0.23%	0.042679	0.042679	0.005808	0.006937	0.008818	0.035155	0.042679	0.050204	0.076541	0.078422	0.079551
516	CHEMICALS AND ALLIED PRODUCTS	5	4.26%	0.789616	0.851833	0.246772	0.282393	0.341762	0.837785	0.851833	0.884311	1.085390	1.104435	1.115862
5162	Plastics Materials And Basic Forms And Shapes	1	1.20%	0.223024	0.223024	0.223024	0.223024	0.223024	0.223024	0.223024	0.223024	0.223024	0.223024	0.223024
5169	Chemicals And Allied Products, Not Elsewhere Classified	4	5.03%	0.931264	0.892431	0.817768	0.819348	0.821982	0.868072	0.892431	0.916790	1.094912	1.109196	1.117766
517	PETROLEUM AND PETROLEUM PRODUCTS	7	4.41%	0.815870	0.932846	0.546209	0.560142	0.583363	0.806389	0.932846	0.932846	0.953127	0.957473	0.960081

Down-market Betas of Common Stocks by SIC Codes as of September 28, 2018

SIC Code	Description	Number of Companies	Equity Risk Premium	Mean	Median	1st Percentile	2.5th Percentile	5th Percentile	40th Percentile	50th Percentile	60th Percentile	95th Percentile	97.5th Percentile	99th Percentile
5172	Petroleum And Petroleum Products Wholesalers, Except Bulk Station	7	4.41%	0.815870	0.932846	0.546209	0.560142	0.583363	0.806389	0.932846	0.932846	0.953127	0.957473	0.960081
518	BEER, WINE, AND DISTILLED ALCOHOLIC BEVERAGES	1	6.50%	1.203550	1.203550	1.203550	1.203550	1.203550	1.203550	1.203550	1.203550	1.203550	1.203550	1.203550
5180	WHOLESALE-BEER, WINE & DISTILLED ALCOHOLIC BEVERAGES	1	6.50%	1.203550	1.203550	1.203550	1.203550	1.203550	1.203550	1.203550	1.203550	1.203550	1.203550	1.203550
519	MISCELLANEOUS NONDURABLE GOODS	6	1.85%	0.343052	0.508486	-1.453451	-1.313216	-1.079493	0.422702	0.508486	0.594269	1.148103	1.155796	1.160413
5190	WHOLESALE-MISCELLANEOUS NONDURABLE GOODS	1	2.28%	0.422702	0.422702	0.422702	0.422702	0.422702	0.422702	0.422702	0.422702	0.422702	0.422702	0.422702
5191	Farm Supplies	2	-2.57%	-0.476336	-0.476336	-1.525528	-1.493410	-1.439880	-0.690456	-0.476336	-0.262215	0.487209	0.540739	0.572857
5192	Books, Periodicals, And Newspapers	1	6.28%	1.163490	1.163490	1.163490	1.163490	1.163490	1.163490	1.163490	1.163490	1.163490	1.163490	1.163490
5199	Nondurable Goods, Not Elsewhere Classified	2	3.85%	0.712395	0.712395	0.330640	0.342326	0.361804	0.634485	0.712395	0.790304	1.062985	1.082463	1.094149
	RETAIL TRADE													
52	RETAIL TRADE	14	4.41%	0.816934	0.978612	-0.035190	0.013495	0.094637	0.899960	0.978612	1.026362	1.285667	1.303148	1.313637
521	LUMBER AND OTHER BUILDING MATERIALS DEALERS	12	4.64%	0.859183	1.024925	-0.040183	0.001012	0.069670	0.969828	1.024925	1.030356	1.291046	1.305838	1.314713
5211	Lumber And Other Building Materials Dealers	12	4.64%	0.859183	1.024925	-0.040183	0.001012	0.069670	0.969828	1.024925	1.030356	1.291046	1.305838	1.314713
523	PAINT, GLASS, AND WALLPAPER STORES	1	4.81%	0.891277	0.891277	0.891277	0.891277	0.891277	0.891277	0.891277	0.891277	0.891277	0.891277	0.891277
5231	Paint, Glass, And Wallpaper Stores	1	4.81%	0.891277	0.891277	0.891277	0.891277	0.891277	0.891277	0.891277	0.891277	0.891277	0.891277	0.891277
526	RETAIL NURSERIES, LAWN AND GARDEN SUPPLY STORES	1	1.27%	0.235605	0.235605	0.235605	0.235605	0.235605	0.235605	0.235605	0.235605	0.235605	0.235605	0.235605
5261	Retail Nurseries, Lawn And Garden Supply Stores	1	1.27%	0.235605	0.235605	0.235605	0.235605	0.235605	0.235605	0.235605	0.235605	0.235605	0.235605	0.235605
53	GENERAL MERCHANDISE STORES	18	4.09%	0.757614	0.815659	0.143447	0.147867	0.155232	0.743840	0.815659	0.849614	1.285387	1.391119	1.454557
531	DEPARTMENT STORES	8	4.98%	0.922472	0.908401	0.288213	0.332860	0.407271	0.867402	0.908401	0.961230	1.409777	1.453314	1.479435
5311	Department Stores	8	4.98%	0.922472	0.908401	0.288213	0.332860	0.407271	0.867402	0.908401	0.961230	1.409777	1.453314	1.479435
533	VARIETY STORES	8	3.17%	0.587605	0.779726	0.141714	0.143534	0.146567	0.639565	0.779726	0.820782	0.896753	0.905141	0.910175
5331	Variety Stores	8	3.17%	0.587605	0.779726	0.141714	0.143534	0.146567	0.639565	0.779726	0.820782	0.896753	0.905141	0.910175
539	MISCELLANEOUS GENERAL MERCHANDISE STORES	2	4.20%	0.778217	0.778217	0.740460	0.741615	0.743542	0.770511	0.778217	0.785923	0.812892	0.814819	0.815974
5399	Miscellaneous General Merchandise Stores	2	4.20%	0.778217	0.778217	0.740460	0.741615	0.743542	0.770511	0.778217	0.785923	0.812892	0.814819	0.815974
54	FOOD STORES	23	1.71%	0.317399	0.446442	-1.156823	-1.060363	-0.903244	0.363587	0.446442	0.549071	1.174520	1.235445	1.267356
541	GROCERY STORES	18	2.33%	0.432105	0.520362	-1.053469	-0.801977	-0.382824	0.436420	0.520362	0.632953	1.043945	1.117938	1.162333
5411	Grocery Stores	18	2.33%	0.432105	0.520362	-1.053469	-0.801977	-0.382824	0.436420	0.520362	0.632953	1.043945	1.117938	1.162333
544	CANDY, NUT, AND CONFECTIONERY STORES	1	2.17%	0.402599	0.402599	0.402599	0.402599	0.402599	0.402599	0.402599	0.402599	0.402599	0.402599	0.402599
5441	Candy, Nut, And Confectionery Stores	1	2.17%	0.402599	0.402599	0.402599	0.402599	0.402599	0.402599	0.402599	0.402599	0.402599	0.402599	0.402599
546	RETAIL BAKERIES	1	-5.02%	-0.928827	-0.928827	-0.928827	-0.928827	-0.928827	-0.928827	-0.928827	-0.928827	-0.928827	-0.928827	-0.928827
5461	Retail Bakeries	1	-5.02%	-0.928827	-0.928827	-0.928827	-0.928827	-0.928827	-0.928827	-0.928827	-0.928827	-0.928827	-0.928827	-0.928827
549	MISCELLANEOUS FOOD STORES	3	0.09%	0.016170	-0.567120	-0.670882	-0.667706	-0.662412	-0.588296	-0.567120	-0.195970	1.103055	1.195843	1.251515
5499	Miscellaneous Food Stores	3	0.09%	0.016170	-0.567120	-0.670882	-0.667706	-0.662412	-0.588296	-0.567120	-0.195970	1.103055	1.195843	1.251515
55	AUTOMOTIVE DEALERS AND GASOLINE SERVICE STATIONS	20	4.50%	0.832610	0.912525	-0.274368	-0.217399	-0.122450	0.847226	0.912525	0.973391	1.314188	1.389694	1.434998
5500	RETAIL-AUTO DEALERS & GASOLINE STATIONS	2	6.39%	1.184005	1.184005	1.065606	1.069231	1.075272	1.159842	1.184005	1.208168	1.292739	1.298779	1.302404

Down-market Betas of Common Stocks by SIC Codes as of September 28, 2018

SIC Code	Description	Number of Companies	Equity Risk Premium	Mean	Median	1st Percentile	2.5th Percentile	5th Percentile	40th Percentile	50th Percentile	60th Percentile	95th Percentile	97.5th Percentile	99th Percentile
551	MOTOR VEHICLE DEALERS (NEW AND USED)	8	5.37%	0.994440	0.921125	0.697073	0.707692	0.725390	0.859993	0.921125	0.985949	1.409564	1.437382	1.454073
5511	Motor Vehicle Dealers (New And Used)	8	5.37%	0.994440	0.921125	0.697073	0.707692	0.725390	0.859993	0.921125	0.985949	1.409564	1.437382	1.454073
552	MOTOR VEHICLE DEALERS (USED ONLY)	2	1.80%	0.333448	0.333448	-0.299432	-0.280058	-0.247768	0.204289	0.333448	0.462607	0.914664	0.946954	0.966328
5521	Motor Vehicle Dealers (Used Only)	2	1.80%	0.333448	0.333448	-0.299432	-0.280058	-0.247768	0.204289	0.333448	0.462607	0.914664	0.946954	0.966328
553	AUTO AND HOME SUPPLY STORES	3	4.62%	0.854999	0.918469	0.420883	0.436115	0.461502	0.816921	0.918469	0.981935	1.204067	1.219933	1.229453
5531	Auto And Home Supply Stores	3	4.62%	0.854999	0.918469	0.420883	0.436115	0.461502	0.816921	0.918469	0.981935	1.204067	1.219933	1.229453
554	GASOLINE SERVICE STATIONS	4	3.14%	0.581260	0.584632	-0.101201	-0.084320	-0.056184	0.391463	0.584632	0.777801	1.213983	1.241106	1.257381
5541	Gasoline Service Stations	4	3.14%	0.581260	0.584632	-0.101201	-0.084320	-0.056184	0.391463	0.584632	0.777801	1.213983	1.241106	1.257381
555	BOAT DEALERS	1	4.17%	0.771732	0.771732	0.771732	0.771732	0.771732	0.771732	0.771732	0.771732	0.771732	0.771732	0.771732
5551	Boat Dealers	1	4.17%	0.771732	0.771732	0.771732	0.771732	0.771732	0.771732	0.771732	0.771732	0.771732	0.771732	0.771732
56	APPAREL AND ACCESSORY STORES	34	4.60%	0.852530	0.858407	-0.420440	-0.133011	0.176857	0.739346	0.858407	1.003108	1.441191	1.650698	2.003499
5600	RETAIL-APPAREL & ACCESSORY STORES	1	3.90%	0.723076	0.723076	0.723076	0.723076	0.723076	0.723076	0.723076	0.723076	0.723076	0.723076	0.723076
561	MEN'S AND BOYS' CLOTHING AND ACCESSORY STORES	2	4.02%	0.744930	0.744930	0.674699	0.676849	0.680432	0.730597	0.744930	0.759262	0.809427	0.813010	0.815160
5611	Men's And Boys' Clothing And Accessory Stores	2	4.02%	0.744930	0.744930	0.674699	0.676849	0.680432	0.730597	0.744930	0.759262	0.809427	0.813010	0.815160
562	WOMEN'S CLOTHING STORES	8	3.68%	0.682046	0.854071	-0.547800	-0.451412	-0.290766	0.620879	0.854071	1.059840	1.287828	1.341684	1.373998
5621	Women's Clothing Stores	8	3.68%	0.682046	0.854071	-0.547800	-0.451412	-0.290766	0.620879	0.854071	1.059840	1.287828	1.341684	1.373998
563	WOMEN'S ACCESSORY AND SPECIALTY STORES	1	6.24%	1.155240	1.155240	1.155240	1.155240	1.155240	1.155240	1.155240	1.155240	1.155240	1.155240	1.155240
5632	Women's Accessory And Specialty Stores	1	6.24%	1.155240	1.155240	1.155240	1.155240	1.155240	1.155240	1.155240	1.155240	1.155240	1.155240	1.155240
565	FAMILY CLOTHING STORES	15	4.60%	0.851849	0.850644	0.013459	0.080741	0.192877	0.758239	0.850644	0.915326	1.449688	1.844194	2.080898
5651	Family Clothing Stores	15	4.60%	0.851849	0.850644	0.013459	0.080741	0.192877	0.758239	0.850644	0.915326	1.449688	1.844194	2.080898
566	SHOE STORES	6	5.78%	1.069781	1.113775	0.611337	0.615986	0.623735	1.031150	1.113775	1.196400	1.491153	1.508561	1.519007
5661	Shoe Stores	6	5.78%	1.069781	1.113775	0.611337	0.615986	0.623735	1.031150	1.113775	1.196400	1.491153	1.508561	1.519007
569	MISCELLANEOUS APPAREL AND ACCESSORY STORES	1	5.21%	0.965050	0.965050	0.965050	0.965050	0.965050	0.965050	0.965050	0.965050	0.965050	0.965050	0.965050
5699	Miscellaneous Apparel And Accessory Stores	1	5.21%	0.965050	0.965050	0.965050	0.965050	0.965050	0.965050	0.965050	0.965050	0.965050	0.965050	0.965050
57	HOME FURNITURE, FURNISHINGS, AND EQUIPMENT STORES	11	4.14%	0.767522	0.859274	0.184554	0.188935	0.196237	0.741329	0.859274	0.879470	1.263650	1.327455	1.365738
5700	RETAIL-HOME FURNITURE, FURNISHINGS & EQUIPMENT STORES	1	0.98%	0.181633	0.181633	0.181633	0.181633	0.181633	0.181633	0.181633	0.181633	0.181633	0.181633	0.181633
571	HOME FURNITURE AND FURNISHINGS STORES	6	4.43%	0.820044	0.819107	0.488198	0.491656	0.497419	0.741329	0.819107	0.896884	1.134060	1.135050	1.135644
5712	Furniture Stores	3	3.82%	0.708035	0.741329	0.491002	0.498665	0.511437	0.690242	0.741329	0.772440	0.881329	0.889106	0.893773
5713	Floor Covering Stores	1	2.87%	0.531997	0.531997	0.531997	0.531997	0.531997	0.531997	0.531997	0.531997	0.531997	0.531997	0.531997
5719	Miscellaneous Homefurnishings Stores	2	6.11%	1.132080	1.132080	1.128199	1.128318	1.128516	1.131288	1.132080	1.132872	1.135644	1.135842	1.135961
572	HOUSEHOLD APPLIANCE STORES	1	1.14%	0.210841	0.210841	0.210841	0.210841	0.210841	0.210841	0.210841	0.210841	0.210841	0.210841	0.210841
5722	Household Appliance Stores	1	1.14%	0.210841	0.210841	0.210841	0.210841	0.210841	0.210841	0.210841	0.210841	0.210841	0.210841	0.210841
573	RADIO, TELEVISION, CONSUMER ELECTRONICS, AND MUSIC STORES	3	5.63%	1.043335	0.879470	0.859678	0.860284	0.861294	0.875431	0.879470	0.981828	1.340081	1.365671	1.381024
5731	Radio, Television, And Consumer Electronics Stores	2	6.13%	1.135365	1.135365	0.884588	0.892265	0.905060	1.084186	1.135365	1.186544	1.365671	1.378465	1.386142
5735	Record And Prerecorded Tape Stores	1	4.64%	0.859274	0.859274	0.859274	0.859274	0.859274	0.859274	0.859274	0.859274	0.859274	0.859274	0.859274
58	EATING AND DRINKING PLACES	66	3.70%	0.684592	0.702961	-0.708778	-0.447103	0.034486	0.619102	0.702961	0.801068	1.254740	1.532948	1.828384

Down-market Betas of Common Stocks by SIC Codes as of September 28, 2018

SIC Code	Description	Number of Companies	Equity Risk Premium	Mean	Median	1st Percentile	2.5th Percentile	5th Percentile	40th Percentile	50th Percentile	60th Percentile	95th Percentile	97.5th Percentile	99th Percentile
581	EATING AND DRINKING PLACES	66	3.70%	0.684592	0.702961	-0.708778	-0.447103	0.034486	0.619102	0.702961	0.801068	1.254740	1.532948	1.828384
5810	RETAIL-EATING & DRINKING PLACES	2	3.15%	0.584195	0.584195	-0.373525	-0.344207	-0.295344	0.388742	0.584195	0.779648	1.463734	1.512597	1.541915
5812	Eating Places	63	3.73%	0.690353	0.702967	-0.723488	-0.228804	0.081085	0.621684	0.702967	0.801370	1.254740	1.372235	1.822979
5813	Drinking Places (Alcoholic Beverages)	1	2.82%	0.522430	0.522430	0.522430	0.522430	0.522430	0.522430	0.522430	0.522430	0.522430	0.522430	0.522430
59	MISCELLANEOUS RETAIL	73	2.96%	0.547603	0.741932	-2.579527	-1.615176	-0.986195	0.686932	0.741932	0.798293	1.596240	2.059136	2.318653
5900	RETAIL-MISCELLANEOUS RETAIL	1	-4.15%	-0.768550	-0.768550	-0.768550	-0.768550	-0.768550	-0.768550	-0.768550	-0.768550	-0.768550	-0.768550	-0.768550
591	DRUG STORES AND PROPRIETARY STORES	8	5.35%	0.991061	0.916545	0.660740	0.665670	0.673885	0.853151	0.916545	0.955408	1.662783	1.839222	1.945085
5912	Drug Stores And Proprietary Stores	8	5.35%	0.991061	0.916545	0.660740	0.665670	0.673885	0.853151	0.916545	0.955408	1.662783	1.839222	1.945085
592	LIQUOR STORES	1	2.22%	0.411434	0.411434	0.411434	0.411434	0.411434	0.411434	0.411434	0.411434	0.411434	0.411434	0.411434
5921	Liquor Stores	1	2.22%	0.411434	0.411434	0.411434	0.411434	0.411434	0.411434	0.411434	0.411434	0.411434	0.411434	0.411434
593	USED MERCHANDISE STORES	3	3.76%	0.696637	0.669790	0.576156	0.579022	0.583800	0.650681	0.669790	0.705007	0.828267	0.837072	0.842354
5932	Used Merchandise Stores	3	3.76%	0.696637	0.669790	0.576156	0.579022	0.583800	0.650681	0.669790	0.705007	0.828267	0.837072	0.842354
594	MISCELLANEOUS SHOPPING GOODS STORES	14	4.23%	0.783312	0.840524	-0.035171	0.023540	0.121390	0.784020	0.840524	0.885888	1.373280	1.638015	1.796856
5941	Sporting Goods Stores And Bicycle Shops	3	2.52%	0.466353	0.300520	0.228243	0.230456	0.234143	0.285770	0.300520	0.414770	0.814645	0.843208	0.860345
5942	Book Stores	2	4.30%	0.795901	0.795901	0.693311	0.696451	0.701685	0.774964	0.795901	0.816838	0.890117	0.895351	0.898491
5943	Stationery Stores	1	10.27%	1.902750	1.902750	1.902750	1.902750	1.902750	1.902750	1.902750	1.902750	1.902750	1.902750	1.902750
5944	Jewelry Stores	3	3.18%	0.589071	0.889417	-0.055036	-0.026125	0.022062	0.696671	0.889417	0.901955	0.945838	0.948973	0.950853
5945	Hobby, Toy, And Game Shops	3	4.89%	0.906187	0.891781	0.741663	0.746258	0.753917	0.861145	0.891781	0.931061	1.068540	1.078360	1.084252
5947	Gift, Novelty, And Souvenir Shops	2	4.28%	0.793492	0.793492	0.778022	0.778495	0.779285	0.790334	0.793492	0.796649	0.807698	0.808488	0.808961
596	NONSTORE RETAILERS	30	2.64%	0.489091	0.734583	-3.182950	-2.572510	-1.786672	0.692532	0.734583	0.820915	1.853407	2.317124	2.450130
5960	RETAIL-NONSTORE RETAILERS	2	3.19%	0.591278	0.591278	0.469621	0.473345	0.479552	0.566450	0.591278	0.616105	0.703003	0.709210	0.712934
5961	Catalog And Mail-Order Houses	28	2.60%	0.481792	0.763825	-3.211016	-2.642676	-1.875545	0.703116	0.763825	0.864717	1.937770	2.332412	2.456245
598	FUEL DEALERS	4	-0.27%	-0.049839	-0.052427	-0.138339	-0.136645	-0.133821	-0.082065	-0.052427	-0.022788	0.037766	0.041366	0.043526
5983	Fuel Oil Dealers	4	-0.27%	-0.049839	-0.052427	-0.138339	-0.136645	-0.133821	-0.082065	-0.052427	-0.022788	0.037766	0.041366	0.043526
599	RETAIL STORES, NOT ELSEWHERE CLASSIFIED	12	2.19%	0.406169	0.740896	-1.359067	-1.189188	-0.906057	0.536964	0.740896	0.745643	1.118860	1.255380	1.337292
5992	Florists	1	4.04%	0.748117	0.748117	0.748117	0.748117	0.748117	0.748117	0.748117	0.748117	0.748117	0.748117	0.748117
5995	Optical Goods Stores	1	4.56%	0.843592	0.843592	0.843592	0.843592	0.843592	0.843592	0.843592	0.843592	0.843592	0.843592	0.843592
5999	Miscellaneous Retail Stores, Not Elsewhere Classified	10	1.77%	0.328232	0.570780	-1.379659	-1.240667	-1.009014	0.297222	0.570780	0.740688	1.168503	1.280202	1.347221
	FINANCE, INSURANCE, AND REAL ESTATE													
60	DEPOSITORY INSTITUTIONS	382	3.58%	0.662276	0.722937	-0.180920	-0.053918	-0.024704	0.622445	0.722937	0.807908	1.238245	1.365489	1.498984
602	COMMERCIAL BANKS	292	3.68%	0.680981	0.769248	-0.194521	-0.090465	-0.008258	0.679287	0.769248	0.827366	1.227202	1.312457	1.356687
6021	National Commercial Banks	106	3.92%	0.725806	0.824189	-0.194720	-0.068209	0.012599	0.711919	0.824189	0.908315	1.256793	1.340671	1.345137
6022	State Commercial Banks	161	3.63%	0.671692	0.752363	-0.148474	-0.035327	0.002564	0.683135	0.752363	0.801644	1.198720	1.244090	1.365478
6029	Commercial Banks, Not Elsewhere Classified	25	2.97%	0.550744	0.655084	-0.207749	-0.134919	-0.049380	0.602837	0.655084	0.689708	1.035976	1.068556	1.093086
603	SAVINGS INSTITUTIONS	80	3.03%	0.562034	0.523219	-0.058981	-0.037923	-0.030591	0.374549	0.523219	0.715677	1.231468	1.499810	1.830913
6035	Savings Institutions, Federally Chartered	60	3.02%	0.560046	0.507764	-0.063870	-0.046089	-0.034619	0.363238	0.507764	0.722647	1.236461	1.499810	2.146249
6036	Savings Institutions, Not Federally Chartered	20	3.07%	0.567998	0.536326	-0.004023	0.035524	0.101435	0.463121	0.536326	0.593443	1.155477	1.277714	1.351055
606	CREDIT UNIONS	1	9.39%	1.738730	1.738730	1.738730	1.738730	1.738730	1.738730	1.738730	1.738730	1.738730	1.738730	1.738730
6061	Credit Unions, Federally Chartered	1	9.39%	1.738730	1.738730	1.738730	1.738730	1.738730	1.738730	1.738730	1.738730	1.738730	1.738730	1.738730
608	FOREIGN BANKING AND BRANCHES AND AGENCIES OF FOREIGN BANKS	2	2.14%	0.396534	0.396534	0.385938	0.386263	0.386803	0.394372	0.396534	0.398696	0.406265	0.406805	0.407130

Down-market Betas of Common Stocks by SIC Codes as of September 28, 2018

SIC Code	Description	Number of Companies	Equity Risk Premium	Mean	Median	1st Percentile	2.5th Percentile	5th Percentile	40th Percentile	50th Percentile	60th Percentile	95th Percentile	97.5th Percentile	99th Percentile
6081	Branches And Agencies Of Foreign Banks	2	2.14%	0.396534	0.396534	0.385938	0.386263	0.386803	0.394372	0.396534	0.398696	0.406265	0.406805	0.407130
609	FUNCTIONS RELATED TO DEPOSITORY BANKING	7	5.13%	0.949802	0.920109	0.381463	0.392864	0.411867	0.874942	0.920109	1.031074	1.470782	1.484786	1.493188
6099	Functions Related To Depository Banking, Not Elsewhere Classified	7	5.13%	0.949802	0.920109	0.381463	0.392864	0.411867	0.874942	0.920109	1.031074	1.470782	1.484786	1.493188
61	NONDEPOSITORY CREDIT INSTITUTIONS	46	2.98%	0.552727	0.616850	-1.329562	-0.428373	-0.259494	0.460563	0.616850	0.706969	1.166878	1.207920	1.688919
611	FEDERAL AND FEDERALLY-SPONSORED CREDIT AGENCIES	5	3.55%	0.657175	0.586359	0.393990	0.403216	0.418591	0.568453	0.586359	0.631879	0.995968	1.032944	1.055130
6111	Federal And Federally-Sponsored Credit Agencies	5	3.55%	0.657175	0.586359	0.393990	0.403216	0.418591	0.568453	0.586359	0.631879	0.995968	1.032944	1.055130
614	PERSONAL CREDIT INSTITUTIONS	16	4.29%	0.795178	0.917171	0.115922	0.171588	0.264364	0.917171	0.917171	0.943321	1.122290	1.168010	1.195442
6141	Personal Credit Institutions	16	4.29%	0.795178	0.917171	0.115922	0.171588	0.264364	0.917171	0.917171	0.943321	1.122290	1.168010	1.195442
615	BUSINESS CREDIT INSTITUTIONS	12	1.45%	0.268268	0.303558	-1.875684	-1.610654	-1.168938	0.224455	0.303558	0.384492	1.166431	1.166840	1.167086
6153	Short-Term Business Credit Institutions, Except Agricultural	8	0.30%	0.055979	0.203833	-1.939933	-1.771278	-1.490186	0.149149	0.203833	0.274434	1.067723	1.116741	1.146153
6159	Miscellaneous Business Credit Institutions	4	3.74%	0.692847	0.696174	0.216348	0.223183	0.234573	0.496670	0.696174	0.895677	1.146465	1.156857	1.163093
616	MORTGAGE BANKERS AND BROKERS	10	3.02%	0.558460	0.514190	-0.121294	-0.114606	-0.103460	0.443347	0.514190	0.605953	1.489411	1.783561	1.960050
6162	Mortgage Bankers And Loan Correspondents	6	2.34%	0.434043	0.540341	-0.066280	-0.051381	-0.026549	0.417524	0.540341	0.663158	0.754527	0.762453	0.767209
6163	Loan Brokers	4	4.02%	0.745084	0.514190	-0.108163	-0.081778	-0.037805	0.482014	0.514190	0.546365	1.851226	1.964468	2.032413
6199	FINANCE SERVICES	3	1.10%	0.204293	-0.065169	-0.299296	-0.292129	-0.280183	-0.112950	-0.065169	0.144290	0.877393	0.929757	0.961176
62	SECURITY AND COMMODITY BROKERS, DEALERS, EXCHANGES, AND SERVICES	100	4.34%	0.804422	0.878923	-0.258742	-0.062815	0.009599	0.674905	0.878923	1.000136	1.448234	1.573561	1.913310
621	SECURITY BROKERS, DEALERS, AND FLOTATION COMPANIES	33	5.14%	0.950988	1.090240	0.087723	0.092146	0.141820	0.892841	1.090240	1.167204	1.452112	1.551452	1.773913
6211	Security Brokers, Dealers, And Flotation Companies	33	5.14%	0.950988	1.090240	0.087723	0.092146	0.141820	0.892841	1.090240	1.167204	1.452112	1.551452	1.773913
622	COMMODITY CONTRACTS BROKERS AND DEALERS	2	4.98%	0.921532	0.921532	0.241100	0.261930	0.296646	0.782668	0.921532	1.060396	1.546418	1.581134	1.601964
6221	Commodity Contracts Brokers And Dealers	2	4.98%	0.921532	0.921532	0.241100	0.261930	0.296646	0.782668	0.921532	1.060396	1.546418	1.581134	1.601964
623	SECURITY AND COMMODITY EXCHANGES	6	3.67%	0.679896	0.740222	0.235375	0.256387	0.291407	0.695425	0.740222	0.785018	0.938767	0.939141	0.939365
6231	Security And Commodity Exchanges	6	3.67%	0.679896	0.740222	0.235375	0.256387	0.291407	0.695425	0.740222	0.785018	0.938767	0.939141	0.939365
628	SERVICES ALLIED WITH THE EXCHANGE OF SECURITIES OR COMMODITIES	59	3.95%	0.731137	0.711698	-0.451133	-0.170683	-0.057469	0.572182	0.711698	0.947167	1.366082	1.463366	1.689108
6282	Investment Advice	58	4.00%	0.739909	0.743450	-0.455825	-0.175314	-0.058098	0.576735	0.743450	0.948958	1.367178	1.466891	1.692972
6289	Services Allied With The Exchange Of Securities Or Commodities	1	1.20%	0.222408	0.222408	0.222408	0.222408	0.222408	0.222408	0.222408	0.222408	0.222408	0.222408	0.222408
63	INSURANCE CARRIERS	142	3.09%	0.571398	0.675693	-0.880491	-0.196264	-0.033702	0.486551	0.675693	0.769950	1.297594	1.422491	1.533970
631	LIFE INSURANCE	35	3.61%	0.668149	0.753836	-0.165467	-0.162447	-0.072798	0.587949	0.753836	0.801317	1.489948	1.528546	1.561818
6311	Life Insurance	35	3.61%	0.668149	0.753836	-0.165467	-0.162447	-0.072798	0.587949	0.753836	0.801317	1.489948	1.528546	1.561818
632	ACCIDENT AND HEALTH INSURANCE AND MEDICAL SERVICE PLANS	18	4.19%	0.776040	0.853542	0.214261	0.220776	0.231634	0.735396	0.853542	0.939476	1.274013	1.323322	1.352907
6321	Accident And Health Insurance	9	4.08%	0.756194	0.783549	0.211962	0.215028	0.220137	0.646030	0.783549	0.899287	1.326222	1.349426	1.363348
6324	Hospital And Medical Service Plans	9	4.30%	0.795887	0.923535	0.400345	0.400937	0.401922	0.797773	0.923535	0.972301	1.134594	1.170092	1.191391

Down-market Betas of Common Stocks by SIC Codes as of September 28, 2018

SIC Code	Description	Number of Companies	Equity Risk Premium	Mean	Median	1st Percentile	2.5th Percentile	5th Percentile	40th Percentile	50th Percentile	60th Percentile	95th Percentile	97.5th Percentile	99th Percentile
633	FIRE, MARINE, AND CASUALTY INSURANCE	73	2.80%	0.518907	0.622327	-1.447202	-0.108284	0.007749	0.481906	0.622327	0.724215	1.214898	1.312170	1.383598
6331	Fire, Marine, And Casualty Insurance	73	2.80%	0.518907	0.622327	-1.447202	-0.108284	0.007749	0.481906	0.622327	0.724215	1.214898	1.312170	1.383598
635	SURETY INSURANCE	8	2.02%	0.374357	0.572748	-1.211027	-1.039138	-0.752656	0.448522	0.572748	0.694129	0.878954	0.893900	0.902868
6351	Surety Insurance	8	2.02%	0.374357	0.572748	-1.211027	-1.039138	-0.752656	0.448522	0.572748	0.694129	0.878954	0.893900	0.902868
636	TITLE INSURANCE	5	3.24%	0.599368	0.785253	0.154812	0.166873	0.186974	0.610266	0.785253	0.800938	0.878947	0.885757	0.889843
6361	Title Insurance	5	3.24%	0.599368	0.785253	0.154812	0.166873	0.186974	0.610266	0.785253	0.800938	0.878947	0.885757	0.889843
637	PENSION, HEALTH, AND WELFARE FUNDS	1	0.83%	0.154391	0.154391	0.154391	0.154391	0.154391	0.154391	0.154391	0.154391	0.154391	0.154391	0.154391
6371	Pension, Health, And Welfare Funds	1	0.83%	0.154391	0.154391	0.154391	0.154391	0.154391	0.154391	0.154391	0.154391	0.154391	0.154391	0.154391
639	INSURANCE CARRIERS, NOT ELSEWHERE CLASSIFIED	2	-0.65%	-0.120856	-0.120856	-0.225934	-0.222717	-0.217356	-0.142301	-0.120856	-0.099412	-0.024357	-0.018995	-0.015779
6399	Insurance Carriers, Not Elsewhere Classified	2	-0.65%	-0.120856	-0.120856	-0.225934	-0.222717	-0.217356	-0.142301	-0.120856	-0.099412	-0.024357	-0.018995	-0.015779
64	INSURANCE AGENTS, BROKERS, AND SERVICE	14	4.38%	0.811325	0.832604	0.208417	0.255493	0.333952	0.807299	0.832604	0.846362	1.203963	1.481162	1.647481
641	INSURANCE AGENTS, BROKERS, AND SERVICE	14	4.38%	0.811325	0.832604	0.208417	0.255493	0.333952	0.807299	0.832604	0.846362	1.203963	1.481162	1.647481
6411	Insurance Agents, Brokers, And Service	14	4.38%	0.811325	0.832604	0.208417	0.255493	0.333952	0.807299	0.832604	0.846362	1.203963	1.481162	1.647481
65	REAL ESTATE	43	3.23%	0.598204	0.557070	-0.211886	-0.119315	-0.071657	0.425369	0.557070	0.584543	1.516440	1.544593	1.910684
6500	REAL ESTATE	3	5.04%	0.933198	0.349787	0.276061	0.278318	0.282079	0.334741	0.349787	0.714880	1.992704	2.083977	2.138741
651	REAL ESTATE OPERATORS (EXCEPT DEVELOPERS) AND LESSORS	16	2.74%	0.507637	0.562182	-0.246578	-0.200700	-0.124236	0.505391	0.562182	0.571045	1.142355	1.343843	1.464735
6510	REAL ESTATE OPERATORS (NO DEVELOPERS) & LESSORS	2	5.54%	1.025361	1.025361	0.515790	0.531389	0.557388	0.921367	1.025361	1.129354	1.493333	1.519332	1.534931
6512	Operators Of Nonresidential Buildings	9	2.33%	0.430990	0.557070	-0.259569	-0.233176	-0.189189	0.489000	0.557070	0.568537	0.862197	0.886316	0.900787
6513	Operators Of Apartment Buildings	3	1.10%	0.204496	0.119454	-0.069406	-0.063625	-0.053989	0.080911	0.119454	0.209022	0.522510	0.544902	0.558337
6519	Lessors Of Real Property, Not Elsewhere Classified	2	4.26%	0.789538	0.789538	0.575415	0.581970	0.592894	0.745839	0.789538	0.833236	0.986181	0.997105	1.003660
653	REAL ESTATE AGENTS AND MANAGERS	20	3.56%	0.659392	0.599517	0.152924	0.158066	0.166636	0.420443	0.599517	0.690421	1.396165	1.463378	1.503705
6531	Real Estate Agents And Managers	20	3.56%	0.659392	0.599517	0.152924	0.158066	0.166636	0.420443	0.599517	0.690421	1.396165	1.463378	1.503705
655	LAND SUBDIVIDERS AND DEVELOPERS	4	2.18%	0.403287	0.338363	-0.112785	-0.099355	-0.076971	0.241375	0.338363	0.435350	0.974437	1.016299	1.041415
6552	Land Subdividers And Developers, Except Cemeteries	4	2.18%	0.403287	0.338363	-0.112785	-0.099355	-0.076971	0.241375	0.338363	0.435350	0.974437	1.016299	1.041415
67	HOLDING AND OTHER INVESTMENT OFFICES	242	2.83%	0.524573	0.488785	-0.878096	-0.305924	-0.155064	0.395430	0.488785	0.567638	1.388181	1.602265	2.529463
671	HOLDING OFFICES	54	2.88%	0.534115	0.555817	-0.315496	-0.258212	-0.159398	0.426318	0.555817	0.708565	1.070816	1.192614	1.313209
6712	Offices Of Bank Holding Companies	44	3.18%	0.588648	0.631932	-0.251886	-0.210835	-0.125042	0.493868	0.631932	0.747368	1.083496	1.231619	1.328079
6719	Offices Of Holding Companies, Not Elsewhere Classified	10	1.59%	0.294168	0.256639	-0.328719	-0.284779	-0.211547	0.202787	0.256639	0.320745	0.879849	0.943715	0.982034
672	INVESTMENT OFFICES	27	2.18%	0.403497	0.441371	-0.561815	-0.281414	-0.002451	0.362918	0.441371	0.491999	0.910845	1.105953	1.223869
6722	Management Investment Offices, Open-End	2	4.60%	0.851322	0.851322	0.705489	0.709953	0.717394	0.821560	0.851322	0.881083	0.985249	0.992690	0.997154
6726	Unit Investment Trusts, Face-Amount Certificate Offices	25	1.99%	0.367671	0.386091	-0.576195	-0.317363	-0.011558	0.348898	0.386091	0.457358	0.567631	0.861742	1.126185
673	TRUSTS	8	3.11%	0.575988	0.413511	0.061911	0.083943	0.120662	0.374963	0.413511	0.476094	1.416164	1.592862	1.698881

Down-market Betas of Common Stocks by SIC Codes as of September 28, 2018

SIC Code	Description	Number of Companies	Equity Risk Premium	Mean	Median	1st Percentile	2.5th Percentile	5th Percentile	40th Percentile	50th Percentile	60th Percentile	95th Percentile	97.5th Percentile	99th Percentile
6733	Trusts, Except Educational, Religious, And Charitable	8	3.11%	0.575988	0.413511	0.061911	0.083943	0.120662	0.374963	0.413511	0.476094	1.416164	1.592862	1.698881
6770	BLANK CHECKS	6	1.30%	0.240155	0.046337	-0.023557	-0.022445	-0.020592	0.043407	0.046337	0.049268	0.955268	1.087394	1.166670
679	MISCELLANEOUS INVESTING	147	2.98%	0.552118	0.498140	-1.404306	-0.412774	-0.155064	0.411102	0.498140	0.603757	1.523449	2.277366	2.738591
6794	Patent Owners And Lessors	10	0.63%	0.117231	0.480313	-2.485969	-2.119082	-1.507604	0.310495	0.480313	0.538080	0.775253	0.800057	0.814939
6798	Real Estate Investment Trusts	58	2.71%	0.502371	0.468881	-0.155064	-0.155064	-0.075614	0.407137	0.468881	0.555268	1.203098	1.223340	1.307119
6799	Investors, Not Elsewhere Classified	79	3.48%	0.643690	0.546079	-1.145744	-0.627778	-0.253031	0.426272	0.546079	0.725878	2.187876	2.561074	2.925687
	SERVICES													
70	HOTELS, ROOMING HOUSES, CAMPS, AND OTHER LODGING PLACES	29	4.47%	0.827705	0.835510	0.046959	0.073893	0.231799	0.818549	0.835510	0.918733	1.278970	1.297048	1.308749
7000	HOTELS, ROOMING HOUSES, CAMPS & OTHER LODGING PLACES	1	3.30%	0.610437	0.610437	0.610437	0.610437	0.610437	0.610437	0.610437	0.610437	0.610437	0.610437	0.610437
701	HOTELS AND MOTELS	28	4.51%	0.835464	0.845488	0.046317	0.072290	0.214465	0.823026	0.845488	0.927232	1.280185	1.297745	1.309028
7011	Hotels And Motels	28	4.51%	0.835464	0.845488	0.046317	0.072290	0.214465	0.823026	0.845488	0.927232	1.280185	1.297745	1.309028
72	PERSONAL SERVICES	16	5.42%	1.004485	0.906509	0.266633	0.282796	0.309734	0.870712	0.906509	0.913992	1.972255	2.633433	3.030139
7200	SERVICES-PERSONAL SERVICES	4	8.15%	1.509147	0.913992	0.913992	0.913992	0.913992	0.913992	0.913992	0.913992	2.937517	3.116064	3.223191
721	LAUNDRY, CLEANING, AND GARMENT SERVICES	3	4.55%	0.843495	0.899026	0.562948	0.573236	0.590383	0.830439	0.899026	0.934295	1.057736	1.066553	1.071843
7211	Power Laundries, Family And Commercial	1	3.00%	0.556089	0.556089	0.556089	0.556089	0.556089	0.556089	0.556089	0.556089	0.556089	0.556089	0.556089
7215	Coin-Operated Laundries And Drycleaning	1	4.85%	0.899026	0.899026	0.899026	0.899026	0.899026	0.899026	0.899026	0.899026	0.899026	0.899026	0.899026
7218	Industrial Launderers	1	5.81%	1.075370	1.075370	1.075370	1.075370	1.075370	1.075370	1.075370	1.075370	1.075370	1.075370	1.075370
723	BEAUTY SHOPS	2	4.70%	0.871067	0.871067	0.391981	0.406647	0.431090	0.773294	0.871067	0.968840	1.311044	1.335487	1.350153
7231	Beauty Shops	2	4.70%	0.871067	0.871067	0.391981	0.406647	0.431090	0.773294	0.871067	0.968840	1.311044	1.335487	1.350153
726	FUNERAL SERVICE AND CREMATORIES	2	3.20%	0.593236	0.593236	0.333004	0.340970	0.354247	0.540127	0.593236	0.646344	0.832224	0.845501	0.853467
7261	Funeral Service And Crematories	2	3.20%	0.593236	0.593236	0.333004	0.340970	0.354247	0.540127	0.593236	0.646344	0.832224	0.845501	0.853467
729	MISCELLANEOUS PERSONAL SERVICES	5	4.94%	0.915218	0.870712	0.269147	0.289081	0.322304	0.757663	0.870712	1.054411	1.491168	1.511319	1.523410
7299	Miscellaneous Personal Services, Not Elsewhere Classified	5	4.94%	0.915218	0.870712	0.269147	0.289081	0.322304	0.757663	0.870712	1.054411	1.491168	1.511319	1.523410
73	BUSINESS SERVICES	451	3.96%	0.732868	0.777756	-1.234455	-0.722338	-0.181682	0.660451	0.777756	0.874357	1.588825	2.071393	3.080210
731	ADVERTISING	18	3.33%	0.617490	0.525508	-0.312509	-0.150174	0.120383	0.474573	0.525508	0.553337	1.685537	1.776363	1.830859
7311	Advertising Agencies	12	3.69%	0.683759	0.508979	-0.333293	-0.202135	0.016462	0.465787	0.508979	0.628868	1.749650	1.808420	1.843682
7312	Outdoor Advertising Services	3	2.28%	0.422389	0.512025	0.221797	0.230682	0.245489	0.452795	0.512025	0.517473	0.536543	0.537905	0.538722
7313	Radio, Television, And Publishers' Advertising Representatives	2	2.37%	0.439540	0.439540	0.272864	0.277966	0.286470	0.405524	0.439540	0.473556	0.592610	0.601114	0.606216
7319	Advertising, Not Elsewhere Classified	1	4.12%	0.763455	0.763455	0.763455	0.763455	0.763455	0.763455	0.763455	0.763455	0.763455	0.763455	0.763455
732	CONSUMER CREDIT REPORTING AGENCIES, MERCANTILE REPORTING AGENCIES	9	4.21%	0.780525	0.834090	0.115306	0.172148	0.266885	0.830886	0.834090	0.860424	1.046267	1.061888	1.071261
7320	SERVICES-CONSUMER CREDIT REPORTING, COLLECTION AGENCIES	1	5.82%	1.077510	1.077510	1.077510	1.077510	1.077510	1.077510	1.077510	1.077510	1.077510	1.077510	1.077510
7322	Adjustment And Collection Services	2	3.83%	0.709052	0.709052	0.554255	0.558994	0.566892	0.677461	0.709052	0.740643	0.851212	0.859110	0.863849
7323	Credit Reporting Services	6	4.08%	0.754851	0.832088	0.114735	0.170721	0.264032	0.830085	0.832088	0.834090	0.990608	0.995005	0.997643
733	MAILING, REPRODUCTION, COMMERCIAL ART AND PHOTOGRAPHY, AND STENOGRAPHY	4	-4.54%	-0.841491	0.637878	-6.153518	-5.852946	-5.351992	0.450442	0.637878	0.825314	1.597894	1.655037	1.689323

Down-market Betas of Common Stocks by SIC Codes as of September 28, 2018

SIC Code	Description	Number of Companies	Equity Risk Premium	Mean	Median	1st Percentile	2.5th Percentile	5th Percentile	40th Percentile	50th Percentile	60th Percentile	95th Percentile	97.5th Percentile	99th Percentile
7331	Direct Mail Advertising Services	2	5.50%	1.018833	1.018833	0.339352	0.360152	0.394820	0.880163	1.018833	1.157502	1.642845	1.677513	1.698313
7336	Commercial Art And Graphic Design	1	-34.31%	-6.353900	-6.353900	-6.353900	-6.353900	-6.353900	-6.353900	-6.353900	-6.353900	-6.353900	-6.353900	-6.353900
7338	Secretarial And Court Reporting Services	1	5.13%	0.950271	0.950271	0.950271	0.950271	0.950271	0.950271	0.950271	0.950271	0.950271	0.950271	0.950271
734	SERVICES TO DWELLINGS AND OTHER BUILDINGS	3	2.52%	0.465914	1.081140	-0.732359	-0.676844	-0.584318	0.711038	1.081140	1.082106	1.085487	1.085729	1.085873
7342	Disinfecting And Pest Control Services	1	5.84%	1.081140	1.081140	1.081140	1.081140	1.081140	1.081140	1.081140	1.081140	1.081140	1.081140	1.081140
7349	Building Cleaning And Maintenance Services, Not Elsewhere Classified	2	0.85%	0.158301	0.158301	-0.750816	-0.722986	-0.676602	-0.027233	0.158301	0.343834	0.993203	1.039587	1.067417
735	MISCELLANEOUS EQUIPMENT RENTAL AND LEASING	19	3.72%	0.689344	0.731402	-1.117670	-0.712310	-0.036710	0.669755	0.731402	0.987466	1.357715	1.365883	1.370783
7350	SERVICES-MISCELLANEOUS EQUIPMENT RENTAL & LEASING	1	-7.49%	-1.387910	-1.387910	-1.387910	-1.387910	-1.387910	-1.387910	-1.387910	-1.387910	-1.387910	-1.387910	-1.387910
7353	Heavy Construction Equipment Rental And Leasing	1	3.95%	0.731402	0.731402	0.731402	0.731402	0.731402	0.731402	0.731402	0.731402	0.731402	0.731402	0.731402
7359	Equipment Rental And Leasing, Not Elsewhere Classified	17	4.37%	0.809062	0.843331	0.122521	0.136169	0.158915	0.684579	0.843331	1.087760	1.359530	1.366790	1.371146
736	PERSONNEL SUPPLY SERVICES	24	3.61%	0.668663	0.669314	-0.173947	-0.138308	-0.083031	0.511416	0.669314	0.879634	1.280282	1.380942	1.452533
7361	Employment Agencies	5	4.06%	0.751918	0.690357	0.595844	0.599121	0.604582	0.673522	0.690357	0.776627	0.918222	0.919746	0.920660
7363	Help Supply Services	19	3.49%	0.646754	0.490855	-0.179112	-0.151221	-0.104735	0.420928	0.490855	0.879634	1.313501	1.406881	1.462908
737	COMPUTER PROGRAMMING, DATA PROCESSING, AND OTHER COMPUTER RELATED	285	4.19%	0.775283	0.802190	-0.738093	-0.684217	-0.152596	0.685040	0.802190	0.887092	1.551730	2.082011	2.956237
7370	SERVICES-COMPUTER PROGRAMMING, DATA PROCESSING, ETC.	3	1.78%	0.329743	0.898525	-0.786417	-0.734838	-0.648871	0.554659	0.898525	0.901122	0.910210	0.910859	0.911248
7371	Computer Programming Services	54	3.81%	0.704737	0.739467	-1.428265	-0.227733	-0.141893	0.641611	0.739467	0.800903	1.758994	2.631351	3.079843
7372	Prepackaged Software	136	4.03%	0.746288	0.802217	-0.722338	-0.718558	-0.234475	0.705214	0.802217	0.884363	1.494533	1.957028	2.262420
7373	Computer Integrated Systems Design	34	5.33%	0.987815	0.832250	-0.125393	0.083712	0.280773	0.696886	0.832250	0.870932	1.317808	2.762732	6.365743
7374	Computer Processing And Data Preparation And Processing Services	41	4.02%	0.745338	0.779214	-0.356386	-0.165657	-0.094455	0.660451	0.779214	0.844762	1.521550	1.671760	1.879684
7375	Information Retrieval Services	11	6.08%	1.125675	1.450740	-0.112047	-0.056134	0.037054	1.175140	1.450740	1.486050	1.604230	1.630480	1.646230
7376	Computer Facilities Management Services	1	0.86%	0.159348	0.159348	0.159348	0.159348	0.159348	0.159348	0.159348	0.159348	0.159348	0.159348	0.159348
7379	Computer Related Services, Not Elsewhere Classified	5	4.03%	0.745836	0.911401	0.120368	0.154580	0.211600	0.813943	0.911401	0.951053	1.035650	1.038790	1.040674
738	MISCELLANEOUS BUSINESS SERVICES	89	3.90%	0.721922	0.721120	-1.794832	-1.076052	-0.209830	0.627501	0.721120	0.870345	1.749960	2.492922	3.359325
7380	SERVICES-MISCELLANEOUS BUSINESS SERVICES	1	6.62%	1.226780	1.226780	1.226780	1.226780	1.226780	1.226780	1.226780	1.226780	1.226780	1.226780	1.226780
7381	Detective, Guard, And Armored Car Services	2	9.38%	1.736787	1.736787	0.236218	0.282154	0.358713	1.430548	1.736787	2.043026	3.114861	3.191420	3.237356
7382	Security Systems Services	2	5.31%	0.983983	0.983983	0.940974	0.942290	0.944485	0.975206	0.983983	0.992760	1.023481	1.025676	1.026992
7384	Photofinishing Laboratories	1	2.79%	0.516933	0.516933	0.516933	0.516933	0.516933	0.516933	0.516933	0.516933	0.516933	0.516933	0.516933
7389	Business Services, Not Elsewhere Classified	83	3.71%	0.687540	0.715649	-1.913364	-1.079763	-0.256623	0.621089	0.715649	0.842212	1.739515	2.124042	2.841043
75	AUTOMOTIVE REPAIR, SERVICES, AND PARKING	6	4.00%	0.740651	0.999740	-0.738373	-0.637733	-0.470001	0.899299	0.999740	1.100180	1.389500	1.405875	1.415700
751	AUTOMOTIVE RENTAL AND LEASING, WITHOUT DRIVERS	4	5.60%	1.037299	1.095275	0.547282	0.563613	0.590831	0.977689	1.095275	1.212860	1.402600	1.412425	1.418320

Down-market Betas of Common Stocks by SIC Codes as of September 28, 2018

SIC Code	Description	Number of Companies	Equity Risk Premium	Mean	Median	1st Percentile	2.5th Percentile	5th Percentile	40th Percentile	50th Percentile	60th Percentile	95th Percentile	97.5th Percentile	99th Percentile
7510	SERVICES-AUTO RENTAL & LEASING (NO DRIVERS)	1	4.86%	0.899299	0.899299	0.899299	0.899299	0.899299	0.899299	0.899299	0.899299	0.899299	0.899299	0.899299
7513	Truck Rental And Leasing, Without Drivers	2	4.93%	0.913823	0.913823	0.543944	0.555266	0.574138	0.838337	0.913823	0.989308	1.253507	1.272379	1.283701
7514	Passenger Car Rental	1	7.68%	1.422250	1.422250	1.422250	1.422250	1.422250	1.422250	1.422250	1.422250	1.422250	1.422250	1.422250
753	AUTOMOTIVE REPAIR SHOPS	1	5.94%	1.100180	1.100180	1.100180	1.100180	1.100180	1.100180	1.100180	1.100180	1.100180	1.100180	1.100180
7538	General Automotive Repair Shops	1	5.94%	1.100180	1.100180	1.100180	1.100180	1.100180	1.100180	1.100180	1.100180	1.100180	1.100180	1.100180
754	AUTOMOTIVE SERVICES, EXCEPT REPAIR	1	-4.35%	-0.805466	-0.805466	-0.805466	-0.805466	-0.805466	-0.805466	-0.805466	-0.805466	-0.805466	-0.805466	-0.805466
7542	Carwashes	1	-4.35%	-0.805466	-0.805466	-0.805466	-0.805466	-0.805466	-0.805466	-0.805466	-0.805466	-0.805466	-0.805466	-0.805466
76	MISCELLANEOUS REPAIR SERVICES	2	3.54%	0.656100	0.656100	-0.040787	-0.019454	0.016102	0.513878	0.656100	0.798322	1.296099	1.331655	1.352988
762	ELECTRICAL REPAIR SHOPS	2	3.54%	0.656100	0.656100	-0.040787	-0.019454	0.016102	0.513878	0.656100	0.798322	1.296099	1.331655	1.352988
7623	Refrigeration And Air-Conditioning Service And Repair Shops	2	3.54%	0.656100	0.656100	-0.040787	-0.019454	0.016102	0.513878	0.656100	0.798322	1.296099	1.331655	1.352988
78	MOTION PICTURES	18	4.16%	0.771035	0.550830	-1.730562	-1.145626	-0.170732	0.423099	0.550830	0.565942	2.458849	3.530555	4.173578
781	MOTION PICTURE PRODUCTION AND ALLIED SERVICES	13	3.96%	0.733587	0.565942	-1.845256	-1.432360	-0.744199	0.513885	0.565942	0.565942	2.876750	3.739505	4.257158
7812	Motion Picture And Video Tape Production	11	4.16%	0.770053	0.565942	-1.871571	-1.498148	-0.875776	0.535717	0.565942	0.565942	3.164335	3.883298	4.314675
7819	Services Allied To Motion Picture Production	2	2.88%	0.533024	0.533024	0.180542	0.191332	0.209316	0.461089	0.533024	0.604959	0.856732	0.874716	0.885506
782	MOTION PICTURE DISTRIBUTION AND ALLIED SERVICES	1	11.24%	2.080600	2.080600	2.080600	2.080600	2.080600	2.080600	2.080600	2.080600	2.080600	2.080600	2.080600
7822	Motion Picture And Video Tape Distribution	1	11.24%	2.080600	2.080600	2.080600	2.080600	2.080600	2.080600	2.080600	2.080600	2.080600	2.080600	2.080600
783	MOTION PICTURE THEATERS	3	1.78%	0.328885	0.394052	0.187550	0.193872	0.204408	0.351909	0.394052	0.397095	0.407746	0.408506	0.408963
7832	Motion Picture Theaters, Except Drive-In	3	1.78%	0.328885	0.394052	0.187550	0.193872	0.204408	0.351909	0.394052	0.397095	0.407746	0.408506	0.408963
784	VIDEO TAPE RENTAL	1	6.88%	1.274740	1.274740	1.274740	1.274740	1.274740	1.274740	1.274740	1.274740	1.274740	1.274740	1.274740
7841	Video Tape Rental	1	6.88%	1.274740	1.274740	1.274740	1.274740	1.274740	1.274740	1.274740	1.274740	1.274740	1.274740	1.274740
79	AMUSEMENT AND RECREATION SERVICES	33	2.70%	0.499975	0.570150	-1.244218	-1.243556	-0.993639	0.498354	0.570150	0.743827	1.243614	1.614104	2.369850
7900	SERVICES-AMUSEMENT & RECREATION SERVICES	3	-1.82%	-0.336327	-0.090885	-0.812485	-0.790396	-0.753579	-0.238150	-0.090885	-0.090885	-0.090885	-0.090885	-0.090885
792	THEATRICAL PRODUCERS (EXCEPT MOTION PICTURE), BANDS, ORCHESTRAS	3	1.32%	0.243951	0.791222	-1.203942	-1.142866	-1.041072	0.384046	0.791222	0.870036	1.145883	1.165587	1.177409
7922	Theatrical Producers (Except Motion Picture) And Miscellaneous Theater	2	-0.16%	-0.029685	-0.029685	-1.220361	-1.183911	-1.123163	-0.272680	-0.029685	0.213310	1.063793	1.124541	1.160991
7929	Bands, Orchestras, Actors, And Other Entertainers And Entertainment	1	4.27%	0.791222	0.791222	0.791222	0.791222	0.791222	0.791222	0.791222	0.791222	0.791222	0.791222	0.791222
793	BOWLING CENTERS	1	-0.17%	-0.032022	-0.032022	-0.032022	-0.032022	-0.032022	-0.032022	-0.032022	-0.032022	-0.032022	-0.032022	-0.032022
7933	Bowling Centers	1	-0.17%	-0.032022	-0.032022	-0.032022	-0.032022	-0.032022	-0.032022	-0.032022	-0.032022	-0.032022	-0.032022	-0.032022
794	COMMERCIAL SPORTS	8	2.53%	0.467752	0.589037	-0.623749	-0.521889	-0.352121	0.534712	0.589037	0.647634	0.931641	0.981555	1.011504
7941	Professional Sports Clubs And Promoters	2	3.48%	0.644812	0.644812	0.545409	0.548452	0.553523	0.624525	0.644812	0.665098	0.736100	0.741171	0.744214
7948	Racing, Including Track Operation	6	2.21%	0.408732	0.567368	-0.643151	-0.570394	-0.449131	0.500041	0.567368	0.634694	0.948452	0.989961	1.014866
799	MISCELLANEOUS AMUSEMENT AND RECREATION SERVICES	18	3.92%	0.725907	0.766504	-1.075872	-0.824760	-0.406241	0.562600	0.766504	0.827420	1.535381	2.204530	2.606020
7990	SERVICES-MISCELLANEOUS AMUSEMENT & RECREATION	3	4.38%	0.810390	0.806138	0.335427	0.349837	0.373853	0.710075	0.806138	0.904752	1.249903	1.274556	1.289349

Down-market Betas of Common Stocks by SIC Codes as of September 28, 2018

SIC Code	Description	Number of Companies	Equity Risk Premium	Mean	Median	1st Percentile	2.5th Percentile	5th Percentile	40th Percentile	50th Percentile	60th Percentile	95th Percentile	97.5th Percentile	99th Percentile
7993	Coin-Operated Amusement Devices	1	6.52%	1.206550	1.206550	1.206550	1.206550	1.206550	1.206550	1.206550	1.206550	1.206550	1.206550	1.206550
7996	Amusement Parks	3	3.63%	0.672501	0.743223	0.489670	0.497431	0.510368	0.691477	0.743223	0.752535	0.785128	0.787456	0.788853
7997	Membership Sports And Recreation Clubs	3	3.14%	0.582127	0.977238	-0.233813	-0.196740	-0.134951	0.730085	0.977238	0.987324	1.022627	1.025148	1.026661
7999	Amusement And Recreation Services, Not Elsewhere Classified	8	3.82%	0.708091	0.551276	-1.126085	-0.950292	-0.657304	0.524243	0.551276	0.638630	2.251730	2.562705	2.749290
80	HEALTH SERVICES	80	3.84%	0.711224	0.707205	-0.765737	-0.375196	-0.035918	0.606065	0.707205	0.797529	1.587696	1.784211	2.179282
801	OFFICES AND CLINICS OF DOCTORS OF MEDICINE	15	4.84%	0.897085	0.970622	-0.053019	0.044787	0.207796	0.872462	0.970622	1.023760	1.644188	1.712879	1.754094
8011	Offices And Clinics Of Doctors Of Medicine	15	4.84%	0.897085	0.970622	-0.053019	0.044787	0.207796	0.872462	0.970622	1.023760	1.644188	1.712879	1.754094
804	OFFICES AND CLINICS OF OTHER HEALTH PRACTITIONERS	1	4.54%	0.840508	0.840508	0.840508	0.840508	0.840508	0.840508	0.840508	0.840508	0.840508	0.840508	0.840508
8041	Offices And Clinics Of Chiropractors	1	4.54%	0.840508	0.840508	0.840508	0.840508	0.840508	0.840508	0.840508	0.840508	0.840508	0.840508	0.840508
805	NURSING AND PERSONAL CARE FACILITIES	8	2.86%	0.529727	0.443856	0.288739	0.300361	0.319731	0.435515	0.443856	0.498334	0.780935	0.782587	0.783579
8051	Skilled Nursing Care Facilities	8	2.86%	0.529727	0.443856	0.288739	0.300361	0.319731	0.435515	0.443856	0.498334	0.780935	0.782587	0.783579
806	HOSPITALS	16	4.16%	0.770074	0.714353	0.152795	0.156173	0.161805	0.692649	0.714353	0.947212	1.354953	1.457571	1.519143
8062	General Medical And Surgical Hospitals	11	3.91%	0.723203	0.712695	0.180354	0.202546	0.239533	0.692649	0.712695	0.716011	1.162690	1.224615	1.261770
8069	Specialty Hospitals, Except Psychiatric	5	4.72%	0.873189	0.978509	0.167989	0.194160	0.237778	0.821794	0.978509	1.023097	1.466148	1.513169	1.541382
807	MEDICAL AND DENTAL LABORATORIES	18	2.35%	0.434406	0.495806	-0.779054	-0.773577	-0.764448	0.222492	0.495806	0.722557	1.350176	1.491603	1.576459
8071	Medical Laboratories	18	2.35%	0.434406	0.495806	-0.779054	-0.773577	-0.764448	0.222492	0.495806	0.722557	1.350176	1.491603	1.576459
808	HOME HEALTH CARE SERVICES	7	2.45%	0.453010	0.457213	-0.013282	0.014176	0.059939	0.450837	0.457213	0.554261	0.720833	0.734058	0.741994
8082	Home Health Care Services	7	2.45%	0.453010	0.457213	-0.013282	0.014176	0.059939	0.450837	0.457213	0.554261	0.720833	0.734058	0.741994
809	MISCELLANEOUS HEALTH AND ALLIED SERVICES, NOT ELSEWHERE CLASSIFIED	15	5.42%	1.003451	0.941828	0.158564	0.203391	0.278104	0.836073	0.941828	0.978652	2.304456	2.791243	3.083315
8090	SERVICES-MISC HEALTH & ALLIED SERVICES, NEC	1	6.49%	1.201450	1.201450	1.201450	1.201450	1.201450	1.201450	1.201450	1.201450	1.201450	1.201450	1.201450
8093	Specialty Outpatient Facilities, Not Elsewhere Classified	6	6.11%	1.131475	0.810304	0.345915	0.351573	0.361002	0.681461	0.810304	0.939147	2.741145	3.009588	3.170653
8099	Health And Allied Services, Not Elsewhere Classified	8	4.77%	0.882683	0.954293	0.153551	0.190858	0.253038	0.866009	0.954293	0.972705	1.609506	1.748358	1.831669
81	LEGAL SERVICES	1	3.51%	0.649653	0.649653	0.649653	0.649653	0.649653	0.649653	0.649653	0.649653	0.649653	0.649653	0.649653
811	LEGAL SERVICES	1	3.51%	0.649653	0.649653	0.649653	0.649653	0.649653	0.649653	0.649653	0.649653	0.649653	0.649653	0.649653
8111	Legal Services	1	3.51%	0.649653	0.649653	0.649653	0.649653	0.649653	0.649653	0.649653	0.649653	0.649653	0.649653	0.649653
82	EDUCATIONAL SERVICES	15	1.62%	0.300030	0.563829	-1.525043	-1.408077	-1.213134	0.529310	0.563829	0.687296	0.979716	0.984491	0.987355
8200	SERVICES-EDUCATIONAL SERVICES	3	2.67%	0.494167	0.772152	-0.146738	-0.118609	-0.071727	0.584623	0.772152	0.792890	0.865472	0.870657	0.873767
821	ELEMENTARY AND SECONDARY SCHOOLS	4	3.54%	0.655564	0.738205	0.181881	0.199369	0.228515	0.630582	0.738205	0.845828	0.966917	0.971270	0.973883
8211	Elementary And Secondary Schools	4	3.54%	0.655564	0.738205	0.181881	0.199369	0.228515	0.630582	0.738205	0.845828	0.966917	0.971270	0.973883
822	COLLEGES, UNIVERSITIES, PROFESSIONAL SCHOOLS, AND JUNIOR COLLEGES	3	-1.00%	-0.184723	0.485023	-1.561259	-1.498618	-1.394216	0.067414	0.485023	0.500784	0.555948	0.559889	0.562253
8221	Colleges, Universities, And Professional Schools	3	-1.00%	-0.184723	0.485023	-1.561259	-1.498618	-1.394216	0.067414	0.485023	0.500784	0.555948	0.559889	0.562253
823	LIBRARIES	1	3.41%	0.630726	0.630726	0.630726	0.630726	0.630726	0.630726	0.630726	0.630726	0.630726	0.630726	0.630726
8231	Libraries	1	3.41%	0.630726	0.630726	0.630726	0.630726	0.630726	0.630726	0.630726	0.630726	0.630726	0.630726	0.630726

Down-market Betas of Common Stocks by SIC Codes as of September 28, 2018

SIC Code	Description	Number of Companies	Equity Risk Premium	Mean	Median	1st Percentile	2.5th Percentile	5th Percentile	40th Percentile	50th Percentile	60th Percentile	95th Percentile	97.5th Percentile	99th Percentile
824	VOCATIONAL SCHOOLS	3	-1.16%	-0.215502	-0.589730	-1.036914	-1.023225	-1.000409	-0.680992	-0.589730	-0.273931	0.831366	0.910315	0.957685
8249	Vocational Schools, Not Elsewhere Classified	3	-1.16%	-0.215502	-0.589730	-1.036914	-1.023225	-1.000409	-0.680992	-0.589730	-0.273931	0.831366	0.910315	0.957685
829	SCHOOLS AND EDUCATIONAL SERVICES, NOT ELSEWHERE CLASSIFIED	1	5.21%	0.965632	0.965632	0.965632	0.965632	0.965632	0.965632	0.965632	0.965632	0.965632	0.965632	0.965632
8299	Schools And Educational Services, Not Elsewhere Classified	1	5.21%	0.965632	0.965632	0.965632	0.965632	0.965632	0.965632	0.965632	0.965632	0.965632	0.965632	0.965632
83	SOCIAL SERVICES	4	4.76%	0.881667	1.005754	0.335775	0.358610	0.396670	0.899106	1.005754	1.112402	1.192944	1.193777	1.194277
832	INDIVIDUAL AND FAMILY SOCIAL SERVICES	1	6.39%	1.183500	1.183500	1.183500	1.183500	1.183500	1.183500	1.183500	1.183500	1.183500	1.183500	1.183500
8322	Individual And Family Social Services	1	6.39%	1.183500	1.183500	1.183500	1.183500	1.183500	1.183500	1.183500	1.183500	1.183500	1.183500	1.183500
833	JOB TRAINING AND VOCATIONAL REHABILITATION SERVICES	1	6.45%	1.194610	1.194610	1.194610	1.194610	1.194610	1.194610	1.194610	1.194610	1.194610	1.194610	1.194610
8331	Job Training And Vocational Rehabilitation Services	1	6.45%	1.194610	1.194610	1.194610	1.194610	1.194610	1.194610	1.194610	1.194610	1.194610	1.194610	1.194610
835	CHILD DAY CARE SERVICES	1	4.47%	0.828008	0.828008	0.828008	0.828008	0.828008	0.828008	0.828008	0.828008	0.828008	0.828008	0.828008
8351	Child Day Care Services	1	4.47%	0.828008	0.828008	0.828008	0.828008	0.828008	0.828008	0.828008	0.828008	0.828008	0.828008	0.828008
836	RESIDENTIAL CARE	1	1.73%	0.320551	0.320551	0.320551	0.320551	0.320551	0.320551	0.320551	0.320551	0.320551	0.320551	0.320551
8361	Residential Care	1	1.73%	0.320551	0.320551	0.320551	0.320551	0.320551	0.320551	0.320551	0.320551	0.320551	0.320551	0.320551
87	ENGINEERING, ACCOUNTING, RESEARCH, MANAGEMENT, AND RELATED SERVICES	167	3.94%	0.730255	0.715840	-1.085007	-0.764834	-0.276639	0.598346	0.715840	0.858592	1.752881	2.137996	2.612442
871	ENGINEERING, ARCHITECTURAL, AND SURVEYING SERVICES	19	4.34%	0.804380	0.706871	-0.166209	-0.099891	0.010640	0.646245	0.706871	1.037738	1.637837	1.732954	1.790023
8711	Engineering Services	19	4.34%	0.804380	0.706871	-0.166209	-0.099891	0.010640	0.646245	0.706871	1.037738	1.637837	1.732954	1.790023
872	ACCOUNTING, AUDITING, AND BOOKKEEPING SERVICES	4	3.32%	0.614417	0.761276	-0.245023	-0.208874	-0.148626	0.625019	0.761276	0.897532	1.171859	1.188050	1.197764
8721	Accounting, Auditing, And Bookkeeping Services	4	3.32%	0.614417	0.761276	-0.245023	-0.208874	-0.148626	0.625019	0.761276	0.897532	1.171859	1.188050	1.197764
873	RESEARCH, DEVELOPMENT, AND TESTING SERVICES	95	4.53%	0.838145	0.768546	-0.829639	-0.643517	-0.365117	0.616956	0.768546	0.957971	1.976939	2.432060	2.814465
8731	Commercial Physical And Biological Research	79	4.71%	0.872020	0.768546	-0.851894	-0.633241	-0.276907	0.660392	0.768546	0.992477	1.918373	2.306253	2.843090
8732	Commercial Economic, Sociological, And Educational Research	8	3.95%	0.731268	0.820529	-0.620663	-0.570089	-0.485800	0.642132	0.820529	0.908708	2.100347	2.307124	2.431189
8733	Noncommercial Research Organizations	6	2.84%	0.525087	0.400077	-0.259252	-0.228340	-0.176818	0.282502	0.400077	0.517652	1.272245	1.283888	1.290873
8734	Testing Laboratories	2	4.68%	0.866744	0.866744	0.597522	0.605764	0.619500	0.811801	0.866744	0.921687	1.113988	1.127724	1.135966
874	MANAGEMENT AND PUBLIC RELATIONS SERVICES	49	2.71%	0.501794	0.701355	-3.432572	-1.218393	-0.527940	0.598115	0.701355	0.760372	1.328620	1.348192	1.572863
8741	Management Services	12	2.92%	0.541079	0.656863	-0.689477	-0.547203	-0.310080	0.560133	0.656863	0.770906	1.062837	1.084579	1.097623
8742	Management Consulting Services	33	2.41%	0.445468	0.701355	-4.080468	-2.136780	-0.616781	0.596259	0.701355	0.760256	1.340736	1.436898	1.640845
8743	Public Relations Services	1	3.71%	0.687225	0.687225	0.687225	0.687225	0.687225	0.687225	0.687225	0.687225	0.687225	0.687225	0.687225
8744	Facilities Support Management Services	1	4.65%	0.860551	0.860551	0.860551	0.860551	0.860551	0.860551	0.860551	0.860551	0.860551	0.860551	0.860551
8748	Business Consulting Services, Not Elsewhere Classified	2	4.99%	0.923371	0.923371	0.559193	0.570341	0.588922	0.849049	0.923371	0.997692	1.257819	1.276400	1.287548
88	PRIVATE HOUSEHOLDS	3	2.64%	0.489753	0.419585	0.202345	0.208996	0.220079	0.375250	0.419585	0.506020	0.808544	0.830153	0.843118
8880	AMERICAN DEPOSITARY RECEIPTS	3	2.64%	0.489753	0.419585	0.202345	0.208996	0.220079	0.375250	0.419585	0.506020	0.808544	0.830153	0.843118
89	SERVICES, NOT ELSEWHERE CLASSIFIED	15	8.86%	1.640240	0.730856	-1.556177	-1.302476	-0.879643	0.365747	0.730856	0.888365	6.848985	12.656693	16.141317

Down-market Betas of Common Stocks by SIC Codes as of September 28, 2018

SIC Code	Description	Number of Companies	Equity Risk Premium	Mean	Median	1st Percentile	2.5th Percentile	5th Percentile	40th Percentile	50th Percentile	60th Percentile	95th Percentile	97.5th Percentile	99th Percentile
899	SERVICES, NOT ELSEWHERE CLASSIFIED	15	8.86%	1.640240	0.730856	-1.556177	-1.302476	-0.879643	0.365747	0.730856	0.888365	6.848985	12.656693	16.141317
8999	Services, Not Elsewhere Classified	15	8.86%	1.640240	0.730856	-1.556177	-1.302476	-0.879643	0.365747	0.730856	0.888365	6.848985	12.656693	16.141317
	PUBLIC ADMINISTRATION													
94	ADMINISTRATION OF HUMAN RESOURCE PROGRAMS	1	6.86%	1.270480	1.270480	1.270480	1.270480	1.270480	1.270480	1.270480	1.270480	1.270480	1.270480	1.270480
943	ADMINISTRATION OF PUBLIC HEALTH PROGRAMS	1	6.86%	1.270480	1.270480	1.270480	1.270480	1.270480	1.270480	1.270480	1.270480	1.270480	1.270480	1.270480
9431	Administration Of Public Health Programs	1	6.86%	1.270480	1.270480	1.270480	1.270480	1.270480	1.270480	1.270480	1.270480	1.270480	1.270480	1.270480
96	ADMINISTRATION OF ECONOMIC PROGRAMS	2	5.41%	1.001869	1.001869	0.808279	0.814205	0.824082	0.962361	1.001869	1.041377	1.179656	1.189533	1.195459
961	ADMINISTRATION OF GENERAL ECONOMIC PROGRAMS	1	4.34%	0.804328	0.804328	0.804328	0.804328	0.804328	0.804328	0.804328	0.804328	0.804328	0.804328	0.804328
9611	Administration Of General Economic Programs	1	4.34%	0.804328	0.804328	0.804328	0.804328	0.804328	0.804328	0.804328	0.804328	0.804328	0.804328	0.804328
963	REGULATION AND ADMINISTRATION OF COMMUNICATIONS, ELECTRIC, GAS	1	6.48%	1.199410	1.199410	1.199410	1.199410	1.199410	1.199410	1.199410	1.199410	1.199410	1.199410	1.199410
9631	Regulation And Administration Of Communications, Electric, Gas	1	6.48%	1.199410	1.199410	1.199410	1.199410	1.199410	1.199410	1.199410	1.199410	1.199410	1.199410	1.199410
	NONCLASSIFIABLE ESTABLISHMENTS													
99	NONCLASSIFIABLE ESTABLISHMENTS	70	1.19%	0.220713	0.553990	-9.994425	-1.454570	-1.214812	0.373517	0.553990	0.647027	2.662020	2.685079	3.368998
999	NONCLASSIFIABLE ESTABLISHMENTS	70	1.19%	0.220713	0.553990	-9.994425	-1.454570	-1.214812	0.373517	0.553990	0.647027	2.662020	2.685079	3.368998
9995	NON-OPERATING ESTABLISHMENTS	2	-1.60%	-0.295892	-0.295892	-0.678664	-0.666947	-0.647418	-0.374009	-0.295892	-0.217776	0.055633	0.075162	0.086879
9999	Nonclassifiable Establishments	68	1.27%	0.235907	0.558630	-10.526575	-1.474676	-1.228425	0.449625	0.558630	0.701902	2.662020	2.689271	3.409200

Up-market Betas of Common Stocks by SIC Codes as of September 28, 2018

Details:
Benchmark: S&P 500 Index
Returns period and frequency: 1 year of daily returns
Risk-free rate for betas: Federal Funds Rate
Expected US Equity Risk Premium: 5.40% (Fernandez, Pablo and Pershin, Vitaly and Fernández Acín, Isabel, Market Risk Premium and Risk-Free Rate used for 59 Countries in 2018: A Survey (April 3, 2018). Available at SSRN: https://ssrn.com/abstract=3155709)

SIC Code	Description	Number of Companies	Equity Risk Premium	Mean	Median	1st Percentile	2.5th Percentile	5th Percentile	40th Percentile	50th Percentile	60th Percentile	95th Percentile	97.5th Percentile	99th Percentile
	AGRICULTURE, FORESTRY, AND FISHING													
01	AGRICULTURAL PRODUCTION-CROPS	9	0.44%	0.080733	-0.021668	-0.815334	-0.757119	-0.660094	-0.125124	-0.021668	0.223074	0.790079	0.843115	0.874937
011	CASH GRAINS	2	3.95%	0.731550	0.731550	0.570239	0.575177	0.583407	0.698629	0.731550	0.764470	0.879692	0.887922	0.892860
0115	Corn	1	4.84%	0.896152	0.896152	0.896152	0.896152	0.896152	0.896152	0.896152	0.896152	0.896152	0.896152	0.896152
0116	Soybeans	1	3.06%	0.566947	0.566947	0.566947	0.566947	0.566947	0.566947	0.566947	0.566947	0.566947	0.566947	0.566947
013	FIELD CROPS, EXCEPT CASH GRAINS	1	-0.12%	-0.021668	-0.021668	-0.021668	-0.021668	-0.021668	-0.021668	-0.021668	-0.021668	-0.021668	-0.021668	-0.021668
0131	Cotton	1	-0.12%	-0.021668	-0.021668	-0.021668	-0.021668	-0.021668	-0.021668	-0.021668	-0.021668	-0.021668	-0.021668	-0.021668
016	VEGETABLES AND MELONS	1	-0.82%	-0.150988	-0.150988	-0.150988	-0.150988	-0.150988	-0.150988	-0.150988	-0.150988	-0.150988	-0.150988	-0.150988
0161	Vegetables And Melons	1	-0.82%	-0.150988	-0.150988	-0.150988	-0.150988	-0.150988	-0.150988	-0.150988	-0.150988	-0.150988	-0.150988	-0.150988
017	FRUITS AND TREE NUTS	2	2.47%	0.457614	0.457614	0.287726	0.292927	0.301595	0.422943	0.457614	0.492285	0.613634	0.622301	0.627502
0174	Citrus Fruits	2	2.47%	0.457614	0.457614	0.287726	0.292927	0.301595	0.422943	0.457614	0.492285	0.613634	0.622301	0.627502
018	HORTICULTURAL SPECIALTIES	1	-1.38%	-0.255914	-0.255914	-0.255914	-0.255914	-0.255914	-0.255914	-0.255914	-0.255914	-0.255914	-0.255914	-0.255914
0181	Ornamental Floriculture And Nursery Products	1	-1.38%	-0.255914	-0.255914	-0.255914	-0.255914	-0.255914	-0.255914	-0.255914	-0.255914	-0.255914	-0.255914	-0.255914
019	GENERAL FARMS, PRIMARILY CROP	1	-1.99%	-0.369020	-0.369020	-0.369020	-0.369020	-0.369020	-0.369020	-0.369020	-0.369020	-0.369020	-0.369020	-0.369020
0191	General Farms, Primarily Crop	1	-1.99%	-0.369020	-0.369020	-0.369020	-0.369020	-0.369020	-0.369020	-0.369020	-0.369020	-0.369020	-0.369020	-0.369020
02	AGRICULTURAL PRODUCTION-LIVESTOCK AND ANIMAL SPECIALTIES	2	-2.90%	-0.537830	-0.537830	-1.418086	-1.391139	-1.346228	-0.717474	-0.537830	-0.358186	0.270568	0.315479	0.342426
021	LIVESTOCK, EXCEPT DAIRY AND POULTRY	1	-7.75%	-1.436050	-1.436050	-1.436050	-1.436050	-1.436050	-1.436050	-1.436050	-1.436050	-1.436050	-1.436050	-1.436050
0213	Hogs	1	-7.75%	-1.436050	-1.436050	-1.436050	-1.436050	-1.436050	-1.436050	-1.436050	-1.436050	-1.436050	-1.436050	-1.436050
025	POULTRY AND EGGS	1	1.95%	0.360390	0.360390	0.360390	0.360390	0.360390	0.360390	0.360390	0.360390	0.360390	0.360390	0.360390
0252	Chicken Eggs	1	1.95%	0.360390	0.360390	0.360390	0.360390	0.360390	0.360390	0.360390	0.360390	0.360390	0.360390	0.360390
07	AGRICULTURAL SERVICES	5	1.35%	0.249728	0.497716	-1.263157	-1.183983	-1.052025	0.300083	0.497716	0.594478	1.206812	1.265211	1.300250
074	VETERINARY SERVICES	1	0.02%	0.003633	0.003633	0.003633	0.003633	0.003633	0.003633	0.003633	0.003633	0.003633	0.003633	0.003633
0742	Veterinary Services For Animal Specialties	1	0.02%	0.003633	0.003633	0.003633	0.003633	0.003633	0.003633	0.003633	0.003633	0.003633	0.003633	0.003633
075	ANIMAL SERVICES, EXCEPT VETERINARY	1	-7.11%	-1.315940	-1.315940	-1.315940	-1.315940	-1.315940	-1.315940	-1.315940	-1.315940	-1.315940	-1.315940	-1.315940
0752	Animal Specialty Services, Except Veterinary	1	-7.11%	-1.315940	-1.315940	-1.315940	-1.315940	-1.315940	-1.315940	-1.315940	-1.315940	-1.315940	-1.315940	-1.315940
076	FARM LABOR AND MANAGEMENT SERVICES	1	2.69%	0.497716	0.497716	0.497716	0.497716	0.497716	0.497716	0.497716	0.497716	0.497716	0.497716	0.497716
0762	Farm Management Services	1	2.69%	0.497716	0.497716	0.497716	0.497716	0.497716	0.497716	0.497716	0.497716	0.497716	0.497716	0.497716
078	LANDSCAPE AND HORTICULTURAL SERVICES	1	3.99%	0.739622	0.739622	0.739622	0.739622	0.739622	0.739622	0.739622	0.739622	0.739622	0.739622	0.739622
0782	Lawn And Garden Services	1	3.99%	0.739622	0.739622	0.739622	0.739622	0.739622	0.739622	0.739622	0.739622	0.739622	0.739622	0.739622
08	FORESTRY	1	0.28%	0.052143	0.052143	0.052143	0.052143	0.052143	0.052143	0.052143	0.052143	0.052143	0.052143	0.052143
085	FORESTRY SERVICES	1	0.28%	0.052143	0.052143	0.052143	0.052143	0.052143	0.052143	0.052143	0.052143	0.052143	0.052143	0.052143
0851	Forestry Services	1	0.28%	0.052143	0.052143	0.052143	0.052143	0.052143	0.052143	0.052143	0.052143	0.052143	0.052143	0.052143
09	FISHING, HUNTING, AND TRAPPING	2	2.73%	0.506175	0.506175	-1.253449	-1.199583	-1.109807	0.147068	0.506175	0.865282	2.122157	2.211933	2.265799
	MINING													
10	METAL MINING	218	1.75%	0.324248	0.462939	-3.369758	-2.128718	-1.238845	0.327484	0.462939	0.581579	1.589052	1.751427	1.843314
1000	METAL MINING	5	-3.20%	-0.593460	-0.041235	-3.349007	-3.159267	-2.843034	-0.150010	-0.041235	-0.033922	0.703855	0.794706	0.849217
101	IRON ORES	6	3.10%	0.574037	0.356344	-0.176903	-0.146887	-0.096860	0.300310	0.356344	0.412377	1.571566	1.676063	1.738761
1011	Iron Ores	6	3.10%	0.574037	0.356344	-0.176903	-0.146887	-0.096860	0.300310	0.356344	0.412377	1.571566	1.676063	1.738761
102	COPPER ORES	20	3.44%	0.637123	0.621755	-0.785701	-0.733340	-0.646072	0.523643	0.621755	0.735056	1.636879	1.727779	1.782320
1021	Copper Ores	20	3.44%	0.637123	0.621755	-0.785701	-0.733340	-0.646072	0.523643	0.621755	0.735056	1.636879	1.727779	1.782320
103	LEAD AND ZINC ORES	2	2.70%	0.500465	0.500465	0.031432	0.045791	0.069721	0.404744	0.500465	0.596186	0.931209	0.955139	0.969497

Up-market Betas of Common Stocks by SIC Codes as of September 28, 2018

SIC Code	Description	Number of Companies	Equity Risk Premium	Mean	Median	1st Percentile	2.5th Percentile	5th Percentile	40th Percentile	50th Percentile	60th Percentile	95th Percentile	97.5th Percentile	99th Percentile
1031	Lead And Zinc Ores	2	2.70%	0.500465	0.500465	0.031432	0.045791	0.069721	0.404744	0.500465	0.596186	0.931209	0.955139	0.969497
104	GOLD AND SILVER ORES	123	1.80%	0.333637	0.462892	-2.245617	-1.310736	-1.129233	0.310474	0.462892	0.558285	1.531093	1.637419	1.703570
1040	GOLD AND SILVER ORES	3	1.55%	0.287681	0.281018	0.091061	0.096876	0.106568	0.242251	0.281018	0.323782	0.473457	0.484148	0.490563
1041	Gold Ores	110	1.69%	0.312318	0.462795	-2.319748	-1.446436	-1.196563	0.308171	0.462795	0.563490	1.545330	1.647808	1.709574
1044	Silver Ores	10	3.14%	0.581932	0.606649	-0.244254	-0.201890	-0.131284	0.502766	0.606649	0.695873	1.253975	1.256672	1.258291
106	FERROALLOY ORES, EXCEPT VANADIUM	6	1.65%	0.305794	-0.153970	-0.776832	-0.741428	-0.682421	-0.225905	-0.153970	-0.082034	1.742060	1.795210	1.827100
1061	Ferroalloy Ores, Except Vanadium	6	1.65%	0.305794	-0.153970	-0.776832	-0.741428	-0.682421	-0.225905	-0.153970	-0.082034	1.742060	1.795210	1.827100
108	METAL MINING SERVICES	27	1.51%	0.279834	0.448304	-2.297844	-1.979955	-1.637700	0.229875	0.448304	0.564712	1.667268	2.286512	2.736229
1081	Metal Mining Services	27	1.51%	0.279834	0.448304	-2.297844	-1.979955	-1.637700	0.229875	0.448304	0.564712	1.667268	2.286512	2.736229
109	MISCELLANEOUS METAL ORES	29	1.12%	0.208210	0.522211	-4.273611	-3.445207	-2.093934	0.423922	0.522211	0.707042	1.544028	1.610279	1.671738
1090	MISCELLANEOUS METAL ORES	1	8.46%	1.566380	1.566380	1.566380	1.566380	1.566380	1.566380	1.566380	1.566380	1.566380	1.566380	1.566380
1094	Uranium-Radium-Vanadium Ores	14	0.30%	0.055692	0.578368	-4.322614	-3.567714	-2.309549	0.455088	0.578368	0.707042	1.413510	1.435220	1.448246
1099	Miscellaneous Metal Ores, Not Elsewhere Classified	14	1.42%	0.263716	0.468242	-2.580886	-2.171979	-1.490468	0.356065	0.468242	0.520555	1.581274	1.646992	1.686423
12	COAL MINING	9	4.36%	0.808137	0.571171	-0.017333	0.032612	0.115854	0.544885	0.571171	0.599568	1.874634	2.089482	2.218391
122	BITUMINOUS COAL AND LIGNITE MINING	8	4.94%	0.915483	0.588919	0.373552	0.385509	0.405437	0.564599	0.588919	0.730986	1.928346	2.116338	2.229133
1220	BITUMINOUS COAL & LIGNITE MINING	2	3.18%	0.588919	0.588919	0.571526	0.572058	0.572946	0.585369	0.588919	0.592469	0.604892	0.605780	0.606312
1221	Bituminous Coal And Lignite Surface Mining	6	5.53%	1.024338	0.883287	0.371275	0.379815	0.394049	0.538313	0.883287	1.228260	2.035770	2.170050	2.250618
124	COAL MINING SERVICES	1	-0.27%	-0.050630	-0.050630	-0.050630	-0.050630	-0.050630	-0.050630	-0.050630	-0.050630	-0.050630	-0.050630	-0.050630
1241	Coal Mining Services	1	-0.27%	-0.050630	-0.050630	-0.050630	-0.050630	-0.050630	-0.050630	-0.050630	-0.050630	-0.050630	-0.050630	-0.050630
13	OIL AND GAS EXTRACTION	216	2.90%	0.536760	0.777781	-3.094621	-1.976949	-1.091518	0.672165	0.777781	0.895942	1.562763	1.704083	1.901933
131	CRUDE PETROLEUM AND NATURAL GAS	147	2.72%	0.504588	0.761605	-4.075850	-2.337592	-0.576234	0.654738	0.761605	0.880777	1.574053	1.704775	1.976634
1311	Crude Petroleum And Natural Gas	147	2.72%	0.504588	0.761605	-4.075850	-2.337592	-0.576234	0.654738	0.761605	0.880777	1.574053	1.704775	1.976634
132	NATURAL GAS LIQUIDS	4	6.20%	1.148673	1.150245	1.019702	1.021339	1.024069	1.093098	1.150245	1.207392	1.271075	1.273333	1.274687
1321	Natural Gas Liquids	4	6.20%	1.148673	1.150245	1.019702	1.021339	1.024069	1.093098	1.150245	1.207392	1.271075	1.273333	1.274687
138	OIL AND GAS FIELD SERVICES	65	3.09%	0.571863	0.805354	-2.167744	-1.659026	-1.335174	0.691654	0.805354	0.898316	1.485776	1.651110	1.766094
1381	Drilling Oil And Gas Wells	19	2.94%	0.544718	0.772887	-1.357409	-1.078887	-0.614683	0.688655	0.772887	0.839604	1.331826	1.469868	1.552693
1382	Oil And Gas Field Exploration Services	19	2.09%	0.387749	0.458034	-2.595563	-2.344452	-1.925934	0.346916	0.458034	0.816237	1.524236	1.689773	1.789095
1389	Oil And Gas Field Services, Not Elsewhere Classified	27	3.89%	0.720526	0.847115	-1.327267	-1.275873	-1.174457	0.814468	0.847115	0.965054	1.452158	1.561971	1.654334
14	MINING AND QUARRYING OF NONMETALLIC MINERALS, EXCEPT FUELS	28	1.38%	0.255756	0.476593	-1.650689	-1.573829	-1.502984	0.328928	0.476593	0.627716	1.442784	1.763150	2.014436
1400	MINING & QUARRYING OF NONMETALLIC MINERALS (NO FUELS)	2	4.28%	0.792440	0.792440	0.371166	0.384063	0.405556	0.706465	0.792440	0.878414	1.179323	1.200816	1.213713
141	DIMENSION STONE	2	-0.41%	-0.075135	-0.075135	-1.188048	-1.153979	-1.097198	-0.302260	-0.075135	0.151990	0.946928	1.003709	1.037778
1411	Dimension Stone	2	-0.41%	-0.075135	-0.075135	-1.188048	-1.153979	-1.097198	-0.302260	-0.075135	0.151990	0.946928	1.003709	1.037778
142	CRUSHED AND BROKEN STONE, INCLUDING RIPRAP	2	4.44%	0.821786	0.821786	0.646244	0.651618	0.660574	0.785961	0.821786	0.857611	0.982998	0.991954	0.997328
1422	Crushed And Broken Limestone	1	5.40%	1.000910	1.000910	1.000910	1.000910	1.000910	1.000910	1.000910	1.000910	1.000910	1.000910	1.000910
1423	Crushed And Broken Granite	1	3.47%	0.642662	0.642662	0.642662	0.642662	0.642662	0.642662	0.642662	0.642662	0.642662	0.642662	0.642662
144	SAND AND GRAVEL	5	3.89%	0.721039	0.726902	0.178649	0.211621	0.266575	0.718624	0.726902	0.782928	1.092154	1.120302	1.137191
1442	Construction Sand And Gravel	2	2.39%	0.441785	0.441785	0.162369	0.170923	0.185179	0.384761	0.441785	0.498808	0.698390	0.712646	0.721200
1446	Industrial Sand	3	4.90%	0.907208	0.866968	0.709421	0.714244	0.722282	0.834816	0.866968	0.923264	1.120302	1.134376	1.142820
147	CHEMICAL AND FERTILIZER MINERAL MINING	8	0.20%	0.036508	0.363244	-1.510317	-1.507567	-1.502984	0.160599	0.363244	0.496231	1.233368	1.397434	1.495874

Up-market Betas of Common Stocks by SIC Codes as of September 28, 2018

SIC Code	Description	Number of Companies	Equity Risk Premium	Mean	Median	1st Percentile	2.5th Percentile	5th Percentile	40th Percentile	50th Percentile	60th Percentile	95th Percentile	97.5th Percentile	99th Percentile
1474	Potash, Soda, And Borate Minerals	5	1.83%	0.339798	0.505575	-1.406766	-1.287975	-1.089989	0.500903	0.505575	0.552937	1.373996	1.467748	1.523999
1479	Chemical And Fertilizer Mineral Mining, Not Elsewhere Classified	3	-2.53%	-0.468977	-0.127372	-1.484454	-1.442911	-1.373672	-0.404328	-0.127372	-0.055379	0.196596	0.214594	0.225393
148	NONMETALLIC MINERALS SERVICES, EXCEPT FUELS	2	-1.71%	-0.316940	-0.316940	-1.077645	-1.054358	-1.015547	-0.472186	-0.316940	-0.161693	0.381668	0.420479	0.443766
1481	Nonmetallic Minerals Services, Except Fuels	2	-1.71%	-0.316940	-0.316940	-1.077645	-1.054358	-1.015547	-0.472186	-0.316940	-0.161693	0.381668	0.420479	0.443766
149	MISCELLANEOUS NONMETALLIC MINERALS, EXCEPT FUELS	7	0.63%	0.117087	-0.175679	-1.630052	-1.522234	-1.342538	-0.276706	-0.175679	0.141536	1.830450	2.006205	2.111658
1499	Miscellaneous Nonmetallic Minerals, Except Fuels	7	0.63%	0.117087	-0.175679	-1.630052	-1.522234	-1.342538	-0.276706	-0.175679	0.141536	1.830450	2.006205	2.111658
	CONSTRUCTION													
15	CONSTRUCTION	24	3.69%	0.682436	0.553262	0.064764	0.121654	0.220379	0.519507	0.553262	0.586117	1.214126	1.236268	1.253459
152	GENERAL BUILDING CONTRACTORS-RESIDENTIAL BUILDINGS	2	2.81%	0.519990	0.519990	0.461511	0.463302	0.466285	0.508056	0.519990	0.531924	0.573695	0.576678	0.578469
1521	General Contractors-Single-Family Houses	2	2.81%	0.519990	0.519990	0.461511	0.463302	0.466285	0.508056	0.519990	0.531924	0.573695	0.576678	0.578469
153	OPERATIVE BUILDERS	16	2.97%	0.549341	0.520295	0.051572	0.088674	0.150512	0.518937	0.520295	0.545094	0.957452	1.086271	1.163562
1531	Operative Builders	16	2.97%	0.549341	0.520295	0.051572	0.088674	0.150512	0.518937	0.520295	0.545094	0.957452	1.086271	1.163562
154	GENERAL BUILDING CONTRACTORS-NONRESIDENTIAL BUILDINGS	6	5.89%	1.091506	1.208660	0.537778	0.586326	0.667240	1.208660	1.208660	1.208660	1.250855	1.257888	1.262107
1541	General Contractors-Industrial Buildings And Warehouses	5	6.53%	1.208724	1.208660	1.154958	1.158314	1.163908	1.208660	1.208660	1.208660	1.253668	1.259294	1.262670
1542	General Contractors-Nonresidential Buildings, Other Than Industrial	1	2.73%	0.505413	0.505413	0.505413	0.505413	0.505413	0.505413	0.505413	0.505413	0.505413	0.505413	0.505413
16	HEAVY CONSTRUCTION OTHER THAN BUILDING CONSTRUCTION-CONTRACTORS	20	3.58%	0.662794	0.740968	-0.258464	-0.139829	0.057894	0.585978	0.740968	0.781598	1.081457	1.778058	2.196019
161	HIGHWAY AND STREET CONSTRUCTION, EXCEPT ELEVATED HIGHWAYS	3	7.38%	1.366953	0.861564	0.766575	0.769482	0.774329	0.842178	0.861564	1.184183	2.313350	2.394005	2.442398
1611	Highway And Street Construction, Except Elevated Highways	3	7.38%	1.366953	0.861564	0.766575	0.769482	0.774329	0.842178	0.861564	1.184183	2.313350	2.394005	2.442398
162	HEAVY CONSTRUCTION, EXCEPT HIGHWAY AND STREET CONSTRUCTION	17	2.91%	0.538530	0.685634	-0.270951	-0.171049	-0.004545	0.429197	0.685634	0.749885	0.960453	0.984292	0.998595
1622	Bridge, Tunnel, And Elevated Highway Construction	1	2.29%	0.424332	0.424332	0.424332	0.424332	0.424332	0.424332	0.424332	0.424332	0.424332	0.424332	0.424332
1623	Water, Sewer, Pipeline, And Communications And Power Line Construction	9	2.53%	0.467985	0.436495	-0.304252	-0.254301	-0.171049	0.363705	0.436495	0.724565	0.903887	0.926210	0.939605
1629	Heavy Construction, Not Elsewhere Classified	7	3.49%	0.645545	0.717299	0.140559	0.161521	0.196459	0.698300	0.717299	0.749885	0.960709	0.984420	0.998646
17	CONSTRUCTION-SPECIAL TRADE CONTRACTORS	9	3.97%	0.735470	0.723615	0.338895	0.362686	0.402336	0.619455	0.723615	0.827125	1.097715	1.159217	1.196119
171	PLUMBING, HEATING AND AIR-CONDITIONING	1	3.18%	0.589173	0.589173	0.589173	0.589173	0.589173	0.589173	0.589173	0.589173	0.589173	0.589173	0.589173
1711	Plumbing, Heating And Air-Conditioning	1	3.18%	0.589173	0.589173	0.589173	0.589173	0.589173	0.589173	0.589173	0.589173	0.589173	0.589173	0.589173
173	ELECTRICAL WORK	5	3.86%	0.714333	0.593415	0.330965	0.342860	0.362686	0.564564	0.593415	0.721332	1.159217	1.189969	1.208419
1731	Electrical Work	5	3.86%	0.714333	0.593415	0.330965	0.342860	0.362686	0.564564	0.593415	0.721332	1.159217	1.189969	1.208419

Up-market Betas of Common Stocks by SIC Codes as of September 28, 2018

SIC Code	Description	Number of Companies	Equity Risk Premium	Mean	Median	1st Percentile	2.5th Percentile	5th Percentile	40th Percentile	50th Percentile	60th Percentile	95th Percentile	97.5th Percentile	99th Percentile
174	MASONRY, STONEWORK, TILE SETTING, AND PLASTERING	2	4.26%	0.788309	0.788309	0.724909	0.726850	0.730084	0.775370	0.788309	0.801247	0.846533	0.849767	0.851708
1742	Plastering, Drywall, Acoustical, And Insulation Work	2	4.26%	0.788309	0.788309	0.724909	0.726850	0.730084	0.775370	0.788309	0.801247	0.846533	0.849767	0.851708
177	CONCRETE WORK	1	4.76%	0.881773	0.881773	0.881773	0.881773	0.881773	0.881773	0.881773	0.881773	0.881773	0.881773	0.881773
1771	Concrete Work	1	4.76%	0.881773	0.881773	0.881773	0.881773	0.881773	0.881773	0.881773	0.881773	0.881773	0.881773	0.881773
	MANUFACTURING													
20	FOOD AND KINDRED PRODUCTS	87	4.20%	0.777995	0.578002	-1.817540	-1.156643	-0.464136	0.480445	0.578002	0.689050	1.121167	1.235275	5.470403
2000	FOOD AND KINDRED PRODUCTS	2	-1.02%	-0.188105	-0.188105	-0.536030	-0.525380	-0.507628	-0.259110	-0.188105	-0.117100	0.131418	0.149170	0.159820
201	MEAT PRODUCTS	7	2.18%	0.403911	0.551295	-0.286504	-0.240091	-0.162734	0.413359	0.551295	0.598979	0.729165	0.734878	0.738306
2011	Meat Packing Plants	2	2.24%	0.414516	0.414516	0.202588	0.209076	0.219888	0.371265	0.414516	0.457766	0.609143	0.619955	0.626443
2013	Sausages And Other Prepared Meat Products	2	0.01%	0.001977	0.001977	-0.311059	-0.301476	-0.285505	-0.061908	0.001977	0.065862	0.289459	0.305430	0.315013
2015	Poultry Slaughtering And Processing	3	3.59%	0.664797	0.702505	0.554319	0.558856	0.566416	0.672263	0.702505	0.710122	0.736782	0.738687	0.739829
202	DAIRY PRODUCTS	7	1.01%	0.187173	0.480105	-1.679466	-1.503989	-1.211528	0.444816	0.480105	0.538843	0.748565	0.757249	0.762459
2022	Natural, Processed, And Imitation Cheese	2	3.98%	0.736987	0.736987	0.708620	0.709488	0.710936	0.731198	0.736987	0.742776	0.763038	0.764486	0.765354
2023	Dry, Condensed, And Evaporated Dairy Products	1	0.83%	0.153291	0.153291	0.153291	0.153291	0.153291	0.153291	0.153291	0.153291	0.153291	0.153291	0.153291
2024	Ice Cream And Frozen Desserts	1	3.12%	0.578002	0.578002	0.578002	0.578002	0.578002	0.578002	0.578002	0.578002	0.578002	0.578002	0.578002
2026	Fluid Milk	3	-1.61%	-0.298352	0.421290	-1.752095	-1.685563	-1.574676	-0.022258	0.421290	0.433053	0.474224	0.477164	0.478929
203	CANNED, FROZEN, AND PRESERVED FRUITS, VEGETABLES, AND FOOD SPECIAL	9	3.55%	0.656536	0.668868	0.446012	0.454644	0.469031	0.603004	0.668868	0.711702	0.841955	0.846954	0.849953
2030	CANNED, FROZEN & PRESERVD FRUIT, VEG & FOOD SPECIALTIES	2	4.38%	0.812007	0.812007	0.772859	0.774057	0.776055	0.804017	0.812007	0.819996	0.847958	0.849956	0.851154
2032	Canned Specialties	2	3.42%	0.633608	0.633608	0.444124	0.449925	0.459592	0.594938	0.633608	0.672278	0.807624	0.817291	0.823092
2033	Canned Fruits, Vegetables, Preserves, Jams, And Jellies	3	3.31%	0.612177	0.586538	0.528763	0.530532	0.533479	0.574747	0.586538	0.613712	0.708823	0.715616	0.719693
2034	Dried And Dehydrated Fruits, Vegetables, And Soup Mixes	1	3.61%	0.668868	0.668868	0.668868	0.668868	0.668868	0.668868	0.668868	0.668868	0.668868	0.668868	0.668868
2037	Frozen Fruits, Fruit Juices, And Vegetables	1	2.77%	0.512193	0.512193	0.512193	0.512193	0.512193	0.512193	0.512193	0.512193	0.512193	0.512193	0.512193
204	GRAIN MILL PRODUCTS	7	4.19%	0.776210	0.780720	0.487665	0.497728	0.514500	0.672790	0.780720	0.828593	1.065064	1.069732	1.072533
2041	Flour And Other Grain Mill Products	2	3.41%	0.630838	0.630838	0.483954	0.488450	0.495944	0.600862	0.630838	0.660814	0.765732	0.773226	0.777722
2043	Cereal Breakfast Foods	1	3.24%	0.600837	0.600837	0.600837	0.600837	0.600837	0.600837	0.600837	0.600837	0.600837	0.600837	0.600837
2044	Rice Milling	1	5.80%	1.074400	1.074400	1.074400	1.074400	1.074400	1.074400	1.074400	1.074400	1.074400	1.074400	1.074400
2046	Wet Corn Milling	2	3.92%	0.726639	0.726639	0.595445	0.599462	0.606155	0.699864	0.726639	0.753413	0.847122	0.853815	0.857832
2047	Dog And Cat Food	1	5.63%	1.043280	1.043280	1.043280	1.043280	1.043280	1.043280	1.043280	1.043280	1.043280	1.043280	1.043280
205	BAKERY PRODUCTS	5	3.85%	0.712297	0.743064	-0.040035	0.008269	0.088777	0.738974	0.743064	0.852482	1.116290	1.128750	1.136226
2051	Bread And Other Bakery Products, Except Cookies And Crackers	2	5.06%	0.937024	0.937024	0.736922	0.743047	0.753257	0.896187	0.937024	0.977861	1.120791	1.131001	1.137126
2052	Cookies And Crackers	3	3.04%	0.562479	0.743064	-0.055932	-0.031473	0.009292	0.580004	0.743064	0.797773	0.989255	1.002933	1.011139
206	SUGAR AND CONFECTIONERY PRODUCTS	4	2.01%	0.371644	0.498046	-0.065686	-0.041156	-0.000273	0.477060	0.498046	0.519032	0.566600	0.569562	0.571340
2061	Cane Sugar, Except Refining	1	2.88%	0.533023	0.533023	0.533023	0.533023	0.533023	0.533023	0.533023	0.533023	0.533023	0.533023	0.533023
2066	Chocolate And Cocoa Products	2	1.03%	0.190515	0.190515	-0.076588	-0.068412	-0.054784	0.136004	0.190515	0.245026	0.435814	0.449441	0.457618
2068	Salted And Roasted Nuts And Seeds	1	3.09%	0.572525	0.572525	0.572525	0.572525	0.572525	0.572525	0.572525	0.572525	0.572525	0.572525	0.572525
207	FATS AND OILS	2	3.34%	0.618250	0.618250	0.342040	0.350495	0.364588	0.561880	0.618250	0.674619	0.871911	0.886004	0.894459
2075	Soybean Oil Mills	1	1.82%	0.336403	0.336403	0.336403	0.336403	0.336403	0.336403	0.336403	0.336403	0.336403	0.336403	0.336403
2077	Animal And Marine Fats And Oils	1	4.86%	0.900096	0.900096	0.900096	0.900096	0.900096	0.900096	0.900096	0.900096	0.900096	0.900096	0.900096

Up-market Betas of Common Stocks by SIC Codes as of September 28, 2018

SIC Code	Description	Number of Companies	Equity Risk Premium	Mean	Median	1st Percentile	2.5th Percentile	5th Percentile	40th Percentile	50th Percentile	60th Percentile	95th Percentile	97.5th Percentile	99th Percentile
208	BEVERAGES	32	1.76%	0.325978	0.354111	-1.488782	-0.801321	-0.460351	0.187794	0.354111	0.504562	1.198167	1.268329	1.307881
2080	BEVERAGES	1	4.12%	0.763347	0.763347	0.763347	0.763347	0.763347	0.763347	0.763347	0.763347	0.763347	0.763347	0.763347
2082	Malt Beverages	5	2.78%	0.514099	0.647593	0.096755	0.104943	0.118590	0.479663	0.647593	0.683473	0.840695	0.853621	0.861376
2084	Wines, Brandy, And Brandy Spirits	5	0.23%	0.042567	0.004321	-0.314809	-0.298101	-0.270255	-0.016401	0.004321	0.067050	0.368870	0.394836	0.410416
2085	Distilled And Blended Liquors	5	3.60%	0.666435	0.834770	0.107196	0.125629	0.156350	0.661711	0.834770	0.838443	1.093927	1.125173	1.143921
2086	Bottled And Canned Soft Drinks And Carbonated Waters	14	0.48%	0.089647	0.182798	-1.754896	-1.466606	-0.986122	0.107879	0.182798	0.293306	1.070583	1.202416	1.281517
2087	Flavoring Extracts And Flavoring Syrups, Not Elsewhere Classified	2	6.20%	1.148700	1.148700	1.050220	1.053235	1.058259	1.128602	1.148700	1.168798	1.239141	1.244166	1.247180
209	MISCELLANEOUS FOOD PREPARATIONS AND KINDRED PRODUCTS	12	16.14%	2.988836	0.759321	-1.128131	-0.922962	-0.581015	0.667666	0.759321	0.792411	14.348842	22.613521	27.572328
2095	Roasted Coffee	5	3.43%	0.634286	0.807912	0.010161	0.057598	0.136661	0.792411	0.807912	0.807912	0.807912	0.807912	0.807912
2097	Manufactured Ice	1	-6.83%	-1.264910	-1.264910	-1.264910	-1.264910	-1.264910	-1.264910	-1.264910	-1.264910	-1.264910	-1.264910	-1.264910
2099	Food Preparations, Not Elsewhere Classified	6	30.56%	5.659918	0.681302	0.324205	0.344661	0.378755	0.613121	0.681302	0.749483	23.364855	27.121528	29.375531
21	TOBACCO PRODUCTS	9	1.96%	0.362457	0.515970	-0.988951	-0.863133	-0.653437	0.397404	0.515970	0.544871	1.146723	1.276637	1.354585
2100	TOBACCO PRODUCTS	2	-1.90%	-0.352534	-0.352534	-1.058424	-1.036815	-1.000800	-0.496593	-0.352534	-0.208475	0.295732	0.331747	0.353356
211	CIGARETTES	7	3.06%	0.566740	0.552096	-0.012992	0.004040	0.032426	0.530420	0.552096	0.577857	1.211680	1.309115	1.367576
2111	Cigarettes	7	3.06%	0.566740	0.552096	-0.012992	0.004040	0.032426	0.530420	0.552096	0.577857	1.211680	1.309115	1.367576
22	TEXTILE MILL PRODUCTS	11	3.58%	0.662742	0.620874	0.231194	0.239910	0.254436	0.619587	0.620874	0.654300	1.264810	1.285975	1.298674
221	BROADWOVEN FABRIC MILLS, COTTON	2	2.53%	0.468894	0.468894	0.287195	0.292757	0.302028	0.431812	0.468894	0.505975	0.635759	0.645030	0.650592
2211	Broadwoven Fabric Mills, Cotton	2	2.53%	0.468894	0.468894	0.287195	0.292757	0.302028	0.431812	0.468894	0.505975	0.635759	0.645030	0.650592
222	BROADWOVEN FABRIC MILLS, MANMADE FIBER AND SILK	2	5.35%	0.991616	0.991616	0.682401	0.691867	0.707643	0.928511	0.991616	1.054720	1.275588	1.291364	1.300830
2221	Broadwoven Fabric Mills, Manmade Fiber And Silk	2	5.35%	0.991616	0.991616	0.682401	0.691867	0.707643	0.928511	0.991616	1.054720	1.275588	1.291364	1.300830
225	KNITTING MILLS	3	3.96%	0.733670	0.753147	0.235939	0.251772	0.278160	0.647594	0.753147	0.847014	1.175547	1.199013	1.213093
2252	Hosiery, Not Elsewhere Classified	1	1.22%	0.225384	0.225384	0.225384	0.225384	0.225384	0.225384	0.225384	0.225384	0.225384	0.225384	0.225384
2253	Knit Outerwear Mills	2	5.33%	0.987814	0.987814	0.757840	0.764880	0.776614	0.940880	0.987814	1.034747	1.199013	1.210747	1.217787
227	CARPETS AND RUGS	3	2.79%	0.516182	0.501548	0.427632	0.429895	0.433666	0.486463	0.501548	0.525413	0.608941	0.614908	0.618487
2273	Carpets And Rugs	3	2.79%	0.516182	0.501548	0.427632	0.429895	0.433666	0.486463	0.501548	0.525413	0.608941	0.614908	0.618487
228	YARN AND THREAD MILLS	1	3.35%	0.619587	0.619587	0.619587	0.619587	0.619587	0.619587	0.619587	0.619587	0.619587	0.619587	0.619587
2282	Yarn Texturizing, Throwing, Twisting, And Winding Mills	1	3.35%	0.619587	0.619587	0.619587	0.619587	0.619587	0.619587	0.619587	0.619587	0.619587	0.619587	0.619587
23	APPAREL AND OTHER FINISHED PRODUCTS MADE FROM FABRICS AND SIMILAR MATERIAL	19	4.31%	0.797809	0.735376	0.288176	0.289619	0.292025	0.661350	0.735376	0.855794	1.366825	1.682433	1.871797
2300	APPAREL & OTHER FINISHD PRODS OF FABRICS & SIMILAR MATL	2	7.38%	1.366708	1.366708	0.748003	0.766943	0.798509	1.240442	1.366708	1.492974	1.934907	1.966473	1.985413
232	MEN'S AND BOYS' FURNISHINGS, WORK CLOTHING, AND ALLIED GARMENTS	6	4.35%	0.805939	0.896970	0.312576	0.350618	0.414023	0.871131	0.896970	0.922809	0.999213	1.008811	1.014571
2321	Men's And Boys' Shirts, Except Work Shirts	2	3.32%	0.614417	0.614417	0.293758	0.303574	0.319934	0.548976	0.614417	0.679858	0.908900	0.925260	0.935076
2325	Men's And Boys' Separate Trousers And Slacks	1	4.29%	0.794448	0.794448	0.794448	0.794448	0.794448	0.794448	0.794448	0.794448	0.794448	0.794448	0.794448
2326	Men's And Boys' Work Clothing	1	5.50%	1.018410	1.018410	1.018410	1.018410	1.018410	1.018410	1.018410	1.018410	1.018410	1.018410	1.018410
2329	Men's And Boys' Clothing, Not Elsewhere Classified	2	4.84%	0.896970	0.896970	0.871648	0.872423	0.873715	0.891802	0.896970	0.902138	0.920225	0.921517	0.922292
233	WOMEN'S, MISSES', AND JUNIORS' OUTERWEAR	8	4.15%	0.767684	0.612238	0.394125	0.407229	0.429069	0.564034	0.612238	0.733948	1.239301	1.267995	1.285212

Up-market Betas of Common Stocks by SIC Codes as of September 28, 2018

SIC Code	Description	Number of Companies	Equity Risk Premium	Mean	Median	1st Percentile	2.5th Percentile	5th Percentile	40th Percentile	50th Percentile	60th Percentile	95th Percentile	97.5th Percentile	99th Percentile
2330	WOMEN'S, MISSES', AND JUNIORS OUTERWEAR	1	6.12%	1.132720	1.132720	1.132720	1.132720	1.132720	1.132720	1.132720	1.132720	1.132720	1.132720	1.132720
2337	Women's, Misses', And Juniors' Suits, Skirts, And Coats	1	3.51%	0.649090	0.649090	0.649090	0.649090	0.649090	0.649090	0.649090	0.649090	0.649090	0.649090	0.649090
2339	Women's, Misses', And Juniors' Outerwear, Not Elsewhere Classified	6	3.92%	0.726610	0.547007	0.391629	0.400989	0.416589	0.518628	0.547007	0.575386	1.240863	1.268776	1.285525
234	WOMEN'S, MISSES', CHILDREN'S, AND INFANTS' UNDERGARMENTS	1	1.58%	0.292559	0.292559	0.292559	0.292559	0.292559	0.292559	0.292559	0.292559	0.292559	0.292559	0.292559
2341	Women's, Misses', Children's, And Infants' Underwear And Nightwear	1	1.58%	0.292559	0.292559	0.292559	0.292559	0.292559	0.292559	0.292559	0.292559	0.292559	0.292559	0.292559
238	MISCELLANEOUS APPAREL AND ACCESSORIES	2	3.12%	0.577642	0.577642	0.447550	0.451532	0.458170	0.551093	0.577642	0.604191	0.697114	0.703752	0.707734
2385	Waterproof Outerwear	1	2.40%	0.444895	0.444895	0.444895	0.444895	0.444895	0.444895	0.444895	0.444895	0.444895	0.444895	0.444895
2389	Apparel And Accessories, Not Elsewhere Classified	1	3.84%	0.710389	0.710389	0.710389	0.710389	0.710389	0.710389	0.710389	0.710389	0.710389	0.710389	0.710389
24	LUMBER AND WOOD PRODUCTS, EXCEPT FURNITURE	12	3.87%	0.716859	0.835516	-0.269102	-0.191197	-0.061355	0.727082	0.835516	0.937426	1.309540	1.381345	1.424428
2400	LUMBER & WOOD PRODUCTS (NO FURNITURE)	1	5.46%	1.010290	1.010290	1.010290	1.010290	1.010290	1.010290	1.010290	1.010290	1.010290	1.010290	1.010290
241	LOGGING	1	1.53%	0.283311	0.283311	0.283311	0.283311	0.283311	0.283311	0.283311	0.283311	0.283311	0.283311	0.283311
2411	Logging	1	1.53%	0.283311	0.283311	0.283311	0.283311	0.283311	0.283311	0.283311	0.283311	0.283311	0.283311	0.283311
242	SAWMILLS AND PLANING MILLS	2	0.28%	0.052027	0.052027	-0.313578	-0.302386	-0.283732	-0.022586	0.052027	0.126640	0.387786	0.406440	0.417632
2421	Sawmills And Planing Mills, General	2	0.28%	0.052027	0.052027	-0.313578	-0.302386	-0.283732	-0.022586	0.052027	0.126640	0.387786	0.406440	0.417632
243	MILLWORK, VENEER, PLYWOOD, AND STRUCTURAL WOOD MEMBERS	3	3.28%	0.607381	0.743568	0.162962	0.180736	0.210359	0.625077	0.743568	0.780347	0.909074	0.918268	0.923785
2430	MILLWOOD, VENEER, PLYWOOD, & STRUCTURAL WOOD MEMBERS	1	0.82%	0.151113	0.151113	0.151113	0.151113	0.151113	0.151113	0.151113	0.151113	0.151113	0.151113	0.151113
2434	Wood Kitchen Cabinets	1	5.01%	0.927463	0.927463	0.927463	0.927463	0.927463	0.927463	0.927463	0.927463	0.927463	0.927463	0.927463
2439	Structural Wood Members, Not Elsewhere Classified	1	4.02%	0.743568	0.743568	0.743568	0.743568	0.743568	0.743568	0.743568	0.743568	0.743568	0.743568	0.743568
245	WOOD BUILDINGS AND MOBILE HOMES	2	7.14%	1.322595	1.322595	1.194651	1.198568	1.205096	1.296484	1.322595	1.348706	1.440095	1.446622	1.450539
2451	Mobile Homes	2	7.14%	1.322595	1.322595	1.194651	1.198568	1.205096	1.296484	1.322595	1.348706	1.440095	1.446622	1.450539
249	MISCELLANEOUS WOOD PRODUCTS	3	4.93%	0.912440	0.944068	0.720652	0.727491	0.738890	0.898473	0.944068	0.970686	1.063851	1.070505	1.074498
2491	Wood Preserving	1	3.87%	0.716092	0.716092	0.716092	0.716092	0.716092	0.716092	0.716092	0.716092	0.716092	0.716092	0.716092
2493	Reconstituted Wood Products	1	5.82%	1.077160	1.077160	1.077160	1.077160	1.077160	1.077160	1.077160	1.077160	1.077160	1.077160	1.077160
2499	Wood Products, Not Elsewhere Classified	1	5.10%	0.944068	0.944068	0.944068	0.944068	0.944068	0.944068	0.944068	0.944068	0.944068	0.944068	0.944068
25	FURNITURE AND FIXTURES	20	3.36%	0.621769	0.598267	-0.221806	-0.088659	0.133252	0.564394	0.598267	0.671919	1.125281	1.240140	1.309056
251	HOUSEHOLD FURNITURE	12	3.36%	0.621606	0.596741	-0.247645	-0.153257	0.004055	0.555422	0.596741	0.765184	1.217319	1.286159	1.327464
2511	Wood Household Furniture, Except Upholstered	7	2.74%	0.506847	0.537479	0.264091	0.268013	0.274549	0.403568	0.537479	0.564394	0.838646	0.887397	0.916647
2512	Wood Household Furniture, Upholstered	1	-1.68%	-0.310570	-0.310570	-0.310570	-0.310570	-0.310570	-0.310570	-0.310570	-0.310570	-0.310570	-0.310570	-0.310570
2515	Mattresses, Foundations, And Convertible Beds	3	5.16%	0.955638	0.894367	0.868407	0.869202	0.870526	0.889069	0.894367	0.936428	1.083640	1.094155	1.100464
2519	Household Furniture, Not Elsewhere Classified	1	7.32%	1.355000	1.355000	1.355000	1.355000	1.355000	1.355000	1.355000	1.355000	1.355000	1.355000	1.355000
252	OFFICE FURNITURE	7	3.72%	0.688499	0.628718	0.357650	0.363804	0.374059	0.602720	0.628718	0.693519	1.073237	1.093214	1.105199

Up-market Betas of Common Stocks by SIC Codes as of September 28, 2018

SIC Code	Description	Number of Companies	Equity Risk Premium	Mean	Median	1st Percentile	2.5th Percentile	5th Percentile	40th Percentile	50th Percentile	60th Percentile	95th Percentile	97.5th Percentile	99th Percentile
2521	Wood Office Furniture	3	3.45%	0.639650	0.585388	0.358185	0.365140	0.376732	0.539020	0.585388	0.664313	0.940551	0.960283	0.972121
2522	Office Furniture, Except Wood	4	3.92%	0.725137	0.682719	0.428122	0.437428	0.452938	0.650318	0.682719	0.715120	1.056720	1.084955	1.101896
253	PUBLIC BUILDING AND RELATED FURNITURE	1	0.85%	0.156611	0.156611	0.156611	0.156611	0.156611	0.156611	0.156611	0.156611	0.156611	0.156611	0.156611
2531	Public Building And Related Furniture	1	0.85%	0.156611	0.156611	0.156611	0.156611	0.156611	0.156611	0.156611	0.156611	0.156611	0.156611	0.156611
26	PAPER AND ALLIED PRODUCTS	27	2.86%	0.530350	0.655173	-1.478827	-0.733624	-0.062364	0.495567	0.655173	0.738688	1.150271	1.270101	1.373462
261	PULP MILLS	2	2.72%	0.503510	0.503510	-0.053484	-0.036433	-0.008015	0.389838	0.503510	0.617182	1.015034	1.043452	1.060503
2611	Pulp Mills	2	2.72%	0.503510	0.503510	-0.053484	-0.036433	-0.008015	0.389838	0.503510	0.617182	1.015034	1.043452	1.060503
262	PAPER MILLS	10	3.24%	0.599452	0.583592	0.044344	0.070594	0.114345	0.508823	0.583592	0.695075	1.136737	1.157038	1.169219
2621	Paper Mills	10	3.24%	0.599452	0.583592	0.044344	0.070594	0.114345	0.508823	0.583592	0.695075	1.136737	1.157038	1.169219
263	PAPERBOARD MILLS	4	2.97%	0.550633	0.590893	-0.040824	-0.017215	0.022133	0.517202	0.590893	0.664584	1.022770	1.050040	1.066402
2631	Paperboard Mills	4	2.97%	0.550633	0.590893	-0.040824	-0.017215	0.022133	0.517202	0.590893	0.664584	1.022770	1.050040	1.066402
265	PAPERBOARD CONTAINERS AND BOXES	2	5.60%	1.037325	1.037325	1.009459	1.010312	1.011734	1.031638	1.037325	1.043012	1.062917	1.064338	1.065191
2655	Fiber Cans, Tubes, Drums, And Similar Products	2	5.60%	1.037325	1.037325	1.009459	1.010312	1.011734	1.031638	1.037325	1.043012	1.062917	1.064338	1.065191
267	CONVERTED PAPER AND PAPERBOARD PRODUCTS, EXCEPT CONTAINERS AND BOXES	9	1.82%	0.337858	0.489919	-1.818067	-1.581722	-1.187813	0.451438	0.489919	0.688934	1.160897	1.301634	1.386075
2671	Packaging Paper And Plastics Film, Coated And Laminated	5	2.85%	0.528448	0.738688	0.011446	0.037747	0.081583	0.616119	0.738688	0.738688	0.738688	0.738688	0.738688
2673	Plastics, Foil, And Coated Paper Bags	2	-1.44%	-0.266630	-0.266630	-1.941450	-1.890180	-1.804730	-0.608430	-0.266630	0.075170	1.271470	1.356920	1.408190
2679	Converted Paper And Paperboard Products, Not Elsewhere Classified	2	2.52%	0.465869	0.465869	0.442299	0.443021	0.444223	0.461058	0.465869	0.470679	0.487514	0.488716	0.489438
27	PRINTING, PUBLISHING, AND ALLIED INDUSTRIES	40	2.68%	0.496037	0.540175	-0.362830	-0.355288	-0.305101	0.444525	0.540175	0.661945	1.154679	1.178875	1.372276
271	NEWSPAPERS: PUBLISHING, OR PUBLISHING AND PRINTING	18	2.02%	0.373346	0.449843	-0.365666	-0.362378	-0.356900	0.375727	0.449843	0.532141	0.859543	0.861780	0.863122
2711	Newspapers: Publishing, Or Publishing And Printing	18	2.02%	0.373346	0.449843	-0.365666	-0.362378	-0.356900	0.375727	0.449843	0.532141	0.859543	0.861780	0.863122
272	PERIODICALS: PUBLISHING, OR PUBLISHING AND PRINTING	2	4.12%	0.762086	0.762086	0.715238	0.716672	0.719062	0.752525	0.762086	0.771646	0.805109	0.807499	0.808933
2721	Periodicals: Publishing, Or Publishing And Printing	2	4.12%	0.762086	0.762086	0.715238	0.716672	0.719062	0.752525	0.762086	0.771646	0.805109	0.807499	0.808933
273	BOOKS	4	3.78%	0.699301	0.732013	0.328727	0.341024	0.361519	0.649083	0.732013	0.814943	0.991287	1.001968	1.008377
2731	Books: Publishing, Or Publishing And Printing	4	3.78%	0.699301	0.732013	0.328727	0.341024	0.361519	0.649083	0.732013	0.814943	0.991287	1.001968	1.008377
274	MISCELLANEOUS PUBLISHING	5	3.56%	0.658653	0.447502	-0.237054	-0.194790	-0.124349	0.444171	0.447502	0.736745	1.435090	1.468150	1.487986
2741	Miscellaneous Publishing	5	3.56%	0.658653	0.447502	-0.237054	-0.194790	-0.124349	0.444171	0.447502	0.736745	1.435090	1.468150	1.487986
275	COMMERCIAL PRINTING	8	2.72%	0.503288	0.600361	-0.251987	-0.230468	-0.194603	0.473441	0.600361	0.693723	1.088280	1.121060	1.140728
2750	COMMERCIAL PRINTING	1	6.23%	1.153840	1.153840	1.153840	1.153840	1.153840	1.153840	1.153840	1.153840	1.153840	1.153840	1.153840
2752	Commercial Printing, Lithographic	2	1.25%	0.230692	0.230692	-0.055549	-0.046787	-0.032183	0.172275	0.230692	0.289109	0.493567	0.508171	0.516933
2754	Commercial Printing, Gravure	3	2.62%	0.485674	0.756829	-0.245870	-0.215175	-0.164017	0.552197	0.756829	0.798769	0.945557	0.956042	0.962333
2759	Commercial Printing, Not Elsewhere Classified	2	2.58%	0.477027	0.477027	0.280125	0.286153	0.296199	0.436843	0.477027	0.517211	0.657855	0.667901	0.673929
276	MANIFOLD BUSINESS FORMS	1	5.13%	0.949883	0.949883	0.949883	0.949883	0.949883	0.949883	0.949883	0.949883	0.949883	0.949883	0.949883
2761	Manifold Business Forms	1	5.13%	0.949883	0.949883	0.949883	0.949883	0.949883	0.949883	0.949883	0.949883	0.949883	0.949883	0.949883
277	GREETING CARDS	1	-1.63%	-0.302477	-0.302477	-0.302477	-0.302477	-0.302477	-0.302477	-0.302477	-0.302477	-0.302477	-0.302477	-0.302477
2771	Greeting Cards	1	-1.63%	-0.302477	-0.302477	-0.302477	-0.302477	-0.302477	-0.302477	-0.302477	-0.302477	-0.302477	-0.302477	-0.302477

Up-market Betas of Common Stocks by SIC Codes as of September 28, 2018

SIC Code	Description	Number of Companies	Equity Risk Premium	Mean	Median	1st Percentile	2.5th Percentile	5th Percentile	40th Percentile	50th Percentile	60th Percentile	95th Percentile	97.5th Percentile	99th Percentile
278	BLANKBOOKS, LOOSELEAF BINDERS, AND BOOKBINDING AND RELATED WORK	1	4.50%	0.832888	0.832888	0.832888	0.832888	0.832888	0.832888	0.832888	0.832888	0.832888	0.832888	0.832888
2782	Blankbooks, Looseleaf Binders And Devices	1	4.50%	0.832888	0.832888	0.832888	0.832888	0.832888	0.832888	0.832888	0.832888	0.832888	0.832888	0.832888
28	CHEMICALS AND ALLIED PRODUCTS	503	3.49%	0.646981	0.738968	-2.903091	-1.385420	-0.923250	0.554977	0.738968	0.893250	2.149836	2.534406	3.206688
2800	CHEMICALS & ALLIED PRODUCTS	1	6.27%	1.161510	1.161510	1.161510	1.161510	1.161510	1.161510	1.161510	1.161510	1.161510	1.161510	1.161510
281	INDUSTRIAL INORGANIC CHEMICALS	15	3.03%	0.561566	0.874505	-0.664886	-0.604238	-0.503157	0.776396	0.874505	1.004483	1.164359	1.186490	1.199768
2810	INDUSTRIAL INORGANIC CHEMICALS	1	5.97%	1.105710	1.105710	1.105710	1.105710	1.105710	1.105710	1.105710	1.105710	1.105710	1.105710	1.105710
2812	Alkalies And Chlorine	1	5.40%	0.999292	0.999292	0.999292	0.999292	0.999292	0.999292	0.999292	0.999292	0.999292	0.999292	0.999292
2813	Industrial Gases	2	5.62%	1.041563	1.041563	0.877846	0.882858	0.891211	1.008151	1.041563	1.074974	1.191914	1.200267	1.205279
2816	Inorganic Pigments	4	1.78%	0.330381	0.296325	-0.410782	-0.402180	-0.387843	-0.016684	0.296325	0.609334	1.096282	1.120836	1.135568
2819	Industrial Inorganic Chemicals, Not Elsewhere Classified	7	2.25%	0.416263	0.713980	-0.685799	-0.656520	-0.607722	0.399976	0.713980	0.892954	1.048889	1.054705	1.058194
282	PLASTICS MATERIALS AND SYNTHETIC RESINS, SYNTHETIC RUBBER, CELLULOSIC MANMADE FIBERS	14	3.86%	0.714652	1.013070	-2.439640	-1.814965	-0.773840	0.855133	1.013070	1.103286	1.356008	1.384179	1.401082
2821	Plastics Materials, Synthetic Resins, And Nonvulcanizable Elastomers	14	3.86%	0.714652	1.013070	-2.439640	-1.814965	-0.773840	0.855133	1.013070	1.103286	1.356008	1.384179	1.401082
283	DRUGS	403	3.54%	0.655558	0.737189	-3.242163	-1.351469	-0.903802	0.535224	0.737189	0.905038	2.168525	2.545046	3.147297
2833	Medicinal Chemicals And Botanical Products	12	3.06%	0.566408	0.782466	-0.826960	-0.705459	-0.502957	0.630205	0.782466	0.907426	1.142836	1.209438	1.249399
2834	Pharmaceutical Preparations	308	3.21%	0.595275	0.686831	-3.315955	-1.953421	-0.974145	0.479924	0.686831	0.870033	2.115457	2.481000	3.203759
2835	In Vitro And In Vivo Diagnostic Substances	22	3.92%	0.726574	0.759340	-1.302443	-1.117498	-0.832014	0.585383	0.759340	0.969058	2.524043	2.684687	2.790697
2836	Biological Products, Except Diagnostic Substances	61	5.14%	0.951861	0.902152	-1.050195	-0.713289	-0.386824	0.794305	0.902152	1.045080	2.231830	2.538550	2.821872
284	SOAP, DETERGENTS, AND CLEANING PREPARATIONS; PERFUMES, COSMETICS	20	1.13%	0.208666	0.286847	-2.377616	-1.587966	-0.271882	0.174578	0.286847	0.462721	0.866715	0.969148	1.030607
2841	Soap And Other Detergents, Except Specialty Cleaners	5	2.92%	0.540845	0.495522	0.278258	0.290104	0.309847	0.484430	0.495522	0.586619	0.742482	0.744884	0.746325
2842	Specialty Cleaning, Polishing, And Sanitation Preparations	4	-3.70%	-0.685145	-0.016020	-2.820929	-2.696247	-2.488445	-0.086416	-0.016020	0.054377	0.181378	0.188443	0.192682
2844	Perfumes, Cosmetics, And Other Toilet Preparations	11	2.07%	0.382697	0.303333	-0.022541	-0.021118	-0.018746	0.143183	0.303333	0.459340	0.963757	1.017668	1.050015
285	PAINTS, VARNISHES, LACQUERS, ENAMELS, AND ALLIED PRODUCTS	4	5.04%	0.933012	0.936068	0.766898	0.772531	0.781921	0.907426	0.936068	0.964710	1.079825	1.088298	1.093381
2851	Paints, Varnishes, Lacquers, Enamels, And Allied Products	4	5.04%	0.933012	0.936068	0.766898	0.772531	0.781921	0.907426	0.936068	0.964710	1.079825	1.088298	1.093381
286	INDUSTRIAL ORGANIC CHEMICALS	21	4.02%	0.743928	0.667993	-0.739520	-0.457676	0.012066	0.555505	0.667993	0.713111	1.294040	2.913285	3.884832
2860	INDUSTRIAL ORGANIC CHEMICALS	1	24.48%	4.532530	4.532530	4.532530	4.532530	4.532530	4.532530	4.532530	4.532530	4.532530	4.532530	4.532530
2861	Gum And Wood Chemicals	2	1.27%	0.234907	0.234907	0.016523	0.023208	0.034350	0.190339	0.234907	0.279476	0.435465	0.446607	0.453292
2865	Cyclic Organic Crudes And Intermediates, And Organic Dyes And Pigments	1	3.20%	0.593093	0.593093	0.593093	0.593093	0.593093	0.593093	0.593093	0.593093	0.593093	0.593093	0.593093
2869	Industrial Organic Chemicals, Not Elsewhere Classified	17	3.19%	0.589827	0.701433	-0.769440	-0.532475	-0.137533	0.600500	0.701433	0.785553	1.094632	1.194336	1.254158
287	AGRICULTURAL CHEMICALS	13	5.09%	0.941868	1.046780	-1.171349	-1.016428	-0.758227	0.886390	1.046780	1.152064	2.616286	2.918203	3.099353
2870	AGRICULTURAL CHEMICALS	3	4.40%	0.815231	0.898558	0.109528	0.133682	0.173939	0.737531	0.898558	1.009588	1.398195	1.425952	1.442607

Up-market Betas of Common Stocks by SIC Codes as of September 28, 2018

SIC Code	Description	Number of Companies	Equity Risk Premium	Mean	Median	1st Percentile	2.5th Percentile	5th Percentile	40th Percentile	50th Percentile	60th Percentile	95th Percentile	97.5th Percentile	99th Percentile
2873	Nitrogenous Fertilizers	5	2.95%	0.546396	0.837717	-1.240203	-1.188563	-1.102496	0.337047	0.837717	1.050278	2.044808	2.129269	2.179946
2874	Phosphatic Fertilizers	2	5.79%	1.072290	1.072290	1.047290	1.048056	1.049331	1.067188	1.072290	1.077392	1.095249	1.096525	1.097290
2879	Pesticides And Agricultural Chemicals, Not Elsewhere Classified	3	8.86%	1.640679	1.528170	0.200836	0.241469	0.309190	1.257286	1.528170	1.866560	3.050925	3.135523	3.186281
289	MISCELLANEOUS CHEMICAL PRODUCTS	12	2.65%	0.489935	0.971435	-2.450178	-2.195385	-1.770730	0.827607	0.971435	1.097489	1.578290	1.652760	1.697442
2890	MISCELLANEOUS CHEMICAL PRODUCTS	2	-3.14%	-0.581805	-0.581805	-2.579275	-2.518128	-2.416217	-0.989452	-0.581805	-0.174158	1.252607	1.354518	1.415665
2891	Adhesives And Sealants	1	6.98%	1.292950	1.292950	1.292950	1.292950	1.292950	1.292950	1.292950	1.292950	1.292950	1.292950	1.292950
2893	Printing Ink	1	6.35%	1.175190	1.175190	1.175190	1.175190	1.175190	1.175190	1.175190	1.175190	1.175190	1.175190	1.175190
2895	Carbon Black	1	5.19%	0.961931	0.961931	0.961931	0.961931	0.961931	0.961931	0.961931	0.961931	0.961931	0.961931	0.961931
2899	Chemicals And Chemical Preparations, Not Elsewhere Classified	7	2.79%	0.516108	0.738058	-1.054041	-1.021341	-0.966843	0.659685	0.738058	0.883786	1.613296	1.670263	1.704443
29	PETROLEUM REFINING AND RELATED INDUSTRIES	20	4.80%	0.889139	0.940355	0.083249	0.234847	0.487510	0.828655	0.940355	1.072546	1.302939	1.333425	1.351716
291	PETROLEUM REFINING	17	5.09%	0.943344	1.059170	0.072363	0.207631	0.433078	0.939229	1.059170	1.094824	1.312566	1.338238	1.353641
2911	Petroleum Refining	17	5.09%	0.943344	1.059170	0.072363	0.207631	0.433078	0.939229	1.059170	1.094824	1.312566	1.338238	1.353641
295	ASPHALT PAVING AND ROOFING MATERIALS	1	3.08%	0.571248	0.571248	0.571248	0.571248	0.571248	0.571248	0.571248	0.571248	0.571248	0.571248	0.571248
2951	Asphalt Paving Mixtures And Blocks	1	3.08%	0.571248	0.571248	0.571248	0.571248	0.571248	0.571248	0.571248	0.571248	0.571248	0.571248	0.571248
299	MISCELLANEOUS PRODUCTS OF PETROLEUM AND COAL	2	3.17%	0.587342	0.587342	0.515571	0.517768	0.521430	0.572694	0.587342	0.601989	0.653253	0.656915	0.659112
2990	MISCELLANEOUS PRODUCTS OF PETROLEUM & COAL	1	2.78%	0.514106	0.514106	0.514106	0.514106	0.514106	0.514106	0.514106	0.514106	0.514106	0.514106	0.514106
2999	Products Of Petroleum And Coal, Not Elsewhere Classified	1	3.57%	0.660577	0.660577	0.660577	0.660577	0.660577	0.660577	0.660577	0.660577	0.660577	0.660577	0.660577
30	RUBBER AND MISCELLANEOUS PLASTICS PRODUCTS	39	3.72%	0.689483	0.596106	-1.312418	-1.054955	-0.805537	0.546745	0.596106	0.791672	1.910966	2.500195	2.513926
301	TIRES AND INNER TUBES	2	4.32%	0.800019	0.800019	0.747826	0.749424	0.752087	0.789367	0.800019	0.810671	0.847951	0.850614	0.852212
3011	Tires And Inner Tubes	2	4.32%	0.800019	0.800019	0.747826	0.749424	0.752087	0.789367	0.800019	0.810671	0.847951	0.850614	0.852212
302	RUBBER AND PLASTICS FOOTWEAR	5	3.63%	0.672033	0.658094	0.531770	0.531770	0.531770	0.607564	0.658094	0.716016	0.829084	0.832357	0.834321
3021	Rubber And Plastics Footwear	5	3.63%	0.672033	0.658094	0.531770	0.531770	0.531770	0.607564	0.658094	0.716016	0.829084	0.832357	0.834321
305	GASKETS, PACKING, AND SEALING DEVICES AND RUBBER AND PLASTICS HOSE	3	6.49%	1.201112	0.585628	0.496449	0.499179	0.503729	0.567428	0.585628	0.973118	2.329335	2.426207	2.484331
3052	Rubber And Plastics Hose And Belting	1	13.62%	2.523080	2.523080	2.523080	2.523080	2.523080	2.523080	2.523080	2.523080	2.523080	2.523080	2.523080
3053	Gaskets, Packing, And Sealing Devices	2	2.92%	0.540129	0.540129	0.495539	0.496904	0.499179	0.531029	0.540129	0.549228	0.581078	0.583353	0.584718
306	FABRICATED RUBBER PRODUCTS, NOT ELSEWHERE CLASSIFIED	3	0.07%	0.013617	0.255559	-1.006611	-0.967974	-0.903577	-0.002027	0.255559	0.367979	0.761451	0.789556	0.806419
3069	Fabricated Rubber Products, Not Elsewhere Classified	3	0.07%	0.013617	0.255559	-1.006611	-0.967974	-0.903577	-0.002027	0.255559	0.367979	0.761451	0.789556	0.806419
308	MISCELLANEOUS PLASTICS PRODUCTS	26	3.80%	0.703286	0.590749	-1.308128	-1.044231	-0.591265	0.541130	0.590749	0.828753	1.832533	2.090640	2.335650
3081	Unsupported Plastics Film And Sheet	3	2.78%	0.515433	0.828753	-0.748151	-0.699879	-0.619424	0.506936	0.828753	0.962578	1.430967	1.464424	1.484497
3084	Plastics Pipe	1	5.22%	0.967076	0.967076	0.967076	0.967076	0.967076	0.967076	0.967076	0.967076	0.967076	0.967076	0.967076
3086	Plastics Foam Products	3	3.35%	0.621018	0.596106	-0.011659	0.006946	0.037954	0.472072	0.596106	0.735087	1.221520	1.256265	1.277112
3089	Plastics Products, Not Elsewhere Classified	19	3.95%	0.732053	0.569207	-1.195703	-0.763167	-0.042274	0.502796	0.569207	0.610073	1.910966	2.204978	2.381385
31	LEATHER AND LEATHER PRODUCTS	7	6.00%	1.112033	0.905102	-0.065660	0.011964	0.141337	0.872832	0.905102	1.033663	2.517167	2.799754	2.969305

Up-market Betas of Common Stocks by SIC Codes as of September 28, 2018

SIC Code	Description	Number of Companies	Equity Risk Premium	Mean	Median	1st Percentile	2.5th Percentile	5th Percentile	40th Percentile	50th Percentile	60th Percentile	95th Percentile	97.5th Percentile	99th Percentile
314	FOOTWEAR, EXCEPT RUBBER	4	8.04%	1.489533	1.012236	0.852932	0.855352	0.859386	0.947956	1.012236	1.076516	2.787895	2.935117	3.023451
3142	House Slippers	1	4.89%	0.905102	0.905102	0.905102	0.905102	0.905102	0.905102	0.905102	0.905102	0.905102	0.905102	0.905102
3143	Men's Footwear, Except Athletic	1	6.04%	1.119370	1.119370	1.119370	1.119370	1.119370	1.119370	1.119370	1.119370	1.119370	1.119370	1.119370
3149	Footwear, Except Rubber, Not Elsewhere Classified	2	10.62%	1.966829	1.966829	0.873628	0.907094	0.962869	1.743727	1.966829	2.189931	2.970789	3.026564	3.060030
317	HANDBAGS AND OTHER PERSONAL LEATHER GOODS	1	4.02%	0.745079	0.745079	0.745079	0.745079	0.745079	0.745079	0.745079	0.745079	0.745079	0.745079	0.745079
3171	Women's Handbags And Purses	1	4.02%	0.745079	0.745079	0.745079	0.745079	0.745079	0.745079	0.745079	0.745079	0.745079	0.745079	0.745079
319	LEATHER GOODS, NOT ELSEWHERE CLASSIFIED	2	2.92%	0.540511	0.540511	-0.104251	-0.084513	-0.051617	0.408927	0.540511	0.672094	1.132638	1.165534	1.185272
3199	Leather Goods, Not Elsewhere Classified	2	2.92%	0.540511	0.540511	-0.104251	-0.084513	-0.051617	0.408927	0.540511	0.672094	1.132638	1.165534	1.185272
32	STONE, CLAY, GLASS, AND CONCRETE PRODUCTS	14	3.48%	0.644027	0.491883	-0.260115	-0.207000	-0.118476	0.455435	0.491883	0.572080	1.753726	1.826113	1.869545
322	GLASS AND GLASSWARE, PRESSED OR BLOWN	3	1.93%	0.357972	0.448949	0.043732	0.056137	0.076811	0.366252	0.448949	0.477060	0.575449	0.582476	0.586693
3221	Glass Containers	2	1.69%	0.312483	0.312483	0.041003	0.049313	0.063164	0.257079	0.312483	0.367887	0.561802	0.575653	0.583964
3229	Pressed And Blown Glass And Glassware, Not Elsewhere Classified	1	2.42%	0.448949	0.448949	0.448949	0.448949	0.448949	0.448949	0.448949	0.448949	0.448949	0.448949	0.448949
323	GLASS PRODUCTS, MADE OF PURCHASED GLASS	1	4.44%	0.821663	0.821663	0.821663	0.821663	0.821663	0.821663	0.821663	0.821663	0.821663	0.821663	0.821663
3231	Glass Products, Made Of Purchased Glass	1	4.44%	0.821663	0.821663	0.821663	0.821663	0.821663	0.821663	0.821663	0.821663	0.821663	0.821663	0.821663
324	CEMENT, HYDRAULIC	2	3.77%	0.697564	0.697564	0.133793	0.151051	0.179815	0.582508	0.697564	0.812619	1.215312	1.244076	1.261334
3241	Cement, Hydraulic	2	3.77%	0.697564	0.697564	0.133793	0.151051	0.179815	0.582508	0.697564	0.812619	1.215312	1.244076	1.261334
325	STRUCTURAL CLAY PRODUCTS	1	-1.60%	-0.295525	-0.295525	-0.295525	-0.295525	-0.295525	-0.295525	-0.295525	-0.295525	-0.295525	-0.295525	-0.295525
3253	Ceramic Wall And Floor Tile	1	-1.60%	-0.295525	-0.295525	-0.295525	-0.295525	-0.295525	-0.295525	-0.295525	-0.295525	-0.295525	-0.295525	-0.295525
326	POTTERY AND RELATED PRODUCTS	1	7.11%	1.317110	1.317110	1.317110	1.317110	1.317110	1.317110	1.317110	1.317110	1.317110	1.317110	1.317110
3264	Porcelain Electrical Supplies	1	7.11%	1.317110	1.317110	1.317110	1.317110	1.317110	1.317110	1.317110	1.317110	1.317110	1.317110	1.317110
327	CONCRETE, GYPSUM, AND PLASTER PRODUCTS	6	4.23%	0.784015	0.491883	-0.013524	0.000901	0.024943	0.481381	0.491883	0.502385	1.842818	1.870659	1.887364
3272	Concrete Products, Except Block And Brick	3	1.73%	0.320208	0.481381	-0.013051	0.002085	0.027311	0.380477	0.481381	0.485582	0.500285	0.501335	0.501965
3273	Ready-Mixed Concrete	1	9.05%	1.675770	1.675770	1.675770	1.675770	1.675770	1.675770	1.675770	1.675770	1.675770	1.675770	1.675770
3274	Lime	1	0.91%	0.169195	0.169195	0.169195	0.169195	0.169195	0.169195	0.169195	0.169195	0.169195	0.169195	0.169195
3275	Gypsum Products	1	10.25%	1.898500	1.898500	1.898500	1.898500	1.898500	1.898500	1.898500	1.898500	1.898500	1.898500	1.898500
33	PRIMARY METAL INDUSTRIES	37	4.47%	0.827214	0.889473	-1.942201	-0.943036	-0.203524	0.855633	0.889473	0.984521	1.581746	1.741934	2.507244
331	STEEL WORKS, BLAST FURNACES, AND ROLLING AND FINISHING MILLS	18	4.81%	0.891602	1.034322	-0.579954	-0.312877	0.132253	0.926670	1.034322	1.099004	1.324833	1.450982	1.526671
3312	Steel Works, Blast Furnaces (Including Coke Ovens), And Rolling Mills	13	4.67%	0.865095	1.090420	-0.632322	-0.443797	-0.129588	0.926670	1.090420	1.099004	1.349670	1.463400	1.531638
3313	Electrometallurgical Products, Except Steel	1	5.28%	0.978223	0.978223	0.978223	0.978223	0.978223	0.978223	0.978223	0.978223	0.978223	0.978223	0.978223
3315	Steel Wiredrawing And Steel Nails And Spikes	1	2.95%	0.547101	0.547101	0.547101	0.547101	0.547101	0.547101	0.547101	0.547101	0.547101	0.547101	0.547101
3317	Steel Pipe And Tubes	3	5.90%	1.092429	1.122840	0.879110	0.886571	0.899006	1.073099	1.122840	1.154334	1.264563	1.272437	1.277161
332	IRON AND STEEL FOUNDRIES	1	4.16%	0.770497	0.770497	0.770497	0.770497	0.770497	0.770497	0.770497	0.770497	0.770497	0.770497	0.770497
3324	Steel Investment Foundries	1	4.16%	0.770497	0.770497	0.770497	0.770497	0.770497	0.770497	0.770497	0.770497	0.770497	0.770497	0.770497
333	PRIMARY SMELTING AND REFINING OF NONFERROUS METALS	6	2.52%	0.467247	0.919652	-2.441449	-2.191158	-1.774006	0.850584	0.919652	0.988719	1.511000	1.555605	1.582368
3334	Primary Production Of Aluminum	3	5.33%	0.986999	0.988719	0.734103	0.741898	0.754888	0.936757	0.988719	1.039649	1.217905	1.230637	1.238277

Up-market Betas of Common Stocks by SIC Codes as of September 28, 2018

SIC Code	Description	Number of Companies	Equity Risk Premium	Mean	Median	1st Percentile	2.5th Percentile	5th Percentile	40th Percentile	50th Percentile	60th Percentile	95th Percentile	97.5th Percentile	99th Percentile
3339	Primary Smelting And Refining Of Nonferrous Metals, Except Copper	3	-0.28%	-0.052505	0.850584	-2.539132	-2.435365	-2.262421	0.158805	0.850584	1.000509	1.525247	1.562729	1.585217
334	SECONDARY SMELTING AND REFINING OF NONFERROUS METALS	1	16.29%	3.017450	3.017450	3.017450	3.017450	3.017450	3.017450	3.017450	3.017450	3.017450	3.017450	3.017450
3341	Secondary Smelting And Refining Of Nonferrous Metals	1	16.29%	3.017450	3.017450	3.017450	3.017450	3.017450	3.017450	3.017450	3.017450	3.017450	3.017450	3.017450
335	ROLLING, DRAWING, AND EXTRUDING OF NONFERROUS METALS	11	3.91%	0.724242	0.844029	-0.053673	-0.036827	-0.008751	0.704080	0.844029	0.844590	1.298290	1.422750	1.497426
3351	Rolling, Drawing, And Extruding Of Copper	3	4.31%	0.798446	0.704080	0.643133	0.644999	0.648108	0.691642	0.704080	0.773138	1.014841	1.032106	1.042464
3353	Aluminum Sheet, Plate, And Foil	1	4.66%	0.863207	0.863207	0.863207	0.863207	0.863207	0.863207	0.863207	0.863207	0.863207	0.863207	0.863207
3356	Rolling, Drawing, And Extruding Of Nonferrous Metals, Except Copper	1	4.56%	0.844590	0.844590	0.844590	0.844590	0.844590	0.844590	0.844590	0.844590	0.844590	0.844590	0.844590
3357	Drawing And Insulating Of Nonferrous Wire	6	3.48%	0.643922	0.722175	-0.059288	-0.050865	-0.036827	0.600320	0.722175	0.844029	1.382776	1.464993	1.514323
34	FABRICATED METAL PRODUCTS, EXCEPT MACHINERY AND TRANSPORTATION EQUIPMENT	48	3.19%	0.590361	0.570725	-1.807249	-0.540234	-0.421678	0.457300	0.570725	0.698293	1.202340	1.299806	4.090207
341	METAL CANS AND SHIPPING CONTAINERS	7	3.77%	0.698702	0.604683	0.042451	0.055530	0.077327	0.521729	0.604683	0.963277	1.202340	1.202340	1.202340
3411	Metal Cans	6	4.24%	0.785310	0.903512	0.055367	0.087819	0.141906	0.604683	0.903512	1.202340	1.202340	1.202340	1.202340
3412	Metal Shipping Barrels, Drums, Kegs, And Pails	1	0.97%	0.179050	0.179050	0.179050	0.179050	0.179050	0.179050	0.179050	0.179050	0.179050	0.179050	0.179050
342	CUTLERY, HANDTOOLS, AND GENERAL HARDWARE	7	2.73%	0.504904	0.767810	-0.448175	-0.404415	-0.331480	0.653379	0.767810	0.782599	0.950621	0.964050	0.972107
3421	Cutlery	2	0.85%	0.157555	0.157555	-0.464651	-0.445604	-0.413859	0.030574	0.157555	0.284536	0.728969	0.760714	0.779761
3423	Hand And Edge Tools, Except Machine Tools And Handsaws	1	3.12%	0.577092	0.577092	0.577092	0.577092	0.577092	0.577092	0.577092	0.577092	0.577092	0.577092	0.577092
3429	Hardware, Not Elsewhere Classified	4	3.57%	0.660531	0.827883	0.031648	0.065800	0.122720	0.791839	0.827883	0.863927	0.964050	0.970764	0.974792
343	HEATING EQUIPMENT, EXCEPT ELECTRIC AND WARM AIR; AND PLUMBING FIXTURES	2	-7.01%	-1.297831	-1.297831	-2.886577	-2.837942	-2.756883	-1.622065	-1.297831	-0.973597	0.161221	0.242280	0.290915
3433	Heating Equipment, Except Electric And Warm Air Furnaces	2	-7.01%	-1.297831	-1.297831	-2.886577	-2.837942	-2.756883	-1.622065	-1.297831	-0.973597	0.161221	0.242280	0.290915
344	FABRICATED STRUCTURAL METAL PRODUCTS	10	4.61%	0.853039	0.947126	0.410429	0.412225	0.415217	0.887879	0.947126	0.968749	1.189715	1.255097	1.294327
3441	Fabricated Structural Metal	2	2.25%	0.415882	0.415882	0.409365	0.409565	0.409897	0.414552	0.415882	0.417212	0.421867	0.422200	0.422399
3442	Metal Doors, Sash, Frames, Molding, And Trim	3	4.99%	0.924825	0.804606	0.652493	0.657150	0.664911	0.773563	0.804606	0.907781	1.268893	1.294686	1.310163
3443	Fabricated Plate Work (Boiler Shops)	3	5.20%	0.963280	0.950856	0.943544	0.943768	0.944141	0.949364	0.950856	0.959803	0.991116	0.993352	0.994694
3448	Prefabricated Metal Buildings And Components	2	5.49%	1.017155	1.017155	1.004675	1.005057	1.005694	1.014608	1.017155	1.019702	1.028617	1.029253	1.029635
345	SCREW MACHINE PRODUCTS, AND BOLTS, NUTS, SCREWS, RIVETS, AND WASHERS	4	0.49%	0.089848	0.045899	-0.172769	-0.168308	-0.160873	-0.027605	0.045899	0.119403	0.402098	0.422718	0.435090
3451	Screw Machine Products	1	0.91%	0.168406	0.168406	0.168406	0.168406	0.168406	0.168406	0.168406	0.168406	0.168406	0.168406	0.168406
3452	Bolts, Nuts, Screws, Rivets, And Washers	3	0.34%	0.063662	-0.076608	-0.173760	-0.170786	-0.165829	-0.096435	-0.076608	0.027381	0.391343	0.417341	0.432939

Up-market Betas of Common Stocks by SIC Codes as of September 28, 2018

SIC Code	Description	Number of Companies	Equity Risk Premium	Mean	Median	1st Percentile	2.5th Percentile	5th Percentile	40th Percentile	50th Percentile	60th Percentile	95th Percentile	97.5th Percentile	99th Percentile
346	METAL FORGINGS AND STAMPINGS	5	9.63%	1.782911	0.515441	0.321947	0.327358	0.336376	0.472673	0.515441	0.759613	5.462278	6.004329	6.329560
3463	Nonferrous Forgings	1	2.21%	0.408522	0.408522	0.408522	0.408522	0.408522	0.408522	0.408522	0.408522	0.408522	0.408522	0.408522
3465	Automotive Stampings	2	4.43%	0.820656	0.820656	0.521545	0.530702	0.545962	0.759613	0.820656	0.881698	1.095349	1.110609	1.119766
3469	Metal Stampings, Not Elsewhere Classified	2	18.53%	3.432360	3.432360	0.380620	0.474041	0.629742	2.809556	3.432360	4.055164	6.234978	6.390679	6.484100
347	COATING, ENGRAVING, AND ALLIED SERVICES	2	1.34%	0.248846	0.248846	0.144930	0.148111	0.153413	0.227639	0.248846	0.270053	0.344279	0.349581	0.352762
3471	Electroplating, Plating, Polishing, Anodizing, And Coloring	1	0.77%	0.142809	0.142809	0.142809	0.142809	0.142809	0.142809	0.142809	0.142809	0.142809	0.142809	0.142809
3479	Coating, Engraving, And Allied Services, Not Elsewhere Classified	1	1.92%	0.354883	0.354883	0.354883	0.354883	0.354883	0.354883	0.354883	0.354883	0.354883	0.354883	0.354883
348	ORDNANCE AND ACCESSORIES, EXCEPT VEHICLES AND GUIDED MISSILES	2	2.60%	0.481468	0.481468	0.461205	0.461825	0.462859	0.477332	0.481468	0.485603	0.500076	0.501110	0.501730
3484	Small Arms	2	2.60%	0.481468	0.481468	0.461205	0.461825	0.462859	0.477332	0.481468	0.485603	0.500076	0.501110	0.501730
349	MISCELLANEOUS FABRICATED METAL PRODUCTS	9	1.95%	0.360310	0.602719	-0.534750	-0.506516	-0.459459	0.572029	0.602719	0.672073	0.852611	0.880770	0.897665
3490	MISCELLANEOUS FABRICATED METAL PRODUCTS	2	-1.27%	-0.235504	-0.235504	-0.316632	-0.314149	-0.310010	-0.252060	-0.235504	-0.218947	-0.160997	-0.156858	-0.154375
3491	Industrial Valves	3	3.72%	0.688771	0.733823	0.567746	0.572830	0.581304	0.699930	0.733823	0.740685	0.764702	0.766418	0.767447
3495	Wire Springs	1	4.91%	0.908929	0.908929	0.908929	0.908929	0.908929	0.908929	0.908929	0.908929	0.908929	0.908929	0.908929
3499	Fabricated Metal Products, Not Elsewhere Classified	3	1.33%	0.246186	0.602719	-0.530447	-0.495758	-0.437944	0.371461	0.602719	0.620057	0.680742	0.685076	0.687677
35	INDUSTRIAL AND COMMERCIAL MACHINERY AND COMPUTER EQUIPMENT	168	3.94%	0.730034	0.743564	-1.590546	-0.807063	-0.252313	0.684520	0.743564	0.853913	1.588108	1.739721	2.104063
351	ENGINES AND TURBINES	10	4.88%	0.903355	0.896317	0.542462	0.558882	0.586248	0.833620	0.896317	0.913822	1.320432	1.362381	1.387550
3510	ENGINES & TURBINES	1	5.55%	1.027740	1.027740	1.027740	1.027740	1.027740	1.027740	1.027740	1.027740	1.027740	1.027740	1.027740
3511	Steam, Gas, And Hydraulic Turbines, And Turbine Generator Set Units	5	4.81%	0.891025	0.886664	0.539321	0.551029	0.570542	0.822657	0.886664	0.894386	1.304658	1.354494	1.384396
3519	Internal Combustion Engines, Not Elsewhere Classified	4	4.79%	0.887671	0.839826	0.656170	0.660711	0.668280	0.788362	0.839826	0.891290	1.174046	1.195968	1.209121
352	FARM AND GARDEN MACHINERY AND EQUIPMENT	9	3.70%	0.684723	0.723867	-0.102409	-0.016964	0.125444	0.676228	0.723867	0.734200	1.163210	1.176220	1.184026
3523	Farm Machinery And Equipment	7	4.29%	0.795259	0.723867	0.554053	0.556132	0.559598	0.688138	0.723867	0.731617	1.169715	1.179473	1.185327
3524	Lawn And Garden Tractors And Home Lawn And Garden Equipment	2	1.61%	0.297846	0.297846	-0.150228	-0.136511	-0.113650	0.206402	0.297846	0.389290	0.709342	0.732203	0.745920
353	CONSTRUCTION, MINING, AND MATERIALS HANDLING MACHINERY AND EQUIPMENT	24	4.22%	0.781289	0.856848	-0.238497	-0.229098	-0.174939	0.699812	0.856848	0.948870	1.419270	1.573484	1.684787
3531	Construction Machinery And Equipment	7	2.88%	0.533390	0.660458	-0.226096	-0.198096	-0.151428	0.570605	0.660458	0.704808	1.056681	1.096716	1.120736
3532	Mining Machinery And Equipment, Except Oil And Gas Field Machinery	2	6.48%	1.199972	1.199972	0.652133	0.668904	0.696855	1.088168	1.199972	1.311775	1.703088	1.731039	1.747810
3533	Oil And Gas Field Machinery And Equipment	9	5.05%	0.934565	0.950747	0.555615	0.562154	0.573054	0.943238	0.950747	0.961682	1.275230	1.298800	1.312942
3535	Conveyors And Conveying Equipment	1	5.69%	1.054260	1.054260	1.054260	1.054260	1.054260	1.054260	1.054260	1.054260	1.054260	1.054260	1.054260
3536	Overhead Traveling Cranes, Hoists, And Monorail Systems	1	7.76%	1.436370	1.436370	1.436370	1.436370	1.436370	1.436370	1.436370	1.436370	1.436370	1.436370	1.436370

Up-market Betas of Common Stocks by SIC Codes as of September 28, 2018

SIC Code	Description	Number of Companies	Equity Risk Premium	Mean	Median	1st Percentile	2.5th Percentile	5th Percentile	40th Percentile	50th Percentile	60th Percentile	95th Percentile	97.5th Percentile	99th Percentile
3537	Industrial Trucks, Tractors, Trailers, And Stackers	4	2.32%	0.428888	0.389007	-0.208389	-0.194693	-0.171866	0.207708	0.389007	0.570306	1.085477	1.120268	1.141143
354	METALWORKING MACHINERY AND EQUIPMENT	8	2.37%	0.439357	0.648252	-0.293886	-0.289651	-0.282593	0.465890	0.648252	0.773076	0.894185	0.909203	0.918213
3541	Machine Tools, Metal Cutting Types	4	1.00%	0.185854	0.136250	-0.295499	-0.293684	-0.290659	-0.099327	0.136250	0.371826	0.731815	0.749721	0.760465
3542	Machine Tools, Metal Forming Types	1	4.29%	0.794873	0.794873	0.794873	0.794873	0.794873	0.794873	0.794873	0.794873	0.794873	0.794873	0.794873
3545	Cutting Tools, Machine Tool Accessories, And Machinists' Precision Tools	1	4.53%	0.838406	0.838406	0.838406	0.838406	0.838406	0.838406	0.838406	0.838406	0.838406	0.838406	0.838406
3546	Power-Driven Handtools	1	1.16%	0.213941	0.213941	0.213941	0.213941	0.213941	0.213941	0.213941	0.213941	0.213941	0.213941	0.213941
3549	Metalworking Machinery, Not Elsewhere Classified	1	4.99%	0.924220	0.924220	0.924220	0.924220	0.924220	0.924220	0.924220	0.924220	0.924220	0.924220	0.924220
355	SPECIAL INDUSTRY MACHINERY, EXCEPT METALWORKING MACHINERY	18	4.37%	0.809907	0.765575	-0.313986	-0.300121	-0.277014	0.632112	0.765575	0.910691	1.696382	1.995671	2.175244
3554	Paper Industries Machinery	1	2.44%	0.451451	0.451451	0.451451	0.451451	0.451451	0.451451	0.451451	0.451451	0.451451	0.451451	0.451451
3555	Printing Trades Machinery And Equipment	1	5.45%	1.009020	1.009020	1.009020	1.009020	1.009020	1.009020	1.009020	1.009020	1.009020	1.009020	1.009020
3556	Food Products Machinery	1	-1.45%	-0.268858	-0.268858	-0.268858	-0.268858	-0.268858	-0.268858	-0.268858	-0.268858	-0.268858	-0.268858	-0.268858
3559	Special Industry Machinery, Not Elsewhere Classified	15	4.82%	0.892448	0.811696	-0.279141	-0.213010	-0.102791	0.686026	0.811696	0.962797	1.802013	2.048487	2.196371
356	GENERAL INDUSTRIAL MACHINERY AND EQUIPMENT	29	3.34%	0.618437	0.698365	-1.775149	-0.814234	-0.093396	0.646061	0.698365	0.780152	1.391136	1.672829	1.903254
3560	GENERAL INDUSTRIAL MACHINERY & EQUIPMENT	1	6.18%	1.145150	1.145150	1.145150	1.145150	1.145150	1.145150	1.145150	1.145150	1.145150	1.145150	1.145150
3561	Pumps And Pumping Equipment	9	4.41%	0.817546	0.850431	0.641124	0.646045	0.654247	0.801717	0.850431	0.864138	0.990970	1.014280	1.028266
3562	Ball And Roller Bearings	4	4.04%	0.747655	0.666971	0.446342	0.454060	0.466924	0.634413	0.666971	0.699529	1.141343	1.178412	1.200653
3564	Industrial And Commercial Fans And Blowers And Air Purification Equipment	6	1.54%	0.285344	0.664761	-2.295031	-2.113937	-1.812114	0.637863	0.664761	0.691658	1.728304	1.892587	1.991157
3566	Speed Changers, Industrial High-Speed Drives, And Gears	1	-0.23%	-0.041693	-0.041693	-0.041693	-0.041693	-0.041693	-0.041693	-0.041693	-0.041693	-0.041693	-0.041693	-0.041693
3568	Mechanical Power Transmission Equipment, Not Elsewhere Classified	1	2.84%	0.525183	0.525183	0.525183	0.525183	0.525183	0.525183	0.525183	0.525183	0.525183	0.525183	0.525183
3569	General Industrial Machinery And Equipment, Not Elsewhere Classified	7	3.28%	0.606493	0.527332	-0.110114	-0.083487	-0.039108	0.500022	0.527332	0.712346	1.311444	1.409842	1.468881
357	COMPUTER AND OFFICE EQUIPMENT	55	4.65%	0.860894	0.782308	-0.962362	-0.666632	-0.063850	0.690302	0.782308	1.069070	1.646528	1.843718	2.064205
3571	Electronic Computers	12	4.05%	0.749468	0.905274	-0.935204	-0.801726	-0.579262	0.618266	0.905274	1.084490	1.790180	1.995030	2.117940
3572	Computer Storage Devices	7	5.02%	0.930200	1.058850	0.080016	0.127333	0.206195	0.880518	1.058850	1.126548	1.458445	1.466073	1.470649
3576	COMPUTER COMMUNICATIONS EQUIPMENT	7	5.66%	1.048244	0.775071	0.686075	0.686283	0.686629	0.725032	0.775071	0.926150	1.820425	1.884528	1.922989
3577	Computer Peripheral Equipment, Not Elsewhere Classified	22	4.34%	0.803488	0.725527	-0.693441	-0.369062	0.127903	0.594249	0.725527	0.900384	1.642404	1.647116	1.648174
3578	Calculating And Accounting Machines, Except Electronic Computers	5	5.43%	1.004647	1.086190	0.141057	0.171499	0.222236	0.902966	1.086190	1.282162	1.604848	1.608439	1.610594
3579	Office Machines, Not Elsewhere Classified	2	4.88%	0.903250	0.903250	0.665424	0.672704	0.684838	0.854714	0.903250	0.951786	1.121662	1.133796	1.141076
358	REFRIGERATION AND SERVICE INDUSTRY MACHINERY	10	3.28%	0.608077	0.647260	0.150620	0.181472	0.232891	0.528299	0.647260	0.743380	0.861686	0.862151	0.862429

Up-market Betas of Common Stocks by SIC Codes as of September 28, 2018

SIC Code	Description	Number of Companies	Equity Risk Premium	Mean	Median	1st Percentile	2.5th Percentile	5th Percentile	40th Percentile	50th Percentile	60th Percentile	95th Percentile	97.5th Percentile	99th Percentile
3580	REFRIGERATION & SERVICE INDUSTRY MACHINERY	2	3.65%	0.676743	0.676743	0.496610	0.502124	0.511315	0.639981	0.676743	0.713504	0.842170	0.851361	0.856875
3585	Air-Conditioning And Warm Air Heating Equipment	3	3.07%	0.568905	0.485515	0.361123	0.364931	0.371277	0.460129	0.485515	0.560935	0.824905	0.843760	0.855073
3589	Service Industry Machinery, Not Elsewhere Classified	5	3.26%	0.604115	0.742644	0.146925	0.172234	0.214417	0.666336	0.742644	0.743380	0.830112	0.840815	0.847238
359	MISCELLANEOUS INDUSTRIAL AND COMMERCIAL MACHINERY AND EQUIPMENT	5	-0.82%	-0.151831	0.694039	-1.954220	-1.919584	-1.861858	-0.143597	0.694039	0.787434	0.982816	0.989728	0.993874
3590	MISC INDUSTRIAL & COMMERCIAL MACHINERY & EQUIPMENT	1	-10.68%	-1.977310	-1.977310	-1.977310	-1.977310	-1.977310	-1.977310	-1.977310	-1.977310	-1.977310	-1.977310	-1.977310
3592	Carburetors, Pistons, Piston Rings, And Valves	1	5.38%	0.996639	0.996639	0.996639	0.996639	0.996639	0.996639	0.996639	0.996639	0.996639	0.996639	0.996639
3594	Fluid Power Pumps And Motors	1	5.01%	0.927526	0.927526	0.927526	0.927526	0.927526	0.927526	0.927526	0.927526	0.927526	0.927526	0.927526
3596	Scales And Balances, Except Laboratory	1	-7.56%	-1.400050	-1.400050	-1.400050	-1.400050	-1.400050	-1.400050	-1.400050	-1.400050	-1.400050	-1.400050	-1.400050
3599	Industrial And Commercial Machinery And Equipment, Not Elsewhere Classified	1	3.75%	0.694039	0.694039	0.694039	0.694039	0.694039	0.694039	0.694039	0.694039	0.694039	0.694039	0.694039
36	ELECTRONIC AND OTHER ELECTRICAL EQUIPMENT AND COMPONENTS, EXCEPT COMPUTER	265	1.88%	0.348034	0.735586	-1.336744	-1.074050	-0.743130	0.550018	0.735586	0.887109	1.886798	2.222224	2.776416
361	ELECTRIC TRANSMISSION AND DISTRIBUTION EQUIPMENT	5	1.85%	0.343405	0.088497	-0.131508	-0.124249	-0.112150	0.046955	0.088497	0.337160	0.998095	1.034088	1.055683
3612	Power, Distribution, And Specialty Transformers	3	-0.11%	-0.021070	-0.015359	-0.133928	-0.130299	-0.124249	-0.039557	-0.015359	0.005412	0.078112	0.083304	0.086420
3613	Switchgear And Switchboard Apparatus	2	4.81%	0.890118	0.890118	0.713754	0.719153	0.728151	0.854125	0.890118	0.926110	1.052084	1.061082	1.066481
362	ELECTRICAL INDUSTRIAL APPARATUS	18	3.81%	0.706172	0.871763	-0.571314	-0.510507	-0.409163	0.806930	0.871763	0.898821	1.136757	1.152304	1.161631
3621	Motors And Generators	13	3.76%	0.696844	0.886573	-0.583237	-0.540315	-0.468777	0.862777	0.886573	0.966000	1.145902	1.156876	1.163460
3625	Relays And Industrial Controls	2	3.33%	0.616807	0.616807	0.364142	0.371877	0.384768	0.565242	0.616807	0.668371	0.848845	0.861736	0.869471
3629	Electrical Industrial Apparatus, Not Elsewhere Classified	3	4.35%	0.806172	0.681503	0.631857	0.633377	0.635910	0.671371	0.681503	0.766436	1.063703	1.084937	1.097677
363	HOUSEHOLD APPLIANCES	7	2.12%	0.392059	0.748205	-1.241106	-1.098479	-0.860769	0.721025	0.748205	0.764735	0.806172	0.808855	0.810464
3630	HOUSEHOLD APPLIANCES	1	-7.22%	-1.336190	-1.336190	-1.336190	-1.336190	-1.336190	-1.336190	-1.336190	-1.336190	-1.336190	-1.336190	-1.336190
3632	Household Refrigerators And Home And Farm Freezers	1	4.29%	0.793655	0.793655	0.793655	0.793655	0.793655	0.793655	0.793655	0.793655	0.793655	0.793655	0.793655
3633	Household Laundry Equipment	2	4.29%	0.793646	0.793646	0.776113	0.776650	0.777544	0.790068	0.793646	0.797224	0.809748	0.810642	0.811179
3634	Electric Housewares And Fans	3	3.06%	0.566552	0.702905	0.257634	0.271265	0.293983	0.612033	0.702905	0.711965	0.743675	0.745940	0.747299
364	ELECTRIC LIGHTING AND WIRING EQUIPMENT	9	1.15%	0.213288	0.185001	-0.891829	-0.856072	-0.796477	0.122362	0.185001	0.421007	1.118317	1.158994	1.183399
3640	ELECTRIC LIGHTING & WIRING EQUIPMENT	3	1.38%	0.255660	0.185001	-0.601638	-0.577557	-0.537423	0.024462	0.185001	0.387935	1.098203	1.148937	1.179377
3641	Electric Lamp Bulbs And Tubes	3	0.34%	0.062441	0.106702	-0.895220	-0.864549	-0.813430	-0.097772	0.106702	0.284619	0.907329	0.951809	0.978496
3643	Current-Carrying Wiring Devices	1	3.34%	0.617633	0.617633	0.617633	0.617633	0.617633	0.617633	0.617633	0.617633	0.617633	0.617633	0.617633
3645	Residential Electric Lighting Fixtures	1	-0.71%	-0.132347	-0.132347	-0.132347	-0.132347	-0.132347	-0.132347	-0.132347	-0.132347	-0.132347	-0.132347	-0.132347
3646	Commercial, Industrial, And Institutional Electric Lighting Fixtures	1	2.59%	0.480008	0.480008	0.480008	0.480008	0.480008	0.480008	0.480008	0.480008	0.480008	0.480008	0.480008
365	HOUSEHOLD AUDIO AND VIDEO EQUIPMENT, AND AUDIO RECORDINGS	7	1.17%	0.216549	0.109803	-0.492928	-0.460451	-0.406322	0.023091	0.109803	0.202369	0.945637	0.962997	0.973413

Up-market Betas of Common Stocks by SIC Codes as of September 28, 2018

SIC Code	Description	Number of Companies	Equity Risk Premium	Mean	Median	1st Percentile	2.5th Percentile	5th Percentile	40th Percentile	50th Percentile	60th Percentile	95th Percentile	97.5th Percentile	99th Percentile
3651	Household Audio And Video Equipment	6	1.83%	0.338404	0.186941	-0.147770	-0.138845	-0.123969	0.109803	0.186941	0.264079	0.951424	0.965890	0.974570
3652	Phonograph Records And Prerecorded Audio Tapes And Disks	1	-2.78%	-0.514580	-0.514580	-0.514580	-0.514580	-0.514580	-0.514580	-0.514580	-0.514580	-0.514580	-0.514580	-0.514580
366	COMMUNICATIONS EQUIPMENT	67	-4.49%	-0.831848	0.525266	-30.864323	-1.124663	-0.788373	0.381662	0.525266	0.762222	1.528893	1.696567	1.928049
3661	Telephone And Telegraph Apparatus	17	3.72%	0.689314	0.797880	-0.591116	-0.538891	-0.451849	0.490036	0.797880	0.956629	1.609640	1.629720	1.641768
3663	Radio And Television Broadcasting And Communications Equipment	35	-10.96%	-2.029118	0.611460	-58.710227	-14.330818	-0.967182	0.439882	0.611460	0.779974	1.208088	1.365490	1.871476
3669	Communications Equipment, Not Elsewhere Classified	15	1.28%	0.237800	0.338857	-0.979827	-0.886463	-0.730856	-0.146701	0.338857	0.548640	1.275598	1.529509	1.681856
367	ELECTRONIC COMPONENTS AND ACCESSORIES	132	4.71%	0.872881	0.885805	-1.272993	-1.054112	-0.434170	0.692212	0.885805	1.076138	2.208623	2.561497	3.141964
3671	Electron Tubes	1	-0.23%	-0.042423	-0.042423	-0.042423	-0.042423	-0.042423	-0.042423	-0.042423	-0.042423	-0.042423	-0.042423	-0.042423
3672	Printed Circuit Boards	14	2.30%	0.425453	0.422922	-0.433095	-0.429953	-0.424717	0.389432	0.422922	0.460964	1.156958	1.237704	1.286152
3674	Semiconductors And Related Devices	96	5.38%	0.995589	1.063380	-1.148201	-1.029418	-0.355756	0.883695	1.063380	1.206230	2.196355	2.538714	3.187377
3675	Electronic Capacitors	1	-0.21%	-0.039618	-0.039618	-0.039618	-0.039618	-0.039618	-0.039618	-0.039618	-0.039618	-0.039618	-0.039618	-0.039618
3676	Electronic Resistors	1	4.24%	0.785909	0.785909	0.785909	0.785909	0.785909	0.785909	0.785909	0.785909	0.785909	0.785909	0.785909
3677	Electronic Coils, Transformers, And Other Inductors	2	4.37%	0.809725	0.809725	0.605556	0.611806	0.622223	0.768057	0.809725	0.851392	0.997226	1.007643	1.013893
3678	Electronic Connectors	4	4.42%	0.819000	0.807604	0.729115	0.731121	0.734464	0.786452	0.807604	0.828756	0.919489	0.926250	0.930307
3679	Electronic Components, Not Elsewhere Classified	13	3.36%	0.622160	0.083660	-1.229203	-1.066412	-0.795094	-0.017319	0.083660	0.917768	2.589694	2.818402	2.955627
369	MISCELLANEOUS ELECTRICAL MACHINERY, EQUIPMENT, AND SUPPLIES	20	3.28%	0.606731	0.739347	-0.847235	-0.815981	-0.763891	0.531301	0.739347	0.943564	1.351780	1.456750	1.519732
3690	MISCELLANEOUS ELECTRICAL MACHINERY, EQUIPMENT & SUPPLIES	2	1.84%	0.339822	0.339822	0.321068	0.321642	0.322599	0.335994	0.339822	0.343649	0.357044	0.358001	0.358575
3691	Storage Batteries	8	3.69%	0.683426	0.790828	-0.037379	-0.028536	-0.013797	0.634194	0.790828	0.935292	1.230764	1.285747	1.318737
3692	Primary Batteries, Dry And Wet	1	-4.10%	-0.758408	-0.758408	-0.758408	-0.758408	-0.758408	-0.758408	-0.758408	-0.758408	-0.758408	-0.758408	-0.758408
3694	Electrical Equipment For Internal Combustion Engines	1	5.35%	0.989820	0.989820	0.989820	0.989820	0.989820	0.989820	0.989820	0.989820	0.989820	0.989820	0.989820
3695	Magnetic And Optical Recording Media	4	2.86%	0.529522	0.712219	-0.834307	-0.783662	-0.699252	0.439320	0.712219	0.985117	1.502520	1.532120	1.549880
3699	Electrical Machinery, Equipment, And Supplies, Not Elsewhere Classified	4	4.91%	0.909516	0.945737	0.562964	0.574413	0.593496	0.864153	0.945737	1.027321	1.174828	1.183044	1.187974
37	TRANSPORTATION EQUIPMENT	102	3.70%	0.685627	0.789328	-2.111011	-0.717664	-0.213284	0.677738	0.789328	0.847278	1.313306	1.389950	1.593473
371	MOTOR VEHICLES AND MOTOR VEHICLE EQUIPMENT	54	4.69%	0.868073	0.894814	-1.462087	-0.644471	-0.156676	0.799731	0.894814	0.987287	1.333394	1.394430	4.450252
3711	Motor Vehicles And Passenger Car Bodies	19	2.99%	0.553058	0.850696	-1.770875	-1.241952	-0.360413	0.793134	0.850696	0.888915	1.152413	1.178842	1.194699
3713	Truck And Bus Bodies	1	2.10%	0.387997	0.387997	0.387997	0.387997	0.387997	0.387997	0.387997	0.387997	0.387997	0.387997	0.387997
3714	Motor Vehicle Parts And Accessories	31	5.78%	1.069813	0.992488	-0.639326	-0.284975	0.077689	0.820130	0.992488	1.077790	1.390510	3.023275	5.942092
3715	Truck Trailers	1	4.29%	0.794631	0.794631	0.794631	0.794631	0.794631	0.794631	0.794631	0.794631	0.794631	0.794631	0.794631
3716	Motor Homes	2	5.46%	1.010526	1.010526	0.967363	0.968684	0.970886	1.001717	1.010526	1.019335	1.050166	1.052368	1.053689
372	AIRCRAFT AND PARTS	29	2.48%	0.458626	0.728290	-3.183254	-1.661659	-0.430887	0.454536	0.728290	0.819107	1.349436	1.444133	1.534899
3721	Aircraft	10	2.16%	0.400727	0.973989	-3.871594	-3.382510	-2.567370	0.837956	0.973989	1.112018	1.464564	1.529987	1.569241
3724	Aircraft Engines And Engine Parts	8	2.03%	0.375968	0.398486	-0.208545	-0.198849	-0.182689	0.314613	0.398486	0.457628	1.000348	1.073594	1.117542

Up-market Betas of Common Stocks by SIC Codes as of September 28, 2018

SIC Code	Description	Number of Companies	Equity Risk Premium	Mean	Median	1st Percentile	2.5th Percentile	5th Percentile	40th Percentile	50th Percentile	60th Percentile	95th Percentile	97.5th Percentile	99th Percentile
3728	Aircraft Parts And Auxiliary Equipment, Not Elsewhere Classified	11	3.09%	0.571377	0.678738	0.043045	0.056115	0.077899	0.266666	0.678738	0.788459	1.141711	1.260506	1.331782
373	SHIP AND BOAT BUILDING AND REPAIRING	5	2.17%	0.401461	0.389551	-0.008302	-0.004802	0.001032	0.252810	0.389551	0.521313	0.833179	0.847457	0.856024
3730	SHIP & BOAT BUILDING & REPAIRING	1	-0.06%	-0.010635	-0.010635	-0.010635	-0.010635	-0.010635	-0.010635	-0.010635	-0.010635	-0.010635	-0.010635	-0.010635
3731	Ship Building And Repairing	2	2.46%	0.454717	0.454717	0.055839	0.068049	0.088400	0.373313	0.454717	0.536120	0.821033	0.841384	0.853595
3732	Boat Building And Repairing	2	2.99%	0.554254	0.554254	0.392845	0.397786	0.406021	0.521313	0.554254	0.587195	0.702487	0.710722	0.715663
374	RAILROAD EQUIPMENT	5	3.78%	0.699601	0.565893	0.525935	0.527905	0.531188	0.562516	0.565893	0.610365	1.073790	1.123380	1.153134
3743	Railroad Equipment	5	3.78%	0.699601	0.565893	0.525935	0.527905	0.531188	0.562516	0.565893	0.610365	1.073790	1.123380	1.153134
375	MOTORCYCLES, BICYCLES, AND PARTS	3	2.62%	0.484554	0.643860	0.002770	0.022396	0.055104	0.513025	0.643860	0.679111	0.802490	0.811302	0.816590
3751	Motorcycles, Bicycles, And Parts	3	2.62%	0.484554	0.643860	0.002770	0.022396	0.055104	0.513025	0.643860	0.679111	0.802490	0.811302	0.816590
376	GUIDED MISSILES AND SPACE VEHICLES AND PARTS	3	0.49%	0.089946	-0.180512	-0.356333	-0.350951	-0.341980	-0.216394	-0.180512	0.017645	0.711193	0.760732	0.790455
3761	Guided Missiles And Space Vehicles	1	4.38%	0.810271	0.810271	0.810271	0.810271	0.810271	0.810271	0.810271	0.810271	0.810271	0.810271	0.810271
3764	Guided Missile And Space Vehicle Propulsion Units And Propulsion	1	-1.94%	-0.359921	-0.359921	-0.359921	-0.359921	-0.359921	-0.359921	-0.359921	-0.359921	-0.359921	-0.359921	-0.359921
3769	Guided Missile And Space Vehicle Parts And Auxiliary Equipment, Not Elsewhere Classified	1	-0.97%	-0.180512	-0.180512	-0.180512	-0.180512	-0.180512	-0.180512	-0.180512	-0.180512	-0.180512	-0.180512	-0.180512
379	MISCELLANEOUS TRANSPORTATION EQUIPMENT	3	4.55%	0.843000	0.649472	0.567649	0.570154	0.574328	0.632773	0.649472	0.782288	1.247142	1.280346	1.300268
3790	MISCELLANEOUS TRANSPORTATION EQUIPMENT	1	3.51%	0.649472	0.649472	0.649472	0.649472	0.649472	0.649472	0.649472	0.649472	0.649472	0.649472	0.649472
3795	Tanks And Tank Components	1	7.09%	1.313550	1.313550	1.313550	1.313550	1.313550	1.313550	1.313550	1.313550	1.313550	1.313550	1.313550
3799	Transportation Equipment, Not Elsewhere Classified	1	3.06%	0.565979	0.565979	0.565979	0.565979	0.565979	0.565979	0.565979	0.565979	0.565979	0.565979	0.565979
38	MEASURING, ANALYZING, AND CONTROLLING INSTRUMENTS; PHOTOGRAPHIC, MEDICAL	263	3.07%	0.567691	0.752550	-2.790034	-1.147530	-0.857708	0.545491	0.752550	0.871158	1.808395	1.907648	2.156778
381	SEARCH, DETECTION, NAVIGATION, GUIDANCE, AERONAUTICAL, AND NAUTICAL	11	4.14%	0.766759	0.713512	0.336747	0.341642	0.349801	0.665504	0.713512	0.912920	1.210905	1.252833	1.277989
3812	Search, Detection, Navigation, Guidance, Aeronautical, And Nautical	11	4.14%	0.766759	0.713512	0.336747	0.341642	0.349801	0.665504	0.713512	0.912920	1.210905	1.252833	1.277989
382	LABORATORY APPARATUS AND ANALYTICAL, OPTICAL, MEASURING, AND CONTROL	91	3.23%	0.598159	0.780567	-3.081961	-0.784517	-0.559453	0.583778	0.780567	0.913142	1.823430	1.923953	2.003894
3821	Laboratory Apparatus And Furniture	3	-1.05%	-0.194665	-0.137786	-0.606304	-0.591962	-0.568058	-0.233402	-0.137786	-0.076297	0.138914	0.154286	0.163509
3822	Automatic Controls For Regulating Residential And Commercial Environment	4	-5.86%	-1.085110	0.589544	-6.229973	-5.925927	-5.419185	0.430156	0.589544	0.748932	0.904449	0.908796	0.911403
3823	Industrial Instruments For Measurement, Display, And Control Of Processes	17	4.51%	0.834566	0.796876	0.204058	0.210219	0.220488	0.690992	0.796876	0.966044	1.570062	1.726626	1.820564
3824	Totalizing Fluid Meters And Counting Devices	1	5.96%	1.104020	1.104020	1.104020	1.104020	1.104020	1.104020	1.104020	1.104020	1.104020	1.104020	1.104020
3825	Instruments For Measuring And Testing Of Electricity And Electric	20	3.06%	0.567018	0.567310	-0.573508	-0.560586	-0.539050	0.373698	0.567310	0.808313	1.819002	1.823676	1.826480

Up-market Betas of Common Stocks by SIC Codes as of September 28, 2018

SIC Code	Description	Number of Companies	Equity Risk Premium	Mean	Median	1st Percentile	2.5th Percentile	5th Percentile	40th Percentile	50th Percentile	60th Percentile	95th Percentile	97.5th Percentile	99th Percentile
3826	Laboratory Analytical Instruments	18	2.22%	0.411851	0.626410	-2.296264	-1.676170	-0.642680	0.398771	0.626410	0.786862	1.408487	1.411848	1.413865
3827	Optical Instruments And Lenses	10	6.55%	1.212286	1.251505	0.392956	0.422417	0.471518	1.048762	1.251505	1.464662	1.944938	1.947964	1.949780
3829	Measuring And Controlling Devices, Not Elsewhere Classified	18	3.96%	0.732704	0.922478	-0.769445	-0.662512	-0.484289	0.798764	0.922478	1.023886	1.553870	2.016950	2.294798
384	SURGICAL, MEDICAL, AND DENTAL INSTRUMENTS AND SUPPLIES	152	2.69%	0.498270	0.710472	-2.312847	-1.343703	-0.945785	0.446095	0.710472	0.836886	1.776309	1.828689	1.988567
3841	Surgical And Medical Instruments And Apparatus	92	3.02%	0.559876	0.757411	-1.851760	-1.216830	-0.940800	0.556917	0.757411	0.866356	1.820316	1.946477	2.033789
3842	Orthopedic, Prosthetic, And Surgical Appliances And Supplies	23	1.88%	0.348141	0.698272	-2.617755	-2.162632	-1.470127	0.423206	0.698272	0.805985	1.472377	1.557868	1.593851
3843	Dental Equipment And Supplies	5	1.87%	0.346519	0.472806	-0.885891	-0.884248	-0.881508	-0.060154	0.472806	0.860304	1.540166	1.552493	1.559889
3844	X-Ray Apparatus And Tubes And Related Irradiation Apparatus	2	5.17%	0.957129	0.957129	0.462913	0.478042	0.503257	0.856268	0.957129	1.057989	1.411000	1.436215	1.451344
3845	Electromedical And Electrotherapeutic Apparatus	30	2.26%	0.419145	0.508091	-0.987138	-0.941086	-0.828230	0.280633	0.508091	0.825645	1.308839	1.447240	1.655644
385	OPHTHALMIC GOODS	2	4.76%	0.882290	0.882290	0.844582	0.845736	0.847660	0.874594	0.882290	0.889985	0.916919	0.918843	0.919997
3851	Ophthalmic Goods	2	4.76%	0.882290	0.882290	0.844582	0.845736	0.847660	0.874594	0.882290	0.889985	0.916919	0.918843	0.919997
386	PHOTOGRAPHIC EQUIPMENT AND SUPPLIES	5	2.72%	0.502887	0.613189	-0.210785	-0.197836	-0.176254	0.366475	0.613189	0.693190	1.211494	1.261282	1.291155
3861	Photographic Equipment And Supplies	5	2.72%	0.502887	0.613189	-0.210785	-0.197836	-0.176254	0.366475	0.613189	0.693190	1.211494	1.261282	1.291155
387	WATCHES, CLOCKS, CLOCKWORK OPERATED DEVICES, AND PARTS	2	17.33%	3.209930	3.209930	1.830208	1.872444	1.942838	2.928354	3.209930	3.491506	4.477022	4.547416	4.589652
3873	Watches, Clocks, Clockwork Operated Devices, And Parts	2	17.33%	3.209930	3.209930	1.830208	1.872444	1.942838	2.928354	3.209930	3.491506	4.477022	4.547416	4.589652
39	MISCELLANEOUS MANUFACTURING INDUSTRIES	29	1.76%	0.325689	0.429920	-2.494493	-1.767448	-1.201842	0.306866	0.429920	0.594539	1.687914	2.175667	2.607255
391	JEWELRY, SILVERWARE, AND PLATED WARE	3	-0.82%	-0.150990	-0.069175	-0.683418	-0.664615	-0.633276	-0.194531	-0.069175	0.007092	0.274026	0.293092	0.304532
3911	Jewelry, Precious Metal	3	-0.82%	-0.150990	-0.069175	-0.683418	-0.664615	-0.633276	-0.194531	-0.069175	0.007092	0.274026	0.293092	0.304532
394	DOLLS, TOYS, GAMES AND SPORTING AND ATHLETIC GOODS	20	1.27%	0.234600	0.440147	-2.650289	-2.156937	-1.334683	0.276720	0.440147	0.592394	0.997785	1.946383	2.515541
3942	Dolls And Stuffed Toys	3	-0.54%	-0.100587	0.225084	-1.218666	-1.174469	-1.100809	-0.069559	0.225084	0.324324	0.671665	0.696475	0.711361
3944	Games, Toys, And Children's Vehicles, Except Dolls And Bicycles	9	2.43%	0.449153	0.305543	-1.048971	-0.923812	-0.715213	0.094524	0.305543	0.533308	2.087606	2.491293	2.733505
3949	Sporting And Athletic Goods, Not Elsewhere Classified	8	0.64%	0.118923	0.533861	-2.754303	-2.416972	-1.854754	0.446282	0.533861	0.618625	0.820881	0.859407	0.882523
399	MISCELLANEOUS MANUFACTURING INDUSTRIES	6	4.69%	0.867658	0.821809	-0.062213	-0.028824	0.026824	0.763297	0.821809	0.880321	1.755218	1.811304	1.844956
3990	MISCELLANEOUS MANUFACTURING INDUSTRIES	1	7.66%	1.418700	1.418700	1.418700	1.418700	1.418700	1.418700	1.418700	1.418700	1.418700	1.418700	1.418700
3993	Signs And Advertising Specialties	1	-0.46%	-0.084472	-0.084472	-0.084472	-0.084472	-0.084472	-0.084472	-0.084472	-0.084472	-0.084472	-0.084472	-0.084472
3996	Linoleum, Asphalted-Felt-Base, And Other Hard Surface Floor Cover	1	1.95%	0.360714	0.360714	0.360714	0.360714	0.360714	0.360714	0.360714	0.360714	0.360714	0.360714	0.360714
3999	Manufacturing Industries, Not Elsewhere Classified	3	6.32%	1.170336	0.880321	0.765637	0.769148	0.774999	0.856916	0.880321	1.077735	1.768683	1.818037	1.847649
	TRANSPORTATION, COMMUNICATIONS, ELECTRIC, GAS, AND SANITARY SERVICE													
40	RAILROAD TRANSPORTATION	7	4.65%	0.860837	0.897635	0.589616	0.600890	0.619682	0.799463	0.897635	0.942688	1.074507	1.080884	1.084709
401	RAILROADS	7	4.65%	0.860837	0.897635	0.589616	0.600890	0.619682	0.799463	0.897635	0.942688	1.074507	1.080884	1.084709
4011	Railroads, Line-Haul Operating	7	4.65%	0.860837	0.897635	0.589616	0.600890	0.619682	0.799463	0.897635	0.942688	1.074507	1.080884	1.084709

Up-market Betas of Common Stocks by SIC Codes as of September 28, 2018

SIC Code	Description	Number of Companies	Equity Risk Premium	Mean	Median	1st Percentile	2.5th Percentile	5th Percentile	40th Percentile	50th Percentile	60th Percentile	95th Percentile	97.5th Percentile	99th Percentile
41	LOCAL AND SUBURBAN TRANSIT AND INTERURBAN HIGHWAY PASSENGER TRANSPORTATION	1	-5.76%	-1.067590	-1.067590	-1.067590	-1.067590	-1.067590	-1.067590	-1.067590	-1.067590	-1.067590	-1.067590	-1.067590
415	SCHOOL BUSES	1	-5.76%	-1.067590	-1.067590	-1.067590	-1.067590	-1.067590	-1.067590	-1.067590	-1.067590	-1.067590	-1.067590	-1.067590
4151	School Buses	1	-5.76%	-1.067590	-1.067590	-1.067590	-1.067590	-1.067590	-1.067590	-1.067590	-1.067590	-1.067590	-1.067590	-1.067590
42	MOTOR FREIGHT TRANSPORTATION AND WAREHOUSING	25	2.41%	0.445953	0.391586	-1.226657	-0.745813	-0.207641	0.298281	0.391586	0.524624	1.485938	1.813688	1.976775
421	TRUCKING AND COURIER SERVICES, EXCEPT AIR	23	2.47%	0.456490	0.391586	-1.253371	-0.812597	-0.177723	0.308348	0.391586	0.503530	1.559209	1.836339	1.985836
4213	Trucking, Except Local	23	2.47%	0.456490	0.391586	-1.253371	-0.812597	-0.177723	0.308348	0.391586	0.503530	1.559209	1.836339	1.985836
422	PUBLIC WAREHOUSING AND STORAGE	2	1.75%	0.324776	0.324776	-0.181705	-0.166200	-0.140359	0.221413	0.324776	0.428139	0.789911	0.815752	0.831257
4221	Farm Product Warehousing And Storage	1	-1.04%	-0.192041	-0.192041	-0.192041	-0.192041	-0.192041	-0.192041	-0.192041	-0.192041	-0.192041	-0.192041	-0.192041
4225	General Warehousing And Storage	1	4.54%	0.841593	0.841593	0.841593	0.841593	0.841593	0.841593	0.841593	0.841593	0.841593	0.841593	0.841593
44	WATER TRANSPORTATION	44	2.28%	0.422505	0.623701	-2.102088	-1.562447	-1.284395	0.488956	0.623701	0.692819	1.421291	1.635443	1.687467
4400	WATER TRANSPORTATION	2	0.20%	0.036178	0.036178	-0.747606	-0.723613	-0.683624	-0.123778	0.036178	0.196134	0.755980	0.795969	0.819962
441	DEEP SEA FOREIGN TRANSPORTATION OF FREIGHT	32	1.93%	0.357691	0.611518	-2.212519	-1.784599	-1.466858	0.474679	0.611518	0.664494	1.285545	1.390051	1.585003
4412	Deep Sea Foreign Transportation Of Freight	32	1.93%	0.357691	0.611518	-2.212519	-1.784599	-1.466858	0.474679	0.611518	0.664494	1.285545	1.390051	1.585003
442	DEEP SEA DOMESTIC TRANSPORTATION OF FREIGHT	1	3.95%	0.732404	0.732404	0.732404	0.732404	0.732404	0.732404	0.732404	0.732404	0.732404	0.732404	0.732404
4424	Deep Sea Domestic Transportation Of Freight	1	3.95%	0.732404	0.732404	0.732404	0.732404	0.732404	0.732404	0.732404	0.732404	0.732404	0.732404	0.732404
444	WATER TRANSPORTATION OF FREIGHT, NOT ELSEWHERE CLASSIFIED	1	5.46%	1.011030	1.011030	1.011030	1.011030	1.011030	1.011030	1.011030	1.011030	1.011030	1.011030	1.011030
4449	Water Transportation Of Freight, Not Elsewhere Classified	1	5.46%	1.011030	1.011030	1.011030	1.011030	1.011030	1.011030	1.011030	1.011030	1.011030	1.011030	1.011030
448	WATER TRANSPORTATION OF PASSENGERS	3	4.91%	0.909433	0.810369	0.481198	0.491274	0.508069	0.743191	0.810369	0.936985	1.380142	1.411796	1.430788
4481	Deep Sea Transportation Of Passengers, Except By Ferry	3	4.91%	0.909433	0.810369	0.481198	0.491274	0.508069	0.743191	0.810369	0.936985	1.380142	1.411796	1.430788
449	SERVICES INCIDENTAL TO WATER TRANSPORTATION	5	2.81%	0.519999	0.515990	-0.302310	-0.275428	-0.230624	0.360718	0.515990	0.559761	1.445892	1.548451	1.609986
4491	Marine Cargo Handling	1	-1.73%	-0.320232	-0.320232	-0.320232	-0.320232	-0.320232	-0.320232	-0.320232	-0.320232	-0.320232	-0.320232	-0.320232
4492	Towing And Tugboat Services	1	3.38%	0.625418	0.625418	0.625418	0.625418	0.625418	0.625418	0.625418	0.625418	0.625418	0.625418	0.625418
4499	Water Transportation Services, Not Elsewhere Classified	3	4.13%	0.764936	0.515990	0.135573	0.147218	0.166627	0.438354	0.515990	0.742994	1.537508	1.594259	1.628310
45	TRANSPORTATION BY AIR	22	1.80%	0.333896	0.459308	-1.675149	-1.311772	-0.727482	0.410125	0.459308	0.560514	0.831665	0.930892	0.996165
451	AIR TRANSPORTATION, SCHEDULED, AND AIR COURIER SERVICES	17	2.35%	0.434336	0.465714	-0.647531	-0.473093	-0.182362	0.431512	0.465714	0.560514	0.873907	0.956794	1.006525
4512	Air Transportation, Scheduled	13	2.42%	0.448128	0.452901	-0.022705	-0.001267	0.034464	0.407816	0.452901	0.556353	0.803360	0.817912	0.826643
4513	Air Courier Services	4	2.10%	0.389511	0.641094	-0.726937	-0.671608	-0.579392	0.535866	0.641094	0.746322	1.006199	1.022940	1.032984
452	AIR TRANSPORTATION, NONSCHEDULED	4	2.54%	0.469852	0.487473	0.274122	0.280211	0.290360	0.438213	0.487473	0.536733	0.624673	0.629535	0.632452
4522	Air Transportation, Nonscheduled	4	2.54%	0.469852	0.487473	0.274122	0.280211	0.290360	0.438213	0.487473	0.536733	0.624673	0.629535	0.632452
458	AIRPORTS, FLYING FIELDS, AND AIRPORT TERMINAL SERVICES	1	-10.35%	-1.917400	-1.917400	-1.917400	-1.917400	-1.917400	-1.917400	-1.917400	-1.917400	-1.917400	-1.917400	-1.917400
4581	Airports, Flying Fields, And Airport Terminal Services	1	-10.35%	-1.917400	-1.917400	-1.917400	-1.917400	-1.917400	-1.917400	-1.917400	-1.917400	-1.917400	-1.917400	-1.917400

Up-market Betas of Common Stocks by SIC Codes as of September 28, 2018

SIC Code	Description	Number of Companies	Equity Risk Premium	Mean	Median	1st Percentile	2.5th Percentile	5th Percentile	40th Percentile	50th Percentile	60th Percentile	95th Percentile	97.5th Percentile	99th Percentile
46	PIPELINES, EXCEPT NATURAL GAS	11	4.36%	0.808301	0.873011	0.435498	0.443062	0.455670	0.632558	0.873011	0.917335	1.211035	1.245103	1.265543
461	PIPELINES, EXCEPT NATURAL GAS	11	4.36%	0.808301	0.873011	0.435498	0.443062	0.455670	0.632558	0.873011	0.917335	1.211035	1.245103	1.265543
4612	Crude Petroleum Pipelines	6	3.68%	0.681727	0.619578	0.438066	0.449484	0.468512	0.606598	0.619578	0.632558	0.942046	0.953552	0.960456
4613	Refined Petroleum Pipelines	1	6.91%	1.279170	1.279170	1.279170	1.279170	1.279170	1.279170	1.279170	1.279170	1.279170	1.279170	1.279170
4619	Pipelines, Not Elsewhere Classified	4	4.75%	0.880444	0.948996	0.493978	0.513618	0.546352	0.929999	0.948996	0.967992	1.118563	1.130732	1.138033
47	TRANSPORTATION SERVICES	20	3.89%	0.720390	0.777291	-0.222862	-0.216250	-0.205229	0.758867	0.777291	0.802852	1.248724	1.519987	1.682745
4700	TRANSPORTATION SERVICES	5	3.75%	0.694166	0.777291	0.099353	0.141724	0.212343	0.777291	0.777291	0.777291	1.009738	1.038794	1.056228
472	ARRANGEMENT OF PASSENGER TRANSPORTATION	3	4.58%	0.848398	0.558937	0.202285	0.213203	0.231399	0.486151	0.558937	0.805400	1.668019	1.729634	1.766604
4724	Travel Agencies	1	3.02%	0.558937	0.558937	0.558937	0.558937	0.558937	0.558937	0.558937	0.558937	0.558937	0.558937	0.558937
4725	Tour Operators	2	5.36%	0.993128	0.993128	0.210968	0.234912	0.274818	0.833504	0.993128	1.152752	1.711438	1.751344	1.775288
473	ARRANGEMENT OF TRANSPORTATION OF FREIGHT AND CARGO	10	4.08%	0.755488	0.806269	-0.136719	-0.035693	0.132683	0.766004	0.806269	0.868565	1.145034	1.182602	1.205143
4731	Arrangement Of Transportation Of Freight And Cargo	10	4.08%	0.755488	0.806269	-0.136719	-0.035693	0.132683	0.766004	0.806269	0.868565	1.145034	1.182602	1.205143
478	MISCELLANEOUS SERVICES INCIDENTAL TO TRANSPORTATION	2	2.26%	0.418450	0.418450	-0.214356	-0.194984	-0.162698	0.289306	0.418450	0.547594	0.999598	1.031884	1.051256
4789	Transportation Services, Not Elsewhere Classified	2	2.26%	0.418450	0.418450	-0.214356	-0.194984	-0.162698	0.289306	0.418450	0.547594	0.999598	1.031884	1.051256
48	COMMUNICATIONS	126	3.90%	0.722041	0.635852	-0.897593	-0.761122	-0.405907	0.537728	0.635852	0.781654	2.057355	2.502991	3.071630
481	TELEPHONE COMMUNICATIONS	55	4.20%	0.777196	0.625257	-1.082905	-0.711585	-0.281121	0.464994	0.625257	0.872873	2.190695	2.859100	3.208883
4812	Radiotelephone Communications	14	3.70%	0.684696	0.527042	-0.472165	-0.331456	-0.096940	0.396641	0.527042	0.661879	1.774879	2.527164	2.978536
4813	Telephone Communications, Except Radiotelephone	41	4.37%	0.808781	0.757349	-1.172053	-0.789992	-0.159042	0.487188	0.757349	0.876390	2.134790	2.321140	2.817718
482	TELEGRAPH AND OTHER MESSAGE COMMUNICATIONS	2	7.65%	1.417076	1.417076	0.955757	0.969879	0.993415	1.322929	1.417076	1.511223	1.840737	1.864273	1.878395
4822	Telegraph And Other Message Communications	2	7.65%	1.417076	1.417076	0.955757	0.969879	0.993415	1.322929	1.417076	1.511223	1.840737	1.864273	1.878395
483	RADIO AND TELEVISION BROADCASTING STATIONS	25	4.20%	0.778618	0.749723	-0.440751	-0.409892	-0.375206	0.604204	0.749723	0.831465	2.407782	2.653466	2.765512
4832	Radio Broadcasting Stations	12	4.45%	0.824475	0.837929	-0.451674	-0.437201	-0.413080	0.710112	0.837929	0.871216	2.195703	2.362337	2.462317
4833	Television Broadcasting Stations	13	3.98%	0.736289	0.745630	-0.300863	-0.188749	-0.001893	0.524462	0.745630	0.753174	1.752374	2.296292	2.622643
484	CABLE AND OTHER PAY TELEVISION SERVICES	25	3.72%	0.688304	0.592841	-0.026212	0.032959	0.131602	0.567355	0.592841	0.730937	1.259948	1.416330	1.531692
4841	Cable And Other Pay Television Services	25	3.72%	0.688304	0.592841	-0.026212	0.032959	0.131602	0.567355	0.592841	0.730937	1.259948	1.416330	1.531692
489	COMMUNICATIONS SERVICES, NOT ELSEWHERE CLASSIFIED	19	2.48%	0.459165	0.569994	-0.907457	-0.868453	-0.803447	0.449307	0.569994	0.656260	1.282785	1.317863	1.338909
4899	Communications Services, Not Elsewhere Classified	19	2.48%	0.459165	0.569994	-0.907457	-0.868453	-0.803447	0.449307	0.569994	0.656260	1.282785	1.317863	1.338909
49	ELECTRIC, GAS, AND SANITARY SERVICES	127	1.91%	0.353341	0.330902	-2.032438	-0.788120	-0.258434	0.264113	0.330902	0.435352	1.070188	1.450872	2.165733
491	ELECTRIC SERVICES	45	1.30%	0.240916	0.251399	-0.482445	-0.329000	-0.229868	0.219499	0.251399	0.273140	0.642720	0.660742	0.766471
4911	Electric Services	45	1.30%	0.240916	0.251399	-0.482445	-0.329000	-0.229868	0.219499	0.251399	0.273140	0.642720	0.660742	0.766471
492	GAS PRODUCTION AND DISTRIBUTION	22	3.46%	0.640327	0.600439	-0.115388	-0.065217	0.025625	0.546734	0.600439	0.659106	1.078441	1.274572	1.402125
4922	Natural Gas Transmission	6	2.77%	0.512868	0.546574	-0.117149	-0.069618	0.009600	0.505041	0.546574	0.588106	0.838715	0.846075	0.850491
4923	Natural Gas Transmission And Distribution	7	4.36%	0.807235	0.617107	0.328061	0.348886	0.383596	0.614505	0.617107	0.841819	1.365681	1.426421	1.462864
4924	Natural Gas Distribution	9	3.22%	0.595482	0.548478	0.043635	0.093431	0.176423	0.514489	0.548478	0.659380	0.980591	0.993515	1.001270
493	COMBINATION ELECTRIC AND GAS, AND OTHER UTILITY SERVICES	24	1.81%	0.335067	0.278288	-1.038752	-0.579635	0.005083	0.248972	0.278288	0.298474	1.157972	1.694516	2.059222

Up-market Betas of Common Stocks by SIC Codes as of September 28, 2018

SIC Code	Description	Number of Companies	Equity Risk Premium	Mean	Median	1st Percentile	2.5th Percentile	5th Percentile	40th Percentile	50th Percentile	60th Percentile	95th Percentile	97.5th Percentile	99th Percentile
4931	Electric And Other Services Combined	18	0.95%	0.176804	0.257939	-1.118598	-0.779251	-0.213672	0.196877	0.257939	0.275677	0.572555	0.618005	0.645274
4932	Gas And Other Services Combined	5	2.76%	0.511355	0.332471	0.121849	0.134320	0.155105	0.328037	0.332471	0.417140	1.105021	1.175130	1.217196
4939	Combination Utilities, Not Elsewhere Classified	1	12.43%	2.302360	2.302360	2.302360	2.302360	2.302360	2.302360	2.302360	2.302360	2.302360	2.302360	2.302360
494	WATER SUPPLY	15	2.20%	0.407039	0.462181	-0.034858	-0.021847	-0.000161	0.406689	0.462181	0.518085	0.724028	0.724320	0.724495
4941	Water Supply	15	2.20%	0.407039	0.462181	-0.034858	-0.021847	-0.000161	0.406689	0.462181	0.518085	0.724028	0.724320	0.724495
495	SANITARY SERVICES	21	1.49%	0.276131	0.499286	-2.380174	-2.340370	-2.274030	0.183032	0.499286	0.600027	1.776870	2.108440	2.307382
4950	SANITARY SERVICES	2	6.60%	1.222646	1.222646	0.029629	0.066150	0.127018	0.979173	1.222646	1.466119	2.318274	2.379142	2.415663
4953	Refuse Systems	16	1.07%	0.197807	0.479800	-2.056162	-1.729360	-1.184690	0.183032	0.479800	0.518863	1.071708	1.116134	1.142790
4955	HAZARDOUS WASTE MANAGEMENT	2	-4.29%	-0.794153	-0.794153	-2.374459	-2.326082	-2.245454	-1.116664	-0.794153	-0.471642	0.657148	0.737776	0.786153
4959	Sanitary Services, Not Elsewhere Classified	1	9.60%	1.776870	1.776870	1.776870	1.776870	1.776870	1.776870	1.776870	1.776870	1.776870	1.776870	1.776870
	WHOLESALE TRADE													
50	WHOLESALE TRADE¨DURABLE GOODS	73	3.17%	0.586579	0.653758	-1.992562	-0.981850	-0.408376	0.531998	0.653758	0.778779	1.646328	1.759998	2.093801
501	MOTOR VEHICLES AND MOTOR VEHICLE PARTS AND SUPPLIES	9	3.59%	0.665688	0.756755	-0.365565	-0.275132	-0.124411	0.682397	0.756755	0.771979	1.243322	1.244826	1.245728
5012	Automobiles And Other Motor Vehicles	2	3.89%	0.719796	0.719796	0.664927	0.666606	0.669406	0.708598	0.719796	0.730994	0.770186	0.772986	0.774665
5013	Motor Vehicle Supplies And New Parts	6	3.69%	0.683466	0.856877	-0.388173	-0.331652	-0.237452	0.756755	0.856877	0.956999	1.244450	1.245390	1.245954
5015	Motor Vehicle Parts, Used	1	2.43%	0.450809	0.450809	0.450809	0.450809	0.450809	0.450809	0.450809	0.450809	0.450809	0.450809	0.450809
503	LUMBER AND OTHER CONSTRUCTION MATERIALS	9	3.75%	0.693839	0.423070	0.334982	0.336427	0.338834	0.407342	0.423070	0.664156	1.430028	1.535414	1.598646
5030	WHOLESALE-LUMBER & OTHER CONSTRUCTION MATERIALS	3	2.90%	0.537742	0.423070	0.335800	0.338472	0.342924	0.405260	0.423070	0.509684	0.812831	0.834485	0.847477
5031	Lumber, Plywood, Millwork, And Wood Panels	4	4.73%	0.876034	0.758640	0.347778	0.350358	0.354660	0.545502	0.758640	0.971778	1.561761	1.601280	1.624992
5033	Roofing, Siding, And Insulation Materials	1	2.17%	0.402764	0.402764	0.402764	0.402764	0.402764	0.402764	0.402764	0.402764	0.402764	0.402764	0.402764
5039	Construction Materials, Not Elsewhere Classified	1	3.91%	0.724427	0.724427	0.724427	0.724427	0.724427	0.724427	0.724427	0.724427	0.724427	0.724427	0.724427
504	PROFESSIONAL AND COMMERCIAL EQUIPMENT AND SUPPLIES	16	3.77%	0.698152	0.942978	-2.356534	-1.716144	-0.648828	0.653758	0.942978	1.141030	1.715638	1.902534	2.014672
5044	Office Equipment	1	0.47%	0.087757	0.087757	0.087757	0.087757	0.087757	0.087757	0.087757	0.087757	0.087757	0.087757	0.087757
5045	Computers And Computer Peripheral Equipment And Software	9	5.27%	0.975913	1.141030	0.342134	0.352830	0.370655	0.950236	1.141030	1.151918	1.488544	1.539792	1.570541
5047	Medical, Dental, And Hospital Equipment And Supplies	6	2.07%	0.383241	0.796581	-2.641151	-2.427688	-2.071916	0.609744	0.796581	0.983418	1.901473	1.995451	2.051839
505	METALS AND MINERALS, EXCEPT PETROLEUM	6	4.41%	0.816119	0.744041	0.037229	0.044295	0.056071	0.419162	0.744041	1.068920	1.864865	1.984953	2.057005
5051	Metals Service Centers And Offices	6	4.41%	0.816119	0.744041	0.037229	0.044295	0.056071	0.419162	0.744041	1.068920	1.864865	1.984953	2.057005
506	ELECTRICAL GOODS	17	1.97%	0.364389	0.639062	-1.468668	-1.144186	-0.603382	0.491522	0.639062	0.680174	0.947806	0.952833	0.955848
5063	Electrical Apparatus And Equipment, Wiring Supplies, And Construction	5	2.93%	0.542532	0.695478	-0.294098	-0.235776	-0.138572	0.672912	0.695478	0.742803	0.880605	0.888957	0.893968
5065	Electronic Parts And Equipment, Not Elsewhere Classified	12	1.57%	0.290163	0.509498	-1.513459	-1.256163	-0.827337	0.299369	0.509498	0.634082	0.950948	0.954403	0.956477
507	HARDWARE, AND PLUMBING AND HEATING EQUIPMENT AND SUPPLIES	3	5.02%	0.929439	0.636793	0.477142	0.482029	0.490175	0.604211	0.636793	0.844962	1.573555	1.625598	1.656823

Up-market Betas of Common Stocks by SIC Codes as of September 28, 2018

SIC Code	Description	Number of Companies	Equity Risk Premium	Mean	Median	1st Percentile	2.5th Percentile	5th Percentile	40th Percentile	50th Percentile	60th Percentile	95th Percentile	97.5th Percentile	99th Percentile
5074	Plumbing And Heating Equipment And Supplies (Hydronics)	2	5.81%	1.075762	1.075762	0.485922	0.503978	0.534072	0.955386	1.075762	1.196138	1.617452	1.647546	1.665602
5075	Warm Air Heating And Air-Conditioning Equipment And Supplies	1	3.44%	0.636793	0.636793	0.636793	0.636793	0.636793	0.636793	0.636793	0.636793	0.636793	0.636793	0.636793
508	MACHINERY, EQUIPMENT, AND SUPPLIES	8	2.39%	0.443224	0.596900	-0.728979	-0.613349	-0.420633	0.579490	0.596900	0.628323	0.802136	0.805200	0.807039
5084	Industrial Machinery And Equipment	6	2.05%	0.380320	0.596900	-0.751003	-0.668411	-0.530756	0.587731	0.596900	0.606068	0.803887	0.806076	0.807389
5085	Industrial Supplies	1	2.95%	0.546527	0.546527	0.546527	0.546527	0.546527	0.546527	0.546527	0.546527	0.546527	0.546527	0.546527
5087	Service Establishment Equipment And Supplies	1	3.87%	0.717343	0.717343	0.717343	0.717343	0.717343	0.717343	0.717343	0.717343	0.717343	0.717343	0.717343
509	MISCELLANEOUS DURABLE GOODS	5	2.15%	0.397734	-0.302644	-0.396124	-0.395225	-0.393725	-0.334279	-0.302644	0.384474	1.606726	1.630673	1.645041
5091	Sporting And Recreational Goods And Supplies	2	8.29%	1.534885	1.534885	1.417545	1.421137	1.427124	1.510938	1.534885	1.558832	1.642647	1.648633	1.652225
5094	Jewelry, Watches, Precious Stones, And Precious Metals	2	-2.10%	-0.389228	-0.389228	-0.396574	-0.396349	-0.395974	-0.390727	-0.389228	-0.387728	-0.382481	-0.382106	-0.381881
5099	Durable Goods, Not Elsewhere Classified	1	-1.63%	-0.302644	-0.302644	-0.302644	-0.302644	-0.302644	-0.302644	-0.302644	-0.302644	-0.302644	-0.302644	-0.302644
51	WHOLESALE TRADE¨NONDURABLE GOODS	63	3.83%	0.709905	0.743855	-2.183018	-1.093168	-0.452378	0.685865	0.743855	0.833510	1.647653	2.077372	2.925354
511	PAPER AND PAPER PRODUCTS	1	-9.82%	-1.819430	-1.819430	-1.819430	-1.819430	-1.819430	-1.819430	-1.819430	-1.819430	-1.819430	-1.819430	-1.819430
5112	Stationery And Office Supplies	1	-9.82%	-1.819430	-1.819430	-1.819430	-1.819430	-1.819430	-1.819430	-1.819430	-1.819430	-1.819430	-1.819430	-1.819430
512	DRUGS, DRUG PROPRIETARIES, AND DRUGGISTS' SUNDRIES	23	3.11%	0.575630	0.790052	-2.275237	-1.523732	-0.484442	0.649820	0.790052	0.824571	1.631463	1.940691	2.150432
5122	Drugs, Drug Proprietaries, And Druggists' Sundries	23	3.11%	0.575630	0.790052	-2.275237	-1.523732	-0.484442	0.649820	0.790052	0.824571	1.631463	1.940691	2.150432
513	APPAREL, PIECE GOODS, AND NOTIONS	2	4.20%	0.777002	0.777002	0.690045	0.692707	0.697143	0.759255	0.777002	0.794748	0.856860	0.861296	0.863958
5136	Men's And Boys' Clothing And Furnishings	1	4.67%	0.865733	0.865733	0.865733	0.865733	0.865733	0.865733	0.865733	0.865733	0.865733	0.865733	0.865733
5139	Footwear	1	3.72%	0.688270	0.688270	0.688270	0.688270	0.688270	0.688270	0.688270	0.688270	0.688270	0.688270	0.688270
514	GROCERIES AND RELATED PRODUCTS	14	3.31%	0.613716	0.671364	-0.386425	-0.271074	-0.078822	0.622532	0.671364	0.730333	1.200375	1.301797	1.362651
5140	WHOLESALE-GROCERIES & RELATED PRODUCTS	2	3.19%	0.590189	0.590189	0.137457	0.151317	0.174415	0.497795	0.590189	0.682583	1.005963	1.029061	1.042921
5141	Groceries, General Line	8	3.22%	0.595544	0.639013	-0.418876	-0.352202	-0.241077	0.576265	0.639013	0.702877	1.293996	1.348608	1.381375
5145	Confectionery	1	4.02%	0.743855	0.743855	0.743855	0.743855	0.743855	0.743855	0.743855	0.743855	0.743855	0.743855	0.743855
5148	Fresh Fruits And Vegetables	1	2.24%	0.414179	0.414179	0.414179	0.414179	0.414179	0.414179	0.414179	0.414179	0.414179	0.414179	0.414179
5149	Groceries And Related Products, Not Elsewhere Classified	2	4.02%	0.744632	0.744632	0.677613	0.679664	0.683084	0.730955	0.744632	0.758309	0.806180	0.809600	0.811651
515	FARM-PRODUCT RAW MATERIALS	4	4.66%	0.863334	0.802786	0.331474	0.340050	0.354344	0.630919	0.802786	0.974652	1.457093	1.489552	1.509027
5153	Grain And Field Beans	2	3.82%	0.707493	0.707493	0.333391	0.344843	0.363930	0.631146	0.707493	0.783840	1.051056	1.070143	1.081595
5159	Farm-Product Raw Materials, Not Elsewhere Classified	2	5.50%	1.019176	1.019176	0.526398	0.541483	0.566624	0.918609	1.019176	1.119742	1.471727	1.496868	1.511953
516	CHEMICALS AND ALLIED PRODUCTS	5	4.75%	0.880209	0.827210	0.455773	0.468562	0.489875	0.760480	0.827210	0.959374	1.278388	1.293484	1.302542
5162	Plastics Materials And Basic Forms And Shapes	1	2.42%	0.447248	0.447248	0.447248	0.447248	0.447248	0.447248	0.447248	0.447248	0.447248	0.447248	0.447248
5169	Chemicals And Allied Products, Not Elsewhere Classified	4	5.34%	0.988449	0.992415	0.665390	0.672897	0.685409	0.893292	0.992415	1.091538	1.285936	1.297258	1.304051
517	PETROLEUM AND PETROLEUM PRODUCTS	7	6.66%	1.232870	0.692196	0.175969	0.225395	0.307771	0.692196	0.692196	0.795588	3.248415	3.604988	3.818931

Up-market Betas of Common Stocks by SIC Codes as of September 28, 2018

SIC Code	Description	Number of Companies	Equity Risk Premium	Mean	Median	1st Percentile	2.5th Percentile	5th Percentile	40th Percentile	50th Percentile	60th Percentile	95th Percentile	97.5th Percentile	99th Percentile
5172	Petroleum And Petroleum Products Wholesalers, Except Bulk Station	7	6.66%	1.232870	0.692196	0.175969	0.225395	0.307771	0.692196	0.692196	0.795588	3.248415	3.604988	3.818931
518	BEER, WINE, AND DISTILLED ALCOHOLIC BEVERAGES	1	-0.66%	-0.122419	-0.122419	-0.122419	-0.122419	-0.122419	-0.122419	-0.122419	-0.122419	-0.122419	-0.122419	-0.122419
5180	WHOLESALE-BEER, WINE & DISTILLED ALCOHOLIC BEVERAGES	1	-0.66%	-0.122419	-0.122419	-0.122419	-0.122419	-0.122419	-0.122419	-0.122419	-0.122419	-0.122419	-0.122419	-0.122419
519	MISCELLANEOUS NONDURABLE GOODS	6	6.12%	1.132649	1.015411	0.432276	0.468200	0.528074	0.941911	1.015411	1.088910	1.818953	1.861071	1.886343
5190	WHOLESALE-MISCELLANEOUS NONDURABLE GOODS	1	10.28%	1.903190	1.903190	1.903190	1.903190	1.903190	1.903190	1.903190	1.903190	1.903190	1.903190	1.903190
5191	Farm Supplies	2	7.17%	1.327575	1.327575	1.093683	1.100843	1.112777	1.279842	1.327575	1.375308	1.542374	1.554307	1.561467
5192	Books, Periodicals, And Newspapers	1	4.79%	0.887314	0.887314	0.887314	0.887314	0.887314	0.887314	0.887314	0.887314	0.887314	0.887314	0.887314
5199	Nondurable Goods, Not Elsewhere Classified	2	3.65%	0.675119	0.675119	0.413663	0.421667	0.435006	0.621761	0.675119	0.728477	0.915232	0.928571	0.936575
	RETAIL TRADE													
52	RETAIL TRADE	14	3.85%	0.712373	0.734431	-0.337205	-0.253567	-0.114170	0.664544	0.734431	0.854353	1.562201	1.630460	1.671416
521	LUMBER AND OTHER BUILDING MATERIALS DEALERS	12	4.31%	0.798469	0.778048	0.038162	0.041480	0.047009	0.669482	0.778048	0.885734	1.583204	1.640962	1.675617
5211	Lumber And Other Building Materials Dealers	12	4.31%	0.798469	0.778048	0.038162	0.041480	0.047009	0.669482	0.778048	0.885734	1.583204	1.640962	1.675617
523	PAINT, GLASS, AND WALLPAPER STORES	1	4.24%	0.784566	0.784566	0.784566	0.784566	0.784566	0.784566	0.784566	0.784566	0.784566	0.784566	0.784566
5231	Paint, Glass, And Wallpaper Stores	1	4.24%	0.784566	0.784566	0.784566	0.784566	0.784566	0.784566	0.784566	0.784566	0.784566	0.784566	0.784566
526	RETAIL NURSERIES, LAWN AND GARDEN SUPPLY STORES	1	-2.12%	-0.392964	-0.392964	-0.392964	-0.392964	-0.392964	-0.392964	-0.392964	-0.392964	-0.392964	-0.392964	-0.392964
5261	Retail Nurseries, Lawn And Garden Supply Stores	1	-2.12%	-0.392964	-0.392964	-0.392964	-0.392964	-0.392964	-0.392964	-0.392964	-0.392964	-0.392964	-0.392964	-0.392964
53	GENERAL MERCHANDISE STORES	18	3.56%	0.659322	0.593772	0.248727	0.260219	0.279374	0.547160	0.593772	0.672441	1.035200	1.380300	1.587360
531	DEPARTMENT STORES	8	4.14%	0.766761	0.632902	0.303716	0.330089	0.374044	0.553100	0.632902	0.745107	1.433578	1.579489	1.667036
5311	Department Stores	8	4.14%	0.766761	0.632902	0.303716	0.330089	0.374044	0.553100	0.632902	0.745107	1.433578	1.579489	1.667036
533	VARIETY STORES	8	2.76%	0.511933	0.512858	0.244876	0.250592	0.260119	0.486067	0.512858	0.543527	0.768468	0.796973	0.814076
5331	Variety Stores	8	2.76%	0.511933	0.512858	0.244876	0.250592	0.260119	0.486067	0.512858	0.543527	0.768468	0.796973	0.814076
539	MISCELLANEOUS GENERAL MERCHANDISE STORES	2	4.42%	0.819123	0.819123	0.726731	0.729559	0.734273	0.800267	0.819123	0.837978	0.903972	0.908686	0.911514
5399	Miscellaneous General Merchandise Stores	2	4.42%	0.819123	0.819123	0.726731	0.729559	0.734273	0.800267	0.819123	0.837978	0.903972	0.908686	0.911514
54	FOOD STORES	23	5.02%	0.930015	0.370917	-2.237396	-1.547104	-0.567014	0.283871	0.370917	0.558253	2.027234	6.575144	9.879438
541	GROCERY STORES	18	1.45%	0.269436	0.290684	-2.341985	-1.808578	-0.919567	0.281704	0.290684	0.402956	1.216674	1.372122	1.465391
5411	Grocery Stores	18	1.45%	0.269436	0.290684	-2.341985	-1.808578	-0.919567	0.281704	0.290684	0.402956	1.216674	1.372122	1.465391
544	CANDY, NUT, AND CONFECTIONERY STORES	1	2.71%	0.502486	0.502486	0.502486	0.502486	0.502486	0.502486	0.502486	0.502486	0.502486	0.502486	0.502486
5441	Candy, Nut, And Confectionery Stores	1	2.71%	0.502486	0.502486	0.502486	0.502486	0.502486	0.502486	0.502486	0.502486	0.502486	0.502486	0.502486
546	RETAIL BAKERIES	1	65.24%	12.082300	12.082300	12.082300	12.082300	12.082300	12.082300	12.082300	12.082300	12.082300	12.082300	12.082300
5461	Retail Bakeries	1	65.24%	12.082300	12.082300	12.082300	12.082300	12.082300	12.082300	12.082300	12.082300	12.082300	12.082300	12.082300
549	MISCELLANEOUS FOOD STORES	3	7.12%	1.318569	1.648730	0.265908	0.308239	0.378791	1.366521	1.648730	1.732842	2.027234	2.048262	2.060879
5499	Miscellaneous Food Stores	3	7.12%	1.318569	1.648730	0.265908	0.308239	0.378791	1.366521	1.648730	1.732842	2.027234	2.048262	2.060879
55	AUTOMOTIVE DEALERS AND GASOLINE SERVICE STATIONS	20	3.87%	0.716404	0.825004	-0.126015	-0.098579	-0.052851	0.474492	0.825004	0.911228	1.517014	1.667627	1.757995
5500	RETAIL-AUTO DEALERS & GASOLINE STATIONS	2	6.43%	1.191467	1.191467	0.964044	0.971006	0.982609	1.145054	1.191467	1.237879	1.400324	1.411927	1.418889

Up-market Betas of Common Stocks by SIC Codes as of September 28, 2018

SIC Code	Description	Number of Companies	Equity Risk Premium	Mean	Median	1st Percentile	2.5th Percentile	5th Percentile	40th Percentile	50th Percentile	60th Percentile	95th Percentile	97.5th Percentile	99th Percentile
551	MOTOR VEHICLE DEALERS (NEW AND USED)	8	3.74%	0.692835	0.679548	0.219502	0.235392	0.261875	0.476488	0.679548	0.901528	1.094392	1.110751	1.120566
5511	Motor Vehicle Dealers (New And Used)	8	3.74%	0.692835	0.679548	0.219502	0.235392	0.261875	0.476488	0.679548	0.901528	1.094392	1.110751	1.120566
552	MOTOR VEHICLE DEALERS (USED ONLY)	2	7.28%	1.348676	1.348676	0.888502	0.902589	0.926067	1.254763	1.348676	1.442588	1.771284	1.794762	1.808849
5521	Motor Vehicle Dealers (Used Only)	2	7.28%	1.348676	1.348676	0.888502	0.902589	0.926067	1.254763	1.348676	1.442588	1.771284	1.794762	1.808849
553	AUTO AND HOME SUPPLY STORES	3	3.23%	0.597874	0.775261	-0.031572	-0.006873	0.034292	0.610601	0.775261	0.833489	1.037286	1.051843	1.060577
5531	Auto And Home Supply Stores	3	3.23%	0.597874	0.775261	-0.031572	-0.006873	0.034292	0.610601	0.775261	0.833489	1.037286	1.051843	1.060577
554	GASOLINE SERVICE STATIONS	4	1.96%	0.362947	0.047466	-0.140455	-0.134680	-0.125053	0.009414	0.047466	0.085518	1.292619	1.396889	1.459452
5541	Gasoline Service Stations	4	1.96%	0.362947	0.047466	-0.140455	-0.134680	-0.125053	0.009414	0.047466	0.085518	1.292619	1.396889	1.459452
555	BOAT DEALERS	1	2.48%	0.459708	0.459708	0.459708	0.459708	0.459708	0.459708	0.459708	0.459708	0.459708	0.459708	0.459708
5551	Boat Dealers	1	2.48%	0.459708	0.459708	0.459708	0.459708	0.459708	0.459708	0.459708	0.459708	0.459708	0.459708	0.459708
56	APPAREL AND ACCESSORY STORES	34	4.50%	0.833035	0.800833	-0.686086	-0.475913	-0.041514	0.661930	0.800833	0.882343	2.027702	2.297175	2.856990
5600	RETAIL-APPAREL & ACCESSORY STORES	1	4.90%	0.906598	0.906598	0.906598	0.906598	0.906598	0.906598	0.906598	0.906598	0.906598	0.906598	0.906598
561	MEN'S AND BOYS' CLOTHING AND ACCESSORY STORES	2	14.39%	2.664730	2.664730	2.110569	2.127534	2.155807	2.551636	2.664730	2.777824	3.173653	3.201927	3.218891
5611	Men's And Boys' Clothing And Accessory Stores	2	14.39%	2.664730	2.664730	2.110569	2.127534	2.155807	2.551636	2.664730	2.777824	3.173653	3.201927	3.218891
562	WOMEN'S CLOTHING STORES	8	2.45%	0.454044	0.522934	-0.747433	-0.629281	-0.432361	0.476819	0.522934	0.586843	1.037364	1.093332	1.126913
5621	Women's Clothing Stores	8	2.45%	0.454044	0.522934	-0.747433	-0.629281	-0.432361	0.476819	0.522934	0.586843	1.037364	1.093332	1.126913
563	WOMEN'S ACCESSORY AND SPECIALTY STORES	1	7.58%	1.403190	1.403190	1.403190	1.403190	1.403190	1.403190	1.403190	1.403190	1.403190	1.403190	1.403190
5632	Women's Accessory And Specialty Stores	1	7.58%	1.403190	1.403190	1.403190	1.403190	1.403190	1.403190	1.403190	1.403190	1.403190	1.403190	1.403190
565	FAMILY CLOTHING STORES	15	3.96%	0.733613	0.743560	-0.324050	-0.207711	-0.013814	0.615888	0.743560	0.891166	1.462350	1.725760	1.883806
5651	Family Clothing Stores	15	3.96%	0.733613	0.743560	-0.324050	-0.207711	-0.013814	0.615888	0.743560	0.891166	1.462350	1.725760	1.883806
566	SHOE STORES	6	4.70%	0.869658	0.772384	0.394108	0.398562	0.405986	0.660940	0.772384	0.883828	1.484778	1.519289	1.539996
5661	Shoe Stores	6	4.70%	0.869658	0.772384	0.394108	0.398562	0.405986	0.660940	0.772384	0.883828	1.484778	1.519289	1.539996
569	MISCELLANEOUS APPAREL AND ACCESSORY STORES	1	4.48%	0.829453	0.829453	0.829453	0.829453	0.829453	0.829453	0.829453	0.829453	0.829453	0.829453	0.829453
5699	Miscellaneous Apparel And Accessory Stores	1	4.48%	0.829453	0.829453	0.829453	0.829453	0.829453	0.829453	0.829453	0.829453	0.829453	0.829453	0.829453
57	HOME FURNITURE, FURNISHINGS, AND EQUIPMENT STORES	11	2.25%	0.416009	0.748115	-1.822721	-1.584584	-1.187687	0.704379	0.748115	0.813340	1.212635	1.220703	1.225543
5700	RETAIL-HOME FURNITURE, FURNISHINGS & EQUIPMENT STORES	1	3.80%	0.704379	0.704379	0.704379	0.704379	0.704379	0.704379	0.704379	0.704379	0.704379	0.704379	0.704379
571	HOME FURNITURE AND FURNISHINGS STORES	6	3.44%	0.636971	0.780728	-0.060841	-0.018635	0.051707	0.748115	0.780728	0.813340	0.994427	1.022744	1.039733
5712	Furniture Stores	3	3.20%	0.591807	0.813340	-0.070932	-0.043862	0.001254	0.632876	0.813340	0.860884	1.027288	1.039174	1.046306
5713	Floor Covering Stores	1	4.45%	0.824528	0.824528	0.824528	0.824528	0.824528	0.824528	0.824528	0.824528	0.824528	0.824528	0.824528
5719	Miscellaneous Homefurnishings Stores	2	3.30%	0.610939	0.610939	0.476507	0.480622	0.487481	0.583504	0.610939	0.638374	0.734397	0.741256	0.745371
572	HOUSEHOLD APPLIANCE STORES	1	-2.13%	-0.393894	-0.393894	-0.393894	-0.393894	-0.393894	-0.393894	-0.393894	-0.393894	-0.393894	-0.393894	-0.393894
5722	Household Appliance Stores	1	-2.13%	-0.393894	-0.393894	-0.393894	-0.393894	-0.393894	-0.393894	-0.393894	-0.393894	-0.393894	-0.393894	-0.393894
573	RADIO, TELEVISION, CONSUMER ELECTRONICS, AND MUSIC STORES	3	0.80%	0.147930	1.196500	-1.917920	-1.822581	-1.663682	0.560904	1.196500	1.202954	1.225543	1.227157	1.228125
5731	Radio, Television, And Consumer Electronics Stores	2	6.55%	1.212635	1.212635	1.196823	1.197307	1.198114	1.209408	1.212635	1.215862	1.227157	1.227963	1.228447
5735	Record And Prerecorded Tape Stores	1	-10.70%	-1.981480	-1.981480	-1.981480	-1.981480	-1.981480	-1.981480	-1.981480	-1.981480	-1.981480	-1.981480	-1.981480
58	EATING AND DRINKING PLACES	66	3.82%	0.707292	0.644516	-0.701383	-0.685033	-0.155651	0.562008	0.644516	0.748260	1.713860	2.048851	2.887283

Up-market Betas of Common Stocks by SIC Codes as of September 28, 2018

SIC Code	Description	Number of Companies	Equity Risk Premium	Mean	Median	1st Percentile	2.5th Percentile	5th Percentile	40th Percentile	50th Percentile	60th Percentile	95th Percentile	97.5th Percentile	99th Percentile
581	EATING AND DRINKING PLACES	66	3.82%	0.707292	0.644516	-0.701383	-0.685033	-0.155651	0.562008	0.644516	0.748260	1.713860	2.048851	2.887283
5810	RETAIL-EATING & DRINKING PLACES	2	-0.57%	-0.106259	-0.106259	-0.153861	-0.152403	-0.149975	-0.115973	-0.106259	-0.096544	-0.062543	-0.060114	-0.058657
5812	Eating Places	63	3.99%	0.738449	0.714088	-0.701948	-0.686204	-0.151596	0.603893	0.714088	0.755627	1.741370	2.057980	2.952628
5813	Drinking Places (Alcoholic Beverages)	1	2.01%	0.371497	0.371497	0.371497	0.371497	0.371497	0.371497	0.371497	0.371497	0.371497	0.371497	0.371497
59	MISCELLANEOUS RETAIL	73	3.12%	0.577457	0.732581	-2.446834	-2.328678	-1.208256	0.656808	0.732581	0.822885	1.495470	1.744248	2.121019
5900	RETAIL-MISCELLANEOUS RETAIL	1	-7.29%	-1.349910	-1.349910	-1.349910	-1.349910	-1.349910	-1.349910	-1.349910	-1.349910	-1.349910	-1.349910	-1.349910
591	DRUG STORES AND PROPRIETARY STORES	8	5.23%	0.967671	0.747117	0.686533	0.689319	0.693962	0.728280	0.747117	0.773740	1.877909	2.133255	2.286462
5912	Drug Stores And Proprietary Stores	8	5.23%	0.967671	0.747117	0.686533	0.689319	0.693962	0.728280	0.747117	0.773740	1.877909	2.133255	2.286462
592	LIQUOR STORES	1	3.58%	0.662388	0.662388	0.662388	0.662388	0.662388	0.662388	0.662388	0.662388	0.662388	0.662388	0.662388
5921	Liquor Stores	1	3.58%	0.662388	0.662388	0.662388	0.662388	0.662388	0.662388	0.662388	0.662388	0.662388	0.662388	0.662388
593	USED MERCHANDISE STORES	3	3.79%	0.701441	0.758333	0.564605	0.570535	0.580419	0.718797	0.758333	0.763734	0.782638	0.783989	0.784799
5932	Used Merchandise Stores	3	3.79%	0.701441	0.758333	0.564605	0.570535	0.580419	0.718797	0.758333	0.763734	0.782638	0.783989	0.784799
594	MISCELLANEOUS SHOPPING GOODS STORES	14	4.73%	0.875868	1.020960	-0.644252	-0.392352	0.027480	0.870520	1.020960	1.057866	1.538933	1.607502	1.648643
5941	Sporting Goods Stores And Bicycle Shops	3	6.24%	1.156384	1.066860	0.733035	0.743254	0.760286	0.998732	1.066860	1.188702	1.615149	1.645610	1.663886
5942	Book Stores	2	5.95%	1.101760	1.101760	1.023487	1.025884	1.029877	1.085786	1.101760	1.117734	1.173643	1.177637	1.180033
5943	Stationery Stores	1	5.82%	1.078010	1.078010	1.078010	1.078010	1.078010	1.078010	1.078010	1.078010	1.078010	1.078010	1.078010
5944	Jewelry Stores	3	0.53%	0.099025	0.479608	-0.786349	-0.747595	-0.683006	0.221249	0.479608	0.509617	0.614647	0.622149	0.626650
5945	Hobby, Toy, And Game Shops	3	5.41%	1.002434	1.020030	0.836881	0.842487	0.851832	0.982653	1.020030	1.046850	1.140720	1.147425	1.151448
5947	Gift, Novelty, And Souvenir Shops	2	5.96%	1.103549	1.103549	0.749239	0.760085	0.778162	1.031241	1.103549	1.175857	1.428936	1.447013	1.457859
596	NONSTORE RETAILERS	30	2.15%	0.398152	0.680164	-2.534438	-2.445816	-2.355415	0.537006	0.680164	0.912075	1.491419	1.671918	1.878943
5960	RETAIL-NONSTORE RETAILERS	2	-7.31%	-1.354177	-1.354177	-2.568733	-2.531553	-2.469586	-1.602046	-1.354177	-1.106308	-0.238768	-0.176801	-0.139621
5961	Catalog And Mail-Order Houses	28	2.83%	0.523318	0.729210	-2.369165	-2.338227	-1.893547	0.624223	0.729210	0.933716	1.502446	1.695714	1.888462
598	FUEL DEALERS	4	-0.37%	-0.068323	-0.089930	-0.097161	-0.097160	-0.097158	-0.094252	-0.089930	-0.085608	-0.009238	-0.002753	0.001137
5983	Fuel Oil Dealers	4	-0.37%	-0.068323	-0.089930	-0.097161	-0.097160	-0.097158	-0.094252	-0.089930	-0.085608	-0.009238	-0.002753	0.001137
599	RETAIL STORES, NOT ELSEWHERE CLASSIFIED	12	4.08%	0.755229	0.738356	0.253566	0.259774	0.270120	0.610184	0.738356	0.861809	1.259556	1.261723	1.263023
5992	Florists	1	6.78%	1.256010	1.256010	1.256010	1.256010	1.256010	1.256010	1.256010	1.256010	1.256010	1.256010	1.256010
5995	Optical Goods Stores	1	2.85%	0.527966	0.527966	0.527966	0.527966	0.527966	0.527966	0.527966	0.527966	0.527966	0.527966	0.527966
5999	Miscellaneous Retail Stores, Not Elsewhere Classified	10	3.93%	0.727877	0.738356	0.252814	0.257893	0.266357	0.586140	0.738356	0.822273	1.237115	1.250503	1.258535
	FINANCE, INSURANCE, AND REAL ESTATE													
60	DEPOSITORY INSTITUTIONS	382	3.03%	0.561200	0.681643	-0.420661	-0.326166	-0.226504	0.546534	0.681643	0.760574	1.121282	1.225591	1.332477
602	COMMERCIAL BANKS	292	3.28%	0.607057	0.727121	-0.411360	-0.298110	-0.195212	0.629542	0.727121	0.803004	1.121874	1.202820	1.332368
6021	National Commercial Banks	106	3.51%	0.650261	0.779242	-0.297845	-0.225869	-0.175625	0.672507	0.779242	0.884592	1.170610	1.221563	1.329294
6022	State Commercial Banks	161	3.18%	0.588385	0.716204	-0.440192	-0.339497	-0.226764	0.625510	0.716204	0.761747	1.106160	1.123140	1.238976
6029	Commercial Banks, Not Elsewhere Classified	25	2.94%	0.544117	0.474001	-0.201213	-0.197843	-0.167945	0.413335	0.474001	0.743940	1.263760	1.313338	1.325351
603	SAVINGS INSTITUTIONS	80	2.28%	0.422492	0.528360	-0.330757	-0.321518	-0.259204	0.371939	0.528360	0.619928	0.945543	1.078455	1.243220
6035	Savings Institutions, Federally Chartered	60	2.12%	0.392387	0.516917	-0.334011	-0.324504	-0.311683	0.295352	0.516917	0.607577	0.951648	1.162950	1.243220
6036	Savings Institutions, Not Federally Chartered	20	2.77%	0.512807	0.572163	-0.050222	-0.035122	-0.009954	0.474563	0.572163	0.668094	0.904455	0.928293	0.942596
606	CREDIT UNIONS	1	-2.07%	-0.383679	-0.383679	-0.383679	-0.383679	-0.383679	-0.383679	-0.383679	-0.383679	-0.383679	-0.383679	-0.383679
6061	Credit Unions, Federally Chartered	1	-2.07%	-0.383679	-0.383679	-0.383679	-0.383679	-0.383679	-0.383679	-0.383679	-0.383679	-0.383679	-0.383679	-0.383679
608	FOREIGN BANKING AND BRANCHES AND AGENCIES OF FOREIGN BANKS	2	1.05%	0.193885	0.193885	-0.097316	-0.088402	-0.073545	0.134456	0.193885	0.253314	0.461315	0.476172	0.485086

Up-market Betas of Common Stocks by SIC Codes as of September 28, 2018

SIC Code	Description	Number of Companies	Equity Risk Premium	Mean	Median	1st Percentile	2.5th Percentile	5th Percentile	40th Percentile	50th Percentile	60th Percentile	95th Percentile	97.5th Percentile	99th Percentile
6081	Branches And Agencies Of Foreign Banks	2	1.05%	0.193885	0.193885	-0.097316	-0.088402	-0.073545	0.134456	0.193885	0.253314	0.461315	0.476172	0.485086
609	FUNCTIONS RELATED TO DEPOSITORY BANKING	7	2.56%	0.473505	0.768166	-1.060697	-0.990268	-0.872886	0.636538	0.768166	0.817449	1.322165	1.346278	1.360745
6099	Functions Related To Depository Banking, Not Elsewhere Classified	7	2.56%	0.473505	0.768166	-1.060697	-0.990268	-0.872886	0.636538	0.768166	0.817449	1.322165	1.346278	1.360745
61	NONDEPOSITORY CREDIT INSTITUTIONS	46	2.70%	0.500807	0.558672	-2.048761	-0.478134	-0.406721	0.432393	0.558672	0.725187	1.292378	1.389715	2.313128
611	FEDERAL AND FEDERALLY-SPONSORED CREDIT AGENCIES	5	0.40%	0.074783	0.041738	-0.205648	-0.203411	-0.199682	-0.042897	0.041738	0.153609	0.374486	0.381120	0.385100
6111	Federal And Federally-Sponsored Credit Agencies	5	0.40%	0.074783	0.041738	-0.205648	-0.203411	-0.199682	-0.042897	0.041738	0.153609	0.374486	0.381120	0.385100
614	PERSONAL CREDIT INSTITUTIONS	16	4.28%	0.792189	0.828470	-0.050018	0.040127	0.190368	0.725187	0.828470	0.958037	1.174750	1.288360	1.356526
6141	Personal Credit Institutions	16	4.28%	0.792189	0.828470	-0.050018	0.040127	0.190368	0.725187	0.828470	0.958037	1.174750	1.288360	1.356526
615	BUSINESS CREDIT INSTITUTIONS	12	3.96%	0.733014	0.608333	-0.430378	-0.389028	-0.320113	0.445419	0.608333	0.884354	2.093541	2.576080	2.865604
6153	Short-Term Business Credit Institutions, Except Agricultural	8	4.62%	0.855829	0.743259	-0.425178	-0.376030	-0.294116	0.427714	0.743259	1.050574	2.444479	2.751549	2.935792
6159	Miscellaneous Business Credit Institutions	4	2.63%	0.487386	0.592051	-0.188150	-0.159362	-0.111382	0.496256	0.592051	0.687845	0.939623	0.956204	0.966153
616	MORTGAGE BANKERS AND BROKERS	10	0.50%	0.092073	0.376533	-3.074920	-2.690111	-2.048761	0.258991	0.376533	0.550581	1.222638	1.240179	1.250704
6162	Mortgage Bankers And Loan Correspondents	6	2.72%	0.504444	0.574664	-0.447004	-0.395984	-0.310950	0.454251	0.574664	0.695076	1.168635	1.213178	1.239903
6163	Loan Brokers	4	-2.84%	-0.526484	0.022882	-3.239108	-3.100579	-2.869699	-0.142679	0.022882	0.188442	1.047618	1.113689	1.153332
6199	FINANCE SERVICES	3	0.49%	0.090429	-0.112341	-0.183481	-0.181303	-0.177674	-0.126859	-0.112341	0.023840	0.500472	0.534517	0.554944
62	SECURITY AND COMMODITY BROKERS, DEALERS, EXCHANGES, AND SERVICES	100	3.53%	0.653172	0.700892	-0.659562	-0.426073	-0.188898	0.538987	0.700892	0.838490	1.452563	1.489306	1.502730
621	SECURITY BROKERS, DEALERS, AND FLOTATION COMPANIES	33	3.86%	0.714925	0.807919	-1.005213	-0.757582	-0.371557	0.502207	0.807919	1.000734	1.490672	1.650558	2.024017
6211	Security Brokers, Dealers, And Flotation Companies	33	3.86%	0.714925	0.807919	-1.005213	-0.757582	-0.371557	0.502207	0.807919	1.000734	1.490672	1.650558	2.024017
622	COMMODITY CONTRACTS BROKERS AND DEALERS	2	3.50%	0.647812	0.647812	0.522412	0.526251	0.532649	0.622220	0.647812	0.673404	0.762975	0.769373	0.773212
6221	Commodity Contracts Brokers And Dealers	2	3.50%	0.647812	0.647812	0.522412	0.526251	0.532649	0.622220	0.647812	0.673404	0.762975	0.769373	0.773212
623	SECURITY AND COMMODITY EXCHANGES	6	3.14%	0.582064	0.642348	-0.019794	-0.018659	-0.016767	0.299907	0.642348	0.984789	1.159073	1.180196	1.192871
6231	Security And Commodity Exchanges	6	3.14%	0.582064	0.642348	-0.019794	-0.018659	-0.016767	0.299907	0.642348	0.984789	1.159073	1.180196	1.192871
628	SERVICES ALLIED WITH THE EXCHANGE OF SECURITIES OR COMMODITIES	59	3.38%	0.626044	0.666763	-0.419881	-0.306037	-0.189333	0.551529	0.666763	0.823672	1.225935	1.411382	1.477519
6282	Investment Advice	58	3.40%	0.630276	0.672194	-0.420471	-0.310985	-0.189768	0.575816	0.672194	0.830192	1.232393	1.414528	1.477745
6289	Services Allied With The Exchange Of Securities Or Commodities	1	2.06%	0.380611	0.380611	0.380611	0.380611	0.380611	0.380611	0.380611	0.380611	0.380611	0.380611	0.380611
63	INSURANCE CARRIERS	142	2.33%	0.431924	0.521717	-0.799344	-0.515414	-0.338211	0.423237	0.521717	0.570498	1.017451	1.178402	1.223898
631	LIFE INSURANCE	35	2.48%	0.459561	0.453217	-0.499429	-0.377907	-0.185753	0.323708	0.453217	0.537652	1.073770	1.176051	1.220594
6311	Life Insurance	35	2.48%	0.459561	0.453217	-0.499429	-0.377907	-0.185753	0.323708	0.453217	0.537652	1.073770	1.176051	1.220594
632	ACCIDENT AND HEALTH INSURANCE AND MEDICAL SERVICE PLANS	18	3.02%	0.559058	0.606330	0.018178	0.033757	0.059723	0.487085	0.606330	0.664597	0.995110	1.040350	1.067494
6321	Accident And Health Insurance	9	2.92%	0.540692	0.645422	0.012679	0.020011	0.032230	0.510724	0.645422	0.722123	1.022737	1.054163	1.073019
6324	Hospital And Medical Service Plans	9	3.12%	0.577424	0.584058	0.170217	0.180707	0.198192	0.508487	0.584058	0.619693	0.943819	0.961481	0.972078

Up-market Betas of Common Stocks by SIC Codes as of September 28, 2018

SIC Code	Description	Number of Companies	Equity Risk Premium	Mean	Median	1st Percentile	2.5th Percentile	5th Percentile	40th Percentile	50th Percentile	60th Percentile	95th Percentile	97.5th Percentile	99th Percentile
633	FIRE, MARINE, AND CASUALTY INSURANCE	73	1.99%	0.369267	0.502125	-1.086014	-0.515854	-0.414400	0.344141	0.502125	0.557123	0.971808	1.043344	1.204728
6331	Fire, Marine, And Casualty Insurance	73	1.99%	0.369267	0.502125	-1.086014	-0.515854	-0.414400	0.344141	0.502125	0.557123	0.971808	1.043344	1.204728
635	SURETY INSURANCE	8	2.77%	0.513306	0.627651	-0.749034	-0.625218	-0.418860	0.532107	0.627651	0.724014	1.091677	1.154468	1.192143
6351	Surety Insurance	8	2.77%	0.513306	0.627651	-0.749034	-0.625218	-0.418860	0.532107	0.627651	0.724014	1.091677	1.154468	1.192143
636	TITLE INSURANCE	5	2.83%	0.524608	0.602037	0.214841	0.227284	0.248023	0.526795	0.602037	0.632682	0.713231	0.717554	0.720148
6361	Title Insurance	5	2.83%	0.524608	0.602037	0.214841	0.227284	0.248023	0.526795	0.602037	0.632682	0.713231	0.717554	0.720148
637	PENSION, HEALTH, AND WELFARE FUNDS	1	5.14%	0.951580	0.951580	0.951580	0.951580	0.951580	0.951580	0.951580	0.951580	0.951580	0.951580	0.951580
6371	Pension, Health, And Welfare Funds	1	5.14%	0.951580	0.951580	0.951580	0.951580	0.951580	0.951580	0.951580	0.951580	0.951580	0.951580	0.951580
639	INSURANCE CARRIERS, NOT ELSEWHERE CLASSIFIED	2	1.48%	0.273956	0.273956	0.130162	0.134563	0.141900	0.244610	0.273956	0.303302	0.406012	0.413349	0.417750
6399	Insurance Carriers, Not Elsewhere Classified	2	1.48%	0.273956	0.273956	0.130162	0.134563	0.141900	0.244610	0.273956	0.303302	0.406012	0.413349	0.417750
64	INSURANCE AGENTS, BROKERS, AND SERVICE	14	4.27%	0.790821	0.777837	0.416718	0.451922	0.510595	0.744894	0.777837	0.822596	1.063870	1.082330	1.093406
641	INSURANCE AGENTS, BROKERS, AND SERVICE	14	4.27%	0.790821	0.777837	0.416718	0.451922	0.510595	0.744894	0.777837	0.822596	1.063870	1.082330	1.093406
6411	Insurance Agents, Brokers, And Service	14	4.27%	0.790821	0.777837	0.416718	0.451922	0.510595	0.744894	0.777837	0.822596	1.063870	1.082330	1.093406
65	REAL ESTATE	43	2.26%	0.419137	0.452211	-1.095857	-0.649589	-0.495620	0.385267	0.452211	0.581793	0.888010	1.264906	1.655768
6500	REAL ESTATE	3	3.43%	0.634847	0.262556	-0.271927	-0.255565	-0.228296	0.153478	0.262556	0.595009	1.758594	1.841707	1.891575
651	REAL ESTATE OPERATORS (EXCEPT DEVELOPERS) AND LESSORS	16	1.93%	0.356895	0.399064	-1.236017	-0.968966	-0.523883	0.337174	0.399064	0.525422	0.920058	1.102139	1.211388
6510	REAL ESTATE OPERATORS (NO DEVELOPERS) & LESSORS	2	-2.71%	-0.502240	-0.502240	-1.395814	-1.368459	-1.322869	-0.684602	-0.502240	-0.319877	0.318390	0.363980	0.391335
6512	Operators Of Nonresidential Buildings	9	3.05%	0.565612	0.525422	0.226803	0.231109	0.238286	0.415930	0.525422	0.597010	1.084764	1.184492	1.244329
6513	Operators Of Apartment Buildings	3	0.31%	0.057403	0.138644	-0.219844	-0.208870	-0.190580	0.065483	0.138644	0.163060	0.248516	0.254620	0.258282
6519	Lessors Of Real Property, Not Elsewhere Classified	2	3.92%	0.726047	0.726047	0.654874	0.657053	0.660684	0.711522	0.726047	0.740571	0.791409	0.795040	0.797219
653	REAL ESTATE AGENTS AND MANAGERS	20	2.74%	0.508203	0.595685	-0.415099	-0.258853	0.001558	0.492895	0.595685	0.621013	0.801776	0.849856	0.878704
6531	Real Estate Agents And Managers	20	2.74%	0.508203	0.595685	-0.415099	-0.258853	0.001558	0.492895	0.595685	0.621013	0.801776	0.849856	0.878704
655	LAND SUBDIVIDERS AND DEVELOPERS	4	0.33%	0.060993	0.222295	-0.633784	-0.599788	-0.543129	0.148326	0.222295	0.296263	0.439292	0.447561	0.452522
6552	Land Subdividers And Developers, Except Cemeteries	4	0.33%	0.060993	0.222295	-0.633784	-0.599788	-0.543129	0.148326	0.222295	0.296263	0.439292	0.447561	0.452522
67	HOLDING AND OTHER INVESTMENT OFFICES	242	12.72%	2.355510	0.290049	-2.258737	-1.128473	-0.705979	0.199287	0.290049	0.455110	1.255654	1.465908	2.338729
671	HOLDING OFFICES	54	2.66%	0.493289	0.642660	-1.089691	-0.443607	-0.215428	0.497982	0.642660	0.711014	1.181483	1.237653	1.558810
6712	Offices Of Bank Holding Companies	44	3.41%	0.632205	0.692954	-0.233110	-0.151710	-0.121669	0.619969	0.692954	0.734131	1.193173	1.252828	1.622944
6719	Offices Of Holding Companies, Not Elsewhere Classified	10	-0.64%	-0.117944	-0.065414	-1.626723	-1.461951	-1.187333	-0.107162	-0.065414	-0.037070	0.721872	0.807724	0.859234
672	INVESTMENT OFFICES	27	1.12%	0.207940	0.146617	-0.591593	-0.436329	-0.209633	0.119880	0.146617	0.215839	0.789140	0.956881	1.037022
6722	Management Investment Offices, Open-End	2	4.20%	0.777196	0.777196	0.470207	0.479605	0.495267	0.714545	0.777196	0.839847	1.059125	1.074787	1.084185
6726	Unit Investment Trusts, Face-Amount Certificate Offices	25	0.88%	0.162400	0.127153	-0.599555	-0.456235	-0.238752	0.114253	0.127153	0.183934	0.544944	0.693321	0.808304
673	TRUSTS	8	2.10%	0.388414	0.142761	-0.261988	-0.247931	-0.224503	-0.043436	0.142761	0.381081	1.424507	1.520474	1.578053

Up-market Betas of Common Stocks by SIC Codes as of September 28, 2018

SIC Code	Description	Number of Companies	Equity Risk Premium	Mean	Median	1st Percentile	2.5th Percentile	5th Percentile	40th Percentile	50th Percentile	60th Percentile	95th Percentile	97.5th Percentile	99th Percentile
6733	Trusts, Except Educational, Religious, And Charitable	8	2.10%	0.388414	0.142761	-0.261988	-0.247931	-0.224503	-0.043436	0.142761	0.381081	1.424507	1.520474	1.578053
6770	BLANK CHECKS	6	-0.35%	-0.064199	-0.041013	-0.337863	-0.316250	-0.280229	-0.054872	-0.041013	-0.027154	0.062828	0.065940	0.067807
679	MISCELLANEOUS INVESTING	147	19.66%	3.639859	0.293708	-3.112941	-1.544125	-1.038066	0.212872	0.293708	0.413865	1.299079	1.758830	24.923541
6794	Patent Owners And Lessors	10	0.65%	0.120798	0.469063	-1.713492	-1.622325	-1.470381	0.423786	0.469063	0.524139	1.073714	1.109752	1.131375
6798	Real Estate Investment Trusts	58	5.44%	1.006481	0.226736	-0.816869	-0.714686	-0.502302	0.186536	0.226736	0.297265	1.173501	1.267677	19.727719
6799	Investors, Not Elsewhere Classified	79	32.50%	6.018676	0.374223	-3.663040	-2.643321	-1.158327	0.238363	0.374223	0.490892	1.332120	2.299374	102.000536
	SERVICES													
70	HOTELS, ROOMING HOUSES, CAMPS, AND OTHER LODGING PLACES	29	3.09%	0.573090	0.527540	-0.143354	0.012422	0.191720	0.484014	0.527540	0.641668	1.075156	1.146727	1.214721
7000	HOTELS, ROOMING HOUSES, CAMPS & OTHER LODGING PLACES	1	2.64%	0.488998	0.488998	0.488998	0.488998	0.488998	0.488998	0.488998	0.488998	0.488998	0.488998	0.488998
701	HOTELS AND MOTELS	28	3.11%	0.576093	0.571520	-0.147063	0.003149	0.183217	0.482194	0.571520	0.644726	1.078032	1.150774	1.216340
7011	Hotels And Motels	28	3.11%	0.576093	0.571520	-0.147063	0.003149	0.183217	0.482194	0.571520	0.644726	1.078032	1.150774	1.216340
72	PERSONAL SERVICES	16	0.06%	0.010306	0.395624	-2.323129	-2.198521	-1.990843	0.196528	0.395624	0.506253	1.217303	1.574326	1.788541
7200	SERVICES-PERSONAL SERVICES	4	-0.95%	-0.175472	-0.877746	-0.877746	-0.877746	-0.877746	-0.877746	-0.877746	-0.877746	1.509986	1.720668	1.847077
721	LAUNDRY, CLEANING, AND GARMENT SERVICES	3	2.28%	0.421565	0.640854	-0.098784	-0.076142	-0.038406	0.489907	0.640854	0.660227	0.728033	0.732876	0.735782
7211	Power Laundries, Family And Commercial	1	-0.61%	-0.113879	-0.113879	-0.113879	-0.113879	-0.113879	-0.113879	-0.113879	-0.113879	-0.113879	-0.113879	-0.113879
7215	Coin-Operated Laundries And Drycleaning	1	3.98%	0.737719	0.737719	0.737719	0.737719	0.737719	0.737719	0.737719	0.737719	0.737719	0.737719	0.737719
7218	Industrial Launderers	1	3.46%	0.640854	0.640854	0.640854	0.640854	0.640854	0.640854	0.640854	0.640854	0.640854	0.640854	0.640854
723	BEAUTY SHOPS	2	2.38%	0.441033	0.441033	0.351972	0.354698	0.359242	0.422857	0.441033	0.459208	0.522823	0.527367	0.530093
7231	Beauty Shops	2	2.38%	0.441033	0.441033	0.351972	0.354698	0.359242	0.422857	0.441033	0.459208	0.522823	0.527367	0.530093
726	FUNERAL SERVICE AND CREMATORIES	2	1.90%	0.351391	0.351391	0.199625	0.204271	0.212014	0.320418	0.351391	0.382363	0.490767	0.498510	0.503156
7261	Funeral Service And Crematories	2	1.90%	0.351391	0.351391	0.199625	0.204271	0.212014	0.320418	0.351391	0.382363	0.490767	0.498510	0.503156
729	MISCELLANEOUS PERSONAL SERVICES	5	-2.14%	-0.396553	0.441093	-2.384048	-2.350819	-2.295438	-0.476300	0.441093	0.606834	0.954519	0.966903	0.974333
7299	Miscellaneous Personal Services, Not Elsewhere Classified	5	-2.14%	-0.396553	0.441093	-2.384048	-2.350819	-2.295438	-0.476300	0.441093	0.606834	0.954519	0.966903	0.974333
73	BUSINESS SERVICES	451	3.89%	0.721133	0.770907	-3.356425	-2.163680	-0.798815	0.609712	0.770907	0.915134	1.822635	2.340118	3.784660
731	ADVERTISING	18	2.54%	0.469808	0.561185	-1.036176	-0.941804	-0.784518	0.507790	0.561185	0.608301	1.386446	1.463018	1.508961
7311	Advertising Agencies	12	2.70%	0.500286	0.561185	-0.998583	-0.847823	-0.596556	0.561185	0.561185	0.702533	1.195922	1.277671	1.326720
7312	Outdoor Advertising Services	3	2.77%	0.513674	0.549538	-0.526152	-0.493223	-0.438341	0.330009	0.549538	0.747548	1.440585	1.490087	1.519789
7313	Radio, Television, And Publishers' Advertising Representatives	2	-1.05%	-0.194103	-0.194103	-0.718307	-0.702260	-0.675515	-0.301083	-0.194103	-0.087122	0.287310	0.314055	0.330102
7319	Advertising, Not Elsewhere Classified	1	7.02%	1.300290	1.300290	1.300290	1.300290	1.300290	1.300290	1.300290	1.300290	1.300290	1.300290	1.300290
732	CONSUMER CREDIT REPORTING AGENCIES, MERCANTILE REPORTING AGENCIES	9	4.25%	0.787443	0.861966	-0.008640	0.063469	0.183651	0.710158	0.861966	0.969470	1.173610	1.180740	1.185018
7320	SERVICES-CONSUMER CREDIT REPORTING, COLLECTION AGENCIES	1	6.41%	1.187870	1.187870	1.187870	1.187870	1.187870	1.187870	1.187870	1.187870	1.187870	1.187870	1.187870
7322	Adjustment And Collection Services	2	4.00%	0.741182	0.741182	0.622813	0.626436	0.632475	0.717025	0.741182	0.765338	0.849888	0.855927	0.859550
7323	Credit Reporting Services	6	3.98%	0.736126	0.834276	-0.026667	0.018401	0.093515	0.672206	0.834276	0.996346	1.141290	1.146755	1.150034
733	MAILING, REPRODUCTION, COMMERCIAL ART AND PHOTOGRAPHY, AND STENOGRAPHY	4	-2.47%	-0.458247	-0.006793	-2.890197	-2.757384	-2.536027	-0.019111	-0.006793	0.005524	0.987499	1.073420	1.124972

Up-market Betas of Common Stocks by SIC Codes as of September 28, 2018

SIC Code	Description	Number of Companies	Equity Risk Premium	Mean	Median	1st Percentile	2.5th Percentile	5th Percentile	40th Percentile	50th Percentile	60th Percentile	95th Percentile	97.5th Percentile	99th Percentile
7331	Direct Mail Advertising Services	2	3.17%	0.586538	0.586538	0.025192	0.042376	0.071016	0.471978	0.586538	0.701098	1.102060	1.130700	1.147884
7336	Commercial Art And Graphic Design	1	-16.09%	-2.978740	-2.978740	-2.978740	-2.978740	-2.978740	-2.978740	-2.978740	-2.978740	-2.978740	-2.978740	-2.978740
7338	Secretarial And Court Reporting Services	1	-0.15%	-0.027323	-0.027323	-0.027323	-0.027323	-0.027323	-0.027323	-0.027323	-0.027323	-0.027323	-0.027323	-0.027323
734	SERVICES TO DWELLINGS AND OTHER BUILDINGS	3	3.27%	0.605971	0.762877	0.170017	0.188166	0.218414	0.641885	0.762877	0.789725	0.883694	0.890406	0.894433
7342	Disinfecting And Pest Control Services	1	4.84%	0.897118	0.897118	0.897118	0.897118	0.897118	0.897118	0.897118	0.897118	0.897118	0.897118	0.897118
7349	Building Cleaning And Maintenance Services, Not Elsewhere Classified	2	2.49%	0.460398	0.460398	0.163968	0.173042	0.188166	0.399902	0.460398	0.520893	0.732629	0.747753	0.756827
735	MISCELLANEOUS EQUIPMENT RENTAL AND LEASING	19	1.86%	0.345039	0.603118	-3.524032	-2.564350	-0.964881	0.584721	0.603118	0.648530	1.292127	1.399259	1.463537
7350	SERVICES-MISCELLANEOUS EQUIPMENT RENTAL & LEASING	1	-22.48%	-4.163820	-4.163820	-4.163820	-4.163820	-4.163820	-4.163820	-4.163820	-4.163820	-4.163820	-4.163820	-4.163820
7353	Heavy Construction Equipment Rental And Leasing	1	3.29%	0.609442	0.609442	0.609442	0.609442	0.609442	0.609442	0.609442	0.609442	0.609442	0.609442	0.609442
7359	Equipment Rental And Leasing, Not Elsewhere Classified	17	3.21%	0.594713	0.603118	-0.574568	-0.522256	-0.435069	0.585095	0.603118	0.778198	1.315934	1.411162	1.468299
736	PERSONNEL SUPPLY SERVICES	24	2.96%	0.548980	0.647981	-0.462452	-0.418760	-0.334632	0.485352	0.647981	0.848092	1.162021	1.375523	1.522779
7361	Employment Agencies	5	4.55%	0.842344	0.921956	0.248375	0.262690	0.286550	0.744143	0.921956	0.934198	1.487272	1.554111	1.594214
7363	Help Supply Services	19	2.55%	0.471779	0.533973	-0.468784	-0.434591	-0.377602	0.405006	0.533973	0.797535	1.001525	1.097823	1.155601
737	COMPUTER PROGRAMMING, DATA PROCESSING, AND OTHER COMPUTER RELATED	285	3.89%	0.720695	0.849328	-3.256348	-2.348534	-0.666145	0.721721	0.849328	0.955378	1.925846	2.348777	3.040488
7370	SERVICES-COMPUTER PROGRAMMING, DATA PROCESSING, ETC.	3	4.73%	0.875083	1.363580	-0.307165	-0.256020	-0.170778	1.022612	1.363580	1.411450	1.578995	1.590963	1.598143
7371	Computer Programming Services	54	3.14%	0.581718	0.797921	-3.635069	-2.370026	-0.424347	0.644741	0.797921	0.880767	1.530171	1.591935	1.610223
7372	Prepackaged Software	136	3.54%	0.655703	0.873845	-3.324666	-2.391170	-1.217385	0.663443	0.873845	0.983371	1.998408	2.420706	2.802858
7373	Computer Integrated Systems Design	34	4.04%	0.747679	0.791277	-0.942445	-0.673653	-0.324500	0.677232	0.791277	0.902927	1.418527	1.536888	1.649233
7374	Computer Processing And Data Preparation And Processing Services	41	5.29%	0.979457	0.841722	-1.308090	-0.323011	-0.230163	0.722332	0.841722	0.915134	2.296820	3.366820	5.519122
7375	Information Retrieval Services	11	5.77%	1.068150	1.301710	-0.317312	-0.159229	0.104243	1.301710	1.301710	1.301710	1.617770	1.685950	1.726858
7376	Computer Facilities Management Services	1	14.65%	2.713670	2.713670	2.713670	2.713670	2.713670	2.713670	2.713670	2.713670	2.713670	2.713670	2.713670
7379	Computer Related Services, Not Elsewhere Classified	5	2.31%	0.428448	0.746452	-1.155604	-1.053971	-0.884582	0.636083	0.746452	0.867831	1.088956	1.093838	1.096767
738	MISCELLANEOUS BUSINESS SERVICES	89	5.13%	0.950262	0.687572	-2.384961	-1.812434	-1.145518	0.563827	0.687572	0.776358	2.142292	3.986176	7.982909
7380	SERVICES-MISCELLANEOUS BUSINESS SERVICES	1	5.47%	1.013450	1.013450	1.013450	1.013450	1.013450	1.013450	1.013450	1.013450	1.013450	1.013450	1.013450
7381	Detective, Guard, And Armored Car Services	2	3.63%	0.671640	0.671640	-1.297337	-1.237062	-1.136604	0.269808	0.671640	1.073472	2.479884	2.580342	2.640617
7382	Security Systems Services	2	6.05%	1.120618	1.120618	0.793551	0.803563	0.820250	1.053870	1.120618	1.187366	1.420986	1.437673	1.447685
7384	Photofinishing Laboratories	1	1.86%	0.344218	0.344218	0.344218	0.344218	0.344218	0.344218	0.344218	0.344218	0.344218	0.344218	0.344218
7389	Business Services, Not Elsewhere Classified	83	5.18%	0.959411	0.687139	-2.462456	-1.891901	-0.851644	0.556396	0.687139	0.771167	1.909748	4.211441	9.650008
75	AUTOMOTIVE REPAIR, SERVICES, AND PARKING	6	4.03%	0.746234	0.799108	0.227966	0.253311	0.295554	0.608315	0.799108	0.989901	1.078078	1.087339	1.092896
751	AUTOMOTIVE RENTAL AND LEASING, WITHOUT DRIVERS	4	3.74%	0.693122	0.769455	0.221207	0.236414	0.261760	0.637187	0.769455	0.901722	1.017619	1.020064	1.021532

Up-market Betas of Common Stocks by SIC Codes as of September 28, 2018

SIC Code	Description	Number of Companies	Equity Risk Premium	Mean	Median	1st Percentile	2.5th Percentile	5th Percentile	40th Percentile	50th Percentile	60th Percentile	95th Percentile	97.5th Percentile	99th Percentile
7510	SERVICES-AUTO RENTAL & LEASING (NO DRIVERS)	1	1.14%	0.211069	0.211069	0.211069	0.211069	0.211069	0.211069	0.211069	0.211069	0.211069	0.211069	0.211069
7513	Truck Rental And Leasing, Without Drivers	2	4.24%	0.785759	0.785759	0.553743	0.560846	0.572683	0.738409	0.785759	0.833109	0.998835	1.010672	1.017775
7514	Passenger Car Rental	1	5.35%	0.989901	0.989901	0.989901	0.989901	0.989901	0.989901	0.989901	0.989901	0.989901	0.989901	0.989901
753	AUTOMOTIVE REPAIR SHOPS	1	5.92%	1.096600	1.096600	1.096600	1.096600	1.096600	1.096600	1.096600	1.096600	1.096600	1.096600	1.096600
7538	General Automotive Repair Shops	1	5.92%	1.096600	1.096600	1.096600	1.096600	1.096600	1.096600	1.096600	1.096600	1.096600	1.096600	1.096600
754	AUTOMOTIVE SERVICES, EXCEPT REPAIR	1	3.28%	0.608315	0.608315	0.608315	0.608315	0.608315	0.608315	0.608315	0.608315	0.608315	0.608315	0.608315
7542	Carwashes	1	3.28%	0.608315	0.608315	0.608315	0.608315	0.608315	0.608315	0.608315	0.608315	0.608315	0.608315	0.608315
76	MISCELLANEOUS REPAIR SERVICES	2	-1.24%	-0.228819	-0.228819	-0.772914	-0.756258	-0.728498	-0.339858	-0.228819	-0.117779	0.270861	0.298621	0.315277
762	ELECTRICAL REPAIR SHOPS	2	-1.24%	-0.228819	-0.228819	-0.772914	-0.756258	-0.728498	-0.339858	-0.228819	-0.117779	0.270861	0.298621	0.315277
7623	Refrigeration And Air-Conditioning Service And Repair Shops	2	-1.24%	-0.228819	-0.228819	-0.772914	-0.756258	-0.728498	-0.339858	-0.228819	-0.117779	0.270861	0.298621	0.315277
78	MOTION PICTURES	18	5.01%	0.928612	0.844301	-0.152299	-0.144821	-0.132356	0.643632	0.844301	0.870901	2.718516	3.177873	3.453487
781	MOTION PICTURE PRODUCTION AND ALLIED SERVICES	13	4.61%	0.852823	0.870901	-0.153766	-0.148487	-0.139688	0.348011	0.870901	0.870901	2.988726	3.312978	3.507529
7812	Motion Picture And Video Tape Production	11	5.50%	1.018525	0.870901	-0.103868	-0.067734	-0.007510	0.870901	0.870901	0.870901	3.096810	3.367020	3.529146
7819	Services Allied To Motion Picture Production	2	-0.32%	-0.058539	-0.058539	-0.155310	-0.152348	-0.147410	-0.078289	-0.058539	-0.038790	0.030332	0.035269	0.038231
782	MOTION PICTURE DISTRIBUTION AND ALLIED SERVICES	1	8.99%	1.665480	1.665480	1.665480	1.665480	1.665480	1.665480	1.665480	1.665480	1.665480	1.665480	1.665480
7822	Motion Picture And Video Tape Distribution	1	8.99%	1.665480	1.665480	1.665480	1.665480	1.665480	1.665480	1.665480	1.665480	1.665480	1.665480	1.665480
783	MOTION PICTURE THEATERS	3	3.45%	0.639460	0.705827	0.401071	0.410400	0.425949	0.643632	0.705827	0.728202	0.806514	0.812107	0.815464
7832	Motion Picture Theaters, Except Drive-In	3	3.45%	0.639460	0.705827	0.401071	0.410400	0.425949	0.643632	0.705827	0.728202	0.806514	0.812107	0.815464
784	VIDEO TAPE RENTAL	1	11.04%	2.044460	2.044460	2.044460	2.044460	2.044460	2.044460	2.044460	2.044460	2.044460	2.044460	2.044460
7841	Video Tape Rental	1	11.04%	2.044460	2.044460	2.044460	2.044460	2.044460	2.044460	2.044460	2.044460	2.044460	2.044460	2.044460
79	AMUSEMENT AND RECREATION SERVICES	33	2.59%	0.480132	0.314301	-2.652977	-2.253252	-1.852736	0.220336	0.314301	0.548968	2.903640	4.538850	5.738946
7900	SERVICES-AMUSEMENT & RECREATION SERVICES	3	3.97%	0.735673	2.146860	-2.002029	-1.875022	-1.663344	1.300148	2.146860	2.146860	2.146860	2.146860	2.146860
792	THEATRICAL PRODUCERS (EXCEPT MOTION PICTURE), BANDS, ORCHESTRAS	3	3.12%	0.578094	0.548333	0.137641	0.150214	0.171167	0.464518	0.548333	0.650004	1.005854	1.031272	1.046523
7922	Theatrical Producers (Except Motion Picture) And Miscellaneous Theater	2	3.20%	0.592975	0.592975	0.138534	0.152446	0.175632	0.500232	0.592975	0.685718	1.010319	1.033504	1.047416
7929	Bands, Orchestras, Actors, And Other Entertainers And Entertainment	1	2.96%	0.548333	0.548333	0.548333	0.548333	0.548333	0.548333	0.548333	0.548333	0.548333	0.548333	0.548333
793	BOWLING CENTERS	1	0.06%	0.010196	0.010196	0.010196	0.010196	0.010196	0.010196	0.010196	0.010196	0.010196	0.010196	0.010196
7933	Bowling Centers	1	0.06%	0.010196	0.010196	0.010196	0.010196	0.010196	0.010196	0.010196	0.010196	0.010196	0.010196	0.010196
794	COMMERCIAL SPORTS	8	-0.06%	-0.011096	0.250745	-1.611610	-1.483884	-1.271008	0.220336	0.250745	0.274065	0.562620	0.565217	0.566775
7941	Professional Sports Clubs And Promoters	2	-3.95%	-0.732222	-0.732222	-1.677469	-1.648533	-1.600306	-0.925129	-0.732222	-0.539314	0.135863	0.184090	0.213026
7948	Racing, Including Track Operation	6	1.24%	0.229280	0.281404	-0.447690	-0.398735	-0.317143	0.269173	0.281404	0.293634	0.564104	0.565959	0.567072
799	MISCELLANEOUS AMUSEMENT AND RECREATION SERVICES	18	3.59%	0.665645	0.412213	-2.669849	-2.295433	-1.671405	0.265820	0.412213	0.573048	4.413840	5.476425	6.113976
7990	SERVICES-MISCELLANEOUS AMUSEMENT & RECREATION	3	5.20%	0.963210	1.770280	-2.825665	-2.684973	-2.450486	0.832332	1.770280	2.223986	3.811957	3.925384	3.993439

Up-market Betas of Common Stocks by SIC Codes as of September 28, 2018

SIC Code	Description	Number of Companies	Equity Risk Premium	Mean	Median	1st Percentile	2.5th Percentile	5th Percentile	40th Percentile	50th Percentile	60th Percentile	95th Percentile	97.5th Percentile	99th Percentile
7993	Coin-Operated Amusement Devices	1	-1.46%	-0.269549	-0.269549	-0.269549	-0.269549	-0.269549	-0.269549	-0.269549	-0.269549	-0.269549	-0.269549	-0.269549
7996	Amusement Parks	3	2.48%	0.458644	0.421873	0.402938	0.403518	0.404484	0.418009	0.421873	0.447800	0.538544	0.545025	0.548914
7997	Membership Sports And Recreation Clubs	3	4.48%	0.829073	0.701388	0.660055	0.661320	0.663429	0.692953	0.701388	0.786434	1.084097	1.105358	1.118115
7999	Amusement And Recreation Services, Not Elsewhere Classified	8	3.71%	0.687297	-0.016811	-1.386148	-1.288629	-1.126098	-0.162418	-0.016811	0.120377	4.615155	5.577082	6.154239
80	HEALTH SERVICES	80	2.43%	0.449235	0.628480	-4.843223	-1.166319	-0.554410	0.483014	0.628480	0.689237	2.392608	2.712111	2.925121
801	OFFICES AND CLINICS OF DOCTORS OF MEDICINE	15	5.07%	0.938883	0.899953	-0.012668	0.008611	0.044076	0.726153	0.899953	0.941647	2.162527	2.274874	2.342281
8011	Offices And Clinics Of Doctors Of Medicine	15	5.07%	0.938883	0.899953	-0.012668	0.008611	0.044076	0.726153	0.899953	0.941647	2.162527	2.274874	2.342281
804	OFFICES AND CLINICS OF OTHER HEALTH PRACTITIONERS	1	2.99%	0.553273	0.553273	0.553273	0.553273	0.553273	0.553273	0.553273	0.553273	0.553273	0.553273	0.553273
8041	Offices And Clinics Of Chiropractors	1	2.99%	0.553273	0.553273	0.553273	0.553273	0.553273	0.553273	0.553273	0.553273	0.553273	0.553273	0.553273
805	NURSING AND PERSONAL CARE FACILITIES	8	2.16%	0.400448	0.351188	-0.385443	-0.352738	-0.298229	0.220763	0.351188	0.478334	1.285502	1.432946	1.521412
8051	Skilled Nursing Care Facilities	8	2.16%	0.400448	0.351188	-0.385443	-0.352738	-0.298229	0.220763	0.351188	0.478334	1.285502	1.432946	1.521412
806	HOSPITALS	16	-2.97%	-0.549924	0.441879	-14.729290	-10.971024	-4.707248	0.279206	0.441879	0.588538	2.333563	2.521246	2.633857
8062	General Medical And Surgical Hospitals	11	2.92%	0.540056	0.588538	-0.360267	-0.354963	-0.346123	0.465321	0.588538	0.602699	1.557728	1.883084	2.078298
8069	Specialty Hospitals, Except Psychiatric	5	-15.92%	-2.947881	-0.100576	-16.566664	-15.564460	-13.894119	-0.272904	-0.100576	0.107029	2.250831	2.479881	2.617310
807	MEDICAL AND DENTAL LABORATORIES	18	3.63%	0.671462	0.710637	-0.854479	-0.648700	-0.305735	0.686289	0.710637	0.811534	1.387359	1.467710	1.515920
8071	Medical Laboratories	18	3.63%	0.671462	0.710637	-0.854479	-0.648700	-0.305735	0.686289	0.710637	0.811534	1.387359	1.467710	1.515920
808	HOME HEALTH CARE SERVICES	7	3.81%	0.706275	0.659415	-0.174714	-0.125095	-0.042396	0.646972	0.659415	0.756535	1.518407	1.648909	1.727209
8082	Home Health Care Services	7	3.81%	0.706275	0.659415	-0.174714	-0.125095	-0.042396	0.646972	0.659415	0.756535	1.518407	1.648909	1.727209
809	MISCELLANEOUS HEALTH AND ALLIED SERVICES, NOT ELSEWHERE CLASSIFIED	15	3.55%	0.657819	0.494809	-1.494274	-1.411794	-1.274328	0.222237	0.494809	0.553435	2.963239	3.111475	3.200416
8090	SERVICES-MISC HEALTH & ALLIED SERVICES, NEC	1	0.65%	0.119745	0.119745	0.119745	0.119745	0.119745	0.119745	0.119745	0.119745	0.119745	0.119745	0.119745
8093	Specialty Outpatient Facilities, Not Elsewhere Classified	6	6.88%	1.273203	0.572502	0.116899	0.130610	0.153461	0.494809	0.572502	0.650194	3.153828	3.206769	3.238534
8099	Health And Allied Services, Not Elsewhere Classified	8	1.42%	0.263540	0.140996	-1.521767	-1.480527	-1.411794	-0.264502	0.140996	0.546405	2.236180	2.365575	2.443212
81	LEGAL SERVICES	1	4.96%	0.919293	0.919293	0.919293	0.919293	0.919293	0.919293	0.919293	0.919293	0.919293	0.919293	0.919293
811	LEGAL SERVICES	1	4.96%	0.919293	0.919293	0.919293	0.919293	0.919293	0.919293	0.919293	0.919293	0.919293	0.919293	0.919293
8111	Legal Services	1	4.96%	0.919293	0.919293	0.919293	0.919293	0.919293	0.919293	0.919293	0.919293	0.919293	0.919293	0.919293
82	EDUCATIONAL SERVICES	15	2.53%	0.468715	0.580378	-0.771558	-0.568252	-0.229409	0.465132	0.580378	0.592960	1.049961	1.052611	1.054200
8200	SERVICES-EDUCATIONAL SERVICES	3	3.66%	0.676956	0.847351	0.278555	0.295967	0.324987	0.731270	0.847351	0.861195	0.909648	0.913109	0.915186
821	ELEMENTARY AND SECONDARY SCHOOLS	4	2.45%	0.454372	0.335336	0.100327	0.102126	0.105124	0.217594	0.335336	0.453077	0.970272	1.008981	1.032206
8211	Elementary And Secondary Schools	4	2.45%	0.454372	0.335336	0.100327	0.102126	0.105124	0.217594	0.335336	0.453077	0.970272	1.008981	1.032206
822	COLLEGES, UNIVERSITIES, PROFESSIONAL SCHOOLS, AND JUNIOR COLLEGES	3	3.60%	0.667037	0.580378	0.369771	0.376218	0.386964	0.537397	0.580378	0.675354	1.007772	1.031516	1.045762
8221	Colleges, Universities, And Professional Schools	3	3.60%	0.667037	0.580378	0.369771	0.376218	0.386964	0.537397	0.580378	0.675354	1.007772	1.031516	1.045762
823	LIBRARIES	1	3.21%	0.593816	0.593816	0.593816	0.593816	0.593816	0.593816	0.593816	0.593816	0.593816	0.593816	0.593816
8231	Libraries	1	3.21%	0.593816	0.593816	0.593816	0.593816	0.593816	0.593816	0.593816	0.593816	0.593816	0.593816	0.593816

Up-market Betas of Common Stocks by SIC Codes as of September 28, 2018

SIC Code	Description	Number of Companies	Equity Risk Premium	Mean	Median	1st Percentile	2.5th Percentile	5th Percentile	40th Percentile	50th Percentile	60th Percentile	95th Percentile	97.5th Percentile	99th Percentile
824	VOCATIONAL SCHOOLS	3	-0.01%	-0.001648	0.061027	-0.887733	-0.858689	-0.810283	-0.132597	0.061027	0.217046	0.763113	0.802118	0.825521
8249	Vocational Schools, Not Elsewhere Classified	3	-0.01%	-0.001648	0.061027	-0.887733	-0.858689	-0.810283	-0.132597	0.061027	0.217046	0.763113	0.802118	0.825521
829	SCHOOLS AND EDUCATIONAL SERVICES, NOT ELSEWHERE CLASSIFIED	1	3.20%	0.592389	0.592389	0.592389	0.592389	0.592389	0.592389	0.592389	0.592389	0.592389	0.592389	0.592389
8299	Schools And Educational Services, Not Elsewhere Classified	1	3.20%	0.592389	0.592389	0.592389	0.592389	0.592389	0.592389	0.592389	0.592389	0.592389	0.592389	0.592389
83	SOCIAL SERVICES	4	2.78%	0.515240	0.499048	-0.401329	-0.364704	-0.303664	0.432498	0.499048	0.565598	1.356813	1.422712	1.462251
832	INDIVIDUAL AND FAMILY SOCIAL SERVICES	1	2.10%	0.388131	0.388131	0.388131	0.388131	0.388131	0.388131	0.388131	0.388131	0.388131	0.388131	0.388131
8322	Individual And Family Social Services	1	2.10%	0.388131	0.388131	0.388131	0.388131	0.388131	0.388131	0.388131	0.388131	0.388131	0.388131	0.388131
833	JOB TRAINING AND VOCATIONAL REHABILITATION SERVICES	1	8.04%	1.488610	1.488610	1.488610	1.488610	1.488610	1.488610	1.488610	1.488610	1.488610	1.488610	1.488610
8331	Job Training And Vocational Rehabilitation Services	1	8.04%	1.488610	1.488610	1.488610	1.488610	1.488610	1.488610	1.488610	1.488610	1.488610	1.488610	1.488610
835	CHILD DAY CARE SERVICES	1	3.29%	0.609965	0.609965	0.609965	0.609965	0.609965	0.609965	0.609965	0.609965	0.609965	0.609965	0.609965
8351	Child Day Care Services	1	3.29%	0.609965	0.609965	0.609965	0.609965	0.609965	0.609965	0.609965	0.609965	0.609965	0.609965	0.609965
836	RESIDENTIAL CARE	1	-2.30%	-0.425745	-0.425745	-0.425745	-0.425745	-0.425745	-0.425745	-0.425745	-0.425745	-0.425745	-0.425745	-0.425745
8361	Residential Care	1	-2.30%	-0.425745	-0.425745	-0.425745	-0.425745	-0.425745	-0.425745	-0.425745	-0.425745	-0.425745	-0.425745	-0.425745
87	ENGINEERING, ACCOUNTING, RESEARCH, MANAGEMENT, AND RELATED SERVICES	167	3.57%	0.660722	0.673437	-1.612568	-1.240508	-0.824722	0.514495	0.673437	0.764131	1.901188	2.564264	2.797974
871	ENGINEERING, ARCHITECTURAL, AND SURVEYING SERVICES	19	4.37%	0.808733	0.734194	-0.433215	-0.210808	0.159872	0.636530	0.734194	0.892030	1.757223	1.850072	1.905781
8711	Engineering Services	19	4.37%	0.808733	0.734194	-0.433215	-0.210808	0.159872	0.636530	0.734194	0.892030	1.757223	1.850072	1.905781
872	ACCOUNTING, AUDITING, AND BOOKKEEPING SERVICES	4	4.44%	0.821411	0.820772	0.448216	0.454692	0.465485	0.680990	0.820772	0.960553	1.178231	1.189216	1.195806
8721	Accounting, Auditing, And Bookkeeping Services	4	4.44%	0.821411	0.820772	0.448216	0.454692	0.465485	0.680990	0.820772	0.960553	1.178231	1.189216	1.195806
873	RESEARCH, DEVELOPMENT, AND TESTING SERVICES	95	3.59%	0.664670	0.716983	-2.043032	-1.295195	-0.893044	0.477182	0.716983	0.928519	2.003143	2.493242	2.687631
8731	Commercial Physical And Biological Research	79	3.54%	0.655182	0.736160	-2.179359	-1.393116	-1.069315	0.428659	0.736160	0.965568	2.206611	2.621028	2.688007
8732	Commercial Economic, Sociological, And Educational Research	8	3.55%	0.656533	0.638999	-0.477260	-0.389949	-0.244431	0.572618	0.638999	0.703762	1.605896	1.762248	1.856059
8733	Noncommercial Research Organizations	6	4.35%	0.805166	0.603969	0.279884	0.281429	0.284005	0.431977	0.603969	0.775960	1.542583	1.552686	1.558749
8734	Testing Laboratories	2	3.51%	0.650502	0.650502	0.573053	0.575424	0.579375	0.634696	0.650502	0.666308	0.721629	0.725581	0.727951
874	MANAGEMENT AND PUBLIC RELATIONS SERVICES	49	3.15%	0.582560	0.656083	-1.338176	-1.179029	-0.861089	0.459780	0.656083	0.702105	1.768888	2.760624	4.638740
8741	Management Services	12	2.66%	0.491950	0.688048	-0.193911	-0.175852	-0.145753	0.513829	0.688048	0.700637	0.905654	0.944879	0.968414
8742	Management Consulting Services	33	3.15%	0.583869	0.565253	-1.364500	-1.285526	-1.031848	0.441280	0.565253	0.676169	2.266112	3.635134	5.140544
8743	Public Relations Services	1	5.83%	1.079320	1.079320	1.079320	1.079320	1.079320	1.079320	1.079320	1.079320	1.079320	1.079320	1.079320
8744	Facilities Support Management Services	1	-1.43%	-0.265568	-0.265568	-0.265568	-0.265568	-0.265568	-0.265568	-0.265568	-0.265568	-0.265568	-0.265568	-0.265568
8748	Business Consulting Services, Not Elsewhere Classified	2	6.91%	1.280305	1.280305	1.155301	1.159128	1.165506	1.254794	1.280305	1.305816	1.395105	1.401482	1.405309
88	PRIVATE HOUSEHOLDS	3	0.91%	0.168540	0.146599	0.087079	0.088901	0.091938	0.134452	0.146599	0.171910	0.260500	0.266828	0.270625
8880	AMERICAN DEPOSITARY RECEIPTS	3	0.91%	0.168540	0.146599	0.087079	0.088901	0.091938	0.134452	0.146599	0.171910	0.260500	0.266828	0.270625
89	SERVICES, NOT ELSEWHERE CLASSIFIED	15	3.03%	0.560528	0.409431	-2.489241	-2.460579	-2.412807	0.313553	0.409431	0.549673	3.891494	5.493052	6.453987

Up-market Betas of Common Stocks by SIC Codes as of September 28, 2018

SIC Code	Description	Number of Companies	Equity Risk Premium	Mean	Median	1st Percentile	2.5th Percentile	5th Percentile	40th Percentile	50th Percentile	60th Percentile	95th Percentile	97.5th Percentile	99th Percentile
899	SERVICES, NOT ELSEWHERE CLASSIFIED	15	3.03%	0.560528	0.409431	-2.489241	-2.460579	-2.412807	0.313553	0.409431	0.549673	3.891494	5.493052	6.453987
8999	Services, Not Elsewhere Classified	15	3.03%	0.560528	0.409431	-2.489241	-2.460579	-2.412807	0.313553	0.409431	0.549673	3.891494	5.493052	6.453987
	PUBLIC ADMINISTRATION													
94	ADMINISTRATION OF HUMAN RESOURCE PROGRAMS	1	2.74%	0.506904	0.506904	0.506904	0.506904	0.506904	0.506904	0.506904	0.506904	0.506904	0.506904	0.506904
943	ADMINISTRATION OF PUBLIC HEALTH PROGRAMS	1	2.74%	0.506904	0.506904	0.506904	0.506904	0.506904	0.506904	0.506904	0.506904	0.506904	0.506904	0.506904
9431	Administration Of Public Health Programs	1	2.74%	0.506904	0.506904	0.506904	0.506904	0.506904	0.506904	0.506904	0.506904	0.506904	0.506904	0.506904
96	ADMINISTRATION OF ECONOMIC PROGRAMS	2	8.13%	1.505193	1.505193	0.665953	0.691644	0.734463	1.333920	1.505193	1.676466	2.275923	2.318742	2.344433
961	ADMINISTRATION OF GENERAL ECONOMIC PROGRAMS	1	3.50%	0.648826	0.648826	0.648826	0.648826	0.648826	0.648826	0.648826	0.648826	0.648826	0.648826	0.648826
9611	Administration Of General Economic Programs	1	3.50%	0.648826	0.648826	0.648826	0.648826	0.648826	0.648826	0.648826	0.648826	0.648826	0.648826	0.648826
963	REGULATION AND ADMINISTRATION OF COMMUNICATIONS, ELECTRIC, GAS	1	12.75%	2.361560	2.361560	2.361560	2.361560	2.361560	2.361560	2.361560	2.361560	2.361560	2.361560	2.361560
9631	Regulation And Administration Of Communications, Electric, Gas	1	12.75%	2.361560	2.361560	2.361560	2.361560	2.361560	2.361560	2.361560	2.361560	2.361560	2.361560	2.361560
	NONCLASSIFIABLE ESTABLISHMENTS													
99	NONCLASSIFIABLE ESTABLISHMENTS	70	1.64%	0.303110	0.241506	-6.159588	-3.716408	-2.460346	0.172348	0.241506	0.394862	2.725568	4.781958	7.637076
999	NONCLASSIFIABLE ESTABLISHMENTS	70	1.64%	0.303110	0.241506	-6.159588	-3.716408	-2.460346	0.172348	0.241506	0.394862	2.725568	4.781958	7.637076
9995	NON-OPERATING ESTABLISHMENTS	2	5.03%	0.931323	0.931323	0.546617	0.558394	0.578022	0.852812	0.931323	1.009834	1.284624	1.304252	1.316029
9999	Nonclassifiable Establishments	68	1.54%	0.284633	0.235175	-6.259193	-3.778430	-2.537447	0.136624	0.235175	0.343387	2.740853	4.787074	7.816491

Preferred Stocks by SIC Codes

Betas of Preferred Stocks by SIC Codes as of September 28, 2018

Details:
Benchmark: S&P 500 Index
Returns period and frequency: 1 year of daily returns
Risk-free rate for betas: Federal Funds Rate
Expected US Equity Risk Premium: 5.40% (Fernandez, Pablo and Pershin, Vitaly and Fernández Acín, Isabel, Market Risk Premium and Risk-Free Rate used for 59 Countries in 2018: A Survey (April 3, 2018). Available at SSRN: https://ssrn.com/abstract=3155709)

SIC Code	Description	Number of Companies	Equity Risk Premium	Mean	Median	1st Percentile	2.5th Percentile	5th Percentile	40th Percentile	50th Percentile	60th Percentile	95th Percentile	97.5th Percentile	99th Percentile
	MINING													
13	OIL AND GAS EXTRACTION	3	0.80%	0.147481	0.029049	-0.037830	-0.035782	-0.032370	0.015400	0.029049	0.113757	0.410236	0.431413	0.444119
131	CRUDE PETROLEUM AND NATURAL GAS	2	1.30%	0.240819	0.240819	0.033284	0.039637	0.050226	0.198465	0.240819	0.283173	0.431413	0.442001	0.448355
1311	Crude Petroleum And Natural Gas	2	1.30%	0.240819	0.240819	0.033284	0.039637	0.050226	0.198465	0.240819	0.283173	0.431413	0.442001	0.448355
132	NATURAL GAS LIQUIDS	1	-0.21%	-0.039195	-0.039195	-0.039195	-0.039195	-0.039195	-0.039195	-0.039195	-0.039195	-0.039195	-0.039195	-0.039195
1321	Natural Gas Liquids	1	-0.21%	-0.039195	-0.039195	-0.039195	-0.039195	-0.039195	-0.039195	-0.039195	-0.039195	-0.039195	-0.039195	-0.039195
	CONSTRUCTION													
15	CONSTRUCTION	1	3.06%	0.566261	0.566261	0.566261	0.566261	0.566261	0.566261	0.566261	0.566261	0.566261	0.566261	0.566261
153	OPERATIVE BUILDERS	1	3.06%	0.566261	0.566261	0.566261	0.566261	0.566261	0.566261	0.566261	0.566261	0.566261	0.566261	0.566261
1531	Operative Builders	1	3.06%	0.566261	0.566261	0.566261	0.566261	0.566261	0.566261	0.566261	0.566261	0.566261	0.566261	0.566261
	MANUFACTURING													
20	FOOD AND KINDRED PRODUCTS	1	0.53%	0.098197	0.098197	0.098197	0.098197	0.098197	0.098197	0.098197	0.098197	0.098197	0.098197	0.098197
207	FATS AND OILS	1	0.53%	0.098197	0.098197	0.098197	0.098197	0.098197	0.098197	0.098197	0.098197	0.098197	0.098197	0.098197
2075	Soybean Oil Mills	1	0.53%	0.098197	0.098197	0.098197	0.098197	0.098197	0.098197	0.098197	0.098197	0.098197	0.098197	0.098197
28	CHEMICALS AND ALLIED PRODUCTS	4	1.75%	0.324698	0.111734	0.044087	0.047107	0.052139	0.110196	0.111734	0.113272	0.895407	0.964329	1.005681
282	PLASTICS MATERIALS AND SYNTHETIC RESINS, SYNTHETIC RUBBER, CELLULOSIC MANMADE FIBERS	1	5.58%	1.033250	1.033250	1.033250	1.033250	1.033250	1.033250	1.033250	1.033250	1.033250	1.033250	1.033250
2821	Plastics Materials, Synthetic Resins, And Nonvulcanizable Elastomers	1	5.58%	1.033250	1.033250	1.033250	1.033250	1.033250	1.033250	1.033250	1.033250	1.033250	1.033250	1.033250
283	DRUGS	1	0.23%	0.042074	0.042074	0.042074	0.042074	0.042074	0.042074	0.042074	0.042074	0.042074	0.042074	0.042074
2834	Pharmaceutical Preparations	1	0.23%	0.042074	0.042074	0.042074	0.042074	0.042074	0.042074	0.042074	0.042074	0.042074	0.042074	0.042074
287	AGRICULTURAL CHEMICALS	2	0.60%	0.111734	0.111734	0.109222	0.109299	0.109427	0.111221	0.111734	0.112247	0.114041	0.114169	0.114246
2879	Pesticides And Agricultural Chemicals, Not Elsewhere Classified	2	0.60%	0.111734	0.111734	0.109222	0.109299	0.109427	0.111221	0.111734	0.112247	0.114041	0.114169	0.114246
29	PETROLEUM REFINING AND RELATED INDUSTRIES	1	5.83%	1.079830	1.079830	1.079830	1.079830	1.079830	1.079830	1.079830	1.079830	1.079830	1.079830	1.079830
291	PETROLEUM REFINING	1	5.83%	1.079830	1.079830	1.079830	1.079830	1.079830	1.079830	1.079830	1.079830	1.079830	1.079830	1.079830
2911	Petroleum Refining	1	5.83%	1.079830	1.079830	1.079830	1.079830	1.079830	1.079830	1.079830	1.079830	1.079830	1.079830	1.079830
33	PRIMARY METAL INDUSTRIES	1	4.15%	0.769053	0.769053	0.769053	0.769053	0.769053	0.769053	0.769053	0.769053	0.769053	0.769053	0.769053
331	STEEL WORKS, BLAST FURNACES, AND ROLLING AND FINISHING MILLS	1	4.15%	0.769053	0.769053	0.769053	0.769053	0.769053	0.769053	0.769053	0.769053	0.769053	0.769053	0.769053
3312	Steel Works, Blast Furnaces (Including Coke Ovens), And Rolling Mills	1	4.15%	0.769053	0.769053	0.769053	0.769053	0.769053	0.769053	0.769053	0.769053	0.769053	0.769053	0.769053
34	FABRICATED METAL PRODUCTS, EXCEPT MACHINERY AND TRANSPORTATION EQUIPMENT	1	0.01%	0.001923	0.001923	0.001923	0.001923	0.001923	0.001923	0.001923	0.001923	0.001923	0.001923	0.001923
341	METAL CANS AND SHIPPING CONTAINERS	1	0.01%	0.001923	0.001923	0.001923	0.001923	0.001923	0.001923	0.001923	0.001923	0.001923	0.001923	0.001923
3412	Metal Shipping Barrels, Drums, Kegs, And Pails	1	0.01%	0.001923	0.001923	0.001923	0.001923	0.001923	0.001923	0.001923	0.001923	0.001923	0.001923	0.001923

Betas of Preferred Stocks by SIC Codes as of September 28, 2018

SIC Code	Description	Number of Companies	Equity Risk Premium	Mean	Median	1st Percentile	2.5th Percentile	5th Percentile	40th Percentile	50th Percentile	60th Percentile	95th Percentile	97.5th Percentile	99th Percentile
37	TRANSPORTATION EQUIPMENT	1	4.24%	0.784821	0.784821	0.784821	0.784821	0.784821	0.784821	0.784821	0.784821	0.784821	0.784821	0.784821
371	MOTOR VEHICLES AND MOTOR VEHICLE EQUIPMENT	1	4.24%	0.784821	0.784821	0.784821	0.784821	0.784821	0.784821	0.784821	0.784821	0.784821	0.784821	0.784821
3711	Motor Vehicles And Passenger Car Bodies	1	4.24%	0.784821	0.784821	0.784821	0.784821	0.784821	0.784821	0.784821	0.784821	0.784821	0.784821	0.784821
	TRANSPORTATION, COMMUNICATIONS, ELECTRIC, GAS, AND SANITARY SERVICE													
40	RAILROAD TRANSPORTATION	1	-0.41%	-0.075974	-0.075974	-0.075974	-0.075974	-0.075974	-0.075974	-0.075974	-0.075974	-0.075974	-0.075974	-0.075974
401	RAILROADS	1	-0.41%	-0.075974	-0.075974	-0.075974	-0.075974	-0.075974	-0.075974	-0.075974	-0.075974	-0.075974	-0.075974	-0.075974
4011	Railroads, Line-Haul Operating	1	-0.41%	-0.075974	-0.075974	-0.075974	-0.075974	-0.075974	-0.075974	-0.075974	-0.075974	-0.075974	-0.075974	-0.075974
44	WATER TRANSPORTATION	13	0.56%	0.102827	0.080488	-0.020743	-0.019360	-0.017055	0.052640	0.080488	0.116585	0.263312	0.289789	0.305676
441	DEEP SEA FOREIGN TRANSPORTATION OF FREIGHT	12	0.53%	0.098167	0.067229	-0.020819	-0.019552	-0.017439	0.049980	0.067229	0.096293	0.267725	0.291996	0.306559
4412	Deep Sea Foreign Transportation Of Freight	12	0.53%	0.098167	0.067229	-0.020819	-0.019552	-0.017439	0.049980	0.067229	0.096293	0.267725	0.291996	0.306559
449	SERVICES INCIDENTAL TO WATER TRANSPORTATION	1	0.86%	0.158749	0.158749	0.158749	0.158749	0.158749	0.158749	0.158749	0.158749	0.158749	0.158749	0.158749
4499	Water Transportation Services, Not Elsewhere Classified	1	0.86%	0.158749	0.158749	0.158749	0.158749	0.158749	0.158749	0.158749	0.158749	0.158749	0.158749	0.158749
45	TRANSPORTATION BY AIR	2	3.17%	0.587450	0.587450	0.277759	0.287240	0.303040	0.524247	0.587450	0.650652	0.871859	0.887659	0.897140
451	AIR TRANSPORTATION, SCHEDULED, AND AIR COURIER SERVICES	2	3.17%	0.587450	0.587450	0.277759	0.287240	0.303040	0.524247	0.587450	0.650652	0.871859	0.887659	0.897140
4512	Air Transportation, Scheduled	2	3.17%	0.587450	0.587450	0.277759	0.287240	0.303040	0.524247	0.587450	0.650652	0.871859	0.887659	0.897140
47	TRANSPORTATION SERVICES	1	-0.03%	-0.006220	-0.006220	-0.006220	-0.006220	-0.006220	-0.006220	-0.006220	-0.006220	-0.006220	-0.006220	-0.006220
473	ARRANGEMENT OF TRANSPORTATION OF FREIGHT AND CARGO	1	-0.03%	-0.006220	-0.006220	-0.006220	-0.006220	-0.006220	-0.006220	-0.006220	-0.006220	-0.006220	-0.006220	-0.006220
4731	Arrangement Of Transportation Of Freight And Cargo	1	-0.03%	-0.006220	-0.006220	-0.006220	-0.006220	-0.006220	-0.006220	-0.006220	-0.006220	-0.006220	-0.006220	-0.006220
48	COMMUNICATIONS	2	0.52%	0.096579	0.096579	0.026143	0.028299	0.031893	0.082204	0.096579	0.110954	0.161265	0.164858	0.167015
481	TELEPHONE COMMUNICATIONS	1	0.13%	0.024706	0.024706	0.024706	0.024706	0.024706	0.024706	0.024706	0.024706	0.024706	0.024706	0.024706
4813	Telephone Communications, Except Radiotelephone	1	0.13%	0.024706	0.024706	0.024706	0.024706	0.024706	0.024706	0.024706	0.024706	0.024706	0.024706	0.024706
484	CABLE AND OTHER PAY TELEVISION SERVICES	1	0.91%	0.168452	0.168452	0.168452	0.168452	0.168452	0.168452	0.168452	0.168452	0.168452	0.168452	0.168452
4841	Cable And Other Pay Television Services	1	0.91%	0.168452	0.168452	0.168452	0.168452	0.168452	0.168452	0.168452	0.168452	0.168452	0.168452	0.168452
49	ELECTRIC, GAS, AND SANITARY SERVICES	18	1.08%	0.200169	0.109754	-0.057602	-0.050104	-0.037607	0.084756	0.109754	0.139084	0.757062	1.012851	1.166324
491	ELECTRIC SERVICES	6	0.77%	0.142772	0.125179	0.051549	0.051864	0.052390	0.112512	0.125179	0.137845	0.300085	0.325279	0.340395
4911	Electric Services	6	0.77%	0.142772	0.125179	0.051549	0.051864	0.052390	0.112512	0.125179	0.137845	0.300085	0.325279	0.340395
492	GAS PRODUCTION AND DISTRIBUTION	2	1.91%	0.353487	0.353487	0.046456	0.055855	0.071520	0.290828	0.353487	0.416146	0.635454	0.651119	0.660518
4923	Natural Gas Transmission And Distribution	1	3.60%	0.666784	0.666784	0.666784	0.666784	0.666784	0.666784	0.666784	0.666784	0.666784	0.666784	0.666784
4924	Natural Gas Distribution	1	0.22%	0.040190	0.040190	0.040190	0.040190	0.040190	0.040190	0.040190	0.040190	0.040190	0.040190	0.040190
493	COMBINATION ELECTRIC AND GAS, AND OTHER UTILITY SERVICES	10	1.10%	0.203943	0.099527	-0.059955	-0.055985	-0.049369	0.077369	0.099527	0.121813	0.821407	1.045024	1.179193
4931	Electric And Other Services Combined	10	1.10%	0.203943	0.099527	-0.059955	-0.055985	-0.049369	0.077369	0.099527	0.121813	0.821407	1.045024	1.179193
	WHOLESALE TRADE													
50	WHOLESALE TRADE¨DURABLE GOODS	1	-0.90%	-0.165944	-0.165944	-0.165944	-0.165944	-0.165944	-0.165944	-0.165944	-0.165944	-0.165944	-0.165944	-0.165944

Betas of Preferred Stocks by SIC Codes as of September 28, 2018

SIC Code	Description	Number of Companies	Equity Risk Premium	Mean	Median	1st Percentile	2.5th Percentile	5th Percentile	40th Percentile	50th Percentile	60th Percentile	95th Percentile	97.5th Percentile	99th Percentile
507	HARDWARE, AND PLUMBING AND HEATING EQUIPMENT AND SUPPLIES	1	-0.90%	-0.165944	-0.165944	-0.165944	-0.165944	-0.165944	-0.165944	-0.165944	-0.165944	-0.165944	-0.165944	-0.165944
5072	Hardware	1	-0.90%	-0.165944	-0.165944	-0.165944	-0.165944	-0.165944	-0.165944	-0.165944	-0.165944	-0.165944	-0.165944	-0.165944
	RETAIL TRADE													
59	MISCELLANEOUS RETAIL	1	0.52%	0.095694	0.095694	0.095694	0.095694	0.095694	0.095694	0.095694	0.095694	0.095694	0.095694	0.095694
598	FUEL DEALERS	1	0.52%	0.095694	0.095694	0.095694	0.095694	0.095694	0.095694	0.095694	0.095694	0.095694	0.095694	0.095694
5983	Fuel Oil Dealers	1	0.52%	0.095694	0.095694	0.095694	0.095694	0.095694	0.095694	0.095694	0.095694	0.095694	0.095694	0.095694
	FINANCE, INSURANCE, AND REAL ESTATE													
60	DEPOSITORY INSTITUTIONS	65	0.36%	0.065965	0.052500	-0.130177	-0.041635	-0.030149	0.039278	0.052500	0.069325	0.156447	0.270968	0.616320
602	COMMERCIAL BANKS	65	0.36%	0.065965	0.052500	-0.130177	-0.041635	-0.030149	0.039278	0.052500	0.069325	0.156447	0.270968	0.616320
6021	National Commercial Banks	45	0.26%	0.048019	0.052500	-0.163115	-0.018900	-0.010388	0.039278	0.052500	0.066353	0.132856	0.139394	0.151476
6022	State Commercial Banks	18	0.52%	0.095577	0.054950	-0.046345	-0.043552	-0.038896	0.043358	0.054950	0.078416	0.283235	0.616352	0.816222
6029	Commercial Banks, Not Elsewhere Classified	2	1.10%	0.203254	0.203254	-0.017903	-0.011133	0.000151	0.158120	0.203254	0.248388	0.406357	0.417640	0.424411
61	NONDEPOSITORY CREDIT INSTITUTIONS	32	1.76%	0.325777	0.340609	-0.029579	-0.017851	-0.008840	0.253284	0.340609	0.411102	0.638765	0.659888	0.683959
611	FEDERAL AND FEDERALLY-SPONSORED CREDIT AGENCIES	31	1.80%	0.333205	0.393102	-0.029832	-0.018482	-0.009143	0.258579	0.393102	0.416432	0.639627	0.661182	0.684477
6111	Federal And Federally-Sponsored Credit Agencies	31	1.80%	0.333205	0.393102	-0.029832	-0.018482	-0.009143	0.258579	0.393102	0.416432	0.639627	0.661182	0.684477
614	PERSONAL CREDIT INSTITUTIONS	1	0.52%	0.095509	0.095509	0.095509	0.095509	0.095509	0.095509	0.095509	0.095509	0.095509	0.095509	0.095509
6141	Personal Credit Institutions	1	0.52%	0.095509	0.095509	0.095509	0.095509	0.095509	0.095509	0.095509	0.095509	0.095509	0.095509	0.095509
62	SECURITY AND COMMODITY BROKERS, DEALERS, EXCHANGES, AND SERVICES	22	1.86%	0.344384	0.071165	0.002646	0.018375	0.042109	0.063280	0.071165	0.074126	0.174269	2.993074	4.859828
621	SECURITY BROKERS, DEALERS, AND FLOTATION COMPANIES	17	2.27%	0.419759	0.071447	0.000149	0.012134	0.032107	0.063280	0.071447	0.074126	1.301628	3.702979	5.143790
6211	Security Brokers, Dealers, And Flotation Companies	17	2.27%	0.419759	0.071447	0.000149	0.012134	0.032107	0.063280	0.071447	0.074126	1.301628	3.702979	5.143790
628	SERVICES ALLIED WITH THE EXCHANGE OF SECURITIES OR COMMODITIES	5	0.48%	0.088108	0.070882	0.047905	0.047970	0.048079	0.062107	0.070882	0.080418	0.161447	0.169787	0.174792
6282	Investment Advice	5	0.48%	0.088108	0.070882	0.047905	0.047970	0.048079	0.062107	0.070882	0.080418	0.161447	0.169787	0.174792
63	INSURANCE CARRIERS	20	0.68%	0.126018	0.081560	-0.007640	-0.006549	-0.004730	0.052039	0.081560	0.148398	0.361364	0.362309	0.362876
631	LIFE INSURANCE	1	0.08%	0.014994	0.014994	0.014994	0.014994	0.014994	0.014994	0.014994	0.014994	0.014994	0.014994	0.014994
6311	Life Insurance	1	0.08%	0.014994	0.014994	0.014994	0.014994	0.014994	0.014994	0.014994	0.014994	0.014994	0.014994	0.014994
632	ACCIDENT AND HEALTH INSURANCE AND MEDICAL SERVICE PLANS	4	0.34%	0.063878	0.056594	-0.007500	-0.006199	-0.004029	0.034971	0.056594	0.078217	0.141983	0.146338	0.148950
6321	Accident And Health Insurance	4	0.34%	0.063878	0.056594	-0.007500	-0.006199	-0.004029	0.034971	0.056594	0.078217	0.141983	0.146338	0.148950
633	FIRE, MARINE, AND CASUALTY INSURANCE	15	0.81%	0.149991	0.146868	-0.002099	0.001559	0.007656	0.065734	0.146868	0.189847	0.361861	0.362558	0.362975
6331	Fire, Marine, And Casualty Insurance	15	0.81%	0.149991	0.146868	-0.002099	0.001559	0.007656	0.065734	0.146868	0.189847	0.361861	0.362558	0.362975
67	HOLDING AND OTHER INVESTMENT OFFICES	91	0.30%	0.054671	0.041869	-0.052942	-0.044835	-0.033085	0.030935	0.041869	0.051142	0.163374	0.266147	0.302287
671	HOLDING OFFICES	2	0.38%	0.069530	0.069530	0.041657	0.042510	0.043932	0.063841	0.069530	0.075218	0.095128	0.096550	0.097403
6712	Offices Of Bank Holding Companies	2	0.38%	0.069530	0.069530	0.041657	0.042510	0.043932	0.063841	0.069530	0.075218	0.095128	0.096550	0.097403
672	INVESTMENT OFFICES	14	0.11%	0.019852	0.025975	-0.045336	-0.044522	-0.043167	0.008716	0.025975	0.040394	0.067136	0.073193	0.076828
6726	Unit Investment Trusts, Face-Amount Certificate Offices	14	0.11%	0.019852	0.025975	-0.045336	-0.044522	-0.043167	0.008716	0.025975	0.040394	0.067136	0.073193	0.076828
679	MISCELLANEOUS INVESTING	75	0.33%	0.060774	0.048264	-0.060655	-0.039024	-0.028279	0.031017	0.048264	0.057688	0.189552	0.278348	0.308412
6798	Real Estate Investment Trusts	74	0.33%	0.061984	0.048768	-0.061137	-0.039291	-0.026100	0.031491	0.048768	0.058751	0.193169	0.278940	0.308795

Betas of Preferred Stocks by SIC Codes as of September 28, 2018

SIC Code	Description	Number of Companies	Equity Risk Premium	Mean	Median	1st Percentile	2.5th Percentile	5th Percentile	40th Percentile	50th Percentile	60th Percentile	95th Percentile	97.5th Percentile	99th Percentile
6799	Investors, Not Elsewhere Classified	1	-0.16%	-0.028751	-0.028751	-0.028751	-0.028751	-0.028751	-0.028751	-0.028751	-0.028751	-0.028751	-0.028751	-0.028751
	SERVICES													
70	HOTELS, ROOMING HOUSES, CAMPS, AND OTHER LODGING PLACES	1	0.43%	0.080327	0.080327	0.080327	0.080327	0.080327	0.080327	0.080327	0.080327	0.080327	0.080327	0.080327
701	HOTELS AND MOTELS	1	0.43%	0.080327	0.080327	0.080327	0.080327	0.080327	0.080327	0.080327	0.080327	0.080327	0.080327	0.080327
7011	Hotels And Motels	1	0.43%	0.080327	0.080327	0.080327	0.080327	0.080327	0.080327	0.080327	0.080327	0.080327	0.080327	0.080327
73	BUSINESS SERVICES	1	-0.76%	-0.141601	-0.141601	-0.141601	-0.141601	-0.141601	-0.141601	-0.141601	-0.141601	-0.141601	-0.141601	-0.141601
736	PERSONNEL SUPPLY SERVICES	1	-0.76%	-0.141601	-0.141601	-0.141601	-0.141601	-0.141601	-0.141601	-0.141601	-0.141601	-0.141601	-0.141601	-0.141601
7363	Help Supply Services	1	-0.76%	-0.141601	-0.141601	-0.141601	-0.141601	-0.141601	-0.141601	-0.141601	-0.141601	-0.141601	-0.141601	-0.141601

Down-market Betas of Preferred Stocks by SIC Codes as of September 28, 2018

Details:
Benchmark: S&P 500 Index
Returns period and frequency: 1 year of daily returns
Risk-free rate for betas: Federal Funds Rate
Expected US Equity Risk Premium: 5.40% (Fernandez, Pablo and Pershin, Vitaly and Fernández Acín, Isabel, Market Risk Premium and Risk-Free Rate used for 59 Countries in 2018: A Survey (April 3, 2018). Available at SSRN: https://ssrn.com/abstract=3155709)

SIC Code	Description	Number of Companies	Equity Risk Premium	Mean	Median	1st Percentile	2.5th Percentile	5th Percentile	40th Percentile	50th Percentile	60th Percentile	95th Percentile	97.5th Percentile	99th Percentile
	MINING													
13	OIL AND GAS EXTRACTION	3	1.35%	0.250128	0.115478	0.022560	0.025405	0.030146	0.096515	0.115478	0.215231	0.564367	0.589305	0.604268
131	CRUDE PETROLEUM AND NATURAL GAS	2	1.97%	0.364861	0.364861	0.120466	0.127947	0.140416	0.314984	0.364861	0.414737	0.589305	0.601774	0.609255
1311	Crude Petroleum And Natural Gas	2	1.97%	0.364861	0.364861	0.120466	0.127947	0.140416	0.314984	0.364861	0.414737	0.589305	0.601774	0.609255
132	NATURAL GAS LIQUIDS	1	0.11%	0.020664	0.020664	0.020664	0.020664	0.020664	0.020664	0.020664	0.020664	0.020664	0.020664	0.020664
1321	Natural Gas Liquids	1	0.11%	0.020664	0.020664	0.020664	0.020664	0.020664	0.020664	0.020664	0.020664	0.020664	0.020664	0.020664
	CONSTRUCTION													
15	CONSTRUCTION	1	3.50%	0.648407	0.648407	0.648407	0.648407	0.648407	0.648407	0.648407	0.648407	0.648407	0.648407	0.648407
153	OPERATIVE BUILDERS	1	3.50%	0.648407	0.648407	0.648407	0.648407	0.648407	0.648407	0.648407	0.648407	0.648407	0.648407	0.648407
1531	Operative Builders	1	3.50%	0.648407	0.648407	0.648407	0.648407	0.648407	0.648407	0.648407	0.648407	0.648407	0.648407	0.648407
	MANUFACTURING													
20	FOOD AND KINDRED PRODUCTS	1	-0.14%	-0.025151	-0.025151	-0.025151	-0.025151	-0.025151	-0.025151	-0.025151	-0.025151	-0.025151	-0.025151	-0.025151
207	FATS AND OILS	1	-0.14%	-0.025151	-0.025151	-0.025151	-0.025151	-0.025151	-0.025151	-0.025151	-0.025151	-0.025151	-0.025151	-0.025151
2075	Soybean Oil Mills	1	-0.14%	-0.025151	-0.025151	-0.025151	-0.025151	-0.025151	-0.025151	-0.025151	-0.025151	-0.025151	-0.025151	-0.025151
28	CHEMICALS AND ALLIED PRODUCTS	4	2.41%	0.447183	0.300969	0.010142	0.022377	0.042769	0.284716	0.300969	0.317222	1.056297	1.120554	1.159107
282	PLASTICS MATERIALS AND SYNTHETIC RESINS, SYNTHETIC RUBBER, CELLULOSIC MANMADE FIBERS	1	6.40%	1.184810	1.184810	1.184810	1.184810	1.184810	1.184810	1.184810	1.184810	1.184810	1.184810	1.184810
2821	Plastics Materials, Synthetic Resins, And Nonvulcanizable Elastomers	1	6.40%	1.184810	1.184810	1.184810	1.184810	1.184810	1.184810	1.184810	1.184810	1.184810	1.184810	1.184810
283	DRUGS	1	0.01%	0.001985	0.001985	0.001985	0.001985	0.001985	0.001985	0.001985	0.001985	0.001985	0.001985	0.001985
2834	Pharmaceutical Preparations	1	0.01%	0.001985	0.001985	0.001985	0.001985	0.001985	0.001985	0.001985	0.001985	0.001985	0.001985	0.001985
287	AGRICULTURAL CHEMICALS	2	1.63%	0.300969	0.300969	0.274423	0.275235	0.276590	0.295551	0.300969	0.306387	0.325348	0.326703	0.327515
2879	Pesticides And Agricultural Chemicals, Not Elsewhere Classified	2	1.63%	0.300969	0.300969	0.274423	0.275235	0.276590	0.295551	0.300969	0.306387	0.325348	0.326703	0.327515
29	PETROLEUM REFINING AND RELATED INDUSTRIES	1	4.93%	0.912816	0.912816	0.912816	0.912816	0.912816	0.912816	0.912816	0.912816	0.912816	0.912816	0.912816
291	PETROLEUM REFINING	1	4.93%	0.912816	0.912816	0.912816	0.912816	0.912816	0.912816	0.912816	0.912816	0.912816	0.912816	0.912816
2911	Petroleum Refining	1	4.93%	0.912816	0.912816	0.912816	0.912816	0.912816	0.912816	0.912816	0.912816	0.912816	0.912816	0.912816
33	PRIMARY METAL INDUSTRIES	1	1.59%	0.295292	0.295292	0.295292	0.295292	0.295292	0.295292	0.295292	0.295292	0.295292	0.295292	0.295292
331	STEEL WORKS, BLAST FURNACES, AND ROLLING AND FINISHING MILLS	1	1.59%	0.295292	0.295292	0.295292	0.295292	0.295292	0.295292	0.295292	0.295292	0.295292	0.295292	0.295292
3312	Steel Works, Blast Furnaces (Including Coke Ovens), And Rolling Mills	1	1.59%	0.295292	0.295292	0.295292	0.295292	0.295292	0.295292	0.295292	0.295292	0.295292	0.295292	0.295292
34	FABRICATED METAL PRODUCTS, EXCEPT MACHINERY AND TRANSPORTATION EQUIPMENT	1	0.12%	0.022835	0.022835	0.022835	0.022835	0.022835	0.022835	0.022835	0.022835	0.022835	0.022835	0.022835
341	METAL CANS AND SHIPPING CONTAINERS	1	0.12%	0.022835	0.022835	0.022835	0.022835	0.022835	0.022835	0.022835	0.022835	0.022835	0.022835	0.022835
3412	Metal Shipping Barrels, Drums, Kegs, And Pails	1	0.12%	0.022835	0.022835	0.022835	0.022835	0.022835	0.022835	0.022835	0.022835	0.022835	0.022835	0.022835

Down-market Betas of Preferred Stocks by SIC Codes as of September 28, 2018

SIC Code	Description	Number of Companies	Equity Risk Premium	Mean	Median	1st Percentile	2.5th Percentile	5th Percentile	40th Percentile	50th Percentile	60th Percentile	95th Percentile	97.5th Percentile	99th Percentile
37	TRANSPORTATION EQUIPMENT	1	5.67%	1.049670	1.049670	1.049670	1.049670	1.049670	1.049670	1.049670	1.049670	1.049670	1.049670	1.049670
371	MOTOR VEHICLES AND MOTOR VEHICLE EQUIPMENT	1	5.67%	1.049670	1.049670	1.049670	1.049670	1.049670	1.049670	1.049670	1.049670	1.049670	1.049670	1.049670
3711	Motor Vehicles And Passenger Car Bodies	1	5.67%	1.049670	1.049670	1.049670	1.049670	1.049670	1.049670	1.049670	1.049670	1.049670	1.049670	1.049670
	TRANSPORTATION, COMMUNICATIONS, ELECTRIC, GAS, AND SANITARY SERVICE													
40	RAILROAD TRANSPORTATION	1	-0.22%	-0.039944	-0.039944	-0.039944	-0.039944	-0.039944	-0.039944	-0.039944	-0.039944	-0.039944	-0.039944	-0.039944
401	RAILROADS	1	-0.22%	-0.039944	-0.039944	-0.039944	-0.039944	-0.039944	-0.039944	-0.039944	-0.039944	-0.039944	-0.039944	-0.039944
4011	Railroads, Line-Haul Operating	1	-0.22%	-0.039944	-0.039944	-0.039944	-0.039944	-0.039944	-0.039944	-0.039944	-0.039944	-0.039944	-0.039944	-0.039944
44	WATER TRANSPORTATION	13	0.64%	0.117911	0.025334	-0.061691	-0.052283	-0.036603	0.021693	0.025334	0.086507	0.447862	0.567474	0.639241
441	DEEP SEA FOREIGN TRANSPORTATION OF FREIGHT	12	0.62%	0.115277	0.024688	-0.062214	-0.053590	-0.039217	0.016997	0.024688	0.061455	0.467797	0.577442	0.643228
4412	Deep Sea Foreign Transportation Of Freight	12	0.62%	0.115277	0.024688	-0.062214	-0.053590	-0.039217	0.016997	0.024688	0.061455	0.467797	0.577442	0.643228
449	SERVICES INCIDENTAL TO WATER TRANSPORTATION	1	0.81%	0.149513	0.149513	0.149513	0.149513	0.149513	0.149513	0.149513	0.149513	0.149513	0.149513	0.149513
4499	Water Transportation Services, Not Elsewhere Classified	1	0.81%	0.149513	0.149513	0.149513	0.149513	0.149513	0.149513	0.149513	0.149513	0.149513	0.149513	0.149513
45	TRANSPORTATION BY AIR	2	2.52%	0.467332	0.467332	0.359089	0.362403	0.367925	0.445242	0.467332	0.489422	0.566739	0.572261	0.575575
451	AIR TRANSPORTATION, SCHEDULED, AND AIR COURIER SERVICES	2	2.52%	0.467332	0.467332	0.359089	0.362403	0.367925	0.445242	0.467332	0.489422	0.566739	0.572261	0.575575
4512	Air Transportation, Scheduled	2	2.52%	0.467332	0.467332	0.359089	0.362403	0.367925	0.445242	0.467332	0.489422	0.566739	0.572261	0.575575
47	TRANSPORTATION SERVICES	1	0.12%	0.021394	0.021394	0.021394	0.021394	0.021394	0.021394	0.021394	0.021394	0.021394	0.021394	0.021394
473	ARRANGEMENT OF TRANSPORTATION OF FREIGHT AND CARGO	1	0.12%	0.021394	0.021394	0.021394	0.021394	0.021394	0.021394	0.021394	0.021394	0.021394	0.021394	0.021394
4731	Arrangement Of Transportation Of Freight And Cargo	1	0.12%	0.021394	0.021394	0.021394	0.021394	0.021394	0.021394	0.021394	0.021394	0.021394	0.021394	0.021394
48	COMMUNICATIONS	2	-1.25%	-0.231613	-0.231613	-0.435058	-0.428830	-0.418450	-0.273133	-0.231613	-0.190094	-0.044776	-0.034396	-0.028168
481	TELEPHONE COMMUNICATIONS	1	-0.13%	-0.024016	-0.024016	-0.024016	-0.024016	-0.024016	-0.024016	-0.024016	-0.024016	-0.024016	-0.024016	-0.024016
4813	Telephone Communications, Except Radiotelephone	1	-0.13%	-0.024016	-0.024016	-0.024016	-0.024016	-0.024016	-0.024016	-0.024016	-0.024016	-0.024016	-0.024016	-0.024016
484	CABLE AND OTHER PAY TELEVISION SERVICES	1	-2.37%	-0.439210	-0.439210	-0.439210	-0.439210	-0.439210	-0.439210	-0.439210	-0.439210	-0.439210	-0.439210	-0.439210
4841	Cable And Other Pay Television Services	1	-2.37%	-0.439210	-0.439210	-0.439210	-0.439210	-0.439210	-0.439210	-0.439210	-0.439210	-0.439210	-0.439210	-0.439210
49	ELECTRIC, GAS, AND SANITARY SERVICES	18	1.41%	0.260589	0.281381	-0.094458	-0.089513	-0.081270	0.242327	0.281381	0.336324	0.687211	0.703274	0.712911
491	ELECTRIC SERVICES	6	1.05%	0.193540	0.245367	-0.096785	-0.095331	-0.092907	0.103622	0.245367	0.387112	0.429355	0.432377	0.434190
4911	Electric Services	6	1.05%	0.193540	0.245367	-0.096785	-0.095331	-0.092907	0.103622	0.245367	0.387112	0.429355	0.432377	0.434190
492	GAS PRODUCTION AND DISTRIBUTION	2	2.06%	0.380671	0.380671	0.048779	0.058939	0.075873	0.312938	0.380671	0.448404	0.685470	0.702403	0.712563
4923	Natural Gas Transmission And Distribution	1	3.88%	0.719336	0.719336	0.719336	0.719336	0.719336	0.719336	0.719336	0.719336	0.719336	0.719336	0.719336
4924	Natural Gas Distribution	1	0.23%	0.042006	0.042006	0.042006	0.042006	0.042006	0.042006	0.042006	0.042006	0.042006	0.042006	0.042006
493	COMBINATION ELECTRIC AND GAS, AND OTHER UTILITY SERVICES	10	1.49%	0.276801	0.281381	-0.017607	-0.004488	0.017377	0.263092	0.281381	0.312612	0.541949	0.611746	0.653623
4931	Electric And Other Services Combined	10	1.49%	0.276801	0.281381	-0.017607	-0.004488	0.017377	0.263092	0.281381	0.312612	0.541949	0.611746	0.653623
	WHOLESALE TRADE													
50	WHOLESALE TRADE¨DURABLE GOODS	1	-0.76%	-0.139946	-0.139946	-0.139946	-0.139946	-0.139946	-0.139946	-0.139946	-0.139946	-0.139946	-0.139946	-0.139946

Down-market Betas of Preferred Stocks by SIC Codes as of September 28, 2018

SIC Code	Description	Number of Companies	Equity Risk Premium	Mean	Median	1st Percentile	2.5th Percentile	5th Percentile	40th Percentile	50th Percentile	60th Percentile	95th Percentile	97.5th Percentile	99th Percentile
507	HARDWARE, AND PLUMBING AND HEATING EQUIPMENT AND SUPPLIES	1	-0.76%	-0.139946	-0.139946	-0.139946	-0.139946	-0.139946	-0.139946	-0.139946	-0.139946	-0.139946	-0.139946	-0.139946
5072	Hardware	1	-0.76%	-0.139946	-0.139946	-0.139946	-0.139946	-0.139946	-0.139946	-0.139946	-0.139946	-0.139946	-0.139946	-0.139946
	RETAIL TRADE													
59	MISCELLANEOUS RETAIL	1	-0.25%	-0.045807	-0.045807	-0.045807	-0.045807	-0.045807	-0.045807	-0.045807	-0.045807	-0.045807	-0.045807	-0.045807
598	FUEL DEALERS	1	-0.25%	-0.045807	-0.045807	-0.045807	-0.045807	-0.045807	-0.045807	-0.045807	-0.045807	-0.045807	-0.045807	-0.045807
5983	Fuel Oil Dealers	1	-0.25%	-0.045807	-0.045807	-0.045807	-0.045807	-0.045807	-0.045807	-0.045807	-0.045807	-0.045807	-0.045807	-0.045807
	FINANCE, INSURANCE, AND REAL ESTATE													
60	DEPOSITORY INSTITUTIONS	65	0.29%	0.054360	0.033574	-0.126742	-0.085341	-0.067466	0.016476	0.033574	0.050511	0.187270	0.345839	0.581846
602	COMMERCIAL BANKS	65	0.29%	0.054360	0.033574	-0.126742	-0.085341	-0.067466	0.016476	0.033574	0.050511	0.187270	0.345839	0.581846
6021	National Commercial Banks	45	0.24%	0.043553	0.025716	-0.040920	-0.032795	-0.028761	0.013336	0.025716	0.048915	0.172417	0.188716	0.198552
6022	State Commercial Banks	18	0.33%	0.060643	0.043652	-0.160451	-0.142162	-0.111681	0.031982	0.043652	0.050235	0.227183	0.426705	0.546417
6029	Commercial Banks, Not Elsewhere Classified	2	1.30%	0.240964	0.240964	-0.068635	-0.059157	-0.043362	0.177781	0.240964	0.304148	0.525290	0.541086	0.550564
61	NONDEPOSITORY CREDIT INSTITUTIONS	32	2.57%	0.475997	0.528256	-0.058903	-0.023376	0.013758	0.438613	0.528256	0.579094	0.842401	0.859846	0.871942
611	FEDERAL AND FEDERALLY-SPONSORED CREDIT AGENCIES	31	2.64%	0.488578	0.538356	-0.059667	-0.025286	0.011945	0.474512	0.538356	0.597188	0.843455	0.860496	0.872202
6111	Federal And Federally-Sponsored Credit Agencies	31	2.64%	0.488578	0.538356	-0.059667	-0.025286	0.011945	0.474512	0.538356	0.597188	0.843455	0.860496	0.872202
614	PERSONAL CREDIT INSTITUTIONS	1	0.46%	0.085991	0.085991	0.085991	0.085991	0.085991	0.085991	0.085991	0.085991	0.085991	0.085991	0.085991
6141	Personal Credit Institutions	1	0.46%	0.085991	0.085991	0.085991	0.085991	0.085991	0.085991	0.085991	0.085991	0.085991	0.085991	0.085991
62	SECURITY AND COMMODITY BROKERS, DEALERS, EXCHANGES, AND SERVICES	22	2.12%	0.393348	0.042590	-0.050424	-0.031064	-0.001655	0.033412	0.042590	0.055716	0.170289	3.650341	5.956716
621	SECURITY BROKERS, DEALERS, AND FLOTATION COMPANIES	17	2.66%	0.492108	0.050327	-0.001183	-0.000153	0.001564	0.034338	0.050327	0.055716	1.601893	4.548096	6.315819
6211	Security Brokers, Dealers, And Flotation Companies	17	2.66%	0.492108	0.050327	-0.001183	-0.000153	0.001564	0.034338	0.050327	0.055716	1.601893	4.548096	6.315819
628	SERVICES ALLIED WITH THE EXCHANGE OF SECURITIES OR COMMODITIES	5	0.31%	0.057564	0.031431	-0.059714	-0.054290	-0.045248	0.029691	0.031431	0.066925	0.162012	0.167242	0.170381
6282	Investment Advice	5	0.31%	0.057564	0.031431	-0.059714	-0.054290	-0.045248	0.029691	0.031431	0.066925	0.162012	0.167242	0.170381
63	INSURANCE CARRIERS	20	0.69%	0.128425	0.108712	-0.067618	-0.054670	-0.033090	0.097439	0.108712	0.140582	0.303261	0.316310	0.324139
631	LIFE INSURANCE	1	-0.41%	-0.076250	-0.076250	-0.076250	-0.076250	-0.076250	-0.076250	-0.076250	-0.076250	-0.076250	-0.076250	-0.076250
6311	Life Insurance	1	-0.41%	-0.076250	-0.076250	-0.076250	-0.076250	-0.076250	-0.076250	-0.076250	-0.076250	-0.076250	-0.076250	-0.076250
632	ACCIDENT AND HEALTH INSURANCE AND MEDICAL SERVICE PLANS	4	0.48%	0.088486	0.095054	0.055609	0.056820	0.058839	0.087053	0.095054	0.103056	0.108937	0.108986	0.109015
6321	Accident And Health Insurance	4	0.48%	0.088486	0.095054	0.055609	0.056820	0.058839	0.087053	0.095054	0.103056	0.108937	0.108986	0.109015
633	FIRE, MARINE, AND CASUALTY INSURANCE	15	0.82%	0.152721	0.174838	-0.029741	-0.028123	-0.025428	0.113815	0.174838	0.216808	0.310129	0.319744	0.325513
6331	Fire, Marine, And Casualty Insurance	15	0.82%	0.152721	0.174838	-0.029741	-0.028123	-0.025428	0.113815	0.174838	0.216808	0.310129	0.319744	0.325513
67	HOLDING AND OTHER INVESTMENT OFFICES	91	0.45%	0.083297	0.060974	-0.104520	-0.076543	-0.035791	0.042560	0.060974	0.082054	0.299215	0.353372	0.402656
671	HOLDING OFFICES	2	0.74%	0.136244	0.136244	-0.004143	0.000154	0.007317	0.107594	0.136244	0.164895	0.265172	0.272334	0.276632
6712	Offices Of Bank Holding Companies	2	0.74%	0.136244	0.136244	-0.004143	0.000154	0.007317	0.107594	0.136244	0.164895	0.265172	0.272334	0.276632
672	INVESTMENT OFFICES	14	0.26%	0.048892	0.036574	-0.034914	-0.029770	-0.021196	0.029257	0.036574	0.046819	0.165281	0.195437	0.213531
6726	Unit Investment Trusts, Face-Amount Certificate Offices	14	0.26%	0.048892	0.036574	-0.034914	-0.029770	-0.021196	0.029257	0.036574	0.046819	0.165281	0.195437	0.213531
679	MISCELLANEOUS INVESTING	75	0.48%	0.088308	0.070443	-0.116842	-0.088585	-0.036700	0.044285	0.070443	0.098106	0.320963	0.364832	0.442902
6798	Real Estate Investment Trusts	74	0.50%	0.091850	0.071071	-0.089747	-0.052189	-0.028131	0.045169	0.071071	0.099639	0.321301	0.365205	0.445418

Down-market Betas of Preferred Stocks by SIC Codes as of September 28, 2018

SIC Code	Description	Number of Companies	Equity Risk Premium	Mean	Median	1st Percentile	2.5th Percentile	5th Percentile	40th Percentile	50th Percentile	60th Percentile	95th Percentile	97.5th Percentile	99th Percentile
6799	Investors, Not Elsewhere Classified	1	-0.94%	-0.173834	-0.173834	-0.173834	-0.173834	-0.173834	-0.173834	-0.173834	-0.173834	-0.173834	-0.173834	-0.173834
	SERVICES													
70	HOTELS, ROOMING HOUSES, CAMPS, AND OTHER LODGING PLACES	1	0.38%	0.070590	0.070590	0.070590	0.070590	0.070590	0.070590	0.070590	0.070590	0.070590	0.070590	0.070590
701	HOTELS AND MOTELS	1	0.38%	0.070590	0.070590	0.070590	0.070590	0.070590	0.070590	0.070590	0.070590	0.070590	0.070590	0.070590
7011	Hotels And Motels	1	0.38%	0.070590	0.070590	0.070590	0.070590	0.070590	0.070590	0.070590	0.070590	0.070590	0.070590	0.070590
73	BUSINESS SERVICES	1	-0.33%	-0.061966	-0.061966	-0.061966	-0.061966	-0.061966	-0.061966	-0.061966	-0.061966	-0.061966	-0.061966	-0.061966
736	PERSONNEL SUPPLY SERVICES	1	-0.33%	-0.061966	-0.061966	-0.061966	-0.061966	-0.061966	-0.061966	-0.061966	-0.061966	-0.061966	-0.061966	-0.061966
7363	Help Supply Services	1	-0.33%	-0.061966	-0.061966	-0.061966	-0.061966	-0.061966	-0.061966	-0.061966	-0.061966	-0.061966	-0.061966	-0.061966

Up-market Betas of Preferred Stocks by SIC Codes as of September 28, 2018

Details:
Benchmark: S&P 500 Index
Returns period and frequency: 1 year of daily returns
Risk-free rate for betas: Federal Funds Rate
Expected US Equity Risk Premium: 5.40% (Fernandez, Pablo and Pershin, Vitaly and Fernández Acín, Isabel, Market Risk Premium and Risk-Free Rate used for 59 Countries in 2018: A Survey (April 3, 2018). Available at SSRN: https://ssrn.com/abstract=3155709)

SIC Code	Description	Number of Companies	Equity Risk Premium	Mean	Median	1st Percentile	2.5th Percentile	5th Percentile	40th Percentile	50th Percentile	60th Percentile	95th Percentile	97.5th Percentile	99th Percentile
	MINING													
13	OIL AND GAS EXTRACTION	3	0.15%	0.028198	0.083953	-0.132936	-0.126296	-0.115231	0.039690	0.083953	0.094763	0.132597	0.135300	0.136921
131	CRUDE PETROLEUM AND NATURAL GAS	2	0.60%	0.110978	0.110978	0.084493	0.085304	0.086655	0.105573	0.110978	0.116382	0.135300	0.136651	0.137462
1311	Crude Petroleum And Natural Gas	2	0.60%	0.110978	0.110978	0.084493	0.085304	0.086655	0.105573	0.110978	0.116382	0.135300	0.136651	0.137462
132	NATURAL GAS LIQUIDS	1	-0.74%	-0.137362	-0.137362	-0.137362	-0.137362	-0.137362	-0.137362	-0.137362	-0.137362	-0.137362	-0.137362	-0.137362
1321	Natural Gas Liquids	1	-0.74%	-0.137362	-0.137362	-0.137362	-0.137362	-0.137362	-0.137362	-0.137362	-0.137362	-0.137362	-0.137362	-0.137362
	CONSTRUCTION													
15	CONSTRUCTION	1	0.06%	0.012033	0.012033	0.012033	0.012033	0.012033	0.012033	0.012033	0.012033	0.012033	0.012033	0.012033
153	OPERATIVE BUILDERS	1	0.06%	0.012033	0.012033	0.012033	0.012033	0.012033	0.012033	0.012033	0.012033	0.012033	0.012033	0.012033
1531	Operative Builders	1	0.06%	0.012033	0.012033	0.012033	0.012033	0.012033	0.012033	0.012033	0.012033	0.012033	0.012033	0.012033
	MANUFACTURING													
20	FOOD AND KINDRED PRODUCTS	1	-1.64%	-0.304153	-0.304153	-0.304153	-0.304153	-0.304153	-0.304153	-0.304153	-0.304153	-0.304153	-0.304153	-0.304153
207	FATS AND OILS	1	-1.64%	-0.304153	-0.304153	-0.304153	-0.304153	-0.304153	-0.304153	-0.304153	-0.304153	-0.304153	-0.304153	-0.304153
2075	Soybean Oil Mills	1	-1.64%	-0.304153	-0.304153	-0.304153	-0.304153	-0.304153	-0.304153	-0.304153	-0.304153	-0.304153	-0.304153	-0.304153
28	CHEMICALS AND ALLIED PRODUCTS	4	1.85%	0.342804	0.043363	-0.050664	-0.047607	-0.042512	0.026483	0.043363	0.060244	1.147336	1.242263	1.299219
282	PLASTICS MATERIALS AND SYNTHETIC RESINS, SYNTHETIC RUBBER, CELLULOSIC MANMADE FIBERS	1	7.22%	1.337190	1.337190	1.337190	1.337190	1.337190	1.337190	1.337190	1.337190	1.337190	1.337190	1.337190
2821	Plastics Materials, Synthetic Resins, And Nonvulcanizable Elastomers	1	7.22%	1.337190	1.337190	1.337190	1.337190	1.337190	1.337190	1.337190	1.337190	1.337190	1.337190	1.337190
283	DRUGS	1	-0.28%	-0.052702	-0.052702	-0.052702	-0.052702	-0.052702	-0.052702	-0.052702	-0.052702	-0.052702	-0.052702	-0.052702
2834	Pharmaceutical Preparations	1	-0.28%	-0.052702	-0.052702	-0.052702	-0.052702	-0.052702	-0.052702	-0.052702	-0.052702	-0.052702	-0.052702	-0.052702
287	AGRICULTURAL CHEMICALS	2	0.23%	0.043363	0.043363	0.015792	0.016636	0.018043	0.037736	0.043363	0.048990	0.068684	0.070091	0.070935
2879	Pesticides And Agricultural Chemicals, Not Elsewhere Classified	2	0.23%	0.043363	0.043363	0.015792	0.016636	0.018043	0.037736	0.043363	0.048990	0.068684	0.070091	0.070935
29	PETROLEUM REFINING AND RELATED INDUSTRIES	1	5.17%	0.958258	0.958258	0.958258	0.958258	0.958258	0.958258	0.958258	0.958258	0.958258	0.958258	0.958258
291	PETROLEUM REFINING	1	5.17%	0.958258	0.958258	0.958258	0.958258	0.958258	0.958258	0.958258	0.958258	0.958258	0.958258	0.958258
2911	Petroleum Refining	1	5.17%	0.958258	0.958258	0.958258	0.958258	0.958258	0.958258	0.958258	0.958258	0.958258	0.958258	0.958258
33	PRIMARY METAL INDUSTRIES	1	2.13%	0.394909	0.394909	0.394909	0.394909	0.394909	0.394909	0.394909	0.394909	0.394909	0.394909	0.394909
331	STEEL WORKS, BLAST FURNACES, AND ROLLING AND FINISHING MILLS	1	2.13%	0.394909	0.394909	0.394909	0.394909	0.394909	0.394909	0.394909	0.394909	0.394909	0.394909	0.394909
3312	Steel Works, Blast Furnaces (Including Coke Ovens), And Rolling Mills	1	2.13%	0.394909	0.394909	0.394909	0.394909	0.394909	0.394909	0.394909	0.394909	0.394909	0.394909	0.394909
34	FABRICATED METAL PRODUCTS, EXCEPT MACHINERY AND TRANSPORTATION EQUIPMENT	1	-0.29%	-0.053411	-0.053411	-0.053411	-0.053411	-0.053411	-0.053411	-0.053411	-0.053411	-0.053411	-0.053411	-0.053411
341	METAL CANS AND SHIPPING CONTAINERS	1	-0.29%	-0.053411	-0.053411	-0.053411	-0.053411	-0.053411	-0.053411	-0.053411	-0.053411	-0.053411	-0.053411	-0.053411
3412	Metal Shipping Barrels, Drums, Kegs, And Pails	1	-0.29%	-0.053411	-0.053411	-0.053411	-0.053411	-0.053411	-0.053411	-0.053411	-0.053411	-0.053411	-0.053411	-0.053411

Up-market Betas of Preferred Stocks by SIC Codes as of September 28, 2018

SIC Code	Description	Number of Companies	Equity Risk Premium	Mean	Median	1st Percentile	2.5th Percentile	5th Percentile	40th Percentile	50th Percentile	60th Percentile	95th Percentile	97.5th Percentile	99th Percentile
37	TRANSPORTATION EQUIPMENT	1	1.62%	0.300175	0.300175	0.300175	0.300175	0.300175	0.300175	0.300175	0.300175	0.300175	0.300175	0.300175
371	MOTOR VEHICLES AND MOTOR VEHICLE EQUIPMENT	1	1.62%	0.300175	0.300175	0.300175	0.300175	0.300175	0.300175	0.300175	0.300175	0.300175	0.300175	0.300175
3711	Motor Vehicles And Passenger Car Bodies	1	1.62%	0.300175	0.300175	0.300175	0.300175	0.300175	0.300175	0.300175	0.300175	0.300175	0.300175	0.300175
	TRANSPORTATION, COMMUNICATIONS, ELECTRIC, GAS, AND SANITARY SERVICE													
40	RAILROAD TRANSPORTATION	1	-2.02%	-0.374538	-0.374538	-0.374538	-0.374538	-0.374538	-0.374538	-0.374538	-0.374538	-0.374538	-0.374538	-0.374538
401	RAILROADS	1	-2.02%	-0.374538	-0.374538	-0.374538	-0.374538	-0.374538	-0.374538	-0.374538	-0.374538	-0.374538	-0.374538	-0.374538
4011	Railroads, Line-Haul Operating	1	-2.02%	-0.374538	-0.374538	-0.374538	-0.374538	-0.374538	-0.374538	-0.374538	-0.374538	-0.374538	-0.374538	-0.374538
44	WATER TRANSPORTATION	13	0.20%	0.036864	0.000705	-0.431412	-0.361382	-0.244664	-0.022755	0.000705	0.040880	0.396881	0.411740	0.420656
441	DEEP SEA FOREIGN TRANSPORTATION OF FREIGHT	12	0.22%	0.039877	0.009369	-0.435303	-0.371108	-0.264117	-0.025126	0.009369	0.042027	0.399357	0.412979	0.421151
4412	Deep Sea Foreign Transportation Of Freight	12	0.22%	0.039877	0.009369	-0.435303	-0.371108	-0.264117	-0.025126	0.009369	0.042027	0.399357	0.412979	0.421151
449	SERVICES INCIDENTAL TO WATER TRANSPORTATION	1	0.00%	0.000705	0.000705	0.000705	0.000705	0.000705	0.000705	0.000705	0.000705	0.000705	0.000705	0.000705
4499	Water Transportation Services, Not Elsewhere Classified	1	0.00%	0.000705	0.000705	0.000705	0.000705	0.000705	0.000705	0.000705	0.000705	0.000705	0.000705	0.000705
45	TRANSPORTATION BY AIR	2	3.54%	0.656041	0.656041	0.179712	0.194293	0.218596	0.558831	0.656041	0.753250	1.093485	1.117788	1.132369
451	AIR TRANSPORTATION, SCHEDULED, AND AIR COURIER SERVICES	2	3.54%	0.656041	0.656041	0.179712	0.194293	0.218596	0.558831	0.656041	0.753250	1.093485	1.117788	1.132369
4512	Air Transportation, Scheduled	2	3.54%	0.656041	0.656041	0.179712	0.194293	0.218596	0.558831	0.656041	0.753250	1.093485	1.117788	1.132369
47	TRANSPORTATION SERVICES	1	-0.81%	-0.150350	-0.150350	-0.150350	-0.150350	-0.150350	-0.150350	-0.150350	-0.150350	-0.150350	-0.150350	-0.150350
473	ARRANGEMENT OF TRANSPORTATION OF FREIGHT AND CARGO	1	-0.81%	-0.150350	-0.150350	-0.150350	-0.150350	-0.150350	-0.150350	-0.150350	-0.150350	-0.150350	-0.150350	-0.150350
4731	Arrangement Of Transportation Of Freight And Cargo	1	-0.81%	-0.150350	-0.150350	-0.150350	-0.150350	-0.150350	-0.150350	-0.150350	-0.150350	-0.150350	-0.150350	-0.150350
48	COMMUNICATIONS	2	0.50%	0.091728	0.091728	0.073330	0.073893	0.074832	0.087973	0.091728	0.095482	0.108624	0.109562	0.110126
481	TELEPHONE COMMUNICATIONS	1	0.60%	0.110501	0.110501	0.110501	0.110501	0.110501	0.110501	0.110501	0.110501	0.110501	0.110501	0.110501
4813	Telephone Communications, Except Radiotelephone	1	0.60%	0.110501	0.110501	0.110501	0.110501	0.110501	0.110501	0.110501	0.110501	0.110501	0.110501	0.110501
484	CABLE AND OTHER PAY TELEVISION SERVICES	1	0.39%	0.072954	0.072954	0.072954	0.072954	0.072954	0.072954	0.072954	0.072954	0.072954	0.072954	0.072954
4841	Cable And Other Pay Television Services	1	0.39%	0.072954	0.072954	0.072954	0.072954	0.072954	0.072954	0.072954	0.072954	0.072954	0.072954	0.072954
49	ELECTRIC, GAS, AND SANITARY SERVICES	18	0.94%	0.173541	0.081458	-0.312847	-0.269659	-0.197679	-0.016703	0.081458	0.113122	0.756133	1.126677	1.349003
491	ELECTRIC SERVICES	6	0.68%	0.125289	0.047601	-0.045439	-0.044862	-0.043900	-0.011346	0.047601	0.106548	0.439616	0.474302	0.495114
4911	Electric Services	6	0.68%	0.125289	0.047601	-0.045439	-0.044862	-0.043900	-0.011346	0.047601	0.106548	0.439616	0.474302	0.495114
492	GAS PRODUCTION AND DISTRIBUTION	2	2.17%	0.401151	0.401151	0.181432	0.188158	0.199368	0.356310	0.401151	0.445991	0.602933	0.614143	0.620869
4923	Natural Gas Transmission And Distribution	1	3.38%	0.625353	0.625353	0.625353	0.625353	0.625353	0.625353	0.625353	0.625353	0.625353	0.625353	0.625353
4924	Natural Gas Distribution	1	0.96%	0.176948	0.176948	0.176948	0.176948	0.176948	0.176948	0.176948	0.176948	0.176948	0.176948	0.176948
493	COMBINATION ELECTRIC AND GAS, AND OTHER UTILITY SERVICES	10	0.85%	0.156971	0.012105	-0.326396	-0.303532	-0.265425	-0.077335	0.012105	0.081362	1.080988	1.289104	1.413974
4931	Electric And Other Services Combined	10	0.85%	0.156971	0.012105	-0.326396	-0.303532	-0.265425	-0.077335	0.012105	0.081362	1.080988	1.289104	1.413974
	WHOLESALE TRADE													
50	WHOLESALE TRADE"DURABLE GOODS	1	-1.25%	-0.231312	-0.231312	-0.231312	-0.231312	-0.231312	-0.231312	-0.231312	-0.231312	-0.231312	-0.231312	-0.231312

Up-market Betas of Preferred Stocks by SIC Codes as of September 28, 2018

SIC Code	Description	Number of Companies	Equity Risk Premium	Mean	Median	1st Percentile	2.5th Percentile	5th Percentile	40th Percentile	50th Percentile	60th Percentile	95th Percentile	97.5th Percentile	99th Percentile
507	HARDWARE, AND PLUMBING AND HEATING EQUIPMENT AND SUPPLIES	1	-1.25%	-0.231312	-0.231312	-0.231312	-0.231312	-0.231312	-0.231312	-0.231312	-0.231312	-0.231312	-0.231312	-0.231312
5072	Hardware	1	-1.25%	-0.231312	-0.231312	-0.231312	-0.231312	-0.231312	-0.231312	-0.231312	-0.231312	-0.231312	-0.231312	-0.231312
	RETAIL TRADE													
59	MISCELLANEOUS RETAIL	1	0.30%	0.056097	0.056097	0.056097	0.056097	0.056097	0.056097	0.056097	0.056097	0.056097	0.056097	0.056097
598	FUEL DEALERS	1	0.30%	0.056097	0.056097	0.056097	0.056097	0.056097	0.056097	0.056097	0.056097	0.056097	0.056097	0.056097
5983	Fuel Oil Dealers	1	0.30%	0.056097	0.056097	0.056097	0.056097	0.056097	0.056097	0.056097	0.056097	0.056097	0.056097	0.056097
	FINANCE, INSURANCE, AND REAL ESTATE													
60	DEPOSITORY INSTITUTIONS	65	0.20%	0.037842	0.015741	-0.294736	-0.161879	-0.123587	0.008832	0.015741	0.037207	0.225485	0.303737	0.680985
602	COMMERCIAL BANKS	65	0.20%	0.037842	0.015741	-0.294736	-0.161879	-0.123587	0.008832	0.015741	0.037207	0.225485	0.303737	0.680985
6021	National Commercial Banks	45	0.03%	0.005068	0.015081	-0.364579	-0.167830	-0.144014	0.003222	0.015081	0.018642	0.097870	0.111040	0.191269
6022	State Commercial Banks	18	0.56%	0.103738	0.040725	-0.123762	-0.122275	-0.119797	0.029960	0.040725	0.055406	0.393644	0.805207	1.052145
6029	Commercial Banks, Not Elsewhere Classified	2	0.98%	0.182192	0.182192	-0.011274	-0.005352	0.004519	0.142709	0.182192	0.221675	0.359865	0.369735	0.375658
61	NONDEPOSITORY CREDIT INSTITUTIONS	32	0.77%	0.141850	0.145495	-0.778880	-0.651493	-0.521206	0.031075	0.145495	0.259833	0.664196	0.908786	1.308808
611	FEDERAL AND FEDERALLY-SPONSORED CREDIT AGENCIES	31	0.77%	0.142603	0.172476	-0.781620	-0.658342	-0.527447	0.018210	0.172476	0.260147	0.668835	0.930293	1.317411
6111	Federal And Federally-Sponsored Credit Agencies	31	0.77%	0.142603	0.172476	-0.781620	-0.658342	-0.527447	0.018210	0.172476	0.260147	0.668835	0.930293	1.317411
614	PERSONAL CREDIT INSTITUTIONS	1	0.64%	0.118514	0.118514	0.118514	0.118514	0.118514	0.118514	0.118514	0.118514	0.118514	0.118514	0.118514
6141	Personal Credit Institutions	1	0.64%	0.118514	0.118514	0.118514	0.118514	0.118514	0.118514	0.118514	0.118514	0.118514	0.118514	0.118514
62	SECURITY AND COMMODITY BROKERS, DEALERS, EXCHANGES, AND SERVICES	22	1.72%	0.318717	0.021167	-0.114818	-0.092504	-0.058588	0.010802	0.021167	0.027063	0.093442	3.265940	5.369552
621	SECURITY BROKERS, DEALERS, AND FLOTATION COMPANIES	17	2.18%	0.404276	0.011374	-0.117503	-0.099217	-0.068739	0.000675	0.011374	0.022044	1.429454	4.100707	5.703459
6211	Security Brokers, Dealers, And Flotation Companies	17	2.18%	0.404276	0.011374	-0.117503	-0.099217	-0.068739	0.000675	0.011374	0.022044	1.429454	4.100707	5.703459
628	SERVICES ALLIED WITH THE EXCHANGE OF SECURITIES OR COMMODITIES	5	0.15%	0.027815	0.049588	-0.055465	-0.050378	-0.041900	0.040122	0.049588	0.052694	0.063526	0.064298	0.064761
6282	Investment Advice	5	0.15%	0.027815	0.049588	-0.055465	-0.050378	-0.041900	0.040122	0.049588	0.052694	0.063526	0.064298	0.064761
63	INSURANCE CARRIERS	20	-0.12%	-0.022701	-0.008315	-0.277410	-0.235783	-0.166405	-0.020878	-0.008315	0.019802	0.083436	0.101868	0.112926
631	LIFE INSURANCE	1	-0.35%	-0.064142	-0.064142	-0.064142	-0.064142	-0.064142	-0.064142	-0.064142	-0.064142	-0.064142	-0.064142	-0.064142
6311	Life Insurance	1	-0.35%	-0.064142	-0.064142	-0.064142	-0.064142	-0.064142	-0.064142	-0.064142	-0.064142	-0.064142	-0.064142	-0.064142
632	ACCIDENT AND HEALTH INSURANCE AND MEDICAL SERVICE PLANS	4	-0.04%	-0.007878	-0.012500	-0.078256	-0.076525	-0.073641	-0.029569	-0.012500	0.004569	0.064357	0.068628	0.071191
6321	Accident And Health Insurance	4	-0.04%	-0.007878	-0.012500	-0.078256	-0.076525	-0.073641	-0.029569	-0.012500	0.004569	0.064357	0.068628	0.071191
633	FIRE, MARINE, AND CASUALTY INSURANCE	15	-0.13%	-0.023891	-0.007364	-0.284713	-0.254040	-0.202920	-0.011738	-0.007364	0.030644	0.093137	0.106718	0.114867
6331	Fire, Marine, And Casualty Insurance	15	-0.13%	-0.023891	-0.007364	-0.284713	-0.254040	-0.202920	-0.011738	-0.007364	0.030644	0.093137	0.106718	0.114867
67	HOLDING AND OTHER INVESTMENT OFFICES	91	0.05%	0.008575	0.001589	-0.227326	-0.184716	-0.151787	-0.018618	0.001589	0.037390	0.135702	0.154024	0.226886
671	HOLDING OFFICES	2	-0.28%	-0.051193	-0.051193	-0.117777	-0.115739	-0.112342	-0.064782	-0.051193	-0.037605	0.009955	0.013352	0.015391
6712	Offices Of Bank Holding Companies	2	-0.28%	-0.051193	-0.051193	-0.117777	-0.115739	-0.112342	-0.064782	-0.051193	-0.037605	0.009955	0.013352	0.015391
672	INVESTMENT OFFICES	14	0.08%	0.015111	-0.003111	-0.146532	-0.131575	-0.106646	-0.014090	-0.003111	0.025049	0.138518	0.153738	0.162871
6726	Unit Investment Trusts, Face-Amount Certificate Offices	14	0.08%	0.015111	-0.003111	-0.146532	-0.131575	-0.106646	-0.014090	-0.003111	0.025049	0.138518	0.153738	0.162871
679	MISCELLANEOUS INVESTING	75	0.05%	0.008949	0.010436	-0.257891	-0.189716	-0.156804	-0.019052	0.010436	0.037800	0.134524	0.144882	0.311336
6798	Real Estate Investment Trusts	74	0.05%	0.009321	0.011908	-0.259801	-0.190260	-0.158426	-0.017900	0.011908	0.038164	0.134818	0.145262	0.317240

Up-market Betas of Preferred Stocks by SIC Codes as of September 28, 2018

SIC Code	Description	Number of Companies	Equity Risk Premium	Mean	Median	1st Percentile	2.5th Percentile	5th Percentile	40th Percentile	50th Percentile	60th Percentile	95th Percentile	97.5th Percentile	99th Percentile
6799	Investors, Not Elsewhere Classified	1	-0.10%	-0.018618	-0.018618	-0.018618	-0.018618	-0.018618	-0.018618	-0.018618	-0.018618	-0.018618	-0.018618	-0.018618
	SERVICES													
70	HOTELS, ROOMING HOUSES, CAMPS, AND OTHER LODGING PLACES	1	-0.08%	-0.014548	-0.014548	-0.014548	-0.014548	-0.014548	-0.014548	-0.014548	-0.014548	-0.014548	-0.014548	-0.014548
701	HOTELS AND MOTELS	1	-0.08%	-0.014548	-0.014548	-0.014548	-0.014548	-0.014548	-0.014548	-0.014548	-0.014548	-0.014548	-0.014548	-0.014548
7011	Hotels And Motels	1	-0.08%	-0.014548	-0.014548	-0.014548	-0.014548	-0.014548	-0.014548	-0.014548	-0.014548	-0.014548	-0.014548	-0.014548
73	BUSINESS SERVICES	1	-2.35%	-0.434931	-0.434931	-0.434931	-0.434931	-0.434931	-0.434931	-0.434931	-0.434931	-0.434931	-0.434931	-0.434931
736	PERSONNEL SUPPLY SERVICES	1	-2.35%	-0.434931	-0.434931	-0.434931	-0.434931	-0.434931	-0.434931	-0.434931	-0.434931	-0.434931	-0.434931	-0.434931
7363	Help Supply Services	1	-2.35%	-0.434931	-0.434931	-0.434931	-0.434931	-0.434931	-0.434931	-0.434931	-0.434931	-0.434931	-0.434931	-0.434931

Mutual Funds by Peer Groups

Betas of Mutual Funds by Peer Groups as of September 28, 2018

Details:
Benchmark: S&P 500 Index
Returns period and frequency: 1 year of daily returns
Risk-free rate for betas: Federal Funds Rate
Expected US Equity Risk Premium: 5.40% (Fernandez, Pablo and Pershin, Vitaly and Fernández Acín, Isabel, Market Risk Premium and Risk-Free Rate used for 59 Countries in 2018: A Survey (April 3, 2018). Available at SSRN: https://ssrn.com/abstract=3155709)

Peer Group	Number of Mutual Funds	Equity Risk Premium	Mean	Median	1st Percentile	2.5th Percentile	5th Percentile	40th Percentile	50th Percentile	60th Percentile	95th Percentile	97.5th Percentile	99th Percentile
Allocation--15% to 30% Equity	153	0.98%	0.180625	0.174820	0.052463	0.053473	0.055068	0.157632	0.174820	0.198429	0.344203	0.506816	0.508635
Allocation--30% to 50% Equity	435	1.78%	0.329958	0.328646	0.086231	0.120913	0.147026	0.316155	0.328646	0.362049	0.480795	0.499351	0.569664
Allocation--50% to 70% Equity	702	2.87%	0.531507	0.547341	0.231921	0.261404	0.301724	0.517069	0.547341	0.566053	0.674277	0.699956	0.749933
Allocation--70% to 85% Equity	310	3.60%	0.665927	0.675443	0.296365	0.404436	0.479471	0.646641	0.675443	0.702216	0.810027	0.893723	0.904903
Allocation--85%+ Equity	132	4.35%	0.804869	0.821287	0.494702	0.571996	0.689638	0.815797	0.821287	0.834340	0.902275	0.951448	0.954799
Bank Loan	16	0.14%	0.026281	0.021902	0.001993	0.002032	0.002097	0.020578	0.021902	0.033885	0.047755	0.057184	0.062841
Bear Market	63	-8.06%	-1.491971	-1.218540	-2.443600	-2.443344	-2.438724	-1.790414	-1.218540	-1.175324	-0.860818	-0.603169	-0.598473
China Region	50	4.86%	0.899881	0.954490	0.552516	0.595083	0.596271	0.825649	0.954490	0.971162	1.178607	1.192033	1.192700
Commodities Broad Basket	96	1.21%	0.223234	0.203622	0.009896	0.045599	0.115237	0.198225	0.203622	0.210162	0.399308	0.475362	0.520972
Commodities Precious Metals	2	0.27%	0.049918	0.049918	0.049783	0.049787	0.049794	0.049891	0.049918	0.049946	0.050042	0.050049	0.050053
Communications	27	4.15%	0.769359	0.751505	0.620725	0.621259	0.622423	0.723247	0.751505	0.751993	1.004652	1.030802	1.059853
Consumer Cyclical	24	4.67%	0.863901	0.925755	0.630238	0.630621	0.631100	0.833014	0.925755	0.932815	0.964163	0.991865	1.013990
Consumer Defensive	19	3.55%	0.658240	0.630652	0.583568	0.583598	0.583649	0.630073	0.630652	0.649576	0.737612	0.757364	0.769215
Convertibles	79	2.97%	0.549832	0.617667	0.014798	0.017076	0.288592	0.581012	0.617667	0.624019	0.678168	0.679940	0.685296
Corporate Bond	133	-0.14%	-0.026490	-0.029731	-0.070933	-0.068127	-0.066264	-0.033583	-0.029731	-0.026471	-0.005186	0.074591	0.182770
Diversified Emerging Mkts	668	3.94%	0.729666	0.764998	0.214590	0.310436	0.368663	0.727941	0.764998	0.795545	0.940983	0.974202	0.982137
Diversified Pacific/Asia	30	3.84%	0.711173	0.736715	0.378223	0.378403	0.468211	0.682231	0.736715	0.785387	0.842818	0.843950	0.844241
Emerging Markets Bond	224	0.52%	0.097064	0.091760	-0.081481	-0.032630	0.010221	0.083225	0.091760	0.100063	0.171167	0.204888	0.524156
Emerging-Markets Local-Currency Bond	69	1.19%	0.219570	0.248681	0.054790	0.056660	0.073658	0.228517	0.248681	0.253798	0.305445	0.319636	0.322697
Energy Limited Partnership	91	4.06%	0.752651	0.762052	0.553009	0.557103	0.573970	0.749588	0.762052	0.777757	0.983075	1.021748	1.028939
Equity Energy	77	5.22%	0.967487	0.967708	0.699709	0.736796	0.757979	0.964589	0.967708	1.009580	1.109408	1.142896	1.421120
Equity Precious Metals	52	1.97%	0.365509	0.352922	0.296049	0.299386	0.300465	0.329272	0.352922	0.376834	0.466889	0.486989	0.506341
Europe Stock	86	3.47%	0.643458	0.669367	0.296327	0.315707	0.424621	0.631742	0.669367	0.687331	0.799950	0.801907	0.805854
Financial	71	4.52%	0.837444	0.864410	0.429592	0.431635	0.520416	0.845809	0.864410	0.876511	1.052785	1.104628	1.119230
Foreign Large Blend	683	3.68%	0.681791	0.686637	0.337486	0.432564	0.539211	0.666023	0.686637	0.702155	0.813665	0.827975	0.895581
Foreign Large Growth	291	3.91%	0.723816	0.714627	0.614280	0.616092	0.618138	0.698151	0.714627	0.728769	0.882267	0.891292	0.940961
Foreign Large Value	270	3.49%	0.646323	0.663619	0.253780	0.315795	0.437682	0.648576	0.663619	0.694424	0.755370	0.759705	0.880560
Foreign Small/Mid Blend	79	2.99%	0.554395	0.583951	0.336607	0.338336	0.382891	0.522250	0.583951	0.596080	0.699256	0.703110	0.704860
Foreign Small/Mid Growth	115	3.28%	0.607625	0.621057	0.379636	0.389877	0.470065	0.573625	0.621057	0.652206	0.735761	0.779447	0.781733
Foreign Small/Mid Value	52	2.90%	0.536773	0.593709	0.132841	0.134527	0.154315	0.567706	0.593709	0.594583	0.714830	0.717079	0.718708
Global Real Estate	196	2.64%	0.488424	0.503133	0.324770	0.337872	0.368019	0.490765	0.503133	0.507354	0.562746	0.566768	0.596362
Health	101	5.25%	0.972679	0.952241	0.828016	0.836725	0.849954	0.933584	0.952241	0.954994	1.165000	1.229170	1.229580
High Yield Bond	377	0.43%	0.078910	0.074954	0.019826	0.028616	0.034819	0.070800	0.074954	0.078792	0.146333	0.161824	0.270760
High Yield Muni	96	0.01%	0.002056	0.000146	-0.013622	-0.011459	-0.009787	-0.000584	0.000146	0.001721	0.016545	0.020621	0.020815
India Equity	14	2.11%	0.390264	0.391292	0.313776	0.313858	0.313996	0.387967	0.391292	0.420044	0.447352	0.447868	0.448177
Industrials	23	5.28%	0.977224	0.979967	0.850734	0.885568	0.934346	0.978276	0.979967	0.994314	1.007087	1.008338	1.009011
Inflation-Protected Bond	181	-0.16%	-0.029196	-0.035136	-0.090224	-0.088762	-0.087474	-0.037393	-0.035136	-0.032473	0.018914	0.093941	0.146187
Infrastructure	65	2.88%	0.534207	0.529644	0.337762	0.403963	0.441717	0.527232	0.529644	0.535858	0.640322	0.642019	0.643571
Intermediate Government	229	-0.25%	-0.046450	-0.044801	-0.081783	-0.079958	-0.075658	-0.048847	-0.044801	-0.041719	-0.024102	-0.016626	-0.008655
Intermediate-Term Bond	855	-0.18%	-0.032684	-0.036392	-0.079411	-0.063396	-0.059511	-0.040673	-0.036392	-0.031740	-0.003535	0.022384	0.058777
Japan Stock	27	3.59%	0.664911	0.700791	0.506446	0.508078	0.509881	0.683801	0.700791	0.705968	0.738094	0.746216	0.747081
Large Blend	1201	5.22%	0.966655	0.980048	0.616782	0.754366	0.801013	0.957862	0.980048	0.992832	1.058650	1.073960	1.084880
Large Growth	1211	5.71%	1.056681	1.074630	0.818451	0.863710	0.897694	1.055280	1.074630	1.090730	1.202650	1.217695	1.239598
Large Value	1074	4.82%	0.891690	0.909657	0.540850	0.601289	0.704718	0.896600	0.909657	0.924585	0.992710	1.007926	1.173340
Latin America Stock	13	4.38%	0.811871	0.826357	0.744901	0.750252	0.759171	0.777487	0.826357	0.827918	0.876345	0.876509	0.876607
Long Government	24	-0.78%	-0.144727	-0.149899	-0.188994	-0.188977	-0.188164	-0.151182	-0.149899	-0.146747	-0.093414	-0.089383	-0.086138
Long-Short Credit	25	0.24%	0.043671	0.019761	-0.017258	-0.017129	-0.016897	0.016729	0.019761	0.070579	0.097139	0.097411	0.097532
Long-Short Equity	217	2.90%	0.536772	0.541168	-0.086063	-0.054394	0.103220	0.513633	0.541168	0.594025	0.951597	1.063988	1.254246
Long-Term Bond	18	-0.23%	-0.042287	-0.027661	-0.098660	-0.098653	-0.098642	-0.047979	-0.027661	-0.025673	0.010615	0.011973	0.012787

Betas of Mutual Funds by Peer Groups as of September 28, 2018

Peer Group	Number of Mutual Funds	Equity Risk Premium	Mean	Median	1st Percentile	2.5th Percentile	5th Percentile	40th Percentile	50th Percentile	60th Percentile	95th Percentile	97.5th Percentile	99th Percentile
Managed Futures	94	1.72%	0.319097	0.315422	-0.102978	-0.092837	-0.029346	0.251016	0.315422	0.342539	0.628732	0.915738	0.957190
Market Neutral	127	0.57%	0.104710	0.086727	-0.294550	-0.266255	-0.095878	0.034247	0.086727	0.096839	0.530448	0.606659	0.857738
Mid-Cap Blend	343	4.65%	0.861335	0.875610	0.317778	0.522464	0.706662	0.862096	0.875610	0.884688	1.026166	1.075869	1.255990
Mid-Cap Growth	552	5.14%	0.952007	0.964564	0.601702	0.739547	0.801627	0.944140	0.964564	0.979885	1.095521	1.163070	1.200733
Mid-Cap Value	369	4.50%	0.832426	0.839869	0.562983	0.641503	0.699076	0.827657	0.839869	0.849394	0.952168	0.983045	1.049261
Miscellaneous Region	30	3.26%	0.604408	0.606729	0.423382	0.423469	0.424408	0.581589	0.606729	0.629714	0.751466	0.823084	0.832546
Miscellaneous Sector	6	9.36%	1.734013	1.733010	1.622794	1.622889	1.623048	1.625380	1.733010	1.840640	1.845983	1.846141	1.846237
Multialternative	321	1.47%	0.272514	0.231076	-0.110873	-0.042088	-0.001904	0.197539	0.231076	0.255216	0.731606	0.770664	1.448273
Multicurrency	37	0.26%	0.048809	0.078629	-0.255236	-0.204020	-0.194520	0.063690	0.078629	0.129364	0.203110	0.203206	0.203327
Multisector Bond	221	0.27%	0.049780	0.027697	-0.145380	-0.143527	-0.142127	0.015927	0.027697	0.059140	0.187015	0.252635	0.426683
Muni California Intermediate	40	0.01%	0.002217	0.000762	-0.010103	-0.008766	-0.004505	0.000463	0.000762	0.001557	0.017623	0.018185	0.018898
Muni California Long	71	0.00%	0.000268	-0.000091	-0.009480	-0.009286	-0.007971	-0.001176	-0.000091	0.000988	0.012159	0.016665	0.019545
Muni Massachusetts	39	-0.02%	-0.003348	-0.002908	-0.010500	-0.010353	-0.009686	-0.003691	-0.002908	-0.001887	0.001241	0.002257	0.003215
Muni Minnesota	36	-0.02%	-0.003586	-0.003751	-0.011485	-0.010636	-0.009072	-0.004286	-0.003751	-0.003199	0.002418	0.003411	0.007465
Muni National Interm	147	0.00%	0.000732	-0.001090	-0.011732	-0.010117	-0.008254	-0.002079	-0.001090	-0.000166	0.018278	0.029308	0.030438
Muni National Long	118	-0.01%	-0.001976	-0.002003	-0.016122	-0.011260	-0.009873	-0.003272	-0.002003	-0.001317	0.008341	0.014386	0.015315
Muni National Short	12	0.09%	0.016539	0.018815	-0.000881	-0.000310	0.000641	0.013514	0.018815	0.023620	0.028508	0.028955	0.029223
Muni New Jersey	40	0.00%	-0.000206	-0.001760	-0.009709	-0.009574	-0.006831	-0.002831	-0.001760	-0.000465	0.021681	0.024383	0.026336
Muni New York Intermediate	31	0.01%	0.001221	-0.001378	-0.008642	-0.008401	-0.008031	-0.002220	-0.001378	-0.000732	0.021231	0.022686	0.023264
Muni New York Long	56	0.01%	0.001040	-0.001076	-0.006317	-0.005911	-0.005524	-0.001685	-0.001076	0.000199	0.015429	0.017600	0.018470
Muni Ohio	22	-0.01%	-0.001872	-0.001988	-0.009328	-0.009236	-0.009073	-0.002260	-0.001988	-0.001590	0.005847	0.006793	0.007387
Muni Pennsylvania	42	0.00%	-0.000001	-0.000775	-0.004919	-0.003637	-0.003536	-0.001066	-0.000775	-0.000193	0.006080	0.008312	0.013696
Muni Single State Interm	69	-0.01%	-0.001376	-0.001916	-0.009640	-0.008709	-0.007096	-0.002554	-0.001916	-0.000817	0.005518	0.006831	0.009347
Muni Single State Long	164	-0.01%	-0.002004	-0.002292	-0.010213	-0.008872	-0.007738	-0.003330	-0.002292	-0.001255	0.005204	0.005621	0.006443
Muni Single State Short	4	0.00%	-0.000379	-0.000065	-0.003414	-0.003328	-0.003185	-0.000962	-0.000065	0.000833	0.001986	0.002035	0.002064
Natural Resources	94	4.92%	0.910862	0.950679	0.101554	0.282472	0.648653	0.922489	0.950679	0.955497	1.129375	1.129749	1.144197
Nontraditional Bond	181	0.29%	0.053657	0.048087	-0.061259	-0.042890	-0.009938	0.040414	0.048087	0.057487	0.155937	0.164558	0.172527
Option Writing	88	2.78%	0.515080	0.542278	0.031959	0.053256	0.208301	0.456065	0.542278	0.588152	0.755916	0.771890	0.785561
Pacific/Asia ex-Japan Stk	61	3.76%	0.696291	0.709098	0.270368	0.367078	0.465299	0.665973	0.709098	0.759555	0.962276	0.962749	0.963831
Preferred Stock	37	0.36%	0.067557	0.048496	0.022331	0.023636	0.024116	0.045206	0.048496	0.060427	0.205664	0.205818	0.206466
Real Estate	206	2.83%	0.524088	0.528357	0.151115	0.174333	0.473305	0.525665	0.528357	0.532899	0.565263	0.738726	0.766296
Short Government	24	-0.20%	-0.036118	-0.033835	-0.056128	-0.055137	-0.053424	-0.036757	-0.033835	-0.033198	-0.025756	-0.021570	-0.018240
Short-Term Bond	65	-0.10%	-0.018190	-0.035005	-0.050458	-0.050060	-0.049967	-0.040170	-0.035005	-0.030308	0.128291	0.151967	0.152402
Small Blend	650	4.58%	0.847876	0.869738	0.584434	0.659852	0.709625	0.852529	0.869738	0.880436	0.943261	0.949439	0.990611
Small Growth	590	5.01%	0.927365	0.933787	0.686476	0.745314	0.794041	0.914401	0.933787	0.957565	1.035533	1.060884	1.085492
Small Value	376	4.36%	0.807440	0.820812	0.433456	0.513573	0.654826	0.809862	0.820812	0.832552	0.909019	0.946208	0.966960
Tactical Allocation	231	2.67%	0.494985	0.477342	-0.042280	0.010091	0.133293	0.424079	0.477342	0.538830	0.922746	0.973197	1.011930
Target-Date 2000-2010	100	1.71%	0.316737	0.332065	0.174456	0.252639	0.261372	0.323713	0.332065	0.336218	0.355677	0.356360	0.358409
Target-Date 2015	122	1.83%	0.339626	0.368833	0.079293	0.083121	0.146008	0.358519	0.368833	0.382369	0.428778	0.470449	0.476790
Target-Date 2020	210	2.11%	0.390151	0.412701	0.129609	0.138218	0.143722	0.397298	0.412701	0.425554	0.511548	0.514545	0.548555
Target-Date 2025	183	2.62%	0.485027	0.508956	0.214024	0.263553	0.321441	0.491659	0.508956	0.535260	0.581933	0.602732	0.621650
Target-Date 2030	209	3.08%	0.569625	0.611855	0.199107	0.216581	0.223474	0.603871	0.611855	0.618523	0.665880	0.672091	0.698182
Target-Date 2035	181	3.58%	0.662107	0.691302	0.310831	0.359175	0.435667	0.678153	0.691302	0.703992	0.757333	0.774867	0.779404
Target-Date 2040	209	3.78%	0.700613	0.747456	0.254065	0.259042	0.279737	0.733725	0.747456	0.755203	0.804401	0.808070	0.808683
Target-Date 2045	182	4.05%	0.750282	0.772894	0.358302	0.437505	0.501851	0.760270	0.772894	0.783687	0.827393	0.843501	0.854796
Target-Date 2050	207	4.01%	0.742165	0.786192	0.292825	0.296368	0.328299	0.770235	0.786192	0.794758	0.855175	0.861062	0.868768
Target-Date 2055	187	4.13%	0.765736	0.783772	0.373310	0.462837	0.536133	0.773191	0.783772	0.791014	0.847588	0.853281	0.882205
Target-Date 2060+	118	4.31%	0.797694	0.794528	0.685638	0.687384	0.705425	0.787824	0.794528	0.810393	0.854628	0.889245	0.890437
Target-Date Retirement	150	1.46%	0.269583	0.270773	0.124230	0.125617	0.128790	0.252234	0.270773	0.284566	0.371049	0.375969	0.378097
Technology	149	6.38%	1.181547	1.185430	0.852729	0.960683	0.999231	1.168664	1.185430	1.195482	1.338730	1.391488	1.391876
Trading--Inverse Commodities	4	-3.47%	-0.642859	-0.642432	-0.938977	-0.938893	-0.938753	-0.819274	-0.642432	-0.465589	-0.347562	-0.347551	-0.347544
Trading--Inverse Debt	15	0.30%	0.055051	0.148493	-0.165593	-0.164468	-0.162595	0.118243	0.148493	0.149785	0.200041	0.200090	0.200119
Trading--Inverse Equity	7	-10.86%	-2.010244	-2.093310	-2.104659	-2.103967	-2.102813	-2.095314	-2.093310	-2.092686	-1.674619	-1.585485	-1.532004
Trading--Leveraged Debt	9	-0.78%	-0.145028	-0.186180	-0.201175	-0.201051	-0.200845	-0.194926	-0.186180	-0.186118	0.066392	0.150369	0.200755

Betas of Mutual Funds by Peer Groups as of September 28, 2018

Peer Group	Number of Mutual Funds	Equity Risk Premium	Mean	Median	1st Percentile	2.5th Percentile	5th Percentile	40th Percentile	50th Percentile	60th Percentile	95th Percentile	97.5th Percentile	99th Percentile
Trading--Leveraged Equity	97	8.96%	1.658896	1.762890	0.373256	0.522542	0.785239	1.531432	1.762890	1.802780	2.437182	2.461450	2.461982
Trading--Miscellaneous	8	-0.70%	-0.130097	-0.132659	-0.522056	-0.522027	-0.521978	-0.133403	-0.132659	-0.078967	0.134615	0.134752	0.134834
Utilities	49	2.04%	0.376908	0.375022	0.255994	0.256439	0.256939	0.360018	0.375022	0.430138	0.445240	0.452396	0.459801
Volatility	3	-8.26%	-1.530497	-1.525310	-1.540559	-1.540092	-1.539314	-1.528422	-1.525310	-1.525310	-1.525310	-1.525310	-1.525310
World Allocation	430	2.74%	0.508146	0.498826	0.118680	0.178474	0.247776	0.462830	0.498826	0.539967	0.765228	0.796430	0.825440
World Bond	257	0.25%	0.045401	0.021939	-0.023878	-0.016002	-0.006655	0.014887	0.021939	0.033445	0.166771	0.188654	0.189695
World Stock	901	4.25%	0.786619	0.817353	0.329003	0.467051	0.539583	0.785928	0.817353	0.836260	0.985915	1.011485	1.072540

Down-market Betas of Mutual Funds by Peer Groups as of September 28, 2018

Details:
Benchmark: S&P 500 Index
Returns period and frequency: 1 year of daily returns
Risk-free rate for betas: Federal Funds Rate
Expected US Equity Risk Premium: 5.40% (Fernandez, Pablo and Pershin, Vitaly and Fernández Acín, Isabel, Market Risk Premium and Risk-Free Rate used for 59 Countries in 2018: A Survey (April 3, 2018). Available at SSRN: https://ssrn.com/abstract=3155709)

Peer Group	Number of Mutual Funds	Equity Risk Premium	Mean	Median	1st Percentile	2.5th Percentile	5th Percentile	40th Percentile	50th Percentile	60th Percentile	95th Percentile	97.5th Percentile	99th Percentile
Allocation--15% to 30% Equity	153	0.95%	0.175777	0.169691	0.029979	0.031875	0.037658	0.162961	0.169691	0.195683	0.348748	0.514618	0.517735
Allocation--30% to 50% Equity	435	1.79%	0.330917	0.334486	0.084188	0.095498	0.103583	0.315509	0.334486	0.358412	0.485402	0.495528	0.561827
Allocation--50% to 70% Equity	702	2.89%	0.534558	0.545146	0.219571	0.252555	0.344164	0.527343	0.545146	0.568108	0.679495	0.691618	0.744020
Allocation--70% to 85% Equity	310	3.60%	0.667166	0.671484	0.278127	0.462506	0.482884	0.652093	0.671484	0.702391	0.820593	0.864926	0.934272
Allocation--85%+ Equity	132	4.30%	0.796466	0.816095	0.514138	0.590166	0.594259	0.808191	0.816095	0.824761	0.901645	0.926887	0.931232
Bank Loan	16	0.15%	0.027142	0.023168	-0.003473	-0.002601	-0.001147	0.021321	0.023168	0.035824	0.055479	0.057579	0.058839
Bear Market	63	-7.73%	-1.430714	-1.317440	-2.194506	-2.192708	-2.191290	-1.687192	-1.317440	-1.088352	-0.837722	-0.616220	-0.612886
China Region	50	4.26%	0.788866	0.792452	0.542107	0.579837	0.580234	0.703428	0.792452	0.842848	0.981153	0.988444	0.990729
Commodities Broad Basket	96	0.94%	0.173678	0.154489	-0.091036	-0.014780	0.106226	0.147321	0.154489	0.159553	0.394310	0.430194	0.463522
Commodities Precious Metals	2	0.05%	0.008633	0.008633	0.007047	0.007096	0.007177	0.008309	0.008633	0.008956	0.010089	0.010170	0.010218
Communications	27	4.12%	0.762958	0.759384	0.664523	0.664739	0.665042	0.750731	0.759384	0.760446	0.912517	0.934111	0.958022
Consumer Cyclical	24	4.72%	0.874077	0.916025	0.666479	0.666777	0.667274	0.893465	0.916025	0.932208	0.959759	0.978361	0.991824
Consumer Defensive	19	3.61%	0.669363	0.667226	0.591281	0.591659	0.592290	0.666085	0.667226	0.667482	0.721818	0.744397	0.757944
Convertibles	79	2.82%	0.522707	0.569490	0.047282	0.049554	0.256344	0.546493	0.569490	0.585968	0.664722	0.667134	0.675473
Corporate Bond	133	-0.18%	-0.032710	-0.035205	-0.085346	-0.075333	-0.073393	-0.038060	-0.035205	-0.030734	-0.010126	0.010414	0.170287
Diversified Emerging Mkts	668	3.48%	0.644694	0.675770	0.189301	0.306719	0.371819	0.652185	0.675770	0.697356	0.803693	0.827965	0.845701
Diversified Pacific/Asia	30	3.76%	0.695472	0.717492	0.412247	0.415073	0.480336	0.704495	0.717492	0.744246	0.781270	0.782240	0.782471
Emerging Markets Bond	224	0.43%	0.079938	0.077662	-0.088168	-0.041067	0.004953	0.069894	0.077662	0.086902	0.126694	0.142215	0.426773
Emerging-Markets Local-Currency Bond	69	0.80%	0.147424	0.159398	0.038305	0.041332	0.085086	0.152550	0.159398	0.162566	0.184637	0.189745	0.194700
Energy Limited Partnership	91	3.95%	0.731783	0.735408	0.566804	0.569776	0.571594	0.728487	0.735408	0.746955	0.961519	0.982465	0.997332
Equity Energy	77	5.06%	0.937817	0.948376	0.611012	0.679416	0.729015	0.923691	0.948376	0.970359	1.100516	1.128532	1.360386
Equity Precious Metals	52	1.29%	0.239045	0.232273	0.119646	0.149758	0.157829	0.199510	0.232273	0.241463	0.362719	0.418516	0.428762
Europe Stock	86	3.70%	0.684975	0.709948	0.361634	0.375905	0.450504	0.697399	0.709948	0.724846	0.803670	0.825767	0.826478
Financial	71	5.02%	0.929639	0.968871	0.547506	0.548759	0.588641	0.927154	0.968871	0.987792	1.162180	1.186458	1.187845
Foreign Large Blend	683	3.79%	0.702327	0.712063	0.398224	0.471704	0.569431	0.694024	0.712063	0.724313	0.791465	0.799004	0.829816
Foreign Large Growth	291	4.01%	0.742983	0.746861	0.620793	0.625817	0.637690	0.726613	0.746861	0.761383	0.839197	0.854900	0.871433
Foreign Large Value	270	3.63%	0.672005	0.697057	0.310605	0.348685	0.486890	0.677936	0.697057	0.705960	0.788997	0.792571	0.889939
Foreign Small/Mid Blend	79	3.40%	0.630503	0.651155	0.406198	0.407261	0.417246	0.648046	0.651155	0.656002	0.771475	0.776119	0.780026
Foreign Small/Mid Growth	115	3.71%	0.686616	0.704006	0.455793	0.515540	0.519229	0.686524	0.704006	0.714837	0.811354	0.863604	0.866311
Foreign Small/Mid Value	52	3.11%	0.575134	0.629679	-0.001106	0.045312	0.202483	0.593139	0.629679	0.639601	0.775983	0.780534	0.782950
Global Real Estate	196	2.84%	0.525084	0.536574	0.339979	0.351877	0.431985	0.531137	0.536574	0.546301	0.592718	0.595138	0.603956
Health	101	5.34%	0.989694	0.960841	0.837846	0.841981	0.845914	0.950206	0.960841	0.970135	1.189480	1.237805	1.239110
High Yield Bond	377	0.45%	0.083760	0.080735	0.024907	0.032864	0.041146	0.075983	0.080735	0.086196	0.128710	0.161733	0.255910
High Yield Muni	96	0.03%	0.005867	0.006157	-0.012715	-0.011419	-0.006976	0.001662	0.006157	0.008413	0.023897	0.029892	0.031664
India Equity	14	1.37%	0.254136	0.264358	0.196812	0.197622	0.198974	0.263958	0.264358	0.265396	0.296959	0.297380	0.297633
Industrials	23	5.51%	1.019704	1.053970	0.897488	0.929301	0.972755	1.007272	1.053970	1.056066	1.061159	1.062078	1.062721
Inflation-Protected Bond	181	-0.17%	-0.030961	-0.037858	-0.087386	-0.084887	-0.083044	-0.040825	-0.037858	-0.033308	0.020690	0.095167	0.135416
Infrastructure	65	3.09%	0.571476	0.564261	0.364215	0.453534	0.484927	0.560316	0.564261	0.569442	0.695040	0.696214	0.698658
Intermediate Government	229	-0.27%	-0.050791	-0.049119	-0.086880	-0.082989	-0.078393	-0.051989	-0.049119	-0.046429	-0.028922	-0.026503	-0.024411
Intermediate-Term Bond	855	-0.20%	-0.037652	-0.041629	-0.080347	-0.070622	-0.065855	-0.046301	-0.041629	-0.037468	-0.000243	0.026608	0.048322
Japan Stock	27	4.16%	0.769664	0.761569	0.690486	0.699359	0.710946	0.752194	0.761569	0.782634	0.835191	0.839198	0.839769
Large Blend	1201	5.18%	0.959969	0.980124	0.652551	0.716137	0.797654	0.961425	0.980124	0.994094	1.047090	1.061860	1.084100
Large Growth	1211	5.45%	1.008690	1.026090	0.813976	0.858704	0.881981	1.007050	1.026090	1.037710	1.102600	1.120733	1.143238
Large Value	1074	4.96%	0.919434	0.939081	0.485641	0.639102	0.736555	0.922448	0.939081	0.956310	1.028831	1.044822	1.244274
Latin America Stock	13	3.67%	0.678761	0.686698	0.594345	0.603130	0.617770	0.682835	0.686698	0.688791	0.723877	0.724184	0.724368
Long Government	24	-0.90%	-0.166818	-0.169501	-0.226867	-0.226697	-0.225276	-0.170647	-0.169501	-0.167318	-0.102080	-0.101941	-0.101869
Long-Short Credit	25	0.25%	0.045831	0.021697	-0.006549	-0.006366	-0.005929	0.010589	0.021697	0.080803	0.106622	0.108522	0.110009
Long-Short Equity	217	2.92%	0.541085	0.542155	-0.342592	-0.195335	0.021062	0.504582	0.542155	0.595543	0.992278	1.316838	1.406570
Long-Term Bond	18	-0.29%	-0.053079	-0.044567	-0.108151	-0.108150	-0.108148	-0.063491	-0.044567	-0.037988	0.018086	0.019650	0.020589

Down-market Betas of Mutual Funds by Peer Groups as of September 28, 2018

Peer Group	Number of Mutual Funds	Equity Risk Premium	Mean	Median	1st Percentile	2.5th Percentile	5th Percentile	40th Percentile	50th Percentile	60th Percentile	95th Percentile	97.5th Percentile	99th Percentile
Managed Futures	94	2.12%	0.392324	0.352923	-0.046334	0.017461	0.133905	0.329390	0.352923	0.389991	0.666860	0.953519	0.961982
Market Neutral	127	0.59%	0.109729	0.082030	-0.537039	-0.477635	-0.078888	0.068603	0.082030	0.102662	0.556302	0.795072	0.813180
Mid-Cap Blend	343	4.68%	0.865868	0.883840	0.313873	0.527451	0.711229	0.872534	0.883840	0.889577	1.025317	1.043025	1.152325
Mid-Cap Growth	552	5.07%	0.938382	0.948192	0.735269	0.767417	0.787434	0.925819	0.948192	0.958186	1.079522	1.115548	1.185863
Mid-Cap Value	369	4.56%	0.844815	0.857560	0.594845	0.623111	0.683389	0.847342	0.857560	0.874066	0.977164	0.992796	1.013198
Miscellaneous Region	30	3.10%	0.573435	0.556831	0.445197	0.446228	0.447496	0.537358	0.556831	0.616450	0.728425	0.785546	0.790405
Miscellaneous Sector	6	9.06%	1.677822	1.680110	1.623145	1.623616	1.624403	1.636170	1.680110	1.724050	1.727655	1.727793	1.727875
Multialternative	321	1.54%	0.285614	0.249480	-0.146351	-0.076608	-0.053777	0.204289	0.249480	0.293788	0.743229	0.769613	1.676654
Multicurrency	37	0.20%	0.037707	0.097231	-0.254924	-0.228670	-0.223123	0.075149	0.097231	0.131800	0.152959	0.153962	0.154249
Multisector Bond	221	0.27%	0.049260	0.032638	-0.142705	-0.139382	-0.133191	0.016902	0.032638	0.055683	0.191159	0.252646	0.355559
Muni California Intermediate	40	0.04%	0.006806	0.003441	-0.010630	-0.006554	-0.003835	0.002180	0.003441	0.004270	0.034198	0.034564	0.035495
Muni California Long	71	0.04%	0.007256	0.005358	-0.005708	-0.004915	-0.003349	0.004598	0.005358	0.006736	0.025672	0.033039	0.036895
Muni Massachusetts	39	0.02%	0.003282	0.002710	-0.007772	-0.005882	-0.003530	0.001634	0.002710	0.003114	0.011203	0.013280	0.015123
Muni Minnesota	36	0.01%	0.001183	0.000324	-0.011314	-0.010121	-0.008309	0.000001	0.000324	0.001797	0.011084	0.014434	0.015624
Muni National Interm	147	0.03%	0.004747	0.003649	-0.012546	-0.009792	-0.007591	0.002334	0.003649	0.004893	0.023006	0.026564	0.035138
Muni National Long	118	0.02%	0.003563	0.004241	-0.014087	-0.010575	-0.007210	0.002094	0.004241	0.005554	0.016583	0.020866	0.021237
Muni National Short	12	0.11%	0.019632	0.019852	0.008682	0.008768	0.008913	0.016660	0.019852	0.023648	0.031257	0.031512	0.031665
Muni New Jersey	40	0.00%	0.000666	0.001509	-0.023004	-0.022501	-0.017899	0.000656	0.001509	0.003574	0.010666	0.012377	0.013439
Muni New York Intermediate	31	0.04%	0.006935	0.002902	-0.006483	-0.006359	-0.006239	0.001663	0.002902	0.004025	0.039810	0.042698	0.044626
Muni New York Long	56	0.02%	0.004136	0.004265	-0.009139	-0.007376	-0.007139	0.001497	0.004265	0.004926	0.014798	0.016311	0.016748
Muni Ohio	22	0.02%	0.003700	0.004131	-0.004645	-0.004453	-0.004131	0.002283	0.004131	0.005350	0.011874	0.012744	0.013245
Muni Pennsylvania	42	0.01%	0.002248	0.002716	-0.017141	-0.015341	-0.015024	0.002396	0.002716	0.005114	0.009852	0.010489	0.011682
Muni Single State Interm	69	0.00%	0.000566	-0.000176	-0.010368	-0.009158	-0.008483	-0.000523	-0.000176	0.001622	0.011702	0.015831	0.024224
Muni Single State Long	164	0.01%	0.002214	0.002204	-0.011520	-0.009030	-0.007312	0.000863	0.002204	0.003419	0.010469	0.011294	0.014989
Muni Single State Short	4	0.02%	0.003037	0.001722	-0.000170	-0.000120	-0.000036	0.001238	0.001722	0.002206	0.007950	0.008429	0.008716
Natural Resources	94	4.58%	0.847939	0.886386	0.006817	0.214745	0.658236	0.873236	0.886386	0.890818	1.006397	1.121037	1.121575
Nontraditional Bond	181	0.28%	0.051961	0.049800	-0.059100	-0.040677	-0.027580	0.040072	0.049800	0.058536	0.121447	0.127891	0.151545
Option Writing	88	2.99%	0.553988	0.615399	0.032054	0.107470	0.132208	0.523501	0.615399	0.649429	0.854784	0.884477	0.908469
Pacific/Asia ex-Japan Stk	61	3.46%	0.641635	0.688000	0.238199	0.361875	0.487759	0.644485	0.688000	0.694830	0.832249	0.833548	0.834303
Preferred Stock	37	0.41%	0.075990	0.060031	0.028828	0.030744	0.031871	0.052911	0.060031	0.064772	0.226290	0.227349	0.228714
Real Estate	206	2.88%	0.533469	0.536096	0.146364	0.177993	0.494185	0.530252	0.536096	0.540706	0.582490	0.782986	0.820193
Short Government	24	-0.22%	-0.040989	-0.039194	-0.061442	-0.058226	-0.054251	-0.046256	-0.039194	-0.036655	-0.025708	-0.020533	-0.016594
Short-Term Bond	65	-0.06%	-0.011160	-0.036532	-0.048386	-0.047432	-0.046833	-0.039331	-0.036532	-0.031112	0.201709	0.234673	0.234960
Small Blend	650	4.61%	0.854314	0.874360	0.616869	0.681367	0.701203	0.857343	0.874360	0.883250	0.957609	0.966881	1.000316
Small Growth	590	4.86%	0.899171	0.903013	0.647795	0.693267	0.769865	0.879051	0.903013	0.933065	0.997700	1.034398	1.038498
Small Value	376	4.44%	0.821782	0.844564	0.383330	0.520452	0.647587	0.823700	0.844564	0.857602	0.927107	0.956895	0.991946
Tactical Allocation	231	2.63%	0.486277	0.451815	-0.044963	0.003708	0.136339	0.404192	0.451815	0.517040	0.964978	1.007740	1.060911
Target-Date 2000-2010	100	1.68%	0.311872	0.332193	0.183644	0.212540	0.218521	0.324081	0.332193	0.335391	0.352656	0.354098	0.354682
Target-Date 2015	122	1.84%	0.340215	0.371679	0.079554	0.084637	0.167870	0.352019	0.371679	0.379702	0.437298	0.495920	0.501870
Target-Date 2020	210	2.09%	0.387810	0.409681	0.124309	0.127391	0.136428	0.394672	0.409681	0.427376	0.515750	0.530107	0.576817
Target-Date 2025	183	2.63%	0.486992	0.510450	0.220377	0.283131	0.325538	0.495236	0.510450	0.525300	0.576365	0.615624	0.649955
Target-Date 2030	209	3.05%	0.565676	0.608999	0.180547	0.203083	0.209216	0.589052	0.608999	0.620016	0.671127	0.676446	0.731449
Target-Date 2035	181	3.56%	0.659495	0.684050	0.301622	0.415357	0.496152	0.676949	0.684050	0.697933	0.782608	0.786344	0.793893
Target-Date 2040	209	3.75%	0.694645	0.741990	0.241104	0.245646	0.259526	0.729989	0.741990	0.746800	0.800795	0.812928	0.828834
Target-Date 2045	182	4.04%	0.747641	0.766246	0.342139	0.532284	0.573686	0.761459	0.766246	0.773492	0.830549	0.842973	0.854916
Target-Date 2050	207	3.99%	0.739544	0.780894	0.271327	0.277633	0.304111	0.770792	0.780894	0.796152	0.847276	0.850959	0.853411
Target-Date 2055	187	4.13%	0.764354	0.777790	0.344533	0.558246	0.604073	0.773808	0.777790	0.794114	0.835858	0.856112	0.864323
Target-Date 2060+	118	4.31%	0.797777	0.794429	0.684439	0.715323	0.722317	0.782586	0.794429	0.804002	0.880708	0.899021	0.904274
Target-Date Retirement	150	1.44%	0.265855	0.265493	0.112413	0.118274	0.119247	0.257649	0.265493	0.283423	0.373297	0.388619	0.394899
Technology	149	5.67%	1.049515	1.064920	0.732950	0.855549	0.862731	1.055574	1.064920	1.078898	1.168300	1.209945	1.211754
Trading--Inverse Commodities	4	-3.27%	-0.605000	-0.605051	-0.948999	-0.948948	-0.948863	-0.810761	-0.605051	-0.399341	-0.261066	-0.260966	-0.260906
Trading--Inverse Debt	15	0.46%	0.084843	0.172144	-0.123827	-0.120865	-0.115929	0.130290	0.172144	0.172483	0.225622	0.226275	0.226666
Trading--Inverse Equity	7	-10.05%	-1.861384	-1.712230	-2.202873	-2.202324	-2.201407	-2.000542	-1.712230	-1.710130	-1.427875	-1.367928	-1.331959
Trading--Leveraged Debt	9	-0.94%	-0.174559	-0.217575	-0.225408	-0.225405	-0.225400	-0.218350	-0.217575	-0.217549	0.026589	0.107738	0.156427

Down-market Betas of Mutual Funds by Peer Groups as of September 28, 2018

Peer Group	Number of Mutual Funds	Equity Risk Premium	Mean	Median	1st Percentile	2.5th Percentile	5th Percentile	40th Percentile	50th Percentile	60th Percentile	95th Percentile	97.5th Percentile	99th Percentile
Trading--Leveraged Equity	97	8.62%	1.596048	1.678300	0.323047	0.394194	0.791031	1.503276	1.678300	1.771474	2.198648	2.223312	2.223790
Trading--Miscellaneous	8	-0.71%	-0.131735	-0.157215	-0.531191	-0.530557	-0.529501	-0.158434	-0.157215	-0.093307	0.159476	0.159605	0.159682
Utilities	49	2.03%	0.376691	0.388662	0.223610	0.229438	0.232746	0.362899	0.388662	0.413757	0.464319	0.464995	0.469820
Volatility	3	-8.66%	-1.604137	-1.598350	-1.615363	-1.614842	-1.613974	-1.601822	-1.598350	-1.598350	-1.598350	-1.598350	-1.598350
World Allocation	430	2.76%	0.511976	0.494150	0.077434	0.197111	0.237729	0.465514	0.494150	0.548496	0.753905	0.801724	0.837871
World Bond	257	0.22%	0.039860	0.024708	-0.024646	-0.018935	-0.012619	0.016617	0.024708	0.039920	0.129215	0.132813	0.144298
World Stock	901	4.29%	0.793969	0.824112	0.359775	0.525773	0.574479	0.804925	0.824112	0.836984	0.954771	0.969607	0.978470

Up-market Betas of Mutual Funds by Peer Groups as of September 28, 2018

Details:
Benchmark: S&P 500 Index
Returns period and frequency: 1 year of daily returns
Risk-free rate for betas: Federal Funds Rate
Expected US Equity Risk Premium: 5.40% (Fernandez, Pablo and Pershin, Vitaly and Fernández Acín, Isabel, Market Risk Premium and Risk-Free Rate used for 59 Countries in 2018: A Survey (April 3, 2018). Available at SSRN: https://ssrn.com/abstract=3155709)

Peer Group	Number of Mutual Funds	Equity Risk Premium	Mean	Median	1st Percentile	2.5th Percentile	5th Percentile	40th Percentile	50th Percentile	60th Percentile	95th Percentile	97.5th Percentile	99th Percentile
Allocation--15% to 30% Equity	153	0.85%	0.157906	0.158902	0.023367	0.028509	0.032711	0.130950	0.158902	0.174295	0.288079	0.428944	0.435821
Allocation--30% to 50% Equity	435	1.62%	0.300512	0.302172	0.043473	0.067924	0.094776	0.279619	0.302172	0.327104	0.453992	0.488951	0.532563
Allocation--50% to 70% Equity	702	2.71%	0.501822	0.520168	0.159892	0.202477	0.252450	0.484062	0.520168	0.544789	0.652060	0.694633	0.744283
Allocation--70% to 85% Equity	310	3.35%	0.620811	0.631501	0.178087	0.316924	0.412158	0.606642	0.631501	0.664364	0.776867	0.867000	0.906118
Allocation--85%+ Equity	132	4.06%	0.752290	0.768987	0.309397	0.494150	0.640046	0.742834	0.768987	0.782494	0.866792	0.912431	0.918804
Bank Loan	16	-0.37%	-0.067961	-0.000393	-0.989853	-0.730117	-0.297224	-0.002608	-0.000393	0.001426	0.022529	0.024218	0.025231
Bear Market	63	-7.82%	-1.448515	-1.325620	-2.652333	-2.650880	-2.647320	-1.663882	-1.325620	-1.034364	-0.793528	-0.602969	-0.592869
China Region	50	3.97%	0.734633	0.817655	0.269781	0.357934	0.394255	0.689929	0.817655	0.841827	1.047560	1.069270	1.072022
Commodities Broad Basket	96	0.48%	0.089275	0.071370	-0.019806	0.005713	0.017301	0.062984	0.071370	0.077328	0.219397	0.368161	0.437054
Commodities Precious Metals	2	0.59%	0.109634	0.109634	0.107746	0.107803	0.107900	0.109248	0.109634	0.110019	0.111367	0.111464	0.111521
Communications	27	3.81%	0.705383	0.684028	0.558629	0.560468	0.563082	0.606782	0.684028	0.686903	0.914814	0.979893	1.052275
Consumer Cyclical	24	4.47%	0.827318	0.857748	0.712745	0.713588	0.714659	0.795181	0.857748	0.884172	0.928492	0.953893	0.974325
Consumer Defensive	19	3.37%	0.623378	0.626013	0.588890	0.588976	0.589121	0.625682	0.626013	0.627163	0.650835	0.674940	0.689403
Convertibles	79	2.74%	0.506995	0.583838	-0.003689	0.004330	0.248336	0.544250	0.583838	0.586787	0.615024	0.616257	0.633603
Corporate Bond	133	-0.26%	-0.048843	-0.048651	-0.118713	-0.109972	-0.096055	-0.058184	-0.048651	-0.042455	-0.021374	-0.004317	0.185686
Diversified Emerging Mkts	668	3.38%	0.626521	0.663867	0.026265	0.089605	0.285584	0.623836	0.663867	0.696337	0.866524	0.912632	0.920983
Diversified Pacific/Asia	30	3.08%	0.569771	0.602662	0.220755	0.223407	0.278352	0.568755	0.602662	0.630843	0.720296	0.723174	0.724608
Emerging Markets Bond	224	0.28%	0.051605	0.025394	-0.089599	-0.059915	-0.039128	0.015801	0.025394	0.035210	0.166564	0.228315	0.545333
Emerging-Markets Local-Currency Bond	69	1.33%	0.245939	0.286750	-0.006494	-0.003105	0.002210	0.252145	0.286750	0.298164	0.373851	0.403537	0.408623
Energy Limited Partnership	91	3.51%	0.650506	0.672294	0.445582	0.450116	0.454199	0.652895	0.672294	0.687826	0.821640	0.841247	0.844594
Equity Energy	77	4.80%	0.889444	0.902090	0.570804	0.602624	0.693945	0.896165	0.902090	0.910832	1.007912	1.035836	1.180476
Equity Precious Metals	52	2.56%	0.473639	0.474941	0.345267	0.354161	0.378800	0.458644	0.474941	0.484434	0.557741	0.560998	0.581595
Europe Stock	86	2.94%	0.543777	0.548611	0.239065	0.241439	0.266802	0.538244	0.548611	0.586172	0.723190	0.774011	0.791568
Financial	71	4.48%	0.829518	0.845759	0.457487	0.460769	0.476939	0.821441	0.845759	0.881918	1.061195	1.114593	1.119520
Foreign Large Blend	683	3.15%	0.584158	0.597929	0.054655	0.331375	0.406540	0.576298	0.597929	0.613787	0.729949	0.749373	0.780921
Foreign Large Growth	291	3.44%	0.636186	0.638077	0.474293	0.482610	0.499291	0.609156	0.638077	0.653686	0.813858	0.835306	0.862606
Foreign Large Value	270	3.00%	0.554887	0.582570	-0.022957	0.124443	0.216597	0.567068	0.582570	0.601711	0.679255	0.689312	0.813237
Foreign Small/Mid Blend	79	2.49%	0.461643	0.478650	0.228671	0.230113	0.303636	0.427946	0.478650	0.492839	0.601060	0.605449	0.607121
Foreign Small/Mid Growth	115	2.75%	0.508927	0.503409	0.224461	0.281842	0.354159	0.479187	0.503409	0.558462	0.653692	0.704732	0.708097
Foreign Small/Mid Value	52	2.31%	0.428220	0.494703	-0.090382	-0.073979	-0.003331	0.472112	0.494703	0.514418	0.599195	0.605064	0.607953
Global Real Estate	196	1.96%	0.363231	0.377678	0.154791	0.202872	0.223756	0.371587	0.377678	0.385978	0.442315	0.460206	0.465823
Health	101	4.95%	0.916976	0.889720	0.759227	0.771956	0.786189	0.867231	0.889720	0.902402	1.196640	1.207765	1.210970
High Yield Bond	377	0.20%	0.037416	0.031320	-0.016045	-0.004019	0.001152	0.025497	0.031320	0.035771	0.100262	0.165310	0.209738
High Yield Muni	96	0.04%	0.006906	0.001000	-0.018700	-0.014762	-0.013560	-0.002307	0.001000	0.003442	0.042778	0.068979	0.075722
India Equity	14	2.32%	0.430209	0.481071	0.266421	0.267114	0.268270	0.454045	0.481071	0.483648	0.494382	0.499492	0.502558
Industrials	23	4.64%	0.858385	0.864504	0.744562	0.745190	0.751644	0.846593	0.864504	0.865674	0.921821	0.924607	0.926497
Inflation-Protected Bond	181	-0.10%	-0.018089	-0.017289	-0.087987	-0.085159	-0.083185	-0.024812	-0.017289	-0.013489	0.027823	0.082290	0.133237
Infrastructure	65	2.40%	0.443555	0.455829	0.269798	0.293420	0.312501	0.424739	0.455829	0.463172	0.527469	0.533413	0.535694
Intermediate Government	229	-0.21%	-0.038631	-0.040040	-0.073451	-0.069724	-0.067950	-0.045013	-0.040040	-0.033773	-0.007940	0.014933	0.017835
Intermediate-Term Bond	855	-0.18%	-0.034199	-0.036748	-0.079548	-0.069993	-0.063999	-0.041121	-0.036748	-0.032539	0.005107	0.013826	0.056672
Japan Stock	27	2.93%	0.542247	0.575401	0.321157	0.322238	0.346654	0.562613	0.575401	0.579673	0.650494	0.659273	0.669050
Large Blend	1201	5.24%	0.970150	0.974393	0.573766	0.684244	0.756724	0.953915	0.974393	0.991581	1.063210	1.082170	1.107470
Large Growth	1211	5.71%	1.057216	1.078380	0.758307	0.820179	0.865746	1.053500	1.078380	1.096060	1.216240	1.236035	1.298825
Large Value	1074	4.72%	0.873736	0.901236	0.485924	0.568481	0.663577	0.880612	0.901236	0.915843	0.985911	1.005685	1.155068
Latin America Stock	13	4.49%	0.830931	0.823953	0.735068	0.735212	0.735453	0.822644	0.823953	0.824938	0.962817	0.963253	0.963514
Long Government	24	-0.69%	-0.127241	-0.136481	-0.166787	-0.166727	-0.165272	-0.137148	-0.136481	-0.129038	-0.077914	-0.065468	-0.055483
Long-Short Credit	25	0.13%	0.024183	0.006184	-0.054881	-0.054326	-0.053183	-0.003947	0.006184	0.035828	0.123935	0.124589	0.124611
Long-Short Equity	217	2.72%	0.504615	0.505295	-0.200704	-0.049106	0.094793	0.459025	0.505295	0.559806	0.978917	1.103430	1.254029
Long-Term Bond	18	-0.30%	-0.056013	-0.051980	-0.120844	-0.120844	-0.120844	-0.074220	-0.051980	-0.028052	-0.000593	0.000955	0.001884

Up-market Betas of Mutual Funds by Peer Groups as of September 28, 2018

Peer Group	Number of Mutual Funds	Equity Risk Premium	Mean	Median	1st Percentile	2.5th Percentile	5th Percentile	40th Percentile	50th Percentile	60th Percentile	95th Percentile	97.5th Percentile	99th Percentile
Managed Futures	94	0.40%	0.073644	0.075126	-0.427530	-0.416271	-0.219451	0.045428	0.075126	0.120467	0.437406	0.508534	0.538795
Market Neutral	127	0.46%	0.084711	0.056773	-0.270170	-0.253278	-0.154072	0.022547	0.056773	0.075484	0.480972	0.507144	0.743339
Mid-Cap Blend	343	4.30%	0.795634	0.805475	0.279356	0.476349	0.591094	0.796457	0.805475	0.818670	0.973467	1.063195	1.195751
Mid-Cap Growth	552	4.82%	0.893083	0.908439	0.501028	0.677439	0.711477	0.892079	0.908439	0.927331	1.033151	1.073921	1.140863
Mid-Cap Value	369	4.19%	0.776140	0.787106	0.506518	0.588210	0.650282	0.773655	0.787106	0.796523	0.899467	0.932416	0.974680
Miscellaneous Region	30	2.64%	0.488478	0.471195	0.208128	0.210731	0.214686	0.458261	0.471195	0.487241	0.775993	0.850794	0.863985
Miscellaneous Sector	6	9.92%	1.836953	1.837215	1.601711	1.601966	1.602393	1.607560	1.837215	2.066870	2.071065	2.071398	2.071597
Multialternative	321	1.18%	0.218520	0.177796	-0.159785	-0.116487	-0.040985	0.166370	0.177796	0.215079	0.597530	0.727404	1.159089
Multicurrency	37	0.39%	0.071551	0.129363	-0.405658	-0.243996	-0.212399	0.092754	0.129363	0.148556	0.264095	0.264418	0.265202
Multisector Bond	221	0.14%	0.026695	0.006397	-0.157313	-0.152031	-0.146745	-0.008959	0.006397	0.024074	0.166031	0.176424	0.482656
Muni California Intermediate	40	0.01%	0.000945	0.000253	-0.013214	-0.013151	-0.007649	-0.000972	0.000253	0.003059	0.012637	0.013449	0.013757
Muni California Long	71	0.01%	0.002531	0.000241	-0.012156	-0.010343	-0.008813	-0.001694	0.000241	0.000817	0.016605	0.048511	0.065909
Muni Massachusetts	39	-0.03%	-0.004809	-0.004076	-0.019172	-0.018932	-0.018422	-0.005115	-0.004076	-0.001573	0.003555	0.004188	0.005451
Muni Minnesota	36	0.00%	-0.000226	-0.000421	-0.010470	-0.009116	-0.008217	-0.002165	-0.000421	0.001774	0.010481	0.012841	0.012919
Muni National Interm	147	0.01%	0.002110	-0.000238	-0.011205	-0.010729	-0.009492	-0.001891	-0.000238	0.002656	0.023017	0.027949	0.039610
Muni National Long	118	-0.01%	-0.001395	-0.002179	-0.018772	-0.015494	-0.013751	-0.003470	-0.002179	0.000198	0.012712	0.014352	0.016256
Muni National Short	12	0.12%	0.021618	0.023899	-0.003440	-0.003257	-0.002952	0.016624	0.023899	0.030320	0.043117	0.044182	0.044821
Muni New Jersey	40	0.04%	0.006878	-0.002706	-0.012511	-0.011499	-0.011064	-0.004129	-0.002706	-0.001571	0.131798	0.131959	0.132275
Muni New York Intermediate	31	-0.01%	-0.001161	-0.001478	-0.017257	-0.016596	-0.014504	-0.004356	-0.001478	-0.000206	0.015380	0.018029	0.019618
Muni New York Long	56	0.04%	0.008010	-0.001436	-0.011391	-0.011216	-0.010600	-0.003177	-0.001436	0.001051	0.078392	0.091064	0.094774
Muni Ohio	22	-0.02%	-0.004609	-0.005406	-0.013979	-0.013465	-0.012673	-0.006647	-0.005406	-0.003666	0.002535	0.006867	0.009726
Muni Pennsylvania	42	0.03%	0.006349	-0.000421	-0.012391	-0.011891	-0.009383	-0.002509	-0.000421	0.002092	0.098582	0.104512	0.106325
Muni Single State Interm	69	0.00%	0.000474	-0.000403	-0.012199	-0.009374	-0.008667	-0.001085	-0.000403	0.000577	0.012752	0.015337	0.016752
Muni Single State Long	164	0.00%	-0.000866	-0.000373	-0.015508	-0.015031	-0.012844	-0.001710	-0.000373	0.001256	0.011186	0.017007	0.019951
Muni Single State Short	4	0.00%	-0.000367	-0.000046	-0.005015	-0.004795	-0.004428	-0.000181	-0.000046	0.000089	0.003247	0.003518	0.003680
Natural Resources	94	4.54%	0.840195	0.880012	0.096132	0.244831	0.538074	0.867894	0.880012	0.908476	1.082789	1.121383	1.123864
Nontraditional Bond	181	0.19%	0.035953	0.027578	-0.061679	-0.042347	-0.025687	0.017534	0.027578	0.038514	0.177687	0.197798	0.201650
Option Writing	88	2.74%	0.507063	0.538235	0.050668	0.083642	0.224676	0.482098	0.538235	0.559075	0.722134	0.735949	0.751682
Pacific/Asia ex-Japan Stk	61	3.03%	0.560608	0.551373	0.193842	0.237965	0.281153	0.505510	0.551373	0.576485	0.818735	0.821342	0.822328
Preferred Stock	37	0.09%	0.017524	0.001293	-0.020308	-0.018663	-0.016201	-0.002924	0.001293	0.004899	0.127101	0.128122	0.131367
Real Estate	206	2.16%	0.399895	0.401453	0.109133	0.129333	0.321708	0.396720	0.401453	0.408748	0.499374	0.513252	0.579716
Short Government	24	-0.13%	-0.024659	-0.022484	-0.047397	-0.046187	-0.043903	-0.026481	-0.022484	-0.020345	-0.009721	-0.007923	-0.006567
Short-Term Bond	65	-0.12%	-0.021412	-0.036764	-0.058571	-0.056420	-0.053811	-0.041406	-0.036764	-0.027890	0.122147	0.150098	0.151114
Small Blend	650	4.22%	0.781302	0.796839	0.523511	0.578601	0.641432	0.783010	0.796839	0.815936	0.884974	0.907682	0.944744
Small Growth	590	4.65%	0.860654	0.869638	0.663835	0.678229	0.717939	0.846390	0.869638	0.886717	0.981454	1.041650	1.055144
Small Value	376	4.05%	0.750910	0.767387	0.343218	0.451510	0.564824	0.748560	0.767387	0.784656	0.886931	0.917994	0.957641
Tactical Allocation	231	2.39%	0.441693	0.397437	-0.077172	-0.070016	0.064147	0.366813	0.397437	0.508158	0.928121	0.955737	0.968815
Target-Date 2000-2010	100	1.52%	0.280854	0.312969	0.019318	0.022574	0.026245	0.301588	0.312969	0.315321	0.344021	0.346758	0.347729
Target-Date 2015	122	1.58%	0.293486	0.347781	-0.066290	-0.056805	0.058505	0.327812	0.347781	0.361028	0.405989	0.416244	0.433907
Target-Date 2020	210	1.87%	0.346325	0.388644	0.048427	0.052696	0.066911	0.362550	0.388644	0.400426	0.481292	0.493127	0.498275
Target-Date 2025	183	2.41%	0.445910	0.490851	0.088936	0.146023	0.221709	0.434844	0.490851	0.497253	0.547823	0.564845	0.572432
Target-Date 2030	209	2.75%	0.509245	0.572238	0.075716	0.083364	0.094963	0.541454	0.572238	0.588375	0.632284	0.641849	0.645857
Target-Date 2035	181	3.21%	0.595330	0.639301	0.086941	0.103612	0.187014	0.618833	0.639301	0.661846	0.712342	0.733925	0.739073
Target-Date 2040	209	3.41%	0.630751	0.698617	0.091582	0.099335	0.143714	0.673155	0.698617	0.712145	0.768994	0.786154	0.789279
Target-Date 2045	182	3.66%	0.678468	0.727204	0.153173	0.208143	0.239803	0.706574	0.727204	0.738757	0.792477	0.826873	0.827260
Target-Date 2050	207	3.68%	0.680787	0.741547	0.113296	0.118950	0.161093	0.713224	0.741547	0.753288	0.824879	0.838637	0.840390
Target-Date 2055	187	3.79%	0.701900	0.741613	0.178392	0.288604	0.360278	0.724903	0.741613	0.756631	0.820393	0.839423	0.850646
Target-Date 2060+	118	4.02%	0.745341	0.758231	0.627750	0.629687	0.632242	0.745034	0.758231	0.763779	0.816359	0.853934	0.861007
Target-Date Retirement	150	1.26%	0.234200	0.231637	-0.012208	-0.005414	0.034888	0.220003	0.231637	0.264726	0.342754	0.362010	0.365183
Technology	149	6.60%	1.222463	1.220070	0.718069	1.027511	1.056858	1.210938	1.220070	1.228246	1.395948	1.456323	1.504371
Trading--Inverse Commodities	4	-3.52%	-0.651902	-0.651741	-0.885930	-0.885767	-0.885495	-0.790145	-0.651741	-0.513337	-0.418535	-0.418312	-0.418177
Trading--Inverse Debt	15	0.17%	0.031782	0.137328	-0.203241	-0.202616	-0.201575	0.104611	0.137328	0.138185	0.177739	0.177742	0.177744
Trading--Inverse Equity	7	-10.36%	-1.918396	-1.948580	-2.008457	-2.008108	-2.007526	-1.980362	-1.948580	-1.947188	-1.684948	-1.629079	-1.595558
Trading--Leveraged Debt	9	-0.70%	-0.129456	-0.177277	-0.186337	-0.185634	-0.184461	-0.177555	-0.177277	-0.176588	0.087694	0.175085	0.227520

Up-market Betas of Mutual Funds by Peer Groups as of September 28, 2018

Peer Group	Number of Mutual Funds	Equity Risk Premium	Mean	Median	1st Percentile	2.5th Percentile	5th Percentile	40th Percentile	50th Percentile	60th Percentile	95th Percentile	97.5th Percentile	99th Percentile
Trading--Leveraged Equity	97	8.72%	1.614845	1.651750	0.380329	0.568472	0.627026	1.499818	1.651750	1.709348	2.643048	2.716364	2.720176
Trading--Miscellaneous	8	-0.50%	-0.092986	-0.276870	-0.374902	-0.374582	-0.374050	-0.277206	-0.276870	-0.165946	0.279072	0.279247	0.279352
Utilities	49	1.83%	0.338261	0.341943	0.255841	0.257840	0.260568	0.332069	0.341943	0.344172	0.426841	0.427334	0.427782
Volatility	3	-4.10%	-0.758415	-0.749843	-0.775045	-0.774273	-0.772987	-0.754986	-0.749843	-0.749843	-0.749843	-0.749843	-0.749843
World Allocation	430	2.48%	0.458528	0.470437	0.100561	0.139252	0.165000	0.424966	0.470437	0.485859	0.740371	0.749460	0.831437
World Bond	257	0.33%	0.060720	0.042798	-0.035739	-0.029042	-0.020613	0.034756	0.042798	0.052788	0.225374	0.236026	0.238181
World Stock	901	3.94%	0.730309	0.762937	0.227638	0.414662	0.448677	0.730321	0.762937	0.795351	0.942603	1.011535	1.037630

Appendix: Suggested Reading

The paper printed in the following section, "Measuring Risk for Cost of Capital: The Downside Beta Approach" by James Chong and G. Michael Phillips, was first published in the *Journal of Corporate Treasury Management,* 4(4), on pages 344-352, and has been re-published in *Beta Estimates for Valuation & Cost of Capital* with the permission of Henry Stewart Publications http://www.henrystewartpublications.com/.

Measuring risk for cost of capital: The downside beta approach

Received (in revised form): 14th December, 2011

James Chong
is an associate professor and Associate Director of the Center for Financial Planning and Investment at California State University, Northridge. He also serves as the Research Economist for MacroRisk Analytics. James received his MS in financial mathematics from the University of Chicago and his PhD in finance from the ICMA Centre at the University of Reading.

G. Michael Phillips
is the Director of the Center for Financial Planning and Investment, and a professor of Finance, Real Estate, and Insurance at California State University, Northridge. He also serves as Chief Scientist for MacroRisk Analytics. Michael received his BS in mathematics and economics from Illinois State University and his PhD from the University of California, San Diego, with specialisations in econometrics and applied economics.

James Chong, Department of Finance, Real Estate, & Insurance, California State University, Northridge, 18111 Nordhoff Street, Northridge, CA 91330-8379, USA
Tel: +1 (818) 677-2459; E-mail: jchong@macrorisk.com.
G. Michael Phillips, Department of Finance, Real Estate, & Insurance, California State University, Northridge, 18111 Nordhoff Street, Northridge, CA 91330-8379, USA
Tel: +1 (818) 677-2459; E-mail: mphillips@macrorisk.com.

Abstract The cost of capital is partly determined by a cost of equity which centres on the concepts of the 'capital asset pricing model' (CAPM) and, ultimately, beta. Beta traditionally assumes that risks are linear, but according to findings from behavioural finance, they are not; especially downside risks which are not reflected correctly in the traditional CAPM beta. In this paper, the authors discuss the down-market beta and its growing importance as an alternative to the traditional CAPM beta in computing cost of capital and making capital budgeting and valuation decisions. In addition, they demonstrate that equity rates based on CAPM betas can be quite different from those based on down-market beta, leading to significantly different value estimates. In their sample computations, valuations based on CAPM betas would lead to excessive value when there was greater downside risk and lower values when there was less downside risk.

KEYWORDS: valuation, downside risk, WACC, capital budgeting, dual beta

INTRODUCTION

By and large, behavioural finance studies have consistently found that economic decision-makers try to avoid 'pain', including that of disastrous economic loss. Business valuation analysts, corporate decision-makers, and investors try to include measures of risk in their calculations to help account for the possibility that a project might fail, a loan might not be repaid, or that an investment could lose value. On the other hand, these same analysts, investors, and decision-makers hope that their projects succeed beyond their expectations, that all their loans are repaid on schedule, and that various investments produce spectacular profits.

In a sense, both unexpectedly low profits and unexpectedly high profits are 'risk'. But the risk of losing money is generally a bad thing, while the risk of making extra profits is generally a good thing.

The Capital Asset Pricing Model (CAPM) estimate of beta, often used as a component of investment risk, is based on assumptions of symmetry such that the risk of losing money or the risk of making extra profits are viewed as equivalent.

This paper discusses the dual-beta model, which separately accounts for these two types of risk and provides an empirical analysis of how confusing the two types of risk can generate markedly different estimates of required return and, for the business valuation analyst, quite different computations of value.

The authors begin with a discussion of the importance of beta in computing the cost of capital and making capital budgeting and valuation decisions, and then discuss historically significant, but often forgotten, research that highlights the importance of separately assessing the risk of profits and losses. They then discuss the growing importance of the dual-beta model as an alternative. In the empirical section of this paper, the authors compute the equity component of the cost of capital using traditional beta and also a down-market beta estimated using a dual-beta model. They find that traditional beta underestimates equity risk about half the time, compared with the dual-beta estimate and that this can translate into large differences in present value computations. The paper concludes with several suggestions for practitioners.

CONTEXT AND LITERATURE

Investors, business valuation analysts, and corporate decision-makers are frequently faced with the problem of placing a current value on a future payment stream. Investors may be concerned with valuing a stock or mutual fund, corporate decision-makers may be concerned with evaluating a potential acquisition or new product line, and business valuation analysts focus on the current value of an ownership interest in businesses which may range from small personal service firms to large multinationals. In each case, however, there is usually a reduction of expected cash flows to present value.

CAPM in corporate finance

The challenge of forecasting cash flows is not the topic of this paper; rather, it focuses on the discount rate used to compute the present value of equity. In typical corporate finance and investment textbooks, the determination of this discount rate begins with the CAPM equation:

$$(r_j - r_f)_t = \alpha_j + \beta_j(r_m - r_f)_t + \varepsilon_t \qquad (1)$$

in which the excess return (the risk premium) for stock j is linearly related to the excess return (the risk premium) of the market index. The slope of this line, β_j, or simply beta, is perhaps the most commonly used measure of equity risk. The intercept, α_j, is known as 'Treynor's alpha' and represents the sustained economic profit, if any, associated with the investment. In most cases, α_j is assumed to be zero.

With slight modification to (1), the more common equation for the equity discount rate is obtained:

$$r_{jt} = r_{ft} + \beta_j(r_m - r_f)_t + \varepsilon_t. \qquad (2)$$

The riskless rate has added to it a systematic risk component, obtained by multiplying an equity risk premium by an estimate of beta. If there is any sustained economic profit, then one could add an estimate of additional alpha (α_j), if any. In such a case, the resulting equation would be:

$$r_{jt} = r_{ft} + \alpha_j + \beta_j(r_m - r_f)_t + \varepsilon_t. \qquad (2')$$

The CAPM has been found to be widely used in business settings for establishing a cost of capital for discounting purposes. Graham and Harvey[1] found that 73.5 per cent of financial executives they surveyed 'always or almost always use the CAPM' for estimating the cost of capital. Bruner *et al.*[2] found that 80 per cent of financial advisers they surveyed rely on the CAPM; they also found that at least 85 per cent of corporate representatives, and at least 90 per cent of financial planners they surveyed, view the α term as not a part of the CAPM calculation.

Adjustments to the CAPM

With a few exceptions, business valuation texts tend to disagree with the above consensus and routinely discuss firm-specific risk premiums and other added factors that are analogous to the term. Pratt *et al.*[3] are typical in that they present the simple CAPM and then identify a number of additional risk factors, premiums, and discounts that are used to manually adjust the CAPM estimate to obtain discount rates. Hitchner[4] discusses various general premiums to be added to the CAPM and states 'the final component of the discount rate is the risk specific to the company being valued and/or the industry in which it operates'. McKinsey & Company[5] proceeds straight from the CAPM to the weighted average cost of capital (WACC) estimate without other premiums, discounts, or firm-specific adjustments. At the other extreme, Trugman[6] discusses the 'build up method', essentially adding risk premiums to a version of the CAPM in which β_j is assumed to equal 1, as well as the CAPM with estimated coefficients and no additional terms. He then discusses (2) as 'CAPM for the closely held business' in which α_j is identified as unsystematic risk, a specific company risk adjustment, or perhaps a size adjustment.

However, whether one is looking at college texts or professional valuation references, the preponderance that were reviewed are planted firmly on a behavioural theory in which rational economic agents have preferences over the expected outcomes of their investments and also the variance of those outcomes. This is the standard 'modern portfolio theory' approach closely associated with Markowitz[7,8] and Sharpe[9].

Downside risk approach

At about the same time that Markowitz was developing mean-variance theory, an alternative was being developed, which has been termed 'safety first'. Rather than on the entire distribution of possible returns, focus was placed on the probability of disaster or downside loss. First modelled by Roy,[10,11] the 'safety first' criterion has led to an alternative approach to viewing risk and return and, consequently, discount rates and capital budgeting.[12] This alternative approach is the 'mean-semivariance' or 'downside risk' approach, which defines risk in terms of the distribution of possible unfavourable outcomes, instead of all possible outcomes. Semi-variance is the variance determined by the lower portion of a statistical distribution; in the 'safety first' paradigm, it is a measure of the spread of outcomes below a critical value. The square root of the semi-variance is the semideviation, just as the standard deviation is the square root of variance. Curiously, Markowitz also discussed a mean-semivariance approach, but chose to use mean-variance for computational reasons even though he grants that 'semi-variance is the more plausible measure of risk'.[13]

In 1970, focus groups of executives in eight industries exploring their definitions of risk found 'the executives' emphasis on downside risk indicates that their concept of risk is better described by semi-variance than by ordinary variance'.[14] In a companion paper Mao analysed a framework for making capital budgeting decisions based on specific probabilities of outcomes, but concludes that in practical applications 'to work out such a distribution will be very difficult indeed'.[15]

Soon after, a theoretical analysis of capital market values by Hogan and Warren[16] demonstrated that 'the fundamental structure of the "capital-asset pricing model is retained when standard semideviation is substituted for standard deviation to measure portfolio risk."' This suggested that the computationally simpler CAPM type models could be revised to focus on downside risk rather than both upside and downside as measured by the variance. Presumably such revised models would better reflect the view of risk actually held by people.

Non-normal distribution

Development of capital budgeting, based on downside risk measures, slowed down following the 1979 demonstration by Nantell and Price: when the forecasted cash flows of the asset being valued and the returns from the overall market are related, following a bivariate normal distribution, then the equilibrium rates of return (discount rates) computed from the traditional CAPM or from the form using semideviation are equal and therefore there is little need to use semideviation methods.[17]

Intuitively, the normal distributions have a strong symmetry, so that if one knows the left-hand shape of the statistical distribution, one also knows the right-hand shape; the lower semideviation would be half the standard deviation and optimal behaviour with respect to one would be the same as the other. Unfortunately, asset returns series are not normally distributed but follow more complicated statistical distributions such that the probability of loss is not symmetric with the probability of gain.[18]

The investment performance literature actively discussed the impact of non-normality and downside risk, as in Sortino and Price;[19] and, in a series of papers, Estrada[20–22] developed applications of the downside CAPM (D-CAPM) and showed how that measure provides superior estimates of the cost of equity for purposes of present value computations of cash flows in developing markets.

Equity rates reflecting downside risk have also been tested using data from developed countries. An application to US stocks was performed by Post and Van Vliet,[23] who found that the model 'strongly outperforms the traditional ...

CAPM in terms of its ability to explain the cross-section of US stock returns.' The D-CAPM model was successfully applied to stocks on the London Stock Exchange and the Paris Stock Exchange in Artavanis *et al.*[24]

There is a conundrum. A wide range of academic research has confirmed that while the CAPM treats positive surprises (windfalls) and negative surprises (disasters) as equivalent risks, investors and business owners do not. The various measurements of alternative asset pricing models, based on downside risk, have generally proven superior to the symmetric CAPM in terms of their ability to explain the differences in equity returns across assets.[25] Theoretically the downside models provide a 'more plausible' approach to risk.[26] Statistically, they explain the differences in stock returns better than the traditional CAPM. But does it really matter to a business valuation analyst, corporate decision-maker, or investor which model provides the estimated beta, so long as one is provided? The authors provide an initial answer in the next section of this paper, focusing exclusively on down-market beta, in line with business owners' concern over downside risk.

THE DUAL-BETA MODEL AND THE DATA

The version of dual-beta model addressed in this paper is more precisely an 'up-market/down-market' model in which separate model parameters are estimated for times when the market benchmark goes up and for when it goes down, as shown in equation (3).

$$(r_j - r_f)_t = \alpha_j^+ D + \beta_j^+ (r_m^+ - r_f)_t D + \alpha_j^- (1 - D) + \beta_j^- (r_m^- - r_f)_t (1 - D) + \varepsilon_t. \quad (3)$$

In this equation, the dependent variable is the asset return in excess of the riskless rate, the two intercepts are α_j^+ and α_j^-, for the 'up-market' and 'down-market' regime respectively, and $\beta_j^+ (r_m^+ - r_f)_t$ is the product of the 'up-market beta' and the up-market excess return, and similarly $\beta_j^- (r_m^- - r_f)_t$ is the product of the 'down-market beta' and the down-market excess return. D is a dummy variable, which takes the value of 1 when the market index daily return is non-negative, and zero otherwise. The final term, ε_t, reflects the idiosyncratic information not proportional to either the up-market or down-market excess returns. For this paper, 'down-market' days are when the market went down and 'up-market' days are the others. Parameter estimates for β_j, β_j^+, and β_j^- were provided by MacroRisk Analytics, a commercial provider of these estimates, from their database as of 29th October, 2010 for 4,500 common stocks traded on the NYSE, NASDAQ, and AMEX. A graph showing average up-market and down-market beta values per unit of average CAPM beta, by 2-digit SIC code, is provided in Figure 1 — this is to illustrate that seldom would up- and down-market betas equal CAPM beta. Indeed, the authors found that they were lower than those based on the down-market beta about 48 per cent of the time. The down-market equity rates are an average of 7.4 per cent higher than the CAPM equity rates. For those cases where the down-market beta is greater than the CAPM beta, the down-market equity rates are an average of 23.9 per cent higher.

The next exercise is to actually construct 'equity rates' for each of the 4,500 observations as a user might in

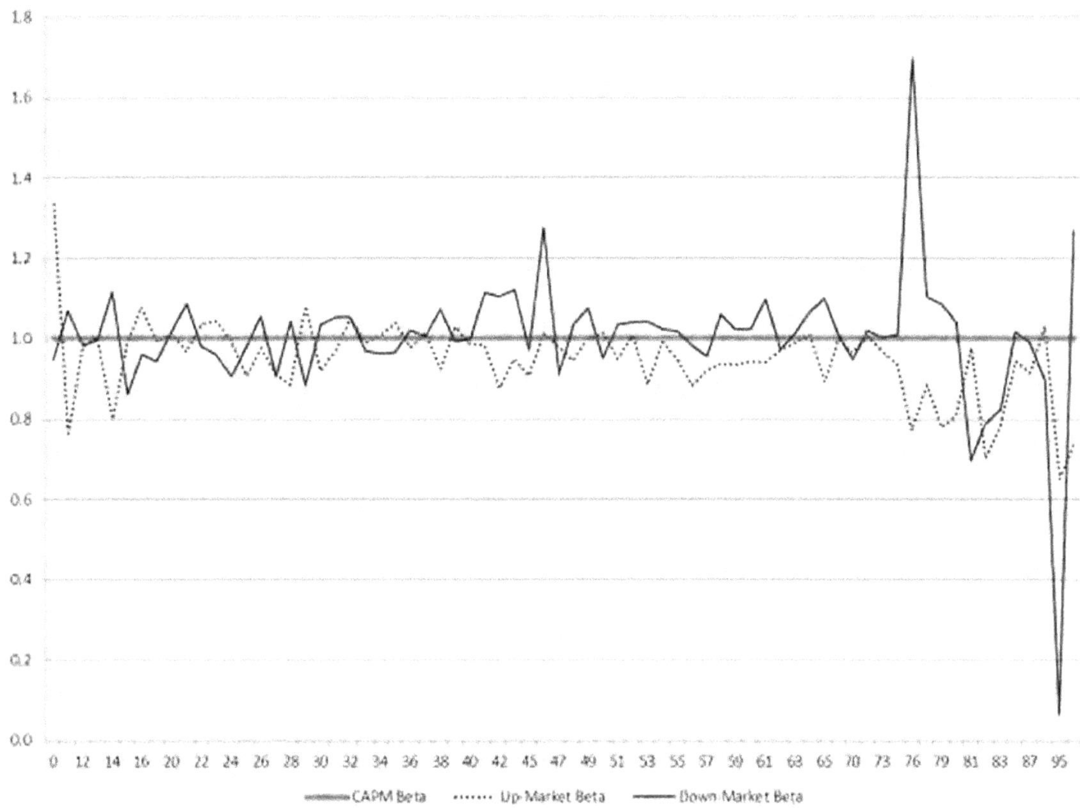

Source: MacroRisk Analytics, data as of 29/10/2010

Figure 1: Average up-market and down-market betas per unit of average CAPM beta, by industry (2-digit SIC)

practice by taking a measure of the riskless rate and adding to it the equity risk premium scaled by the estimated beta. Certainly there are differences regarding the selection of these inputs (see, for example, Fama and French[27]). For this computation, the authors use 3.41 per cent as the riskless rate, based on the forecast values of the 10-year Treasury bond from the third quarter 2010 Survey of Professional Forecasters from the Philadelphia Federal Reserve, and 6.2 per cent as a representative expected equity premium. For each of the approximately 4,500 observed companies the authors compute

$$k_{js} = 0.341 + \beta_{js} * (0.0620) \qquad (4)$$

where 's' refers to the style of beta being used (CAPM, up-market, down-market) and k_{js} is the estimated equity discount rate.

In Table 1, the authors show the average present values of a hypothetical earnings stream of US$100,000 per year for 10 years. The table gives the average results separately for those times when the down-market beta is no greater than the CAPM beta, when the down-market beta exceeds the CAPM beta, and overall without regard to which beta estimate is larger.

On average, using the CAPM beta or the down-market beta produced present values that were fairly close (US$629,817 for the average result using

Table 1: Sample impact of different betas on present value computations

	Present value of US$100,000 per year for 10 years		
	CAPM Beta (US$)	Down-market Beta (US$)	Up-market Beta (US$)
Down-market beta ≤ CAPM beta	609,229.20	646,446.19	609,196.34
Down-market beta > CAPM beta	651,884.44	608,914.08	680,220.75
Overall average	629,816.81	628,331.27	643,476.36

CAPM beta and US$628,331 for the down-market beta). However, that average is based on over-estimated values about half of the time and under-estimated values for the other half. When the CAPM beta exceeds the down-market beta, it is being 'pulled up' by higher upside volatility; the relatively higher chance of profits is being misinterpreted as risk, resulting in too high a discount rate and consequently too low an estimated value. The average value was US$609,229.20 when using the CAPM beta, but would have been estimated as US$646,446.19 if only the down-market beta, reflecting downside risk rather than profit potential, had been used. Similarly, when the CAPM beta is lower than the down-market beta, there is a situation where the downside risk exceeds the upside profit volatility. Using the CAPM beta would have resulted in an overestimated average value of US$651,884.44 compared with the average of US$608,914.08 obtained using the downside beta. In those rare instances when the down-market beta and CAPM beta were practically the same, which the authors did not separately report, the estimated values would be essentially the same using any of the beta estimates. However, as graphically represented in Figure 1, this would be a rare event.

Table 1 reflects that about half the time a financial analyst using CAPM betas for estimating cost of capital would be overstating value and about half the time understating value; while overall 4,500 companies might cancel those errors, they certainly would not for any given analyst. In the Table 1 example, an average financial analyst using CAPM betas would be making approximately a 7 per cent error, but would not know in advance whether that was an error causing an overestimate or an underestimate of value. That error is readily corrected by using downside betas when computing cost of capital.

CONCLUSIONS

"Come to the downside ... we have cookies."

— paraphrase of a bumpersticker, *circa* 2010

That investors, analysts, and decision-makers do not value financial disasters and windfalls as equivalent risks seems a matter of common sense and has been confirmed repeatedly in the financial literature. A long tradition of considering 'safety first' and focusing on the risk of having losses, or having returns below some designated target, points to the use of downside risk measures. Commercial banks, with value-at-risk, and pensions and hedge funds, with return to semideviation ratios ('Sortino ratios'), have begun focusing on downside risk measures as part of their standard analytical practice.

For corporate treasurers, business owners, business valuation analysts, and investors without the resources of a large investment bank, the difference in estimated value caused by using CAPM betas, instead of downside betas, has not been widely understood.

This paper has demonstrated that equity rates based on traditional CAPM betas can be quite different from those based on down-market betas and can lead to significantly different value estimates. In the sample computations, valuations based on traditional betas would lead to excessive value when there was greater downside risk and lower values when there was less downside risk.

The authors do not believe this is the final word on the use of downside risk measures in business valuation. Much additional research remains to be done. The empirical work in this paper, while employing a broad sample of companies, reflects only one point in time. It is not yet known how these values change with the business cycle or credit conditions, or how alternative specifications such as the Fama-French three-factor model would work in a dual-beta formulation.[28] Even so, whether one uses commercially provided values, as used here, or one computes one's own with spreadsheet or regression software, down-market estimates of beta are readily available and can be used at least to provide an alternative calculation of value as part of model 'stress-testing'and perhaps to avoid substantial mispricing of businesses, projects, and investment assets.

Acknowledgments

The authors thank an anonymous reviewer for helpful suggestions, MacroRisk Analytics for providing data used in this paper, and Robert Neff, Sean Chasworth, and Nhat Ho for assistance and comments throughout this project.

References

1 Graham, J.R. and Harvey, C.R. (2001) 'The theory and practice of corporate finance: Evidence from the field', *Journal of Financial Economics*, Vol. 60, No. 2, pp. 187–243.
2 Bruner, R.F., Eades, K.M., Harris, R.S. and Higgins, R.C. (1998) 'Best practices in estimating the cost of capital: Survey and synthesis', *Financial Practice and Education*, Spring/Summer, pp. 13–28.
3 Pratt, S.P., Reilly, R.F. and Schweihs, R.P. (2000) 'Valuing a Business: The analysis and appraisal of closely held companies (4e)', McGraw-Hill, New York, NY.
4 Hitchner, J. R. (2006) 'Financial Valuation: Applications and Models (2e)', John Wiley & Sons, Hoboken, NJ.
5 McKinsey & Company (2011) 'Valuation workbook: Step-by-step exercises and tests to help you master valuation', John Wiley & Sons, Hoboken, NJ.
6 Trugman, G.R. (2008) 'Understanding business valuation: A practical guide to valuing small to medium-sized businesses', AICPA, New York, NY.
7 Markowitz, H. (1952) 'The utility of wealth', *Journal of Political Economy*, Vol. 60, No. 2, pp. 151–158.
8 Markowitz, H. (1991) 'Portfolio selection: Efficient diversification of investment (2e)', Blackwell Publishers Inc., Malden, MA.
9 Sharpe, W.F. (1964) 'Capital asset prices: A theory of market equilibrium under conditions of risk', *Journal of Finance*,

Vol. 19, No. 3, pp. 425–442.
10 Roy, A.D. (1952) 'Safety first and the holding of assets', *Econometrica*, Vol. 20, No. 3, pp. 431–449.
11 Roy, A.D. (1956) 'Risk and rank or safety first generalised', *Economica*, Vol. 23, No. 91, pp. 214–228.
12 Thompson, J.R., Williams, E.E., and Findlay, M.C. (2003) 'Models for investors in real world Markets', John Wiley & Sons, Hoboken, NJ.
13 Markowitz, ref. 8 above.
14 Mao, J.C.T. (1970) 'Survey of capital budgeting: Theory and practice', *Journal of Finance*, Vol. 25, No. 2, pp. 349–360.
15 Mao, J.C.T. (1970) 'Models of capital budgeting, E-V vs E-S', *Journal of Financial and Quantitative Analysis*, Vol. 4, No. 5, pp. 657–675.
16 Hogan, W.W. and Warren, J.M. (1974) 'Toward the development of an equilibrium capital-market model based on semivariance', *Journal of Financial and Quantitative Analysis*, Vol. 9, No. 1, pp. 1–11.
17 Nantell, T.J., and Price, B. (1979), 'An analytical comparison of variance and semivariance capital market theories', *Journal of Financial and Quantitative Analysis*, Vol. 14, No. 2, pp. 221–242.
18 Mandelbrot, B. (1963) 'The variation of certain speculative prices', *Journal of Business*, Vol. 36, No. 4, pp. 394–419.
19 Sortino, F.A., and Price, L.N. (1994) 'Performance measurement in a downside risk framework', *Journal of Investing*, Vol. 3, No. 3, pp. 59–64.
20 Estrada, J. (2000) 'The cost of equity in emerging markets: A downside risk approach', *Emerging Markets Quarterly*, Fall, pp.19–30.
21 Estrada, J. (2002), 'Systematic risk in emerging markets: The D-CAPM', *Emerging Markets Review*, Vol. 3, No. 4, pp. 365–379.
22 Estrada, J. (2007) 'Mean-semivariance behavior: Downside risk and capital asset pricing', *International Review of Economics and Finance*, Vol. 16, No. 2, pp. 169–185.
23 Post, T. and Van Vliet, P. (2004) 'Conditional downside risk and the CAPM', ERIM Report Series, available at: http://papers.ssrn.com/sol3/papers.cfm?abstract_id=797286 (accessed 20th December, 2011).
24 Artavanis, N., Diacogiannis, G. and Mylonakis, J. (2010) 'The D-CAPM: The case of Great Britain and France', *International Journal of Economics and Finance*, Vol. 2, No. 3, pp. 25–38.
25 Chong, J., Pfeiffer, S. and Phillips, G.M. (2011) 'Can dual beta filtering improve investor performance?' *Journal of Personal Finance*, Vol. 10, No. 1, pp. 63–86.
26 Chong, J. and Phillips, G. M. (2011) 'Beta measures market risk except when it doesn't: Regime-switching alpha and errors in beta', *Journal of Wealth Management*, Vol. 14, No. 3, pp. 67–72.
27 Fama, E. F. and French, K. R. (2002) 'The equity premium', *Journal of Finance*, Vol. 57, No. 2, pp. 637–659.
28 Fama, E. F. and French, K. R. (1993) 'Common risk factors in the returns on stocks and bonds', *Journal of Financial Economics*, Vol. 33, No. 1, pp. 3–56.

The paper printed in the following section, "The Entrepreneur's Cost of Capital: Incorporating Downside Risk" by James T. Chong, Yanbo Jin, and G. Michael Phillips, was first published in *Business Valuation Review,* 33(3), on pages 81-91, and has been re-published in *Beta Estimates for Valuation & Cost of Capital* with the permission of the American Society of Appraisers.

Business Valuation Review
Volume 33 • Number 3
© 2014, American Society of Appraisers
BVR

The Entrepreneur's Cost of Capital: Incorporating Downside Risk

James T. Chong, PhD, Yanbo Jin, PhD, and G. Michael Phillips, PhD

The capital asset pricing model (CAPM) suggests that an investor's cost of equity capital is determined by beta, a measure of systematic risk based on how returns co-move with the overall market. We propose to replace beta with downside beta, a measure more consistent with investors' perception of risk. Recent empirical evidence suggests that downside beta better captures the risk-return relationship in both emerging markets and developed markets. Grouping companies into industries by two-digit Standard Industrial Classification (SIC) code, we show that the average downside beta can be very different from traditional beta. We discuss the implications of using downside beta on valuation and provide a simple example to illustrate the application in valuation for both diversified and undiversified investors.

Introduction

Investors are risk-averse. That is, they try to avoid losses and would not mind if their investments produced higher than expected returns. However, modern portfolio theory measures risk in terms of standard deviation of asset returns, which treats both positive and negative deviations from expected returns as risk. The positive deviations can be labeled ''upside risk,'' and negative deviations can be labeled ''downside risk.'' The upside risk is not necessarily undesirable. For example, if a project provided better than expected cash flows, or a stock had higher than average return, such outcome from ''upside risk'' would certainly be welcome by investors. On the other hand, investors would avoid downside risk. This asymmetric view on upside risk and downside risk is certainly not reflected by standard deviation.

The concept of beta in the capital asset pricing model (CAPM) faces a similar problem. Beta is a measure of systematic risk. By definition, it measures how an investment co-moves with the market, whether the market is going up (leading to profits), or going down (leading to losses). It is then plugged into an equation for the required return of an investment. This means that if an investment provided large positive returns when the market went up, and limited losses when the market went down, it would still have a high beta, and thus investors should require a higher rate of return for bearing this ''risk.'' However, this is not consistent with how investors view risk.

This paper discusses downside risk and downside beta, and the way in which downside beta can be incorporated in cost of equity capital estimation. We begin by reviewing the CAPM, followed by a discussion of problems with risk measurement in modern portfolio theory. We then discuss the theoretical background on downside risk and recent empirical evidence on downside beta. Empirically, we compute both downside beta and standard beta for US companies and group them into industries by two-digit Standard Industrial Classification (SIC) code. We show that two-thirds of the time, at the industry-average level, standard beta would underestimate downside beta, which would lead to value overestimation, and for the other one-third of the time, standard beta would overestimate downside beta, leading

James T. Chong, PhD, is a Professor of Finance and Associate Director of the Center for Financial Planning and Investment at California State University, Northridge. He also serves as a Research Economist at MacroRisk Analytics. He received his PhD in Finance from the ICMA Centre, The University of Reading.

Yanbo Jin, PhD (corresponding author), is an Associate Professor of Finance and Director of the Center for China Finance and Business Research at California State University, Northridge. She received her PhD in Finance from University of California, Irvine.

G. Michael Phillips, PhD, is the Director of the Center for Financial Planning and Investment and a Professor of Finance, Financial Planning, and Insurance at California State University, Northridge. He also serves as Chief Scientist for MacroRisk Analytics. He received his PhD from the University of California, San Diego, with specializations in econometrics and applied economics.

to value underestimation. Finally, we use a simple example to illustrate how an entrepreneur can incorporate downside beta in the cost of equity estimation.

The CAPM

For investors in large, publicly traded firms, the cost of equity capital can be measured by CAPM, which shows that for an investor with a well-diversified portfolio, the required return on a security can be measured by the following equation:

$$E(R_i) = R_f + \beta * RP_m \quad (1)$$

where:

$E(R_i)$ = required return on security i,
R_f = risk-free rate, and
RP_m = general market risk premium,

and where β measures the systematic risk, or the sensitivity of a security's excess return (over the risk-free rate) to the excess return on the overall market, such as the New York Stock Exchange (NYSE) Composite Index or S&P 500 Index.

CAPM is widely used in large publicly traded corporations in estimating the cost of equity capital. For example, Graham and Harvey (2001)[1] found that 73.5% of financial executives surveyed "always or almost always use the CAPM" for estimating the cost of equity capital. Bruner et al. (1998)[2] also found that CAPM is the dominant model for estimating cost of equity capital: It is used by 80% of the corporations and 81% of the financial advisors surveyed.

Admittedly, for privately held firms, beta cannot be directly measured, since the market price of equity is unobservable. However, one can estimate a proxy beta using comparable firms operating in the same industry. As suggested by Pratt and Grabowski (2010),[3] an average or median industry beta can be estimated using publicly traded firms, which is then adjusted by leverage. The leverage-adjusted beta, via Equation (1), is then employed to compute the estimated cost of equity capital.

There is evidence showing that business appraisers also use CAPM in cost of equity capital estimation. Dukes et al. (1996)[4] surveyed members of the American Society of Appraisers (ASA) and the Institute of Business Appraisers (IBA) on the valuation practice of closely held firms. They found that when estimating the discount rate, the first choice for practitioners was to use the risk-free rate plus a risk premium. Furthermore, the most popular method to estimate the risk premium was to multiply a market risk premium by the beta of the firm, where beta is derived from a group of publicly traded comparable firms.

Additionally, CAPM can be augmented to incorporate size premium and specific risk. This is particularly important for investors in privately held firms who often do not hold a well-diversified portfolio. The resulting equation can be presented as:

$$E(R_i) = R_f + \beta * RP_m + RP_s +/- RP_u{}^{5} \quad (2)$$

where:

RP_s = risk premium for small size, and
RP_u = risk premium due to company-specific risk factor.[6]

Modern Portfolio Theory: Problems

Modern portfolio theory considers risk of an asset in two different settings: If an asset is held in isolation, then the *total risk* measured by *standard deviation* is the relevant measure of risk; if an asset is part of a well-diversified portfolio, then the *systematic risk* is the relevant measure of risk, which is measured by *beta*.

Standard deviation measures how returns deviate from their mean. Both positive and negative deviation will contribute equally to the magnitude of standard deviation. However, as discussed previously, investors would treat upside risk differently from downside risk.

Similarly, the measure of systematic risk (beta) faces the same problem. Beta measures how an asset return co-moves with the market. Consider two hypothetical stocks: U and L. Suppose the returns on U, L, and the market follow the probability distribution in Table 1.

The distribution from Table 1 shows that, when the market goes down, U goes down half as much as the market while L goes down twice as much as the market, and when the market goes up, U goes up twice as much as the market, while L goes up only half as much as the market. Most investors would probably agree L is riskier than U, and therefore require a higher return to hold L.

[1]J. R. Graham and C. R. Harvey, "The theory and practice of corporate finance: Evidence from the field," *Journal of Financial Economics* 60(2) (2001):187–243.
[2]R. F. Bruner, K. M. Eades, R. S. Harris, and R. C. Higgins, "Best practices in estimating the cost of capital: Survey and synthesis," *Financial Practice and Education* Spring/Summer (1998):13–28.
[3]S. P. Pratt and R. J. Grabowski, *Cost of Capital: Applications and Examples*, 4th ed. (New York: Wiley Finance, 2010), chap. 11.
[4]W. P. Dukes, O. D. Bowlin, and C. K. Ma, "Valuation of closely-held firms: A survey," *Journal of Business Finance and Accounting* 23(3) (1996):419–438.
[5]S. P. Pratt and R. J. Grabowski, *Cost of Capital: Applications and Examples*, 4th ed. (New York: Wiley Finance, 2010), 110.
[6]Examples include industry risk factor, country risk factor, or other "specific risk" factors for investors who do not hold a perfectly diversified portfolio.

Table 1
Returns on the Market and Stocks U and L

Probability	Market	U	L
0.25	−20%	−10%	−40%
0.25	−10%	−5%	−20%
0.25	10%	20%	5%
0.25	20%	40%	10%

However, according to CAPM, U and L would have the same beta, and thus investors would require the same rate of return.

This example highlights the important difference between investor's perception of risk and the measure of beta. Investors focus on the downside risk, while beta measures both upside and downside risk. Next, we discuss the measure of downside risk, its theoretical background, and recent empirical evidence.

Downside Risk

The measure of downside risk was developed at about the same time that Markowitz developed the mean-variance theory.[7] Roy (1952)[8] was the first to formally model downside risk. In his model, an investor would prefer safety of principal first, and the resulting technique is termed the "safety-first" technique. The measure focuses on the downside loss, rather than on the entire distribution of returns.

Downside risk of a single asset

Generally speaking, downside risk for a single asset can be measured relative to the mean, or to any benchmark return. The resulting statistic is known as semivariance, for which the square root is termed semideviation.

Denote semideviation with respect to a benchmark B as $\sum_B$, we have:

$$\sum_B = \sqrt{\left(\frac{1}{T}\right) * \sum_{t=1}^{T}[\min(R_t - B), 0]^2} \qquad (3)$$

When B is the mean return, semideviation measures the spread of outcomes below the mean. However, semideviation can also be measured relative to any benchmark returns, thus making it an effective tool in risk analysis. In fact, this measure of downside risk has been widely used in the investment community to evaluate fund performance.[9]

As can be seen from the formula, only returns below a certain threshold would be considered in semideviation. Thus, the focus is on the downside of asset returns. This is consistent with investors' perception of risk. In fact, Markowitz himself admitted that "semi-variance is the more plausible measure of risk."[10] However, he chose to use the mean-variance framework for computational reasons.

Another reason for using the downside risk measure is that security distributions may not be normal or symmetrical. Markowitz (1959)[11] shows that when distributions are normal, both the semivariance and the variance measure are equivalent. Intuitively, since the normal distribution is symmetrical, the upper-tail and lower-tail would provide the same information. Thus, semivariance would simply be one-half of variance. However, empirical research has shown that security distributions are non-normal, and nonsymmetrical.[12] Therefore, focusing on the part of the distribution below the threshold value gives a more accurate portrait of downside risk.

Empirically, researchers have shown that this measure of downside risk is more consistent with investors' perception of risk. For example, in a survey of business executives in medium and large companies, when asked what they understood by the term "investment risk," the typical answers were:

> *"Risk is the prospect of not meeting the target rate of return. That is the risk, isn't it? If you are one hundred percent sure of making the target return, then it is a zero risk proposition."*
> *"...I never worry about the project return going above the target return. Risk is what might happen when the return is going to be less."*[13]

[7]H. Markowitz, "The utility of wealth," *Journal of Political Economy* 60(2) (1952):151–158; H. Markowitz, "Portfolio selection," *Journal of Finance* 7(1) (1952):77–91.

[8]A. D. Roy, "Safety first and the holding of assets," *Econometrica* 20(3) (1952):431–449.

[9]See, for example, F. A. Sortino and R. V. Meer, "Downside risk," *Journal of Portfolio Management* 17(4) (1991):27–31; F. A. Sortino, and L. N. Price, "Performance measurement in a downside risk framework," *Journal of Investing* 3(3) (1994):59–64; C. Mamoghli and S. Daboussi, "Performance measurement of hedge fund portfolios in a downside risk framework," *Journal of Wealth Management* 12(2) (2007):101–112.

[10]H. Markowitz, *Portfolio Selection: Efficient Diversification of Investment*, 2nd ed. (Malden, MA: Blackwell Publishers Inc., 1991).

[11]H. Markowitz, *Portfolio Selection*, 1st ed. (New York: John Wiley & Sons, 1959).

[12]B. Mandelbrot, "The variation of certain speculative prices," *Journal of Business* 36(4) (1963):394–419; G. Bekaert, C. Erb, C. Harvey, and T. Viskanta, "Distributional characteristics of emerging market returns, and asset allocation," *Journal of Portfolio Management* 24(1998):102–116; F. Aparicio and J. Estrada, "Empirical distributions of stock returns: European securities markets, 1990–95," *European Journal of Finance* 7(2001):1–21.

[13]J. C. T. Mao, "Survey of capital budgeting: Theory and practice," *Journal of Finance* 25(2) (1970):349–360.

These statements clearly show that investors view risk as the probability of loss. Consistent with this view, investors would require higher return to hold assets with higher downside risk.

Downside beta

According to CAPM, when an asset is held in a portfolio, asset risk can be measured by its risk contribution to the market portfolio, also known as market beta. Extending the notion of downside risk to modern portfolio theory, one can measure the downside risk of an asset by downside beta.

In fact, Hogan and Warren (1974)[14] showed that CAPM can be revised with semi-standard deviation in place of standard deviation to measure portfolio risk. Bawa and Lindenberg (1977)[15] demonstrated that CAPM can be naturally extended to incorporate the measure of downside beta as:

$$\beta^{-} = \frac{cov(r_i, r_m | r_m < u_m)}{var(r_m | r_m < u_m)} \tag{4}$$

where r_i and r_m are the excess returns to security i and market m, and u_m is the average market excess return.

Similarly, an upside beta can be measured as follows:

$$\beta^{+} = \frac{cov(r_i, r_m | r_m > u_m)}{var(r_m | r_m > u_m)} \tag{5}$$

Therefore, β^- and β^+ can be estimated with a regression of excess return of security i on excess return of the market, conditional on excess market return being below the mean (downside beta) and above the mean (upside beta).

Recent empirical studies have shown increasing support for using downside beta. In the US market, Ang et al. (2006)[16] showed that investors are rewarded with higher returns for bearing downside risks. The authors estimated that the cross section of stock returns exhibits a downside risk premium of about 6% annually. More importantly, they showed that the reward for bearing downside risk cannot be explained by standard market beta, size, or value, nor can it be explained by liquidity risk or momentum characteristics. They also illustrated that individual stocks with higher downside betas have higher average returns over the same period. More recently, Botshekan et al. (2012)[17] further confirmed that downside risk is priced consistently across different samples, periods, and decomposition methods, using individual US stocks over the period 1963–2008. They also found that downside risks carry higher risk premiums compared to other risk measures.

In addition, downside beta has been shown to explain the cross-section returns better than standard beta among other developed markets.[18] In emerging markets, Alles and Murray (2013)[19] studied eight Asian markets[20] and found that downside beta is priced by investors.

A series of studies by Estrada[21] supported the use of downside beta in both emerging markets and developed markets. In a comprehensive study,[22] he computed standard betas and downside betas for stocks across twenty-three developed markets and twenty-seven emerging markets included in the Morgan Stanley Capital Indices (MSCI). He found that downside beta outperformed standard beta in explaining the variations of cross-section returns in both types of markets. In particular, across emerging market companies, downside beta alone explained 55% of the variability in mean returns.

Estrada also showed that standard beta and downside beta could differ significantly, especially in emerging markets, where stock returns are more skewed than those in developed markets. For example, average standard beta for Brazilian firms is 1.44, while downside beta is 2.16; Indian firms' average standard beta is 0.54, while downside beta is 1.10.

Furthermore, Estrada computed the required return on equity based on both measures of beta. Using downside beta, the mean required annual return[23] of firms across developed markets is 74 basis points higher than that measured by standard beta. However, in emerging markets, required return based on downside beta is 254 basis points higher than the standard beta counterpart. Such a big difference will no doubt affect the valuation of

[14] W. W. Hogan and J. M. Warren, "Toward the development of an equilibrium capital-market model based on semi-variance," *Journal of Financial and Quantitative Analysis* 9(1) (1974):1–11.

[15] V. Bawa and E. Lindenberg, "Capital market equilibrium in a mean-lower partial moment framework," *Journal of Financial Economics* 5 (1977):189–200.

[16] A. Ang, J. Chen, and Y. Xing, "Downside risk." *Review of Financial Studies* 19(4) (2006):1191–1239.

[17] M. Botshekan, R. Kraeussl, and A. Lucas, "Cash flow and discount rate risk in up and down markets: What is actually priced?" *Journal of Financial and Quantitative Analysis* 47(6) (2012):1279–1301.

[18] For an analysis on UK individual stocks, see: C. Pedersen and S. Huang, "Does downside beta matter in asset pricing?" *Applied Financial Economics* 17(2007):961–978. For an application on stocks listed on the London Stock Exchange and Paris Stock Exchange, see: N. Artavanis, G. Diacogiannis, and J. Mylonakis, "The D-CAPM: The case of Great Britain and France," *International Journal of Economics and Finance* 2(3) (2010):25–38.

[19] L. Alles and L. Murray, "Rewards for downside risk in Asian markets," *Journal of Banking and Finance* 37(7) (2013):2501–2509.

[20] The eight Asian markets are: China, India, Indonesia, Korea, Malaysia, Pakistan, Taiwan and Thailand.

[21] J. Estrada, "The cost of equity in emerging markets: A downside risk approach," *Emerging Markets Quarterly* Fall (2000):19–30; J. Estrada, "Systematic risk in emerging markets: The D-CAPM," *Emerging Markets Review* 3(4) (2002):365–379; and J. Estrada, "Mean-semivariance behavior: Downside risk and capital asset pricing," *International Review of Economics and Finance* 16 (2007):169–185.

[22] J. Estrada, "Mean-semivariance behavior: Downside risk and capital asset pricing," *International Review of Economics and Finance* 16 (2007):169–185.

[23] The author used a risk-free rate of 5.03% and market risk premium of 5.5%.

companies significantly, private or public. As the author argued in the paper, "Differences of this magnitude are simply too large for practitioners to ignore" (Estrada 2007, 184).

In fact, Pratt and Grabowski (2010) also discussed downside risk as one of the risk measures beyond beta.[24] The authors noted that downside risk measures such as semivariance are more consistent with the common concept of risk. In addition to reviewing the literature, they also computed standard betas and downside betas for five industries as of December 2008. Interestingly, it appears that downside betas are almost always higher than standard betas during this time period, possibly due to investors' sentiment at the time of the financial crisis.

More recently, Chong and Phillips (2012)[25] discussed implications of using downside beta on corporate valuation. They showed that even at the industry level, the average downside beta can be quite different from that of the standard beta. About half of the time, the average downside beta is higher than the standard beta. Under these occasions, a financial analyst using CAPM betas would underestimate the cost of capital and overestimate the project or corporate value.

Other measures of downside risk

In addition to downside beta, researchers have also looked at skewness as a measure of downside risk. As discussed before, asset return distributions are rarely symmetrical. When an asset return has negative skewness, the asset will tend to have more downside returns than upside gains. In a portfolio setting, risk-averse investors will prefer to hold securities that have positive co-skewness with the market, and they will require higher returns to hold securities with negative co-skewness with the market.

Harvey and Siddique (2000)[26] examined an extended CAPM that incorporates conditional skewness. They show that systematic skewness is economically important and requires an average annual risk premium of 3.6%. They also show that systematic skewness helps explain the cross-section variation of expected returns beyond factors like size and book-to-market.

Galagedera and Brooks (2007)[27] used downside co-skewness as an alternative measure of downside risk to examine the explanatory power of this measure to cross-section returns in emerging markets. They found evidence that downside co-skewness is a better explanatory variable of emerging market monthly returns than downside beta.

Both downside beta and downside co-skewness measure the downside risk consistent with investors' perception of risk. However, so far, there seems to be much more empirical evidence supporting the use of downside beta, across both developed markets and emerging markets.

In the next section, we use a simple model to illustrate the application of downside beta and to compare the valuation difference between standard beta and downside beta.

The Dual-beta Model and the Data

To illustrate the difference in standard beta and downside beta, we follow the model used in Chong and Phillips (2012). We estimate the following regression using daily stock returns:

$$(r_j - r_f)_t = \alpha_j^+ D + \beta_j^+ \left(r_m^+ - r_f\right)_t D + \alpha_j^- (1-D) + \beta_j^- \left(r_m^- - r_f\right)_t (1-D) + \varepsilon_t \quad (6)$$

In this equation, D is a dummy variable that takes a value of 1 when the daily market return is non-negative. Thus, two sets of intercept and beta are estimated separately: α_j^- and β_j^- during market downturns (when market return is negative), and α_j^+ and β_j^+ when the market goes up. We label β_j^- as "down-market beta" and β_j^+ as "up-market beta," to be precise.[28]

We computed down-market and up-market beta for 4,500 stocks traded on NYSE, NASDAQ, and AMEX, using daily returns over the past year. We also computed the standard beta using the same data.[29] We then grouped the companies into industries by two-digit SIC code and computed the average and median standard beta and downside beta by industry.

Table 2 presents the results. As shown from the calculated difference, the down-market beta seldom equals the standard beta at the industry level. Roughly two-thirds of the time, the down-market beta is higher than the standard beta. In some cases, the difference can

[24] S. P. Pratt, and R. J. Grabowski, *Cost of Capital: Applications and Examples*, 4th ed. (New York: Wiley Finance, 2010), 222–225.

[25] J. Chong, and G. M. Phillips, "Measuring risk for cost of capital: The downside beta approach," *Journal of Corporate Treasury Management* 4(4) (2012):344–352.

[26] C. Harvey and A. Siddique, "Conditional skewness in asset pricing," *Journal of Finance* 65(3) (2000):1263–1295.

[27] D. Galagedera and R. Brooks, "Is co-skewness a better measure of risk in a downside than downside beta? Evidence in emerging market data," *Journal of Multinational Financial Management* 17 (2007):214–230.

[28] Notice here that the down-market and up-market betas are slightly different from those estimated in Equations (4) and (5). The downside beta in Equation (4) is estimated conditional on when the market excess return is lower than the mean excess return. Similarly, the upside beta in Equation (5) is conditional on when the market excess return is above the mean excess return.

[29] Parameter estimates were provided by MacroRisk Analytics, a commercial provider of these estimates, from their database as of February 22, 2013.

Table 2
Standard Beta and Downside Beta by Two-Digit SIC Code

Two-Digit SIC	Label	Standard Beta (Mean)	Down-market Beta (Mean)	Difference (Mean)	Standard Beta (Median)	Down-market Beta (Median)	Difference (Median)
1	Agricultural production—crops	0.873	0.692	0.181	1.000	0.686	0.315
2	Agricultural production—livestock and animal specialties	0.386	1.002	−0.617	0.476	0.618	−0.142
7	Agricultural services	0.830	1.039	−0.210	0.830	1.039	−0.210
8	Forestry	0.450	0.479	−0.029	0.450	0.479	−0.029
10	Metal mining	1.263	0.485	0.778	1.232	0.293	0.940
12	Coal mining	1.464	1.500	−0.036	1.549	1.419	0.130
13	Oil and gas extraction	1.439	1.371	0.068	1.467	1.387	0.080
14	Mining and quarrying of nonmetallic minerals, except fuels	1.284	0.856	0.428	1.321	0.807	0.513
15	Building construction—general contractors & operative builders	1.430	1.417	0.013	1.599	1.524	0.075
16	Heavy construction, except building construction—contractors	1.243	1.364	−0.121	1.341	1.449	−0.108
17	Construction—special trade contractors	1.281	1.356	−0.075	1.100	1.173	−0.072
20	Food and kindred products	0.743	0.747	−0.003	0.689	0.704	−0.015
21	Tobacco products	0.751	0.874	−0.123	0.547	0.604	−0.057
22	Textile mill products	0.976	1.005	−0.029	1.108	1.075	0.033
23	Apparel, finished products from fabrics & similar materials	1.097	1.288	−0.191	1.150	1.335	−0.185
24	Lumber and wood products, except furniture	1.691	1.569	0.121	1.546	1.458	0.088
25	Furniture and fixtures	1.009	1.189	−0.180	1.157	1.284	−0.127
26	Paper and allied products	1.083	1.100	−0.018	1.047	1.172	−0.126
27	Printing, publishing, and allied industries	0.956	0.987	−0.030	1.028	1.006	0.022
28	Chemicals and allied products	0.960	1.088	−0.128	1.009	1.103	−0.094
29	Petroleum refining and related industries	1.368	1.359	0.009	1.188	1.133	0.055
30	Rubber and miscellaneous plastic products	1.006	0.999	0.007	1.045	1.139	−0.093
31	Leather and leather products	0.946	1.099	−0.153	1.101	1.068	0.033
32	Stone, clay, glass, and concrete products	1.322	1.218	0.104	1.518	1.214	0.304
33	Primary metal industries	1.380	1.200	0.179	1.488	1.338	0.150
34	Fabricated metal products, except machinery & transport equipment	1.026	1.138	−0.112	1.192	1.165	0.027
35	Industrial and commercial machinery and computer equipment	1.220	1.180	0.039	1.300	1.232	0.068
36	Electronic, electrical equipment & components, except computer equipment	1.138	1.049	0.089	1.195	1.053	0.142
37	Transportation equipment	1.370	1.333	0.037	1.362	1.235	0.127
38	Mesr/anlyz/cntrl instruments; photo/med/opt gds; watches/clocks	0.917	1.040	−0.123	0.973	1.060	−0.087
39	Miscellaneous manufacturing industries	0.879	0.976	−0.097	0.907	0.974	−0.067
40	Railroad transportation	0.927	0.907	0.020	1.100	0.880	0.220
41	Local, suburban transit & interurban highway passenger transport	0.429	0.994	−0.564	0.429	0.994	−0.564
42	Motor freight transportation	1.160	1.270	−0.110	1.060	1.210	−0.150
44	Water transportation	1.061	0.990	0.071	1.080	0.986	0.094
45	Transportation by air	0.954	1.021	−0.068	0.859	0.957	−0.098
46	Pipelines, except natural gas	0.572	0.596	−0.024	0.589	0.485	0.105
47	Transportation services	0.937	0.951	−0.013	0.909	0.811	0.099
48	Communications	0.878	1.021	−0.143	0.875	1.075	−0.201
49	Electric, gas, and sanitary services	0.523	0.629	−0.106	0.526	0.593	−0.067
50	Wholesale trade—durable goods	0.957	0.906	0.051	1.006	1.032	−0.025
51	Wholesale trade—nondurable goods	0.898	0.916	−0.018	0.848	0.915	−0.067
52	Building materials, hardware, garden supply & mobile home dealers	1.116	1.197	−0.081	1.016	1.213	−0.196
53	General merchandise stores	0.903	0.955	−0.053	0.896	0.880	0.016
54	Food stores	0.967	0.895	0.072	0.917	0.931	−0.014

Table 2
Continued

Two-Digit SIC	Label	Standard Beta (Mean)	Down-market Beta (Mean)	Difference (Mean)	Standard Beta (Median)	Down-market Beta (Median)	Difference (Median)
55	Automotive dealers and gasoline service stations	0.988	0.972	0.017	1.217	1.524	−0.307
56	Apparel and accessory stores	1.065	1.045	0.021	1.105	1.156	−0.051
57	Home furniture, furnishings and equipment stores	0.978	0.875	0.103	1.048	0.975	0.073
58	Eating and drinking places	0.834	0.931	−0.097	0.924	0.893	0.032
59	Miscellaneous retail	0.909	0.941	−0.032	0.953	1.037	−0.084
60	Depository institutions	0.620	0.719	−0.099	0.498	0.701	−0.203
61	Nondepository credit institutions	0.627	0.722	−0.095	0.575	0.631	−0.056
62	Security & commodity brokers, dealers, exchanges & services	0.630	0.666	−0.035	0.757	0.835	−0.078
63	Insurance carriers	0.792	0.877	−0.085	0.724	0.783	−0.059
64	Insurance agents, brokers and service	0.834	0.740	0.094	0.741	0.785	−0.044
65	Real estate	0.806	0.968	−0.161	0.775	0.978	−0.203
67	Holding and other investment offices	0.602	0.649	−0.047	0.744	0.839	−0.095
70	Hotels, rooming houses, camps, and other lodging places	1.132	1.189	−0.057	1.291	1.278	0.013
72	Personal services	1.013	1.057	−0.043	0.971	1.110	−0.140
73	Business services	1.003	1.025	−0.022	1.036	1.043	−0.007
75	Automotive repair, services and parking	1.294	1.407	−0.114	1.319	1.301	0.018
76	Miscellaneous repair services	0.981	2.324	−1.343	0.981	2.324	−1.343
78	Motion pictures	0.821	0.835	−0.015	0.873	0.870	0.002
79	Amusement and recreation services	0.735	0.718	0.017	0.827	0.857	−0.030
80	Health services	0.947	1.010	−0.063	0.976	1.118	−0.142
81	Legal services	1.023	1.335	−0.312	1.023	1.335	−0.312
82	Educational services	0.861	1.103	−0.243	0.845	1.126	−0.280
83	Social services	0.806	−0.381	1.187	0.806	0.505	0.301
86	Membership organizations	1.389	1.253	0.135	1.389	1.253	0.135
87	Engineering, accounting, research, management & related services	0.866	1.037	−0.171	0.834	0.890	−0.056
89	Services, not elsewhere classified	1.136	1.118	0.018	1.215	1.074	0.141
95	Administration of environmental quality and housing programs	1.161	2.721	−1.560	1.161	2.721	−1.560
96	Administration of economic programs	1.210	1.540	−0.330	1.210	1.540	−0.330
99	Nonclassifiable establishments	0.773	0.817	−0.045	0.900	0.924	−0.023

be quite significant. Take for example, the ''agricultural production—livestock and animal specialties'' industry (SIC = 2): The average standard beta is 0.386, while the downside beta is 1.002, i.e., more than twice the estimate of standard beta. In the cases when down-market beta is higher than the standard beta, the down-market beta is higher by about 21.3% on average.

We also computed equity rates using both down-market and standard beta. We used a risk-free rate of 2%, which is close to the ten-year US Treasury note yield as of the end of February 2013, and equity risk premium of 6%, as suggested in Ang et al. (2006). Thus, the equity rates are computed using:

$$k_{is} = 2\% + \beta_{is} * 6\% \qquad (7)$$

where i stands for the industry, and s refers to the style of beta used (down-market or standard beta).

The equity rates are presented in Table 3. In addition, assuming a hypothetical annual perpetual cash flow of $100,000, we computed the value of the cash flows using both equity rates. PV(std) shows the present value of cash flows using equity rates with standard beta, while PV(down) shows the value using equity rates with down-market beta. The last column shows the value difference. Since about two-thirds of the time the standard beta is lower than the down-market beta, using equity rates based on standard beta would overestimate the value of the cash flows about two-thirds of the time. The average overvaluation is about 14%. For the other one-third of the time, standard beta is higher than down-market beta. This leads to value underestimation by 7.3% on average.

Next, we use a simple example to illustrate the valuation impact to an entrepreneur. For simplification,

Table 3

Equity Rates and Present Value of Cash Flows Based on Standard Beta and Down-market Beta

Equity Risk Premium	6%
Riskless Rate	2%
Annual Cash Flow	$ 100,000

Two-Digit SIC	Label	Standard Beta (Mean)	Base Rate (Standard Beta)	Down-market Beta (Mean)	Base Rate (Down Beta)	PV (Std)	PV (Down)	(PV[Std] − PV[Down])	As % of Std
1	Agricultural production—crops	0.873	7.2%	0.692	6.2%	$ 1,381,802	$ 1,625,062	$ (243,260)	−17.60%
2	Agricultural production—livestock and animal specialties	0.386	4.3%	1.002	8.0%	$ 2,317,940	$ 1,247,894	$ 1,070,046	46.16%
7	Agricultural services	0.830	7.0%	1.039	8.2%	$ 1,433,244	$ 1,214,413	$ 218,831	15.27%
8	Forestry	0.450	4.7%	0.479	4.9%	$ 2,127,345	$ 2,051,690	$ 75,654	3.56%
10	Metal mining	1.263	9.6%	0.485	4.9%	$ 1,044,148	$ 2,036,063	$ (991,915)	−95.00%
12	Coal mining	1.464	10.8%	1.500	11.0%	$ 927,207	$ 909,233	$ 17,974	1.94%
13	Oil and gas extraction	1.439	10.6%	1.371	10.2%	$ 940,378	$ 977,916	$ (37,538)	−3.99%
14	Mining and quarrying of nonmetallic minerals, except fuels	1.284	9.7%	0.856	7.1%	$ 1,030,499	$ 1,401,812	$ (371,313)	−36.03%
15	Building construction—general contractors & operative builders	1.430	10.6%	1.417	10.5%	$ 945,070	$ 952,144	$ (7,074)	−0.75%
16	Heavy construction, except building construction—contractors	1.243	9.5%	1.364	10.2%	$ 1,057,105	$ 982,010	$ 75,095	7.10%
17	Construction—special trade contractors	1.281	9.7%	1.356	10.1%	$ 1,032,657	$ 986,846	$ 45,812	4.44%
20	Food and kindred products	0.743	6.5%	0.747	6.5%	$ 1,548,045	$ 1,543,053	$ 4,992	0.32%
21	Tobacco products	0.751	6.5%	0.874	7.2%	$ 1,536,729	$ 1,380,446	$ 156,283	10.17%
22	Textile mill products	0.976	7.9%	1.005	8.0%	$ 1,272,792	$ 1,245,607	$ 27,185	2.14%
23	Apparel, finished products from fabrics & similar materials	1.097	8.6%	1.288	9.7%	$ 1,165,366	$ 1,027,970	$ 137,395	11.79%
24	Lumber and wood products, except furniture	1.691	12.1%	1.569	11.4%	$ 823,450	$ 875,920	$ (52,471)	−6.37%
25	Furniture and fixtures	1.009	8.1%	1.189	9.1%	$ 1,241,776	$ 1,094,704	$ 147,072	11.84%
26	Paper and allied products	1.083	8.5%	1.100	8.6%	$ 1,176,978	$ 1,162,573	$ 14,404	1.22%
27	Printing, publishing and allied industries,	0.956	7.7%	0.987	7.9%	$ 1,292,576	$ 1,262,717	$ 29,860	2.31%
28	Chemicals and allied products	0.960	7.8%	1.088	8.5%	$ 1,288,427	$ 1,172,573	$ 115,854	8.99%
29	Petroleum refining and related industries	1.368	10.2%	1.359	10.2%	$ 979,462	$ 984,840	$ (5,378)	−0.55%
30	Rubber and miscellaneous plastic products	1.006	8.0%	0.999	8.0%	$ 1,244,356	$ 1,250,604	$ (6,249)	−0.50%
31	Leather and leather products	0.946	7.7%	1.099	8.6%	$ 1,302,577	$ 1,163,756	$ 138,820	10.66%
32	Stone, clay, glass, and concrete products	1.322	9.9%	1.218	9.3%	$ 1,007,065	$ 1,074,342	$ (67,277)	−6.68%
33	Primary metal industries	1.380	10.3%	1.200	9.2%	$ 972,862	$ 1,086,709	$ (113,848)	−11.70%
34	Fabricated metal products, except machinery & transport equipment	1.026	8.2%	1.138	8.8%	$ 1,226,432	$ 1,132,974	$ 93,457	7.62%

Table 3
Continued

Two-Digit SIC	Label	Standard Beta (Mean)	Base Rate (Standard Beta)	Down-market Beta (Mean)	Base Rate (Down Beta)	PV (Std)	PV (Down)	(PV[Std] − PV[Down])	As % of Std
35	Industrial and commercial machinery and computer equipment	1.220	9.3%	1.180	9.1%	$ 1,073,285	$ 1,101,246	$ (27,961)	−2.61%
36	Electronic, electrical equipment & components, except computer equipment	1.138	8.8%	1.049	8.3%	$ 1,132,839	$ 1,205,575	$ (72,736)	−6.42%
37	Transportation equipment	1.370	10.2%	1.333	10.0%	$ 978,461	$ 1,000,370	$ (21,909)	−2.24%
38	Mesr/anlyz/cntrl instruments; photo/med/opt gds; watches/clocks	0.917	7.5%	1.040	8.2%	$ 1,333,118	$ 1,213,593	$ 119,524	8.97%
39	Miscellaneous manufacturing industries	0.879	7.3%	0.976	7.9%	$ 1,374,484	$ 1,272,984	$ 101,500	7.38%
40	Railroad transportation	0.927	7.6%	0.907	7.4%	$ 1,322,213	$ 1,343,712	$ (21,499)	−1.63%
41	Local, suburban transit & interurban highway passenger transport	0.429	4.6%	0.994	8.0%	$ 2,185,376	$ 1,255,994	$ 929,382	42.53%
42	Motor freight transportation	1.160	9.0%	1.270	9.6%	$ 1,116,175	$ 1,039,822	$ 76,353	6.84%
44	Water transportation	1.061	8.4%	0.990	7.9%	$ 1,195,613	$ 1,259,540	$ (63,927)	−5.35%
45	Transportation by air	0.954	7.7%	1.021	8.1%	$ 1,294,867	$ 1,230,278	$ 64,589	4.99%
46	Pipelines, except natural gas	0.572	5.4%	0.596	5.6%	$ 1,840,985	$ 1,792,958	$ 48,027	2.61%
47	Transportation services	0.937	0.076	0.951	0.077	$ 1,311,559	$ 1,298,055	$ 13,504	1.03%
48	Communications	0.878	0.073	1.021	0.081	$ 1,375,891	$ 1,230,688	$ 145,203	10.55%
49	Electric, gas and sanitary services	0.523	0.051	0.629	0.058	$ 1,946,198	$ 1,731,549	$ 214,648	11.03%
50	Wholesale trade—durable goods	0.957	0.077	0.906	0.074	$ 1,292,067	$ 1,345,090	$ (53,024)	−4.10%
51	Wholesale trade—nondurable goods	0.898	0.074	0.916	0.075	$ 1,352,997	$ 1,333,582	$ 19,415	1.43%
52	Building materials, hardware, garden supply & mobile home dealers	1.116	0.087	1.197	0.092	$ 1,150,202	$ 1,089,120	$ 61,082	5.31%
53	General merchandise stores	0.903	0.074	0.955	0.077	$ 1,348,331	$ 1,293,372	$ 54,959	4.08%
54	Food stores	0.967	0.078	0.895	0.074	$ 1,281,851	$ 1,356,711	$ (74,860)	−5.84%
55	Automotive dealers and gasoline service stations	0.988	0.079	0.972	0.078	$ 1,261,054	$ 1,277,161	$ (16,107)	−1.28%
56	Apparel and accessory stores	1.065	0.084	1.045	0.083	$ 1,191,688	$ 1,209,458	$ (17,771)	−1.49%
57	Home furniture, furnishings and equipment stores	0.978	0.079	0.875	0.073	$ 1,271,051	$ 1,379,006	$ (107,955)	−8.49%
58	Eating and drinking places	0.834	0.070	0.931	0.076	$ 1,428,257	$ 1,318,356	$ 109,901	7.69%
59	Miscellaneous retail	0.909	0.075	0.941	0.076	$ 1,341,547	$ 1,308,369	$ 33,178	2.47%
60	Depository institutions	0.620	0.057	0.719	0.063	$ 1,748,077	$ 1,584,223	$ 163,855	9.37%
61	Nondepository credit institutions	0.627	0.058	0.722	0.063	$ 1,735,717	$ 1,578,887	$ 156,830	9.04%
62	Security & commodity brokers, dealers, exchanges & services	0.630	0.058	0.666	0.060	$ 1,729,787	$ 1,668,390	$ 61,397	3.55%
63	Insurance carriers	0.792	0.068	0.877	0.073	$ 1,481,042	$ 1,377,551	$ 103,491	6.99%
64	Insurance agents, brokers and service	0.834	0.070	0.740	0.064	$ 1,427,276	$ 1,552,399	$ (125,124)	−8.77%
65	Real estate	0.806	0.068	0.968	0.078	$ 1,462,278	$ 1,281,165	$ 181,113	12.39%

Table 3
Continued

Two-Digit SIC	Label	Standard Beta (Mean)	Base Rate (Standard Beta)	Down-market Beta (Mean)	Base Rate (Down Beta)	PV (Std)	PV (Down)	(PV[Std] − PV[Down])	As % of Std
67	Holding and other investment offices	0.602	0.056	0.649	0.059	$ 1,781,693	$ 1,697,051	$ 84,642	4.75%
70	Hotels, rooming houses, camps, and other lodging places	1.132	0.088	1.189	0.091	$ 1,137,444	$ 1,094,716	$ 42,728	3.76%
72	Personal services	1.013	0.081	1.057	0.083	$ 1,237,498	$ 1,199,005	$ 38,493	3.11%
73	Business services	1.003	0.080	1.025	0.081	$ 1,247,487	$ 1,227,027	$ 20,460	1.64%
75	Automotive repair, services and parking	1.294	0.098	1.407	0.104	$ 1,024,412	$ 957,513	$ 66,899	6.53%
76	Miscellaneous repair services	0.981	0.079	2.324	0.159	$ 1,268,101	$ 627,200	$ 640,901	50.54%
78	Motion pictures	0.821	0.069	0.835	0.070	$ 1,444,394	$ 1,425,975	$ 18,419	1.28%
79	Amusement and recreation services	0.735	0.064	0.718	0.063	$ 1,559,968	$ 1,584,869	$ (24,901)	−1.60%
80	Health services	0.947	0.077	1.010	0.081	$ 1,302,047	$ 1,240,797	$ 61,250	4.70%
81	Legal services	1.023	0.081	1.335	0.100	$ 1,229,111	$ 999,211	$ 229,901	18.70%
82	Educational services	0.861	0.072	1.103	0.086	$ 1,395,811	$ 1,160,094	$ 235,717	16.89%
83	Social services	0.806	0.068	−0.381	−0.003	$ 1,462,779	$ (34,838,593)	$ 36,301,372	2481.67%
86	Membership organizations	1.389	0.103	1.253	0.095	$ 967,809	$ 1,050,316	$ (82,508)	−8.53%
87	Engineering, accounting, research, management & related services	0.866	0.072	1.037	0.082	$ 1,389,458	$ 1,216,283	$ 173,175	12.46%
89	Services, not elsewhere classified	1.136	0.088	1.118	0.087	$ 1,134,405	$ 1,148,598	$ (14,193)	−1.25%
95	Administration of environmental quality and housing programs	1.161	0.090	2.721	0.183	$ 1,115,683	$ 545,716	$ 569,967	51.09%
96	Administration of economic programs	1.210	0.093	1.540	0.112	$ 1,079,599	$ 889,594	$ 190,005	17.60%
99	Nonclassifiable establishments	0.773	0.066	0.817	0.069	$ 1,507,031	$ 1,448,662	$ 58,369	3.87%

we assume the entrepreneur does not have any debt, and the annual projected cash flow is $100,000 for ten years. The entrepreneur uses the CAPM model to estimate the cost of capital. The comparable industry is the *miscellaneous repair service* with SIC = 76. We chose this industry because it gives an example where downside beta is significantly higher than the standard beta.

Table 4 shows the cost of equity capital and present value calculation. We assume the size premium is 6.36%.[30] For a diversified investor, we assume there is no additional risk premium ($RP_u = 0$ in Equation [2]). Based on downside beta, the estimated present value is $388,480. If the entrepreneur used the standard beta instead, he would have estimated the present value to be $516,642, leading to an overestimation of $128,162, or about a 33% value overestimation.

If the entrepreneur is undiversified, the required return would be higher to reflect the investor's lack of diversification.[31] For illustration purposes, we add a risk premium of 5% for the owner's lack of diversification. The cost of equity capital based on downside beta and standard beta is 27.3% and 19.25%, respectively. The present value based on downside beta is $333,486, while that based on standard beta is $430,212. Again, using standard beta would overestimate value by about 30%.

This example illustrates how downside beta can improve the accuracy of cost of capital estimation, compared to standard beta. It is important to note that downside beta applies to both diversified and undiversified investors, as long as the investors are risk averse. However, for undiversified investors, it is important to add additional

[30]Ibbotson SSBI 2011 Valuation Yearbook, Decile 10.

[31]For a more detailed discussion on cost of capital adjustment to reflect investors' lack of diversification, see: D. McConaughy and V. Covrig, "Owner's lack of diversification and the cost of equity capital for a closely-held firm," *Business Valuation Review* 26(4) (2007):115–120.

Table 4
Sample Impact of Downside and Standard Beta on Valuation

Build-Up Model (Assuming Comparable Industry SIC = 76)		
Risk-Free Rate	2%	
Equity Risk Premium	6%	
Size Premium*	6.36%	
Lack-of-Diversification Premium**	5%	
Annual Cash Flow (for 10 Years)	$100,000	
Downside Beta	2.324	
Standard Beta	0.981	
Diversified Investor	**Downside Beta**	**Standard Beta**
Cost of Equity	22.30%	14.25%
Present Value	$388,480	$516,642
Value Difference (Standard-Down)	$128,162	
Undiversified Investor	**Downside Beta**	**Standard Beta**
Cost of Equity	27.30%	19.25%
Present Value	$333,486	$430,212
Value Difference (Standard-Down)	$96,726	

* Size premium, group 10, last page of SBBI Valuation Edition 2011.
** For a more detailed discussion on diversification discount, see McConaughy and Covrig (2007).[31]

risk premium to compensate for the investor's lack of diversification.

Admittedly, not all industries experience such a big difference between standard beta and downside beta. However, for most of the industries, the difference is still quite significant. Thus, using downside beta could potentially lead to more accurate valuation estimation. Besides, the estimation procedure on downside beta requires no additional information beyond that required by standard beta. At a minimum, it would provide an alternative, and arguably better, valuation measure than those derived from standard beta.

Conclusion

There is now increasing evidence showing that downside risk is priced by investors. Downside risk focuses on the risk of losses, instead of the entire distribution of investment returns. Theoretically, this measure is more consistent with investors' perception of risk. Empirically, studies have shown that investment with higher downside risk is rewarded with higher returns, both in emerging markets and in developed markets. The reward for bearing downside risk is significant and cannot be explained by the standard beta.

This paper reviewed the theoretical and empirical literature on downside beta. More importantly, using daily returns of about 4,500 stocks over February 2012–February 2013, we showed that downside beta can be quite different from standard beta, even at the industry-average level. More specifically, we find that around two-thirds of the time, standard beta would underestimate the downside risk. Under these scenarios, valuation based on standard beta would lead to overestimation.

Using a simple example, we illustrated how an entrepreneur could incorporate downside beta in the cost of equity capital estimation, and how using standard beta would lead to significant value overestimation when downside beta is much higher than standard beta.

Downside beta is readily available through commercial data providers or by using a spreadsheet.[32] At a minimum, valuation based on downside beta would provide an alternative measure to the entrepreneur, perhaps leading to a more accurate valuation of the business.

[32]See, for example, Pratt, S.P. and Grabowski, R.J. (2010) *The Cost of Capital: Applications and Examples 4th ed. Workbook and Technical Supplement*, Chapter 4, which contains an example of computing downside beta.

The paper printed in the following section, "Why Downside Beta is Better: An Educational Example" by James T. Chong, William P. Jennings, and G. Michael Phillips, was first published in the *American Journal of Business Education,* 6(3), on pages 371-374, and has been re-published in *Beta Estimates for Valuation & Cost of Capital* with the permission of the authors and The Clute Institute.

American Journal Of Business Education – May/June 2013 *Volume 6, Number 3*

Why Downside Beta Is Better: An Educational Example

James T. Chong, California State University, USA
William P. Jennings, California State University, USA
G. Michael Phillips, California State University, USA

ABSTRACT

An educational example is presented that is an effective teaching illustration to help students understand the difference between traditional CAPM beta and downside (or down-market) beta and why downside beta is a superior measure for use in personal financial planning investment policy statements.

Keywords: CAPM; Downside Beta; Investment Policy Statements; Teaching Illustration

INTRODUCTION

Beta is ubiquitous in investment planning as a measure of the relative riskiness of an asset or portfolio compared to the overall market risk. Beta is often used as a limit on acceptable investments in investment policy statements. Beta is provided as a statistic in numerous printed and electronic databases and is widely used to summarize portfolio risk characteristics.

This paper proposes that downside beta - a beta estimated just from those data points of the asset or portfolio return when the benchmark return is negative - is a superior measure. This is because traditional beta includes any observations when the asset or portfolio outperforms the benchmark. If there is any asymmetry in the returns process, this could result in a misstatement of beta and lead to the incorrect exclusion of assets from consideration.

THE BASIC EXAMPLE

Consider the follow simple example: Suppose you have an investment policy statement in which a client specifies that she only wants assets with beta less than or equal to 1. That is, she only wants assets that are no riskier than the market portfolio.

Now, suppose that there are two assets to consider. Mutual fund A is identical to the market portfolio and has a beta of 1 regardless of whether the market is rising or falling. Mutual fund B is identical to the market portfolio on days that the market goes down, but goes up twice as much as the benchmark on up-days in the market. Figure 1 shows a comparison of these two investments in returns space, with the market index return as the horizontal axis. Note that P1SIM1 and P1SPX are essentially identical in returns.

Figure 1: Returns For Two Simulated Series (Y-axis) Against Returns For S&P Index (X-axis)

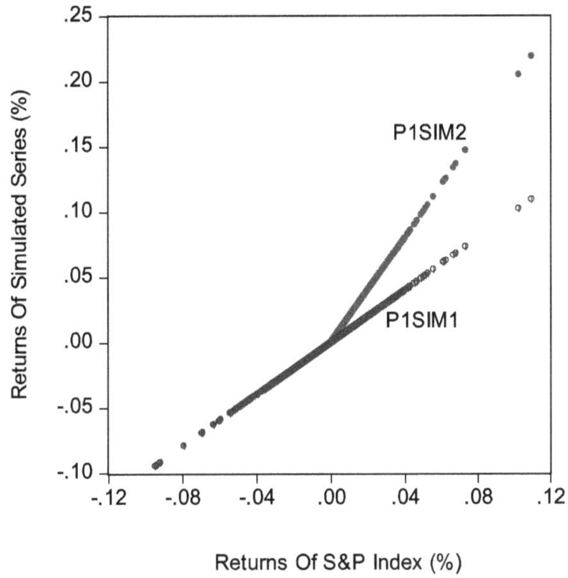

When the two returns series are plotted against each other, the difference between the two simulated portfolios becomes more apparent (Figure 2).

Figure 2: Comparison Of Two Simulated Series (Same Downside Beta, Series 1 With Lower Upside Beta, Series 2 With Higher Upside Beta)

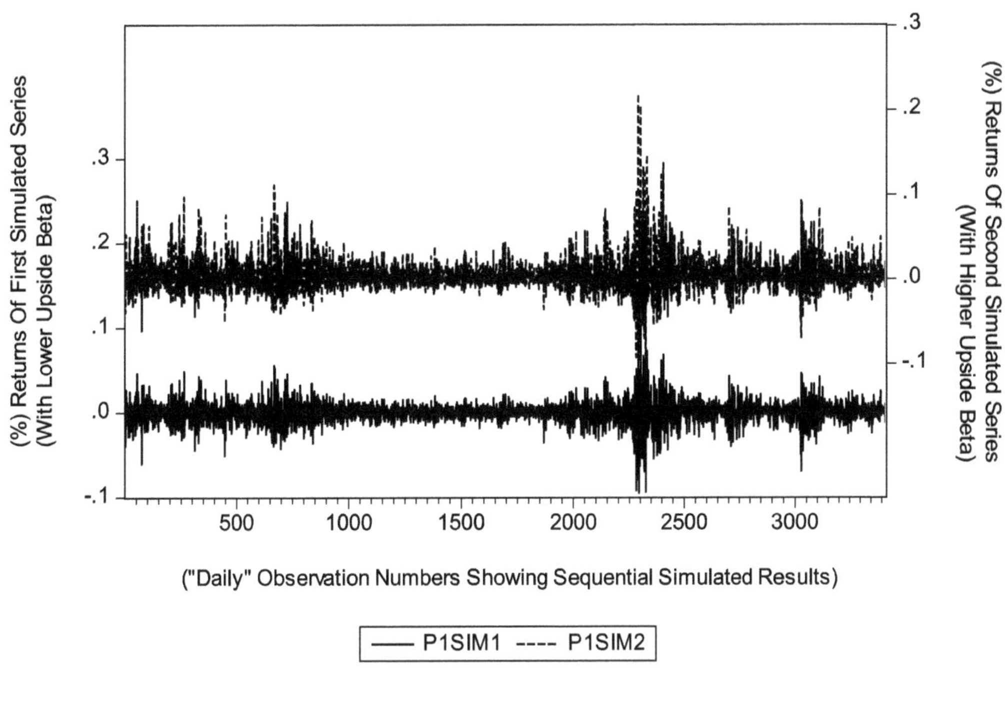

One can see that the P1SIM2 line, the second simulation, exceeds the first but is never less.

When converting from returns space into price space, the real difference in these portfolios is apparent (Figure 3).

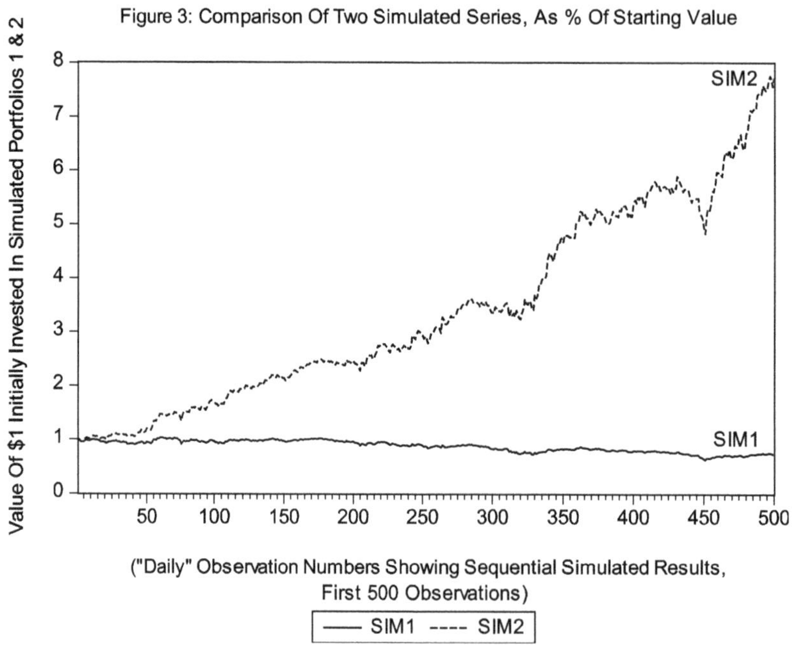

Now, one asks the students which portfolio is preferred: The dashed one (PISIM2) or the solid one (P1SIM1)? Virtually everybody would prefer the dashed-line since the two portfolios have the same downside movement, but the dashed-line portfolio shows substantially greater gain.

Running a basic market model equation against each of the two simulated portfolios verifies that the estimated beta for P1SIM1 is 1 and the estimated beta for P1SIM2 is 1.489.

According to the investment policy statement's guidelines, the dominant portfolio would not be acceptable because the beta exceeds the market.

If instead a downside beta measure was used, finding the beta using just those days when the market return was negative, then both investments would have the same downside beta, 1. At that point, other criteria such as upside beta (1 for P1SIM1 and 2 for P1SIM2) could be used to determine which investment is most appropriate.

CONCLUSION

Downside beta is not a hard concept, but it is unfamiliar to many financial professionals and students and is seldom discussed in textbooks. For purposes of investment policy statements, it is superior to traditional beta because it does not confuse positive return—profits—with loss.

This simple, yet effective, example quickly illustrates these differences and the problem with an investment policy statement designed to use beta limits.

Additional information on downside beta is available in Chong, Halcoussis, and Phillips (2012), Chong, Pfeiffer, and Phillips (2011), and Chong and Phillips (2011).

AUTHOR INFORMATION

James T. Chong, Ph.D., is a Professor and Associate Director of the Center for Financial Planning and Investment at California State University, Northridge. He also serves as a Research Economist at MacroRisk Analytics. He received his Ph.D. in Finance from the ICMA Centre, The University of Reading. E-mail: jchong@csun.edu

William P. Jennings, Ph.D., is Professor of Finance and Emeritus Dean of Business at California State University, Northridge, where he currently serves as Interim Vice President of University Advancement. He received his Ph.D. from the University of California, Los Angeles. E-mail: william.jennings@csun.edu

G. Michael Phillips, Ph.D., is the Director of the Center for Financial Planning and Investment and a Professor of Finance, Real Estate, and Insurance at California State University, Northridge. He also serves as Chief Scientist for MacroRisk Analytics. He received his Ph.D. from the University of California, San Diego, with specializations in econometrics and applied economics. E-mail: mphillips@csun.edu (Corresponding author)

REFERENCES

1. Chong, James, Dennis Halcoussis, and G. Michael Phillips. (2012). Misleading Betas: An Educational Example. *American Journal of Business Education, 5*(5), 617-622.
2. Chong, James, Shawn Pfeiffer, and G. Michael Phillips. (2011). Can Dual Beta Filtering Improve Investor Performance? *Journal of Personal Finance, 10*(1), 63-86.
3. Chong, James, and G. Michael Phillips. (2011). Beta Measures Market Risk Except When It Doesn't: Regime-Switching Alpha and Errors in Beta. *The Journal of Wealth Management*, *14*(3), 67-72.

The paper printed in the following section, "Misleading Betas: An Educational Example" by James Chong, Dennis Halcoussis, and G. Michael Phillips, was first published in the *American Journal of Business Education,* 5(5), on pages 617-622, and has been re-published in *Beta Estimates for Valuation & Cost of Capital* with the permission of the authors and The Clute Institute.

American Journal Of Business Education – September/October 2012 Volume 5, Number 5

Misleading Betas: An Educational Example

James Chong, California State University-Northridge, USA
Dennis Halcoussis, California State University-Northridge, USA
G. Michael Phillips, California State University-Northridge, USA

ABSTRACT

The dual-beta model is a generalization of the CAPM model. In the dual-beta model, separate beta estimates are provided for up-market and down-market days. This paper uses the historical "Anscombe quartet" results which illustrated how very different datasets can produce the same regression coefficients to motivate a discussion of the dual-beta model. Using data from 39 mutual funds, it is shown how very different dual-beta models can lead to the same CAPM beta estimates, much like the Anscombe quartet scenarios.

Keywords: CAPM; Beta; Dual-Beta; Anscombe

INTRODUCTION

The use of the standard Capital Asset Pricing Model (CAPM) beta to measure risk is well known and widely discussed in the finance literature (see, for example, Scholes and Williams, 1977; Todorov and Bollerslev, 2010). Lesser known is the concept of using asymmetric betas—estimating one value for an upswing in the market and another different value for downswings in the market (Chong, Pfeiffer, and Phillips, 2011). In fact, there is no reason to believe that one value for beta will accurately capture market risk for both an up- and down-market. The prevalent use of one estimate of a beta per stock or mutual fund for both up- and downturns in the market can lead investors to oversimplify the risk characteristics of the investment.

The misleading impression given to investors by the use of a single beta estimate for both up- and down-markets is analogous to Anscombe's quartet, four very different data sets that produce the same set of regression results (Anscombe, 1973). In fact, the comparison of the two problems is more than analogous. The concept of dual-betas exploits the fact that data used to estimate a single overall beta can be divided into two separate, distinct subsets. One subset is from the up-market and another from the down-market, giving two different beta estimates that capture different levels of market risk for the stock or fund. Ignoring these differences in the data by estimating a single beta gives a misleading portrait of asset risk in the same way that different data sets can lead to the same regression results (as demonstrated by Anscombe's quartet).

STANDARD CAPM MODEL

Beta has been shown by Fama and French (1992) to be an imperfect measure of investment risk. However, the standard CAPM model, which originally developed the idea of beta, is still popular among investment professionals and can be expressed as:

$$(r_j - r_f)_t = \alpha_j + \beta_j (r_m - r_f)_t + \varepsilon_t, \tag{1}$$

where r_f is the risk-free rate (the overnight U.S. Federal funds rate is used as proxy), r_j is the return on asset j, $(r_j - r_f)_t$ is the observed excess return on asset j, α_j is the estimated regression intercept, called alpha, $(r_m - r_f)_t$ is the estimated excess return on the market index (here, the S&P 500 Index), and ε_t is the unexplained portion of the model.

DUAL-BETA MODEL

As an extension of the standard CAPM model, the dual-beta model estimates separately the parameters for up-market when the daily return for the market index is non-negative and down-market when the daily return for the market index is negative. The dual-beta model can thus be expressed as:

$$\left(r_j - r_f\right)_t = \alpha_j^+ D + \beta_j^+ (r_m^+ - r_f)_t D + \alpha_j^- (1 - D) + \beta_j^- (r_m^- - r_f)_t (1 - D) + \varepsilon_t, \quad (2)$$

where α_j^+, β_j^+, α_j^-, and β_j^- are the estimated parameters for up-market and down-market days, respectively; $r_m^+ = r_m$ on days the market index did not decline and $r_m^- = r_m$ on days it did; *D* is a dummy variable, which takes the value of 1 when the market index daily return is non-negative and zero otherwise. If there is no asymmetry in beta, then the dual-beta model is identical to the standard CAPM model. In this study, the standard CAPM beta, up-market beta, and down-market beta are estimated using one-year daily returns as of September 16, 2011.

Chong, Pfeiffer, and Phillips (2011) had explored the dual-beta model's efficacy in containing risk during stock market downturns and found it superior to the standard CAPM beta, while Chong and Phillips (2011) provided the theoretical basis for the relevance of the dual-beta model.

ANSCOMBE'S QUARTET

Anscombe (1973) gives four different data sets which all produce the same regression results. Figures 1 through 4 show the four different data sets for Anscombe's quartet. All four data sets give the following results:

$$Y = 3 + 0.5X \quad (3)$$

Figure 1: Anscombe (1973) Data Set 1

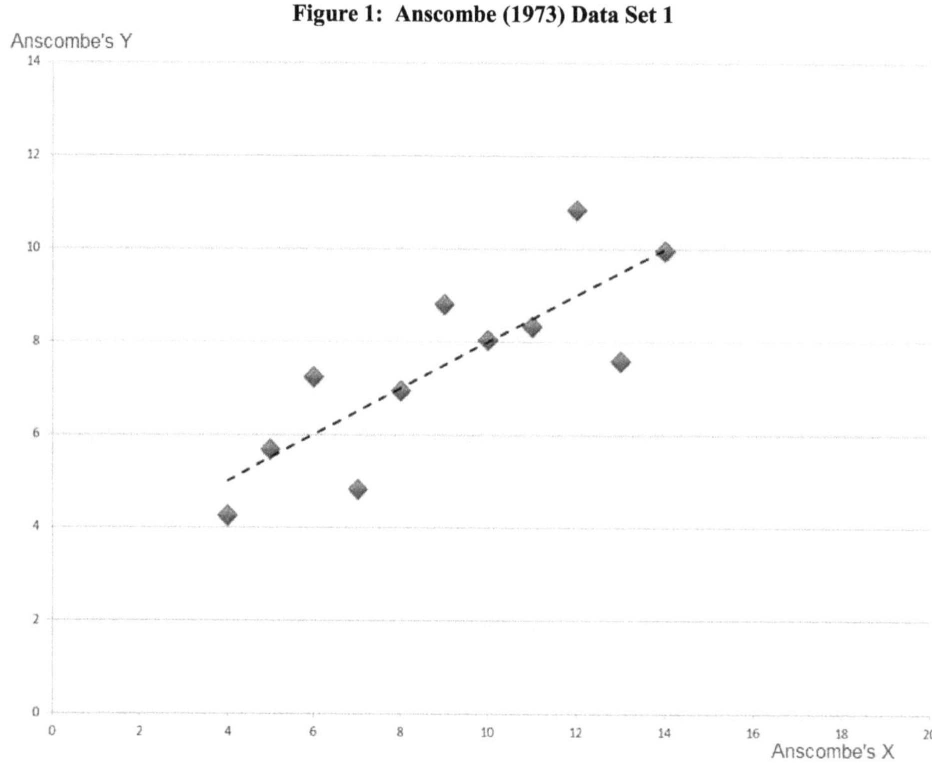

Clearly, Equation (3) does not adequately describe the data displayed in Figures 2 to 4, even though the results are accurate for all four figures. The data in Figure 2 would be better described by a non-linear equation than a simple linear regression model. If you take away the outlier in Figure 3, it looks like the intercept would be higher than 3 and the slope lower than 0.5. In Figure 4, most of the data points have the same X value and form a vertical line. Like Figure 3, only one point or outlier forces the regression to have the same outcome as the others. Only Figure 1 displays data that one would typically imagine after seeing Equation (3). Anscombe's point is that just looking at regression results without a data plot or more information can mislead the reader.

Figure 2: Anscombe (1973) Data Set 2

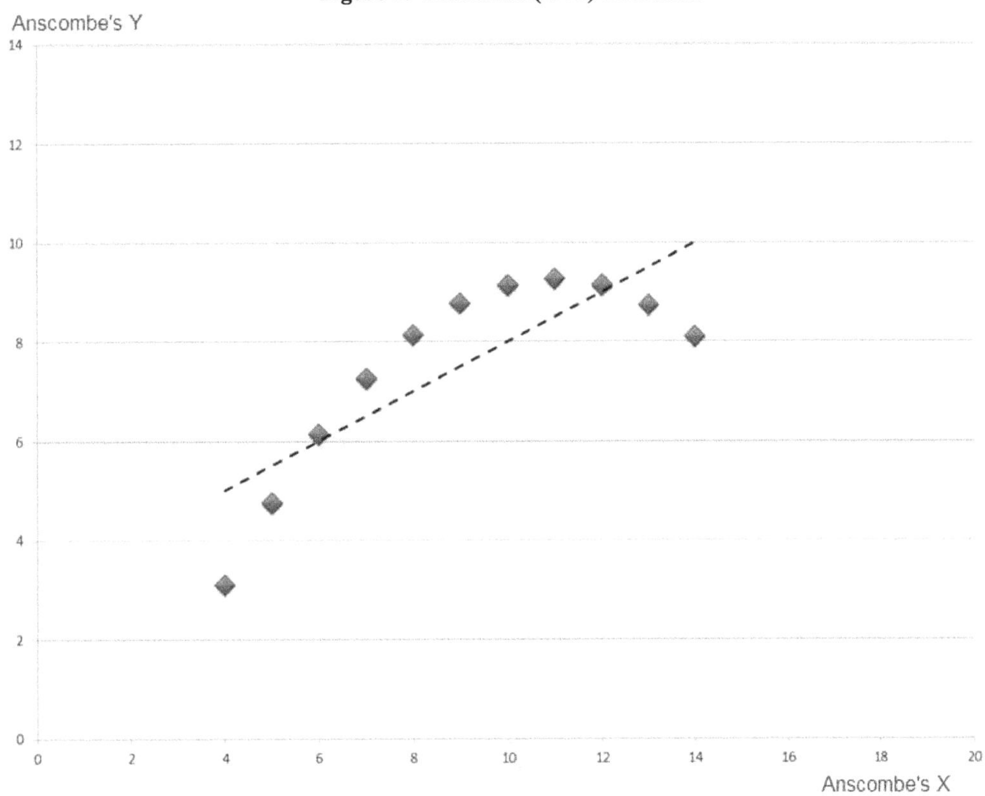

Figure 3: Anscombe (1973) Data Set 3

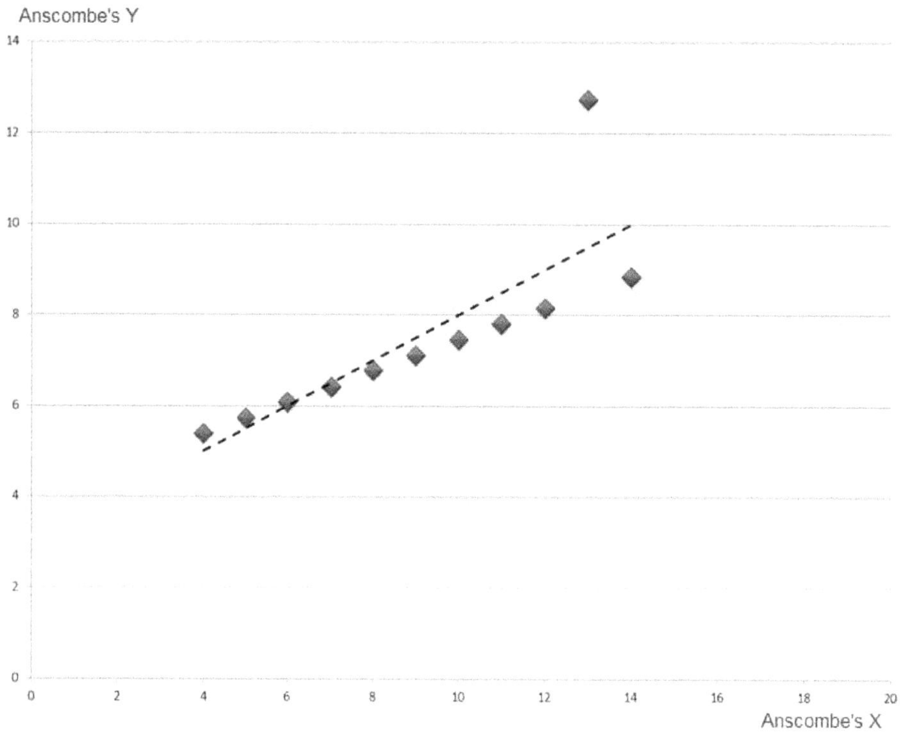

Figure 4: Anscombe (1973) Data Set 4

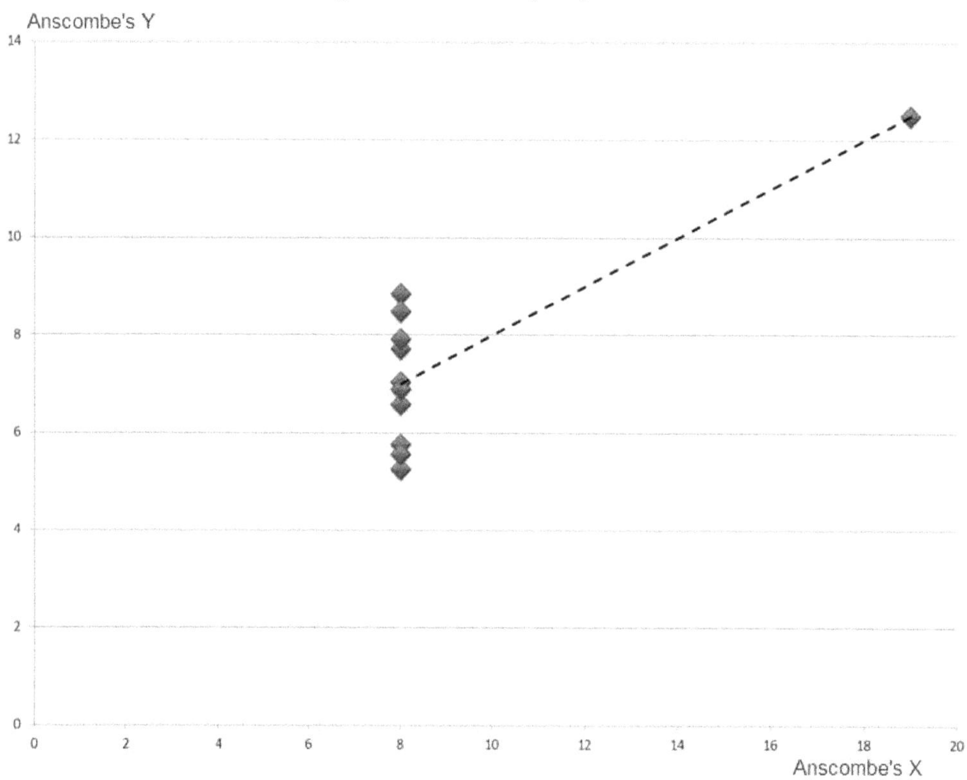

Figure 5 shows the up-market and down-market betas for 39 mutual funds. All 39 funds have an overall standard CAPM beta of 1.1. Figure 5 shows the great variety of up- and down-market betas that can result in a traditional beta with the same value. As discussed above, similar to Anscombe's quartet, investors considering a stock or mutual fund can be misled by examining one value for beta for both up- and downturns in the economy. Consider two mutual funds - MCVIX (MFS Mid Cap Value Fund) and SSMAX (SEI Institutional Investment Trust-Small/Mid Cap Equity Fund). MCVIX and SSMAX are observations 8 and 9 in Figure 5, respectively. Both these mutual funds have an estimated beta of 1.1. Both funds have the same alphas - 0.02. MCVIX has both an up-market beta and down-market beta of 1.1, so, in this case, the overall beta estimate of 1.1 gives an accurate picture for both up- and down-markets. SSMAX has an up-market beta of 1.28 and a down-market beta of 0.086. An investor who just looked at the typical beta estimate for each fund would think they are the same in terms of risk. MCVIX exhibits the same risk whether it is an up- or down-market with a beta of 1.1, but SSMAX is a very different investment, even though it also has a standard CAPM beta of 1.1. Note that the differences in betas here are relatively conservative since mutual funds rather than stocks are being used.

Figure 5: CAPM Beta, Up-Market Beta, and Down-Market Beta for 39 Mutual Funds

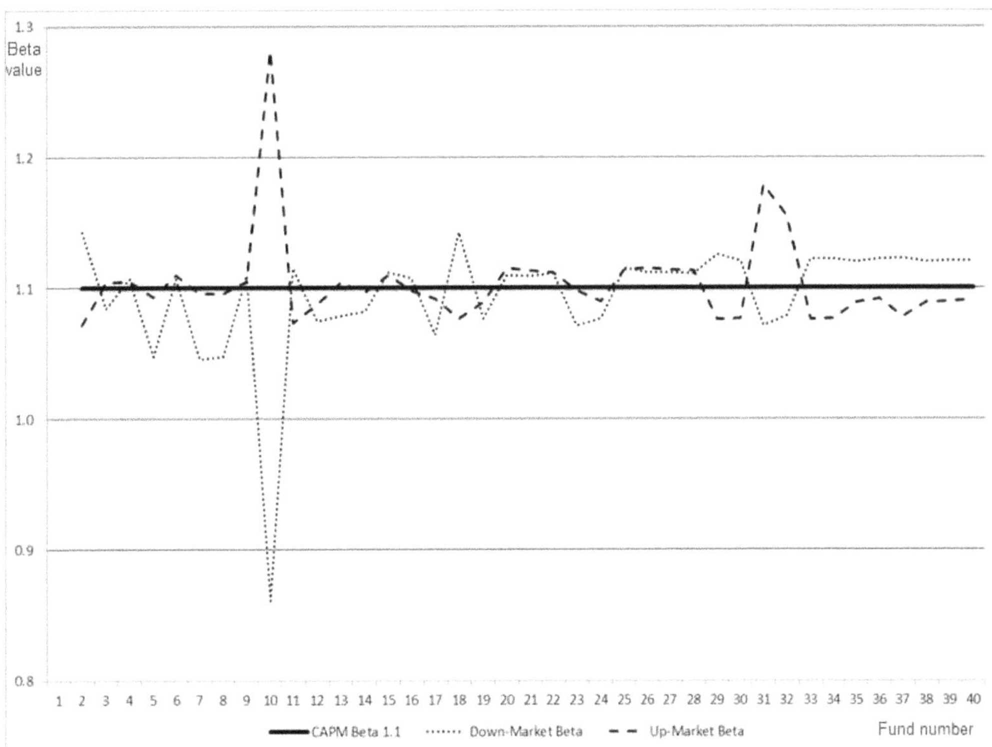

CONCLUSION

In finance, the use of beta as a measure of risk is well-known. Not as well-known is the use of separate beta estimates for up- and down-markets. Using one beta estimate to measure risk, rather than looking at both an up-market beta estimate and a down-market beta estimate, can mislead investors. We provide mutual fund examples showing how the possible confusion arises and how this problem is analogous to the problem explored in Anscombe (1973) that very different data sets can lead to the exact same regression results.

Using these examples, investment professors may be able to better motivate the discussion of dual-beta models while reinforcing better data analysis practices, such as looking at data charts rather than simply numerical summaries.

AUTHOR INFORMATION

James Chong, Ph.D., is a Professor and Associate Director of the Center for Financial Planning and Investment at California State University, Northridge. He also serves as a Research Economist at MacroRisk Analytics. He received his Ph.D. in Finance from the ICMA Centre, The University of Reading. E-mail: jchong@csun.edu

Dennis Halcoussis, Ph.D., is Professor of Economics at California State University, Northridge, where he teaches courses in econometrics and data analysis. He is the author of the popular textbook "*Understanding Econometrics*" and is the author of numerous papers applying econometric methods to diverse economic topics. He received his Ph.D. from the University of Pennsylvania in 1992. E-mail: dhalcoussis@csu.edu

G. Michael Phillips, Ph.D., is the Director of the Center for Financial Planning and Investment and a Professor of Finance, Real Estate, and Insurance at California State University, Northridge. He also serves as Chief Scientist for MacroRisk Analytics. He received his Ph.D. from the University of California, San Diego, with specializations in econometrics and applied economics. E-mail: mphillips@csun.edu (Corresponding author)

REFERENCES

1. Anscombe, Francis J. 1973. "Graphs in Statistical Analysis", *The American Statistician* 27(1), 17-21.
2. Chong, James, Shawn Pfeiffer, and G. Michael Phillips. 2011. "Can Dual Beta Filtering Improve Investor Performance?" *Journal of Personal Finance* 10 (1), 63-86.
3. Chong, James, and G. Michael Phillips. 2011. "Beta Measures Market Risk Except When It Doesn't: Regime-Switching Alpha and Errors in Beta", *Journal of Wealth Management* 14(3), 67-72.
4. Fama, Eugene F., and Kenneth French. 1992. "The Cross-Section of Expected Stock Returns", *Journal of Finance* 47(2), 427-465.
5. Scholes, Myron, and Joseph Williams. 1977. "Estimating Betas from Nonsynchronous Data", *Journal of Financial Economics* 5(3), 309-327.
6. Todorov, Viktor, and Tim Bollerslev. 2010. "Jumps and Betas: A New Framework for Disentangling and Estimating Systematic Risks", *Journal of Econometrics* 157(2), 220-235.

Walnut Oak Press Valuation Reference Series

Financial Data Estimates

Beta Estimates for Valuation and Cost of Capital: CAPM, Down-Market, and Up-Market Betas by Industry is a series of books published quarterly that provides betas, up-market betas and down-market betas of common stocks, preferred stocks, and mutual funds. The data for common stocks and preferred stocks are grouped by SIC codes. The data for mutual funds are provided by peer groups. Unlike other reference books that usually include only the average or median betas, these books also include different percentiles to provide the reader with additional information to value companies. Valuation analysts would find these books helpful when conducting valuation of companies in different industries.

*(Volumes are available with quarterly updates **beginning with** End of 4th Quarter, 2016.)*

Beta Estimates for Valuation and Cost of Capital: CAPM, Down-Market, and Up-Market Betas by Industry (G. Michael Phillips, William P. Jennings, James Chong, George Arzumanyan)

Book sections available as separate eBook purchases include tables for

Common Stocks
Preferred Stocks
Mutual Funds

Sample Size Illustrations, Confidence Intervals, & Margins of Error

The *Sample Size Illustrations, Confidence Intervals, & Margins of Error* volumes provide sample size illustrations with corresponding confidence intervals and margins of error at the 80, 85, 90, 95, and 99 percent confidence levels. These books will help you determine the sample size, for a particular population size, which would not result in the margin of error exceeding your prespecified margin of error. For instance, what sample size should be taken from a population of 100 so that the sample results do not exceed 10 percent margin of error at the 80 percent confidence level?

The tables are calculated using the "population adjusted hypergeometric distribution" (sometimes called "hypergeometric distribution"). The calculations are performed using a variation of the Clopper-Pearson exact method to calculate confidence intervals.

Population sizes in these books range from one to 500. All integer population sizes are included between one to 250 after which the population size increases by 10 up to 500.

Tables for 80, 85, 90, 95 and 99 percent confidence levels can be purchased as separate volumes from Walnut Oak Press.

Sample Size Illustrations, Confidence Intervals, & Margins of Error: Hypergeometric Distributions Tables for Attorneys & Experts (George Arzumanyan, Dennis Halcoussis, G. Michael Phillips)

Sample Size Illustrations, Confidence Intervals, & Margins of Error: Jeffreys Method Tables for Attorneys & Experts (George Arzumanyan, Dennis Halcoussis, G. Michael Phillips)

Sample Size Illustrations, Confidence Intervals, & Margins of Error: Agresti-Coull Tables for Attorneys & Experts (George Arzumanyan, Dennis Halcoussis, G. Michael Phillips)

Walnut Oak Press Valuation Reference Series

Mortality Adjusted Valuation Factors

This series of reference works specializes in probabilities and factors which forensic economists, valuation experts, and attorneys will frequently find useful. Encompassing everything from age-based conditional probabilities of death and cumulative survival probabilities to factors made specifically for calculating the present values of remainder perpetuities and life annuities, this series provides professionals with estimators which cannot be found elsewhere.

(Volumes are available ***beginning with*** *2012 life table data, published in 2016.)*

Mortality Factors for Valuation: Age-Based Cumulative Probabilities of Survival
(G. Michael Phillips, David Fractor, Dennis Halcoussis, Edward T. Garcia, Laurel J. Fish)

Mortality Factors for Valuation: Age-Based Conditional Probabilities of Death
(G. Michael Phillips, David Fractor, Dennis Halcoussis, Edward T. Garcia, Laurel J. Fish)

Mortality Factors for Valuation: Life Expectancy Based Remainder Perpetuity Present Value Factors
(G. Michael Phillips, David Fractor, Dennis Halcoussis, Edward T. Garcia, Laurel J. Fish)

Mortality Factors for Valuation: Probability Adjusted Remainder Perpetuity Present Value Factors
(G. Michael Phillips, David Fractor, Dennis Halcoussis, Edward T. Garcia, Laurel J. Fish)

Mortality Factors for Valuation: Single Life Annuity Present Value Factors
(G. Michael Phillips, David Fractor, Dennis Halcoussis, Edward T. Garcia, Laurel J. Fish)

For each Mortality Adjusted Valuation Factor series, sections available for separate eBook purchases include

United States Total Population
United States Male Population
United States Female Population
United States White Population
United States White Male Population
United States White Female Population
United States Black Population
United States Black Male Population
United States Black Female Population
United States Hispanic Population
United States Hispanic Male Population
United States Hispanic Female Population
United States Non-Hispanic White Population
United States Non-Hispanic White Male Population
United States Non-Hispanic White Female Population
United States Non-Hispanic Black Population
United States Non-Hispanic Black Male Population
United States Non-Hispanic Black Female Population

www.ingramcontent.com/pod-product-compliance
Ingram Content Group UK Ltd.
Pitfield, Milton Keynes, MK11 3LW, UK
UKHW051508290926
15471UKWH00008B/1506

9 781947 572317